T&T Clark Social Identity Commentaries on the New Testament

Series Editors

Kathy Ehrensperger
University of Potsdam, Abraham Geiger College, Germany

Philip F. Esler
University of Gloucestershire, UK

Gabriella Gelardini
Nord University, Norway

Aaron Kuecker
Trinity Christian College, USA

Petri Luomanen
University of Helsinki, Finland

J. Brian Tucker
Moody Theological Seminary, USA

2 Corinthians

A Social Identity Commentary

Philip F. Esler

LONDON • NEW YORK • OXFORD • NEW DELHI • SYDNEY

T&T CLARK
Bloomsbury Publishing Plc
50 Bedford Square, London, WC1B 3DP, UK
1385 Broadway, New York, NY 10018, USA
29 Earlsfort Terrace, Dublin 2, Ireland

BLOOMSBURY, T&T CLARK and the T&T Clark logo are trademarks of Bloomsbury Publishing Plc

First published in Great Britain 2022
This paperback edition published 2023

Copyright © Philip Esler, 2022

Philip Esler has asserted his right under the Copyright, Designs and Patents Act, 1988, to be identified as Author of this work.

For legal purposes the Acknowledgements on p. xi constitute an extension of this copyright page.

Cover design: Charlotte James
Cover image © Shutterstock

All rights reserved. No part of this publication may be reproduced or transmitted in any form or by any means, electronic or mechanical, including photocopying, recording, or any information storage or retrieval system, without prior permission in writing from the publishers.

Bloomsbury Publishing Plc does not have any control over, or responsibility for, any third-party websites referred to or in this book. All internet addresses given in this book were correct at the time of going to press. The author and publisher regret any inconvenience caused if addresses have changed or sites have ceased to exist, but can accept no responsibility for any such changes.

A catalogue record for this book is available from the British Library.

Library of Congress Cataloging-in-Publication Data
Names: Esler, Philip Francis, author.
Title: Second Corinthians : a social identity commentary / by Philip F. Esler.
Description: London ; New York : T&T Clark, 2021. | Series: T&T Clark social identity commentaries on the New Testament | Includes bibliographical references and indexes. | Summary: "Philip Esler provides a commentary on Paul's second letter to the Corinthians considering it from the perspective of social identity theory"– Provided by publisher.
Identifiers: LCCN 2021012610 (print) | LCCN 2021012611 (ebook) | ISBN 9780567668721 (hardback) | ISBN 9780567668738 (pdf) | ISBN 9780567668745 (epub)
Subjects: LCSH: Identity (Psychology)–Religious aspects–Christianity. | Identification (Religion) | Bible. Corinthians, 2nd–Commentaries.
Classification: LCC BS2675.6.I33 E85 2021 (print) | LCC BS2675.6.I33 (ebook) | DDC 227/.307—dc23
LC record available at https://lccn.loc.gov/2021012610
LC ebook record available at https://lccn.loc.gov/2021012611

ISBN: HB: 978-0-5676-6872-1
PB: 978-0-5677-0333-0
ePDF: 978-0-5676-6873-8
ePUB: 978-0-5676-6874-5

Typeset by Deanta Global Publishing Services, Chennai, India

To find out more about our authors and books visit www.bloomsbury.com and sign up for our newsletters.

To Patricia

Contents

Series preface	ix
Preface and acknowledgements	xi
List of abbreviations	xiii
Introduction	1
1 Setting the scene	3
2 The social identity approach to leadership	30
Commentary: Part A	
2 Corinthians 1–7: Paul re-establishes his leadership	47
3 Reconnecting with the Corinthians (1.1-22)	49
4 Paul explains himself to the Corinthians (1.23–2.13)	75
5 Pauline leadership and the new covenant (2.14–3.18)	94
6 The signs, trials and triumph of leadership (4.1-15)	132
7 The future destiny of Christ-followers (4.16–5.10)	149
8 The foundation and exercise of Pauline leadership (5.11–6.2)	161
9 Leadership and ingroup identity (6.3–7.4)	181
10 Paul, Titus and the Corinthians (7.5-16)	205
Commentary: Part B	
2 Corinthians 8–9: The collection	227
11 The collection (2 Corinthians 8–9): Introductory issues	229
12 The collection (2 Corinthians 8–9)	239
Commentary: Part C	
2 Corinthians 10–13: Paul defends his leadership against his opponents and stiffens the Corinthians' identity in Christ	269
13 Paul's opponents and his response in a social identity perspective	271

14	Paul's assertion of his leadership against the claims of his opponents (2 Corinthians 10)	287
15	Claiming honour as a fool (2 Corinthians 11)	306
16	Paul's vision and his impending visit to Corinth: (2 Corinthians 12)	331
17	Confrontation in Corinth and conclusion: (2 Corinthians 13)	356

References	373
Index of authors	399
Index of ancient and biblical references	405

Series preface

The T&T Clark Social Identity Commentaries on the New Testament (SICNT) is a series that presents readings of the NT focused on identity. In the last three decades biblical studies have seen a marked upsurge of interest in questions of identity in the ancient world, both of groups and of individuals. The Hebrew Bible and the New Testament are replete with phenomena that are embedded in and have an impact on issues of identity. A primary narrative of the New Testament concerns the processes in the first century CE by which a new socioreligious Christ-movement formed within the populous and long-established Judean/Jewish group and developed, interacting with Greek, Roman and other traditions, on trajectories of its own until, at some stage, to be both Judean/Jewish and a Christ-follower became difficult, resulting in rapidly increasing social and intergroup complexity. Central to that process was the way participation in various Christ-following assemblies cultivated in the minds and hearts of their members an identity that eventually became distinct from Judean/Jewish identity. This identity was manifested in distinctive beliefs, attitudes, and behavior, which Christ-followers traced back to the ministry, teaching, death, and resurrection of Jesus Christ. Since the 1990s that branch of social psychology known as social identity theory, originally developed by Henri Tajfel and John Turner in the University of Bristol in the 1970s and 1980s—now deployed by hundreds if not thousands of psychologists across the world—has proven a remarkably rich theoretical resource for probing these inter- and intra-group dimensions of the identity of the Christ-movement as exposed in the books of the New Testament. A torrent of books, articles, and essays has appeared and continues to appear applying social identity theory to the biblical texts, not least, the *T&T Clark Handbook to Social Identity in the New Testament* (Bloomsbury, 2014) and the *T&T Clark Social Identity Commentary on the New Testament* (Bloomsbury, 2020). This series of commentaries testifies to the extent to which the application of social identity theory has become established as one of the liveliest subfields of New Testament research and to the resulting need to make available to scholars, students, and the general public detailed treatments of each text from this perspective. The authors of each volume, all well-recognized scholars in the area, while engaging with existing scholarship as they move through the text seriatim in commentary style, will apply distinctive social identity ideas and other perspectives on group behavior generating fresh but well-founded interpretations of the New

Testament's twenty-seven constituent books. The series aims to demonstrate how much New Testament interpretation can benefit from the application of the expert investigation into the social realities of groups, and group and individual identities undertaken by social identity psychologists and other social-scientific specialists.

Series editors

Kathy Ehrensperger
   University of Potsdam, Abraham Geiger College, Germany
Philip Esler
   University of Gloucestershire, UK
Gabriella Gelardini
   Nord University, Norway
Aaron Kuecker
   Trinity Christian College, USA
Petri Luomanen
   University of Helsinki, Finland
J. Brian Tucker
   Moody Theological Seminary, USA

Preface and acknowledgements

Prior to commencing this project, I had used social identity theory as an aid to Pauline interpretation, especially in relation to Galatians (1998) and Romans (2003), and that previous research has shaped the way I understood how Paul had sought to shape the identity of his Christ-groups, especially vis-à-vis the millions-strong Judean ethnic group in which it had arisen. Early in 2009 I was reviewing recent developments in social psychology that might be relevant to my New Testament research when I came upon an article by John Turner in the 2005 volume of the *European Journal of Social Psychology*. Turner had worked with Henri Tajfel, the founder of social identity theory, at the University of Bristol in the 1970s and 1980s and played a major role in the formulation of the theory. His article was entitled 'Explaining the Nature of Power: A Three-Process Theory', and it offered a new position on how leaders exercise power in groups from a social identity perspective. Turner's ideas seemed to me to have the potential to stimulate new thinking about Paul's relationships with his communities, especially as evident in 2 Corinthians. That realization led me to work through 2 Corinthians in 2009 with Turner's article (and social identity theory generally) in mind.

In November 2009, I was able to give the approach its first public airing at a meeting of the Society of Biblical Literature in New Orleans. Soon after, in February 2010, I presented on the subject at the Graduate Seminar in the University of Durham, courtesy of an invitation from Professor Francis Watson. The course of my career then kept me away from 2 Corinthians until 2014, when I delivered a paper on the letter at the meeting of the Society of New Testament Studies in Szeged, Hungary. My social identity analysis of the text has proceeded since then somewhat intermittently, as other projects demanded attention. Nevertheless, in September 2017 I had a long conversation with Professor Steve Reicher of the School of Psychology in the University of St Andrews on the current state of social identity research, especially in relation to leadership, and soon after he provided me with a collection of social identity works he had co-authored that were then in publication. His help has been invaluable in relation to the social identity spine of this commentary. Discussions with my colleagues and friends Kathy Ehrensperger, Aaron Kuecker, Petri Luomanen and Brian Tucker, series editors for the T&T Clark Social Identity Commentaries on the New Testament series, led me to undertake this book. In recent years, the series editors have held sessions on Writing Social-Scientific Commentaries on the

New Testament at Annual Meetings of the Society of Biblical Literature and I presented at some of those sessions. I spoke on the project at the Seminar of the International Centre for Biblical Interpretation in the University of Gloucestershire in January 2019 and at the International SBL meeting in Rome in July 2019. On all of these occasions I have benefited from the discussions with those present. Christopher Stanley assisted me greatly in understanding the 'oracular' nature of Paul's use of scripture and carefully read and commented on an offshoot from this commentary dealing with 2 Cor. 6.14–7.1 that has now appeared separately (in the *Biblical Theology Bulletin*). I have also profited greatly from discussions with other researchers who in many cases have provided me with published or unpublished work of their own, in particular John Barclay, David Horrell, John Kloppenborg, Frederick Long, Kar Yong Lim, Andrew Lincoln, Margaret Mitchell, Robert Morgan, Ludvig Nyman, Christopher Porter, Volker Rabens, Gregory Sterling, Brian Tucker and Larry Welborn. Finally, I have greatly benefited from a careful review of the entire manuscript by Kathy Ehrensperger and Brian Tucker. It goes without saying that many of the topics raised in this volume are matters of lively debate, and I alone am responsible for the views expressed.

Although I had come to the letter without a position in the ongoing debate about its unity, as I spent time thinking about it in terms of the social identity approach to leadership I became convinced of its literary integrity, that we have its text as Paul intended. I also started with no fixed views on the character of the opponents Paul refers to in the letter. Only in the last few years, as I worked through the text using social identity theory at the forefront of my mind, yet in constant interaction with the magnificent scholarship undertaking historical investigation of 2 Corinthians not using that theory, have I arrived at a settled position on the nature of Paul's opponents.

At Bloomsbury T&T Clark, Dominic Mattos, editorial director and publisher, and Sarah Blake, assistant editor, have been very helpful in advising me on the project and in their patience while I completed the manuscript. Mohammed Raffi carefully oversaw the copy-editing, type-setting, proofing and indexing of the manuscript. Finally, I dedicate this commentary to my wife, Patricia, who, in addition to her usual, constant support and lively humour during our thirty-eight years of married life, spent three months in early 2020 nursing me back to excellent health after major heart surgery. *Mulierem fortem quis inveniet?*

Abbreviations

ABR	*Australian Biblical Review*
ARP	*Annual Review of Psychology*
BDAG	Danker, Frederick William (ed.) (2000) *A Greek-English Lexicon of the New Testament and Other Early Christian Literature. Third Edition.* Chicago and London: University of Chicago Press.
BDF	Blass, F., A. Debrunner and Robert W. Funk (1961) *A Greek Grammar of the New Testament and Other Early Christian Literature.* A translation and revision of the ninth-tenth German edition. Chicago and London: The University of Chicago Press.
BJSP	*British Journal of Social Psychology*
BTB	*Biblical Theology Bulletin*
BJRL	*Bulletin of the John Rylands Library*
CBQ	*Catholic Biblical Quarterly*
EJSP	*European Journal of Social Psychology*
ER	*Epworth Review*
ERSP	*European Review of Social Psychology*
ETL	*Ephemerides Theologicae Lovanienses*
EvT	*Evangelische Theologie*
HTR	*Harvard Theological Review*
JBL	*Journal of Biblical Literature*
JESP	*Journal of Experimental Social Psychology*
JGRCJ	*Journal of Greco-Roman Christianity and Judaism*
JPSP	*Journal of Personality and Social Psychology*
JSJ	*Journal for the Study of Judaism*
JSNT	*Journal for the Study of the New Testament*
JSOT	*Journal for the Study of the Old Testament*
JTS	*Journal of Theological Studies*

LQ	*The Leadership Quarterly*
NEB	*The New English Bible*
NovT	*Novum Testamentum*
NTS	*New Testament Studies*
PP	*Political Psychology*
PSPR	*Personality and Social Psychology Review*
PSPB	*Personality and Social Psychology Bulletin*
RB	*Revue Biblique*
RQ	*Restoration Quarterly*
RSV	*Revised Standard Version*
SJT	*Scottish Journal of Theology*
SPPC	*Social and Personality Psychology Compass*
SNTSMS	*Society of New Testament Studies Monograph Series*
TDNT	*Theological Dictionary of the New Testament, Volume V,* edited by Gerhard Friedrich, trans. and ed. Geoffrey W. Bromiley (1967) Grand Rapids, MI: Eerdmans.
ZNTW	*Zeitschrift für die Neutestamentliche Wissenschaft*

Introduction

1

Setting the scene

Opening 2 Corinthians

It will be useful to begin this commentary by summarizing the context in which Paul wrote 2 Corinthians, the various details of which are not presuppositions but results based on later argument provided in the text. When Paul, located somewhere in Macedonia around 55 CE,[1] began to compose what we call his second letter to the Corinthians, he faced a complex communicative task. Paul knew this because Titus had recently returned to him from visiting the Christ-followers of Corinth and had briefed him on the changing situation of the Christ-movement in the city. There were four major issues that Paul needed to address and in relation to which he wanted the Corinthians to follow his advice. They were important in themselves but would also impact upon the success or otherwise of the visit Paul himself was soon to make to Corinth, his third to the city.

The first of these issues was his relationship with the Corinthian Christ-followers. This had been damaged by his failing to visit them on the way to Macedonia, as he had earlier undertaken to do, and by the continuing reverberations of an unpleasant incident that had occurred during his second visit to the city, which were amplified by a severe letter on the matter he had subsequently sent to them. Secondly, he wanted them to complete the collection for the poor Christ-followers of Jerusalem that he had initiated the previous year but which now required urgent resolution. Thirdly, and this is a matter argued for in considerable detail later in the volume, since he had last visited Corinth, Christ-followers had arrived there, most likely from Jerusalem, preaching a different Gospel to his – probably in that they insisted on his converts' adherence to the law of Moses – and heavily criticizing him for the nature of his apostleship. Fourthly, he was concerned that the adherence of the Corinthians to their new orientation to and identity in Christ was potentially shaky and needed strengthening. The first three issues are the focus, respectively, of chs 1–7, 8–9 and 10–13, although there are

---

[1] For the dating of 2 Corinthians, see Thrall 1994: 74–7.

linkages across the sections in what is a carefully unified letter, as discussed later in the volume. The fourth issue appears mainly, but not exclusively, in chs 10–13.

Not surprisingly, Paul's attention to these issues meant that the resulting letter was long and complex. Yet such a communication was not unheard of in the ancient Greek east. Orators intent on persuading the assemblies of the city states frequently needed to make speeches addressing several issues. As one example, Andocides' *On the Mysteries*, like 2 Corinthians, also dealt with four (Long 2004: 81).

This commentary does not, however, involve itself in the detailed nature of ancient rhetoric and leaves that task to others – very successfully accomplished in some cases (e.g. Long 2004), but not so successfully in others where his letters are pressed into elaborate rhetorical structures rather artificially (e.g. Betz 1985). Nevertheless, Paul must have had a general familiarity with the ways in which ancient speakers crafted their arguments from having heard many of them speak in the marketplaces of the various Greek cities he visited. Above all, he must have realized that the whole point of rhetoric was to move an audience to a particular point of view. That is precisely the task he has undertaken in 2 Corinthians. The very success of his ministry in Corinth depended on his persuading the Christ-group there to adopt his viewpoint in a number of areas. Accordingly, my interest lies in what some scholars call the 'original meaning' of the text, that is, the meaning Paul was trying to communicate to an actual group of ancient people in a particular place and time. Caution is necessary here. Clearly, we can never have a complete grasp of what Paul was trying to communicate. All an interpreter can hope for is a rough approximation influenced by his or her knowledge, understanding and perspective. Nevertheless, use of the phrase 'original meaning' underlines the fact that this is not an exercise in reader response but an attempt to respect the alterity of an ancient writer by investigating the practical message or messages (Esler 2005: 88–93) Paul was seeking to convey to the Corinthian Christ-followers, who were (by and large) illiterate non-Judeans, by writing and despatching this letter. This consideration means that throughout this commentary I will seek to interpret 2 Corinthians in terms of what Paul was attempting to communicate to his audience and not what he may have had in this head (e.g. an encyclopaedic grasp of Israelite scripture) but did not deploy to make his case.

In addition, the occasional nature of Paul's letters – with the resulting close linkages between context and message – means that one must always take care when seeking to adduce evidence from one of his letters to understand another. Sometimes, however, this becomes necessary. Thus, 1 Corinthians bears directly on 2 Corinthians in many significant respects. At significant points in the commentary, moreover, I will adduce evidence from other Pauline letters – Galatians especially, which I also interpret from a social identity perspective (1996, 1998, 2006b) – to assist in the interpretation of 2 Corinthians. Using Romans, however, to interpret 2 Corinthians is more difficult. Romans is the one letter where Paul is writing into a situation where Judean Christ-followers are being treated negatively (Rom. 11.17-24), and this induces him to come to the defence of his people, for whom he shows notable warmth, not least in Rom. 9.1-5, 10.1-2 and 11.1-2.[2] Thus, in Romans 4 he draws back from his virtual exclusion of Judeans from Abrahamic ancestry in Galatians 3 and, at various points, makes positive remarks regarding the Mosaic law that stand in sharp contrast to his very negative assessment of the law in 2 Corinthians 3. To my mind, Paul's deepest feelings and considered judgement about his own people and its magnificent institutions and traditions are to be found in Romans and not in 2 Corinthians.

The existing secondary literature on 2 Corinthians offers many ways to encapsulate its purpose. Here are a few recent examples: a study of renewal through suffering (Harvey 1996), an expression of Paul's ministry as antithetical to the spirit of his age (Savage 1996), an apology for failing to visit them as he had promised (Long 2004), an expression of the character of Jesus (Stegman 2005), a bid for reconciliation (Vegge 2008) and an enactment of church leadership by Paul and Timothy (Land 2015). All of these approaches fruitfully engage with data in the text, even if, as we will see later, they are also susceptible to critical scrutiny.

This commentary, however, charts a fresh course by arguing that the letter represents an effort by Paul to encourage the Corinthian Christ-followers to embody and to act in accordance with the new identity that they had obtained by becoming Christ-followers through baptism. In particular, in line with the perspective of the Series in which this commentary appears, the particular perspective on identity adopted is the social identity approach. This is not the first time that the social identity approach has been applied to 2 Corinthians. This letter has attracted important monographs by Jack Barentsen (*Emerging Leadership in the Pauline Mission: A Social Identity Perspective on Local Leadership in Corinth and Ephesus* in 2011) and Kar Yong Lim (*Metaphors and Social Identity Formation in Paul's Letters to the Corinthians* in 2017). Lim has also authored the chapter on 2 Corinthians in the *T & T Clark Social Identity Commentary on the New Testament* (Tucker and Kuecker 2020). I will refer to these writings in what follows.

The social identity approach is a branch of social psychology. It comprises social identity theory, which focuses on intergroup relations, and was

---

[2] See Esler 2003a: 270–3.

articulated by Henri Tajfel and others at Bristol University in the 1970s, and the closely related self-categorization theory, which is a fundamental theory of how groups form and exist and was developed by John Turner (a doctoral student and then colleague of Tajfel at Bristol) and others in the 1980s. I have explained the general nature of the social identity approach in other publications and will not repeat that material here (Esler 2014a; also cf. Barentsen 2011: 32–52). Nevertheless, detailed aspects of it are introduced where appropriate in commenting on particular sections of the letter. The social identity approach is probably the most influential branch of social psychology today, not least because of the number of its practitioners. Thus, Tajfel's original doctoral students and the generations of psychologists thereafter who gained doctorates in this vibrant tradition now number over 700 (Brown 2020: 241), and there are many more social psychologists around the world who apply the social identity approach who are not in this line of academic descent.

One particular aspect of the social identity approach, its position on leadership, will play a particularly prominent role. This is because Paul's attempt in the letter to influence the Christ-group that he founded in Corinth into thinking, feeling and behaving in particular ways in relation to the four issues mentioned earlier is a paradigmatic attempt at exercising leadership, and the social identity approach offers a rich array of insights for understanding the dynamics of this process.

There already exists a considerable body of scholarship on Paul's use of power and authority in relation to his communities. Milestones in this research include works by John Schütz in 1975, Bengt Holmberg in 1978, Graham Shaw in 1983, Elizabeth Castelli in 1991, Sandra Polaski in 1999, Kathy Ehrensperger in 2007 and Andrew Clarke in 2008. John Goodrich has recently reviewed scholarship in this area (2012: 1–12). The works by Schütz and Holmberg were not so much concerned with the question of leadership, with influencing others so that they help to achieve group goals, but with Pauline authority, in the sense of the character and basis of Paul's rights in relation to Christ-movement communities, especially connected with his claim to be an apostle commissioned by God to preach the Gospel (Esler 2003a: 33). As we will see later in the chapter, even in a commentary pursuing a social identity approach that remains an important issue.

Some of the scholarship on Paul's use of power and authority, however, evinces a quite negative interpretation of Paul's exercise of power. Graham Shaw, for example, has argued that Paul engaged in an abusive exercise of power, manipulating his communities, while concealing his dependence on them, and alienating believers who failed to toe his line (1983: 181–4). In her hard-hitting 1991 work *Imitating Paul: A Discourse of Power*, Castelli focused especially on Paul's exhortations to imitate him and she criticized some earlier studies for either spiritualizing or naturalizing the Pauline idea of mimesis (1991: 32). In so doing, she suggested that such commentators have either 'ignored the implicit articulation of power present in the advocacy of mimetic relations or have rendered the power relationship unproblematic and self-evident' (1991: 33). Sandra Polaski, while not wishing to offer a hostile reading of Paul, or to vilify his approach to the exercise of power or to dismiss him for being deceptively self-serving, nevertheless employed a Foucaudian hermeneutic of suspicion to discern his use of power relations that the surface meaning of the text may disguise (1999: 21). On the other hand, Kathy Ehrensperger has proposed a much more sympathetic reading of Paul on power, arguing that he uses his authority in a constructive way, to help his communities move towards a more mature grip on their faith and Christ-movement identity. In a statement very close to my own view, she writes that the aim of Paul's teaching was 'to *empower* those within his communities to *support each other*' (2007: 136, emphasis original). While acknowledging the rich insights to be gained from reading these works, the social identity approach offers a new way to approach the textual data in 2 Corinthians on the question of how Paul seeks to lead the Corinthians Christ-followers in particular directions.

Although perhaps insufficiently appreciated by modern readers of 2 Corinthians, we have firm evidence that Paul's attempt to exercise leadership in relation to the Corinthians was ultimately successful. We know this from what he says towards the end of his epistle to the Romans. Writing from Corinth towards the end of the third visit that he foreshadows in 2 Corinthians, Paul makes clear both that his work in those regions is complete and that he has successfully gathered the collection for the poor Christ-followers of Jerusalem in Achaia (which included Corinth) and Macedonia and is about to convey it to them (Rom. 15.23-27). This means, in effect, that he had successfully accomplished his aims in writing 2 Corinthians. As we work through Paul's strenuous endeavours to address and solve the challenging complexities of his leadership role with the Corinthian Christ-followers, it will assist if we know at the outset that this will be a story with a happy ending.

The detailed work on the text of 2 Corinthians undertaken in writing this commentary from a social identity perspective (beginning in 2009) has disclosed what is, to my mind, a tightly integrated communication across all of its thirteen chapters. This result stands in stark contradistinction to the view of many commentators who, since S. Semler's commentary of 1776, have argued that 2 Corinthians is a collection of Pauline letter fragments. If correct, the partition theories (and they are many, varied and mutually contradictory) exclude making sense of canonical 2 Corinthians as a unified Pauline composition. For this reason, if mistaken, they represent what is arguably the greatest error of interpretation in the entire course of critical New Testament scholarship and a serious obstacle to understanding Paul historically and theologically. Accordingly, while it is not the primary focus of this commentary, throughout its length I will argue for the literary integrity of the letter. I will consider this issue in a general way in the third section of this chapter, reserving consideration of specific issues for discussion in the commentary as and when they arise. First of all, I will explain my understanding of the historical context in which 1 and 2 Corinthians were written. This section represents a result of my engagement with 2 Corinthians, not the presuppositions with which I began.

The course of events evidenced by 1 and 2 Corinthians

Most commentaries on 2 Corinthians contain an extensive coverage of the history and archaeology of Corinth. There are also a number of excellent works on Corinth from these perspectives (e.g. Schowalter and Friesen 2005). To keep this commentary within reasonable compass – given the need to explore and apply the social identity approach to leadership – that readily available material will not be canvassed in this Introduction. On the other hand, it will assist anyone reading the commentary to know at the outset how I understand the course of events in Paul's interaction with the Christ-followers of Corinth that can be discerned from 1 and 2 Corinthians. The following is a summary of the situation, with argument in support of the various positions taken on disputed issues appearing at the relevant places in the commentary.

Paul founded the Christ-movement in Corinth; he states that 'I planted' (ἐφύτευσα; 1 Cor. 3.6) and 'I laid the foundation' (θεμέλιον ἔθηκα; 1 Cor. 3.10). Specific support for this subsists in the fact that he baptized the household of Stephanas (1 Cor. 1.16) and they were the first fruits (ἀπαρχή), that is, the first Christ-followers, in Achaia (1 Cor. 16.15). He was aided by Timothy and Silvanus (2 Cor. 1.19).[3] In all likelihood this was Paul's first visit to the city. The particular date of this visit is not critical to this discussion of Paul's interaction with the Corinthians, which relies rather on getting the sequence of events and their overall character correct. Nevertheless, we are

---

[3] Acts 18.5 also has Timothy and Silvanus (there called 'Silas') assisting Paul in his initial evangelism in Corinth, which is a significant confirmation of Luke's having had access to accurate information about Paul's initial stay in the city (see note no. 4).

in the unusual position of being able to date his initial period in Corinth with some degree of accuracy. It almost certainly occurred while L. Iunius Gallio was proconsul of Achaia, during the period from 1 July 51 to 1 July 52 CE.[4]

Although there is no evidence for how long Paul stayed in Corinth, at some point he left the city. Later he wrote them a letter – we know not when or from where – which is now lost but which he summarizes in 1 Cor. 5.9-13 to the effect that he did not want them to associate with 'immoral people' (πόρνοι) who were members of the Christ-group but, rather, to drive them out of their midst.

Following the despatch of that letter, he received further information from Corinth that prompted him to write another letter to the Christ-followers in the city, a long letter we know as 1 Corinthians. He was at Ephesus (1 Cor. 16.8), and he had recently been visited by Stephanas, the first Corinthian Christ-follower, and two other Corinthian believers, Fortunatus and Achaicus (1 Cor. 16.17), who were no doubt the source of his new information about affairs in the city.

Among the various problems that Paul addresses in 1 Corinthians 5-14 as he responds to the news from the city – the first mentioned (which underlines its significance for him) – was that there was an egregious instance of 'immorality' (πορνεία) among them in that a man was living with his father's wife. He directed that this man be removed from among them (1 Cor. 5.1-8). No doubt Paul had been stung by the fact that in permitting this situation to persist, the Corinthians were disobeying the direction in his earlier letter that they should not associate with immoral people (πόρνοι) among the Christ-followers but should drive them out (1 Cor. 5.9-13).

Towards the end of 1 Corinthians, Paul gave his addressees directions concerning the 'collection for the saints' (ἡ λογεία ἡ εἰς τοὺς ἁγίους). Each of them was to put something aside on the first day of every week, so that collections need not be made when he came to Corinth (16.1-2). The force of this statement is that Paul wanted the Corinthian Christ-followers to start

---

[4] While acknowledging the insight of John Knox that the primary sources for Paul's life are his letters and that, in cases of conflict with Acts, the letters should govern interpretation (1989), Acts provides a valuable piece of information, the historicity of which there is little reason to doubt. It is that during Paul's initial stay in the city he was taken by local Judeans before Gallio, the proconsul of Achaia (Acts 18.12-17). Even a commentator as sceptical of details in Acts as Ernst Haenchen comments that 'although we may not regard the text as an exact reproduction of events, we can view the report as a whole with confidence' (1971: 541). Epigraphic evidence for L. Iunius Gallio's year in post exists in the form of an inscription found in Delphi in the early twentieth century. For a detailed discussion of this inscription and its relevance to the dating of Gallio's proconsulship, see Murphy-O'Connor 1983: 141–52. Careful consideration of the inscription and ancient literary evidence strongly suggests that the most likely date for Gallio's proconsulship is 1 July 51 to 1 July 52 CE (Jewett 1979: 38–40; Murphy-O'Connor 1983: 146–50).

the collection immediately, that is, upon receipt of 1 Corinthians. He also suggested arrangements for sending their gift (χάρις) to Jerusalem (16.3-4).

In 1 Cor. 4.19-21, just after he has mentioned sending Timothy to remind them of his ways in Christ, Paul tells the Corinthians that he will visit them soon if the Lord wills and will take on any arrogant (literally, 'puffed up' [πεφυσιωμένοι]) believers. He asks them if they want him to come to them 'with a rod (ῥάβδος), or with love (ἀγάπη) in a spirit of gentleness' (4.21). Paul means by this that he will be in receipt of information, no doubt from Timothy (see the following), in advance of his visit that will determine whether he comes with severity or gentleness.

In 1 Cor. 16.5-7, Paul provides concrete details of his statement in 1 Cor. 4.19 by telling the Corinthians that he would visit them after passing through Macedonia (implying after he had left Ephesus) and perhaps would overwinter with them. He added that he did not want to see them just in passing but to spend an extended period of time with them.

At two places in 1 Corinthians, Paul foreshadows that he will be sending Timothy to them (i.e. in advance of his own visit). In 1 Cor. 4.17, he says, 'Therefore I will send (ἔπεμψα; a futuristic aorist) Timothy . . . who will remind (ἀναμνήσει) you of my ways in Christ, as I teach them everywhere in every Christ-group (ἐκκλησία).'[5] In 1 Cor. 16.10-11, Paul asks them to put Timothy at ease when he comes and to send him back to him, since he was expecting him with the brothers. This latter feature suggests that Timothy would soon be in Corinth and would not stay long before returning to Paul.

The fact of Timothy's imminent visit precludes his being the bearer of 1 Corinthians to Corinth. Nevertheless, good grounds exist for identifying who brought this letter to the Corinthians – Titus. In 2 Corinthians 8, where Paul is speaking of the collection, he says in v. 6, 'we have urged Titus that just as he had previously made a beginning, so he should also complete among you this work-of-grace' (χάρις). In 2 Cor. 8.10, Paul also states that he began the collection a year previously (ἀπὸ πέρυσι). This suggests that Titus was in Corinth to supervise the inauguration of the collection, and to do that he must have been there when the letter arrived with its instructions on the matter. These factors indicate that he brought 1 Corinthians to Corinth. Further support for this comes from 2 Cor. 12.17-18 where, in a context in which Paul is denying he took (what appears to be financial) advantage of the Corinthians, he asserts, 'Did I take advantage of you through any of those whom I sent to you? I urged Titus (to visit you) and sent the brother with him. Surely Titus did not take advantage of you?' It is highly probable that

---

[5] For a discussion of the origin and significance of the term ἐκκλησία to the Christ-movement, see Esler 2021c.

Paul is denying that Titus took (financial) advantage of the Corinthians in relation to the collection a year before, when Paul sent him and, we now learn, another (unnamed) Christ-follower to deliver 1 Corinthians and commence the collection.

After initiating the collection, which would probably not have taken much time, Titus (and no doubt the brother with him) must have left Corinth. Around this time Timothy presumably arrived in the city, as prepared for in 1 Cor. 4.17 and 16.10-11 (discussed earlier), for a very different purpose and then returned to Paul, certainly with the latest information on the state of the Christ-movement there.

Paul made a visit to Corinth that caused the Corinthian Christ-followers pain (λύπη; see 2 Cor. 2.1). This must have been his second visit, since the one he foreshadows making in 2 Corinthians will be his third (2 Cor. 12.14 and 13.1). We do not know what the reason for the pain was. It is most likely that he had heard of a major problem from someone, Timothy perhaps (Furnish 1984: 151), in advance of his making his visit so that he came, as it were, with a rod as he had previously threatened (1 Cor. 4.19-21). There is some further, and valuable, information about this visit in 2 Cor. 13.2-3, when Paul says, 'I have warned (προείρηκα) and I am forewarning (προλέγω) those who have previously sinned and all the rest, as I did when present the second time and now when I am absent, that if I come again I will not spare them.' This provides, very late in the letter, some unexpected illumination of what Paul said during this visit and the atmosphere in which it was conducted. This was probably a short and unanticipated visit from Ephesus to address one particular problem, not the sort of extended visit he had previously announced (1 Cor. 16.7).

It has occasionally been argued that the second, severe visit that Paul mentions in 2 Corinthians 2 actually occurred before 1 Corinthians had been written. Solid reasons exist for rejecting this hypothesis. There is no sign of such a visit in 1 Corinthians, and the information he has of problems in Corinth has come from Chloe's people (1.11), not from his personal knowledge (Thrall 1994: 50-3). Moreover, in 1 Cor. 2.1 Paul 'refers to only one occasion of his presence in Corinth. Had there been more than one, he would have had to use πρότερον (as in Gal. 4.13) to indicate the first of them' (Thrall 1994: 52).

At some point prior to writing 2 Corinthians, Paul informed the Corinthian Christ-followers of his travel plans (2 Cor. 1.15-16) He intended travelling from Ephesus, then to Corinth, then to Macedon, and back to Corinth (thus meaning that they will see him twice). This represented an improvement on the travel plans he announced in 1 Corinthians in which he only envisaged visiting them on the way back from Macedonia. Paul probably told the Corinthians this during his second visit to soften the blow of whatever action he had been forced to take. 'This has only been a short visit, as I have interrupted my work in Ephesus', he must have said, 'but I will make up for it by making not one, but two visits to you'. This was the only occasion on which he could have told them this, because it could not have been in the severe letter he later sent them for the reason mentioned in the following. On the other hand, we cannot exclude the possibility that Paul told them of this new travel agenda in some other letter not mentioned in his two extant letters and now lost.

Back in Ephesus, Paul hears that something else has gone wrong among the members of the Corinthian Christ-movement (2 Cor. 1.23–2.1). This is a new issue that has cropped up. The idea that it occurred during Paul's second visit to Corinth (Barrett 1973: 89; Thrall 1994: 171) is not credible. The issue occurred in Paul's absence. Although he rejected the idea of making another painful visit (2 Cor. 1.23–2.1), he had obviously considered it after receiving word that a problem had arisen in Corinth when he was not there. Moreover, if it had happened in his presence, would Paul not have sorted it out while he was there? Why wait to a later time in order to address it afresh?

But Paul resolves not to make another painful visit (2 Cor. 2.1-2). He decides to send them a letter instead (2.3-4), with anguish of heart and tears, not wanting to cause them pain (λυπεῖν). He charges Titus to carry this letter to Corinth and to return to him in Troas or Macedon when he has delivered it (2 Cor. 2.12-13; 7.5-16). The main evidence for Titus being the bearer of the letter is that Paul couples the Corinthians' grief at the letter so closely with their acceptance of it that it seems that Titus was there during the whole period (2 Cor. 7.8-11). In the event, Paul does cause them pain (λυπεῖν), but only for a time, since because of this pain they repent (2 Cor. 7.8-9).

What was the subject of his painful letter? The actual situation is that some ἀδικία ('wrong-doing') had occurred in Corinth. Paul was not there at that time, and we do not know how he heard about it. There was an offender (ἀδικήσας; 7.12) and a victim (ἀδικήθεις; 7.12), but since the Corinthians were grieved into repentance (2 Cor. 7.9), they must somehow have been complicit in the ἀδικία.

As suggested initially by Hausrath in 1870, many commentators who believe that 2 Corinthians is a composite of letter fragments have regarded chs 10–13 as this severe letter. Our reasons for rejecting this view appear in Chapter 13 of this volume. The primary issue is that it is not possible to reconcile what Paul says about the focus of his severe letter (involving a single wrongdoer and the man he wronged) with chs 10–13, which focus on another matter entirely, that of people who have arrived in Corinth criticizing Paul and offering a different teaching.

There have been numerous attempts to identify the two relevant parties, the wrongdoer and the one wronged. Patristic interpreters favoured the view that the guilty party was the man living with his father's wife in 1 Corinthians 5, so that the victim would then be the man's apparently still-living father. The major problem with this view is that the problem would surely have been resolved earlier, either by Timothy during his visit to the city envisaged in 1 Corinthians or by Paul himself during his second, severe visit.

Numerous scholars consider that Paul himself was the injured party.[6] Others think it was some unnamed person. As noted earlier, Paul would have been motivated to make a severe visit to Corinth by information he had received from the city; this factor, not taken into account by many commentators, lessens the chances that he was the wronged party for the reason that it excludes any affront offered to Paul in person.

In the severe letter Paul sent to Corinth with Titus, he must have instructed the Corinthians to do something because he was testing their obedience (2 Cor. 2.9). In response to this letter, the majority in Corinth had the offender punished (2 Cor. 2.6). Perhaps the minority wanted a more severe punishment. That Titus was bringing a (harsh) letter from Paul was probably why he was received with fear and trembling (2 Cor. 7.15). They knew they had done wrong. But Paul seems to have told Titus in advance that the Corinthians would react well to the letter (2 Cor. 7.12).

The Corinthian Christ-followers reacted positively to the letter and the presence of Titus, so that Paul considered that he and they were fully reconciled on the matter of the ἀδικία.

During this visit to Corinth, Titus discovered that, since Paul had left the city following his second visit, Judean Christ-followers (probably from Jerusalem) had arrived in Corinth with a programme similar to those who had turned up in Galatia. That is, they were suggesting that non-Judean Christ-followers should take on the law of Moses and become Judeans and attacking Paul's credentials as an apostle. This was clearly a very recent development in Corinth, unbeknown to Paul when he despatched Titus with the severe letter, since otherwise he would have mentioned it in that letter or, more likely, decided that the issue really demanded a personal visit from himself, not just a letter. It is inconceivable that Titus would not have informed Paul of the arrival of these interlopers when next he met him, in Macedon, a conclusion that has attracted surprisingly little attention in scholarship, with honourable exceptions such as Schlatter (1969: 47–8).

Paul has one other problem with the Corinthians. When he is writing 2 Corinthians, his change of travel plans that has upset the Corinthians

---

[6] Welborn 2011 is a superbly argued and innovative expression of this position.

represents a very recent disturbance to his relationship with them, so he needs to deal with it in the letter (1.15-22). It is almost certain on the basis of 2 Cor. 1.13 in the context of his discussing his change of plans that he informed them of the change in a letter. The only candidate (absent another letter of which we have no knowledge) is the severe letter itself or its bearer, Titus. Since Paul has clearly told Titus to meet him in Troas or, if he was not there, in Macedon, it would hardly have been possible for Titus to keep Paul's changed travel plan a secret from the Corinthians. This meant that Paul had to give them the bad news himself, in the letter or via an oral communication from Titus. So in the course of delivering Paul's severe letter to them, on a matter that was successfully resolved, Titus has brought the Corinthians further cause for disappointment that Paul needs to address in 2 Corinthians.

Fully informed by Titus of the complex situation in Corinth, Paul writes 2 Corinthians. As he does so, he is preparing to send him and two brothers back to Corinth to finalize the collection prior to his own arrival in the city (2 Cor. 8.16-24). This will be his third visit to the city (12.14; 13.1), a fact that corresponds closely with the history of his interaction set out earlier.

We know from Rom. 15.22-29 that Paul did make this foreshadowed third visit to Corinth and that it was successful: he gathered the collection for delivery to Jerusalem and completed his work there.

The integrity of 2 Corinthians: General considerations

A central issue of existing research into 2 Corinthians is the belief, widely held among scholars, that the letter as we have it is not as Paul composed it, but is rather a composite of other Pauline letters or letter fragments. This line of thinking was inaugurated by Johann Salomo Semler in his work *Paraphrasis II: Epistolae ad Corinthios* in 1776. Semler divided the letter into three parts: (i) 1–8, plus 13.11-13 and Romans 16; (ii) 9 and (iii) 10–13.10 (Thrall 1994: 3–4). Once the idea of 2 Corinthians being a composite letter was out, there was simply no stopping it: 'With Semler the dam had broken, releasing a mighty flood which swept scholars of all persuasions and schools into a debate on partition theories of 2 Corinthians and other Pauline letters for the next two hundred years' (Betz 1985: 4). Throughout this time, now nearly 250 years, the two (alleged) seams most often detected in the letter have been between 2 Corinthians 1–9 and 10–13 (the most widely accepted discontinuity) and between 2 Corinthians 8 and 9. As noted earlier, both ideas originated with Semler. After Semler, further doubts arose, especially as to the unity of 2 Corinthians 1–7 (with suspicion falling on 2.12–7.4 as an interpolation), while 6.14–7.1 was frequently viewed as a late intruder (possibly not even by Paul).[7] Yet pointing to these four major foci of the discussion hardly does justice to the efflorescence of partition theories concerning 2 Corinthians. Some scholars found two letters in 2 Corinthians, 1–9 and 10–13, with some dating 10–13 after 1–9 and some earlier (the latter often seeing it as the 'severe' letter Paul refers to in chs 1–7). Some found three letters or more (in various and different ways). Margaret Mitchell found five, and has been followed in her division and reordering by Calvin Roetzel in his commentary (Mitchell 2005; Roetzel 2007; Mitchell 2020: 104). Johannes Weiss found six (1959: 356–7). Walter Schmithals found nine (1971). Thrall (1994: 47–9) and Land (2015: 7–30) have usefully summarized the various positions. As far as partitionists are concerned, it is almost a case of *quot homines tot sententiae*, a position that does not inspire confidence in the likelihood of any particular partition theory being correct. On the other hand, there have always been many scholars who have regarded 2 Corinthians as a unity, and that position has been increasing in popularity in the last two decades.[8]

When I began research into 2 Corinthians in 2009, I had no firm view as to whether 2 Corinthians was best viewed as a unified letter existing in the form that Paul had written it, or as a composite work. The initial social-scientific perspective I brought to the text, however, the new theory of how group leadership operated by leading social identity theorist John Turner (2005, discussed later in the chapter), chimed very closely with the organization of 2 Corinthians in its traditional form. Over the years of working with the text, moreover, I have grown increasingly convinced both of its integral character and of the weakness of the arguments advanced to defend central propositions of the partitionists' case, especially the two most prominent partitionist ideas that chs 10–13 do not follow naturally from chs 1–9 and the proposal that chs 8 and 9 do not hang closely together but reflect different letters. Yet since my views have been reached following close engagement with the text, I will leave detailed discussion of the arguments to appropriate places in the commentary, especially in relation to 1–7, 6.14–7.1, 8–9 and 10–13. At this stage, however, I will restrict myself to four general observations on partition theories that underpin my rejection of them, while

---

[7] On the authenticity of 6.14–7.1, see Esler 2021d.
[8] Thrall (1994: 49) lists Klöpper, Hilgenfeld, Holtzmann, Denney, Heinrici, Bousset, Bachmann, Menzies, Goudge, Lietzmann, Allo, Hughes, Kümmel, Stephenson, Bates, Hyldahl, Young and Ford, Wolff. To this list we may now add Bieringer 1994a, 1994b and 1994c, Scott 1998, Garland 1999, Lambrecht 1999, Hafemann 2000, Hall 2003, Matera 2003, Seifrid 2014 and Land 2015. A number of scholars have also begun employing close attention to the rhetorical aspects of the letter, examined within Greco-Roman views on rhetoric, as a way of demonstrating its unity; see, for example, Witherington 1995 and Long 2004.

recognizing the variety of ways that critics appeal to the text of 2 Corinthians to argue for and against its unity, as Land has explained (2015: 7–30).

Firstly, all advocates of partition theories must imagine that at some point in antiquity, quite early in the history of the Christ-movement, someone sat down with a collection of Paul's letters, perhaps as many as nine of them. That person then very carefully cut away from most of them, and discarded, their introductions and closures, even though they would have contained precious information about individuals in the Christ-movement, and then pasted the remaining passages together in the form we now have. The outcome of this exercise obviously made sense to someone in antiquity, for we have '2 Corinthians', and it was presumably adapted to some communicative purpose in some particular context, and this in spite of the discontinuities that the composition is alleged to contain. Yet, if this text did satisfy someone in antiquity in such circumstances, why need we postulate such an outlandish process? Why not simply assume that the ancient person who produced this text and to whom it originally made sense was Paul himself?

Secondly, there is no manuscript evidence that 2 Corinthians and its constituent parts ever existed other than in the form we now have. The history of the text is curious. The failure of Clement of Rome (writing at the end of the first century CE) to cite 2 Corinthians, even though he regularly cites 1 Corinthians is surprising, especially when the revolt against authority in Corinth to which Clement was responding bore similarities to 2 Corinthians. Yet Clement's probable apparent lack of acquaintance with 2 Corinthians does not negate the Pauline composition of the letter as to form, style and content (Furnish 1984: 29–30). Nor is this issue relevant to the question of partition, since Clement's failure to cite any part of 2 Corinthians is also a failure to cite any of the individual letters of which it is allegedly composed. The earliest reference to the letter is in the Muratorian Canon of 140–50 CE, while the oldest textual evidence of 2 Corinthians is found in Papyrus 46. Here the text is complete, although the relevant leaves are shared by the Chester Beatty Library in Dublin and the University of Michigan. Papyrus 46 is probably to be dated to the period 175–225 CE (Griffin 1996). Thereafter every manuscript of 2 Corinthians maintains the contents and order that appear in Papyrus 46. There is no sign in the manuscript tradition of a separate tradition of the two, three, four, five or nine or however many letters are postulated as making up 2 Corinthians. Although the manuscript evidence is often dismissed by those in favour of partition, this is a non-trivial finding. It was quite likely that, if constituent parts of 2 Corinthians had enjoyed some prior existence before ending up in that text via a cut-and-paste operation, some textual trace of them would have survived. After all, this was what happened with Paul's epistle to the

Romans. The manuscript tradition reveals that shorter forms of Romans, some even lacking ch. 16, existed in the early church, as carefully discussed by Harry Gamble (1977). Yet there is no trace of any such major textual variations as far as 2 Corinthians is concerned.

Thirdly, no Patristic writer ever suggested that 2 Corinthians was anything other than an integral Pauline letter. None of them ever discerned the alleged 'literary seams', 'gaps in narrative sequence' or 'the contradictions' that have been detected by some modern interpreters, as Roetzel has described them (2007: 25). Now one might answer this by observing that the whole course of historical criticism of the biblical texts since the seventeenth century has, inevitably, involved uncovering issues not appreciated by ancient authors. Yet there are some circumstances where that rejoinder carries little, if any, sway. Let us take as our example the transition from the end of 2 Corinthians 9 to 2 Corinthians 10–13. This transition is the most popular discontinuity relied upon for the view that 2 Corinthians is a composite. Numerous modern commentators and critics express the view that the shift in 'tone' is so abrupt that chs 10–13 must have come from some other Pauline letter; Paul himself, it is declared, could not have produced this transition where chs 1–9 were followed by these four chapters. I do not need to refer to any of these scholars here; readers of this volume can test the truth of the previous sentence themselves. Just ask a group of people familiar with 2 Corinthians whether it is an integral or composite document. A proportion will reply 'composite' and, when asked why, most will say, in words roughly to the following effect: 'Well, at the very least the abrupt transition in tone at the start of ch. 10 that continues through to ch. 13 shows this section belonged to a different letter.' Indeed, this opinion is a cliché in modern New Testament scholarship. In short, the claim for a shift of 'tone' at the start of ch. 10 is the most common argument advanced for the most widely accepted aspect of the partition theories.[9] A demonstration that this particular argument is untenable should make one highly suspicious of the whole partitionist enterprise.

Let us now attempt such a demonstration. Firstly, we should tidy up our terminology, since 'tone' itself is problematic; indeed, Land was able to comment as late as 2015 that 'nowhere in the debate has anyone attempted to clearly define what is meant by "tone" or how it is manifested in Paul's written

---

[9] I respectfully part company from Welborn's suggestion (2011: xx) that it is not so much the change of tone that causes scholars to doubt the original connection of chs 1–9 to 10–13 as the differences in content; this is certainly Welborn's reasonable position but not that of a majority of scholars. Welborn is, however, right in asserting that the discovery of alleged, serious, particular inconsistencies between what Paul says in chs 1–9 and in chs 10–13 represents a separate area of evidence for partition. In the commentary I will argue that there are no such inconsistencies.

words (2015: 23)'. Unbeknown to Land, Douglas Campbell had addressed the meaning of 'tone' only a year earlier:

> strictly speaking, tone is a nontextual or paralinguistic dimension added to a written text by its presenter at the time of its performance, and we can supply very different tones to the same texts through different performances of them, as any actor will attest. It is more accurate, then, to speak of a *rhetorical* shift in a certain, quite specific sense.

Campbell goes on to suggest that the shift at 10.1 is not merely abrupt, but that it represents a change in textual direction and in persuasive strategy 'with an aggressive and even sarcastic argumentation'.[10] I fully agree. So would many modern critics; it is the reason why they think chs 10–13 must come from another Pauline letter. But let us test this proposition with reference to St John Chrysostom. Chrysostom, who has left the richest literary legacy of any Greek father, was born around 350 CE and died in 407 CE. He studied rhetoric and philosophy as a youth (possibly under Libanius). Ordained a priest in 386 CE, in the next decade he established a reputation as one of the greatest orators the church has ever known (Mayer and Allen 2017). It was precisely because of this eloquence built upon his rhetorical knowledge and expertise that he acquired the name 'Chrysostom' ('golden-mouth'). His set of *Homilies* on 2 Corinthians is 'the oldest preserved continuous expository treatment in Greek' of the text (Mitchell 2020: 112). Yet here is how Chrysostom begins his *Homily 21* on what we call 2 Corinthians 10.1-6.

> When he has completed the discourse about almsgiving in a manner that was fitting, and has showed that he loves them more than he is loved, and has described the particulars of his endurance and trials, he then opportunely (εὐκαίρως) engages in more critical statements, alluding to the false apostles, concluding the discourse with more wearisome matters and recommending himself. For he makes that his concern throughout the letter.[11]

So here we have the greatest rhetorician of the early church describing the transition from ch. 9 to ch. 10 as occurring 'opportunely', or 'at an opportune time' (εὐκαίρως), as Paul 'engages in more critical statements, alluding to the

---

[10] Campbell 2014: 99 (emphasis original). Campbell actually speaks of a 'sudden change' but I will argue in the commentary that Paul has been preparing his audience for this change since ch. 2.
[11] My translation.

false apostles'.[12] Not only did Chrysostom see nothing discordant in Paul's taking up a new subject here but, on the contrary, he praised the apostle for the way he did it – it was executed 'opportunely'. Moreover, Chrysostom makes this statement in a passage where he summarizes the major topics of the letter and obviously finds nothing discordant about their range or combination. He is commending the way Paul has managed the rhetorical structuring of his argument. This is not an area in which modern historical criticism puts New Testament critics in a better position to make a judgement than Chrysostom. On the contrary, he lived and breathed the assessment and creation of successful rhetoric in the ancient Mediterranean and they do not. How can any individual modern interpreter possibly prefer his or her opinion on this matter to that of Chrysostom? This is a contest that only Chrysostom can win. The circumstance that numerous modern critics express views opposite to that of Chrysostom does not affect this conclusion. A negative integer multiplied repeatedly produces a smaller, not a larger, number. Indeed, the sheer number of those who hold this identical view on the transition to chs 10–13 is problematic. It raises the likelihood that the opinion is sustained by groupthink (Janis 1972) that can survive only by ignoring the potent evidence to the contrary provided by Chrysostom. The correct view is that the last four chapters serve a vital role in the letter. Paul is extremely angry, not really with the Corinthians themselves but with the interlopers. He has good reason to be angry – inter alia, they have come to Corinth with a Gospel different from his, criticize him and his ministry, and seek payment for their evangelism. He intimated as early as 2 Cor. 2.17–3.18 that he would attack them and now he does. He has reconciled himself to the Corinthians (chs 1–7) and sorted out the collection (chs 8–9); now, at this εὔκαιρος moment, he proceeds to the third aspect of the four-part exigence of his letter: dealing with the intruders who are putting his mission at Corinth at risk. John Chrysostom saw the good order in all this and so too should we.

Fourthly, it is worth considering how serious a step it is, and therefore perhaps one not lightly undertaken, for an interpreter to treat 2 Corinthians as a composite of letter fragments. Calvin Roetzel, following the courage of his convictions in relation to his acceptance of Mitchell's five-part partition theory, rearranges the order of the letter according to its alleged constituent letters and comments upon its contents as follows (2007: 7–10): (1) letter of appeal for the offering (8.1–24); (2) first letter in defence of Paul's ministry (2.14–7.4); (3) second letter of defence: the letter of tears (10.1–13.10); (4) reconciling letter (1.1–2.13; 7.5–16; 13.11–13); (5) offering letter to the

---

[12] See O'Mahony 2001: 52 for a valuable recognition of the importance of Chrysostom's *Homily 21* for its view on 2 Corinthians 10–13, from which I have greatly benefited.

churches in Achaia (9.1-15). The reader is asked to assimilate a series of Pauline fragments with little, if any, argumentative connection between them, even though Roetzel comments on those fragments with great insight and lucidity. The consequence of this, and other reorderings, some less thoroughgoing (e.g. Bultmann 1985), is that one forfeits any understanding of the totality of the letter, if 2 Corinthians is as Paul wrote it. If this was a letter with a pervasive communicative purpose, we will never know what it might have been. This matters not only on the theological level, in that it challenges the canonical status of the work as a Pauline letter. It is also profoundly worrying for historical reasons. If 2 Corinthians is as Paul left it, it must have conformed to his ongoing relationship with the Corinthian Christ-followers and other sections of the Christ-movement of his day. While disentangling those connections is difficult, once we begin to partition the letter, the prospect of reaching a real understanding of the relationship rapidly recedes or disappears entirely. Nor can we easily appreciate Paul's total communicative aim and strategy in ways that may bear upon the contemporary practice of leadership inside or outside the church.[13]

Margaret Mitchell has recently observed that 'neither unity nor division has an inherent probability or default setting for any Pauline letter but must be argued for' (2020: 106). My general view is that the default setting for 2 Corinthians is that it is a unity, but perhaps I have partially proved her point by needing to argue to reach that conclusion! That argument will continue in the commentary as I critically assess the principal arguments that have been advanced for 2 Corinthians being a composite work and find them all wanting. This will be a subsidiary task to offering a social identity reading of the letter, but yet a related and important one.

The social identity approach in biblical interpretation: Explanation and justification

Prior to applying the social identity approach to 2 Corinthians, it is worthwhile briefly to explain and justify its methodology as a notably useful component within the wider task of social-scientific biblical interpretation. Occasional reflection on the foundations of methodologies we employ is an essential feature of academic research. In addition, even after its twenty-

---

[13] See Esler 2014c for a brief ecclesiological reflection on Paul's exercise of leadership in 2 Corinthians.

five years of use in biblical interpretation, and the numerous publications employing social identity theory that have appeared (in growing numbers in recent years), some interpreters still have reservations about its suitability for the task. Thus, in 2011 John Barclay expressed scepticism towards the use of the social identity approach in biblical interpretation:

> This form of social analysis is based on necessarily artificial experiments on modern subjects, and its applicability across time and culture is extremely uncertain. (2011a: 6–7, fn. 10)

Taking up this challenge will allow me both to set out more clearly the nature of social identity approach within the wider context of social-scientific interpretation and to demonstrate that there is a good answer to be made to this criticism.

There are five major issues with Barclay's view:

1. It assumes that the use of social sciences in biblical interpretation is nomic; that is, it involves the application of social laws to biblical data to explain the latter as an illustration of the former.
2. It assumes that social identity theory involves a direct extrapolation from laboratory experiment to the lived experience of groups, when this is a hotly contested topic among social identity psychologists themselves.
3. It overlooks the fact the social identity theory is not based solely on laboratory experimentation but is multi-methodological.
4. Although much social psychological theory is decontextualized, social identity theory is not like this. It asks what aspects of culture matter in any given situation. It is very interested in context.
5. Like someone insisting it is aerodynamically impossible for bees to fly, it is a meta-critical position that fails to engage with biblical interpretation that applies the social identity approach, thereby avoiding confrontation with the results of the enterprise that might undermine arguments against its usefulness.

I will deal with these issues in turn.

Social-scientific biblical interpretation as heuristic and interpretative, not nomic

Long ago I had occasion to oppose the view of Edwin Judge that 'social models' that had been 'defined in terms of other cultures' should not be imported into

New Testament studies and that social-scientific models should not be used in historical research unless they had been thoroughly tested 'for historical validity' (Esler 1987: 13–14). My main criticism was that Judge was viewing models as 'something akin to social laws' rather than as research tools, or mental constructs (Esler 1987: 14). I suggested that there were no social laws (1987: 6 [citing Mills 1978: 166], 11–12), a position I still hold, and the same point had been made by John Elliott even earlier in the development of social-scientific biblical interpretation (1981: 9). In addition, tools are either useful or not; they cannot be tested for validity, that is, verified. In suggesting that the 'applicability' of social identity theory 'across time and culture is extremely uncertain', Barclay, I submit, is essentially repeating Judge's position. He sees this as a theory in need of verification, and that is to attribute to it a nomic status that does not accord with the way it is used in biblical interpretation. The use of social-scientific ideas (including social identity theory) to interpret biblical texts is a heuristic, not a nomic, exercise (Elliott 1993). It has two aspects: first, it allows us (rather than just relying on folk psychology) to put to biblical data new questions derived from the social sciences; and, secondly, it facilitates our situating the answers the texts provide to those questions within social realistic frameworks of meaning, a process akin to 'drawing lines between the dots'. It certainly does not, however, allow us to use modern social theory to fill holes in ancient data (Esler 1987: 12, 14).

The nature of experiment in social identity theory

Barclay is fully justified in nominating experiment, that is, laboratory experiment, as central to social identity theory. Social psychologists distinguish between experimental and non-experimental methods for conducting the empirical testing of hypotheses. Experiment is now the main way that social psychologists go about gathering empirical information (Hogg and Vaughan 2005: 10). Yet this was not always the case. It was only during the 1950s and 1960s that experiment acquired dominance: whereas in 1949 in the prestigious *Journal of Personality and Social Psychology* 30 per cent of articles were based on experiment, by 1969 this had become 87 per cent (Gergen 1978: 508).

An experiment consists of testing a hypothesis in which one element ('the independent variable') is modified to measure what effect this has on a second element ('the dependent variable'). For example, a researcher might seek to determine the influence of watching violent television programmes (= independent variable) on aggression among children (= dependent variable).

By randomly assigning a group of children into two groups, one of whom watches violent programmes and the other non-violent programmes, one can then test for aggression. Yet it is necessary to filter out all other possible contributors to aggression for the result to be valid (Hogg and Vaughan 2005: 9–10).

In 1981, social identity psychologist John Turner offered a significant defence of experimental method against those who took the view 'that the laboratory experiment is an inherently artificial setting and hence it cannot but produce artificial behaviour'. He suggested this view meant that 'experimental social psychology can neither be generalized to nor applied in the spontaneously complex conditions of social reality'. Hence, according to these critics, 'laboratory experimentation is an intellectually futile activity' and this factor excuses 'any reluctance to learn how its results might be applied' (Turner 1981: 7). Barclay's wariness towards the 'necessarily artificial experiments on modern subjects' conducted by social identity psychologists means he shares this negative view.

Central to Turner's defence of experimentation was the argument that the whole point of experiments was their artificiality. He observed that laboratory experiments 'are constructed to generate singular, artificial events which neither duplicate nor are representative of real-world happenings' (1981: 15). They are 'artificial' in that they tend to be either unnaturally isolated or extremely innovative. This type of causal analysis 'is not intended to simulate reality but to discover the theoretical significance of important variables as a first step towards predicting natural events' (1981: 16). Artificial effects 'play a positive, creative role in disconfirming received wisdom and stimulating new ways of thinking' (1981: 20).

Nevertheless, in an important article on John Turner published in 2012, Steve Reicher and colleagues observed that Turner regarded theoretical debates in social identity as important but that 'External referentiality must always be our ultimate yardstick' (2012: 348). They encapsulated Turner's 1981 essay on experiment as to the effect that he argued:

> the issue is not so much why people behave as they do in any given experiment, but rather whether the models we build to explain that behaviour help us understand what happens outside our experiments. The point is not to understand why people allocate points to each other, but to understand when and why we discriminate or else challenge discrimination. (Reicher et al. 2012: 348)

Social identity theory was developed to explain Tajfel's famous 'minimal group' experiments that are alluded to in the previous quotation; it is a serious error to regard the experiments as a test of the theory (Reicher et al. 2012: 349). The minimal group experiments indicated that merely allocating people to a group, where the members did not know or interact with each other, was enough to produce discrimination against outgroups (Tajfel et al. 1971). At first sight, the minimal group experiments might produce the conclusion that conflict between groups was natural and inevitable. This was soon realized to be wrong. Instead, the findings generated ideas of social categorization and social comparison and the notion of social identity itself: with its cognitive, emotional and evaluative dimensions (Reicher et al. 2012: 350). This can be seen clearly in the way the theory developed. In their joint publication in 1979, Tajfel and Turner noted their strong interest in low-status groups: they regarded the concept of social identity as 'primarily of interest as an intervening variable in the process of social change' (Reicher et al. 2012: 352). This meant that 'An enquiry that starts off looking at discrimination ends up by addressing social change'. Experiments that suggest groups are a problem finally identify them as the solution (Reicher et al. 2012: 353).

Moreover, when one looks at the minimal group experiments, they resist the kind of simplification, or even fetishization, to which they have subsequently been subjected. It was clear, in the experiments themselves, for example, that sometimes a sense of justice held by the participants acted as a restraint on discrimination. In short, the minimal group experiments did not reflect 'some supposed universal principle of group psychology (an understanding of the implications of the minimal group studies routinely encouraged by textbooks)'. Rather, 'differentiation emerges as an interactive product of human motivations and social realities'. Furthermore, 'whether or not differentiation results in negative treatment of the outgroup depends on what is valued within a group's belief system' (Reicher et al. 2012: 351).

This latter factor explains the cultural variation we observe in cross-cultural applications of the minimal group experiments. Attempts in New Zealand in the late 1970s and early 1980s with Maori and Pacific Island children to replicate the minimal group experiment found the children 'chose to maximize the *joint profit* of both groups rather than maximize ingroup profit or the difference between groups. They did not consistently discriminate' (Weatherall 1996: 278–9; emphasis original). This was consistent with the way in which cooperative and competitive patterns are inbuilt in Maori and Pacific Island cultures (1996: 279). Yuki reported similar issues in some East Asian cultures (2003). Yet minimal group experiments still remain a powerful tool in research into social categorization (Otten 2016), including in relation to leadership, so long as the cultural context in which they are being conducted is taken carefully into account (Falk et al. 2014; Lee et al. 2015; van Dick and Kerschreiter 2016). Speaking more generally, Hopkins and Reicher have cogently argued that because social identity theory respects culture and cultural difference, it has a continuing value in exploring the practices of identity in the behaviour of any group (2011).

Some social identity theorists see experiment as a part of a process that ultimately results in the production of 'general laws from the conceptual meanings of the observed effects' (Turner 1981: 17). Tajfel himself aimed at the discovery of 'law-like processes' that he assumed were generating observable social patterns (Weatherall 1996: 275). But many other psychologists in the social identity tradition, while actively conducting experiments, do not aim at the elucidation social laws; they regard that as too mechanical an understanding of what they are doing. In 1996, Margaret Weatherall mounted a critique of Tajfel's dependence on laboratory experiment in an argument devoted to 'breaking the stranglehold of the experimental method in social psychology' (282).

For unlike the position in the natural sciences, it is doubtful that social psychology, through experiment or any other method, can discover laws that are valid across time. The reason for the difference is that in social psychology the objects of the study, human beings, have agency: they are actively attaching meaning and significance to their own actions. This means that social psychology cannot be sharply distinguished from what it studies. What appear to be laws may prove to have very limited temporal validity as people modify both their behaviour and how they understand it (Manstead and Semin 2001: 108).

Yet in the decades since Tajfel's death in 1983, most social identity theorists have continued to find laboratory experiment an essential tool in their research. It is submitted that, although social laws do not exist, this still leaves a wide range of human activities where roughly predictable patterns of human behaviour are observable and susceptible to observation and theory formation. Max Weber, who opposed the notion of laws in sociology (an idea that originated in the positivism of Auguste Comte), nevertheless did subscribe to the idea of 'typical probabilities confirmed by observation to the effect that under certain conditions an expected course of social action will occur, which is understandable in terms of the typical motives and typical subjective intentions of the actors' (1964: 107–8; Esler 2006a: 4–8). Social psychology has proved itself remarkably adept in the identification of such probabilities, and experiment has continued to play a central role in this process.

Finally, those who are sceptical of the value of what Barclay accurately describes as 'necessarily artificial experiments', while disengaged from their practice and results, presumably have some defensible basis for preferring their view to that of the hundreds, if not thousands, of social psychologists across the world who find them useful in the larger task of understanding human nature, for providing cogent reasons for why they know more than those actually engaged in the process.

Social identity theory is multi-methodological

Social identity theory embraces a number of methods in addition to laboratory experimentation. They include field studies, case studies, surveys and archival research (Hogg and Vaughan 2005: 13–14).

Field studies are often used in association with experiment. Van Knippenberg and Hogg have noted that the connection between leadership and prototypicality has been demonstrated not only in the laboratory but in more naturalistic, field settings (2003: 253). Similarly, in their research into prototypicality in leadership Ulrich et al. included a field study 'to strengthen the generalizability of our findings' (2009: 239). So too did Steffens et al. in a similar project, using a natural group consisting of employees questioned about their bosses in an online survey (2015).

Sometimes field studies can be undertaken, however, without laboratory experiment. Thus, social identity psychologists used ethnographic observation, semistructured interviews and questionnaires with pilgrims attending the month-long winter Hindu religious festival, the Magh Mela (Pandey et al. 2014; Khan et al. 2016).

Of the greatest importance is that much social identity research, including in the area of leadership, proceeds by way of the qualitative analysis of documents and not by the direct application of experimental method. The documents can be contemporary (or roughly so) with the research or historical in nature. Stephen Reicher and colleagues have produced a number of studies using this method, for example: on speeches made by Prime Minister Margaret Thatcher and Opposition Leader Neil Kinnock during the British miners' strike in 1984–5 (Reicher and Hopkins 1996); in numerous illustrations in a book on nationalism (Reicher and Hopkins 2001); on Bulgaria's (successful) efforts to protect its Jewish population from the Nazis in the Second World War (Reicher et al. 2006); on the dispute over women's ordination in the Anglican church (Sani and Reicher 2000); on how Donald Trump won the 2016 US presidential election (Reicher and Haslam 2017); and on how British political leaders mobilized people in relation to immigration in the period preceding the vote to leave the European Union (Portice and Reicher 2018). Reicher's highly revealing analysis of historical documentation from the perspective of social identity theory represents a close analogy to the use of this theory in the interpretation of biblical texts.

Social identity theory, culture and context

In the last two decades, there has been some resistance to the utility of talking about group identities, including ethnic groups, a line of thought particularly represented in the writings of Rogers Brubaker (Brubaker and Cooper 2000; Brubaker et al. 2004; Brubaker 2006). To the extent that groups or group identities have in some quarters been essentialized or even reified that is a useful corrective. As Hopkins and Reicher have argued (2011: 36), however, this work is reason to be more careful about how concepts like 'group' or 'identity' are used, not for jettisoning them altogether. What is needed is 'an analytic framework that captures the reality of group life and social identities that groups support without assuming such groups and identities are givens'.

Social identity theory provides such a framework. It shows how identities are dependent on group processes in a manner that highlights the ways that individuals categorize themselves and how these self-categorizations shape cognition and behaviour. In addition, it focuses on how culture and context affect the manner in which self-categorizations are triggered (2011: 37). This will prove to be a highly significant aspect of this commentary since the distinctive culture of the first-century Mediterranean world (speaking at a high level of generality), especially the role of honour as the primary value (Malina 2001; Esler 2011a: 35–76), will appear repeatedly as the context shaping what Paul is seeking to communicate.

The initial phenomenon addressed in social identity theory, intergroup differentiation, is not specific behaviour but a process. The outcomes of such a process depend upon the norms and values of the relevant entity (Reicher 2004). In other words, the behavioural products of the process reflect how the ingroup defines its identity, and here the critical point is that 'identities are neither given nor fixed but constructed in and through argument' (Hopkins and Reicher 2011: 38). The role of argument in social psychology has been subject to illuminating analysis by Michael Billig (1996).

It is also through social processes that the norms and values that provide content to any particular identity are subject to continual reappraisal and contestation. Those advocating such reassessment are often motivated by the desire to bring about change in the way that the group acts in its social context so as to create new modes of living, and being and relating to others, including at the national level (Reicher and Hopkins 2001):

> In other words, people's talk of identity should be understood as having a performative and constitutive dimension, and as organised to encourage the forms of action that would realise a particular vision of how the social world should be. (Hopkins and Reicher 2001: 38)

This position is thoroughly comparable with what Paul was seeking to achieve in all his letters, including 2 Corinthians. So too is the likelihood that the claims of anyone seeking to speak authoritatively in this way 'are always controversial and attract counter-responses' (Hopkins and Reicher 2011: 40).

Biblical interpretation employing social identity theory

Although some critics (like John Barclay) question the use of social identity theory in biblical interpretation, there are many who do not. The earliest extended uses of SIT in NT interpretation appear to have been a paper I delivered at the British New Testament Conference in September 1994 (eventually published as Esler 2014b) and Esler 1996. I followed those with monographs on Galatians (1998) and Romans (2003a) and an article on the Parable of the Good Samaritan (Esler 2000). Meanwhile, other scholars began to pick up on the approach, in relation to both the Old and the New Testament. Particularly prominent were researchers in the Nordic countries, Finland especially, with Jutta Jokiranta, for example, applying the theory to the Dead Sea Scrolls (culminating in Jokiranta 2013) and Petri Luomanen to the New Testament (e.g. Luomanen 2007). Other early adopters were Atsuhiro Asano on Galatians (2005), Matthew Marohl on Hebrews (2008), Coleman Baker on Jeremiah (2008), Jan Bosman on Nahum (2009), Minna Shkul on Ephesians (2010), Brian Tucker on 1 Corinthians (2010a and 2010b), Barentsen on leadership in several New Testament letters (2011), Kuecker on Luke-Acts (2011), Ho on 1 Corinthians (2016) and Lim on 2 Corinthians (2017; 2020). In 2007, I applied the theory to First Cement. Baker (2012) provided an overview of the field.

In the last ten years, there has been something of a boom of interest among biblical researchers in the social identity approach. Brian Tucker has been particularly active during this period. In 2014, Tucker and Baker edited a collection of essays on all twenty-seven books of the New Testament, with most of the authors explicitly using social identity theory. In 2020, he and Kuecker edited a one-volume social identity commentary on the New Testament. But perhaps more indicative of the maturity of this subfield of biblical research is the number of monographs that have been published. In the New Testament, for example, there have been books on Pauline leadership in Corinth and Ephesus (Barentsen 2011), Luke-Acts (Kuecker 2011), Johannine Christianity (Hakola 2015), Paul's Corinthian correspondence (Lim 2017), 1 Corinthians (Tucker 2010a, 2010b, 2017) and Romans (Tucker 2018). In relation to the Old Testament, books have been published on Ruth (Lau 2011) and the Exodus (Stargel 2018). In 2020, Robert Brawley's *Luke: A Social Identity Commentary* appeared as the first volume in the new T & T Clark Social Identity Commentaries on the New Testament Series. Accordingly, there is no sign of biblical research using social identity theory abating, and, since social identity theorists are continually pushing the field in new directions, that circumstance is unlikely to change.

2

The social identity approach to leadership

Overview

Leadership has been defined as 'the process of influencing others in a manner that enhances their contribution to the realization of group goals' (Haslam 2001: 58). So expressed, it is clear that successful leadership depends upon creating followership. It is fundamentally a process of social influence: someone with no influence has no followers and therefore cannot be a leader. The social identity approach to leadership offers a distinctive explanation for how this happens. It has particular application where the group in question is 'a chronically central or situationally salient anchor for one's social identity' (Hogg et al. 2012: 292). It differs from other approaches to leadership that focus on the individual characteristics of the leader and instead proposes that influence comes from having and exhibiting ingroup, and not outgroup, norms and attitudes that form part of the group identity. Since ingroup norms are most likely to be held by ingroup members, such people will be more influential than members of outgroups (Platow et al. 2006: 305). In short, the social identity approach maintains that leadership is a group phenomenon and that successful leaders mobilize followers 'to the extent that they successfully manage a group identity that they share with followers' (Steffens et al. 2015: 181).

From this perspective, the ability to lead depends on the ability to represent a group consensus that itself is produced by a shared identity:

> Where there is no group and no consensus every other voice represents a threat to one's own. But where there is a group and there is a consensus then one voice can speak for all. (Reicher et al. 2005: 555)

This means that leaders and followers are bound together in two ways: first, their relationship is dependent on a shared social identity; and, secondly, their relationship depends on their agreeing to a group consensus and who best represents it. Thus, 'Leadership is a process of mutual influence that revolves around a partnership in a social self-categorical relationship' (Reicher et al. 2005: 555, citing Haslam 2001: 85).

This approach meshes well with the fundamental characteristic of leadership to be a transformative process:

> It involves changes in the self-understanding of people and also in the nature of the social world . . . these two forms of change are interdependent since identities are models of how the world is and how it should be. (Reicher et al. 2005: 564)

Recent social identity literature on leadership has focused on four distinct though interacting aspects of leadership, all of which play a role in its transformative nature. These four aspects are: prototypicality and exemplarity, identity advance, entrepreneurship, and impressarioship.

Yet while ideas of prototypicality have been a major interest in social identity research into leadership since its inception around 2000, less research has been conducted into the other three aspects. These areas, however, although not completely neglected, have recently begun to attract considerable attention and are now regularly added to prototypicality to produce a more rounded explanation of the phenomenon of leadership. One recent publication has even developed an 'Identity Leadership Inventory' to allow a more focused examination of all four aspects (Steffens et al. 2014). I will now consider each in turn, with most attention paid to prototypicality (and the related phenomenon of exemplarity). As we will see in the commentary, there are data in 2 Corinthians that respond to analysis in relation to all four aspects.

Prototypicality and exemplarity

Prototypicality

According to Elizabeth Castelli, the identification of imitation with the 'drive toward unity and nondifference' is apparent in Paul's writings. In addition, the language of imitation 'masks the will to power which one finds in Pauline discourse'. The discourse of mimesis 'identifies the fundamental values of wholeness and unity with Paul's own privileged position vis-à-vis the gospel, the early communities he founded and supervises, and Christ himself. Here is precisely where he makes his coercive move'. To stand for anything else is to opt for difference, which is associated with discord and disorder, and to oppose the gospel, the community and Christ (1991: 87). The role of prototypicality in the social identity perspective on leadership offers a different interpretation to the negative view on Pauline mimesis taken by

Castelli. In this context, Paul's recommendations to imitate him represent one possible mechanism in the very common, indeed necessary, effort made by a leader to present himself or herself as prototypical of the values, beliefs and identity of the group.

The first, and still the most important, focus of the social identity approach to leadership concerns the 'prototypicality' of leaders (Hogg 2001; van Knippenberg and Hogg 2003). 'Exemplarity' has as yet not been a major feature of this research, and I will return to it later in the chapter. One of the major discoveries of social identity theory has been that leaders are more effective at eliciting followership if the members consider that they are 'prototypical' of the group they lead, that is, in manifesting what it means to be a member of the ingroup and in representing it in ways that differentiate it from outgroups.

Underlying this idea of prototypicality is that of self-categorization as originally explained by John Turner (1982). Turner argued that the psychological foundation for being a member of a group was the cognitive act of defining oneself as a member of that group (= the act of social identification). Having taken this step, the member then ascertains the attributes attached to group membership and aligns himself or herself with them. The people who are able to supply reliable information about the definition of group membership, especially those seen as prototypical of the group, are those who wield influence among the membership. These are often the group's leaders (Reicher et al. 2005: 551–2). This insight about the effect of prototypicality has long been part of the social identity theory of leadership and has been confirmed in a number of publications.[1] The evidence for the importance of prototypicality does not originate only in experiments. Van Knippenberg and Hogg (2003: 253) note that the connection between leadership and prototypicality has been demonstrated not only in the laboratory but in more naturalistic, field settings. This notion of prototypicality has already proven useful in understanding what Paul is seeking to achieve by his exercise of leadership in Romans, for example in Romans 7 (Esler 2003a: 222–42), and in various Pauline and pseudo-Pauline letters, including 2 Corinthians (Barentsen 2011).

To respond to the copious data in 2 Corinthians, the nature of prototypicality needs further explanation. Eleanor Rosch has noted that 'prototypes' of categories generally mean 'the clearest cases of category membership defined operationally by people's judgments of goodness of membership in the category'. Yet a prototype should not be reified 'as though

---

[1] As examples, see: Hogg 2001; Platow and van Knippenberg 2001; Turner and Haslam 2001; and Haslam, Reicher and Platow 2011: 77–108 and van Knippenberg 2011.

it meant a specific category member or mental structure' (1978: 36). Her understanding of a prototype as an *assemblage of attributes* emerges when she adds that the 'more prototypical of a category a member is rated, the more attributes it has in common with other members of the category and the fewer attributes in common with members of the contrasting categories' (1978: 37). 'To speak of a prototype at all is simply a convenient grammatical fiction; what is really referred to are judgments of degree of prototypicality. Only in some artificial categories is there by definition a literal single prototype' (Rosch 1978: 40). A prototype can also be defined as 'an abstract concept derived from multiple experiences with category members', a summary representation that captures the central tendency of the category in question (Smith and Zarate 1990: 245). Two social identity psychologists, writing in the initial stages of development of the social identity approach to leadership, offer greater detail of what a prototype means as applied to a group, and in so doing make clear that a prototype is not an average or lowest common denominator:

> The ingroup prototype is an abstract cognitive representation of 'us' that draws on immediate situational information that maximizes intergroup differences and ingroup similarity, but also draws on ingroup and intergroup memory and on past group history. The ingroup prototype describes and prescribes group membership appropriate attributes in a specific context. As such the prototype is closer to a representation of the ideal than typical group member (i.e. the prototypical group member is not the average group member). (van Knippenberg and Hogg 2003: 245)

In the course of a lengthy discussion on prototypes and groups, Michael Hogg and Joanne Smith (2007: 94–6) have made the following observation:

> People cognitively represent a social group (e.g., a nation, a religion, an organisation, a team) as a category prototype – a fuzzy set of attributes that are meaningfully inter-related, and simultaneously capture similarities within the group and differences between the group and other groups, or people who are not in the group.

They note that these 'attributes can include how people look, how they dress, how they speak, what they do, what they feel, and of course their attitudes towards objects, events, people, and so forth' (2007: 94). But they add that prototypes not only *describe* attributes but also *prescribe* what they ought to be. This is the vital normative dimension of prototypes: they embrace norms for behaviour, and one might add, although this has not traditionally been a major focus of the social identity approach (with the exception of the work by Daniel Bar-Tal [1990]), beliefs that members must hold to secure their membership in the group. A group prototype, however, is not a norm, because it is the members' cognitive representation of the normative properties of the group (Hogg et al. 2012: 262). A prototype is not the same as a norm for the further reason that it is an assemblage of a group attributes and will nearly always encompass more than one norm or even several norms, including features such as beliefs, attitudes and feelings characteristic of the group.

Most, if not all, New Testament texts contain data that respond to analysis as identifying attributes that the members would have regarded as prototypical of Christ-group identity. The Matthean beatitudes, for example, offer nine prototypical types of behaviour (Matt. 5.3-12). Some relate to normative actions and dispositions (such as being merciful, hungering and thirsting for righteousness, being pure in heart and making peace), and some to typical attitudes and experiences of the members (being poor in spirit, mourning, being persecuted for righteousness' sake, and being reviled and spoken against). While some of these characteristics were valorized in groups outside the Christ-movement, especially in the Judean ethnic group from which it arose (including the qualities of righteousness and mercy), these beatitudes are very distinctive in being collected together like this and also express prototypical beliefs of the Christ-movement, especially relating to the kingdom of heaven, their status as sons of God, and the coming erasure of their negative experiences and their replacement by various forms of blessedness in the future (Esler 2014b). More relevant to 2 Corinthians, where Christ-movement prototypicality is a lively issue throughout the text, are examples in other Pauline letters. In Rom. 12.9-21 Paul sets out a long sequence of characteristics of Christ-movement identity – which can appropriately be designated 'identity-descriptors' – beginning with ἀγάπη, the characteristic love of the Christ-movement, in which the prominence of aural effects, such as alliteration, assonance and even rhyme, which likely had a mnemonic function, suggests that this is a precious fragment of Paul's oral proclamation (Esler 2003a: 317–19). In Gal. 5.22-23, he lists a number of attributes under the heading 'fruits of the Spirit': love, joy, peace, patience, kindness, goodness, faithfulness, gentleness and self-control (Esler 1998: 226–30). These are all prototypical of the Christ-movement, and their ingroup dimension is reinforced by their being preceded by a list of antithetical 'works of the flesh' (5.19-21). A similar assemblage of prototypical attributes of Christ-movement identity occurs in 1 Thess. 5.12-22.

We will not be surprised, therefore, to find the enunciation of Christ-movement prototypicality a feature of 2 Corinthians. We may, however, not be prepared for the extent to which prototypicality is a field of contestation in the letter, especially in relation to being an apostle (ἀπόστολος). The role of ἀπόστολος is best regarded as a subgroup identity. They were a select few within the wider group of Christ-followers. They seem to have been characterized by certain features – 'the signs of the apostle' (τὰ σημεῖα τοῦ ἀποστόλου; 2 Cor. 12.12). Paul claimed to be an apostle of Christ Jesus (2 Cor. 1.1), but so did his opponents in Corinth. He labelled them 'false apostles' (ψευδαπόστολοι) who were pretending to be 'apostles of Christ' (2 Cor. 11.13). Being an apostle was the foundation for Paul's claim to exercise authoritative leadership; to this extent there is an element of his being a leader which does not depend on group processes but on external warrant from a supernatural source. There is really nothing like this in the social identity approach, except to the extent that the claim only functioned if his Christ-followers considered it was true. This is an instance of the fact, very common in social-scientific interpretation, that sometimes there is not a perfect fit between social theory and empirical data.

Exemplarity

In selecting the idea of prototypicality as the primary means by which members of a group access its unique identity, social identity psychologists have largely neglected an alternative means whereby we can specify the central tendency of a group or category. This is by the use of exemplars.

Robert Nosofsky, building on earlier research, offers an explicit contrast to categorization based on 'abstract summary representations of categories, such as rules or idealized prototypes' in the form of individual exemplars of categories (2011: 18). This means that rather than defining a class or group by assembling a collection of attributes of a typical member, one proffers an actual, existing member of the class or group to illustrate its nature. Nosofsky points out that '(w)hereas exemplar models assume that categories are represented in terms of individually stored exemplars, prototype models assume instead a single summary representation that is the central tendency of the individual exemplars' (2011: 30). There is a lively debate in psychology about which approach is more effective. Recent research, however, has suggested that it is often difficult to resolve the question of which of them provides a more effective access to social categories (Johansen et al. 2013). We do not need to resolve this debate between the two approaches. Earlier research indicated that people use both abstract collections of features and information from particular instances that they have in their memory to assess whether someone (or something) belongs to a particular category (Smith and Zarate 1990: 248–61). Evidence from the New Testament – where both approaches are observable – suggests that it is more helpful to view prototypes and exemplars as simultaneous and parallel ways to achieve this goal, as rightly observed by Porter (2019: 5).

We have already noted how Paul provides lists of identity-descriptors that characterize the prototypical Christ-follower, that is, descriptors possessed by all Christ-followers acting in alignment with the beliefs and values of the movement. Occasionally, however, he directs the attention of his audience to an exemplar of that identity, namely, himself. He does this most clearly when he offers himself up for imitation (1 Cor. 4.16; 11.1). He also proffers his own exemplarity for Christ-movement identity in relation to his attributes and (often very difficult) experiences, as we will see in 2 Corinthians. Another relevant feature of New Testament texts is the use of figures from the past, such as Abraham and Job. These are not exemplars in the full sense since Christ-followers have no actual experience of them, and can only access them through memory in texts or traditions. Nor, with the exception of Abraham (as in Galatians 3, Esler 2006b), are they necessarily enlisted into the Christ-movement. Often they are proposed essentially to illustrate one characteristic of Christ-movement identity, as when the endurance (ὑπομονή) of Job is endorsed as a group identity-descriptor in James 5.11 (Dancy 2021: 154). For this reason, it is perhaps better to regard them as being prototypes of the social identity of Christ-followers or prototypical of one dimension of it.

A difficult question is the extent to which Jesus Christ can be seen as an exemplar of the identity of the movement named after him. Barentsen suggests that Paul presents 'Jesus as the community prototype for every community member' (2011: 127). This seems certainly to be the case in relation to behavioural norms, such as the priority of love. Moreover, to the extent that the suffering of Jesus in a general sense is something shared by Paul and his Corinthian converts, that is accurate. On the other hand, very few Christ-followers would follow Jesus to crucifixion, and even if they did, their death would not have the same significance as his, so his being crucified could not be prototypical of the movement. The idea that Christ's crucifixion could only be experienced by analogy, and not as prototypical,[2] seems to have been recognized by Luke when changed 'let him take up his cross and follow me' (Mk 8.34) to 'let him take up his cross daily and follow me' (9.23). In addition, Christ has a status and role in the economy of salvation – being very close to or identical with God – that he does not share with his human followers, and to that extent he is neither an exemplar nor prototype of the group. The 'two natures' teaching the Council of Chalcedon was the outcome of early Christianity seeking to reconcile his human and divine dimensions.

---

[2] A distinction suggested by Kathy Ehrensperger during the 2020 SBL meeting.

Further dimensions of prototypicality and exemplarity

Subsequent research has further developed our understanding of prototypicality by showing that leaders need to represent and define social identity in context (Ellemers et al. 2004; Platow and van Knippenberg 2001). The most general dimension of context will inevitably be the wider culture in which the group finds itself. By a group's culture is meant

> the total, generally organized way of life, including language, knowledge, beliefs, values, norms, sanctions, institutions, art, custom, traditions, interests, ideologies, and artifacts that is proper to a given people, and that is passed on from generation to generation. (Elliott 1993: 128)

As noted in Chapter 1 of this volume, knowledge of the cultural context in which a group operates is vital to understanding the processes by which it creates and maintains its identity. In the (abundant) literature that relates social identity theory to the workplace, that most general level is the national culture (Lee and Koo 2015: 1052-3, 1056). In exploring 2 Corinthians, however, this dimension consists of the broader patterns of Mediterranean culture, especially those embodying the values of honour and shame and a collectivist, rather than individualist culture (Malina 2001; Esler 2011a: 35-76). In collectivist cultures, people are interdependent within their ingroups (such as family, tribe, ethnic group and so on) rather than autonomous, and they give priority to the goals of their ingroups rather than to their personal goals, act on the basis of ingroup norms, behave in a communal way and are especially concerned with relationships (Triandis 2001: 909). Many nations in the modern world also have a collectivistic culture similar to that of the ancient Mediterranean (Lee and Koo 2015: 1052-3; Triandis 1990, 1995 and 2001). One illustration of this is that there is now strong evidence that in collectivistic cultures staff employed by an organization tend to identify more strongly with it than in individualistic cultures (Lee and Koo 2015).

Finally, so powerful is the effect of a leader's prototypicality for group members that such prototypicality can act as a substitute for both intergroup distributive fairness (Platow and van Knippenberg 2001) and ingroup procedural fairness (Ulrich et al. 2009). This suggests that leaders who embody the group identity have considerable latitude in the way that they distribute resources or treat individual members. In addition, group members are more likely to regard a leader as charismatic if he or she is prototypical of the group (Platow et al. 2006). Thus, 'charisma may, indeed, be a special gift, but it is one bestowed on group members by group members for being representative of, rather than distinct from, the group itself' (Platow et al. 2006: 317). Finally, there is evidence that the performance of a leader in office and his or her prototypicality are interdependent:

> there is a need to recognize that appraisals of leader performance are conditioned by leader prototypicality, just as appraisals of leader prototypicality are conditioned by leader performance... it thus appears that leaders' success hinges upon a dual capacity to be ahead of followers in terms of performance but alongside them in terms of prototypicality. (Steffens et al. 2013: 612)

This view paves the way for the three other dimensions of leadership pursuant to the social identity approach.

Identity advancement

The second aspect of leadership within the social identity approach is 'identity advancement'. It was initially called 'group-oriented behaviour' and described as follows:

> Social identification with a group produces group-oriented motivation, and endorsement of leaders who are trusted to share this motivation. Leader prototypicality may be an important source of such trust in the leader, but it is not the only source. Irrespective of their prototypicality, leaders may display their group-oriented motivation through group-oriented attitudes and behavior. (van Knippenberg and Hogg 2003: 256)

Identity advancement thus refers to the way in which the capacity of leaders to elicit positive responses from followers is 'rooted in their capacity to promote shared social identity by advancing "our" (collective) interests (rather than their personal interests or those of an outgroup)' (Steffens et al. 2015: 182, citing Haslam et al. 2011). The identification of a leader with a group (= prototypicality) and his or her acting to advance its interests are likely to be positively associated but they are distinct. To take university leaders as an example, a vice chancellor or president who was an eminent academic on appointment may fail actively to promote the university's interests, whereas someone brought in from industry with no academic background may prove the university's most passionate defender. Recent research by Niklas Steffens and colleagues (2015) has explored identity advancement with reference to a laboratory experiment but also a field study using a natural group (employees questioned about their bosses in an online survey). This research shows that a leader identifying with a group, that is, demonstrating that he or she is *working for* the group, by standing up for it and by championing collective interests, represents a path to successful leadership in addition to prototypicality (= being *representative of* the group). Indeed, leaders who worked strongly for the interests of the group were able to inspire followership even if they were not particularly prototypical. Only a leader who had the interests of the group at heart, and not his or her personal interests or the interests of an outgroup, could satisfy this requirement. So strong was this effect that leaders who strongly advanced the group's interests were at times able to break its norms or act in ways regarded by the group as deviant without prejudicing their leadership position (Jetten et al. 2011 and 2014; Steffens et al. 2015: 188).

Identity entrepreneurship

The third aspect of leadership from a social identity perspective is identity entrepreneurship. The idea of 'entrepreneurs of identity' goes back to 1996 in research by Steve Reicher and Nick Hopkins into how Margaret Thatcher (then British prime minister) and Neil Kinnock (then leader of the opposition) sought to mobilize opinion in the United Kingdom during the long and bitter miners' strike of 1984–5.[3] The central insight of this aspect is that 'the construction of shared identity and associated notions of prototypicality are both negotiable and actively constructed by leaders'.[4] On this approach, leaders seek through their words and deeds to craft a sense of identity that is shared by the members. They establish and maintain a coherent sense of the group vis-à-vis outgroups. This entails defining the boundaries of the group and fleshing out the content of its identity (Steffens et al. 2014: 1004). The latter may involve invoking particular contexts or comparisons from the past or the present (Reicher et al. 2005).

Hogg et al. (2012: 277) have made the following observation:

> When group membership is salient people spend a great deal of time communicating directly or indirectly about group norms – this is how

---

[3] See Reicher and Hopkins 1996. This idea has been utilized to explain Paul's leadership in Romans (Esler 2003a: 38, 223).
[4] Steffens et al. 2014: 1004. For relevant literature, see Reicher and Hopkins 2001 and 2003 and Reicher et al. 2005.

norms are constructed, conveyed and learned (Hogg and Reid 2006; Hogg and Giles 2012). Prototypical leaders play a pivotal role in 'norm talk' as they have the most influential and effective voice within the group; through their rhetoric, they act as entrepreneurs of prototypicality and identity (Reicher and Hopkins 2003). They shape perceptions of the group's attributes and goals and of their own embodiment of group prototypical attributes, and are thus able to enhance their own leadership position, transform the group and mobilise its members. . . . To support this analysis Reicher and his associates have conducted research on the rhetoric and language that leaders use to exercise their leadership and convey their vision of the group's identity. . .

Barentsen aptly describes this process as painting a verbal picture of social identity (2011: 56).

Identity impresarioship

Identity impresarioship, a concept coined and developed by Haslam, Reicher and Platow (2011: 163–95), is the fourth aspect of leadership identified by the social identity approach. It concerns the necessity for leaders to 'embed' group identity, in particular, by delivering concrete outcomes for the group and acting in such a way as to 'make us matter'. Leaders engage in projects and activities that result in outcomes allowing the members of the group to live out their membership in a meaningful way. Typical means adopted by leaders to embed identity include erecting physical structures, establishing and/or implementing institutions and practices, formalizing rituals and organizing events that are related to the values of the groups they represent. Haslam, Reicher and Platow observe that achieving this will involve hard work. Yet in the end it is worth it. This 'is because those who have control over the definition of reality have a world-making and self-renewing power. The more they exercise that power in making the social world, the more they are able to continue doing so' (2011: 193).

Other dimensions of the social identity approach to leadership

When considering how prototypes (and exemplars) function in leadership, it is important to note that they are not fixed but fluid since they depend upon a context that inevitably changes over time. van Knippenberg and Hogg (2003: 260) express this as follows:

> In their attempts to use the group prototype to mobilize followers for their cause leaders need not accept the group prototype as fixed. The context-dependence of prototypes ensures that what is prototypical of the group may change over time, for instance because the intergroup comparative context has changed ... or because an organization's core business has changed.

The potential fluidity of what is prototypical of a group means that leaders have to actively construe and project themselves as prototypical in changing circumstances to accord with the group members' mobile perception of prototypicality (Reicher and Hopkins 2003). This activity will often involve discursive means, especially dialogue and argument. That will also be necessary in relation to persuading members in relation to matters falling with in identity advance, entrepreneurship and impressarioship. This dimension of leadership from a social identity viewpoint meshes closely with the omni-presence of rhetoric in the ancient Greco-Roman world as the formal means for mounting arguments on every conceivable issue. Although Paul was probably not as invested in the finer points of rhetoric as some scholars suggest (e.g. Betz 1979, 1985), it would have been impossible for him not to have been aware of and been influenced by the ways his contemporaries presented arguments in the varied contexts of the Greek cities of the East.

John Turner's critique of the standard theory of power and his proposal of a new theory

In 2005, John Turner published an article in which he argued that the accepted social psychological theory of power was beset with serious flaws and proposed a new theory in its place. When I first read Turner's article, it struck me that 2 Corinthians contained so much data that was responsive to Turner's theory that a closer investigation was warranted. It soon transpired that Turner's argument was deeply relevant to the question of whether or not 2 Corinthians was a unity as Paul had intended or a collection of letter fragments; the ease with which Turner's approach matched the canonical shape of the letter pushed towards the former option. This commentary seeks to bring Turner's theory, especially in relation to leadership, to service in the interpretation of 2 Corinthians.

Critique of the standard theory

Turner notes that the standard theory of power in social psychology runs like this: a person ('the influencing agent') controls resources (such as positive and negative outcomes; rewards and costs, information, etc.).[5] These resources are desired, valued or needed by others ('the subjects'), and this makes them dependent upon the influencing agent for the satisfaction of their needs or the attainment of their goals. This situation gives the influencing agent the capacity to influence them. The exercise of such influence represents power in action. Where the agent exercises influence by providing information or reducing uncertainty, the subjects may experience private acceptance, for example in the form of a change of attitude. Other kinds of influence are more social or goal-oriented in nature; these embody group pressure or compulsion and may lead only to public compliance by the subjects (2005: 1–2). Although influential for some fifty years, there are significant problems with this theory, and, by setting them out, Turner lays the foundations for his new alternative theory.

First, there is marked disagreement on how the dependence-influence relationships work (in particular whether there are one or more types of influence and what role group cohesion plays in compliance).

Secondly, 'the basic idea that influence reflects dependence is highly problematic'. It attributes a far greater impact to the influencing agent than is suggested by empirical investigations. Just because someone possesses information does not mean he or she will exert influence and thus produce dependence:

> The perceived validity of information is always a function of social and relational factors such as the perceived source of a message, the degree to which it has consensual support and the degree to which the target defines the source as a positive reference group, that is, the degree to which it is in line with ingroup norms. So-called informational influence is not purely cognitive but also social and normative. (3)

Thirdly, the standard theory is not easily reconcilable with the facts of historical and social change, since it seems to exclude social change, innovation and minority influence. It implies influence flows only from the top-down, from the 'haves' to the 'have nots', from those with power to those without it. But history has many examples of movement from the bottom-up. 'New movements can gain adherents despite often lacking resources, expertise and prestige.'

---

[5] See, for example, French and Raven 1959, Bass 1990: 225–73 and Pfeffer 1992.

Fourthly, it is assumed on the standard theory that group formation is a product of this type of power: 'control of resources gives people power, defined as the capacity to influence people's attitudes, beliefs and behaviour, and that influence between people who depend on each other leads to shared social norms and values'. That is, mutual dependence between people is assumed to produce a psychological group. In fact, however, the better view is that 'the psychological group is a precondition of influence, not simply an outcome'. One of the findings of self-categorization theory, largely developed by Turner in the 1980s, is that people 'expect to agree where they define themselves as members of the same group, in terms of the same social identity' and confront the same shared situation that provokes uncertainty. In other words, group formation is a precondition for the experience of uncertainty that sets off the processes of informational influence (i.e. influence based on the possession of information). Hence, the basis of power is not dependence but group formation that itself reflects group identity (4).

Fifthly and finally, nowhere in the standard theory is there a place for the sharp distinction between influence and power that appears in everyday discourse in the antagonism between persuasion on the one hand and naked force or domination on the other. Coercion is not recognized for the deeply conflictual process that it is and, indeed, tends to be viewed in a positive light as a form of influence in which the powerless are shaped by the powerful, as a form of 'going along with the group' (5).

Turner's new approach to influence

Before proceeding to his new approach, John Turner gives some attention to the meaning of power (5-8). He notes that although defining power 'has long been a murky business', its 'most general meaning is the capacity to cause effects, to have an impact on or change things, to do "work", either in the physical or social world'. A subcategory of power is the capacity to affect people or society, to cause them to act in ways they would not otherwise have acted. He regards power as impact (5-6).

Turner's own proposal turns the standard theory on its head. His unifying conceptual framework is self-categorization theory, which explains psychological group formation in terms of self-categorization rather than dependence (Turner et al. 1987). He argues that causality runs in exactly the opposite direction to that espoused by the standard theory. There are three main aspects. First, psychological group formation, which is understood as meaning the development of a shared social identity, produces influence among the group members. Secondly, influence, operating through one or more of the three processes of persuasion, authority and coercion, produces power, meaning the capacity to exert one's will over, to have an impact on, other people. Thirdly, the power so produced allows its holder to gain and control resources and their distribution.

Turner devotes considerable attention to describing the three processes of persuasion, authority and coercion. First, 'Persuasion is the process of influence outlined in self-categorization theory (Turner et al. 1987). It is explained as arising from the collective attempt by the group to develop a consensual response to some stimulus situation.' Since the group will validate any judgement concerning the circumstances that have provoked the uncertainty to the degree to which it embodies an ingroup norm, 'it also follows that where group members seek to influence each other they will tend to be more persuasive to the degree that they are perceived as relatively prototypical of the emerging consensus' (10). Such a situation means that someone who is seeking to gain or to hold on to a leadership position in relation to the group should do so by making a case for his or her prototypicality with respect to group norms, beliefs and aspirations (11).

Authority, secondly, is:

> the power to control ingroup members because they are persuaded that it is right for a certain person to control them in certain matters. Thus legitimate authority is a product of influence and the formation of norms within the group. Authority is based on ingroup norms that a person, role or group has the right to prescribe appropriate beliefs, attitudes or behaviour in certain areas.

It is important to note, however, a 'person's authority varies flexibly with the identity, norms and goals of the group, its beliefs and the situation in which it finds itself, in the same way that conformity to any ingroup norm varies' (11).

Thirdly, coercion is an attempt to control people against their will through the deployment of human and material resources to constrain and manipulate their behaviour. Yet such an attempt to restrict the freedom of the target makes them all too aware of their difference from and disagreement with the person engaging in coercion and leads to increased social distance and disagreement with that person and hence reduces his or her influence and authority (12). 'It is a divisive, destabilizing and counter-productive means of control.' In short, 'Coercion is the power one uses when one does not have power' (13). If coercion is persisted in, it tends 'to produce private attitude change away from the coercer, reactance conflict and the emergence of a countervailing force' (16).

Yet while coercion is never an effective substitute for influence and authority over the group as a whole, it can be vital to preserving the existence of the group 'as a means of neutralizing and excluding the determinedly recalcitrant' (14). To achieve this, it is necessary to negatively categorize and stereotype the target as different from the group as a whole, so that the members will not be able to identify with him or her (17).

Overall then, for Turner power is 'an emergent property of human social relationships, not something that stands outside of them' (18). And as an emergent property of social and psychological relations between people, 'these relations shape the form it takes'. Leaders gain power not by possessing resources in a manner separate from group dynamics but by representing and working for group values and identity (19).

This theory has a very considerable prima facie application to what Paul is attempting in 2 Corinthians. Throughout the letter, in the context of his strong affirmation of their belonging to a group with a distinctive identity in Corinth, Paul seeks to persuade the Corinthians to do, or refrain from doing, certain things or to maintain or adopt certain attitudes and beliefs. To this extent he is seeking to exercise power through people in the basic sense adopted by Turner, meaning the capacity to exert one's will through other people, to affect people and things by getting people to carry out one's will. At the same time, he expressly eschews the use of coercion, stating in 2 Cor. 1.24: 'Not that we lord it (κυριεύομεν) over your faith, but we are fellow-workers for your joy'. Moreover, Paul wishes to exercise power over the Corinthians in relation to a very important resource issue, the collection for the saints in Jerusalem, but he only does so in chs 8 and 9 after an extended effort on his part to strengthen the relationship between himself and the Corinthians. Similarly, only when he has rebuilt his relationship with the Corinthians does he turn his fire on interlopers who have sought to weaken his influence in Corinth, a task that occupies chs 10–13. These correspondences between Turner's theory and the text suggest that it will be a fruitful perspective in the social identity commentary that follows.

Commentary: Part A

2 Corinthians 1–7: Paul re-establishes his leadership

3

Reconnecting with the Corinthians (1.1-22)

The Letter opening (1.1-2)

2 Corinthians 1.1 Ancient Greco-Roman letters almost always began by naming the sender, then his or her recipients and then sending a greeting and a wish for good health (Stowers 1986: 20). Here Paul follows this pattern but with very significant differences. In the first verse of the letter, Paul identifies as its senders himself, 'an apostle of Christ Jesus by the will of God', and Timothy, 'his (lit. 'the') brother'. While Timothy, a close associate of Paul (Malina 2008), was probably with Paul when he dictated the letter and was known to its addressees, it is unlikely that he helped compose it, especially in view of the frequency with which Paul moves to the first-person singular in the letter. When Paul uses the first-person plural in this letter, 'we' or 'us', it is usually the 'literary plural' meaning 'I' or 'me', even though there are times when a genuine plural is in view, such as 1.19 (Paul, Silvanus and Timothy) and possibly 1.20 (the same group) and perhaps certain of the plurals in 2 Corinthians 3–6, where Paul speaks of the apostolic ministry more generally (Thrall 1994: 83, 105–7).

We are so familiar with the specifications of senders and addressees in ancient letter openings that we might read the rest of this letter without giving much thought as to what he is conveying in v. 1. That would be unfortunate here because the twenty-nine words of this verse in Greek are replete with vital information about the social identity of the Christ-followers of Corinth and Paul's intention to exercise leadership over them. The critical feature is Paul's self-designation. In Phil. 1.1, he describes the senders of the letter simply as 'Paul and Timothy, slaves of Christ Jesus'. From the outset of 2 Corinthians, on the other hand, Paul is making an issue of his role and authority, which he sharply differentiates from those of Timothy: himself an apostle, the latter a brother. Moreover, Paul's description of himself as 'an apostle of Christ by the will of God (διὰ θελήματος θεοῦ)' takes its place among the stronger self-designations in his letter openings. In 1 Cor. 1.1, he is more modest, saying he is 'called (κλητός) (to be) an apostle of Christ Jesus through the will of God', so the will of God is more closely connected with the call than with the status of apostle itself. In Rom. 1.1, he is 'called (to be) an apostle, set apart for the Gospel of God', with no mention of the will of God. Neither in 1 Thessalonians nor in Philemon does he make any such statement about his leadership role and warrant. Only in Galatians, a letter written – as here – in a context where his authority was clearly under challenge, do we find anything comparable when he says he is 'an apostle not from men or through a man but through Jesus Christ and God the Father who raised him from the dead' (Gal. 1.1). The strong affirmation of the connection between his status as an apostle and the divine will at the very start of 2 Corinthians is not a matter of Paul identifying himself as an apostle 'because that was who he was' (Garland 1999: 49). Instead, it suggests that his authority and its warrant will be a central issue in the text of the letter, as indeed proves to be the case. Here we have the first indication that 2 Corinthians is a unified composition: Paul begins it knowing that he will later (including in chs 10–13) be defending his apostleship in the face of opposition from false apostles who claim to be superlative (11.5, 13; 12.11), even to the extent of his needing to insist that he demonstrated the signs of the apostle among the Corinthians (12.12). It appears that within the Christ-movement there were norms and practices that were associated with being an apostle; in other words, there was a sense of the prototypical apostle, even though it is evident in 2 Corinthians, in chs 10–13, in particular that precisely what those norms and practices were was hotly contested. That is, the Christ-group contains a subcategory of member known as ἀπόστολος, together with an understanding of prototypicality attached to it (Porter 2019: 12).

Paul then specifies as the letter's addressees 'the Christ-group (ἐκκλησία) of God in Corinth, with all the saints who are in the whole of Achaia'. In this commentary, ἐκκλησία, currently the subject of intense discussion (Trebilco 2011; van Kooten 2012; Park 2015; Korner 2017; Last 2018; Esler 2021c), is regularly translated as 'Christ-group' because it refers to a group (not to a meeting or an assembly) and because the Christ-movement was unique in using this word as a group designation. None of the thousands of voluntary associations – with which the Christ-groups were closely comparable (Kloppenborg 2019) – used this word as a group designation (Esler 2021c). The use of both ἐκκλησία and ἐκκλησία τοῦ θεοῦ probably dates back to the early years of the Greek-speaking branch of the movement in Judea, when it was subject to persecution, notably by Paul (Esler 2021c). It is worth noting that the expression 'the assembly of God' (ἐκκλησία τοῦ θεοῦ) in v. 1, of its very nature, conveys a sense of great privilege and worth. This is not just any group, but actually God's own in Corinth.

Similarly, the members are 'the saints' (οἱ ἅγιοι), a rich expression that conveys divine election and possession, a distinct community, separation from outsiders and holiness, and thus defies adequate rendering in English (Harris 2005: 132). It is somewhat puzzling that the saints specified here are those in Achaia. Why does Paul feel the need to mention them here, especially when he does not do so in the address in 1 Cor. 1.2? The most probable answer is that he does so because in 2 Cor. 9.2 he will note that they have been enthusiastic about the collection, while in 2 Cor. 11.10 he will state that his boast will be heard 'in the regions of Achaia'. Here we see one of the vital links Paul creates across the whole letter that are disregarded by those who favour partition theories.

'Social identity' is an identity possessed by an individual that derives from a sense of belonging to a particular group, a sense that carries with it cognitive implications (the recognition of belonging to the group, with its particular beliefs, norms and practices), emotional dimensions (covering positive or negative connotations of belonging) and evaluative dimensions (referring to attitudes held towards insiders and outsiders). For Paul to refer to the Corinthian Christ-followers as 'the Christ-group of God in Corinth' and as 'the saints' was likely to have triggered a whole range of very positive resonances in relation to these various components of the social identity the members each derived from belonging to it.

The contents of v. 1 also cohere closely with the letter being one in which Paul seeks to exercise leadership over these addressees, meaning to influence them in a manner that will augment their contribution to realizing group ideals. To be successful, Paul will need to persuade them to be, or to become, Christ-followers as he understands the meaning of the identity involved. To that extent, he will lead and they will follow. He needs to change how they understand him but also influence how they act in the world with a changed mind and understanding. He must build a relationship with them based upon their shared group identity. As noted in Chapter 2 of this volume, the social identity approach to social influence enabled John Turner to reformulate how a leader exercised power in a group. Turner viewed authority as 'the power to control ingroup members because they are persuaded that it is right for a certain person to control them in certain matters' (2005: 11). Paul's assertion that he is an apostle of Christ Jesus by the will of God represents, in this context, the strongest imaginable basis for his having power, in some matters, to influence them to act in certain ways, that is, to have legitimate authority over them. By 'this context', I mean the particular group to whom he is writing in a particular place in a particular time, characterized by particular norms that will mean that this claim is likely to be accepted. He will thus have an influence, since, to quote Turner again, 'Authority is based on ingroup norms that a person, role or group has the right to prescribe appropriate beliefs, attitudes or behaviour in certain areas' (2005: 11). Yet Paul is leaving nothing to chance here, since he connects the source of his authority with the very nature of the group they are: just as his authority comes from God, so too are they God's ἐκκλησία in Corinth (and Achaia). As God's people, they should acknowledge Paul as an apostle of Christ Jesus by God's will and respect the authority that flows from that status. The Corinthian Christ-followers are the salient group for Paul as he composes the letter; if he was indeed a Roman citizen (Acts 22.22-29; 25.10-12), his calling himself merely 'Paul' and failing to provide all three names to which such status entitled one (Thrall 1994: 79) indicate that the social identity derived from such a citizenship was quite irrelevant here. In short, the theme of Paul's authority, an integral aspect of his capacity for influencing and hence for leadership within the context of a very distinctive group with its own characteristic psychological processes, is firmly established in the first verse of the letter.

2 Corinthians 1.2 The blessing in 2 Cor. 1.2, 'Grace to you and peace from God our Father and Lord Jesus Christ', has attracted attention in terms of an 'apostolic greeting' in existing scholarship (Lieu 1985). It also provides a rich seam of data for the approach being pursued here, even if our natural tendency might be to rush on to the text of the letter, so inured have we become to such a formula, with identical expressions appearing in Rom. 1.7, 1 Cor. 1.3, Gal. 1.3, Phil. 1.2 and Philemon 3, while 1 Thess. 1.1, Paul's oldest extant letter, carries the briefer form, 'Grace to you and peace'. Paul himself seems to have formulated this blessing (Lieu 1985: 167–70). He has probably adapted the first word, χάρις ('grace'), from Greek culture (although in letter openings the verbal form χαίρειν was employed) and the second, εἰρήνη ('peace'), from Judean tradition (Thrall 1994: 94–5). The words probably convey that God's bestowal of his grace leads to peace. Χάρις is a major Pauline designator for the operation of divine gift recently explored by John Barclay (2015).

Some regard this expression as a prayer: 'May grace and peace be yours from God' (Harris 2005: 135). But this is an under-interpretation of what is said here. Paul is not just any Christ-follower praying to God to bestow grace and peace on other members of the movement. As an apostle of Christ Jesus by God's will, he is in a very privileged position from his closeness to God that this status implies. By use of the formula, Paul impliedly designates himself as someone with an unparalleled capacity to effect a channelling of divine grace and peace in the direction of his addressees, even if he does not go so far as to suggest such a result will necessarily follow. This indicates that part of the role of apostle was to be a broker mediating mutual benefits between patron and clients.

Seen in this light, grace and peace here represent the first resources, but by no means the last, to be mentioned in the letter. But we must note that Paul is not saying divine grace and peace are his to bestow, nor even promising that he can ensure their delivery. For this reason, he is not seeking to exercise power on the basis of such a faculty, in the manner prescribed by the standard theory of power that Turner critiques. Yet he is establishing a context in which resources with a divine origin are part of the reality in which he and his addressees exist and comprise an incident of belonging to a group whose character and status are as exalted as he portrays the Christ-group in Corinth to be by virtue of their being 'God's' (1.1). He is also staking a claim for his closeness to these resources. But as we will soon see, in this letter they figure in the play of social interactions between Paul and the Corinthians under God in a manner close to Turner's approach to power, influence and leadership.

Comfort in affliction (1.3-7)

The next section of the letter is probably best defined as beginning at v. 3 and ending at v. 11. This delineation can be defended for reasons largely tied to ancient epistolary form (Thrall 1994: 98–100), but is perhaps more firmly suggested by the content of the passage, in that Paul first outlines a partnership approach to comfort in affliction (vv. 3-7) and then offers a specific example to trigger that process (vv. 8-11).

2 Corinthians 1.3-4 Paul begins this section of the letter by invoking a blessing on God or – the distinction being rather inconsequential (Barrett 1973: 58) – making a statement about God, who is, in a striking parallel, both the father of 'our Lord Jesus Christ' and also 'the father of mercies and the God of all comfort' (παράκλησις; v. 3). But whereas this is the only occurrence of 'mercies' (οἰκτιρμοί) in the letter, the mention of comfort inaugurates a section of the text that is notable for its concentration of the words παράκλησις and παρακαλεῖν. Here they have the meaning of 'comfort/ consolation', one of three broad areas of meaning for these words, the other two being 'appeal/request' and 'encouragement/exhortation', senses that also appear in 2 Corinthians.[1]

This meaning of 'comfort' is strikingly prominent in 2 Corinthians (Ehrensperger 2007: 101; Kaplan 2011). In 2 Cor. 1.3-7, the meaning 'comfort/ consolation' occurs via the verb (παρακαλεῖν) and the noun (παράκλησις). Paul uses the verb on thirty-eight occasions in his letters, with twelve, possibly thirteen (if we include the instance in 1 Cor. 4.13) of them

---

[1] For an extended discussion of these words, see Schmitz and Stählin 1967.

meaning 'to comfort, console', and a full nine of those are in 2 Corinthians, five in 2 Cor. 1.4-7 and four in 2 Corinthians 7. He deploys the noun eighteen times, with the meaning of 'comfort, consolation' on ten occasions, and nine of those are in 2 Corinthians, of which six occur in 1 Cor. 1.3-7 and three in 2 Corinthians 7. In fact, 2 Cor. 1.3-7 'are the five verses of the New Testament with the highest density of παρακαλέω or παράκλησις terminology' (Bieringer 2011). While the idea of comfort will recur later in the letter (in ch. 7), vv. 3-7 lay the foundation for its meaning throughout. This is a phenomenon deserving our close attention. While there could be an allusion to παρακαλεῖν as a translation of נחם in Deutero-Isaiah (e.g., Isa. 40.1 and 51.12), where God will 'comfort his people', thus possibly evoking a messianic connection (Thrall 1994: 103; Bieringer 2011), our task here is to explain the use of these words in relation to Paul's exercise of leadership in the letter.

The theoretical framework I am utilizing, of leadership and the influence it brings in a social identity and social categorization context, also raises the question of whether in the notion of 'comfort' we are dealing with another valuable resource that is available to the Christ-followers in Corinth and that becomes a component in the relationships between the members and in the identity of the group. These relationships include those Paul has with his Corinthian addressees that he seeks to repair and to mobilize in his attempt to secure his influence and leadership.

The heart of Paul's understanding of comfort is found in v. 4. Here he sets out a three-stage process by specifying that the 'God of all comfort' mentioned in v. 3:

(a) is the one who comforts (παρακαλεῖν) us in all our affliction (θλῖψις),
(b) so that we may be able to comfort (παρακαλεῖν) those in every affliction (θλῖψις)
(c) through the comfort (παράκλησις) by which we ourselves are comforted (παρακαλεῖν) by God.

What does this amount to? First of all, we must recognize that the 'us' in this verse is Paul himself; he does not seem to be including the Corinthians within its ambit; they do not enter the scene until v. 6. Paul is saying that it has been a feature of his life (as a follower of Christ) to experience afflictions. These would inevitably have a negative impact on the social identity he derives from his belonging to the Christ-movement. But not too negative, or not negative for too long, because in all such afflictions God comforts him, so that the suffering of affliction is matched by the comfort God brings, and the positive neutralizes the negative. But this divine comfort is not just for his benefit; it is bestowed on him so that he may share the comfort he has received with others who are afflicted. Thus, there is a strong relational dimension to what he is saying.

2 Corinthians 1.5 Paul refers to his own experience again in v. 5: 'For just as the sufferings (παθήματα) of Christ abound upon us, so through Christ our comfort also abounds.' The experience described in the previous verse as 'affliction' is now further specified as 'the sufferings of Christ'. Paul's claim to share Christ's sufferings further augments the high authority he asserted at the beginning of the letter. Similarly, the negative experience of these sufferings (clearly very distinctive to this particular group, since they bear Christ's name) elicits a matching abundance of comfort. There is much discussion as the meaning of the 'sufferings of Christ' (e.g. Barrett 1973: 61-2; Thrall 1994: 107-10; Garland 1999: 65-7 and Harris 2005: 145-7). The most likely candidate is the sufferings that Christ himself endured. This view coheres well with what Paul says in Gal. 6.17 (he bears the marks of Jesus [τὰ στίγματα τοῦ Ἰησοῦ] on his body), Rom. 6.3 (Christ-followers are baptized into his death) and Phil. 3.10-11 (he wants to share Christ's sufferings and become like him in his death). On one view, this means that the solidarity between Christ and his followers extends to his sufferings (Garland 1999: 66). Although this certainly applies to the examples in Rom. 6.3 and Phil. 3.10-11, the example in Gal. 6.17 seems to go further. Is this a claim that all Christ-followers would make, or only an apostle like Paul? Dunn notes, in commenting on Gal. 6.17, that there is 'a strong consensus that by "the marks of Jesus" themselves Paul means the scars and physical effects of the various beatings and severe hardships (including being stoned) which Paul had already experienced in the course of his missionary work' (1993: 347). Accordingly, Paul is speaking of his experience as an apostle, not just a Christ-follower. He is, in effect, suggesting that such suffering is prototypical for an apostle, but not necessarily for every Christ-follower. So while Christ-followers share in the sufferings of Christ, in another context Paul was willing to claim that he exhibited the (additional) features of the στίγματα τοῦ Ἰησοῦ that reflected his apostolic status and authority.

2 Corinthians 1.6 Only in this verse do we find Paul expressly addressing both his experience and that of the Corinthians. Here Paul announces a theme that he will develop strongly in chs 10–13 in the context of rebutting the claims of the interlopers (which is another sign that Paul had the whole letter in mind from the outset). Whatever he experiences, whether negative or positive, it is not for him but for them, both their immediate comfort and their (ultimate) salvation. In the last section of the letter, he will employ the word οἰκοδομή ('building up, edification') to express both dimensions (10.8; 12.19; 13.10). Although in v. 6 Paul only explicitly attributes ὑπομονή to the Corinthians, it is implied as part of his own experience, and this becomes explicit later in the text (6.4; 12.12).

2 Corinthians 1.7 Verse 7 serves as a recapitulation:

Our hope for you is firmly established; for we know that just as you are partners (κοινωνοί) in suffering (παθήματα), so also you are partners in comfort (παράκλησις).

Most translations introduce a future tense into the last clause of v. 7, but there is no good reason to do so. The previous verse treats their comfort as a present reality (as seen in its effectiveness in generating endurance), and the present tense persists in v. 7. The reference to Paul's firm hope in this verse is not an indication that their comfort is yet to arrive, but that the current position, where they are both partners in affliction but also, happily, partners in comfort, will continue. This view is confirmed by evidence later in the letter (7.7), considered in the following, which shows that the Corinthians are already adept at the giving of comfort by the time Paul writes this letter. Great significance attaches to Paul's description of himself and the Corinthians as κοινωνοί. This links with but transcends his assertion that he and they share sufferings and comfort since it allows Paul to temper the strong claims to leadership he will make later in this letter. It is of a piece with the remarkable statement in 1.24: 'We do not lord it over your faith, but are fellow-workers (συνεργοί) of your joy', where συνεργοί is very close in meaning to κοινωνοί. We will soon see that Paul needs to rebuild his relationship with the Corinthians in the early stages of the letter and emphasizing that they are partners (and fellow-workers) contributes to this end.

The theoretical framework applied in this volume, of leadership in a social identity and social categorization context, raises the question of whether any of the four aspects of leadership discussed in Chapter 2 of this volume comes into play here: prototypicality, identity advancement, identity entrepreneurship and identity impresarioship.

First, features of prototypicality, but not exemplarity, are in evidence. Paul is proposing that there are a number of characteristics of Christ-movement identity – that we are describing as prototypical – sharing the same sufferings, affliction, comfort, endurance and salvation. Paul exhibits these characteristics and, with his help, so do the Corinthians. That Paul wants to align himself with his addressees in these respects emerges unequivocally when, in v. 6, he acknowledges that they experience 'the same sufferings' (τὰ αὐτὰ παθήματα) that he does. We thus witness Paul acting in accordance with the key insight of the social identity approach to leadership: a leader must share the prototypical values, behaviour and experience of the group. And yet Paul is also leaving space for himself to be, as it were, at the front of the line. The sufferings and the comfort of Christ no doubt extend to the Corinthians, but they 'abound' (περισσεύειν; v. 5) in him. This is not surprising, since he, after all, is an 'apostle of Christ Jesus by the will of God' (v. 1) and they are not.

The second aspect of leadership, identity advancement, is also relevant to this passage. What Paul has suffered, he has suffered for them; he has their interests at heart, not his personal interests. This issue also indicates that Paul is here engaging in identity entrepreneurship, since to evoke the sufferings of Christ which he (and the rest of the membership) experiences is to raise the spectre of the threatening world beyond the ingroup, the outgroups who have in the past and will continue to afflict them with such suffering. To invoke the figure of Christ in this connection is to define a critical boundary that separates 'us' from 'them'. Paul does not, however, appear to be engaging in the fourth aspect, identity impresarioship, in this passage. That will come later, in chs 8–9.

If we dig a little more deeply into the manner in which Paul is seeking to win influence over his addressees, we are led to ask if the data in 2 Cor. 1.3-7 relate to the two theories of power and influence under consideration? In considering this issue, we will see the value of such a social-scientific interpretative framework in prompting fresh and important questions to put to the text. At first sight, these verses seem to support the standard theory. As noted earlier, it holds that a person ('the influencing agent') controls resources, these resources are desired, valued or needed by others, and this makes them dependent upon the influencing agent for the satisfaction of their needs or the attainment of their goals. This situation gives the influencing agent the capacity to influence them.

Here the resource in question is comfort that neutralizes the effects of affliction or suffering. While God is the source of this comfort, is Paul presenting it as a transferable good and himself as the agent of the transfer? Is the picture one in which (a) Paul controls the 'comfort-in-affliction' resource; (b) he offers to provide it to the Corinthians so (c) they become dependent upon him for satisfying this particular need and (d) he can use this dependence to exercise influence over them? We must answer these questions in the negative.

Harris suggests, especially on the basis of v. 6, that the effect of what Paul writes is that 'it was not simply a matter of Corinthian suffering followed automatically and directly by divine comfort, but rather of Paul's mediating God's comfort to the Corinthians in their suffering' (2005: 150). Yet Thrall cautions against seeing Paul as a mediator of divine comfort, since Paul could not have supposed that the Corinthians were unable to receive comfort directly from God (1994: 104), and it is probably the case that 'mediation' is too active a role for what Paul has in mind. To reach a view on this, we need to take a closer look at the entirety of vv. 3-7, especially v. 6. Paul does claim that God has comforted him in every affliction in order that he may be able to comfort others so afflicted with that same divine comfort (v. 4) and that his abundant affliction has given him abundant comfort (v. 5). Care needs to be taken with v. 6. Certainly Paul is linking his affliction and comfort to theirs, and it is likely from v. 4 that this involved him comforting them. Yet, while in v. 6 his comfort is for the sake of (ὑπέρ) theirs, the precise meaning of this is not made clear. Paul does not claim to be the agent of a simple transfer of comfort from God to the Corinthians. But is he asserting some influence in the Corinthians receiving comfort?

The most we can say is that Paul envisages that his comforting the Corinthians induces in them, sparks the generation of, their own comfort. Exposure to Paul's divinely sourced comforting allows them to develop their own, no doubt by opening themselves to the same divine source of all comfort. Perhaps Paul has some mimetic process in mind here. In any event, he has stimulated their opening themselves to God in this regard, the father and hence the source of all comfort. Just as Paul and they must suffer their own afflictions (even if they are similar in nature as linked to Christ's), so too will they experience their own comfort, a comfort necessarily just as separable from his as the afflictions to which he and they are respectively subject. This comfort of theirs already has such a defined and potent reality that it is taking effect (ἐνεργουμένη; v. 6) in their endurance of sufferings. In other words, at the time Paul is writing to them they have already received comfort; it is not something in his control, and for which they are dependent on him in such a way that he can use this dependence to influence them.

That his firm hope is not to establish a dependency relationship in the area of comfort, but a partnership, finds confirmation in v. 7. Just as they are currently partners (κοινωνοί) in suffering, so will they be in comfort. This entails that their capacity for receiving and giving comfort is on par with his. There is explicit confirmation that this was, in fact, Paul's view later in the 2 Corinthians when he notes how effectively they had comforted Titus (2 Cor. 7.7) and even himself (2 Cor. 7.13). They have already acquired a capacity in this area independent of Paul, and they will not be dependent on him for the satisfaction of this need. Instead, they will experience comfort as partners with him, and this begins a theme of partnership that will be very prominent in the letter, as noted earlier.

Paul's affliction in Asia (1.8-11)

Having spoken of afflictions generally in vv. 3-7, in 2 Cor. 1.8-11 Paul recounts one particular affliction and its resolution that he has (fairly recently, it seems) experienced in Asia. At a general level, the problem he encountered in Asia illustrates the catalogues of hardships he lists later in the letter (4.7-11; 6.3-10). More specifically, however, the subject matter of vv. 8-11 and the nature of the opening statement, 'For (γάρ) we do not want you to be ignorant, brothers, concerning . . .', indicate that this section is connected to what precedes. In fact, it serves as a detailed vignette of the coupling of affliction and comfort that Paul has just been discussing in a general way. In addition, just as the previous section had concluded with an expression of the partnership between him and his Corinthian addressees in relation to these two phenomena, this passage ends with a request by Paul that will give practical reality to that partnership.

2 Corinthians 1.8-10 The nature of Paul's affliction in Asia, meaning the Roman province of which Ephesus was the capital, remains uncertain (vv. 8-10). It was a deadly peril, which left Paul utterly crushed and despairing of life itself, as if he had received a sentence of death (τὸ ἀπόκριμα τοῦ θανάτου; v. 9). Several possibilities have been suggested, including encountering violent opposition, imprisonment, a severe illness or even being exposed to wild beasts (Harris 2005: 164–82). Rather than illness (Barrett 1973: 64), some form of persecution or violence is perhaps more likely, so as to illustrate the alignment of this experience with the παθήματα of Christ mentioned in v. 5. Whatever its nature, which is not of great moment for present purposes, Paul was delivered from it by God 'who raises the dead' and learned the lesson that we must not rely on ourselves but on him, on whom Paul has set his hope that, having delivered him from such a death, he will deliver him again.[2]

2 Corinthians 1.11 Paul's hope of future deliverance is accompanied by his expression of an assumption about their behaviour that he specifies in v. 11, a verse that is both important yet also syntactically taxing. God will save him, Paul says at the end of v. 10,

> so long as you are cooperating (συνυπουργούντων καὶ ὑμῶν) in prayer for us, so that many will give thanks on our behalf for the favour (χάρισμα) to be granted to us on account of many.

Although χάρισμα is difficult here, it probably refers to an anticipated act of divine rescue to which Paul looks forward. But that rescue will come as a result of cooperative prayer activity. This is the only occurrence in the New Testament of the rare verb συνυπουργεῖν, and it does not appear in the Septuagint. Liddell and Scott cite two instances (Hippocrates, *Art.* 58 and Lucian, *Bis Accusatus* 17) in addition to 2 Cor. 1.11. Accordingly, it

---

[2] For a discussion of the three textual issues in v. 10, see Thrall 1994: 120-2.

makes quite a splash here and needs to be given due weight. It comprises two elements, namely ὑπουργεῖν, meaning 'assist', itself a compound of ὑπό and ἐργεῖν, and σύν, meaning ('with', or 'in conjunction with'), so the verb carries the meaning 'join in assisting' or 'cooperate with'. Thus, we have a combination of σύν – ὑπό – ἐργεῖν, which is very close to being a verbal form of συνεργοί that we are about to encounter in 1.24. The only plausible candidate for whom Paul wants them to cooperate is himself. Bultmann (1985: 29) points to the very similar expression in Rom. 15.30, 'to contest together with me' (συναγωνίσασθαι μοι). If the Corinthians go along with his request, the partnership that Paul has envisaged in v. 7 will take a specific form, as the Corinthians cooperate with him by joining him in prayer that he will be saved and that will encourage others to give thanks for his deliverance following the prayers of many. While Paul appears to have in mind what we would call a chain reaction of prayer, the central feature of v. 11 is the role of the Corinthians in cooperating with him in prayer. As his partners (κοινωνοί; v. 7), he calls on them to express their close relationship by aligning their prayer with his at a time of possible future crisis.

At a general level, to recall the discussion of the social identity approach in the Introduction, we see an example of leadership being a process of mutual influence that revolves around a partnership embedded in a particular social category or group. Paul's statement in v. 11 is also an example of identity impresarioship: the embedding of the group identity in a particular activity, in this case, joint prayer in a time of crisis. For Paul, to introduce this practice represents an exercise in world-making, even if only at the microcosmic level of the group. Additionally, in line with Turner's redescription of power in groups, Paul certainly sees 'the nature of power as having more to do with the basis of organized, collective action than with a dependence relationship' (2005: 2). Whatever influence Paul is seeking to exercise, he is bent on doing so by working with the members of the Christ-movement in Corinth, building a partnership relationship with them that touches upon their shared beliefs, norms and practices, and not by imposing his will in any coercive way.

An explanation of recent events to rebuild the relationship (1.12–2.13)

Introduction (1.12-14)

2 Corinthians 1.12-14 These verses open the body of the letter and have been described as 'the theme statement of the letter' (Garland 1999: 83).

This is going too far, however. These verses do not mention major aspects of the letter and cannot, therefore, constitute its theme statement. Rather, they represent an apt beginning for 2 Cor. 1.12–2.13, a section of the letter in which Paul begins to repair or even rebuild a relationship with the Corinthians that has recently come under serious strain because of sharp criticism directed at him. In v. 12, Paul moves from the rather generalized discussion of their partnership in affliction and comfort and begins a section of the letter extending to 2 Cor. 2.13 that deals with recent difficulties that have arisen in his relationship with the Corinthians.

As we have seen, according to Turner a person's authority 'varies flexibly with the identity, norms and goals of the group, its beliefs and the situation in which it finds itself, in the same way that conformity to any ingroup norm varies' (2005: 11). In a manner closely cognate with this perspective, Paul is using persuasion to reinforce his authority with the Corinthians in view of the particular circumstances he is facing. It is clear from what follows that specific complaints have been made about him and that he needs to get these out of the way before moving on to the more general issues relating to the apostolic ministry in 2.14–7.4. This strategy shows that Paul is not in a position to use coercive force over the Corinthians. Rather, he needs to base his authority on persuasion, of a form closely related to group norms and group beliefs. As we have seen, in a social identity perspective, seeking to lead by the exercise of influence will often depend on someone providing proof of being prototypical of group identity and/or of working in its interests. This imperative emerges as early as vv. 12-14.

2 Corinthians 1.12 Paul begins with a provocative assertion: 'For this is our καύχησις – the testimony of our conscience – that we have behaved in the world, and especially towards you, with straightforwardness[3] and with the sincerity of God, and not by human wisdom but by the grace of God.' The common translation of καύχησις is 'boast' or 'boasting' (Forbes 1986, Marshall 1987: 353-4). But these translations are inappropriate since they convey negative connotations that may be at home in our culture but were out of place in Paul's. In fact, καύχησις transports us straight into the honour culture of the first-century Mediterranean world. An 'act of claiming honour' or a 'claim-to-honour' better catches Paul's meaning. Those who valued their reputation acted within social conventions by drawing attention to circumstances that portrayed it in a good light. Not surprisingly, then, the

---

[3] There is a very difficult textual issue as to whether the reading should be 'simplicity' (ἁπλότητι) or 'holiness' (ἁγιότητι). The latter is more strongly attested but the former makes better sense in this context, where Paul is being charged with having been deceptive in relation to this travel plans. Note, however, that ἁγνότητι occurs at 2 Cor. 6.6, where the context requires it.

Vulgate (a version written in a culture similar in this respect) translates the word as *gloria*. It was not problematic to make a claim of this sort, as long as it had a solid foundation; otherwise one made oneself a fool and thus became shamed. An illustration of this perspective appears in Plutarch's work, *On Inoffensive Self-Praise*. First, he lays down the general principle that making honour-claims can be acceptable:

> Yet in spite of all this there are times when the statesman might venture on self-glorification (περαυτολογία), as it is called, not for any personal glory or pleasure, but when the occasion and the matter in hand demand that the truth be told about himself, as it might about another – especially when by permitting himself to mention his good accomplishments and character he is enabled to achieve some similar good. (*Moralia*, 539EF. ET Lacy and Einarson 1959: 109–67)

Next Plutarch offers a specific example of this where a person is defending his good name, in circumstances very similar to those in which Paul found himself in relation to Corinth (where the Corinthians do seem to have been angry with him):

> In the first place self-praise goes unresented if you are defending your good name or answering a charge . . . For not only is there nothing puffed up, vainglorious, or proud in taking a high tone about oneself at such a moment, but it displays as well a lofty spirit and greatness of character, which by refusing to be humbled humbles and overpowers envy. For men no longer think it fit even to pass judgement on such as these, but exult and rejoice and catch the inspiration of the swelling speech, when it is well-founded and true. The facts confirm this. (*Moralia*, 540CE. ET Lacy and Einarson 1959: 123)

Since this social dynamic is plainly visible later in the text, in 2 Cor. 7.14, it is reasonable to discern its presence in what Paul is trying to communicate here.

A major point to be made concerning the use of καύχησις in v. 12 is that it inaugurates the prominent theme of Paul's honour-claims, sometimes in conflict with those of others, which will stretch across the entirety of the letter, meaning in each of the three major sections comprising chs 1–7, 8–9 and 10–13, sections which are often treated by those arguing against the unity of 2 Corinthians as being, or as originating in, separate letters. The prominence of this semantic field – which covers the verb καυχάομαι, and the nouns καύχησις and καύχημα – is evident in the following chart:

	καυχάομαι	καύχησις	καύχημα	Total
Instances in the NT	37	11	11	59
Instances In Paul	34	10	10	54
Instances In 2 Cor.	20	6	3	29
Instances In 2 Cor. 1–7	2	3	2	7
Instances In 2 Cor. 8–9	1	1	1	3
Instances In 2 Cor. 10–13	17	2		19

'Paul' meaning Romans, 1 and 2 Corinthians, Galatians, Philippians, 1 Thessalonians and Philemon.

Thus, 92 per cent of the New Testament examples of this semantic field appear in the Pauline corpus and 54 per cent of the Pauline examples are in 2 Corinthians. Also, 2 Corinthians 10–13 contain a spike in instances of the verb. Of the seventeen uses of καυχάομα in 2 Corinthians 10–13, fourteen relate to Paul himself, two are in general form (2 Cor. 10.17) and one relates to Paul's opponents (2 Cor. 11.18). Just as Plutarch suggested, Paul felt it necessary to resort to honour-claims about himself 'when by permitting himself to mention his good accomplishments and character he is enabled to achieve some similar good', or, in order to defend his good name and to answer a charge. The critical point here is that in all three major sections of the letter Paul senses that his authority and his mission are under threat and resorts to honour-claims in response to that pressure. The intensity of the case he is mounting in chs 10–13, which I will address later in this volume, largely explains the concentration of the semantic field (especially in its verbal form) in that part of the letter. This letter-wide response to opposition using the semantic field of honour-claims, which is rather unusual in the broad context of his writings, is nicely compatible with the letter's being a unified composition. It is incompatible with the idea that the three major sections of letter were originally separate letters that, by a strange coincidence, just happened to share an unusually high concentration of Pauline honour-claims.

Standing immediately after the phrase 'For this is our καύχησις' in v. 12 are the words 'the witness of our conscience' (τὸ μαρτύριον τῆς συνειδήσεως). Many commentators interpret συνειδήσεως as a subjective genitive, so the phrase means 'the testimony our conscience gives'. This is probably correct, since an objective genitive (as at Acts 4.33 or 1 Cor. 1.6) would mean 'testimony about our conscience', which does not fit the context. But some of these commentators regard this subjective genitive as defining what Paul is proud of (Harris 2005: 184). This is a strained interpretation, since that issue is covered in the remainder of the verse. Rather, by the words 'the witness of my conscience', Paul actually specifies a warrant he has for his honour-claim: 'For this is my claim-to-honour, as my conscience bears witness, that . . .'.

In fact, τὸ μαρτύριον τῆς συνειδήσεως make perfectly good sense as a parenthesis, 'a grammatically independent thought thrown into the midst of the sentence' (BDF §458). A parenthesis 'usually originates in a need which suddenly crops up to enlarge upon a concept or a thought where it appears in a sentence'. The New Testament, 'especially the Epistles of Paul, contains a variety of harsher parentheses, harsher than a careful stylist would allow'. Paul's thought is often interrupted (BDF §465). In v. 12, having announced that he was about to give the content of his boast, he interrupts this thought briefly to provide warrant for it in a parenthetical statement in the nominative case to the effect that it is testified to by his conscience. Harris notices the possibility of a parenthesis here but discards it, alleging that Greek word order makes this unlikely and that a genitive case might have been expected (2005: 185). But this means he is arguing that Paul is not saying he is proud of how he behaved but of the fact that his conscience gave testimony concerning his behaviour. So on this view Paul is not making an honour-claim in relation to what he has done among people in the world who provide the court of public opinion to confirm or reject this claim, but in relation to what his conscience testifies (he has done). This is socially unrealistic in relegating a matter of honour to the private sphere.

Yet we also need to consider the meaning of 'conscience' (συνείδησις) in the very different cultural setting of the ancient Mediterranean. Bruce Malina had the creative idea of re-examining the meaning of συνείδησις as part of his investigations into a culture that was group-oriented and committed to honour as its primary value. The Greek word and its Latin translation, *conscientia*, stand for 'with-knowledge', 'that is, a knowledge with others, individualized common knowledge, commonly shared meaning, common sense'. Accordingly:

> Conscience then refers to a person's sensitive awareness to one's public ego-image along with the purpose of striving to align one's behavior and self-assessment with that publicly perceived image. A person with a conscience is a respectable, reputable, and honorable person.

Respectability, in this social context, would be the characteristic of a person who needs other people in order to grasp his or her own identity. Conscience is a sort of internalization of what others say, do, and think about oneself since these others play the role of witness and judge. (2001: 58-9)

On this view, 'conscience' has an internal dimension, but one that is closely tied to what significant others think of a person's behaviour and how it measures up against socially accepted standards. This is immediately appealing, since in 1.12 (and also in the use of συνείδησις in 4.2 and 5.11) Paul is proffering his behaviour very publicly to the assessment of others and looking for a favourable view of it from them.

Modern views of conscience are more likely to reflect our need for independence from the views of others. At the Second Vatican Council, for example, the Catholic Church insisted that conscience involved recognition of God's law written deep within a person, 'the interior space in which we can listen to and hear the truth, the good, the voice of God'. There a person is alone with God 'whose voice echoes in his depths'.[4] Conscience means to act in accordance with that echoing divine voice. There is not much room here for how one's views are assessed by others, which is also reflected in the way in which Robert Bolt dramatized Thomas More's refusal to give way to Henry VIII in *A Man for All Seasons*.

The use of συνείδησις in 2 Cor. 1.12 aligns closely with Malina's explanation. It is also an outward directed faculty because it speaks of the witness of his συνείδησις, a genitive meaning the witness his συνείδησις gives, in the context of his making a claim to honour. Paul is looking to a public verdict in his favour in an honour-obsessed world. Nevertheless, even here συνείδησις does have an internal dimension.

Let us return to the substance of his honour-claim: 'that we have behaved in the world, and especially towards you, with simplicity and with the sincerity of God, and not by human wisdom but by the grace of God'.[5] As we will soon see, Paul had been charged with insincerity and wanted to fend off that charge. If it were true, it would damage his reputation and also reduce his capacity to persuade the Corinthians to his point of view. That is why he prefixes this material with the statement that it comprises his honour-claim. This brings home the relevance of a particular cultural context to the way that the social dynamics postulated by the old theory

---

[4] *Gaudium et Spes: The Pastoral Constitution on the Church in the Modern World* (7 December 1965), 16.
[5] As noted in footnote 3, there is a textual issue here but the meaning 'simplicity' is preferable to 'holiness'.

of influence and Turner's new one function, an important point that has been made in relation to the social identity approach generally by Hopkins and Reicher (2011), as noted in Chapter 1 of this volume. In addition, Paul knows that the critical thing is the state of his relationship with the Corinthians. If they take a dim view of him, especially if they consider that he does not live by what they regard as group norms, his chances of presenting himself as prototypical of their shared values, or of acting on their behalf, will be diminished or destroyed. All of this aligns very closely with Turner's proposal.

2 Corinthians 1.13 Paul's assertion, 'For we do not write to you anything different from what you read or understand' must be a response to a charge along the lines, 'Paul writes to us differently from what we read and understand'. Rejection of such a possibility on the ground that it would constitute an illicit form of 'mirror reading' (Barclay 1987) would be most unwise. Ancient rhetoricians well understood (and acknowledged in their works) that it is vital to answer in advance any case that is likely to be made against one's own. This was called 'anticipation' (προκατάληψις or πρόληψις; *praesumptio*). The author of the *Rhetorica ad Alexandrum* described this as 'the method by which we shall counteract the ill-feeling which is against us by anticipating the adverse criticisms of our audience and the arguments of those who are going to speak against us' (1432b) and further observed:

> If then one is under suspicion of wrongdoing in the past, one must employ anticipation in addressing one's audience and say, 'I am well aware that a prejudice exists against me, but I will prove that it is groundless.' You must then make a brief defence in your proem, if you have anything to say on your own behalf, or raise objections to the arguments which have been passed against you. (*Rhetorica ad Alexandrum*, 1436b–1437a)[6]

Modern advocates also appreciate the importance of anticipating and answering the case likely to be made against one's client.[7]

Nevertheless, the precise nature of the problem Paul is referring to in this verse is unclear (Garland 1999: 91–2; Thrall 1994: 133–4; Matera 2003: 49). Paul appears to be saying that he is not inconsistent or unclear in what he says in his letters to them. It is what he has said in a letter in the broader context

---

[6] ET by Forster 1924.
[7] I once had the privilege of working on a case in Sydney as a barrister assisting a Queen's Counsel who was famous for spending nearly as much time on the arguments his opponent would run against his as on his own; he had a large and very successful practice!

of his correspondence with them that has caused the problem. Probably the best course is to draw guidance from what he says shortly afterwards in this chapter – that the Corinthians are complaining about his changing his plans to visit them. They consider that there is a gap between his language and his real intentions, as when he sometimes means 'no' when he says 'yes', and 'yes' when he says 'no' (v. 17). Such behaviour would also mean he was not acting in a straightforward way or with sincerity (v. 12), as he has just asserted he is. In Chapter 1 of this volume, the likely course of events explaining their unhappiness is set out. During his severe visit (or possibly in some other letter not mentioned and now lost), Paul promised them to visit the Corinthians on his way to and from Macedonia. In his severe letter, he had reneged on this undertaking.

2 Corinthians 1.14 This verse contains an acknowledgement by Paul, who now for the first time moves to first-person singular discourse, that they have understood him partially (ἀπὸ μέρους). When coupled with the previous sentence – 'I hope that you will understand fully (ἕως τέλους)' (v. 13) – this can only mean that this is due to a failure of understanding on their part, not misstatement on his. This is a reasonable tactic in persuasion, especially as it provides a basis for renewing the conversation, for building the relationship, to make sure they get things right this time. His hope is that they will come to understand him ἕως τέλους matching ἀπὸ μέρους.

Paul continues with notions of reciprocity such as have appeared earlier in the letter, notably in the reference to their being partners in v. 7: 'so that we will be your claim-to-honour and you will be ours on the Day of our Lord Jesus' (v. 14). In other words, on the Lord's Day the Corinthians will point to Paul and say words to the effect, 'We claim honour from Paul and his work that has enhanced our reputation', while Paul will say, 'I claim honour from the Corinthian Christ-followers and their work that has enhanced my reputation'. Here he mentions a vital and very distinctive group belief, the coming Day of the Lord, and attributes to him and the Corinthians a similar role in relation to it: they will all be there and they will be equally proud of one another. Here we have further evidence that Paul is out to stress that he and the Corinthians are partners in a common enterprise with common beliefs and values. At the same time, this is the first mention in the letter of the glorious future in store for them; this contributes to the social identity they derive from membership by situating their biographies and integrating their experience within a narrative having a past, a present and a future (Condor 1996; Esler 2003a: 22–4; Lim 2020: 329–30). Paul is thus engaged in psychological group formation, by further developing their shared group identity, to produce influence among the Christ-followers in Corinth.

Answering a charge of fickleness (1.15-22)

2 Corinthians 1.15-16 Paul now progresses to the specific issue of his recent dealings with the Corinthians. In reliance on the matter he has just mentioned (ταύτῃ τῇ πεποιθήσει) – presumably meaning their understanding of the pride he and they would take in one another on the Day of the Lord (v. 14) – he will seek to explain his changing travel plans. In other words, he writes hoping they will be able to make honour-claims in relation to one another.

To understand the accusation against him that Paul will answer in 2 Cor. 1.15-22, it is necessary to bear in mind the course of his relationship with the Corinthians, as set out in Chapter 1 of this volume. The immediate problem was his apparently reneging on his promise to visit them on the way to Macedonia and on the way back, a promise probably made during the course of his severe visit. These two visits would have constituted a 'double gift' (δευτέρα χάρις; 2 Cor. 1.15). Instead, he had gone to Macedonia without stopping in Corinth. This looks like he had reverted to the journey he had originally told them in 1 Cor. 16.5-9 that he intended to make. No doubt this was a disappointment to the Corinthians, and they would naturally have conceived the idea that Paul was vacillating in relation to them. His change of plan happened in the recent past, probably being announced in his severe letter that Paul sent to Corinth with Titus, since he has to deal with the consequences in 2 Corinthians itself.

A probable explanation suggests itself, as outlined in Chapter 1. During the painful visit, Paul informed the Corinthians of a change of plan. He would leave Corinth (probably to travel back to Ephesus), but that then he would return to Corinth and travel thence to Macedonia, back to Corinth and then on to Jerusalem (the 'double gift'). He may have offered them this divergence from his original plan as a means of softening the impact of his painful visit. But later, when he had returned from the visit, he decided against this itinerary. This formed an important part of what he communicated in his painful letter that preceded 2 Corinthians (2 Cor. 2.3 and 7.12-13). In this letter he informed them that he would not, after all, be visiting them on the way to Macedonia. When Titus took this severe letter to Corinth, this issue ranked next to that concerning the incident of ἀδικία (mentioned in 2.5-11 and 7.12) and in relation to which Paul was eagerly looking forward to meeting up with him, to learn of the Corinthians' reaction to his letter. While the letter and Titus' mediation did secure a satisfactory outcome in relation to the ἀδικία, Paul's change of travel plans continued to rankle with the Corinthian Christ-followers.

2 Corinthians 1.17-18 Although he will offer an explanation for his change of plans in 2 Cor. 1.23–2.4, he wants first to neutralize attacks that are being made on his character because he has changed his plan and not visited Corinth first (and, as just noted, this necessitates that the Corinthians knew of his original plan and that he had changed it). He begins with a question (in v. 17), 'With this in mind did I indulge in fickleness (ἐλαφρία)?' This is the only occurrence of this word in the New Testament, although ἐλαφρός, meaning 'light', appears in 2 Cor. 4.17 (and Mt. 11.30). At its core, ἐλαφρός means 'light' and then, by extension, 'frivolous', 'fickle', 'vacillating' (BDAG 314). It has been suggested that the charge against Paul was not one of fickleness but of being blasé about his relationship with them (Garland 1999: 99). Yet this is difficult to square with what comes next. For he asks, 'Or when I make plans, do I plan in a human way (κατὰ σάρκα), so that with me it is "Yes, yes" and then "No, no"' (v. 17)? Presumably, some Christ-followers in Corinth were complaining that this was how he had behaved (Barnett 1997: 102; Guthrie 2015: 109). It represents an understandable response to Paul's saying in succession: 'I am going to Macedonia before visiting you'; then 'I will visit you going to and coming from Macedonia'; and, lastly, 'I am reverting to my original plan'. Moreover, since fickleness of this sort is very close to insincerity, we see that he had good reason for his asserting simplicity and godly sincerity in 2 Cor. 1.12 and for solemnly insisting in v. 18 that the language (λόγος) he uses to them is not 'Yes and no'. The solemnity of the insistence consists of Paul's tying his reliability to God's: either 'God is faithful with respect to my discourse not being "yes and no"', or (if Paul is uttering an oath), 'As surely as God is faithful . . .' (Thrall 1994: 144).

2 Corinthians 1.19-22 These verses represent an argument supporting this assertion. The logic is quite challenging but highly revealing. Paul begins (v. 19) with 'For God's son, Jesus Christ' (thus picking up the reference to God at the start of the previous verse), who was proclaimed among you by us (διὰ ἡμῶν) – by me, Silvanus and Timothy[8] – was (ἐγένετο; aorist tense) not "Yes and no", but in him "Yes" has occurred (γέγονεν; perfect tense)'. In Jesus Christ an ongoing affirmation has come into existence, not a mixture of affirmation and negation. As Thrall notes, however, v. 19 does not logically follow from v. 18. Jesus Christ could be a model of faithful reliability even though Paul, Silvanus and Timothy were not (1994: 147). But let us not despair at this point! Rather, we need some connection between Christ and Paul if he is to benefit from the argument and that means following its course a little further. 'For as many (ὅσαι) promises of God as exist', Paul continues in v. 20, 'their "yes" (is) in him'. The generality of ὅσαι warns us against limiting these promises to those made only to Israel (*contra*, Garland 1999: 103). It

---

[8] Cf. Acts 18.5.

is likely, however, that Paul had taken some steps to inform his non-Judean converts of the promises God had made to Israel (Lambrecht 1999: 29).

In v. 20, Paul adds, 'Therefore, also through him (δι' αὐτοῦ) (there is) Amen to God for glory through us' (διὰ ἡμῶν). The reappearance here of 'through us' (διὰ ἡμῶν), after its use in relation to Paul, Silvanus and Timothy in v. 19, is the link. It is by their activity that the Amen, now presented as a critically important specific component of the Yes, goes up to God for (his) glory. Harris argues that ἡμῶν refers not to Paul and his colleagues but to all 'Christians' (2005: 204). The problem with this view is that it would also entail that ἡμῶν means Paul, Silvanus and Timothy in vv. 18, 19 and 21, but all Christ-followers in v. 20 without any indication that the referent had changed (Thrall 1994: 150). More importantly, it is the words in v. 20 that establish the link Paul needs between Christ's 'Yes' and his own work in Corinth. That connection subsists in the fact that the Amen to God for his glory that occurs through Jesus Christ (δι' αὐτοῦ) also has another cause: it is 'by us' (διὰ ἡμῶν), meaning through the preaching (that made Christ known in Corinth) undertaken by Paul, Silvanus and Timothy. The use of the same preposition, διά, in relation to what Christ did and what Paul, Silvanus and Timothy has done is quite striking here. Underlying Paul's argument is the reality that some at least of the Corinthians would not even have heard of Christ without his preaching, something he prided himself on: 'For Christ did not send me to baptise but to preach the gospel' (1 Cor. 1.17). So Paul is arguing that the reality of the Yes of Jesus has been enabled by their preaching, and, therefore, it is implied, there can be no separation between how he has behaved and how Jesus Christ behaved. Jesus Christ is consistent and so is he.

Although this argument may not appear a very convincing answer to the complaint of the Corinthians, its purport is unmistakable. In relation to the question of leadership, moreover, it continues the idea Paul has already begun in the claim that he shares Christ's sufferings (2 Cor. 1.5) by now attaching himself closely to the great Yes that Christ uttered to the divine will. This is another venture in claiming his alignment to a central belief of the group and therefore of asserting his role as, given the wide-ranging significance of this attachment, an exemplar of that identity. In addition, his mention of the work undertaken by himself with help from Timothy and Silvanus serves to reinforce his claim to be an apostle of Christ Jesus by the will of God (2 Cor. 1.1), a claim developed with remarkable force in the next two verses.

For this section concludes, in vv. 21-22, with four statements about what God has done for 'us':

(a) It is God himself who is establishing (βεβαιῶν) us together with you in Christ,

(b) and anointed (χρίσας) us,
(c) and who sealed (σφραγισάμενος) us,
(d) and gave (δοὺς) the pledge (ἀρραβών) of the Spirit in our hearts.

Our starting point must be that Dunn's interpretation of vv. 21-22 in terms of the baptism of the Spirit and not water baptism is surely correct (1970a: 131–4). Paul is referring back to the type of experience with the Spirit he has dealt with at length in 1 Corinthians 12–14, as I have discussed elsewhere (1994: 43–9). The failure of commentators to see this may lie in their lack of enthusiasm for charismatic phenomena. It is difficult to see why Harris (2005: 210) should assert that the following features 'would have been naturally evocative of baptism':

1. References to the receipt of the Spirit,
2. Divine ownership and protection, and
3. Commissioning and endowment for service.

As to 1., 1 Corinthians 12–14 has a very rich array of Spirit experiences but with no reference to baptism. As to 2., the word βεβαιόω at the start of v. 21 appears on three other occasions in Paul. At Rom. 15.8, it is used in relation to confirming/fulfilling the promises made to the fathers, not baptism; this is very appropriate here given Paul's references to the fulfilment of promises in 2 Cor. 1.20 (although there not just those to the fathers). Most tellingly, however, in 1 Cor. 1.6 Paul uses βεβαιόω to claim that the witness of Christ has been strong among the Corinthians, so that, he adds in the very next verse, they do not lack any spiritual gift (χάρισμα) and he then returns to the word in 1 Cor. 1.8 in relation to Jesus Christ continuing to keep them safe. So in 1 Cor. 1.6-8, βεβαιόω has the strongest connection to the experience of the Spirit. Also, the only other place where σφραγισάμενος appears in Paul is at Rom. 15.28, where it has nothing to do with baptism. As to 3., χρίω ('anoint') only appears here in Paul, so has no necessary connection with baptism. In addition, whereas Paul certainly saw himself as closely connected with their gifts of the Spirit, he himself had not been much of a baptizer (1 Cor. 1.14-16).

The major interpretative question posed by vv. 21-22 is the referent of the various instances of 'us'. Certainly the first of the two occurrences of 'us' in v. 21 refers only to Paul or, perhaps, to Paul and Timothy, not to the Corinthians, since they are differentiated by the expression 'together with you'. But when 'us' appears again in v. 21 and in v. 22, with 'our' also in v. 22, do these instances still refer to Paul (and Timothy) or do they also embrace the Corinthians? While scholarship is divided on this question, the former alternative is more likely. Four considerations support this view. First, since Paul feels it necessary in v. 21 specifically to add 'together with you' to the establishing in Christ process, which is ongoing as shown by the present tense of βεβαιῶν, but not to 'and anointed us', nor 'sealed us', nor 'in our hearts' suggests it would be an error to understand that the 'us' in these three instances also included the Corinthians. That is, the fact that Paul included the Corinthians expressly in the first instance of 'us' or 'our' but not in the next three suggests it would be an error to assume their presence. This reflects the common-sense logic underlying the rule of legal interpretation: *unius expressio est alterius exclusio* ('The expression of one thing means the exclusion of another'), which is commonly applied where one item in a list is qualified in a way the others are not. Secondly, and strengthening this conclusion, is that whereas the participle in which he does include the Corinthians, βεβαιῶν, is in the present tense, the next three are in the aorist, referring to a single event in the past (χρίσας, σφραγισάμενος and δούς). Once the focus shifts from the present back into the past, the case for understanding 'anointed us' and so on as also including the Corinthians becomes even less plausible. Thirdly, it is very difficult to give χρίσας, 'having anointed', any other meaning when applied to a human being than what we find in the Old Testament: the conferment of an exalted leadership role, there of priest, or prophet or king. Paul might well attribute such an ascribed honour to himself, since he presumably has in mind something like the overwhelming event in his life that he describes in Gal. 1.11-17. He might also do so for Silvanus and Timothy, who also worked with him proclaiming the Gospel for the first time among the Corinthians. But it is not credible that he should do so for the Corinthians themselves. Fourthly, the whole point of this section of the letter is to answer a charge that has been made against Paul, that he is inconsistent, and his case will not be helped if at this climactic point in his argument in reply he shifts the spotlight away from his own character and leadership credentials to the Corinthians (other than in relation to one point about their current experience: that God is establishing all of them in Christ [v. 21]).

One counterargument by Margaret Thrall, however, needs to be addressed. Thrall argued that the instances of 'us' and 'our' in question in vv. 21-22 also embrace the Corinthians. She was especially inclined to this view for the reason that restricting their ambit to Paul, Silvanus and Timothy 'cannot possibly fit the allusion to the gift of the Spirit as the "advance instalment" of future salvation' (1994: 154), where by 'advance instalment' she is referring to ἀρραβών (though see Kwon 2008 for the argument that ἀρραβών means 'pledge' not 'down payment'). No doubt underlying Thrall's suggestion is the fact that later in this very letter Paul presents the ἀρραβών of the Spirit as a characteristic of all Christ-followers (2 Cor. 5.1-5). Certainly the Corinthians manifested the gifts of the Spirit themselves (1 Corinthians 12–14; Esler 1994: 43–9). Yet Thrall's argument is not persuasive. Admittedly, Paul, like all Christ-followers, had received the ἀρραβών of the Spirit. But as far as the Spirit was concerned, Paul and the Corinthians were hardly on equal terms, for he had received the Spirit (which must be understood in charismatic terms) in far greater abundance than them. This was the man, after all, who not long before had reminded them that his initial preaching to the Corinthians was accompanied by 'a demonstration of spirit and power' (1 Cor. 2.4), and who, in the midst of a long discussion of charismatic phenomena, had asserted, 'I thank God that I speak in tongues more than all of you' (1 Cor. 14.18). In Galatians, he also claimed (without any obvious fear of contradiction) that his addressees received the Spirit when he preached the Gospel to them (Gal. 3.2). More to the point, later in this letter (in 2 Cor. 12.12) he will go even further, asserting that he showed he was a true apostle by the fact that he performed among them signs (σημεῖα), wonders (τέρατα) and works of power (δυνάμεις), thus claiming to have produced miracles in their midst. As I have argued previously in relation to the importance of charismatic phenomena in the early stages of the Christ-movement (Esler 1994: 37–51), Paul was very like the travelling charismatic preachers that Felicitas Goodman encountered in Latin America, who had powerful charismatic capacities and who were able to initiate the dynamics of Spirit possession among the members when they founded a new congregation (1972).[9] In addition, and as discussed earlier, unlike the Corinthians, Paul had been anointed and sealed. This is a sign of his exalted leadership role. We might reasonably suppose that his reception of the Spirit, whenever that first occurred, was proof of the anointing and sealing for the mighty task God had in mind for him in choosing to reveal his Son in him (Gal. 1.16). He is a prototypical ἀπόστολος.

We may now summarize how vv. 15–22 support Paul's argument. His chief aim is to reinforce the claim to his godly sincerity (v. 12) and to the fact that he does not devise plans in a human way (κατὰ σάρκα; v. 17), in that he denies saying 'Yes and No' by associating himself with the great 'Yes' represented by Christ. The main mechanism of association is that Christ was preached to the Corinthians through him (and Silvanus and Timothy). This is the burden of vv. 19–20. Verses 21–22 show that the involvement of Paul, Silvanus and Timothy in the great 'Yes' of Christ has been confirmed by their receipt of the Spirit, which applies to them, Paul especially, in a particularly

---

[9] Colleen Shantz has published an important examination of Paul's ecstatic states from a neurobiological perspective (2009).

potent way. Paul is willing to grant that the Corinthians are, like him, Silvanus and Timothy being established by God in Christ. But he will not let up on the importance of his being the one who mediated Christ to the Corinthians, since that is essential for his argument that he is consistent. An incident of that mediation, he reminds them, is his having been anointed and sealed in the Spirit, an area where (they would recall) his capabilities were superior to theirs. Yet at this very juncture, it seems, Paul sensed that he had to be careful, that it would not further his aim of rebuilding his relationship with the Corinthians if he pushed too hard on his own authority and power. Time, then, for him to re-emphasize the partnership that exists between him and them that he has been striving to propound earlier in the letter.

In addition, within the framework of Turner's argument (2005), only if the Corinthians are confident that Paul is a leader who shares prototypical values of the Christ-movement and, we might add, of the subgroup of that movement consisting of the apostles, will he be able to control the deployment of resources, as he will need to do in relation to the collection in chs 8–9. To that extent, the argument he runs in 1.1-22 is fully integrated with what is to come in chs 8–9.

This brings us to vv. 23-24, which are more naturally read with what follows (in ch. 2), than with the passage that immediately precedes them (in ch. 1), since they move from the question of whether he had been inconsistent or not to the actual reason for his change of plans.

4

Paul explains himself to the Corinthians (1.23–2.13)

In 2 Cor. 1.23, Paul advances to a new stage in his argument. He needs to explain why he cancelled a visit to Corinth and sent a letter (at the hand of Titus) instead. He also seeks to delve into the facts underlying these events, involving an incident of 'wrongful conduct' (ἀδικία) in the Christ-movement, which, coupled with his reaction to it, had threatened to damage his relationship with the Corinthian believers. In the result, fortunately, it did not. These matters occupy 2 Cor. 1.23–2.13 and 7.5-16. In 2 Cor. 2.13, Paul describes heading for Macedonia to meet Titus, and in 7.5 he mentions his arriving there. The material of a quite different character that Paul includes as 2 Cor. 2.24–7.4 has inevitably fuelled arguments that this section is an interpolation of Pauline material from some other letter that breaks an originally unified text running from 2.13 to 7.5. The case for Paul having introduced the material in 2 Cor. 2.14–7.4 after 2.13 and before 7.5 as part of his original conception for the letter – that is, the case for its not being an interpolation – will appear in the next chapter of this commentary.

Paul's cancelled visit to Corinth and his severe letter (2 Cor. 1.23–2.4)

2 Corinthians 1.23 In spite of all the careful arguments as to his sincerity that occupy 2 Cor. 1.12-22, Paul still faced the particular problem that he had cancelled a visit. So now he needed to convince the Corinthians that, in this case, he did have a good reason for doing so. He takes the bull by the horns at the outset: 'I appeal to God as witness on my own life that I refrained from coming (οὐκέτι ἦλθον) to Corinth in order that I might spare you.' The phrase οὐκέτι ἦλθον 'implies the abandonment of a previous intention or plan to visit Corinth' (Harris 2005: 13). Paul has previously called his conscience to witness (1.12) and that he should now solemnly invoke God as his witness shows the extent to which he regards himself as on trial as far as the Corinthians are concerned (Garland 1999: 109). But this gambit also helps him rebut the specific charge of insincerity.

2 Corinthians 1.24 What was Paul sparing them from? We learn in 2 Cor. 2.1 that it was another painful visit like the one he had previously made to them, presumably associated with the type of severe chastisement with which he had threatened them in 1 Cor. 4.19-21: 'Shall I come to you with a whip?' and during which he certainly warned them about their conduct (2 Cor. 13.2-3). Yet having stated it was to spare them produces something of a dilemma for Paul, since this implies something severe that he could have done if he had chosen. In particular, since his approach to leadership hitherto has involved trying to build a partnership with them, the exercise of naked force to achieve his ends is unlikely to be a successful strategy. Accordingly, he engages in what the ancient rhetoricians called *correctio* (or ἐπιδιόρθωσις or ἐπανόρθωσις), 'the correction of the speaker's own utterance, which is recognized to be improper by the speaker himself, or might perhaps be regarded as improper by the audience'.[1] In addition, he does this precisely in the mode of decrying any hegemonic disposition or activity on his part and insisting again on their partnership. He states: 'Not that we lord it over (κυριεύομεν) your faith, but we are co-workers (συνεργοί) of your joy, since you stand by faith.'

Some commentators suggest that the shift from first-person singular in v. 23 to first-person plural in v. 24 indicates that Paul is including Silvanus and Timothy (e.g. Furnish 1984: 152; Matera 2003: 59). This is unlikely; Silvanus and Timothy were mentioned in 1.19 as founders of the Corinthian Christ-movement with Paul. They are not relevant to the point he is making in 1.24. Rather, since Paul uses the first-person singular in 1.23 and 2.1, then κυριεύομεν and ἐσμεν in v. 24 probably also refer to Paul (Harris 2005: 214).

There are four other instances of κυριεύειν in Paul. The word can certainly have a negative connotation, as in 'Death no longer lords it over him' (Rom. 6.9), 'Sin will no longer lord it over you' (Rom. 6.14) and 'Law lords it over a person as long as he or she lives' (Rom. 7.1). In these cases, it is similar to the instance at Lk. 22.25-26: 'The kings of the foreigners lord it over them'. The verb appears as κατακυριεύειν in the parallel passages in Mk. 10.42 and Matt. 20.25. But it can also have a positive connotation, as in 'so that he (Christ) might be lord over the living and the dead' (Rom. 14.9) and also 1 Tim. 6.15 ('the Lord of those who are lords').

In v. 24, κυριεύειν certainly conveys a negative impression, as shown by its contrast with συνεργοί. Paul is disavowing any form of rule (no doubt oppressive) associated with 'lords' (κύριοι) in this context. This comes very

---

[1] Orton and Anderson 1998: 346–9, at para. 784; there is another such *correctio* in 2 Cor. 3.5.

Paul Explains Himself to the Corinthians (1.23–2.13)

close to a disavowal of coercion in his dealings with the Corinthians. To this point in the letter he has been working hard to present his relationship with them as one of partnership. But this is not to say that he does not at times use words that encapsulate the nature of his authority: especially his being like a father to them, involving both authority and affection (Burke 2000), and their need to be obedient to him (for example, and very clearly, at 2 Cor. 12.14).

Commentators have asked with whom, however, does Paul work jointly in his promotion of joy. Who is encompassed in the συν- of συνεργοί? There are a number of possibilities, but his Corinthian audience is the only likely contender. Why assert that he does not lord it over their faith and then talk about joint-working in joy if the Corinthians are not the ones with whom he will be engaging in that joint-working, especially when he has already used similar partnership language of them and him in 2 Cor. 1.7. While Thrall rejects this view (1994: 162), largely because Paul does not employ the word συνεργοί of believers in general, his wide use of the word elsewhere (there are ten other instances) indicates that this is an entirely appropriate way to designate the Corinthians in the current situation. If he can identify them as partners (κοινωνοί) in 2 Cor. 1.7, he can call them joint-workers here. We know that for him these two descriptors fit closely together, since he describes Titus as both κοινωνός and συνεργός in 2 Cor. 8.23, a circumstance that makes it natural to assume that Paul is here using both terms of the Corinthians.

The two other possibilities are unappealing. It is implausible to regard the reference as to Silvanus and Timothy (Thrall 1994: 162), since a shift from the Corinthians to Silvanus and Timothy in the one statement would be inexplicable. The only human beings Paul has in mind in v. 24 are himself and his Corinthian audience. Nor does Paul mean to include God as his συνεργός, since, again, this would entail an unnatural movement away from the Corinthians, and it would mean Paul aligning himself to God at the level of activity.

If the expression 'since you stand by faith' at the end of v. 24 relates to the first clause in v. 24 (which is most likely, given its reference to faith), Paul is implying that there is no need for him to try to lord it over their faith in any event (additionally to his denying he is doing this) as it is strong already. Alternatively (and less likely), if the expression relates to the second clause, Paul implies, 'I am particularly interested in partnering your joy since your faith is firm'. On either view, Paul is paying the Corinthians a high compliment that contributes to his general aim of establishing an even stronger affective bond with them.

2 Corinthians 2.1 In this verse, Paul articulates the underlying reason for his wanting to spare them another visit from him: 'I came to this decision: not to inflict another sorrowful visit on you' (literally: 'not again (πάλιν) in sorrow [λύπῃ]) to come to you'). The aorist case in relation to his making a decision (ἔκρινα) stands in contrast to the imperfect of 'I was intending' in 1.15. The word πάλιν is central to the proper interpretation of the statement yet difficult to interpret. The difficulty arises from determining whether Paul is referring to: (a) his coming back to Corinth, this time with grief (meaning this would be Paul's second visit); or (b) to his coming again with grief, which would imply a previous sorrowful visit, which must be different from Paul's founding visit, so that any further visit would be Paul's third. Option (a) was common in antiquity (it was the view of Theodoret, for example [*Interpretatio in xiv epistulas sancti Pauli*; PG: 82:385]). Option (b), however, is now held by the majority of Pauline interpreters (e.g. Barrett 1973: 85; Lambrecht 1999: 31; Vegge 2008: 88–9; Seifrid 2014: 72–3), having first been suggested by Friedrich Bleek in 1830 (Carlson 2016: 600). It is accepted as correct in this commentary. Some scholars, such as Richard Batey (1965), Douglas Campbell (2014: 83–4) and Stephen Carlson (2016) have challenged that majority view. Carlson has demonstrated that attempts to disambiguate the meaning of πάλιν on syntactic grounds are unconvincing and that the wider context of 2 Corinthians must determine its meaning.

Yet the key elements of that context are: Paul's statement just before (in 2 Cor 1.23) that he did not pay them a visit so as to spare them (φειδόμενος ὑμῶν); his mentioning that his forthcoming visit will be his third (12.14; 13.1); his assurance in 12.14 that (this time, implying unlike the last) he will not cause them trouble (καταναρκάω);[2] the allusions to his second visit in 12.20-21; and the strong indication in 13.2 that on his second visit he was severe with them (i.e. he caused them sorrow). There is, indeed, a very close connection between 13.2 and 1.23 that is only explicable on the basis that Paul was responsible for all of our canonical 2 Corinthians as a unified composition. He reminds them in 13.2 that he had said (on his prior [i.e. second] visit) that if he came again he would not spare them (οὐ φείσομαι), and at 1.23 it is clear this view was still in his mind when he was contemplating such a third visit because he abandoned the idea so as to spare them (φειδόμενος ὑμῶν). This element also suggests, as 2.2 abundantly confirms, that the primary subject of the grief (λύπη) he mentions in 2.1 will be the Corinthians, not him, even though he acknowledges in 2.3 that he too will suffer grief, which is another sign of his solidarity with them.

In his discussion of the contextual features, Carlson eventually moves to Theodoret's position, largely because he is unable to characterize the second visit (13.1-2) as one in which the Corinthians suffered grief. His discussion, however, implausibly constrains the meaning of λύπη to the

---

[2] The verb καταναρκάω probably conveys the meaning expressed in the colloquial phrase 'shake down' (BDAG 522).

results of punishment, when it could also have been triggered among the Corinthians by what Paul describes in 13.1-2, including his warning to 'those who sinned before and all the others', a statement probably linked to 12.20-21, and whatever were the specifics of Paul's actions alluded to in the verb καταναρκάω in 12.14 (which Carlson does not discuss). In short, on the previous visit Paul caused them (and no doubt himself in solidarity with them) sorrow, but he forbore taking some unspecified punitive action against them, while in 2.1 he says he anticipated another sorrowful visit, only this time he would not have spared them.

Two factors suggest that this, second and sorrowful visit, was a visit subsequent to his foundation visit and occurred between his writing of 1 Corinthians and 2 Corinthians. First, the circumstances of his first visit as described in 1 Cor. 2.1-5, 11.2 and 15.1 and elsewhere are not compatible with the painful visit to which he is referring here (Thrall 1994: 53–6). Secondly, there is no indication in 1 Corinthians of a painful visit between the foundation visit and his writing that letter.[3]

2 Corinthians 2.2 What Paul says next is of a piece with this assertion that he is their partner in joy in 2 Cor. 1.24: 'For if I cause you pain, who will make me glad (εὐφραίνων) except the one whom I have pained?' Thrall reasonably explains that in this verse 'The stress is on what he sees as the mutuality of the relationship between himself and his readers' (1994: 165). Nevertheless, her recognition of the mutuality stressed by Paul in this verse further undermines her refusal to see any reference to the Corinthians in συνεργοί (co-workers') used only two verses previously (2 Cor. 1.24). For worthy of note are the lengths to which Paul goes to develop his relationship with the Corinthians by stressing that they are the source of his own happiness. The word εὐφραίνων connotes quite intense gladness. It is not common in Paul, appearing only here and in a biblical quotation in Rom. 15.10 (of the nations rejoicing with the Israelites, from Deut. 32.43 LXX) and in Gal. 4.27 (of the barren woman who has not conceived but who will, from Isa. 54.1 LXX). Moreover, his use of the singular with εὐφραίνων should not be missed. By saying, in effect, 'You are the one who makes me happy', Paul is actually employing the intimate language employed by two people who love another to express how he feels towards the Corinthians. The fact that Paul is writing the Corinthians what is virtually a love letter appears explicitly in the following two verses.

2 Corinthians 2.3 The letter to which Paul refers in this verse is the same as that mentioned in 2.4, 2.9 and 7.8 (and referred to by implication in 10.10). It is almost certain that Titus was the bearer of this letter (see comments on 2 Cor. 7.5-16). As it turned out, the letter caused the Corinthians considerable

---

[3] *Contra*, Campbell (2014: 83–4); Hall 2003: 243–6.

pain (7.8-13) and that is part of the context we must bear in mind in assessing his message to them here. Having said that a further reason for his not paying them a painful visit was that it would have made him unhappy, Paul goes on to express a sentiment similar to that in the previous verse. This is that the Corinthians should make him rejoice (χαίρειν), before continuing the theme of co-workers in joy (χαρά) from v. 24 – that he was confident that his joy (χαρά) was joy for all of them. Once again he is expressing a mutuality of feeling. Thrall wonders at this point whether Paul might have come across as somewhat self-centred to the Corinthians by his insistence that, in effect, they had a duty to make him happy – whether the love he is expressing for them might have seemed to them to be 'demanding and possessive' (1994: 169). But this notion has a touch of anachronism about it. It presupposes a view of personal relationships quite at home in the West where individuals are accustomed to strike off on their own and resist personal claims (from relatives especially) that are seen as contrary to their self-identity. But it is far less plausible in the strongly group-oriented world of the ancient Mediterranean world where tight bonds held groups, families especially, closely together and the interests of one were seen as the interests of all. Paul is appealing precisely to such a view of social relationships when he says, 'my joy is the joy of all of you'. He presupposes that he and the Corinthians are members of a group with the closest of ties to one another.

2 Corinthians 2.4 All of this is reinforced by what follows in v. 4. Paul is emphasizing that his letter was not to cause them pain, but to express his love (ἀγάπη) for them. Although it is possible that Paul is implying that when he wrote the letter, he recognized that such might be the result (Lambrecht 1999: 31), such a concession does not sit easily with his denial of causing pain in 2.5. It is certainly the case, however, that this verse culminates a section of the letter (2.1-4) with a remarkable vocabulary of sorrow and joy: 'Through it Paul emphasizes the bonds that exist between the apostles and his Christians, bonds he wants to strengthen even more' (Lambrecht 1999: 31). Viewed from a social identity approach, Paul is highlighting his commitment to group norms such as ἀγάπη, while couching his closeness with the other members in the strongest affective terms so as to underline the emotional dimension of belonging.

The reason for Paul's severe letter and his journey to Troas and Macedonia (2.5-13)

The precipitating cause for the severe letter being a problem was that an individual had behaved wrongly (ὁ ἀδικήσας; 7.12), someone had suffered from this wrongdoing (ὁ ἀδικηθείς; 7.12) and somehow the community had been implicated in it. But he had now been punished and was repentant, and Paul wanted the Corinthians to forgive him and move on. Paul breaks up the material relating to the incident of ἀδικία and its perpetrator into two sections. In 2.5-13, first, he gives a fleeting indication of why he wrote the letter – to have the Corinthians punish the malefactor in obedience to his (Paul's) wishes – but also, now they have done this, to endorse the punishment imposed at the behest of a majority of the Corinthian believers as sufficient. This endorsement was no doubt dependent on the report Titus had brought back to him of how his severe letter had been received, on which there is rich evidence in 7.5-16. This passage in 2 Corinthians 7 is the second section in the text providing evidence of this incident and how the Corinthians responded to Paul's severe letter. As we will see in discussing 2 Cor. 7.5-16 later in the volume, Paul was heavily dependent on how sensitively Titus handled the issue with the Corinthians when he delivered the letter, and in this regard he was not disappointed.

In the Patristic period, many writers identified the wrongdoer (ὁ ἀδικήσας) with the man charged with incest in 1 Corinthians 5, but there are weighty reasons against that view. The major problem with it is that it is difficult to see why this issue would not have been resolved by Timothy during his visit to the city envisaged in 1 Corinthians or, failing that, by Paul himself during his second, severe visit, as suggested by Thrall (1994: 61–5).

The majority of modern commentators consider that Paul himself was the victim of the wrongdoing.[4] The position taken in this commentary is that the evidence is insufficient to make this identification and that much evidence, when read from a social identity perspective, points towards both victim and assailant being incapable of identification. Since the relevant evidence appears in 2 Cor. 2 and 7, a summary of the position is deferred till Chapter 10 of this commentary. The entire issue, however, is illuminated by a social identity perspective on deviance and its punishment that will now be set out.

A social identity perspective on deviance and its punishment

The social identity approach (especially as it relates to leadership) is well adapted to a social situation such as the one concerning this wrongdoer in

---

[4] Thrall 1987; Murphy-O'Connor (1996: 293): 'a single Christian (2:6; 7:12) made a serious attack (2:1, 3, 4) on Paul personally (2:5, 10)'; Welborn 2011 argues that Gaius was the wrongdoer and Paul the person wronged (being falsely charged with embezzlement in relation to the collection).

Corinth. Some recent research from social identity psychologists has focused precisely on the question of when and to what extent a group determines that one of its members has done wrong – or has acted 'as a deviant' – and, if so, whether and how he or she should be punished. Although the sociology of deviance has already proved illuminating in New Testament research (Barclay 1995), a social identity approach introduces useful psychological dimensions of the case in view. I will proceed by first outlining a social identity approach to deviance (conveniently summarized in an article by Jolanda Jetten et al. in 2011) that holds the promise of allowing a more nuanced discussion of the text than might be possible without it and then considering the textual data in the light of the theory. The social identity approach to deviance, after it has been explained, will be applied to 2 Cor. 2.5-13 in this chapter and to 7.5-16 in Chapter 10.

It is commonplace for a member of a group to make a mistake, to fall from grace. Such an occurrence is likely to cause reverberations among the membership. Yet, somewhat surprisingly perhaps, even when the member concerned has behaved very badly (including damaging the reputation of the group), the response of the membership is not always as harsh as we might expect. Even though deviants can undermine the integrity of the group, so that derogating them and excluding them from the ingroup might serve the important function of maintaining a distinctive and positive identity, at times a much more lenient response might occur. Sometimes, for example, some members may argue that the behaviour was not deviant at all. Alternatively, even if the behaviour is viewed as deviant, it may be just as common for some ingroup members at least to turn a blind eye to the transgression as to punish the deviant harshly. In other words, responses among the members are likely to vary widely (Jetten et al. 2011: 118). The two critical questions in any given case are, first, whether the behaviour should be appraised as deviance and, secondly, if so, should the deviant be punished (Jetten et al. 2011: 118–19).

The question, first, of whether the behaviour is regarded as deviant is complicated by a number of factors. First, what counts as normative within the group is not always clear. This may be the case particularly when it is the first occasion on which the behaviour has appeared and how it relates to group norms has not previously been canvassed. Secondly, even where the relevant norms are settled, there can also be differences in how the individual is appraised. Some members may express strong hostility, while others are more forgiving. Thus, one study in 2004 analysed the results of an online bulletin board maintained by the BBC to assess reactions to British and American soldiers who abused Iraqi prisoners after the Second Gulf War. Nearly all responses from outside the United Kingdom and the United States were strongly negative. Yet while most British and American responses were negative, a minority of them sought to excuse the soldiers' rule-breaking. In other words, there was more variability among ingroup (i.e. British and American) members than among outgroup members (Iyer et al. 2012; Jetten et al. 2011: 120–1). Thirdly, attributions of the motive of the individual can play an important role in determining how other members respond to his or her behaviour. Criticism of the person might be accepted, for example, if it is known that he or she cares for the group, or if it were thought that, put in the same situation, everyone would act as the individual in question did. Fourthly, the wider context of the group could come into play: Did it, for example, possess a norm that encouraged tolerance of diversity or innovation? In groups that reflected a collectivist mindset, group members holding concordant views are more likely to be evaluated positively than those holding dissenting attitudes. On the other hand, in groups that possessed norms encouraging diverse opinions, members could be loyal to the group in the very act of being different (Jetten et al. 2011: 121–3). The result of this analysis is that members may answer the question of whether an individual's behaviour is deviant with a 'no', 'maybe' or 'yes'.

In relation to the second question – should the deviant be punished? – research suggests that when rule-breaking by an individual is regarded as a deviant act, the dominant reactions to him or her are rejection and punishment. But it is wrong to think this is inevitable, since at times group members are quite forgiving of the transgressions of other members, 'even when they have involved extreme acts of deviance'. A number of factors have a bearing on whether the wrongdoer will experience punishment or forgiveness (Jetten et al. 2011: 124).

To begin, communication between the individual and group members can greatly affect the outcome. If the other members speak with the individual and persuade him or her of the need for a change of attitude and behaviour – to accept the majority view – reinstatement can occur quickly. Punishment is less likely to be required if, possibly as a result of a process of communication, the deviants show remorse for their actions and it is their first offence. This factor, therefore, focuses on how interactions occur between the individual concerned and other group members, with responses to him or her developing over time (Jetten et al. 2011: 124–5).

Two other, closely related, factors relevant to whether the individual is punished or forgiven are whether the group regards itself as operating at a high level of morality and rule-keeping and to what extent members identify with the group. Recent research suggests, rather paradoxically, that the members strongly identifying with a group that has high moral standards are more likely than other members of the group to struggle to find the appropriate response to a member's wrongdoing (Iyer et al. 2012; Jetten et al. 2011: 126–7).

A group that regards itself as occupying the high moral ground appears to provide its members with room to manoeuvre in how they appraise the severity of the offence:

> The results suggested that it is low identifiers, and not more highly committed group members, who were more likely to report the inconsistency between the rule-breaker's behaviour and the stance of the group. Compared to low identifiers, high identifiers perceived the rule breaking as less damaging for the group. (Jetten et al. 2011: 127)

Furthermore, in the case of such a group:

> Compared to high identifiers, low identifiers were more negative in their evaluations of the rule-breakers and perceived their behaviour to be more damaging to the group. These negative evaluations had important concrete implications as well: *low identifiers recommended a harsher punishment for the rule-breakers than high identifiers.* (Jetten et al. 2011: 128 [emphasis added])

The researchers explained this on the basis that 'high identifiers appeared to see the rule-breakers as generally good individuals whose rule breaking constituted an isolated action', so that the reputation of the group was not undermined. The high identifiers regarded the group's moral superiority as a 'protective buffer' limiting the negative impact of rule-breaking by group members (Jetten et al. 2011: 128).

A fourth factor that may lead to lenient treatment of an offender is that at times deviance is useful because transgressions, and the soul-searching they produce, help groups to understand and negotiate their identity, to see more clearly what the group is about. In other words, deviant behaviour helps the group as a whole to define what is normative (Jetten et al. 2011: 128–9).

Other factors, not particularly relevant to the wrongdoer mentioned in 2 Corinthians 2 and 7, include the extent to which the actions of the group are exposed to an external audience, whether members were long-time members of the group or had only recently joined and whether the survival of the group depended on one or more of its rules being broken (Jetten et al. 2011: 130–1).

Applying the social identity approach to deviance to 2 Cor. 2.5-11

In answering the first question, whether behaviour should be appraised as deviance, we must initially determine whether a member of the group has breached its norms. We can do that in general terms here, leaving some details – especially the identity of the parties and the precise nature of the wrong – to the discussion of this issue in 2 Cor. 7.5-16, where further evidence exists. While it is clear that Paul (and perhaps the Corinthian Christ-followers close to him, such as Stephanas, Fortunatus and Achaicus [1 Cor. 16.15, 17]) considered a member had behaved wrongly, it appears that this was not the unanimous view of the group. That the Corinthians were later grieved into repenting over the incident (2 Cor. 7.9) means that some of them were probably complicit in it and, therefore, not necessarily of the view that it was wrong. This means that the incident reflects the common situation where there is disagreement in the group over whether the behaviour in question represents deviance or not.

Was the man viewed as a deviant?

To begin with, Paul tells us in 2.5 that someone – a male person as becomes clear in vv. 6-8 – has caused sorrow (λελύπηκεν). It has been suggested (BDAG 604) that the verb λυπεῖν, when used in an absolute sense (as here), goes beyond causing pain or vexation and approaches causing severe humiliation or outrage. This meaning, however, does not accord with the meaning of 'cause sorrow' in 2 Cor. 2.2, and it is difficult to see why Paul would intend so different a connotation for the verb only three verses later. It is also unclear how such a meaning could cohere with Paul's stated wish not to blow the matter out of proportion. Some light falls on the factual substratum of that sorrow-giving in 7.12, when Paul, in relation to the context in which he wrote the stern letter, refers to the (male) person who did wrong (ὁ ἀδικήσας; aorist active participle) and the (male) person who suffered the wrong (ὁ ἀδικηθείς; aorist passive participle). As just noted, however, detailed consideration of the ἀδικία and its perpetrator and victim is deferred until Chapter 10 of this volume. Although this must be how Paul always saw the situation, there were plainly different views held on the matter in Corinth.

2 Corinthians 2.5 Paul begins in a notably circumspect way: 'If (εἰ) anyone (τις) has caused sorrow (λελύπηκεν), he has not caused sorrow to me, but, to a certain extent (ἀπὸ μέρους) – lest I exaggerate (ἵνα μὴ ἐπιβαρῶ) – to all of you' (2 Cor. 2.5). The verse starts with a conditional clause using εἰ and the indicative mood. This means that the condition has been fulfilled. As Harris suggests, it is essentially the same as saying, 'The person who ...' (2005: 223). The word τις refers to a real person known to Paul and his Corinthians addressees but not, unfortunately, to us (though Welborn has argued it was Gaius [2011]). Paul's disavowal in the previous verse of having wanted to cause them sorrow by his letter allows a natural transition to this verse that introduces someone who *has* caused them sorrow. Here Paul tactfully fails to name the offender, but he assumes they will know who it is, and it is certainly the person he will later in the letter describe as ὁ ἀδικήσας (2 Cor. 7.12). Here is further evidence of the extent to which Paul writes into a situation already known to and assumed by him and his audience and of the need to be wary of obsessing over alleged 'mirror' readings of his letters to the extent that it hinders our interpretation of them.

The social identity approach to deviance sensitizes us to look for signs of a diversity of views among the membership as to the behaviour of one of the members. In this context, the meaning of the expression 'to a certain extent lest I exaggerate' (ἀπὸ μέρους ἵνα μὴ ἐπιβαρῶ) as a qualification of 'he has caused sorrow to all of you' becomes a matter of considerable importance. First, when the verb ἐπιβαρεῖν is used transitively (e.g. at 1 Thess. 2.9), it means to lay a burden on someone. Most commentators, however, consider it used intransitively here, thus suggesting the meaning 'exaggerate' (Furnish 1984: 155). Secondly, we need to assess the meaning of ἀπὸ μέρους. Paul employs this expression on three other occasions. In Rom. 11.25-26, he states that πώρωσις ἀπὸ μέρους τῷ Ἰσραὴλ γέγονεν ('a hardening has come upon *part of* Israel') until, he continues, the *full number* (τὸ πλήρωμα) of the non-Judeans come in and *all* Israel will be saved.[5] In Rom. 15.15, he tells his addressees that he wrote to them more boldly ἀπὸ μέρους as a reminder, where the phrase must mean 'in part/s' of the letter. In Rom. 15.24, he uses ἀπὸ μέρους in relation to the time he hopes to have for enjoying the company of the Romans before travelling to Spain, so it probably means 'for a time', 'for a while', presumably meaning for a limited amount of the total time he will be in Rome. Finally, in 2 Cor. 1.13-14 he contrasts the Corinthians' understanding 'fully' (ἕως τέλους) with their understanding in part (ἀπὸ μέρους). As applied to ἀπὸ μέρους in 2 Cor. 2.5, the meaning of the phrase in Rom. 11.25, that is, part of a whole – here meaning some of Paul's Corinthian addressees – is excluded as inconsistent with πάντας ὑμᾶς ('all of you'). Instead, the phrase has an adverbial meaning and modifies 'he has caused sorrow' (λελύπηκεν). Thus, Paul is suggesting that the offender has caused them all grief 'in part', or 'to a certain extent'.[6] Paul thus takes care to emphasize the limited nature of the sorrow the man caused (even though the perfect tense of the verb λελύπηκεν suggests some sorrow persisted into the present): it was limited in some way, and he does not want to exaggerate its

---

[5] In spite of contrary views (e.g. Dunn 1988: 679; BDAG 632), the context requires ἀπὸ μέρους to accompany Ἰσραὴλ not πώρωσις, as does the contradictory character of a partial hardening ('hardening' being like pregnancy in that regard).

[6] Numerous commentators take this view, e.g. Barrett 1973: 89; Thrall 1994: 172; Barnett 1997: 124; Harris 2005: 225; Guthrie 2015: 132.

impact. While it is possible that the sorrow was greater for some members than others, this is not something that Paul foregrounds in this verse.

It must also be emphasized that the sorrow of all the Corinthians only came after the arrival of Titus with Paul's severe letter, something for which we have direct evidence in 7.6-13. Although in these verses Paul indicates that his letter was the immediate cause of their sorrow, the ultimate cause was the offender who precipitated his despatch of the letter, and, in that sense, he 'has caused them sorrow' (λελύπηκεν). Moreover, the sorrow that Paul elicited from the letter was connected with their somehow having been complicit with the malefactor's ἀδικία, otherwise there would have been no need for the repentance he attributes to them in 2.9. In v. 5, Paul also suggests that the offender has caused sorrow not to him but to all the Corinthians. This statement at last indicates some diversity of views among the Corinthians, yet it appears to be a case of Paul vis-à-vis all the rest.

That Paul had to write a severe letter to the Corinthians and that they repented of what they had done in consequence of it relates to the first and second reasons mentioned earlier for why group members might take a different view on someone potentially deviant. In other words, perhaps the norm that has been allegedly breached was not clear or not established in the group or, if it was, members differed on how to appraise the individual in relation to it. That Paul induced the Corinthians to repentance (7.9) seems to exclude the former option, since 'repentance' (μετάνοια) sits more closely with an acknowledgment of one's deliberate breach of an established norm than with the commission of an act one did not know was wrong in the first place. It is, therefore, more likely that the case fell into the second category, in that, for some unknown reason, the Corinthians were prepared to overlook the offence (ἀδικία), but Paul was not. His letter persuaded them they had been wrong to do so. It is possible that the third reason for different views also came into play; the person's motive for so acting encouraged the Corinthians to overlook the offence. The fourth factor, that the Christ-movement in Corinth fostered innovation, is unlikely to have been present, as in a collectivist culture like this, conformity with, rather than dissent from, group norms is more likely to have been accepted.

Paul's statement in 2 Cor. 2.5 that the person in question 'did not cause sorrow to me' (οὐκ ἐμὲ λελύπηκεν) has attracted intense attention from commentators. Most of them consider that when Paul says the offender has not caused him sorrow, he actually means the man has. The debate focuses on whether this is an absolute negative on Paul's part, or whether it is relative, meaning that the man caused more sorrow to the Corinthian Christ-followers than to him. The point is an important one because there are scholars who interpret Paul himself as ὁ ἀδικηθείς of 2 Cor. 7.12, and they need the negative to be relative and not absolute in nature, for how could Paul be the recipient of the ἀδικία if he were in no way caused sorrow by the man's action? Thrall argues that this is a relative negation for the reason that in 2 Cor. 2.10 Paul speaks of his own forgiveness for the man. In support, she cites Harris' view that the negation is a relative one, based on two other alleged examples in Paul (1 Cor. 1.17 and 2 Cor. 7.12) and F. F. Bruce.[7] She also follows several other commentators in asking why make the disclaimer at all unless the incident could be interpreted as a personal offence to Paul.[8]

These are not particularly good reasons, however, for espousing a relative quality to the negative in v. 5. The fact that Paul will indicate his forgiveness of the culprit in v. 10 need not indicate any particular affront to him but merely that, once again, he is expressing his solidarity with his Corinthian addressees as would have been natural in a group-oriented, non-individualistic culture such as this. Paul makes the disclaimer, moreover, because it leads directly to the next point in his argument, that the business of forgiving the man is more the Corinthians' business than his. Nevertheless, it is indeed likely that this is a relative negation (meaning, the man pained him less than he pained the Corinthians), but rather for the reason that, in a letter where Paul is emphasizing his solidarity with the Corinthians, he would not wish to convey the impression to them that where an act of ἀδικία by one member on another had caused them suffering, it had not also occasioned suffering to him. If they are partners in suffering (2 Cor. 1.7) and he is a co-worker in their joy (2 Cor. 1.24), how could he not also share their sorrow? Still, we must not exaggerate the extent of his sorrow. Even the Corinthians' sorrow was limited; if Paul's was less than theirs, it must have been even more limited. The reason that the ἀδικία caused sorrow to Paul was that he cared for the community, a community that had experienced more sorrow by reason of the man's act than he had. But as part of that community and as also experiencing some sorrow, Paul is in a position to be able to forgive him along with the Corinthians.

We must also give due weight to this relative negation. The majority of commentators consider that Paul himself was the injured party, the ἀδικηθείς of 2 Cor. 7.12. Yet if the most Paul is saying to the Corinthians is that 'He caused all of you more sorrow than he caused me, and even then he only caused you sorrow to a limited degree', it is hard to see how this could be the case if Paul himself was the victim of the man's ἀδικία. In this case, Paul

---

[7] Thrall 1994: 171, citing Harris 1976: 330 (now see Harris 2005: 223-4) and Bruce 1971: 185.

[8] Thrall 1994: 171, citing Lietzmann 1949: 105, Bachmann 1909: 112, Allo 1956: 38, Barrett 1973: 89, Furnish 1984: 160, but noting other scholars who take the words literally: Klöpper 1874: 158 and Hughes 1962: 64.

would have suffered more sorrow than they. Here the circumstance that those who highly identify with a group, as Paul does here, tend to be more tolerant of deviance would presumably be cancelled out by the fact that Paul was the direct and personal target of the offender's ἀδικία. To take this further, we need to consider the rest of the passage.

How should the deviant be punished?

2 Corinthians 2.6-8 In the aforementioned discussion concerning deviant behaviour within a group from a social identity perspective, it was noted that the second question, of how to deal with deviance in a group once it has occurred, was also a matter likely to split opinions among the membership. Precisely this issue arises in the next verse of the letter. For when Paul writes next that 'For such a person this punishment imposed by the majority (οἱ πλείονες) is sufficient' (2 Cor. 2.6), he reveals that there must have been a minority who favoured a different punishment for the offender. As a preliminary point, it follows from this statement that, while Paul wrote to the Corinthians to punish the man for his misbehaviour, he did not specify precisely what punishment he wanted imposed. If he had done this, he surely would have expressed satisfaction with the Corinthians for following his advice, or dissatisfaction if they had not. Rather, he merely agrees with what the majority have decided to do. That he was relaxed on this point is not easy to reconcile with the suggestion that he was the aggrieved party in the wrongdoing. Paul must have been broadly happy with the outcome of his writing the painful letter (an outcome reported back to him by Titus). Titus reported what they have done (or at least a majority had done, following what must have been a vote on the matter [Esler 2021c: 126]), something with which Paul was content.

Moreover, Paul's view that now is the time for forgiveness suggests that the minority wanted him to be punished more severely. What was the penalty? Probably it was some sort of exclusion from the community (at Qumran, a member who defamed another was excluded from the community for a limited period: 1 QS 7.17-20). Perhaps the majority had opted for a temporary (or short) punishment, such as exclusion, while the minority wanted a permanent (or longer) punishment. Paul supports the majority position. The details of his attitude are noteworthy. In v. 7, he tells the Corinthians that as opposed to seeking a harsher punishment (which is the force of τοὐναντίον, 'the opposite') 'you should rather forgive and comfort (παρακαλέσαι), lest it happen that this man will be overwhelmed by excessive sorrow'. In v. 8, he beseeches them 'to formally reaffirm (κυρῶσαι)' their love (ἀγάπη) for him. Here κυρῶσαι refers to reaching a decision in some formal process (BDAG

579),⁹ probably a resolution of the members that he has been readmitted to membership (Thrall 1994: 177), where ἀγάπη was a key group norm and identity-descriptor. This reaffirmation of love for him was formal in the sense that it would involve some specific action by the community readmitting him to the privileges (whatever they were) from which he had been excluded. Verses 7-8 make it virtually certain that the offender was a local Corinthian, living in the city, not a casual visitor. With παρακαλέσαι in v. 7, we are back to the 'comfort' language of 2 Corinthians 1. This outcome can be illuminated with respect to the social identity approach to deviance. The very fact that there was disagreement on the matter is comparable to the finding that groups who have high moral standards (as the Christ-movement did) are more likely to fracture on the appropriate punishment for breach of their rules. The finding that those who identify more strongly with a group are more likely to be less severe towards members who breach its rules chimes with the fact that Paul, a high identifier if ever there were one, supported the lenient approach of the majority. Perhaps in that majority there were other high identifiers, people such as Stephanas, Fortunatus and Achaicus who were able to refresh his spirit (1 Cor. 16.17-18) and must therefore have been close to him and accepting of his Gospel. Possibly those who recommended a harsher punishment for the man than the majority were low identifiers, as the social identity approach suggests is likely (Jetten et al. 2011: 128). Other factors that may have come into play in relation to this division of opinion were the degree of communication between the offender and the other members, the length of time those with differing views had been members and whether the issue had caused any reverberations in Corinth beyond the Christ-group in ways that influenced the approach taken among the membership.

At this point in drafting 2 Corinthians, Paul seems to have been struck by the fact that the Corinthians might have yet another cause to accuse him of either obscurity (1.13) or inconsistency (or, even worse, insincerity) of the sort that earlier in the letter he has taken pains to refute (1.17-18). Having previously in his stern letter sought that the offender be punished, he anticipates his addresses might wonder why (in 2 Corinthians) is he now exhorting them to end his punishment and to readmit the man to the privileges from which he has been deprived in consequence of Paul's own urging? Pursuing this thought occupies the next two verses.

2 Corinthians 2.9 'For with this aim I also (καὶ) wrote to you' (ἔγραψα), Paul continues in v. 9, 'that I might put you to the test to know whether you

---

⁹ The sense is revealed by Paul's own use of the word in Gal. 3.15: κεκυρωμένην διαθήκην, a duly executed will.

are obedient (ὑπήκοοί) in everything'. Here ἔγραψα, which is a reference to his previous severe letter,[10] is preceded by καί, and this assists us in understanding Paul's meaning. Paul has already given one reason for his writing the severe letter, to keep them from another painful visit (2 Cor. 2.3). Now he develops the case for his having written a letter by nominating a further reason, namely, to test their obedience. Since he is plainly looking to their obedience in what he is about to say, the καί carries the implication that he is doing the same in this current letter. In other words, in answer to any suggestion that he was being inconsistent, he is claiming that both in the past and now there has been a common theme in the two letters, to test their obedience. Later, in 7.12, he will offer a third, though related, reason, so that their zeal for him might be revealed.

2 Corinthians 2.10-11 So far Paul has suggested (told?) them that they should forgive and comfort the man (v. 7), has urged (but not ordered) them to take him back into their love (v. 8) and has reminded them of how he tested their obedience through a past letter but with obvious reference to the present one (v. 9). Yet now, in vv. 10-11, he immediately reverts to the language of reciprocity that has been characteristic of the letter so far:

> Anyone you forgive for anything, I forgive. What I for my part have forgiven – if I have forgiven anything – has been for your sake in the sight of Christ, so that Satan will not gain the advantage over us, for we are not ignorant of his schemes.

Here, albeit on the telling assumption that they will forgive the man just as he has requested, Paul softens the impact of this result with the idea that he is fully aligned with them in the vital area of forgiveness. At first sight, this may seem an otiose statement, since Paul could hardly not forgive the man when he has just asked the Corinthians to do so. Yet his statement does more than this by setting up a general principle that transcends the present circumstances. Paul is establishing the fact that in relation to any instance of forgiveness he and the Corinthians are of one mind. Nothing could be clearer, therefore, than that Paul is actively seeking to counteract any notion that might be abroad in Corinth that he exercises his authority in a domineering fashion; he is not 'lording it' over their faith (2 Cor. 1.24). Further information relevant to this subject in 2 Cor. 7.5-16 will be considered in the following.

---

[10] Stegman (2012) regards ἔγραψα as an epistolary aorist (meaning 'I am writing'), in a creative argument which nevertheless produces an unacceptably strained dislocation from the same verb and similar expression in 2.3.

In the second clause in v. 10, Paul is telling the Corinthians that he has forgiven the man. Such forgiveness does not entail that Paul himself was the victim. Although many commentators consider that Paul could only have forgiven someone if he had been personally affronted,[11] this opinion fails before the extent to which, in a group-oriented culture such as this, an offence to one of the members was felt by all. In addition, even this shared forgiveness is minimalized when Paul adds a conditional clause – 'if I have forgiven anything' – parenthetically, in the interests of implying that the offence committed was against them not against him (Barrett 1973: 93). It is difficult to see how Paul could thus hypothesize his forgiveness if he were the victim of the ἀδικία, since how could he cast doubt on his forgiveness of the man? Moreover, he adds that what he had forgiven was for their sake (i.e., not his) in the sight of Christ. This is an early announcement of a theme repeated in chs 10–13 (10.8; 13.10).

In relation to v. 11, it is unclear precisely how Paul considers Satan might gain the advantage, but possibly it relates to encouraging discord (Harris 2005: 233–4) or even to depriving the community of one of its members (Thrall 1994: 181). Matera (2003: 63) rightly points to the prominence of Satan (under that or other names) in 2 Corinthians (4.4; 6.15; 11.3, 14; 12.7) and to our need to appreciate the extent to which Paul conceives of Satan in a personal manner. By announcing he is 'not ignorant of his schemes', Paul intimates the important knowledge he possesses by virtue of his role as apostle and lays the foundation for his savage indictment of his opponents later in the letter as the 'servants of Satan' (11.15).

Restlessness in the Troad (2 Cor. 2.12-13)

2 Corinthians 2.12-13 At first sight, the connection of vv. 12-13 to what precedes is not immediately obvious:

> When I came to the Troad to preach the Gospel of Christ a door stood open for me in the Lord, yet I could get no peace of mind when I did not find Titus my brother there, so I said farewell to them and went off to Macedonia.

In fact, these verses perform essential service in carrying forward Paul's chronological account of his travels and how they have borne upon the Corinthians, interspersed with other types of material, that is a dominant

---

[11] For example, Witherington 1995: 364-365; Lambrecht 1999: 32 (Paul is minimalizing 'the injustice he personally experienced'); Harris 2005: 233; Guthrie 2015: 136–7.

feature of this letter. First comes the reference to his problem in Asia (1.8-11); then the mention of his original travel plan (1.15-16), which he implies he has changed in a manner with which they must be familiar (1.17); thirdly, his reasons for that change (1.23–2.11); and now, the next step, his mention of his reaching the Troad, which follows from what he has said in 1.16-17 but contains extra information with which it appears that the Corinthians were familiar. Not only had Paul not visited them on the way to Macedonia but the route he had taken to get there was overland via the Troad and not by boat direct from Ephesus or some other port in Asia. The next steps in the story, told in 2 Corinthians 7, will be his meeting Titus in Corinth and receiving a positive report from him on how his letter was received. From 2 Corinthians 8 onwards, Paul will be focusing more on the future, especially arrangements for the collection and his forthcoming visit (with occasional references to previous events). This concentration of references to his past and future actions is unique in the Pauline correspondence (even though letters like 1 Corinthians and Galatians do have some similar material) and reflects the extent to which Paul and his ministry (past, present and future) are more of an issue in 2 Corinthians than in any other of his extant letters.

In addition, however, vv. 12-13 carry forward the argument that he has just been making in relation to his travel arrangements. As many commentators suggest, these verses exemplify his closeness to, and the love he has for, the Corinthians that he has just been expressing (2.4). That is to say, he was so anxious to get news of them from Titus that he abandoned a promising missionary field and went off to Macedonia to find him. The debate as to whether Paul went to the Troad, the region, or to Troas, the city, does not need to be revisited, let alone settled, here, although the presence of the article before Τρῳάς suggests the former not the latter (BDAG 1019).

5

Pauline leadership and the new covenant (2.14–3.18)

2 Cor. 2.14–7.4 as an integral part of the letter

In 2 Cor. 2.14, Paul moves away from autobiographical details and only returns to them in 7.5, with mention of his arrival in Macedonia (consequent upon the journey he had announced in 2.13). The section of the letter constituted by 2.14–7.4 represents material of a different type and comprises, broadly speaking, an explanation and defence of his apostolic ministry, or, as suggested in this volume, his leadership (2.14–6.10, 7.2-4), and an assertion of Christ-movement identity (6.14–7.1). For numerous commentators, the presence of 2.14–7.4 between 2.13 and 7.5 represents an unsurmountable obstacle to the literary integrity of 2 Corinthians.[1] This position has been well put by Larry Welborn (2011: xxi), who cites the view of Johannes Weiss that 'This separation of what belongs together is unheard of and intolerable from a literary point of view, since 2:13 and 7:5 f. fit onto each other as neatly as the broken pieces of a ring (1937: 1:349)'. Welborn further suggests that an 'excursus of such length (6 pages in Nestle-Aland!) has no parallel in the letters of Paul' and that the 'attempt to construe Paul's apology for his apostolic office in 2:14-7:4 as a "digression" within the narrative fails to convince, since the apology has no point of departure in what precedes, and makes no connection with what follows' (2011: xxi; 1997). In short, he concludes (2011: xxi), the judgement of Dieter Georgi remains valid:

> The seams in 2:13/14 and 7:4/5 are so basic, and the connections between 2:13 and 7:5 so obvious, that the burden of proof now lies with those who

---

[1] In most partition theories where more than two letter fragments are postulated (typically 2 Corinthians 1–9 and 10–13), 2 Cor. 2.14–7.4 is thought to originate in a separate letter. In his discussion of this issue, Harris (2005: 8–14) mentions that those who regard 2 Cor. 2.14–7.4 as an intrusion between 2.13 and 7.5 include (and there are many more): Johannes Weiss, Rudolf Bultmann, Erich Dinkler, Philipp Vielhauer, Günther Bornkamm, Dieter Georgi, R. H. Fuller, Willi Marxsen, Eduard Lohse, Norman Perrin, Helmut Koester, Hans Dieter Betz and Margaret Mitchell.

defend the integrity of the canonical text, and they have not brought any good arguments to support their claims. (Georgi 1986/1987: 335)

It is submitted, however, that there are 'good arguments' in defence of the present arrangement of the text as integral to Paul's original conception for the letter, and I will summon three.

First, I noted in commenting on 2 Cor. 2.12-13 that throughout this letter Paul intersperses details of his past actions or his future plans with other types of discourse and that, in the concentration of such features, 2 Corinthians is unique among the Pauline letters. At the most general level, the presence of 2.14–7.4 between 2.13 and 7.5 is merely the most egregious example of that pattern. This issue – the general ordering of the material in the letter – can be sharpened considerably, however, by conducting the mental experiment of doing what those advocating partition must consider Paul should have done (or perhaps once did do), namely joining 2.12-13 and 7.5-16. This produces the question (a very awkward one for partitionists) as to where – given that Paul obviously wanted the material covered by 2.14–7.4 in the letter and (apart from 6.14–7.1) no one denies it is Pauline – this composite body of text should go. Let us assume we propel the putative 2.12-13 + 7.5-16 to just after 7.4. This produces the effect of moving 2.12-13, which are directly relevant to, and help soften the blow of, his problematic change of travel plans so far forward into the letter that they could make no contribution to his earlier argument on that subject. Why, we must ask, would Paul want to do that? The alternative is to situate 2.12-13 + 7.5-16 immediately after 2.11. This might seem a sensible way to bring all his autobiographical material together in one place, especially given the amount of such material already present in 2 Corinthians 1–2. Yet in its present (canonical) form, the extremely good news of the Corinthians' positive response to the letter and to Titus in ch. 7 comes immediately before Paul starts asking them for money in chs 8–9. Even at the level of folk psychology, one can see why having the climax of Paul's relationship with the Corinthians in 7.5-16 moved backwards to ch. 2 and followed by a long section of text (2.14–7.4) mainly about Paul and his ministry, where some rather tough things are said (e.g. 2.17), might not be an optimal preparation for a major request for money. A similar argument can be raised from the perspective of social identity. To reiterate the main element of the John Turner's understanding of leadership (2005), it is not the case that because leaders have power over the members they are able to control resources. Rather, it is because leaders have persuaded the members that they are prototypical of the group's values and generally act in its best interests in solidarity with the membership that they are able to make arrangements concerning resources. Paul's acute understanding of his ministry has led him to a view similar to that advocated by Turner: he establishes his apostolic and hence leadership credentials (2.14–7.4) and builds the case for his solidarity with the Corinthians (7.5-16), and only then moves on to the collection (chs 8–9). Accordingly, Paul realized that there was no good place in the letter for the material represented in 2.12-13 + 7.5-16 to appear conjoined, so he split it up. It is a very deft separation, since the reference to his having set off for Macedonia in 2.13 creates a broad imaginative space in which to insert the material in 2.14–7.4. Paul's elegant solution, weighed against the numerous New Testament scholars who have failed to appreciate it, may reflect William Blake's apophthegm: 'The tygers of wrath are wiser than the horses of instruction.'

The second reason against regarding 2.14–7.4 as a later insertion is that Weiss errs in his claim that '2:13 and 7:5 f. fit on to each other as neatly as the broken pieces of a ring'. While many commentators find that the transition from 2.13 to the doxology in 2.14 is abrupt, it is readily explicable as the sign of a structural division, namely Paul's transition to a new subject, his discussion of the foundations of his leadership. He is looking forwards not backwards (Thrall 1994: 23), although the previous material provides some of the reason for his doing so. I doubt, however, that it is helpful, with many commentators (who at least regard it as an original part of the letter), to call 2.14–7.4 a 'digression' (e.g. Dean 1938/1939; Bruce 1971: 187; Horrell 1996: 296; Harris 2005: 14; Guthrie 2015: 25), since its subject is so closely tied to the other parts of the letter. Furthermore, there is a very powerful connection between 2.13 and 2.14 that deserves more attention than it receives. Whereas Paul ends 2.13 by saying that he went off to Macedonia, 2.14 is a verse in which thanks are offered to God for (a) leading us in Christ in triumph and (b) spreading the aroma of knowledge concerning him, through Paul, 'in every place' (ἐν παντὶ τόπῳ). Both (a) and (b) refer to Paul's movement through space, and 'every place' must include Macedonia. George Guthrie has very aptly described the situation as follows:

> Paul has great confidence that the events of his life are under the Lord's direction. He is not simply wandering around the Mediterranean, as some of his opponents have probably suggested. Rather, he is led by God, under the triumphant lordship of Christ, for the cause of the Gospel. (2015: 156)

Thus, the movement from 2.13 to 2.14 is not the suspiciously abrupt jump mooted by those who view 2 Corinthians as a composite, but a cleverly executed transition that picks up the theological dimension of his journeying and thereby signals that 2.13 was followed by 2.14 in Paul's composition of the letter.

A strong case can also be made for the transition from 7.4 to 7.5. Here the rather mechanical repetition of language from 2.13 to 7.5 – involving ἄνεσις, ἔσχηκα/ἔσχηκεν and ἐλθεῖν, with minor variations, namely σάρξ instead of πνεῦμα,[2] and the plural ἡμῶν rather than singular μου and ἐλθόντων ἡμῶν rather than ἐξῆλθον – makes it unlikely that Paul ever intended these verses to follow one another. Yet these features correspond very well to what J. M. Robinson astutely described as a 'resumptive repetition' of an earlier remark (1971: 244–5). In addition, the words καὶ γάρ at the start of 7.5 are unsuitable if this verse ever followed immediately after 2.13, for there is nothing in 2.12-13 that provides a causative factor to explain the γάρ. By way of contrast, 7.2-4 relate well to their immediate context. Thus, 7.2-4 connect closely with 7.5-16 in relation to comfort, in that the comfort he says he feels in 7.4 is explained (hence, the γάρ in 7.5) by the arrival of Titus (7.6) after Paul's initial disappointment that he had not arrived (7.5). In addition, other important themes such as claiming honour, joy and affliction in 7.4 reappear in 7.5-16. In this respect, 7.5-6 announce a motif of which 7.5-16 represents a detailed elaboration, and καὶ γάρ are very appropriate as announcing the start of that elaboration.

Thirdly, in answer to Welborn's point that the 2.14-7.4 has 'no point of departure in what precedes, and makes no connection with what follows', it is submitted that the preferable view is that of Frank Matera, who, in rejecting the notion that 2.14-7.4 is a digression, observes that 'it is in fact an integral part of Paul's argument in chapters 1–7, and it lays the groundwork for his critique of the super-apostles in chapters 10–13' (2003: 65). Paul's apostolic authority, using the traditional language, or his leadership credentials in line with the social identity framework of this commentary, are on the line from the first verse of the letter and remain so to the end. The specific issues that occupy 2 Corinthians 1–2 broaden out to a more theoretical discussion and defence of his leadership in 2.14-7.4. Although the numerous aspects of the connection of 2.14-7.4 with chs 10-13 will appear in the comments on particular verses in the following, two illustrative aspects will be offered here. In 2 Cor. 2.17, Paul castigates certain people as 'pedlars of God's word' and implies that they are insincere and not commissioned by God. This is plainly a reference to the interlopers whom he will criticize in chs 10-13, where his contrasting failure to take money from the Corinthians will be a live issue. Next, in 2 Corinthians 3 Paul offers a contrast between the law of Moses and the new ministry of the Spirit (which he represents) that reflects very badly on the former. This material, again, is paving the way for the case

---

[2] That Paul does not sharply distinguish between these two terms is mentioned again in the commentary on 6.14-7.1 in the following.

he will mount in chs 10–13 against his opponents who (as I will argue in the following) were Judean Christ-followers preaching adherence to the law of Moses.

For all of these reasons, 2 Cor. 2.14–7.4 always formed an integral part of 2 Corinthians.

The exalted and genuine nature of Paul's ministry vis-à-vis that of his opponents (2 Cor. 2.14-17)

2 Corinthians 2.14 In this verse, Paul gives thanks to God in relation to phenomena which he describes in terms of two striking metaphors: the first of triumph and the second of an aroma that spreads far. As noted earlier, both metaphors contribute to a theological explanation of the significance of Paul's movement across space and thus tie this verse very closely to 2.13, with its closing statement that he went off to Macedonia.

The first metaphor, where thanks are always given to God θριαμβεύοντι ἡμᾶς ἐν τῷ Χριστῷ, has attracted enormous discussion.[3] It can be roughly translated as 'leading us in triumph in Christ'. The vast majority of scholars consider that this is a reference to a Roman triumph, a phenomenon well known across the ancient Mediterranean world. The complexity of a Roman *triumphus*, especially the fact both enemy captives and victorious Roman soldiers could be said to be led in procession, with the former ahead of and the latter behind the victorious general or emperor's chariot (Versnel 1970: 95), has generated a lively debate that dates back to the Patristic period. It is likely that God is being viewed as the triumphal general. Yet since a triumph was a status elevation ritual for the general and his troops and a status degradation ritual for the captured enemy soldiers (Esler 1995b: 242–4), into what category has Paul set Christ-followers like himself? A strong strand of recent scholarship plumps for the latter option, and thus views Paul as a defeated captive whom God parades through the world.[4] On this view, Paul is saying words to the effect, 'Thanks be to God who, having defeated us in battle, parades us through the streets in ignominious disgrace!' One wonders how many of Paul's original audience would have heard this reference to triumph and imagined that Paul was slotting himself into the losing side.

---

[3] For a lengthy and, to my mind, convincing discussion, see Guthrie 2015: 157–65.
[4] So Marshall 1983; Furnish 1984: 187; Hafemann 1990a: 10–34; Thrall 1994: 194–5; Witherington 1995: 367–8; Garland 1999: 142–3; Lambrecht 1999: 38–9; Matera 2003: 72–3; Harris 2005: 243, 245–6; Wypadlo 2013.

An influential prop for this view has been the idea that θριαμβεύειν with a direct object, as in 2.14, always refers to the one who has been conquered (Hafemann 1990a: 161). As Guthrie has shown, however, this suggestion misstates the ancient evidence (2015: 161–3). With the lexical question capable of being answered in various ways, the matter can be determined only by looking at the usage of the word in its immediate context, especially 2.15-17, and here the emphasis falls on status elevation, not degradation (Guthrie 2015: 163–5). In particular, in vv. 15-16b, Paul is clearly including himself among 'those being saved' and heading towards life, as opposed to 'those being destroyed' and heading towards death'. Furthermore, in v. 16c, he asks, 'Who is suitable for these things (ταῦτα)?', a rhetorical question if ever there was one and to be answered, 'I am' (as argued later), before launching a savage attack on his opponents in v. 17 in such a way as to leave no room for doubt that ταῦτα encapsulate vv. 14-16b and refer to victory and exaltation, not defeat and disgrace. The more likely view, therefore, is that Paul is representing himself 'as one of the victorious general's soldiers sharing in the glory of his triumph' (Barrett 1973: 98, following Allo and Kümmel). Andreas Hock (2007), based on careful consideration of the verb θριαμβεύειν in 2 Cor. 2.14 and Col. 2.15, also reaches the view that the metaphor has a positive connotation, speaking of victory for Christ and his followers, not defeat.

The second metaphor concerns God, through Paul, making known (φανεροῦντι) the odour of knowledge of him (τὴν ὀσμὴν τῆς γνώσεως αὐτοῦ) in every place. In the phrase τὴν ὀσμὴν τῆς γνώσεως αὐτοῦ, the genitive is probably epexegetical, so the meaning is: 'the aroma, the knowledge of him', where him refers to Christ, as becomes apparent in v. 15. The odour is probably not meant to evoke a sacrificial offering, since there the smell was meant to rise to God and not be scattered around the world (Furnish 1984: 187–8). Moreover, in the LXX the common expression for the smell of sacrifice to God or other deities, occurring some fifty times, is ὀσμὴ εὐωδίας.[5] Yet Paul does not use that phrase here, although he does reach for it in Phil. 4.18. It is possible that the reference to odour refers to perfumes burnt during triumphal processions (Barrett 1973: 98), but, again, such a smell was aimed at the gods, according to Horace, *Odes* 4.2.50-51: *dabimusque divis tura benignis* (Furnish 1984: 188). One must also doubt whether Paul or his audience were aware of incense being a feature of Roman triumphs. Another possibility, probably the most likely, is the idea of Wisdom as a perfume in Sir. 24.15 and 39.13-14. It is highly significant, as Guthrie notes (2015: 167),

---

[5] For instances in relation to Yahweh, for example, see Gen. 8.1; Exod. 29.18; Lev. 1.9, 13, 17; 2.2, 9, 12; 3.5; 4.31; Num. 15.3, 7, 10).

that in Sir. 24.15 the two words (ὀσμή and εὐωδία) are not tied together in the usual formula, but in fact appear separately and in a parallel relationship (as in vv. 15-16 here). When the terms are used on their own, in the Septuagint and in Philo, they rarely refer to sacrifice (Guthrie 2015: 168–9).

Paul's aligning himself closely to the divine activity in the manifestation of the knowledge concerning Christ bears directly on his credentials as a leader; in particular, this assertion is relevant to his status as an apostle, a subgroup within the wider Christ-movement that he mentioned in a very prominent manner in 2 Cor. 1.1. In saying this, he is also paving the way for a major criticism he is soon about to make of his opponents in 2 Cor. 2.17.

2 Corinthians 2.15-16b Paul now provides a daring expansion of his mention of the aroma, that is, the knowledge of Christ, that is manifested everywhere through him (v. 14). He now claims that he is the 'sweet odour' (εὐωδία) of Christ for God, both for those who are being saved and for those who are perishing. In v. 16a, he will introduce ὀσμή as a parallel to εὐωδία (as in Sir. 24.15). In making this assertion in v. 15, he turns up the dial on his claim to leadership that he announced in v. 14. It is likely that Paul still has in mind the wisdom connotations of the notion of an aroma; as with v. 14, a sacrificial dimension seems unlikely by virtue of his failure to enlist the stock phrase ὀσμὴ εὐωδίας (Plummer 1915: 71; Furnish 1984: 177).

The distinction in v. 15 between those who are being saved and those who are perishing (which also appears in 1 Cor. 1.18) represents the viewpoint that Paul adopted after he came to recognize Christ and was given a special mission to non-Judeans (Gal. 1.15-16). Paul's interpretation of the Gospel (which was not shared by many Judean Christ-followers who demanded new members become Judeans by adoption of the law of Moses) meant that the basic division in humanity could no longer be drawn between Judeans and non-Judeans. Instead, the boundary now stretched between those who turned to Christ and were saved (which included Judeans and non-Judeans) and those who did not (Harris 2005: 249–50), a situation clearly set forth in Rom. 2.6-11. In social identity terms, this meant that Paul had abandoned ethnic identity as the basis for the most fundamental intergroup differentiation and adopted the distinction between Christ-followers and all the rest.

In v. 16, Paul embellishes the distinction and his role in it by contending that for those who are perishing he is the odour (ὀσμή) from (ἐκ) death that leads onto (εἰς) death and the odour (ὀσμή) from (ἐκ) life that leads onto (εἰς) life. The claim made, a very large one in relation to Paul's status as a leader of a group like none other, is that he forces people to make a fundamental decision: turn to him and his Gospel and live, but disregard him and his Gospel and die. In terms of social identity, this is intergroup differentiation on an existential, even cosmic, scale. 'God's saving work in Christ, communicated through the apostle, bears both judgment and salvation' (Seifrid 2014: 92).

2 Corinthians 2.16c-17 The last clause in v. 16 looks forward to v. 17, as shown by the word 'and' (καί) with which it begins and the contents of the next verse:

> And who is sufficient [ἱκανός] for these things? For we are not like many who peddle (καπηλεύοντες) the word of God, but out of sincerity (ἐξ εἰλικρινείας), commissioned by God and in the sight of God, we speak in Christ.

It is difficult to overstate the importance of this passage for understanding Paul's communicative intention in the letter and for the evidence it offers of the work's literary integrity.

The word ταῦτα refers back to the various triumphant and exalted things that Paul has said God works through him in vv. 14-16b. 'Sufficient' conveys Paul's 'adequacy for the apostolic vocation' (Barrett 1973: 102), or, in social identity terms, full alignment with the prototype of apostle, the key leadership role, within the Christ-movement. His 'sufficiency' is a strong theme in this section of the letter, with the adjective appearing in relation to Paul here and in 3.5, the substantive (ἱκανότης) in 3.5 and the verb (ἱκανόω) in 3.6. Some commentators hold that Paul expected the answer 'no one' to his question (Barrett 1973: 103; Furnish 1984: 190-1; Lambrecht 1999: 40). Yet this is a highly implausible position. We know from 3.5-6 that when Paul wrote 2.16c, he was already of the view that God had rendered him sufficient for the task. The fact that he was not sufficient in himself is beside the point; God had, in the past, made him sufficient. Further support for this view comes from his acknowledging his debt to God in v. 17 and from the fact that his question about self-commendation in 3.1 would hardly make sense if he had not already affirmed his apostolic sufficiency (Thrall 1994: 209). Finally, the logical γάρ in v. 17 favours Paul's answering the question affirmatively as regards himself: '(We are sufficient,) because we are not like . . .' (Harris 2005: 253).

The opening statement in v. 17 sets up a sharp contrast between Paul and the many who peddle (οἱ καπηλεύοντες) the word of God. The word καπηλεύειν (only appearing here in the New Testament) means to operate as a small-scale trader (κάπηλος), to peddle. While Novick (2011) has creatively linked this statement to Paul's references to aroma and fragrance immediately before by arguing on the basis of rabbinic texts that among the pedlars' main merchandise were aromatic products, this overly circumscribes the activities of pedlars. The word is used, for example, of tavern-keepers. Because such people had a reputation for cheating, for example, by watering down wine, it came to mean adulterate (BDAG 508). 'The ancient stereotype of the merchant was of a person concerned only for profit and quite willing to adulterate the product or give short measure for the sake of it' (Furnish 1984: 178). Both dimensions, the profit motive and the sharp practice, are in play in v. 17; Paul is lambasting the many who sell the word of God and adulterate it at the same time. In 4.2, he will deny that he engages in behaviour that is essentially the same as that which he deprecates here when he says that he does not deceitfully falsify the word of God (μηδὲ δολοῦντες τὸν λόγον τοῦ θεοῦ), with 2.17 and 4.2 being the only places in the letter where the expression 'word of God' (ὁ λόγος τοῦ θεοῦ) occurs. There is no doubt to whom he is referring in 2.17. It is the Christ-followers who have arrived in Corinth from outside bearing letters of recommendation mentioned in the next verse. Later he will refer to them as 'false apostles, deceitful workers' (ψευδαπόστολοι, ἐργάται δόλιοι; 11.13) who preached a different Jesus, spirit and gospel (11.4). These people were of the view that ministers of the Gospel were entitled to be paid by the Christ-groups among whom they were working and accepted such payment. In 1 Cor. 9.1-18, Paul had agreed he shared that right but explained that he chose not to exercise it. In 2 Corinthians, he reiterates his position of refusing to take money from communities with whom he was staying. For this, he was strongly criticized by those who did expect payment. This is a very hot issue in 2 Corinthians 10-13 (e.g. 11.7-9; 12.14-18).

Paul's castigating his opponents as 'pedlars of God's word' is a good example of what social identity theorists call outgroup stereotypification. The members of a group in a competitive environment define themselves and delineate their identity by denigrating members of an outgroup who are portrayed as all sharing the same characteristics (this is the 'outgroup homogeneity' effect).

Having said who he was not like, Paul then moves to the differentiating factor that shows his sufficiency for the task (2.17b-c): 'but out of sincerity (ἐξ εἰλικρινείας), commissioned by God (ἐκ θεοῦ) and in the sight of God (κατέναντι θεοῦ), we speak in Christ (ἐν Χριστῷ λαλοῦμεν).' Paul has already insisted on his sincerity, in 1.12, where it featured as part of his answer to the Corinthians' concern that he had changed his mind about visiting them. Although that factor may still have some operation in 2.17, the major purpose of the appeal to his sincerity here is to differentiate himself from his opponents who are insincere in their adulteration of the Gospel. In addition, the chord struck by Paul concerning his connection with the divine plan with his claim in 1.1 that he was an apostle of Christ Jesus by the will of God (διὰ θελήματος θεοῦ) continues to sound here, with his reference to his being commissioned by God.

Paul introduces the question of whether genuine apostles should be paid for preaching the Gospel, but will return with a vengeance to it later, in chs 10–13. In general terms, therefore, the presence of 2.17–3.1 in the letter is as unambiguous a sign one could hope for that Paul always planned this section of the letter to accompany chs 10–13. One particular feature confirms the extent to which 2.17–3.1 is fully integrated into the letter. Exactly the same expression, κατέναντι θεοῦ ἐν Χριστῷ λαλοῦμεν, crops up in 2 Cor. 12.19, but is found nowhere else in the Pauline correspondence. 2 Corinthians 12.19 appears after a passage (12.14-18) in which he has been speaking about this very issue of not taking money for his ministry, nor of defrauding them by guile. In v. 19, Paul steps back a little to make a solemn declaration in this form to the effect that what he has just said was for their benefit, to build them up, not to defend himself, a defence that in this verse has a direct reference to his honest practice in relation to money.

Conclusion on 2.14-17

2 Corinthians 2.14-17 is thus a very carefully drafted passage in which Paul aimed to achieve a number of communicative goals in the unified text that is 2 Corinthians. First, he segued naturally from mention of his journey to Macedonia (2.13) to a general statement of thanks to God for giving him victory and having him spread the knowledge of Christ wherever he went (2.14), so that he was central to a process that divided humanity into those being saved and those being damned. Secondly, these characteristics of his ministry served as an apt introduction for its defence in 2.14–6.13. Thirdly, he also introduced the question of the presence in Corinth of other alleged ministers of the word of God (whose letters of recommendation from other parts of the Christ-movement he would mention in 3.1) who actually falsified that word and did so for payment. This element means that in 2.14-17 he is both prefacing the defence of his leadership in 2.14–6.13 with an attack on the very people who have made it essential, while at the same time reserving a direct onslaught on his critics themselves until the last section of the letter (chs 10–13), after his instructions of the collection (chs 8–9).

The results of ministry 3.1-3

2 Corinthians 3.1 Letters of recommendation were a common phenomenon in the ancient Greco-Roman world (Kim 1972; Yoon 2016). They were tied to relationships of friendship (Marshall 1987: 268). Letters of self-recommendation were also common, were similarly based on friendship and trust and did not necessarily entail inappropriate self-praise (Marshall 1987:

269–70). The notion of recommendation frequently occurs in the letter, and it should be noted, appears in, and thus indicates the connections between chs 1–7 and 10–13; thus, the verb 'recommend' (συνιστάνειν) is found at 3.1; 4.2; 5.12; 6.4; 7.11; 10.12; 10.18 (bis) and 12.11 and the adjective, 'of, pertaining to recommendation' (συστατικός) in 2.3.

Paul's initial statement in 3.1, 'Are we again (πάλιν) beginning to recommend ourselves (ἑαυτοὺς συνιστάνειν)?', which is equivalent to the Latin *commendo me in fidem* (Marshall 1987: 271), probably recalls the time when Paul first arrived in Corinth and had to recommend himself to the Corinthians. Should he repeat that process, he asks, or, like some (ὥς τινες), does he need letters of recommendation? The use of the technical expression 'letters of recommendation' in 3.1b confirms the translation of συνιστάνειν as 'recommend', with its firm context in reciprocity, and not 'praise oneself' (Marshall 1987: 266–8; Garland 1999: 155). It is a false step to suggest, as Harris does (2005: 259), that by placing the pronoun before the verb, as here (and at 3,1; 5.12; 10.12, 18) a pejorative connotation, namely, of self-praise or 'boasting' is produced. The point of Paul's question is to signal his concern at a possible breach of trust between the Corinthians and himself (Marshall 1987: 268), coupled with his annoyance at their entering into such a relationship with others who have arrived waving letters of recommendation from other Christ-groups. Paul is sharply differentiating himself from such missionaries. Moreover, v. 3.1 is 'connected to and continuous with its predecessor' (Barnett 1997: 161). Accordingly, because of this proximity it is extremely likely that the many (πολλοί) pedlars of God's word in 2 Cor. 2.17 should be identified with the τινες of 2 Cor. 3.1 (Furnish 1984: 180; Harris 2005: 260). Paul will designate his opponents as τινες again later, at 10.2. He is therefore referring to a group of missionaries who have come to Corinth bearing letters of recommendation and who preach a false gospel, demanding payment as they do so. These are the people to whom he will return with marked ferocity in chs 10–13, where his refusal to accept payment for his ministry is a very hot issue.

Who would have written the letters to the Corinthians Paul mentions? They could have been hardly been friendly to Paul, since they recommended people who held views antithetic to his, such as by accepting payment for preaching the Gospel. We learn later in the letter, for example, that he was criticized for not accepting such payment in Corinth (11.7-11). Gerd Theissen has persuasively proposed that the right to be supported was a sign of the radical poverty of the itinerant missionaries – originating in Palestine with the words of Jesus himself – and that in renouncing this right Paul was adjusting his mission to the different needs of a community-organizer in the cities of the East yet inevitably bringing himself into conflict on the point with those who held the established view (1982: 42–54). This argument suggests a Palestinian origin for the letters of recommendation. The Christ-movement in Jerusalem is one likely source. Perhaps the letters were sent by the Pillars themselves who had, after all, broken the agreement they reached with Paul, as described in Gal. 2.1-10 by the behaviour of Peter in Antioch as recounted in Gal. 2.11-14.[6]

Another possibility is the group demanding Christ-followers become circumcised, meaning to adopt the law of Moses and become ethnic Judeans, from fear of whom Paul alleges Peter broke off table-fellowship with non-Judeans (Gal. 2.12). Galatians itself reflects a very similar situation, since non-Judean Christ-followers are under pressure to become circumcised and take on the law of Moses. Paul's argument (in ch. 3 especially) that Christ-followers are the real descendants of Abraham and that righteousness comes with faith (not from the law of Moses)[7] only makes sense if the interlopers who have arrived in Galatia are offering his converts Abrahamic descent and (the very Judean) feature of righteousness as benefits of circumcision. In other words, they are offering them Judean ethnic identity. In recent years important works by Christine Hayes (2002) and Matthew Thiessen (2011) have demonstrated a diversity of ways in which Judeans regarded non-Judeans in purity terms and have pointed to 'genealogical impurity' as a factor that led some Judeans to deny the possibility of non-Judean converts entering the people of Israel. Nevertheless, Hayes (2002: 45–67) considers that both Josephus and Philo do not appear to regard non-Judean ancestry as an obstacle to becoming a Judean. In *De Virtutibus* 102, Philo describes what happens when someone becomes a Judean and it is a very positive picture.[8] The reference in *De Virtutibus* 108 to the admittance of such proselytes into the assembly 'in the third generation' is not likely to affect this result.[9] According to Gregory Sterling, the 'inconcinnity between *Virt.* 102-103 and 108' appears to be due to the citation of Deut. 23.8 in the latter chapter. As he reads the text, §§102-103 are Philo's 'summary statement or principle statement. §108 is offering an interpretation of a specific biblical injunction'. Philo 'understands "third generation" here in a positive way, i.e., through the third generation not until the third generation'.[10]

---

[6] See Esler 1995a ('Making and Breaking an Agreement Mediterranean Style: A New Reading of Galatians 2.1-14').
[7] See Esler 1998: 141–77 and 2006b.
[8] Esler 2017b: 16–18.
[9] For an argument that *De Virtutibus* 108 does have this result, see Ehrensperger 2020: 183–5.
[10] Gregory Sterling, personal communication (19 February 2021).

Another possible source of the letters, which has been suggested (Harris 2005: 260), are the assemblies of Christ in Judea (Gal. 1.22); this is highly unlikely, however, as these Christ-followers must have had views that Paul later adopted, which is why they were still being persecuted when Paul wrote 1 Thessalonians (1 Thess. 2.14). On the other hand, the fact that Paul envisages they could leave Corinth with letters from the Corinthians suggests any Christ-group could write one.

2 Corinthians 3.2 In v. 2, Paul pursues the idea of letters of recommendation with the bold claim that the Corinthians are his letter, and it is one that is known and read (γινωσκομένη καὶ ἀναγινωσκομένη) by everyone. By so saying, he implies that he has no need of the letters (on papyrus or perhaps wooden writing tablets) from Christ-groups elsewhere with which his opponents have arrived in Corinth. He also conveys that he has a very high opinion of the Corinthians and has been praising them among Christ-followers elsewhere. This message is central to his rebuilding his relationship with them as a means to exercise leadership. Such a sentiment is in the same vein as their being 'the Christ-group of God in Corinth' (1.1) and his later statement that Christ is powerful among them (13.3; Barnett 1997: 164). Paul's use of the first-person plural is unlikely to refer to himself and Timothy (1.1). This is an epistolary plural in a section of the letter where Paul is inaugurating a major statement of his leadership.

There is a subsidiary question, raised by a textual issue, as to whether Paul is saying that this letter is written on his heart (literally, 'on our hearts'; ἐν καρδίαις ἡμῶν) or on theirs (literally, 'on your hearts'; ὑμῶν for ἡμῶν). The variant ὑμῶν is weakly attested, although Codex Sinaiticus has it, 'and seems to have been introduced for the sake of an easier sense' (Lambrecht 1999: 41). While it is possible to mount a case for the originality of ὑμῶν (see Thrall 1994: 223–4), I will assume in what follows that Paul wrote ἡμῶν. Fortunately, not a great deal hangs on this question because the central issue in what follows is the notion of a letter written on a human heart (or hearts), not whose heart that may be.

2 Corinthians 3.3 Paul proceeds to expand on the meaning of the Corinthians being a letter in three important respects: it was letter from Christ, ministered by Paul and written not on tablets of stone but on tablets of human hearts.

As to the first, the Corinthians are being publicly displayed (φανερούμενοι, here interpreted as a present passive participle paralleling those in the previous verse – as a result of Paul's publicizing efforts – as a letter from Christ (ἐπιστολὴ Χριστοῦ), this being (as most commentators believe) a genitive of origin (BDF §§ 89-90). Alternative explanations, such as 'a letter belonging to Christ' or 'a letter concerning Christ', do not fit the context, where Paul is not suggesting that he was the author of this particular (and very unusual) letter and where the metaphor indeed requires that he is the object of the recommendation it embodies, not its agent or medium.

Secondly, this was also a letter ministered (διακονηθεῖσα) by Paul; so Christ was the principal in the matter and Paul his agent. The word διακονηθεῖσα represents the first instance of a semantic field that will assume increasing significance as the letter proceeds. There are twenty instances altogether, and they occur in all three of the major sections of the letter (chs 1–7, 8–9 and 10–13). Thus, we have διακονεῖν here and in 8.19 and 20, διάκονος in 3.6, 6.4, 11.15 (twice) and 23, and διακονία in 3.7, 8, 9 (twice), 4.1, 5.18, 6.3, 8.4, 9.1, 12 and 13, and 11.8. Such a concentration is unusual in the broader context of the Pauline correspondence. There are only fifteen other examples: eight in Romans (only two of which relate to Paul: 11.13 and 15.31), three in 1 Corinthians, one each in Galatians, Philippians, 1 Thessalonians and Philemon.[11]

While the διακον- stem words have a core meaning concerned with some service rendered by an intermediary (BDAG 229-230), in English the words 'minister' and 'ministry' provide the best translations for these Greek expression in 2 Corinthians (Thrall 1994: 225; Garland 1999: 159), since it is necessary to preserve the circumstance that διακονία is some form of service provided by an agent who is its διάκονος. This link, very prominent in this letter, is obscured in translations and commentaries that use other words such as 'dispensation' for διακονία. It is also desirable that translations reflect the fact that Paul is evoking a particular semantic field by employing related words in English, a *desideratum* regularly ignored in many translations and commentaries. In particular, its use here anticipates Paul's role as διάκονος ('minister') of the new covenant in 3.6 and the διακονία ('ministry') of the Spirit and righteousness in 3.8-9.

The fact that the διακον- words centre on services provided by a διάκονος carries the consequence that they connect easily with notions of leadership, especially when it is understood in a social identity perspective. The reason for this is that, in certain contexts, a leader seeking to have a group move in a particular direction might well find it advantageous to couch his or her activities as acts of service – or as ministry – carried out on behalf of the members. This is an example of the process of 'identity advancement', as explained in the Chapter 2 of this volume, where a leader demonstrates that he or she is *working for* the group, by standing up for it and by championing

---

[11] Διακονεῖν occurs at Rom. 15.5 and Phlm. 13; διακονία at Rom. 11.13, 12.7 and 15.31 and 1 Cor. 12.5 and 16.15; and διάκονος at Rom. 13.4 (twice), 15.8 and 16.1, 1 Cor. 3.5, Gal 2:17, Phil. 1.1 and 1 Thess. 3.2.

collective interests, and this represents a path to successful leadership in addition to prototypicality (= being *representative of* the group) (Steffens et al. 2015). Although such an approach of a leader of a group serving its members represented an inversion of prevailing notions of leadership in the ancient Mediterranean, it was current in the early Christ-movement, probably stemming from its attribution to Jesus in what became the Synoptic tradition. Examples include the statement that 'For the Son of Man came not to be served (διακονηθῆναι) but to serve (διακονῆσαι), and to give his life as a ransom for many' (Mk 10.45; also Mt. 20.28), and Jesus' assertion, 'But I am among you as one who serves' (διακονῶν; Lk. 22.27).[12] Earlier in the letter Paul has insisted that he does not 'lord it' or 'play the lord' (κυριεύειν, from κύριος, 'lord') over the Corinthians' faith (1.24). Having thus disavowed behaving like a typical leader in the local environment early on in the letter, it is not surprising to find Paul reaching for διακονία language a little later to provide a positive characterization of how he understands leadership in the Christ-movement.

It is evident that Paul did not regard himself as the only διάκονος in the movement, since in 1 Cor. 3.5 he applies the word to himself and Apollos and in 1 Thess. 3.2 to himself and Timothy. This circumstance, however, renders all the more noticeable the prominence he attaches to himself as a διάκονος in 2 Corinthians. The reason for such prominence appears to lie close at hand: it is because the people who had turned up in Corinth and against whom he rails in 2 Corinthians 10–13 were using the language of διακονία in relation to their own teaching and activity (and possibly also to that of Moses). Although detailed assessments of the evidence will be offered below in relation to relevant verses, some general remarks are in order here. Claims to διακονία represent an arena of contestation between himself and his opponents. The reality of this competition between them is evident in 11.23, where he notes that the trouble-makers call themselves διάκονοι of Christ but that he is a better one. Thus, he does not deny that role to them but insists upon his own pre-eminence in relation to it. A much darker note is struck, however, when Paul makes the extreme claim that they are διάκονοι of Satan who disguise themselves as διάκονοι of righteousness (11.15). This is highly significant, since earlier in the letter Paul has claimed for himself the διακονία of righteousness (3.9). In other words, Paul's position is that he is a real διάκονος of righteousness but they merely pretend to be such.

The third significant feature of 3.3 comes as quite a shock: this is a letter 'written not with ink but by the Spirit of the living God, not on tablets of

---

[12] Paul does use διάκονος of secular rulers in Rom. 13.4, but only because he wants to say that they are 'God's servant'.

stone but on tablets of fleshly hearts'. These words are utterly unexpected. Everything else fits with the letter of recommendation idea. It is beyond doubt that Paul intended and the Corinthians would have understood that 'tablets of stone' (πλαξὶν λιθίναις) refer to the tablets upon which the law of Moses was inscribed. The expression πλάκες λίθιναι occurs in numerous places in the Septuagint in connection with God's giving the law to Moses (e.g. Exod. 31.18; 32.15; 34.1; Deut. 4.13; 5.22; 9.9, 10, 11; 10: 1, 3). Christopher Stanley has mounted a persuasive case against the view of scholars such as Richard Hays that Paul evokes numerous details of the context of the biblical expressions he cites or to which he alludes (2004; 2008b). Paul's practice is rather minimalist and 'oracular', where the decontextualized scriptural words themselves carry the meaning (Esler 2021d). Nevertheless, even Stanley agrees that there were certain broad features of Israelite scripture that Paul's Christ-groups, composed of largely illiterate non-Judeans, must have known (Stanley 2008b: 134–6). These include the story of Adam's fall, the Abraham narrative and certain key episodes in the Exodus narrative, including Moses receiving the stone tablets of the law from God on Sinai. We know from 1 Cor. 10.1-5, indeed, that Paul had previously instructed the Corinthians on Moses and the story of the Israelites' time in the desert. It is equally certain that Paul, at the very least, in 2 Cor. 3.3 is disparaging those tablets in comparison with the 'letter from Christ' that consists of the Corinthians. In addition, since the immediate setting concerns the contrast Paul has erected between himself and the pedlars of God's word who have come to Corinth with letters of recommendation, it is also beyond doubt that Paul is associating them with the 'tablets of stone'. In other words, they are advocates of the Mosaic law. This is entirely what we could expect of those he later describes as 'Hebrews', 'Israelites' and 'seed of Abraham' (11.22), as well as being 'ministers of Christ' (11.23). They are ethnic Judeans who have turned to Christ while retaining their ethnic identity, at the core of which lay adherence to the law of Moses.

The expression 'on tablets of human hearts' develops the image in 3.2 of the Corinthians being written on 'on our hearts'. While it is likely that Paul was influenced by Israelite scriptural traditions that contrasted such tablets with those written on stone, it is uncertain whether his addressees would have understood this. Perhaps he had mentioned relevant scriptural passages to them before, perhaps he had not. In considering the context for what Paul says here we must hold firm to the fact that he is crafting a communication to the Corinthians in the context of rebuilding his relationship and leadership role with them in a setting where Judean Christ-followers bent on offering a competing version of the Gospel have arrived in Corinth. What Paul is not doing, in spite of the finely crafted view of Richard Hays (1989: 122–53), is offering a disquisition of general application on hermeneutics, for reasons well advanced by Sloan (1995) and Gleason (1997) in response to Hays.

In discussing a possible scriptural background to the phrase 'tablets of human hearts', we must first observe that this combination is not found in the Septuagint. Paul himself appears to have crafted it and to have done so to create a very sharp contrast with 'tablets of stone', the medium of initial promulgation of the law of Moses, that is highly unflattering to those latter tablets. The sheer terms of the comparison require this, with stone set next to human hearts. In addition, however, in v. 3b Paul establishes a parallel between something written in black (ink) – in his day on papyrus or wooden writing tablets – and something written by the spirit of the living God. So ink and stone as means of transmission are contrasted with the spirit of the living God and tablets of human hearts, with the former necessarily and severely derogated in the process. The Corinthians would not have needed to be aware of any passages from Israelite scripture to comprehend this point. Nevertheless, it is worthwhile to see what may have influenced Paul himself to express the contrast this way, and it is not impossible that he had previously explained such scriptural material to the Corinthians.

Two probable sources present themselves; they are not explicit quotations but unmarked allusions or echoes and would have been difficult for the Corinthians to identify (Stanley 2008a: 9), although perhaps not impossible if he had spoken to them about these passages before and they had remembered such teaching. First, in Jer. 38.31-34 (LXX; 31 MT) the prophet foretells that the Lord will make a new covenant (διαθήκη καινή) with Israel and Judah. Paul uses the expression καινὴ διαθήκη of his own ministry shortly after this, in 3.6, so this passage is very likely to have been on his mind as he composed this section of the letter. Paul knew that the notion of καινὴ διαθήκη featured in Christ-movement traditions before him, because he quotes it in the Eucharistic passage in 1 Cor. 11.25 (its only other appearance in his letters, although it is presumably one of the two, starkly contrasted covenants of Gal. 4.24). The new covenant of Jer. 38.31-34 will not be like the previous one, made with their fathers in the wilderness (v. 32), that is, the Mosaic covenant. This time the Lord will put his laws into their mind, and he 'will write them on their hearts' (ἐπὶ καρδίας αὐτῶν; v. 33). Secondly, in Ezek. 11.19 and 36.26-27 the Lord promises he will bestow on them a new spirit (πνεῦμα καινόν) and that he will remove the heart of stone (τὴν καρδίαν τὴν λιθίνην) from their flesh and give them a fleshly heart (καρδίαν σαρκίνην). Ezek. 11.19 and 36.26 are the only places in the Septuagint with the expression 'fleshly heart' (καρδία σαρκίνη), although 'heart of flesh' (καρδία σαρκός) also occurs. Indeed, there are only three other instances of σαρκίνη in the Septuagint (2 Chron. 32.8; Ez. 4.17 and Prov. 24.23). This usage necessitates that Paul's only source for the phrase 'hearts of flesh' καρδίαι σαρκίναι in 2 Cor. 3.3 is Ezek. 11.19 and 36.26, and in those two passages 'hearts of stone' are contrasted very negatively with 'fleshly hearts.' Neither in Jeremiah 38 nor in the Ezekiel passages is there any mention of 'fleshly tablets' (πλάκες) of stone. Indeed, the only πλάκες ever mentioned in the Septuagint are the two tablets of the law.

There seems, therefore, no reason to doubt that Paul himself has contrived the image of 'tablets of fleshly hearts' to create a very sharp contrast with 'tablets of stone' and which conveyed, for him at least, the dual contrasts of 'written in the heart' versus 'written in stone' (Jer. 38.33) and 'fleshly heart' versus 'heart of stone' (Ezek. 11.19; 36.26), to which he added 'written by the spirit of the living God' versus 'written in black (ink)'. Thrall (1994: 227) rightly observes that it is not possible to deny, as Hafemann does (1990a: 204–5), that 'stone tablets' has a negative ring in this context. But Paul not only sets up this contrast, but also compares his 'letter of recommendation', which is 'written by the Spirit of the living God', to what is written 'in black ink'. Now this statement looks back to the letters of recommendation in 3.1 as one negatively viewed comparator, but it also possibly evokes the black ink used to write the law of Moses in Paul's time, writing referred to in 3.6 (as argued in the following). Both the letters of recommendation and the law of Moses have this characteristic in common; they are written with a pen dipped in black ink.

We must ask ourselves the critical question of why Paul has chosen to generate the contrast between tablets of stone and tablets of fleshly hearts that reflects badly on the former. Why has he chosen to say something that subordinates the tablets on which the Mosaic law was written to the tablets of human hearts? Thrall suggests, surely correctly, that Paul is responding to 'a particular situation in Corinth' (1994: 227). Paul is derogating both the letters of recommendation and the Mosaic law, promulgated in black ink and on stone tablets, in such a way as to establish a close relationship between them. Why would he do this unless those who had arrived in Corinth were not also in some way connected with the law of Moses? Georgi's suggestion (1987: 248–9) that the Decalogue was the letter of recommendation carried by the τινες of 3.1 is implausible for want of any evidence the law was ever called a letter (Thrall 1994: 228). The likely view is more straightforward; it is that those who arrived with the letters also advocated adherence to the law of Moses. He will soon go on to describe himself (using the epistolary plural) as 'ministers of a new covenant' (διάκονοι καινῆς διαθήκης; 3.6), and he also describes himself (again using the epistolary plural) as 'God's ministers' (θεοῦ διάκονοι) in 6.4. Both of these statements serve to differentiate him from those who have been describing themselves as διάκονοι δικαιοσύνης and διάκονοι Χριστοῦ, as mentioned in 11.15 and 11.23.

We are driven by this comparison to conclude that there is a close association between the bearers of the letters of recommendation and the Mosaic law; indeed, Paul is suggesting that they are representatives of that law.

Competence for service 3.4-6

2 Corinthians 3.4 Paul moves to a new issue in v. 4: 'Such is the confidence (πεποίθησιν δὲ τοιαύτην) that we have through Christ toward God.' The word πεποίθησις is only used by Paul in 2 Cor. 1.15; 3.4; 8.22 and 10.2, that is, in all three major sections of the letter, and in Phil. 3.4. While Christ is the ultimate enabler for his confidence in 3.4, as Sloan points out, τοιαύτη qualifying 'confidence' requires an antecedent to give it content (1995: 138). Here the antecedent is probably the fact that 'the Corinthians are a letter written by the Spirit and "ministered" by him (vv. 2-3)' (Lambrecht 1999: 42). That is to say, Paul is confident that the very existence of the Christ-group at Corinth provides him with apostolic credentials (Thrall 1994: 228). Yet he will immediately insist on its foundation not in himself but in its divine origin, via a statement of his apostolic authority in vv. 5-6. This is a preferable interpretation to Richard Hays' idea that the Corinthian community is the enfleshment of prophecies in Jeremiah and Ezekiel (1989: 129–31). As Sloan notes (1995: 138), 'Hays does not really include 3.4-6 in his exegesis of this passage.' It is possible that this confidence could also stretch a little further back, so as also to be based on 2.14-17 (Harris 2005: 267). Perhaps it is best to say that the foundation for Paul's confidence through Christ is expressed in 2.14-17 as amplified by 3.1-3.

2 Corinthians 3.5 In this verse, Paul corrects an impression he fears he may have given in the previous statement, that his competence lay in himself, whereas it came from God. The ancient rhetoricians called such a correction ἐπανόρθωσις (Harris 2005: 267). This further confirms that the previous statement was about his own heart, and not that of the Corinthians. He is continuing to speak of his ministry and to emphasize its divine source, a tactic he initiated in 2 Cor. 1.1. He had, however, expressed a similar view in 1 Cor. 15.9-10, where he confessed he was not qualified to be called an apostle (οὐκ εἰμὶ ἱκανὸς καλεῖσθαι ἀπόστολος), while maintaining that by the grace of God he was what he was. The notion of his ministry becomes explicit in v. 6.

2 Corinthians 3.6 Paul's opening statement, 'It is God who has made us competent (ἱκάνωσεν)', repeats the sentiment in the previous verse, but it is now attached to the divine purpose behind that process: to make him a minister (διάκονοι; epistolary plural) of the new covenant (καινῆς διαθήκης).

Many commentators reasonably regard the aorist ἱκάνωσεν as referring to Paul's conversion experience (Gal. 1.15-17). The word διάκονοι connects with and carries forward διακονηθεῖσα in 3.3. In 6.4, he will claim to be a 'minister of God'. Paul wants to make these assertions reasonably early in the letter because later (11.23) he will acknowledge that his opponents in Corinth are calling themselves 'ministers of Christ' (διάκονοι Χριστοῦ).

Contrary to the important argument of Scott Hafemann (1996: 39–91, 102–3), Paul is not portraying himself as the fulfilment of the expectation of a Mosaic prophet in Deut. 18.18 (an idea that never appears in Paul), nor as a fulfilment of Moses in any way. Rather Paul is depicting his ministry as prophetic with a call similar to that of Moses and the prophets. He uses the language of replacement, not fulfilment, in comparing his role to that of Moses.

Paul announces himself as the minister of 'new covenant'. He probably had in mind the appearance of this expression in Jer. 38.31, especially as in v. 3.2 he alluded to Jer. 38.33 in speaking of what was written on human hearts. Although the new covenant was a feature of the Christ-movement's interpretation of the Lord's Supper before Paul joined it (1 Cor. 11.25), when Paul came across the expression 'new covenant' in that context, he would surely have interpreted it in relation to Jer. 38.31, since that is the only place in the LXX where it occurs. Paul could hardly have recollected Jer. 38.31 (LXX) in v. 3 without recalling what came in v. 32, namely that this new covenant would not be like the one he made when he brought the ancestors of Israel and Judah out of the land of Egypt, a tradition with which his audience was familiar (1 Cor. 10.1-5).

There are three main ways to interpret the statement that 'for what is written (lit: 'the letter'; τὸ γράμμα) kills but the Spirit gives life.' The first goes back to Origen, who argued that 'the letter' referred to literal or external sense of scripture, while the 'Spirit' referred to the spiritual, or internal sense of scriptural passages (Garland 1999: 163–4). This view is quite impossible, and not just because (so Thrall 1994: 234–5) it would give 'Spirit' a different meaning from what it has in v. 3. The main problem is that it is irreconcilable with Paul's communicative intention for the Corinthians, both because the complexities of their situation did not include whether they should engage in literal or allegorical interpretation of texts that most of them could not read and because such an idea has no relation to the argument Paul has just been running. Secondly, it has been argued that 'the letter' refers to tying the 'legalistic' practice of the law to human activity rather than to divine initiative (whereas the Spirit relates to the new action of God in Christ (Barrett 1973: 113). That is, 'letter' means using the law in the wrong way. Yet this view, of 'Judaism' as a religion of works-righteousness, long ago succumbed to the effective counterarguments of E. P. Sanders (1977). Moreover, it is clear from the next verse that Paul is speaking of the initial giving of the law, not its subsequent misuse (Thrall 1994: 235; Barnett 1997: 176–7). Thirdly, τὸ γράμμα refers to the law of Moses itself, a position supported by commentators such as Dunn (1970b: 310 and 1998: 147), Thrall (1994: 235), Barnett (1997: 176–7) and Lambrecht (1999: 43). This is the natural interpretation, especially given that in the very next verse Paul uses the same word in relation to the tablets of the law and to death when he mentions 'the ministry of death, carved in letters of stone' (ἡ διακονία τοῦ θανάτου ἐν γράμμασιν ἐνετετυπωμένη ἐν λίθοις). Many commentators seek to resist the obvious here by referring to Paul's admittedly far more nuanced views on the law expressed in Romans, especially in Rom. 7.12, 14 (e.g. Matera 2003: 80–1; Harris 2005: 273). But this is not an acceptable interpretative gambit. As explained in Chapter 1 of this volume, when reading a Pauline letter for its 'original meaning' we must look at the matter in terms of what Paul was seeking to convey to his audience, in this case the Corinthian Christ-followers, and that is an issue on which his later views in Romans are not necessarily relevant. It is hard to conceive of how the Corinthians would have done anything other than regard v. 7 as amplifying v. 6 and concluded that Paul was very sharply criticizing the law of Moses. Keddie (2015) argues that Paul was not castigating the law or the Judeans but seeking to differentiate himself from Moses by critiquing the latter's meditation to bolster his own authority as a mediator of divine revelation. While Paul's stress on the ministry of death necessitates that he was targeting the Mosaic covenant, so that Keddie's view on this point cannot be accepted, there is, as we will see, an element of Paul's argument that does involve depreciating Moses vis-à-vis himself.

It is, moreover, socially unrealistic to suggest that 'Paul is not engaging in polemics against opponents in this section' but just reminding them that he is the minister of a new covenant of the Spirit (Garland 1999: 166; to similar effect, Thrall 1994: 236). Paul began this part of the letter with a bitter attack on unnamed persons who had turned up in Corinth with letters of recommendation; they are the people who demand that Christ-followers adopt the Mosaic law, and in critiquing it Paul is certainly derogating its exponents. Their presence is felt throughout this section of the letter. They are the ones Paul insists will 'enslave' non-Judean Christ-followers if they get a chance, as we see by his use of καταδουλόω in 2 Cor. 11.20 and, to precisely the same point, in Gal. 2.4, whereas the Spirit produces freedom (ἐλευθερία; 3.17). Paul denigrates the law of Moses because the adoption of that law by non-Judean Christ-followers is precisely what his opponents were advocating. From a social identity point of view, all this is a clear example of outgroup stereotypification.

Two contrasting covenants (3.7-11)

2 Corinthians 3.7 In v. 6, Paul had referred to himself, in the plural, as 'ministers (διάκονοι) of a new covenant, one not of writing but of Spirit'. The verses that follow in ch. 3 bear directly upon the new covenant and its contrast with the old,[13] which is not specified as such until v. 14 but is so identified since it is discussed in relation to the receipt of the law by Moses, for even though the word νόμος does not appear in ch. 3 (or elsewhere in the letter), it appears as 'Moses' in 3.15 and is implied, very negatively, in 3.7. Thus, v. 7 begins a section of the letter linked to the narrative of Exodus 34 that continues until the end of the chapter (v. 18) on which there has been lively scholarly discussion (Stockhausen 1989; Cover 2015: 3-28). This passage follows closely upon the previous verse, with its assertion that 'what is written kills but the Spirit gives life' (Seifrid 2014: 150). As Christopher Stanley has noted, 2 Cor. 3.7-18 is one of those instances where Paul 'frames his argument around a passage of Scripture without quoting a specific verse' (2004: 110). The issues, previously discussed, concerning how much Israelite scripture Paul expected his audience to know in relation to explicit quotations are equally relevant here. Stanley's discussion involves assessing the varying amounts of awareness to be expected of three groups: 'informed', 'competent' and 'minimal' audiences (2004: 110-13). Stanley is open to the possibility that the minimal audience may never even have heard of Moses (2004: 112). This seems highly unlikely, however. Moses was the great lawgiver of the Judean ethnic group. As Josephus indicates, just as the Greeks had legislators like Solon (in Athens), Lycurgus (in Sparta) and Zaleucus (in Locri), so too did Israel have Moses (Josephus, *Contra Apionem*, 2.16). If one knew anything about these ethnic groups, such knowledge probably included the person or, as in the case of the Law of the Twelve Tables in Rome, the legal code ultimately generative of many of their distinctive customs and beliefs. But even if Paul's Corinthian converts had never heard of Judeans, which is hardly likely in view of their existence by the millions throughout the Mediterranean world (Barclay 1996), Paul would have had to tell them something about Israel and its traditions, if only to justify the several occasions on which he leans upon the authority of those traditions and the God of whom they spoke. In telling them something about Moses and his transmission of the law to Israel, Paul would have found Exodus 34 perhaps the most useful source. What Paul says in 1 Cor. 10.1-5 makes it highly likely he had told the Corinthians about Moses and the tablets of the law.

---

[13] Campbell, however, argues that the contrast is between the two ministries, not the two covenants (2018: 168-75).

Whether or not Paul had previously told the Corinthians about the high point of the Exodus narrative, the Sinai account, or not (and, if he had told them anything, it was surely this), there was a very particular reason why Paul had to mention the divine transmission of the law of Moses in this letter. Scholars such as Duff (2004: 314) who overlook or underestimate the evidence that Paul was facing opposition in Corinth similar to that he encountered in Galatia and feared in Philippi from Judean Christ-followers insisting on adherence to the law need to come up with some explanation for the whole section of vv. 7-18 in the letter divorced from such 'Judaizing issues'. In response to scepticism as to the presence of Galatians-style opponents in Corinth, we should recall from our earlier discussion that the Mosaic law played a major role in the maintenance and expression of Judean ethnic identity. In a section of the letter that begins with Paul's mentioning people bearing letters of recommendation (3.1), it is highly probable that he is drawing the attention of his audience to members of the Christ-movement who have turned up in Corinth and who advocate the importance of the Mosaic law. It is reasonable to assume that these are Judean Christ-followers, since who else would raise the figure of Moses to such an audience? Furthermore, the argument that the letter is a unity means that we can identify them with the people whom he describes as 'Hebrews', 'Israelites' and 'seed of Abraham' in 2 Cor. 11.22. In other words, they are ethnic Judeans who are also members of the Christ-movement. The law of Moses mattered to them and if, as seems likely, they had begun to sing its praises to the Corinthians, as an initial step in encouraging them to become Judeans, Paul had to provide a counter-narrative, a form of anti-ethnic reasoning.[14] This he did in 2 Corinthians 3.

The initial statement in 2 Cor. 3.7 designates the tablets of the law that Moses inscribed at God's direction (Exod. 34.27-28) as the 'ministry of death' (διακονία τοῦ θανάτου) 'carved in letters in stones'. This is the first of twelve uses of the key concept διακονία in 2 Corinthians, previously discussed. In 2 Cor. 3.7, διακονία denotes 'the whole system of the Mosaic law, along with its agents; personal and impersonal elements are blended in one' (Harris 2005: 281).

Yet here this ministry is labelled as 'of death'. Although this could mean either that the διακονία brings death or is marked by death (Harris 2005: 281), the former alternative is to be preferred here in view of the statement in the verse preceding this one that 'what is written kills'. Duff (2004) has argued that in this passage Paul is arguing that the Mosaic law was a

---

[14] For an argument in favour of alleged 'ethnic reasoning' in early Christianity, see Buell 2005.

ministry of death for primarily for 'gentiles' not for 'Jews'. But that view is built upon his insistence on the impossibility of the glory that attended the giving of the law being associated with death and condemnation, even though he concedes that the law had precisely that effect for some 'Jews' and many 'gentiles'. Having unwisely denied the presence of any 'Judaizing' opponents of Paul in Corinth who make the presence of this passage in the letter readily explicable, he provides no answer as to why Paul should run this argument in the first place, bar the unconvincing one that Paul is seeking to balance the threat of death hanging over him with the death allegedly threatening 'gentiles' under the law, a threat Paul never mentions in the passage. That Paul only had non-Judeans in mind also clashes with the negative reference to Judeans hearing the law in 3.15.

Paul's point is that it was Judeans for whom the law of Moses was a ministry of death. But Judeans (very reasonably) regarded the Mosaic law as a source of life, not death (Lev. 18.5; Deut. 30.15-20). That Paul should denigrate it as a ministry of death is remarkable and shocking, both for the content of the expression and for the fact that it is offered without any explanation that might soften the blow. Elsewhere Paul does explain his views on how the law was caught up with death (e.g. in Gal. 3.10-14; Rom. 7.7-12; 8.1-2). Yet here there is nothing like that. Paul is succinctly and brutally negative. He appears, moreover, to assume that his audience will know what he is conveying by mention of Moses' death-dealing ministry, and he can only make that assumption if he himself (or perhaps a close associate like Timothy or Titus) has already described the Mosaic law in such terms (similarly, Thrall 1994: 249). No one else whom the Corinthians were likely to have encountered would have done so. It is difficult, therefore, to concur with the view that 'Paul does not seek to denigrate the old covenant ministry that Moses exercised' (Matera 2003: 85). That is precisely what he is doing. This forms part of Paul's larger purpose of his mission to preach the Gospel to non-Judeans that entailed their not having to become Judeans to receive it and be saved. Why join the Judean ethnic group when the body of law that played so large a part in maintaining its distinct identity brought death and not life? A social identity perspective views this as an example of pronounced intergroup differentiation, in this case between the Judean ethnic group on the one hand and the Christ-movement, a group of a very different kind, on the other.

Paul is willing to concede, however, that glory attended the original promulgation of the 'ministry of death', but only in a very limited sense. Having noted that this ministry 'came with glory' (ἐγενήθη ἐν δόξῃ), he then goes on to explain the glory he has in mind and immediately to undermine it. For the second statement in v. 7 records 'that the Israelites were not able to gaze upon the face of Moses on account of the glory (τὴν δόξην) of his face, even though it (sc. the glory) was fading away (καταργουμένην).[15] Here the present participle καταργουμένην has a concessive force, like the example appearing in 11.19: 'although being wise'. This description is based on Exod. 34.29-35 that recount how, when Moses came down from the mountain with the two tablets in his hand, unbeknown to him the skin of his face shone. When the people saw this, they were afraid to approach him, yet did so when he called them. When Moses had finished speaking with them he put a veil over his face. So the pattern was: Moses' unveiled face shone when he spoke to God, he then delivered the divine commandment to the people with a shining face, and put the veil on until he was due to speak to God again.

So begins a protracted use of veil imagery by Paul that will continue until 3.18. It is probable that he chose to adopt this image because of claims being made by his opponents that his Gospel was veiled, perhaps in this case meaning obscure or hidden, a charge to which he replies in 4.3. If so, his resort to veil imagery himself constitutes another sign of the fierce intergroup differentiation and conflict caused by the arrival of his opponents in Corinth,

What therefore was the point of the veil for the Exodus author and audience? This question has provoked a variety of possible answers, such as to prevent the glory of God being wasted or profaned, or as an expression of Moses' modesty (Hafemann 1996: 224). According to Scott Hafemann, *'Moses' veiling himself should be seen as an act of mercy to keep the people from being destroyed by the reflected presence of God'* (1996: 223; italics original). Walter Moberly (1983: 108) had previously suggested a similar reason (while noting the speculative nature of any proposed solution). Hafemann further suggests that the veil was necessary because of Israel's sinful state and thus represented an act of divine mercy (1996: 224). While this is an attractive suggestion, it is strange that Moses speaks to the people for a period with his face uncovered. Why were they not destroyed during that process? Are we to assume that the divine power needed something like a warming-up period before it was effective in wreaking death and destruction?

The very fact that it is not possible to pin down the reason for the veil in Exod. 34.29-35 gave Paul the space to offer this own explanation: the veil concealed the circumstance that over time the glory faded from Moses' face. Although the substantive δόξα ('glory') does not appear in Exod. 34.29-35

---

[15] Baker 2000 argues that καταργουμένην means 'being rendered ineffective', 'hindered' or 'blocked', not 'fading away'.

in relation to what happened to Moses' face in the presence of God, perfect passive forms of the verb δοξάζειν ('to glorify') occur thrice (vv. 29, 30 and 35). Paul introduces the substantive δόξα to assist him with his argument. While there is nothing in Exodus 34 about Moses' face ceasing to shine, neither is there anything that excludes that explanation, and it served Paul's purposes well, whether he invented the idea himself or not.[16] Having just described the law as a ministry of death, Paul thus introduces a negative note into his version of how Moses received that law.

2 Corinthians 3.8 Paul now deploys the negative views that he has expressed on the Mosaic 'ministry of death' and on the method of its delivery by Moses in v. 7 as a foil against which to commend the 'ministry of the Spirit' (διακονία τοῦ πνεύματος). To do this, he introduces a typical instance of *qal wahomer* (an *a minore ad maius*) argument: if the ministry of death was associated with glory, by how much more glorious will be the ministry of the Spirit. This sharp differentiation continues the contrast in v. 6 between how what is written brings death, whereas the Spirit brings life. Just as Paul does not explain what he means by 'the ministry of death' so too he fails to offer any explanation of 'the ministry of the Spirit'. But since the Mosaic law stood at the heart of and expressed Judean ethnic identity, it follows from Paul's direct contrast of the two expressions that the ministry of the Spirit must serve a similar role for Christ-movement identity. It has proven all too easy for most commentators to overlook the fact that when Paul refers to the Spirit he is not conveying to his audience a theological concept but a dynamic expression of the divine being frequently expressed in an explosion of charismatic phenomena such as glossolalia, prophecy, interpretation and miracle-working.[17] We know from the profuse data in 1 Corinthians 12–14 just how prominent were such phenomena in the Corinthian Christ-movement.[18] That Paul himself led the way in the manifestation of the gifts of the Spirit emerges from his claim to pre-eminence in 1 Cor. 14.18: 'I give thanks to God that I speak in tongues more than all of you.'

2 Corinthians 3.9 Paul turns once again to a *qal wahomer* argument, very similar to the one in the previous verse. He wants his audience to understand that there is an equivalence between 'ministry of death' (v. 7) and 'ministry of condemnation' (διακονία τῆς κατακρίσεως) there and between 'ministry of Spirit' (v. 8) and 'ministry of righteousness' (διακονία τῆς δικαιοσύνης) in

---

[16] It is possible, as Harris suggests (2005: 285), that Paul may have known another tradition to this effect. But there is nothing along these lines in *Biblical Antiquities* nor in *Jubilees*.
[17] The seminal work for this understanding of the Spirit in the New Testament is Dunn 1970a.
[18] For a discussion of glossolalia and the admission of non-Judeans into early Christ-groups, see Esler 1994: 37–51.

this verse. The first equivalence (of death and condemnation) strengthens the case that Paul has previously explained his problem with the Mosaic law to the Corinthians, for without their previous exposure to an argument along these lines, it would have been virtually impossible for them to connect 'ministry of death' and 'ministry of condemnation'. Later in his career, in Rom. 7.7-11, where he is speaking in relation to his own deeply felt experience,[19] perhaps going far back in his career as an evangelist, he links the condemnation caused by infringement of the law to the death it produces.

For Paul to draw an equivalence between the 'ministry of Spirit' and the 'ministry of righteousness' is immensely revealing of the situation in which he finds himself when he writes this letter. The notion of righteousness is very poorly served by scholarly attempts to explain it as having either a 'forensic' or a 'relational meaning' and that ignore its function in the establishment and maintenance of group identity.[20] Righteousness was regarded by Judeans as a central feature of what we, using useful etic categories, call ethnic identity. While it had a normative dimension, it was above all an identity-descriptor with a very positive character and represented, in effect, a glittering prize of being a Judean (Esler 1998: 159–69). In Galatians, the Judean Christ-followers who were advocating a gospel in competition to Paul's had offered it to his non-Judean converts as an attractive inducement for them to become ethnic Judeans themselves.[21] That is why Paul must insist that righteousness comes from faith in Christ (Esler 1998: 169–76). So righteousness was likely to be an issue wherever and whenever non-Judean Christ-followers encountered teaching from Judean Christ-followers who insisted that they needed to take on the Mosaic law (including circumcision) and become Judeans as well. The converse is also the case: if Paul's converts were not being exposed to, or threatened with, pressure from representatives of the Christ-movement insisting on their undergoing 'ethnic translation' – to cite the useful phrase of Katherine Southwood (2014) – to become Judeans, righteousness was not only irrelevant but might also be confusing. This was precisely the situation in Thessalonica as reflected in 1 Thessalonians. That Paul was writing to an entirely non-Judean, ex-idolatrous audience is revealed when he says: 'you turned to God from idols, to serve a living and true God' (1 Thess. 1.9). Nor

---

[19] For this interpretation of Romans 7, see Esler 2003a: 222–42.
[20] On the role of righteousness in Christ-movement identity, see Esler 1998: 145–51. Harris (2005: 287), for example, says of δικαιοσύνη here that it 'is a relational rather than an ethical term, denoting a right standing before God, given by God, (as in Rom. 1:17; 3:21-22; 10:3; Phil. 3:9), the status of being "in the right" before the court of heaven.'
[21] Attempts to argue that Paul's opponents in Galatia were non-Judeans (e.g. Munck 1959: 87–8) falter in the face of Paul's complete failure to mention such people, whereas in two earlier incidents he describes, in Jerusalem (Gal. 2.1-5) and then in Antioch (Gal. 2.11-14), pressure on non-Judean Christ-followers had come from Judean Christ-followers.

is there any sign in this letter, unlike the situation in Philippians (3.2), that the arrival of Christ-followers teaching the need to become Judeans is on the horizon. Consequently, righteousness language does not feature in the letter barring the use of the adjective δικαίως at 2.10 to describe Paul's initial behaviour among the Thessalonians, an instance not relevant to this discussion as it is not related to the identity of the Thessalonian Christ-followers. Instead, in 1 Thessalonians the language of 'holiness' and 'sanctification' takes the place of righteousness (Esler 1998: 154–9). Thus, ἁγιωσύνη appears in 1 Thess. 3.13, ἁγιασμός in 4.3, 4 and 7 and ἁγιάζω in 5.23. There are also seven instances of the adjective ἅγιος, but these carry less weight. That the omission of righteousness was not just accidental is proved by Paul's deliberate redacting of Isa. 59.17 LXX ('He put on righteousness as a breastplate and placed the helmet of salvation on his head') to remove 'righteousness': Paul has 'let us be sober and put on the breastplate of faith and love, and for a helmet the hope of salvation' (1 Thess. 5.8) (Esler 2001: 1210). In 1 Cor. 1.30, Paul had described Christ Jesus as the wisdom, righteousness (δικαιοσύνη), sanctification (ἁγιασμός) and redemption (ἀπολύτρωσις) of God. The co-existence of righteousness and sanctification here raises the question of whether 1 Cor. 1.30 marks a transitional phase when Judeans were developing, or were (in Paul's view) likely to have, an influence on the community so that Paul could not just rely on ἁγιασμός language as he had in 1 Thessalonians.

Paul reverts to the language of righteousness in relation to his own ministry on a number of occasions later in 2 Corinthians. In 2 Cor. 5.21, he speaks of God's righteousness. In 6.7, he employs a military metaphor ('with weapons of righteousness for right hand and the left') of the sort he deliberately eschewed in 1 Thess. 5.8. At 6.14, he offers righteousness as the antithesis to 'lawlessness' (ἀνομία). In 2 Corinthians 9, he configures righteousness as a reward for generosity in the collection (vv. 9 and 10).

This way of talking about his ministry in Corinth is highly significant, because it indicates, first, the likelihood that Judean persuasion (possibly extending to the necessity of circumcision) has been or is about to be exerted on the non-Judean Christ-followers and, secondly, that Paul wishes to lay claim to righteousness language for his own version of the Christ-movement. Solid evidence that this was a field of contestation between himself and his opponents in Corinth, just as it had been or would be in Galatia (Esler 2006b), exists in 2 Cor. 11.15 where Paul will claim that these people disguise themselves as servants of righteousness; that is, they present themselves as offering righteousness but, in his view, their claims are false.[22] In other

---

[22] Many commentators (e.g. Harris 2005: 287), even those who believe that the letter is a unity, fail to mention 2 Cor. 11.5 when discussing the instance of righteousness at 2 Cor. 3.9.

words, there is a battle going on in Corinth over righteousness and the identity of its genuine ministers. The fact that Paul defends his own ministry of righteousness in a section of the letter that begins with an attack on outsiders who have turned up in Corinth bearing letters of recommendation (3.1) and later claims that these same people are pretending to be ministers of righteousness ties together 2 Corinthians 1–7 and 10–13 and is thus a persuasive indicator of the unity of the letter.[23]

Thrall suggests that the comparison and contrast at this point in the letter is between 'non-Christian Judaism and Christianity (both Jewish and Gentile)' and seeks to fend off the alternative view by claiming that the 'idea that it is two differing forms of the Christian mission that are opposed to each other is read into the text, not out of it' (1994: 248). Yet there are solid exegetical reasons for regarding the whole point of 2 Corinthians 3 as being to launch a pre-emptive strike on the people he will address in more detail in chs 10–13, and they are Judean members of the Christ-movement, not Judeans *simpliciter*. The main factor is that from 2 Cor. 2.17 and then 3.1 Paul is responding to Judean Christ-followers who have turned up in Corinth to make a pitch for their form of the Gospel. Why would Paul move away from this massive problem, which forms one of four aspects of the rhetorical exigency that he addresses in the letter, to raise the different and much more general issue of the broad relationship between the Judean ethnic group and its Mosaic law and his version of the Christ-movement? The Judean ethnic group only causes problems if some Judean Christ-followers want his converts to become Judeans; that is, his negative presentation of the law of Moses is driven by its being advocated by Judean Christ-followers, and if that were not the case, there would be little reason for him to address it (which is the situation in 1 Thessalonians, for example).

2 Corinthians 3.10 This verse functions as an amplification of the conclusion reached in the previous verse. The neuter form, τὸ δεδοξασμένον ('what has been glorified') and the general sense of the passage probably suggest that Paul does not have in mind Moses' face as what was glorified (as in Exod. 34.35) but the ministry (including the law and covenant) associated with him.

What has been glorified (i.e. the ministry of Moses), states Paul, 'is not glorified' ἐν τούτῳ τῷ μέρει 'on account of the surpassing glory'. We may pass over the meaning of the phrase ἐν τούτῳ τῷ μέρει for the moment. Paul is stating quite bluntly that the Mosaic ministry is no longer glorious. Its glory is disappearing with the arrival of the glory attached to the new

---

[23] Matera (2003: 89) recognizes the link between 2 Cor. 3.9 and 6.7 and 2 Corinthians 10–13 on this question of righteousness.

covenant and the ministry of the Holy Spirit and of righteousness. Like many commentators, Frank Matera is very resistant to the meaning of v. 10 when he claims that here Paul 'is not saying God's glory in the new covenant is somehow more glorious than God's glory in the old covenant' (2003: 89). In fact, Paul goes much further: the old covenant has lost or is losing its glory. As Seifrid observes (2014: 158-9), citing K. Barth: 'Because the sun rises, all lights are extinguished.' 'It is not glorified' (οὐ δεδόξασται). But as Seifrid has rightly noted, 'The contrast that Paul sets between them is so radical and difficult that most, if not all, commentators, do away with it' (2014: 159). From a social identity perspective, however, where one group is defining itself in relation to an outgroup in a fraught situation, such dualistic stereotyping of the character of both is entirely to be expected.

Returning to ἐν τούτῳ τῷ μέρει, the phrase probably does not mean 'in part' because Paul employs the phrases ἀπὸ μέρους (2 Cor. 1.14 and 2.5) or ἐκ μέρους (1 Cor. 12.27; 13.9, 10, 12) for that meaning and τούτῳ would be redundant. The meaning is rather 'in this case', 'in this matter' or 'in this regard' (BDAG 633), the same meaning it has in 2 Cor. 9.3. As such it relates more naturally to οὐ δεδόξασται than to τὸ δεδοξασμένον. But whether the phrase 'in this case' points backwards to v. 9 or forwards to the last words of v. 10, it does not have much impact on the meaning of this verse.

2 Corinthians 3.11 Paul here provides a third *qal wahomer* argument: 'For if what is being abolished came with glory, what abides must have much more glory.' The verse represents bleak news for the Mosaic law and covenant: it is described as 'what is being abolished' (τὸ καταργούμενον). A present passive participle of the same verb was used in v. 7, but there in the feminine as applied to the glory (δόξα) of Moses' face that was fading away. Here, on the other hand, the neuter participle must be interpreted more generally 'as applying to the entire ministry of the old covenant symbolized by Moses' (Furnish 1984: 205). 'What abides' (τὸ μένον) is the new covenant and ministry Paul has just been contrasting with his in vv. 6-10. While the proposition that the Mosaic covenant is being abolished is hard to reconcile with what Paul says in Rom. 9.1-5, it is nevertheless the rhetorical position he adopts here for the benefit of his Corinthian converts and that is what counts when we are interpreting 2 Corinthians. On the other hand, the new covenant will abide. Once again the sentiment embodies the processes of ingroup/outgroup differentiation and stereotypification that forms the central interest of social identity theory. And, once again, some commentators seek refuge from the stark reality of this verse by discovering in it, via an eisegetical technique, some more anodyne meaning. Frank Matera, for example, claims that 'Paul does not denigrate Moses, his old covenant ministry, or the glory that attended it' (2003: 89). On the contrary, denigration of the Mosaic covenant (maybe not Moses himself, at least at this point) and the ministry he associates with it is precisely what Paul is engaged in at this point, unless associating a covenant, which has now lost the glory it once had, with death and condemnation can count as praise. Nor is there any justification for Matera's suggestion that 'the new covenant is the old covenant made alive by God's Spirit. To that extent, there is one enduring covenant' (2003: 89).

Moses' veiled old covenant and unveiled Christ-followers (3.12-18)

2 Corinthians 3.12-18 contains a sustained polemic against the significance of Moses and his law (which continues to be present by necessary implication despite the absence of the word νόμος) for which the only plausible explanation is that these were being advocated by Paul's opponents in Corinth. These were the people he had firmly in his sights in 2.17–3.1 and has kept them there throughout 2 Corinthians 3. Harris (2005: 67) resists this conclusion through a misplaced fear of 'mirror-readings' that I have commented upon earlier in this volume.

2 Corinthians 3.12 For a brief moment, Paul now turns to himself and his role, which his aim in the letter of exercising leadership in relation to the Corinthian Christ-movement will not allow him to neglect: 'Having such hope we employ great forthrightness.' The hope to which Paul refers is probably occasioned by the enduring nature of the glorious new covenant. The quality of forthrightness (παρρησία), discussed by Fredrickson (1996), is not particularly common in the Pauline correspondence. It recurs in 2 Cor. 7.4 and also appears in Phil. 1.20 and Phlm. 8. It refers to 'a use of speech that conceals nothing and passes over nothing, outspokenness, frankness, plainness' (BDAG 781). Paul conveys that he is speaking openly, honestly and forthrightly in contrast, we see in the next verse, with Moses. Paul has already insisted on his honesty and sincerity in this letter, in 1.12, where he mentions his sincerity, his freedom from dissimulation (εἰλικρίνεια), because he was being accused of the opposite in connection with this change of travel plans. Moreover, immediately prior to 2 Corinthians 3 with its opening salvo against those who have arrived in Corinth with letters of recommendation, he has again asserted this characteristic (εἰλικρίνεια) in contrast to those who peddle the word of God (2.17).

If, as already argued, these pedlars of the word of God were preaching the importance of Moses and the Mosaic law and covenant, the suggestion of insincerity he is about to make of Moses aligns their hero with the interlopers in relation to this characteristic. Further examples of Paul's forthrightness (although not with the word εἰλικρίνεια) will appear later in the letter (in chs 10–13). In addition, however, Paul employs another word, closely related to εἰλικρίνεια, namely ἁπλότης, meaning 'simplicity, sincerity, uprightness, frankness' (BDAG 104). It is from ἁπλοῦς, meaning 'single', as opposed to διπλοῦς, 'double', and appears a number of times in the letter. The earliest possible appearance of ἁπλότης is in 2 Cor. 1.12, where it is a textual variant for ἁγιότης, 'holiness', which is probably to be preferred as the *lectio difficilior*. In any event, whatever reading is preferred in 1.12, the substantive immediately after it is εἰλικρίνεια, so that the notion of sincerity appears at this early point in the letter. The other instances of ἁπλότης occur at 8.2, 9.11 and 13, and 11.3. Although it is sometimes said that the three instances in 2 Corinthians 8–9 should be translated 'generosity' or 'liberality', it is preferable to see them as conveying the sense of 'sincere concern, simple goodness' (BDAG 104). Sincerity and forthrightness (expressed by παρρησία, εἰλικρίνεια and ἁπλότης) thus feature in all three of the main sections of the letter and constitute one of the themes that bind it together. Sometimes Paul applies this language to himself (1.12; 2.17; 3.12; 7.4) and sometimes to others (8.2; 9.11 and 13; 11.3); in either case it represents an important identity-descriptor for the Christ-movement. Paul seeks to present himself as embodying a value and a practice already possessed by the Corinthians and thus to align his identity with theirs in the manner that social identity theory insists is necessary for successful leaders of groups. His forthrightness distinguishes him from the deceitful ways of others.[24]

2 Corinthians 3.13 As a preliminary point, there is dispute as to what τέλος means in this verse. It either has a temporal sense, meaning 'termination' or 'cessation', or it has the teleological sense of 'goal' or 'final destiny'. The former is to be preferred, since it is odd to speak of the 'goal' of something that is disappearing, whereas 'termination' makes good sense.[25] The entity that is disappearing is the Mosaic ministry, the old covenant (with this very expression, παλαιὰ διαθήκη, about to appear in the next verse).

Paul has previously differentiated the old covenant and ministry from the new. Now he performs the daring gambit of sharply distinguishing himself from Moses. Having just asserted his own forthrightness, he impugns that of Moses (contra, Campbell 2016). For he is not as Moses 'who placed a veil on

---

[24] Furnish 1984: 231, citing with approval Collange (1972: 87) to the same effect.
[25] There is a lively debate on this subject, as thoroughly canvassed by Thrall (1994: 256–61). Those favouring a temporal sense (as here) include Furnish 1984: 207, Witherington 1995: 381 and Kistemaker 1997: 118–19.

his face so that the sons of Israel could not gaze at the end (sc. in the temporal sense) of what was fading away (τὸ τέλος τοῦ καταργουμένου)'. Even in the first century CE, 'sons of Israel' or 'Israelites' was an ingroup designation for the ethnic group known as Judeans when other ethnic groups were in the frame (Elliott 2007: 148). In 2 Cor. 11.22, Paul will record that his opponents prided themselves on being Israelites; this verse forms part of the case he is formulating against their views.

As noted earlier, Exodus 34 offers no explanation for why Moses needed to put a veil on his face. Paul, however, now ventures into this space with a suggestion that denigrates Moses, and there is no other way to interpret it. Whereas Paul has spoken in an open and forthright way, in reliance on his earlier statement that the glory was fading (v. 7) he now proposes that Moses put on the veil to disguise from the Israelites the end (τὸ τέλος) of what was being abolished. Paul has been open and forthright, but Moses was the opposite, since he was concealing something very important. Thus, the negative dimension is demanded by the contrast between Paul's forthrightness in v. 12 and the opposite quality attributed to Moses in v. 13. Harris ventures to suggest that Moses is practising concealment but 'with no necessary implication of duplicity in that concealment' (2005: 296), a view for which there is no evidence in the text and which flies in the face of the contrast with Paul's own behaviour in the previous verse. Nor is this point strengthened by Harris' view (2005: 296) that this part of the text ends with 'an implied similarity between Moses and all Christian believers (3:18)', when the point made in 3.18 is the profound dissimilarity between the two parties.

Therefore, this was not Moses' 'laudable attempt to have the Israelites realize the impermanence of the Sinaitic economy' (Harris 2005: 301). It was, rather, Moses' insincere attempt to cover up that impermanence. Accordingly, Paul is establishing a direct parallel between Moses' behaviour and that of 'the many who peddle (οἱ πολλοὶ καπηλεύοντες) the word of God' mentioned a little earlier, in 2 Cor. 2.17. The parallel subsists not in the sense that Moses did what he did for gain, but that he, like hucksters in the market, was not entirely honest about the quality of the product he was supplying. Indeed, 'because of the tricks of small tradesmen . . . the word (καπηλεύειν) almost comes to mean *adulterate*' (BDAG 508). Later in the letter Paul will expatiate upon the deceptiveness of the Judean Christ-followers who have arrived in Corinth (11.12-15), using the word μετασχηματίζειν, there meaning 'to feign to be what one is not,' 'to disguise oneself' (BDAG 641-642) on three occasions (vv. 13, 14 and 15). It could be said that Moses, by putting a veil on his face, also disguised himself, in particular, by hiding the glory that was disappearing.

In short, as opposed to Paul, who prides himself on his sincerity and forthrightness, we find here an implied *qal wahomer* argument directed towards his opponents: if Moses himself was not open with Israel about what would happen to his covenant, how much more likely is it that his followers today will deceive and cheat you in their evangelizing efforts? Contrary to the scepticism of Harris (2512005: 301), scholars such as Collange (1972: 88–100) and Dalton (1987: 88–94) who argue that Paul is responding to his Christ-movement adversaries in 3.14-16 have every justification for doing so.

2 Corinthians 3.14 The effect of the strong adversative 'But their minds were hardened (ἀλλὰ ἐπωρώθη τὰ νοήματα αὐτῶν)' in the opening clause is challenging. In its immediate context the clause needs to be interpreted as a comment on the previous verse. The reference is to the sons of Israel mentioned in the previous verse and the hardening that happened in the past (as indicated by the aorist ἐπωρώθη, where the passive form may indicate God as the implied agent but without necessarily excluding human agency [Harris 2005: 301]). This must refer to the occasions when Moses was speaking with a veil on his face so that they could not look at the termination of what was fading away. The clause in question appears to provide a further reason for their inability to look at this phenomenon: their hearts were hardened. In other words, if their minds were not hardened, they would have seen the coming end even with a veil on Moses' face; that is, they would have seen through his ruse, which is a more likely explanation than Lambrecht's view that Paul is trying to undo the harshness of how he has just described Moses by putting some of the blame on the Israelites (1999: 52).

With the second clause, Paul progresses to a metaphorical meaning of veil (κάλυμμα). No longer a piece of material resting on Moses' face, it now becomes a barrier over the reading of the old covenant by the Israelites, persisting to the present day.

Doubt attends the referents of 'still not unveiled, since in Christ it is being destroyed' (μὴ ἀνακαλυπτόμενον ὅτι ἐν Χριστῷ καταργεῖται). In particular, is it the veil or the old covenant that is fading away? Interpreters line up on both sides.[26] Although not much turns on the matter for present purposes, it is almost certainly the old covenant that is fading away. Elsewhere in the passage, after all, it is the glory on Moses' face and the old covenant that are said to be fading away (or being annulled), not the veil (vv. 7, 11 and 13), and to speak of a veil that is unveiled is very odd. Admittedly, at first

---

[26] For 'veil': Furnish 1984: 209; Thrall 1994: 265-6 ('The same veil remains . . . unlifted because [only] in Christ is it abolished' (followed by Harris 2005: 303); and Kistemaker 1997: 121. For 'old covenant': Seifrid 2014: 168-71.

sight we might expect that κάλυμμα, also a neuter singular, was the referent of ἀνακαλυπτόμενον. As Seifrid has meticulously shown (2014: 169–70), however, grammatical considerations actually push us in the opposite direction. This is an absolute use of the participle, and its grammatical subject is not κάλυμμα but the ὅτι clause with the passive verb that follows: 'it not being revealed that in Christ it (the old covenant) is fading away/being annulled (ὅτι ἐν Χριστῷ καταργεῖται).' Translators and commentators favouring 'veil' as its referent regularly, as they must, mistranslate καταργεῖται to mean 'removed', since a veil fading away/being annulled makes no sense. Yet BDAG offers no such meaning for καταργεῖν (except possibly here), and this rendering pits such scholars against the rather awkward fact that Paul has just used the same verb three times in the previous seven verses to mean 'fade away' or 'be annulled' (vv. 7, 11 and 13), including in the previous verse in relation to the old covenant! On the other hand, where Paul was certainly referring to removing a veil, as in 2 Cor. 3.16, the verb he used was περιαιρεῖται.

2 Corinthians 3.15 In vv. 15-16, Paul recapitulates and develops the thought of v. 14. In v. 15, he persists with the metaphorical understanding of veil as an obstacle to understanding, while now supplying greater precision as to where this metaphorical veil is placed: on their (i.e. the contemporary Israelites') hearts, whereas in v. 14 it lay on the reading of the old covenant. 'Moses' now stands in for 'the old covenant', and it is probably the Pentateuch that is meant as being read (Thrall 1994: 267).

2 Corinthians 3.16 This verse turns from the negative picture of the veiled old covenant and veiled Israelite hearts to a very positive portrayal of what happens when a person 'turns to the Lord' (ἐπιστρέψῃ πρὸς κύριον). This is an example of extreme ingroup/outgroup differentiation. To determine what this means and who is referred to we need to identify the Lord referred to in this verse, a question somewhat complicated by the fact that κύριος is here anarthrous. Is it God, especially because he is mentioned in Paul's source text (Exod. 34.34) and because Paul uses the same verb in 1 Thess. 1.9 of a turning to God?[27] Or is it Christ (Lambrecht 1999: 54–550)? Or is it the Spirit (Witherington 1995: 382), who is mentioned in v. 17? This is a hotly disputed issue. Some commentators find the issue too finely balanced to decide (Matera 2003: 95). Yet this is the fifth instance of κύριος in the letter, and in each of the previous four examples (1.2, 3 and 14; 2.12); the referent was Christ, not God, and in 2.12 κύριος is anarthrous. 'In Paul's letters Lord (*Kyrios*) generally means Christ, except when the apostle is quoting scripture

---

[27] So Furnish 1984: 211–12; Thrall 1994: 273; Harris 2005: 308; Roetzel 2007: 67; Seifrid 2014: 173.

or working closely with a scriptural text.'[28] Although Paul is probably reliant on Exod. 34.34 here, he has changed it so much that the exception may not apply. Above all, however, the immediate context strongly suggests 'Christ' is correct, since how could it be suggested that those who are listening to the law of Moses are not already turned to God (unlike the ex-idolaters in 1 Thess. 1.9). Any turning can only be to Christ. These considerations push us strongly in the direction of interpreting πρὸς κύριον in 3.16 as a reference to Christ.

The second question to be answered in v. 16 is the subject of the verb ἐπιστρέψῃ. The only other two instances of ἐπιστρέφειν in Paul are in 1 Thess. 1.9 where it is used of idolaters turning to the true and living God and in Gal. 4.9 where the turning is to the weak and destitute elements. Who is the (unspecified) subject of this verb here? A number of commentators have suggested Moses, but as performing the action as a symbol or type of the Christ-following convert, for others (e.g. Thrall 1994: 271 and Seifrid 2014: 173). But this is unlikely as inconsistent with the exegetical details. It is, first, a very odd transition to move from Moses in the previous verse, meaning the Sinaitic covenant being read in the present day, to Moses as the subject of ἐπιστρέφειν. Secondly, the present tense of both ἐπιστρέψῃ and περιαιρεῖται ('is removed') also count against this verse restating what Moses did and rather locate it in the present experience of Paul's contemporaries. Seifrid interprets these verbs as historic present in tense in his translation: 'As often as he turned to the Lord, he removed the veil' (2014: 172); but Paul has been quite careful to use past tenses in vv. 13-14, and from v. 15 he is addressing the present day, not the Sinaitic past. Thirdly, in Exod. 34.34 Moses did not 'turn' to the Lord, that is, from some imperfect prior state; he went into (εἰσεπορεύετο) (the tent) to converse with the Lord. These notable divergences from Exod. 34.34 also add further weight to the case for κύριος here meaning Christ. Above all, moreover, why in a passage where Paul seeks to differentiate himself from Moses (especially in vv. 12-13) would he want to present Moses as a type or symbol of the Christ-follower? Since the entire Mosaic ministry, especially in its substance but also with respect to its agent is portrayed very negatively in 2 Cor. 3.3-15, interpretations seeing Moses as typical or symbolical of Christ-followers would frustrate the whole point of Paul's argument.

The only viable candidate for the one who turns to the Lord (i.e. to Christ) is the Christ-follower, who is baptized into Christ and has faith in him (even though those two features are not expressed in the text). Paul

---

[28] Furnish 1984: 231; so too Matera 2003: 95; contra Harris 2005: 308.

will clarify who is meant here by use of the first-person plural in v. 18: 'we all' (ἡμεῖς δὲ πάντες), an unambiguous ingroup designation.

What is Paul communicating to his Corinthian audience when he says that the veil is taken away? Does it imply that the person continues to read or be interested in the old covenant or has something else entirely taken its place? One answer is that for 'the convert, the true significance of the Mosaic covenant is revealed' (Thrall 1994: 273). But this is a covenant, characterized by death and judgement that is fading away/being annulled (v. 13); in what would its true significance subsist? It is unlikely that Paul meant its negative significance, since that is a point he has already made abundantly in the previous verses. Furnish's suggestion of the true meaning of Paul's ministry (1984: 234) looks far more likely, but perhaps too general. More likely he was conveying either Christ himself (Kistemaker 1997: 124) or, somewhat more amply, the truth about the new covenant and Christ (Harris 2005: 309). That there must be some reference to Christ is required by the contents of v. 17. This consideration also counts against Collange's idea that Paul has his opponents in mind (1972: 101–2), although Furnish's reason for rejecting this proposal, that it 'involves presuming more about their teaching than is justified' (1984: 234) has little to be said for it.

2 Corinthians 3.17 This verse has attracted much commentary, mainly to do with identifying those referred to and how they relate to each other. Most agree the Lord in v. 16 (and in v. 17) is Christ. That conclusion follows from the previous verse, since this must be the same Lord, and to say that God was Spirit would be rather banal. The most debated issue is whether the relationship between the Christ and the Spirit is one of close identification or a looser association. The latter is more likely, as suggested by the other places in Paul's correspondence where he links the two: Rom. 8.9-11; Phil. 1.19; Gal. 4.6; 1 Cor. 6.17 and 12.3 (Furnish 1984: 212).

The more interesting clause in the verse is the second: 'Where the Spirit of the Lord is, there is freedom (ἐλευθερία).' What sort of freedom is this? Lambrecht accurately observes that it 'must certainly be understood as freedom from the negative features of the old covenant (= the abolition of the veil)' while also having positive characteristics such as righteousness, life, boldness and, in line with v. 18, transformation (1999: 55; similarly, Thrall 1994: 275). Yet we need to go further to explain the meaning of freedom in this verse. Elsewhere in Paul's letters, in Galatians especially, Paul connects freedom with the Christ-movement and slavery with the law that Judean Christ-followers want to impose on Paul's converts. Thus, Paul specifically attributes to his opponents the intention to enslave in Galatia (Gal. 2.4). But we have the same sentiment in relation to Corinth

(2 Cor. 11.20). In addition, for the benefit of his addressees in Galatia Paul uses the language of freedom specifically in relation to being free of the Mosaic law (Gal. 2.4; 5.1). In social identity terms, this is important language in his attempt to negatively stereotype these people. It forms a climax to a passage that began with his acidic mention of 'those who peddle God's word' in 2.17 and who come with letters of recommendation (3.1). This is yet another area where Paul establishes a positive case regarding his apostolate in the early sections of the letter and attacks the negative version thereof in chs 10–13. Because many commentators fail to appreciate that Paul's opponents in Corinth are pushing much the same Judean programme that they were in Galatia (and in Jerusalem and Antioch before that), they tend to overlook (Guthrie 2015: 226) or deliberately exclude this dimension to the meaning of freedom here (Garland 1999: 196–7).

2 Corinthians 3.18 Paul ends this section of the letter with a positive theological flourish which speaks of the exalted identity that comes to the whole Christ-group. Like Moses, but via a completely different route, they have an unveiled face and can look at the glory of the Lord. The word κατοπτριζόμενοι, used here for contemplating that glory, is *hapax* (Tack 2015). The verse thus makes a quite remarkable claim: Christ-followers have the same privileged access to God that Moses had, whereas Judeans contemporary with them suffer from a veiled exposure to a covenant that is, in any event, being annulled. In the process Christ-followers are being transformed into the image of God's son by the power of the Spirit, from glory into glory. This is a reference to the ever-increasing glory of the believers (Lambrecht 2009). It also arguably paves the way for Paul's description of his ministry that is to follow (Duff 2008).

In spite of arguments to the contrary (including Witulski 2012), it is difficult to avoid the conclusion that in 2 Corinthians 3.5-18 Paul is communicating a radical dualism between the old and new covenants (Grindheim 2001), and that he is doing so with his opponents in Corinth firmly in view; or, in social identity terms, that he is espousing a pronounced ingroup/outgroup differentiation between his version of the Christ-movement and the ethnically Judean version that they represent.

6

The signs, trials and triumph of leadership (4.1-15)

Paul's reassertion of his leadership credentials (4.1-6)

In 4.1-6, Paul returns to the question of his leadership credentials (in theological terms, the validity of his apostolic ministry) that he had been previously discussing in 2.14-3.6. Between 2.14-3.6 and 4.1-6 there are both thematic links and linguistic similarities. The verbal similarities between 2.14-17 and 4.1-6 prompt Harris to suggest that '4:1-6 is dealing with the effects of the proclamation of the gospel against the backdrop of the activity of Paul's adversaries' (2005: 320). But in several respects this section also refers to and illuminates 3.7-18 (Barnett 1997: 210; Lambrecht 1999: 67; Matera 2003: 98–9). We will see that the agonistic dimension to the discussion that has been present in the criticism of his rivals – expressly in 2.17–3.1 and impliedly thereafter – continues here, with Paul appearing, at least in part, to be responding to negative views that have been expressed about his ministry in Corinth.

2 Corinthians 4.1 The reference to 'ministry' (διακονία) in v. 1 means that Paul is providing further guidance to the Corinthians on this way of describing his own work among them that he has just described as the ministry of the Spirit (3.8) and of righteousness (3.9), with himself the minister (διάκονος) of a new covenant (3.6). The expression ἠλεήθημεν ('we were shown mercy') is a theological passive, meaning that it was God who showed such mercy. By saying this, Paul implies his dependence on God but also the special mission he has received from God. The aorist tense of the verb indicates that this happened at some particular point in the past, probably the occasion of Paul's revelation of his commission to preach God's son among the non-Judeans (Gal. 1.16; Thrall 1994: 298; Lambrecht 1999: 64). Although ἐγκακοῦμεν is usually translated as 'we do not lose heart', Margaret Thrall has suggested the translation 'we do not grow lax', a meaning attested in extra-biblical sources: 'It is more likely that he was charged with being remiss in his duty than that the Corinthians were simply complaining that he seemed tired or despondent' (1994: 298–300). Thrall's suggestion is preferable, especially when the beginning of 4.2, 'but we have renounced the secret and shameful ways . . .', follows much more naturally after it than the alternative.

2 Corinthians 4.2 The first clause of the verse is very striking. The (middle) aorist tense of ἀπειπάμεθα ('we renounced') suggests that at some particular point in the past Paul disowned shameful practice. Here the nature of the behaviour reflects the shame/honour culture that characterized the ancient Mediterranean (Malina 2001: 27-57). Is Paul suggesting that there was a time when he was engaged in shameful acts best hidden, or is he merely asserting that at some point, perhaps at the start of his Christ-movement ministry (with the aorist of ἀπειπάμεθα matching that of ἠλεήθημεν in the previous verse), he resolved never to engage in such things in his ministry? If the former, the only possible reference would appear to be to his actions when he was persecuting and trying to destroy the Christ-movement before he joined that movement (Gal. 1.13; Phil. 3.6). But this is highly unlikely, since there was nothing hidden about Paul's persecution; indeed, it was quite notorious. Thus, even though the communities of the movement in Judea had not seen him in action as a persecutor among them, they had heard of his conversion and that 'He who once persecuted us is now preaching the faith that he once tried to destroy' (Gal. 1.23). This means that the latter alternative is much more plausible: Paul had not engaged in such behaviour before (which is also consistent with his being blameless as far as righteousness under the law of Moses was concerned; Phil. 3.6), and he would certainly not do so now that he had received God's revelation concerning his mission and become a Christ-follower himself.

This view also coheres well with what he says next, that he does not conduct himself with trickery (πανουργία), nor does he deceitfully falsify (δολοῦντες) the word of God. This is, in essence, precisely the behaviour he ascribed to his rivals in 2.17, with the repetition ὁ λόγος τοῦ θεοῦ quite telling in establishing the link. 'Word of God' probably means 'the Gospel' here, in view of its use of the phrase in 2.17 of Paul's rivals and the negative way in which the Mosaic law is presented in 2 Corinthians 3. The implication is that acting in such a way would constitute the sort of shameful behaviour that needed to be hidden. Paul felt compelled to introduce this denial of πανουργία early in the letter because some in Corinth were alleging that he himself was a trickster who got the better of them by deceit: ὑπάρχων πανοῦργος δόλῳ ὑμᾶς ἔλαβον (12.16), where the language of 4.2 is repeated. The fact that the πανουργία alleged of Paul at 12.16 seems primarily related to financial matters, as some commentators point out (e.g. Thrall 1994: 301; Barnett 1997: 213), does not break the connection with the cognate word at 4.2, since trickery to do with money is simply one instance of a wider class of misbehaviour. Yet it was not enough for Paul merely to deny that he practised the misbehaviour attributed to him by the Corinthians; no, he needed also to pin such practices on his opponents. Pressing just beneath the surface of his discourse in 4.2, therefore, is the suggestion that his rivals in Corinth could not make the same claim to innocence as he can. He has already in 2.17 claimed that they peddle the word of God which, given the cultural expectations concerning pedlars, means accusing them of behaviour very close to that which he disavows for himself in 4.2. Later in the letter, moreover, he charges them with directly comparable malpractice, for in 2 Cor. 11.3 he associates his opponents with Satan's πανουργία and at 2 Cor. 11.13 he attacks the false apostles as ἐργάται δόλιοι ('deceitful workers'), thus using language very close to what we find here.[1] In other words, his renunciation of shameful behaviour that is normally hidden coincides with the implication that this is precisely what characterizes his opponents. These close connections between 2.17, 4.2, 11.3, 11.13 and 12.16 clearly testify to the unity of the letter and illustrate, in particular the error in separating 2 Corinthians 1–9 from 10–13.

2 Corinthians 4.2 also contains a contrasting (i.e. beginning with ἀλλά) positive assertion of how Paul does behave: 'by the φανέρωσις ("open proclamation"; BDAG 1049) of the truth we commend ourselves πρὸς πᾶσαν συνείδησιν ἀνθρώπων before God.' As far as the open proclamation of truth is concerned, Paul's assertion here is of a piece with his earlier claim to speak with great forthrightness (3.12). What he says is open and true. This forms the basis of his self-commendation, an important theme in the letter initiated in 3.1 and now expressed by the same verb (συνιστάνοντες ἑαυτούς), as opposed, by implication, to the letters of recommendation employed by his opponents (3.1). There is no real tension here with his implied denial of self-commendation in 3.1, since both there and here he is not simply relying on his own statement but on some external factor that corroborates that view. In 3.2-3, that factor was the commendation offered by the Corinthians themselves, while here it is his open and honest proclamation the truth.

But what about the second half of this statement? The Greek literally means 'to/towards all/the whole συνείδησις of human beings', leaving συνείδησις untranslated for the moment. Translators and commentators frequently transfer the πᾶσα from συνείδησις to ἀνθρώπων and translate συνείδησις as 'conscience'. Thus, we have versions such as the following: 'to every man's conscience (RSV), 'to the conscience of everyone' (NRSV), 'to every human being with a conscience' (New JB), 'to each and every human conscience'

---

[1] Furnish 1984: 246 and Seifrid 2014: 193 notice these connections with 2 Corinthians 11; many other commentators (including Thrall 1994: 301; Lambrecht 1999: 64–5; Matera 2003: 100 and Harris 2005: 325 [also overlooking 12.16]) do not.

(Furnish 1984: 202), 'to every human conscience' (Thrall 1994: 297) and 'to the conscience of each and every person' (Harris 2005: 321). In this context, moreover, it is commonplace to attribute to συνείδησις virtually the same meaning as it has today: for example, 'the inward faculty of distinguishing right and wrong' and 'an inward faculty of judgment which assesses conduct in accordance with given norms'.[2] Almost invariably this means that the person concerned uses his or conscience to assess the rightness or wrongness of his or her actions. Furnish appreciates this in his comment that conscience 'ordinarily refers to the individual's capacity to experience guilt when considering his or her own past acts' (Furnish 1984: 219).

The problems with such a modern approach to the meaning of the word συνείδησις in the group-oriented context of the ancient Mediterranean were raised earlier in the comments on its appearance in 2 Cor. 1.12, and those problems become visible here. Why would Paul commend himself to the conscience (so understood) of anyone else, let alone (on the current majority view) every (i.e. individual) human being, when it is only his actions that are under scrutiny here? If conscience means an individual's inner sense of what is right or wrong, especially in assessing one's own actions, what relevance do Paul's actions have for anyone else? Why is Paul concerned with the reaction of others to his public manifestation (φανέρωσις) of the truth? Furnish realizes that there is a problem here when a little later he adds: 'Paul has expanded the idea to include the function of assessing the actions of others' (1984: 219). But this is a dramatically different explanation of conscience! In reality, it is not that Paul has pushed the meaning of συνείδησις in such a different direction, but that modern translators and commentators have proceeded on the basis of a misconception as to what the word meant in antiquity. Malina's understanding of συνείδησις fits its use in 4.2 well:

> Conscience then refers to a person's sensitive awareness to one's public ego-image along with the purpose of striving to align one's behavior and self-assessment with that publicly perceived image. (2001: 58–9)

Adopting this meaning facilitates a fresh look at its use in 4.2. It initially suggests leaving πᾶσα where it grammatically belongs, with συνείδησις, and not (along with the majority view) seeking to attach it to ἀνθρώπων. Having taken that step, we need to determine the meaning of πᾶσα συνείδησις. It is unlikely that Paul was speaking of the entirety of συνείδησις among human beings, rather than to a multiplicity of individual examples. There are two obstacles to the former interpretation. First, there is Pauline usage: not only

---

[2] The first definition is from BDAG 968 and second from Thrall 1994: 301.

does Paul nowhere speak of such a συνείδησις, but only a little later, in 5.11, he refers to a multiplicity of συνειδήσεις among the Corinthians (and in 5.11 we also have φανέρωσις language). The second obstacle is Greek usage. For this interpretation, we would need πᾶσα συνείδησις to mean, 'the whole συνείδησις'. Such a meaning exists, but it requires the presence of the article: πᾶσα ἡ συνείδησις (BDAG 784). There are some uses of πᾶσα in the sense of 'the whole' without the article, but they are usually in geographic contexts (e.g. πᾶσα Ἱεροσόλυμα; 'the whole of Jerusalem'; Matt. 2.3). There are a handful of other instances: of a people (πᾶς Ἰσραήλ; 'the whole of Israel'; Rom. 11.26) and other entities (ἐπὶ παντὸς προσώπου τῆς γῆς; 'over the whole face of the earth'; Acts 17.26 and πᾶσα οἰκοδομή; 'the whole household'; Eph. 2.21),[3] but they also have a locatival dimension.

So we are left then with a meaning like 'every human συνείδησις'. Is the reference in 4.2 to a body of shared knowledge or to a faculty people possess for assessing behaviour on the basis of social accepted norms? The latter seems the likely meaning in both 4.2 and 5.11. In 4.2, for example, Paul could hardly be recommending himself to shared knowledge; people must be involved in receiving the recommendation. Similarly, in 5.11, Paul argues for a direct parallel between his behaviour being made manifest to God and to the συνειδήσεις of the Corinthians, and this also requires a personal dimension, that is, a human faculty at least, not just a body of knowledge. And yet 'conscience' still seems to be an inapt translation of συνείδησις. Neither in 4.2 nor in 5.11 is Paul thinking in terms of an inner faculty that allows us to judge the rightness or wrongness of our own actions, which is central to how we understand 'conscience'. He is looking to a faculty possessed by human beings (4.2) and by the Corinthians (5.11) for judging between good and evil that will allow them to commend his behaviour, to provide reassurance that he has acted in line with accepted norms. To bring out this meaning, it is best to eschew the use of 'conscience' in translating συνείδησις and to opt instead for a periphrasis along the lines of 'the capacity to assess behaviour against social norms'.

That he is speaking of this faculty among 'human beings' (ἄνθρωποι) and not just the Corinthians at this point means that Paul assumes that 'there is some general human capacity for recognising the Gospel as truth' (Thrall 1994: 302). It is important to note that by invoking every conscience of *human beings* (ἄνθρωποι) Paul is impliedly encompassing members of all ethnic groups and, necessarily, Greeks, like most of the Corinthians, and Judeans. This is really a challenge: he is saying to everyone, 'Here is my truth'! On reflection that truth must include his Jesus, his Spirit and his Gospel (11.4),

---

[3] See BDAG 783-4.

not the others on offer (and he curses the purveyors of different Gospels in Gal. 1.8).

2 Corinthians 4.3 Paul is speaking of 'our Gospel', an expression that appears only here and in 1 Thess. 1.5. It is close in meaning to 'the gospel preached by me' (Gal. 1.11) and 'the Gospel which I proclaim among non-Judeans' (Ga.l 2.2). Both Thrall (1994: 305) and Harris (2005: 327) fall into error in suggesting, respectively, that the possessive adjective 'carries no special emphasis' and entails no 'particular understanding of the Gospel'. Both overlook the highly agonistic nature of this section of the letter, beginning with 2 Cor. 2.17, and fail to mention the rival Gospel of 2 Cor. 11.4. Instead, the possessive pronoun attached to 'Gospel' underlines the point that, unfortunately for Paul, his was not the only Gospel being preached. Later in the letter he will reveal that his opponents in Corinth are preaching a Jesus different from his, a different Spirit and a different Gospel, to which Gospel the Corinthians were submitting 'readily enough' (11.4).

When Paul begins by saying, 'And even if our Gospel is veiled', this sounds like a concession of fact.[4] He is acknowledging that some who hear it do not understand his Gospel, even though he has proclaimed it openly and clearly (4.2). That Paul should use the language of veiling requires explanation. He has not long previously mentioned that Moses veiled his face (3.13), that to this day a veil lies over the reading of the law of Moses (3.14) and that a veil lies over the minds of Israelites (3.15), and now he uses such language of his Gospel. It is possible that Paul adopted the language of the veil and applied it to the law of Moses and, by implication, to his opponents' mission in 3.12-15 as a pre-emptive strike before moving on to his own ministry. In line with the aforementioned comment on 3.13, however, it seems far more likely that his opponents initially accused him of having a veiled message when the cities of the Greco-Roman east were filled each Sabbath with Judeans listening to the law of Moses (a central feature of the Judean Christ-followers' teaching) than that Paul himself would have initiated such an unlikely charge against them. He began to intimate his own adoption of such language in 3.16 ('When a person turns to the Lord, the veil is removed'), which I have previously interpreted as entailing that the turning involved is to Christ and the truth concerning the new covenant.

But Paul's concession only goes so far. In the second clause of 4.3, he insists that his Gospel is veiled 'to those who are perishing' (ἐν τοῖς ἀπολλυμένοις), which is an example of a dative of disadvantage additionally employing ἐν.[5] The expression does not mean 'among those who are perishing' since that would

---

[4] Collange 1972: 131; Furnish 1984: 219; Barnett 1997: 215; Kistemaker 1997: 139.
[5] So Turner 1965: 264, whom Barnett cites but whose view he unfortunately rejects (1997: 217).

imply the existence of some who were perishing to whom Paul's Gospel was not veiled.[6] The phrase means 'for those perishing', 'for those headed for destruction'. So Paul is insisting that those who do not understand his Gospel are heading for destruction. Here we observe the stark ingroup/outgroup differentiation that social identity theory was focused on from the outset. At this point the fact that in the previous verse Paul asserted that he proclaimed the truth to be assessed by the moral faculty of all ἄνθρωποι assumes particular significance. For among this same trans-ethnic category of people are to be found 'those who are heading for destruction' mentioned in the present verse. Those who do not accept the truth he openly proclaimed (4.2), his Gospel (4.3), are doomed. It is probably a misinterpretation of Paul's meaning to restrict οἱ ἀπολλύμενοι to 'unbelieving Jews and Gentiles' and to exclude 'Judaistic Christians'.[7] For οἱ ἀπολλύμενοι includes everyone: idolatrous Greeks, Judeans not connected with the Christ-movement and certain Judeans (Paul's opponents) who were members of it. The latter is required by the connection between his attack on his opponents beginning in 2.17, the general nature of what he says here and the fact that there is a rival Gospel in view, which must have been ample in scope since it is associated with a different Jesus and a different Spirit (11.4) and which he presents as the work of Satan's agents whose end will correspond to their deeds (11.12-15). The tight connection to what Paul is saying here with the particular issues he faced in Corinth must be emphasized. Later in his career, in Romans, Paul's only letter in which he is writing to a context where Judean Christ-followers are under attack (Rom. 11.13-24),[8] he makes clear that Judeans will not ultimately perish but will be saved (Rom. 11.25-32), and I take this to be his final and considered view on the matter.

2 Corinthians 4.4 This verse connects very closely with 4.3. In the opening expression 'to whom the god of this age' the phrase 'in whom' (ἐν οἷς) is rather awkward, but since it closely matches the form of ἐν τοῖς ἀπολλυμένοις, it should probably also be read as a dative of disadvantage meaning 'to whom' and not 'among whom'. It could also conceivably be a dative of respect, 'in relation to whom'. In any event, 'there is general agreement that the group of people to whom the ἐν οἷς refers i. e., the ἀπολλύμενοι of v. 3, is co-extensive with the group who at the end of this clause are designated as "the unbelievers"' (τῶν ἀπίστων; Thrall 1994: 305–6).

---

[6] Many commentators note the unlikelihood of this scenario (e.g. Furnish 1984: 220–1 and Thrall 1994: 306, fn. 805).
[7] As does Harris 2005: 327. Greater sensitivity to accuracy in designating group identities and to the need to avoid anachronism in naming social groups in the ancient Mediterranean would suggest replacing his 'Judaistic Christians' with 'Christ-believing Judeans'.
[8] See Esler 2003a: 298–305.

Accordingly, ἄπιστοι in 4.4 must mean any ἄνθρωποι, Judean or non-Judean, who do not accept his Gospel; this category, therefore, embraces (idolatrous) Greeks, Judeans and Judean Christ-followers who do not accept his Gospel. The 'god of this world', whom most commentators believe refers to Satan, has blinded their minds so that they do not see the light of Christ's glorious Gospel. Satan appears later in the Gospel, in 11.13-15, where Paul's opponents are described as his servants. In 6.14-15, however, ἄπιστοι will be mentioned again in connection with Beliar, another name for an evil spirit. The 'god of this world' in 4.4 could also be a reference to Beliar, who in the *Martyrdom of Isaiah* 2.4 is called 'the angel of lawlessness' who is 'the ruler of this world'.

This conclusion necessitates that ἄπιστοι in 2 Corinthians has a broader reach than in 1 Corinthians. In the latter it occurs eleven times (6.6; 7.12, 13, 14 [bis], 15; 10.27; 14.2 [bis], 23, 24) and essentially means 'outsider', not a member of the community, where the only possible candidates are the idolatrous neighbours of Paul's Corinthian converts. Yet there is little sign that the sort of opponents referred to in 2 Corinthians had made their appearance when Paul wrote 1 Corinthians and we should be wary, therefore, of deciding in advance that Paul could not categorize them as ἄπιστοι once they did.

Many commentators exclude Paul's Christ-movement opponents from the ranks of the ἄπιστοι in 4.4 without taking account of the possibility just mentioned or, indeed, the proper interpretation of the word within the context of 2 Cor. 4.1-4. Thus, Thrall suggests that it is unlikely that the ἄπιστοι of 4.4 are 'Paul's Christian opponents'. For this view she offers two reasons. First, 'In 1 Corinthians the word always denotes non-Christians'. Yet, as just noted, the word's meaning in 1 Corinthians cannot be decisive for a changed situation, and she also begs the question, since Paul's point is precisely that these people are 'non-Christians'. Secondly, Thrall proposes that 'whatever the apostle himself may have thought about the authenticity of his rivals' faith, his readers would not have understood him as referring to them' (1994: 306). Yet Paul's argument in 4.1-4, coupled with his savage criticism of his opponents as pedlars of the word of God and as needing letters of recommendation (2.17-3.1), would have meant that the Corinthians would have understood that his opponents were numbered in the ranks of the ἄπιστοι.

The 'god of this age' has blinded the ἄπιστοι to prevent them from seeing the light of the gospel of the glory of Christ who is the image of God. There is a reference here back to 3.18, with its mention of beholding the glory of the Lord with unveiled face. In 4.4, however, Paul eschews the 'element of eschatological reserve' that was included in 3.18 by virtue of seeing Christ in a mirror and makes a more openly Christological statement (Seifrid 2014:

197). For in 4.4 Paul says that Christ 'is the image (εἰκών) of God'. Christ is called 'the image (εἰκών) of the invisible God' in a Christological hymn in Col. 1.15. Paul and Colossians are both drawing upon the Wisdom tradition (e.g. Wis. 7.25-26, where Wisdom is described as 'the image [εἰκών] of His goodness'). Probably also in view is the creation of humanity in God's image in Gen. 1.26. Perhaps there is a notion here of Christ as the first Adam (as later developed by Paul in Rom. 5.12-21). But we need to relate this theology to Paul's immediate need vis-à-vis the Corinthians. Paul is the one who preaches the true Gospel of Christ and that Christ is a reflection of God. God is therefore lined up with Paul and not his opponents (whom we later learn preach a different Jesus, a different Spirit and a different Gospel; 11.4). Paul's contention is that the exaltation that comes from God and the nature of Christ is a feature of his ministry, not that of his opponents.

2 Corinthians 4.5 The main question here is why Paul says at this point: 'For we do not preach ourselves but Jesus Christ as lord, with ourselves being your slaves on account of Jesus.'[9] The 'For' (γάρ) suggests a connection to the preceding statement, and it is probable that Paul wants to contrast the high status of Jesus Christ with his very lowly status. On this basis, the critical feature is 'Jesus Christ as lord (κύριος)'. This is really a summary of Paul's proclamation, also expressed as κύριος Ἰησοῦς, 'Jesus is Lord' (Rom. 10.9 and 1 Cor. 12.3), with the focus on Jesus as risen from the dead and raised to universal dominion (Phil. 2.11; Harris 2005: 332). By way of contrast, on account of Jesus, Paul is a *slave* of the Corinthians. Yet, once again, this is not just the expression of a theological sentiment, however profound. Paul will later accuse his adversaries in Corinth of precisely the opposite behaviour: he will claim in 11.20 that they *enslave* the Corinthians and the Corinthians put up with it (Kistemaker 1997: 142). So this is a central element of intergroup differentiation. In addition, however, it is an important aspect of Paul's leadership style; as he has already said, he does not lord it over (κυριεύομεν) their faith (1.24). Jesus Christ is κύριος, not him.

2 Corinthians 4.6 In v. 6, we find Paul purporting to speak from Israelite scripture, but not using the more common formula, 'it is written' (e.g. γέγραπται as on numerous occasions in Romans and Galatians; 1 Cor. 1.31; 3.19; 9.9; 10.7; and 15.45 or γεγραμμένον: 2 Cor. 4.13) without saying what book he is citing, but rather the more personal and direct 'God having said' (εἰπών). Perhaps it is a little too close to Paul's criticism of the written law in 2 Corinthians 3 for him to remind his audience of the written nature of Israelite scripture. He does, however, do so in 2 Cor. 4.13, while reverting

---

[9] 'On account of Jesus' (διὰ Ἰησοῦν) has a somewhat stronger claim than the admittedly well-attested variant 'through Jesus' (διὰ Ἰησοῦ).

to the personal form 'Just as God said that' (καθὼς εἶπεν ὁ θεός) in the important passage in 6.16-18. Paul is probably purporting to speak from scripture because there is, in fact, no scriptural statement quite like this. Gen. 1.3-4 ('Let there be light . . .') and Isa. 9.1 ('Behold a great light! Those who dwell in the land and in the shadow of death, a light will shine on you'; LXX) are similar but each differs significantly from this statement. This shows Paul's tendency to play fast and loose with scripture, either deliberately or because his memory is playing tricks on him. In any event, it is not even remotely likely that he would have wanted his addressees to concern themselves with the original context of the statement. This is another instance of his oracular use of scripture (Esler 2021d). It was enough for Paul to cite divine authority for the comforting statement, especially when the Corinthians were not likely to be a position to challenge him.

Furthermore, the meaning of the verse is not really affected by doubt as to the origin of the quotation. Paul is probably making this statement as a way of explaining 4.5. He preaches Jesus Christ as Lord because he has had a revelation to this effect. He has not made this up; God has revealed it to him (Thrall 1994: 314). The aorist tense of 'shone' (ἔλαμψεν) indicates a single event in the past, and this may be a reference to his conversion experience (Gal. 1.16), with what follows in the verse pointing in this direction. Some support for this comes from the accounts of Paul's conversion in Acts that also feature illumination, although there it is external and not internal (Harris 2005: 336). The plural of 'hearts' is epistolary in nature and does not carry a reference to anyone else. Unlike the veiling of Moses, Paul's heart was illuminated with knowledge of the glory of God visible in Christ's face.

4.7-15 The trials and triumph of leadership

2 Corinthians 4.7 marks a new development in Paul's argument, running to 4.15, in which he turns more specifically to his own situation and highlights the difficulties he encounters and yet, in alignment with the Lord Jesus, overcomes to show that God is at work in him. So begins with a sombre note that will run to 5.10 (Barnett 1997: 230). In terms of the social identity approach to leadership, this material coheres closely with 'identity advancement', meaning, in brief, the extent to which a leader has the interests of the group at heart, and not his or her personal interests, as chiefly shown by enduring suffering for the group.

Paul has been prompted to the statement in 4.7 as a qualification ('Yet' [δέ]) of what he has just been saying about the glory that attends his ministry (διακονία) in 4.1-6. The culminating statement – the particularly exalted claim that God has illuminated his heart with the knowledge of His glory on the face of Christ (v. 6) – must have rung a warning bell for Paul, and he sensed the need to pull back a little. Intrinsic to his leadership style were the claims that God was at work in him so that the credit for what he achieved belonged not to Paul but to God. This is part of the important power-in-weakness theme in this letter (cf. 1.8; 4.7; 12.9). Closely connected with this is the idea that he was not someone who lorded it over them (κυριεύομεν; 1.24). In other words, he was not their lord (κύριος) but their slave (δοῦλος; 2 Cor. 4.5). Within this section, vv. 7-12 contain the first of the catalogues of hardships that Paul sets out in the letter (Fitzgerald 1988: 166).

2 Corinthians 4.7 The referent of the 'treasure' is rather general. It could be his ministry (4.1), the Gospel (4.3) or the glory (4.6) or all three; there is no need to be too specific, although the reference to the transcendent power (ἡ ὑπερβολὴ τῆς δυνάμεως), which has to be the power of the treasure, indicates that there must be some reference to the Gospel. Although a number of specific suggestions have been made for the derivation of Paul's metaphor of the treasure in earthenware jars, it is unnecessary to adjudicate among them because the general sense is clear. The dominant reference, as Fitzgerald plausibly suggests, is to their cheapness and fragility (1988: 168). Earthenware jars were, generally speaking, not expensive and broke easily (as the abundant potsherds in any archaeological excavation attest). So when Paul says he has this treasure in earthenware jars, he is both insisting that he does indeed possess it in his person but also acknowledging that as its possessor he is fragile and not worth much. Paul is not disparaging his (or any) human body, just drawing attention to the sharp discrepancy between the treasure that is the Gospel and ordinariness of its container. This is necessary so as to demonstrate that its surpassing power comes from God and not from him.

2 Corinthians 4.8-9 The structure of the passage in the two verses after v.7, in which we have the *peristasis* catalogue, is noteworthy. Paul proceeds to lay out a series of contrasting present participles that contrast lesser with greater adversity but which exhibit increasing seriousness:

ἐν παντί ('in every way')
θλιβόμενοι ('afflicted')   ἀλλ' οὐ στενοχωρούμενοι ('but not crushed')
ἀπορούμενοι ('at a loss')   ἀλλ' οὐκ ἐξαπορούμενοι ('but not driven to despair')[10]

---

[10] Strictly speaking, ἐξαπορούμενοι is an intensification of ἀπορούμενοι (meaning 'completely at a loss').

διωκόμενοι ('persecuted') ἀλλ'οὐκ ἐγκαταλειπόμενοι ('but not abandoned')
καταβαλλόμενοι ('struck down') ἀλλ'οὐκ ἀπολλύμενοι ('but not destroyed')

It seems likely that in crafting these contrasts Paul has been influenced by what since the early twentieth century has been usefully described as a *'peristasis'* (περίστασις) catalogue, a catalogue of circumstances (περίστασις being a Greek word for 'circumstance'), good or bad but mainly bad, which was a mode of discourse developed by Hellenistic moralists and with which Paul was generally familiar even if we cannot conclude he had read any particular example of this trope. There are a number of these catalogues in Paul's correspondence.[11] A line of thought beginning with Rudolf Bultmann's 1910 work on the subject, but possibly inspired by an idea of Johannes Weiss (Fitzgerald 1988: 8), argues that the Pauline *peristasis* catalogues are quite close in style to the Cynic-Stoic diatribe and describe the circumstances in which the philosopher or the preacher finds himself and how he must endure as a representative of his teaching when he is put to the test. A number of scholars have further suggested that the catalogue in 4.8-9 is oriented along the model of Stoic antitheses.[12] A reasonably close example is to be found in Plutarch's *Moralia* 1057 D-E:

> The sage of the Stoics
>   is not impeded when confined
>   and under no compulsion when flung down a precipice
>   and not in torture when on the rack
>   and not injured when mutilated
>   and is invincible when thrown in wrestling
>   and is impregnable when besieged
>   and is uncaptured while his enemies are selling him into slavery.[13]

But we should not push the comparison with Stoic thought too far.[14] Paul was not a Stoic. For while the antithetical structure is similar to the one Paul

---

[11] Rom. 8.35-39; 1 Cor. 4.9-13; 2 Cor. 4.8-9; 6.3-10; 11.23-29; 12.10; Phil. 4.11-12.
[12] Bultmann 1910. Thrall 1994: 326, who notes other instances of antitheses in Epictetus, *Discourses* 2.2.13, 2.19:34 and 4.9.17. Fitzgerald has described the development of this idea in New Testament scholarship (1988: 7-31).
[13] Translation from Fitzgerald 1988: 100.
[14] The works of Troels Engberg-Pedersen (1990, 2000 and 2010) and Runar Thorsteinsson that seek to argue for a strong link between Paul and Stoic thought have been criticized largely on this basis: see Esler 2004, to whom Engberg-Pedersen (2005) and Thorsteinsson (2006; 2010) made elaborate replies; Barclay 2011b and Levison 2011, to

constructs, its point is very different. It is really a description of the Stoic *ataraxia*, the freedom from concern and tranquillity regarding any external disaster shown by the virtuous sage (Striker 1990). Paul, on the other hand, acknowledges the impact of external travails upon him, yet insists that they could be worse. Moreover, while the antithetical structure of this passage is similar to that of Hellenistic *peristasis* catalogues, the vocabulary is quite biblical, and has a particular affinity with the Psalms (Thrall 1994: 326).

Yet identifying an ancient Mediterranean context for such antitheses is not the end of the matter, since we need to ask why Paul chose this form for this particular letter. Although answering this also requires consideration of vv. 10–15, it is useful to note here that the idea of 'affliction' (using passives of the verb θλίβειν) occurs at 2 Cor. 1.6 and 7.5 (where the expression is identical: 'afflicted in every way') as well as here. There is only one other instance of the verb in Paul's letters (1 Thess. 3.4). In addition, the nominal form, 'affliction' (θλῖψις), appears nine times in 2 Corinthians (in 2 Corinthians 1–8), but only five times in Romans, once in 1 Corinthians and twice in Philippians in 1 Thessalonians. Thus, Paul's afflictions are quite a prominent theme in 2 Corinthians 1–7. They all contribute to solidifying his leadership by a demonstration of 'identity advancement' as previously noted.

2 Corinthians 4.10 Verse 10 provides the last of the present participles when he asserts he is 'always carrying around (περιφέροντες) in our body the dying (νέκρωσις) of Jesus, so that the life of Jesus might also be manifested in our body' (or 'bodies', an epistolary plural, in some versions). Yet the participle περιφέροντες does not figure in another antithesis but rather anchors the first of three statements in the powerful and closely integrated conclusion evident in vv. 10-12. While it is reasonable to refer to vv. 10-12 as 'theological' (Harris 2005: 345) given that Paul is aligning his own experience with the dying and then immortal life of Jesus, this should not be to the neglect of the social identity dimensions of this passage. The message Paul is communicating here represents another aspect of his aim of maintaining or securing his leadership of the Corinthian Christ-followers by burnishing his credentials as the person with the closest relationship with Jesus and whose presence he mediates to them. This makes him a prototypical apostle (in contrast to his opponents in Corinth), and this is a central feature of his claims to leadership.

Appropriate regard should be paid to Paul's using 'dying' (νέκρωσις) instead of 'death' (θάνατος). While νέκρωσις can mean 'death' (as at Rom.

whom Engberg-Pedersen replied (2011); and Kim 2016). Many of the major frailties in the Engberg-Pedersen/Thorsteinsson position have been well exposed by Hubbard (2016). Social identity theory provides an alternative approach to the virtuous life (Esler 2003b).

4.19), it can also refer to the process of dying or being put to death, and this is the preferred meaning required to establish the parallel with Paul's experience as described in vv. 11-12.[15] The dying of Jesus could refer to his last day or two, or, less likely, to a longer course of his earthly ministry culminating in his death (I will note later in the chapter how v. 11 supports the former alternative). The 'life' of Jesus cannot, in context, be the earthly life of Jesus but must refer to his immortal life following his resurrection (Harris 2005: 346–7).

Although the notion that the risen life of Jesus is manifested in Paul's body is an extraordinary one, its meaning is clear in a general way. But what does Paul mean when he says he carries around the 'dying of Jesus'? Comparison with Paul's statements elsewhere about the death of Jesus must have a role in answering this question, especially if there is to be any force in the idea that Jesus' dying was a process culminating in his death. Considering this issue takes us into the question of the extent to which Paul had knowledge of Jesus, including of the sort that we find in the Passion narratives in the Gospel (Wenham 1995). The main point is Paul knew that Jesus had been crucified (1 Cor. 1.17, 18, 23; 2.2, 2.8; Gal. 3.1; 5.11; 6.12, 14; Phil. 2.8; 3.18). Everyone in the ancient world knew that crucifixion was a long, painful and dishonourable death. Very often attachment to the cross by nails or ropes was preceded by torture and degradation. Although people sometimes lasted for a day or more on the cross, if Paul knew the Gospel tradition, he would have been aware that Jesus' suffering began before Golgotha and ended before he received a spear to the chest on the same day that showed he was already dead. Crucifixion was itself a process leading to death; that is why Roman citizens condemned to death were killed immediately by decapitation. Explicit confirmation of Paul's understanding that Jesus experienced a drawn-out death comes in Phil. 3.10, where Paul says that he has acted as he has so that, inter alia, he 'may share his sufferings (παθήματα), becoming like him in his death'. Paul also mentions the sufferings (παθήματα) of Christ in 2 Cor. 1.5. Another aspect of Paul's thought is that Christ-followers share the crucifixion of Jesus. Thus, in Rom. 6.3-4 Paul comments that baptized Christ-followers have been 'baptised into his death', so that just as Christ was also raised so too might they 'walk in newness of life'.

Harris cites Phil. 3.10 and interprets the verse to mean 'To suffer for and with Christ is to die with Christ. For the Christian suffering is not a sign of divine disappointment but an opportunity to divine engagement' (2005: 349). Yet there are a number of theories as to what Paul's language might

---

[15] Lambrecht 1986: 309 and Barnett 1997: 235. Get BDAG for process of dying. *Contra*, Thrall 1994: 331–2 (because of the appearance of this sense at Rom. 4.19).

mean. There are three leading candidates (Thrall 1994: 332–5). First, perhaps it has the meaning of Mk 8.34 where would-be followers of Jesus are told to take up his cross (to which Luke adds 'each day'; 9.23). Problematic for this approach is that the language of 'following' and 'imitating' Jesus does not appear in 2 Corinthians, and Paul does not voluntarily seek suffering; it just seems to be an inevitable incident of his vocation.[16] Secondly, there is a close connection between the death of Jesus and the believer in baptism (Rom. 6.3-6). Various ways have been developed to make this argument, none of them being entirely persuasive. Thirdly, the issue is understood in a revelational way: the apostolate is the earthly manifestation of the Gospel, the somatic manifestation of the Christ who has crucified. Offering some support for this view is the repetition of φανερωθῇ in vv. 10 and 11. On this, more plausible, view, the sufferings of Paul are 'in some sense a public portrayal, a visual image, of the death of Jesus himself', possibly coupled with a belief by Paul that in some deep way he participated in a fundamental union with Christ which meant that Christ's death was reproduced in his own apostolic experience (Thrall 1994: 334). To further develop our answer to the meaning of v. 10, we need to move onto v. 11, which is essentially an explanatory restatement of v. 10.

2 Corinthians 4.11 The verb 'we are being handed over' (παρδιδόμεθα) may create a link between Paul and Jesus at the end of his life, since in the Synoptic tradition this word is used of Jesus being handled over to the Judean and Roman authorities. Paul also uses this word of God's handing Jesus over (Rom. 8.32; 1 Cor. 11.23; Gal. 2.20), thus indicating the ultimate power at work in the process. This verse also offers support for the idea that the suffering of Jesus that Paul has in mind (i.e. the period of his being handed over to death) is that which he experienced in the process leading to his crucifixion, not in the more extended period of his ministry.

2 Corinthians 4.12 Paul's lapidary assertion 'So then death is at work in us, but life in you' brings the argument of vv. 7-12 to an end, with 'life in you' creating a connection with what will follow. While Thrall (1994: 337) is probably correct in seeing in the second clause the new life in Christ (Rom. 6.11) that is produced by the Spirit (cf. Rom. 8.2, 6), Paul nominates the Corinthians as the bearers of this life. Thus, he shifts the focus from himself to the strong connection between him and the Corinthian Christ-followers. Matera rightly suggests that this 'terse statement' implies that Paul's apostolic sufferings 'effect life for the community' (2003: 111). So Paul proves he is their leader by suffering on their behalf and thereby advances the identity of the group.

---

[16] So Ehrensperger 2007: 104-16.

2 Corinthians 4.13-14 Paul now moves on to develop the notion of 'life in you' with which he rounded off vv. 7-12 in v. 12. His initial statement, 'But since we have the same spirit of the faith according to what stands written, "I believed and therefore I spoke", we also believe and therefore we speak', prompts the question of with whom Paul has 'the same spirit of the faith (τῆς πίστεως)'? Many commentators believe it is the speaker of the psalm that Paul is about to quote, in that he is referring to the kind of faith that issues in speech.[17] This is reasonable, given that the first word of the quotation is 'I believed' (ἐπίστευσα) and Paul follows on with 'we believe' (πιστεύομεν), even though this means πίστις does not here have the precise meaning of Christ-movement faith (which it does in the other six instances of πίστις in this letter: 1.24 [twice]; 5.7; 8.7; 10.15 and 13.5).[18] The quotation is from Psalm 115 (LXX).1, and the fact that it concerns the righteous sufferer may well have triggered Paul to reach for it here (Matera 2003: 112). Nevertheless, Paul does not mention the source of the statement, and it is unlikely that his addressees would have recognized it. It is enough for his argument that they realize he is quoting the sacred tradition of Israel. It is submitted that Stegman's argument (2007) that in saying ἐπίστευσα Paul was claiming he had the same spirit of faithfulness that animated Jesus is over-interpretation (so, correctly, Lambrecht 2008). The same problem militates against Richard Hays' proposal (2002: 119–207) that the 'faithfulness of Jesus' lies at the heart of Paul's Christology, upon which Stegman relies, and the arguments of Schenck (2008) and Campbell (2009) that the verse supplies evidence for the subjective reading of πίστις Χριστοῦ. As Lambrecht (2010) rightly insists in response to Stegman (2007) and Campbell (2009), when Paul wrote ἐπίστευσα, he was aligning himself with the same state of mind and the same spirit of faith as the psalmist, and not making a statement about Christ.

Verse 13 serves to provide a dramatic foundation for the statement in v.14, to the effect that God who raised the Lord Jesus from the dead will also raise Paul and bring him before (παραστήσει) Jesus along with the Corinthians. This probably suggests a judgement scene, as already implied in 2 Cor. 1.14 and later specified in 2 Cor. 5.10. Although Paul could, alternatively, have a more general notion in mind, that Paul and the Corinthians will come into the presence of Jesus,[19] not a lot turns on which of these is correct. The

---

[17] For example: Thrall 1994: 339; Lambrecht 1999: 74 (perhaps he has David in mind as the speaker); and Matera 2003: 112.
[18] Unless Paul is proleptically attributing πίστις in the technical sense to the psalmist/David, which does not seem likely.
[19] So Lambrecht 1999: 75. Seifrid 2014: 211 rejects the idea of a presentation to Jesus for judgement and opts for the meaning being 'the arrival in the presence of God that constitutes salvation'.

resurrection in mind here is 'eschatological', that is, as referring to the actual resurrection on the Last Day; it is not 'existential', to the effect God will raise us over and over to a full life in Christ in this existence (Lambrecht 1999: 75). Both here and in 1.14, Paul emphasizes the group dimension of that day, even though Christ-followers will be judged as individuals for their good and evil works (5.10). While this statement supplies further details of the 'life in you' mentioned in v. 12, it goes much further. An essential aspect of the social identity of any individual is that it exists in a chronological continuum embracing that person's the past, the present and the future. The connection forged in v. 12 between Paul's present sufferings and the life of the Corinthians is now revealed to possess a future dimension, namely the resurrection that is to come. Inherent in the social identity that the members derive from belonging to the Christ-movement is a glorious future that Paul will assist them to secure. Paul's insistence on the End-time reflects the extent to which the social identity group members derive from the group exists in a chronological continuum with a past, present and future (Condor 1996; Lim 2020: 329–30). The Corinthians' 'possible future selves', to use the helpful expression of social identity theorist Marco Cinnirella (1998), embrace a resurrected state in the presence of the Lord Jesus (as judge) and also of one another.

2 Corinthians 4.15 Here Paul reinforces his assertion in 2 Cor. 4.5 that he preaches Jesus Christ as Lord and himself as their slave and unpicks the tight formulation of 4.12. At the same time, he makes clear that the ultimate purpose is that the expanding thanksgiving of the Corinthians will sound to God's glory. Thus, Paul insists that the supernatural dimension of the identity of Christ-movement must not be forgotten. In light of features such as the wordplay of χάρις and εὐχαριστίαν and the alliteration of πλεονάσασα and πλειόνων in this verse, Lambrecht observes that the 'vocabulary and the redundant, overloaded character' of the purpose clause gives 'the impression that this text unit comes to a close at this point' (1999: 75). With v. 4.16, therefore, we move to a new text unit, and one that extends to 5.10.

7

The future destiny of Christ-followers (4.16–5.10)

In 2 Cor. 4.7-15, Paul has linked his sufferings in the present with the prospect of life that has a strongly futurist dimension, namely the prospect of resurrection for him and the Corinthians that is affirmed in 4.14. In 2 Cor. 4.16–5.10, Paul explains how the present will morph into that future which he and they will share and elaborates on its character. While it is not inaccurate to say that '4.16-5.10 engages in theological reflection on his and their present and future' (Barnett 1997: 246), we must also bear in mind the role that this section of the letter plays in building and maintaining the identity of the Christ-movement and the social identity its members derive from belonging to it. The identity a group provides to its members sometimes contains a strongly futurist dimension, and this was true in a paramount degree with the Christ-movement. Such a dimension allowed the members to integrate their past, present and future existence in a powerfully integrated fashion (Condor 1996). This is another area where social and theological issues are closely integrated.

Glory through suffering (4.16-18)

2 Corinthians 4.16 In Paul's opening statement, 'Therefore we do not grow lax' (Διὸ οὐκ ἐγκακοῦμεν), Διὸ refers back to what he has just said, as providing the reason for his not growing lax in the performance of his apostolic duties. Having said this, Paul proceeds to articulate the sense of renewal he experiences even as his physical strength diminishes, presumably in consequence of the trials he lists in 4.8-9. In particular, at this juncture he formulates a striking contrast between 'our outer self' (ὁ ἔξω ἡμῶν ἄνθρωπος) and 'our inner (self)' (ὁ ἔσω ἡμῶν), with ἄνθρωπος implied in the second phrase. While these notions probably reflect the dualistic thinking of Greek thought of the time (Furnish 1984: 261), pinning down their precise meaning is not easy. Nevertheless, it seems preferable to view these two concepts as referring not to body and soul, and not even to divided selves, but to the same self viewed in two different perspectives (Matera 2003: 115). This is the only instance of the expression ὁ ἔξω ἡμῶν ἄνθρωπος in the Pauline writings. The preferable course is to interpret it in line with its immediate context. On this basis, it represents another way of referring to the earthenware jars that are afflicted in every way, at a loss, persecuted and struck down (4.7-8). The expression is not equivalent to 'the old self' (ὁ παλαιὸς ἄνθρωπος) of Rom. 6.6 that is employed to speak of the condition of human beings under sin, since there is no such moral connotation here, only hardships experienced. The outer self is what the world sees, one's personality and identity (Allo 1956: 135). The immediate context gives less guidance in relation to 'the inner (self)'. But we should not be deflected by the apparently similar expression ὁ ἔσω ἄνθρωπος in Rom. 7.22. For in that case the expression 'the inner self' refers to the mind that delights in God's law. Rather, we need to go back a little further in 2 Corinthians, to 3.18, to find the meaning of 'our inner self' here – that of ourselves as (inwardly) transformed 'from glory to glory,' with glory about to be mentioned in the 4.17. A felicitous way of explaining the inner person is 'the embodied person as viewed from God's point of view, from the perspective of faith', a person who has the possibility of being renewed (Matera 2003: 115). Lambrecht strikes the right balance: 'Both phrases point to the whole person, although from a different angle: outward-visible and inward-hidden' (1999: 81).

2 Corinthians 4.17 Verse 17 is a remarkable statement built around a stark contrast that builds on that in v. 16: 'For the momentary lightness of our affliction is producing for us to an extraordinary degree an eternal weight of glory.' The adverb παραυτίκα, translated as 'momentary', occurs only here in the New Testament. It signifies something in the present in contrast to what will come later on and here is contrasted with αἰώνιον, 'eternal' in the second part of the verse (Furnish 1984: 262). 'Lightness of affliction' translates τὸ . . . ἐλαφρὸν τῆς θλίψεως, where τὸ ἐλαφρὸν is an articular neuter singular adjective serving as an abstract noun to establish a direct contrast with 'weight of glory' later in the verse. The expression 'to an extraordinary degree' renders the unusual phrase καθ' ὑπερβολὴν εἰς ὑπερβολήν. Accessing the meaning of this verse probably requires reference back to 3.18, with is claim of a transformation from glory into glory. While there is a strong emphasis on the future here, there is also a sense in which some of the glory is being experienced in the present (Thrall 1994: 353-4; Harris 2005: 362).

2 Corinthians 4.18 The contrast evoked here – between what is transient and seen and what is unseen and eternal – is not between what is visible and what is invisible, or (in line with Platonic thought) between what appears to be and what actually is, but between 'what is now seen by mortals and what is as yet hidden from mortal gaze because of human mortality and temporality'

(Harris 2005: 364). Paul's meaning in vv. 16-18 is that the inner self or person is not seen but is being transformed by God's glory and will therefore live forever, while the outer self or person who suffers afflictions in the here and now is seen but will pass away.

Confidence in the face of death (5.1-10)

In 2 Cor. 5.1-10, Paul develops the thought of 4.16-18 in considerable detail. The subject matter of these verses, dealing with how Paul understood his ultimate, post-mortem and End-Time destiny and, surely, that of all Christ-followers – although that only becomes clear in 5.10 with its reference to 'all of us' – and the difficulties of interpretation they pose, have made them one of the most intensely studied passages in 2 Corinthians. Once again, however, we must be alert to avoid the idea that all that is at stake here is theology. For the issues raised also bear directly on the future of the Christ-group and the social identity its members gain from belonging to it. In describing the future Paul is communicating at both levels, theological and social. The thought in 5.1-10 is extremely complex and has attracted significant analysis (e.g. Lingård 2005: 106–84; Lambrecht 2013).

2 Corinthians 5.1 A common view of commentators is that in the expression οἰκία τοῦ σκήνους (literally, 'house of the tent'), the genitive τοῦ σκήνους is appositional to οἰκία and that the latter is the dominant word (Furnish 1984: 264). This view, however, is difficult to reconcile with Paul's use of 'tent' (σκῆνος) and not 'house' (οἰκία) in v. 4. While the genitive is appositive, the word σκῆνος is dominant in the sense of providing the specific focus of the expression: it means 'a house that consists of a tent'.[1]

Paul thus establishes a detailed antithesis between two entities:

	a building from God
a house-tent	a house not made by hand
earthly	in the heavens
capable of destruction	eternal

There is little doubt that the destruction of the house-tent continues the thought of the 'earthen vessel' in 4.7 and his outer self that is disappearing in 4.16. The house-tent image conveys an impression of impermanence and flimsiness, of a structure made of fabric and likely to be blown down

---

[1] See BDF §§167–8 on this form of genitive.

in a strong wind. Paul possibly had in mind the expression 'earthly tent' (τὸ γεῶδες σκῆνος) in Wis. 9.15 that burdens the thoughtful mind (although his audience are unlikely to have spotted the allusion). The destruction of the house-tent (especially in view of what has preceded this verse) is surely meant to convey death. Paul might have derived the thought from Isa. 38.12 (LXX): 'I have parted with the remainder of my life; it has gone out and has departed from me like someone who has pitched a tent takes it down.'

The second part of the verse, however, is more contested. The major question is the referent of 'a building' in the phrase οἰκοδομὴν ἐκ θεοῦ. Thrall details nine possible solutions (1994: 363–70). Some of the most unlikely possibilities are: a heavenly habitation, in the sense of John 14.2; the body of Christ; the heavenly temple; the glory of the eschatological age; and the heavenly dimension of present existence. There are two major objections to all of these. First, the strong parallels between the entity in the first half of the verse (Paul's earthly self) and the entity in the second require some fundamental identity between them, and none is provided by these possibilities. Secondly, v. 2, which replays the sentiment in v. 1 in a different key, also requires that a direct personal connection exists between the first half of v. 1 and the second. For reasons such as these, the most popular solution (and it goes back to the Patristic period) is that the 'building from God' refers to the individual resurrection body, the σῶμα πνευματικόν of 1 Cor. 15.44.

This still leaves areas of uncertainty, however, in aligning what Paul says here with what he wrote in 1 Corinthians 15. Does Paul understand what happens after death in the same way as in 2 Corinthians? Some issues can be resolved on the basis that Paul has here represented his thought to accord with the particular argument he is running in 2 Corinthians. The movement from a σῶμα πνευματικόν to a tent-like building is explicable on this basis (Matera 2003: 118–19).

But difficulties remain, and the most prominent of them concerns the timing of these post-mortem events. Some commentators are of the view that 2 Cor. 5.1 suggests that the point at which Paul and other Christ-followers receive their resurrection body is immediately upon death. Yet 1 Cor. 15.23 and 15.52 suggest that the resurrection (implying the provision of the resurrection body) occurs at the parousia (Thrall 1994: 368). 2 Corinthians 5.2 does not assist in answering this question since its reference to longing to put on the dwelling (now called οἰκητήριον rather than οἰκοδομή) from heaven could apply to either the post-mortem or parousia moments. The answer to this question is usually seen to lie in the proper interpretation of 'we have' (ἔχομεν) in 5.1. Must it have a present meaning, or cannot it denote the future? Harris has set out five possibilities (2005: 374–80):

1. The present possession of the spiritual body (σῶμα πνευματικόν; 1 Cor. 15.44) in heaven;
2. The present possession of the spiritual body on earth, in embryonic form;
3. The future acquisition of the spiritual body at death in reality;
4. The future acquisition of the spiritual body at death as an ideal possession actualized at the parousia; and
5. The future acquisition of the spiritual body at the parousia.

The most widely accepted interpretations are 3. and 5., with 5., which is the one most easily reconcilable with 1 Corinthians 15. As Matera has noted, if Paul had changed his view from 1 Corinthians 15 in so dramatic a fashion, one would expect him 'to articulate such an important change in a more explicit manner' (2003: 120). All of them are possible on the basis of Greek syntax. Harris himself favours 4. Yet this solution is ontologically complex: What meaning can be attached to 'the ideal possession' of a 'spiritual body'? This view does, however, necessitate the existence of some aspect of Paul in the intermediate state between death and resurrection at the parousia. Option 5. is capable of reconciliation with this position, and additional evidence – available, as we will see, in 2 Cor. 5.3 – does support his belief in some aspect of his personal existence in the intermediate period.

Finally, is Paul implying here that only Christ-followers have such a dwelling? This would go rather well with 1 Corinthians 15 where resurrection does seem to be closely linked to Christ. Also see later on Josephus, who said that the Pharisees did not believe in resurrection for the unjust but that their souls would be punished.

2 Corinthians 5.2 'For in this one (ἐν τούτῳ) we groan', says Paul, 'longing to put on our dwelling (οἰκητήριον) from heaven over (it)'. The phrase ἐν τούτῳ at the start of the verse is quite difficult. It could mean 'for this reason', which Paul himself uses in 1 Cor. 4.4 (and which also appears in John 16.30 and Acts 24.16; BDF §219; BDAG 741). Other possibilities, such as 'here' or 'now' (Furnish 1984: 266), seem less coordinated to the previous verse, but cannot be ruled out. Many commentators and translators offer 'In this one', meaning 'in the tent', where ἐν τούτῳ is the (neuter) antecedent explaining the dative ἐν τούτῳ. This is very likely to be correct, given the close connection between vv. 2 and 4. As noted earlier, the emphasis in οἰκία τοῦ σκήνους ('house-tent') falls on σκῆνος, which recurs in v. 4. There is also the strong parallel between 'For in this one we groan (στενάζομεν)' of v. 2 and 'being in the tent we groan' (ὄντες ἐν τῷ σκήνει στενάζομεν) of v. 4.

The expression 'to put on over' reflects the fact that the Greek does not have ἐνδύσασθαι, 'to put on', 'to don', but ἐπενδύσασθαι, 'to put on over' (an existing garment) or 'to put on in addition' (BDAG 361 and Furnish 1984: 267). Ἐπενδύσασθαι will reappear in v. 4. If the idea present here is that Paul longs to see his resurrection body put on over his earthly body, this would entail that he hopes to experience the parousia and the resurrection before he dies (Lambrecht 1999: 82). But an alternative explanation is that Paul is aware of the possibility that he will die before the parousia, in which case his resurrection body will necessarily be put on over some aspect of his personality that survives death.

2 Corinthians 5.3 As a preliminary point, two textual issues in this verse require attention. First, and most importantly, some manuscripts read 'taking it off' (ἐκδυσάμενοι) not 'putting it on' (ἐνδυσάμενοι). The latter reading is, however, much better attested (Thrall 1994: 373; Harris 2005: 368–9), while also making good sense in context. Secondly, the translation 'on the basis, that is' reflects the reading εἰ γε καί, favoured by the majority of the witnesses. The alternative reading, εἴπερ, would mean 'if indeed', 'since'.[2] We thus translate the verse: 'on the basis that having put (it) on over we shall not be found naked'.

The content of the verse is difficult. The metaphors being used here, of buildings and donning clothing, are productive of some ambiguity. Yet as the metaphor of 'donning' continues in v. 4, we have no choice but to live with the incongruity. Paul envisages that putting on the resurrection body will remove the nakedness from which he would have suffered without it. The broad sentiment here reflects the antipathy of first-century Judeans to nakedness (an antipathy not shared by Greeks, who performed naked in many sporting contexts). But what sort of nakedness, removed by the resurrection body being put on over something else, did Paul expect his audience to understand here? Possibilities include: the soul stripped of its mortal body (Thrall 1994: 374–5); nakedness in a moral sense, meaning some form of shamefulness (as one appears before the judgement seat of Christ mentioned in v. 10); or death itself, which requires no presence of an intermediate state or a disembodied soul (Matera 2003: 121–2). The first explanation is probably to be preferred.[3] Paul seems to have some expectation of existence prior to the resurrection (1 Cor. 15.37), perhaps with Jesus (2 Cor. 5.8), and some ontic reality is needed to give substance to this hope. A soul would fit the bill and, although Paul does not use any particular word to describe to describe the aspect of his personality that would survive in a disembodied state, such a notion was current in the first century CE in Platonic circles and in the writings of Philo, who, in describing the death of Moses, talks of his body being stripped away

---

[2] For a detailed defence of the originality of εἰ γε καί, see Thrall 1981: 223–9.
[3] This is Thrall's view (1994: 379–80); *contra*, Daugherty 2011–12.

and his soul laid bare (*Virt.* 76). An objection likely to be raised to this view is that it presupposes Paul thought he would die before the parousia. Was that his view at the time he was composing 2 Corinthians? Certainly it is difficult to conclude from 1 Corinthians 15 that Paul was confident we would be alive at the parousia. His survival to that point had been rather haphazard (1 Cor. 15.31-32). Death seems a real possibility (1 Cor. 15.51-58). Very early in 2 Corinthians (1.8) he tells the Corinthians that he nearly died in Asia.

Thus, Paul appears to contemplate, but to strongly discount, the possibility that after donning his resurrection body over something (either his earthly body or some post-mortem aspect of his personality) he will be found naked. For this reason, 2 Cor. 5.3 represents a qualification of the longing to put on this body expressed in the previous verse – what a disaster to get to that point only to discover that we are naked! But, as Lambrecht observes, 'A statement in restrictive form does not necessarily express a real doubt, but can, on the contrary, be a figure of speech for a subjective certainty, for assurance' (1999: 83).

2 Corinthians 5.4 The first clause, 'For while we are still in this tent we sigh being weighed down (βαρούμενοι)', is closely related to v. 2 and is reasonably straightforward. In 2 Cor. 1.8, Paul used a passive form of βαρεῖν of his affliction in Asia. Βαρούμενοι is a circumstantial not a causal participle; it describes what accompanies Paul's sighs, rather than providing a reason for that sighing (Harris 2005: 387). The reason is laid out in the remainder of the verse: 'for the reason that (ἐφ' ᾧ) we do not wish to be become unclothed, but rather further clothed, so that what is mortal may be swallowed up by life.'

The expression ἐφ' ᾧ is probably short for ἐπὶ τούτῳ ὅτι, 'for the reason that', 'because' (Furnish 1984: 269). Paul uses the expression elsewhere in Rom. 5.12 and Phil. 3.12 and 4.10. In saying he does not want to become unclothed, Paul is possibly expressing the apprehension concerning the disembodied state after death that he hopes to avoid (Lambrecht 1999: 84). But since this state held some appeal to Paul (2 Cor. 5.8), perhaps his fear is simply of death itself (Thrall 1994: 382; Garland 1999: 261). In saying what is mortal will then be swallowed up by life, Paul is expressing his fervent hope in the resurrection and probably has in mind Isa. 25.8, which he cites in 1 Cor. 15.54: 'Death has been swallowed up in victory.' Thus, 'Death is not erased but conquered' (Seifrid 2014: 229).

2 Corinthians 5.5 Paul now offers the assurance that he who has prepared us 'for this very thing' (εἰς αὐτὸ τοῦτο), meaning the resurrection, is God, and he has given 'us' the Spirit as a pledge (ἀρραβών). The word ἀρραβών, previously used at 1.22 and also in connection with the Spirit, is a loan word in Greek from the Phoenician word ערב that was used for various forms of security in commercial transactions. Here it probably means a 'pledge' rather than 'down payment' (Kwon 2008). It is wrong to think of the Spirit only in theological terms. Paul's meaning is primarily that the profusion of charismatic gifts bestowed by the Spirit in meetings of the Christ-movement guarantees the resurrection that is to come. Some of the power of this future experience is felt in the present. This tight interlocking of present and future validates the social identity a member derives from belonging to the Christ-movement because it provides a larger framework in which his or her individual life history makes sense (Condor 1996).

2 Corinthians 5.6-8 These three verses build on v. 5 by continuing to paint a picture of how the events expected in the future positively condition the Christ-followers' experience of the present. Verse 6 – using two words, ἐνδημεῖν and ἐκδημεῖν that are found nowhere else in either the New Testament or the Septuagint – begins a particular line of thought that is developed in vv. 7-8. It is the contrast between 'being at home in the body' (ἐνδημοῦντες ἐν τῷ σώματι) and 'away from the Lord' (ἐκδημοῦμεν ἀπὸ τοῦ κυρίου), as opposed to 'go away from the body' (ἐκδημῆσαι ἀπὸ τοῦ σώματι) and to 'make our home with the Lord' (ἐνδημῆσαι πρὸς τὸν κύριον). The antithesis lies between embodied existence (on earth) and disembodied existence (at home with the Lord). Ἐκδημῆσαι is probably not an ingressive aorist and rather has a regular, punctiliar sense, whereas ἐνδημῆσαι is an ingressive aorist, meaning 'to make our home' or 'to take up residence' (Harris 2005: 400).

Two major questions arise. First, what does 'to go away from the body' mean, since this process effects the transition from one state to another. Its natural meaning is 'to die'. This meaning, moreover, connects well with the destruction of Paul's earthly tent in 2 Cor. 5.1; that is, the κατάλυσις of 5.1 and the ἐκδημία of 5.8 occur at death (Harris 2005: 400). The aorist points to a single event, and this makes it a preferable interpretation to the opinion of some that 'going away from the body' has an ethical significance, meaning gradually to restrain one's engagement with the physical realm in preference to engagement with the Lord, which requires a process not a single act (Thrall 1994: 389–90). These considerations also weigh against the suggestion of some commentators that the point of time in view is the parousia,[4] to which event leaving one's body can only be very awkwardly related, if at all. Secondly, is there any interval of time between death and 'making our home' with the Lord? This is highly unlikely. Verse 6 contemplates two antithetical states: being at home in the body and being at home with the Lord. No mediating position is envisaged: one is either in the body or with the Lord. This implies

---

[4] Harris (2005: 400) cites Lietzmann, Schweitzer, Mundle, Brun and Hoffmann as holding this view.

that when the former state ends the latter begins. Verse 8 confirms this implication, with its direct movement from one state to the other. So too does v. 7: 'For we walk by faith (διὰ πίστεως) not by sight (διὰ εἴδους)', where 'sight' means the act of seeing, where the object of that sight is the Lord. This meaning for the verse corresponds to the notion of believing but not yet seeing, as in John 20.29 and 1 Pet. 1.8. The alternative, and more widely attested, meaning of εἶδος is 'that which is seen', 'form', namely of the Lord, although this would not radically transform the burden of the verse. Here walking by faith corresponds to being at home in the body, while walking by sight (or 'on account of his form') corresponds to being at home with the Lord. These are sharp alternatives with no interval between them.

The second part of v. 8 expresses Paul's preference for being at home with the Lord, rather than remaining in his current bodily state. In other words, he is looking forward to his own death. This is rather different from what he will later say in Phil. 1.19-26, where, although he expresses a wish to depart and 'to be with the Lord' (σὺν Χριστῷ; 1:23) (i.e. by death), he recognizes that if he were to die, he would not be able to serve the Philippians (1.24).

Paul's recognition of his possibly imminent death represents a shift away from his earlier expectation that he would be alive at the parousia. This expectation is crystal clear in 1 Thess. 4.15 when he writes, 'we who are alive, who are left until the coming of the Lord', while 4.17 is to similar effect ('we who are alive, who are left'). Possibly the near-death experience he had recently endured (2 Cor. 1.8-9) had alerted him to the possibility he might not live to see the parousia. So too must the hazards to which he was exposed in the course of his ministry (2 Cor. 4.7-12; 6.3-10). Alternatively, he may have reasoned that the time the Lord was taking to return inevitably increased his chance of a pre-parousia death. Whatever the explanation, taking that risk seriously would also have focused his attention on the period of time between his own death and the return of the Lord. In 1 Thessalonians, he described those who had died before the parousia as 'sleeping' (4.14-15); at the sound of God's trumpet, they would rise first (4.16). This view meant that Paul recognized that for these people, too, there was a period of time between death and parousia. But now the possibility that he might find himself in the same position appears to have prompted rather more thought about the matter, beyond the idea that they were sleeping. Hence, he came up with the rather more positive and active idea of 'being at home with the Lord'. The fact that during this intervening period he would either have sight of the Lord or experience his form (v. 7) indicates a conscious state, not one where he is sleeping.

2 Corinthians 5.9 Paul states that 'we aspire to be pleasing to him' whether 'being at home (ἐνδημοῦντες) or away from home (ἐκδημοῦντες)'. In context, this means whether we are dead or alive. This verse cannot be interpreted in such a way that a person who is at home with the Lord can engage in actions that are pleasing to him, for the reason that only bodily actions (the basis for the Lord's approval) will be recognized at the judgement, which is described in v. 10. The preferable option is to take 'to be pleasing to him' with the verb 'we aspire' (φιλοτιμούμεθα), meaning 'our aim (effected by actions in our current life) is to please him, whether we are alive or dead and with him. As Thrall explains, 'During his present life Paul aims so to act that both now and hereafter he will be pleasing to Christ' (1994: 393).

2 Corinthians 5.10 With v. 10 we have a picture of judgement. When Paul says, 'all of us' (τοὺς ... πάντας ὑμᾶς), he certainly means others beyond himself, but are those others in the very limited category of Christ-followers who follow his Gospel (the πιστοί; cf. 2 Cor. 6.15, there in the singular). But are others included (meaning followers of Christ whose Gospel he does not acknowledge and, indeed, everyone else, Judeans and idol-worshipping non-Judeans)? In short, whom does he mean by 'us'? Scholarly opinion is divided. Most commentators favour Christ-followers only, with Margaret Thrall (1994: 394) expressing a blunt view on the basis of the connection with v. 9 and that this is the natural meaning of 'us'. 'The "all of us" is, of course, restricted to believers.'[5] Perhaps a smaller number of commentators see here a general judgement of all humanity (e.g. Seifrid 2014: 236), and this view seems far more likely.

To begin with, the fact that Paul might, at this point, aver that 'all of us' will be judged does not thereby exclude the possibility that on that occasion others would be judged too. This appears to be Barnett's position: Paul is referring to the general resurrection (perhaps the general judgement?) of the dead, but the focus here is on believers. He appeals to 2 Cor. 5.14 and 19 (1997: 274).

Harris suggests that a particular consideration favours the restriction to 'all Christians'. This is that in Rom. 2.6, where the principle of recompense is applied to works of all people, 'there is found a description of two mutually exclusive categories of people (Rom 2:7-10), not a delineation of two types of action . . . which may be predicated of all people.'[6] Thrall agrees with Harris, offering his view as positive support for the restriction of 'all of us' to Christ-followers: 'In Rom. 2.7-10, moreover, where Paul does have in mind a general judgment, he refers to "two mutually exclusive categories" of people,

---

[5] Those who favour a judgement only for Christ-followers (both Paul's converts and his opponents) include: Furnish 1984: 275; Barnett 1997: 274; Kistemaker 1997: 180; Lambrecht 1999: 86: Harris 2005: 406; those who think all human beings will be judged include Seifrid 2014: 236.

[6] He initially expressed this view in Harris 1983: 156 and then in 2005: 406.

not, as here in v. 10b, to two "types of action"' (1994: 394). Yet if Paul only has Christ-followers in mind, it is unlikely that these can only be those who follow his version of the Gospel. At 2 Cor. 11.15, Paul asserts that the end of the interlopers will correspond to their deeds; this suggests that they will be subject to this process of judgement.

For what it is worth, Acts 24:15 has Paul saying to Felix, 'there will be a resurrection of both the just and the unjust'. To similar effect is John 5.28-29 and Matt. 10.28. This is the view of Dan. 12.2-3. But the Pharisees believed that souls have immortal vigour in them but that only the just will be resurrected (*JW* 2.163: 'They say that all souls are incorruptible, but that the souls of good men only are removed into other bodies, but that the souls of bad men are subject to eternal punishment'; *JA* 18.1.3).[7] The problem with this view is that if Paul does believe that everyone will be judged, are we to imagine that there are two separate judgements, one by God for everyone and one by Christ for Christ-followers? But if all must appear at one judgement, does this mean that the unjust will have resurrection bodies too?

Those who see here only a judgement of Christ-followers rely essentially on this being the better view given what Paul has been saying in the preceding section of the latter. Nevertheless, there is some tension between this view and the fact that shortly afterwards, in vv. 5.14-15 (Christ died 'for all') and 19, he is speaking in terms of Christ's mission having been for all humanity.

Although the view has been expressed that v. 10 does not entail that those judged will appear at the one time, but sequentially upon the death of each of them (Allo 1956: 133, 159), this is most unlikely for a number of reasons. First, the use of the article τοὺς with πάντας indicates the sum total, so the expression means 'the sum total of us' (Furnish 1984: 275). Secondly, it produces an unnatural reading of the verse, in that Christ would need to run an eternal assize, rather than resolving the issue at one hearing. Thirdly, it is contrary to the image of a final judgement embedded in so many Judean texts, biblical and non-biblical, and in New Testament passages such as Matt. 25.31-46. For everyone to be present, such a gathering could only occur at the End-Time. It is highly probable that the occasion in view here is what Paul meant in 2 Cor. 4.14 when he said, 'the one who raised the Lord Jesus will also raise us with Jesus and will bring us, together with you, before him'. This also means that some present will have died before judgement, raising the question of what happened to them, if anything, in the meantime.

In Rom. 14.10-11, Paul envisages that every human being will stand before the judgement-dais (βῆμα) of God. Matera considers that 'Paul can speak of

---

[7] As Johnson has noted (1992: 413), the evidence of Josephus, *JA* 18.14, on this matter is less clear.

judgment before God and before Christ' (2003: 125). If this means, as seems intended, that there will be two judgements, one must doubt such a result. Would Christ-followers have to appear before God's judgement-dais and also Christ's? The solution to this issue is that Christ will judge as God's agent (so that the judgement-dais is both that of God and of Christ). In Rom. 2.16, after all, Paul explicitly introduces a principal/agent relationship in this context when he writes, 'on that day, when, according to my Gospel, God judges the secrets of human beings through Christ Jesus (διὰ Χριστοῦ Ἰησοῦ)'.

Perhaps Paul has in mind (like the Pharisees) that all will be judged but that only Christ-followers will be raised.

8

The foundation and exercise of Pauline leadership (5.11–6.2)

Motivation for service (5.11-15)

2 Corinthians 5.11 This verse is both closely connected to v. 10 (via the word οὖν, 'therefore') and also begins a new train of thought. Paul knows the fear of the Lord, particularly because of his awareness of the coming judgement described in the previous verse. The 'Lord' in view is probably Christ rather than the Father, since he is specified as presiding at that judgement. Paul speaks of seeking to persuade a wide audience, designated as 'people' (ἄνθρωποι) – with πείθομεν interpreted here as a conative present ('we try to persuade'; BDF §319), since the mild adversative δὲ in the next clause ('but [δὲ] we are made known to God') suggests that the persuasion may not be fully effective (i.e. he has not been made known to 'people' in general). The aim of his persuasion is no doubt that people should turn to Christ by accepting his Gospel and, importantly, of his own status as a minister of that Gospel (Matera 2003: 129). In social identity terms, he wants to be recognized as the leader of the group and as efficacious in that role.

Just as all of us must be 'made known' (φανερωθῆναι) before Christ on his dais (v. 10), so Paul has been made known to God (πεφανερώμεθα). Paul seems to imply that the process of making known that will be conducted by Christ at the End has proleptically begun before God in this present life, presumably with an implied verdict favourable to Paul. Yet even if his targeting of a general audience has not been fully successful, he has been made known to God, and he wants to succeed with the Corinthians. For he also hopes to be made known to their capacities to judge acceptable behaviour (συνειδήσεσιν). As I have argued in relation to 2 Cor. 4.2, which also features the language of being made known (φανέρωσις), 'consciences' is an inapt translation for συνειδήσεσιν. We need a periphrasis such as 'capacities to judge acceptable behaviour', since although συνειδήσεσιν refers to a capacity internal to a person, it is closely tied to what is socially acceptable in the local context. Paul's openness to God and to the Corinthians is a major theme in the letter, in which at a very early point he was arguing against a perception of him in Corinth that he was a dissembler (2 Cor. 1.17-20). Such a view of him was a major obstacle to his need to be prototypical of Christ-movement values so as to be a trusted leader among the Corinthians.

2 Corinthians 5.12 With this verse Paul aims to dispel any impression from what he has just said that he is engaging in self-commendation here (but this does not mean that he has a negative attitude *tout court* to self-recommendation:[1] it is just not what he is doing here). Rather he is hoping that they will be able to commend him: literally, giving them an opportunity 'of making an honour-claim (καύχημα)' about him.

The people referred to, 'who claim honour for appearances and not what is in the heart', are presumably the same as those he attacks as peddling the word (2.17) and as proffering letters of commendation (3.1). Three considerations support this view. First, Paul is referring to people who have been making claims about themselves to the Corinthians that are based on appearance but not reality, a categorization well matched to both the unscrupulousness of pedlars and to those who rely on what others say about them. Secondly, his denial that he is engaging in self-commendation points back to his original denial on this score in a passage where the 'pedlars' appear (2.17–3.6). Thirdly, the confidence he expresses here resembles his claim to competence in ministry in this same passage (3.6).[2] As already argued, these pedlars of the word are to be identified with his opponents in 2 Corinthians 10–13. A very specific point of connection is that the criticism that Paul levels against his opponents in 2 Cor. 11.13-15, namely that they are deceitful workmen (ἐργάται δόλιοι; 11.13) who disguise themselves (μετασχηματίζονται) as ministers of righteousness (11.15), corresponds closely to those who claim 'honour for appearances and not what is in the heart'. 2 Corinthians 5.12, therefore, is further confirmation of the integration of 2 Corinthians 1–7 with 2 Corinthians 10–13 and the unity of the letter generally.

2 Corinthians 5.13 Paul floats the remarkable possibility that 'we have been out of our senses' (ἐξέστημεν) for God. The verb ἐξέστημεν is the (intransitive) second aorist middle of ἐξίστημι, meaning 'to lose one's mind' or 'to be out of one's senses'. It is uncertain whether the aorist refers to the past or has a 'timeless' force (Furnish 1984: 308). Some dimension of the past is necessary here lest Paul convey that he is out of his senses as he composes the letter! How it aids his argument to introduce at this point the notion of his at times being out of his mind is hardly obvious. That he has been out of his senses for God indicates that he regards it as a positive experience.

---

[1] *Contra* Furnish 1984: 354, who suggests that Paul is here rejecting 'the pretentious boasting in externals (ecstatic experiences and the like) of his rivals'.
[2] See Barnett 1997: 278 for the second and third factors.

Probably the reference is to his experience of the charismatic gifts. In 1 Cor. 14.14, that when he prays in a tongue, his spirit prays but his mind is unfruitful (ἄκαρπος), while in 1 Cor. 14.23 he notes that an outsider coming to a meeting and hearing them speaking in tongues will think they are mad (μαίνεσθαι). These phenomena are not very far from his statement here. Presumably his assertion that he loses his mind for good responds either to a claim that he is deficient in the area of ecstatic states or, alternatively, that he is too prone to them. The former is hardly likely given the evidence for the charismatic dimensions of his Corinthian congregation in 1 Corinthians 12–14. Far more plausible is the latter alternative. After all, Paul was someone who was proud of his ecstatic skills: 'I give thanks to God,' he had recently written to them, 'that I speak in tongues more than all of you' (1 Cor. 14.18). Is the statement in his verse a response to a criticism that was being made against Paul precisely on this score? If so, people who levelled such a charge against Paul are hardly likely to have been strongly charismatic themselves, even if they may have claimed to have had some visionary experiences (12.1). Making the point in this section of the letter that his ecstatic experience has God as its subject also paves the way for his assertion of being taken to heaven that he will describe in 12.2-4.

Paul's alternative to be being out of his mind for God is 'to be of sound mind' (σωφρονεῖν; BDAG 986) for the Corinthians. This provides some confirmation that being out of his mind refers to his charismatic experiences by ἐξέστημεν, since in 1 Cor. 14.19 he contrasts speaking in tongues with speaking 'in his mind' (i.e. rationally). Losing his mind for God is one way in which Paul is 'made known to God', whereas being in his right mind aids him in his activity of persuasion (v. 11).

All of this – both types of action, one for God and the other for them, not out of self-interest (Harris 2005: 417) – gives the Corinthians a basis for making honour-claims in relation to Paul (v. 12). This particular issue, of not living for one's own interests explains the connection to vv. 14-15, which provide a profound theological reflection on this idea.

2 Corinthians 5.14-15 These verses need to be considered together. Paul begins with the notion that the love of God constrains him.[3] In the phrase the 'love of Christ' (ἀγάπη τοῦ Χριστοῦ), the genitive is probably subjective, meaning 'Christ's love (for us)', not objective, which would convey '(our) love for Christ'. Whereas Paul does not elsewhere speak of 'our love for Christ', he repeatedly speaks of Christ's love for us (e.g. Rom. 8.35, 37; Gal. 2.20). In short, he exists within the power of Christ's love. This idea also connects

---

[3] Interpreting ἡμᾶς in the text as Paul himself; but see Boers 2002: 529–31 for arguments that the pronoun could refer to Paul and his readers.

immediately with Christ's dying on behalf of all, as a demonstration of self-sacrificing love, in the remainder of v. 14.

The second and third clauses in the verse, 'we who formed this view (κρίναντας τοῦτο) that one died for all; therefore all died', raise fundamental social and theological issues. The aorist tense of the participle κρίναντας in v. 14 points to a particular time in the past when Paul reached this view, almost certainly when he was converted. The substance of that view expresses the heart of Paul's theological reflection: 'One died for all', where 'One' is Christ Jesus, in a formulation similar to the 'Christ died for us' of Rom. 5.8. The contrast between 'one' and 'all' means it is possible that Paul has in mind the antithesis of Adam and Christ that he will later develop in Rom. 5.15-19 (Harris 2005: 420), although it would be unwise to make too much of this given the different situation Paul was facing when he wrote Romans.

Paul's train of thought in vv. 14-15 can be outlined as follows:

v. 14b. One (εἷς) died for all (ὑπὲρ πάντων);
    therefore (ἄρα)
    all died, and
v. 15 he died for all (ὑπὲρ πάντων)
    so that (ἵνα)
    those living might no longer live for themselves
    but
    for the one who died for them (ὑπὲρ αὐτῶν)
    and was raised.[4]

Initially, given that εἷς is Christ, we must ask, who are the 'all' for whom Christ died (where 'for' translates the Greek ὑπέρ), as Paul states he did at the start of both v. 14b and v. 15? The possible allusion to the sin of Adam in v. 14 may suggest that Paul has in mind all of humanity, since here is how he will later express his view on the matter (Rom. 5.18):

Therefore, just as one person's trespass led to condemnation of all human beings (εἰς πάντας ἀνθρώπους), so one person's act of righteousness leads to righteousing of life for all human beings (εἰς πάντας ἀνθρώπους).

While we must always be cautious in interpreting 2 Corinthians with respect to a letter like Romans that presupposes a different exigence, this interpretation does appear to be corroborated by v. 19 where Paul says that God has in Christ reconciled the cosmos to himself (Rabens 2014: 292).

---

[4] This is a modified version of the structure set out by Matera (2003: 133).

It is no surprise then that Paul can say, 'Christ died for the ungodly' (Rom. 5.6), even if on other occasions he prefers expressions of the form 'Christ died for us' (Rom. 5.8) or 'died for our sins' (1 Cor. 15.3) or 'gave himself for our sins' (Gal. 1.4), where the salvific intention of Christ's death is linked to the ingroup. For Paul is not saying that salvation flows automatically to all. It is also necessary for human beings to accept the divine gift of reconciliation that has been offered (Rabens 2014: 293). This is the theological foundation on which Paul can differentiate a Christ-following ingroup from sinful outgroups (Rabens 2014: 318-19). 'Christ dying for all' inevitably entailed non-Judeans as well as Judeans, and the particular time he realized this was the case (see aforementioned κρίναντας τοῦτο) was likely to have been the moment of his initial revelation, that he should preach Christ to the non-Judeans (Gal. 1.16).

Interpreting the meaning of expression 'therefore all died' in v. 14 is more troublesome. What can it mean to say that all died because Christ died for them? Numerous explanations have been offered.[5] We are guided in our interpretation of the statement by two considerations. First, we need to give 'all' (πάντες) its full force: it must have the same meaning as in the first half of the verse, and hence it must mean all humanity, not just Christ-followers. Secondly, for the death of the one and the death of all, Paul used the aorist of the same verb, ἀπέθανεν and ἀπέθανον respectively, and this suggests that these two 'deaths' occurred at the same time. This timing rules out any connection between the death of all and the baptism of Christ-followers and is, rather, consonant with Christ's death being aimed at all humanity. Paul is insisting that something, to which the word death can be attributed, happened to all when Christ died. But he cannot be speaking of physical death. The idea operates at a general level: in some meaningful sense, 'Paul views humanity as incorporated into its new representative. Consequently, when the representative died, humanity died *in* the representative, thereby dying to the powers of sin, death, and law that the representative overcame' (Matera 2003: 134). This is an attractive view, although since 'Paul is pointing here to what happened in the cross event, not to death in baptism as in Rom. 6.3-11' (Lambrecht 1999: 95), we must acknowledge that the Christ-follower experiences a much deeper experience of dying with Christ in baptism.

Perhaps we should think of a potential death for humanity accompanying Christ's crucifixion that is realized in the baptism of the Christ-movement. Baptism thus becomes the initiating rite for entry into the ingroup of Christ, as opposed to the rest of humanity who had

---

[5] Thrall notes six major possibilities (1994: 409-411)

the benefit of the crucifixion but failed to accept the offer it posed. This ingroup, moreover, should be restricted to those who follow Paul's Gospel. Paul does not have universal salvation in view; as he has already told the Corinthians, he is 'the sweet odour of Christ for God, among both those who are being saved and those who are perishing', to the latter a fragrance from death to death, to the other a fragrance from life to life (2 Cor. 2.15-16). He is also exceptionally hard on those who say they believe in Christ but advocate a different Jesus, a different Spirit and a different Gospel (2 Cor. 11.4; Gal. 1.6-9).

The favoured ingroup comes into focus in v. 15. After repeating that 'he died for all', Paul replaces the language of death with the language of life by specifying people whom he designates as 'those living' (οἱ ζῶντες): 'so that those living might no longer live for themselves but for the one who died for them and was raised'. Christ's death is now presented as having as its purpose (or, possibly but less plausibly, its result) that these people should live not for themselves but for him, who died for them and was raised. Paul probably has in mind 'a new creation of the human being' (Seifrid 2014: 245), although that thought only becomes explicit in v. 17.

The initial question is whether 'those living' is a larger group of which the people who no longer live for themselves constitute a subgroup, or whether the two groups are identical. The former view has its supporters. Thrall suggests, for example, that 'Paul is referring to all those who live, in the natural sense, in the era of the Christ-event' (1994: 412). Yet v. 15 seems to assume that the group designated as 'the living' are identical with those who no longer live for themselves; a notion that some of 'the living' do not so live is difficult to discern here. In addition, while it is possible to imagine that 'those living' could refer to the people alive on earth at the time of the crucifixion some twenty years previously, this would be an odd use of the present participle. And where would it leave those who had been born since that event? In addition, 'the living' has a very commendatory ring to it. It is hard to imagine that in using it Paul did not have in mind people who had turned to Christ. More likely, then, is that they are a subset of humanity. In other words, 'οἱ ζῶντες introduces a new category of persons, distinct from and narrower than (οἱ) πάντες, and refers to those who are "alive to God in Christ Jesus" (Rom. 6.11)'(Furnish 1984: 311). Presumably they can be identified with those 'who are being saved' in 2 Cor. 2.15-16 mentioned earlier.

The reference in the final words of v. 15 to 'the one who died for them and was raised' reminds the reader of the direct connection between the crucifixion and the resurrection, the first an event of Jesus' obedience and the second an act of divine power.

The message of reconciliation (5.16–6.2)

2 Corinthians 5.16 Verses 16-17 begin a new train of thought that extends to 2 Cor. 6.2, although it is consequential on 5.14-15 as indicated by the initial ὥστε ('So that'). Verse 16 focuses on the consequence in a negative way and v. 17 in a positive way. Verse 16 bristles with exegetical issues. To start with, who are the 'we' (ἡμεῖς), the subject of its two clauses, which in the Greek has an emphatic position immediately after ὥστε? The two most likely options are either Paul (using the epistolary plural) or all Christ-followers. Linking this verse to v. 14a and giving weight to the emphatic position of 'we' promote the cause of the former alternative, Paul himself (Lambrecht 1999: 95; Matera 2003: 135), as does the fact that the ingroup in v. 15 are designated using the third- and not the second-person plural. The proximity to v. 15 and the reference to anyone in Christ would suggest the latter alternative, Christ-followers (Furnish 1984: 312). While the case seems stronger for the former option, perhaps the best solution is that Paul is the primary referent but that what he is saying is also applicable to other Christ-followers (Barnett 1997: 294; Matera 2003: 135; Harris 2005: 426). Then follows a temporal expression meaning 'from now on' (ἀπὸ τοῦ νῦν). While this is a common expression in the *koine* Greek of the period, Paul often uses 'now' in reference to the era of salvation inaugurated by the death and resurrection of Jesus. This is evident shortly after this verse, in 6:2, but also in Rom. 3.21, 5.9; 11; 8.1; 11.30; 13.11; Gal. 2.20 and 4.9.

In the balance of the verse we have Paul saying, first, that he now regards no one κατὰ σάρκα, and, if he once knew Christ in this way, he now does so no longer. There is a good case from Paul's usage for attaching κατὰ σάρκα to the verbs of knowing in the verse and not to the nouns 'no one' and 'Christ', respectively (Harris 2005: 428). Doubt surrounds the precise meaning of both elements, especially the latter. Nevertheless, broadly speaking, the first clause means that Paul (and with him, presumably, other Christ-followers) now regard all human beings differently, in a manner charged and influenced by the death and resurrection of Jesus; this means, in line with v. 15, that he (and they) no longer live for themselves but him. He is declaring that he has now abandoned the customary manner of regarding (and treating) other people that he accepted prior to the salvation initiated in Christ. This declaration is echoed earlier in the letter (1.17) when he interrogates the suggestion that he makes plans κατὰ σάρκα, and also later, in 10.2-3, when he denies the suspicion of some that he behaves (literally 'walks') κατὰ σάρκα.

Most challenging is the idea that Paul once regarded Christ κατὰ σάρκα. The Greek reads: εἰ καὶ ἐγνώκαμεν κατὰ σάρκα Χρίστον, ἀλλὰ νῦν οὐκέτι γινώσκαμεν. The ἀλλά that begins the apodosis is fairly straightforward; it means 'yet', 'certainly', 'at least' (BDAG 38), while the whole clause means, 'certainly we now no longer know him in a human way'. The difficulties dwell in the protasis.[6] Broadly speaking, εἰ καί, here used with a verb in the perfect (ἐγνώκαμεν), can introduce a real condition, that is, one specifying an actual situation in the past, or, less commonly, a hypothetical condition, one that expresses a real possibility but with no indication of actuality. In the case of the former, Paul would be saying, 'even though we once regarded Christ from a human point of view'. In the case of the latter, it would mean, 'Even supposing we once knew Christ from a human point of view'. It is worth noting that the apodosis is not an unreal condition, which would mean, 'Even if we had known Christ from a human point of view (but we did not)', since this would require an aorist verb (Thrall 1994: 415). Though much discussed in scholarship, the distinction here between a real and a hypothetical condition is minimized by the array of possibilities posed by κατὰ σάρκα. This could mean, at its highest, that Paul had known Jesus before he was killed, perhaps having seen or heard or even met him in Jerusalem, or it could refer to a much lesser degree of acquaintance, for example, that he had heard of Jesus from other people (before or after Jesus' death). To make this a little more concrete, considering that Paul must have heard something about Jesus when he was persecuting the Christ-movement, that measure of knowledge would satisfy both a real and a hypothetical condition

So when Paul proceeds to say in the apodosis that 'certainly now we no longer regard (him κατὰ σάρκα)' he has in mind the transformation in himself (and other Christ-followers) caused by the salvific effects of Christ's death and resurrection (while allowing all human beings to die in some way to their previous lives) and the fact that he was in the subset of the larger group who turned to Christ and obtained life thereby. If pressed (since the point is not explicitly made here), Paul would presumably have acknowledged that the moment when he moved from knowing Christ in a human way to not knowing him in that way was when Christ appeared to him, last of all, as one untimely born (1 Cor. 15.8) or, in the alternative version of Gal. 1.15-16, when God chose to reveal his son to him in order that he might preach him among the non-Judeans. His point is really a more general one: that in this new era, this 'now', he sees people, especially Jesus entirely differently, a viewpoint he implies will be the case for all Christ-followers. From a social identity point of view, this is primarily a statement of a group belief (Bar-Tal 1990) in relation to Jesus.

It is possible that, in asserting that he once knew Christ in a human way but now knows him in another way (by implication, the appearance of Christ to

---

[6] In her commentary, Margaret Thrall devoted five pages to this issue (1994: 415–20).

him), he also has his sights on his opponents who may also have been making claims to knowledge of Christ (Seifrid 2014: 248-9). After all, later he will appear to imply that they were claiming to have had 'visions and revelations of the Lord' (12.1). Yet rendering this supposition unlikely is circumstance that Paul seems at this point to be speaking in a general way about the effect of Christ's death and resurrection. What he is saying is mainly applicable to himself at this point, but the context, at least from vv. 14-15, also relates to all Christ-followers. That wider applicability blossoms into rich expression in v. 17. Finally, there is no basis for seeing in this verse any suggestion that the knowledge of the earthly Jesus is irrelevant or unimportant; that is simply not the issue with which he is engaged.

2 Corinthians 5.17 After the negative formulation of a consequence of vv. 14-15 in v. 16, we pass to a positive consequence, also beginning with ὥστε, in v. 17, and one considerably easier to interpret. 'If anyone is in Christ' is a potent theological but also social expression. The phrase 'in Christ' has previously appeared in relation to Christ-followers in 2.14,17 and 3.14, and will reappear in 12.2 and 19.[7] It is ubiquitous in the Pauline writings, appearing as such or in the form 'in him' or 'in whom' some 160 times. Although at the core of the idea is no doubt the close bond that exists between Christ and those who have faith in him, it is not possible to offer a straightforward definition. In addition, the precise mechanism by which this bond is achieved is nowhere clearly explained, even though Paul's explanation of the effect of baptism in Rom. 6.1-11 is richly instructive at a theological level. In addition, the phrase appears to carry different connotations in different contexts.[8] Current scholarship provides a rich variety of theological positions on the subject: the 'mystical' participation in Christ and in his dying and rising (the keynote of Albert Schweitzer's work *The Mysticism of the Apostle Paul* [1953]); the ecclesiological; the eschatological; the soteriological; the representative, and the personal.[9] All of these options can find support from data in the letters.

In addition, sometimes Paul writes of individuals being in Christ, himself quite often (especially as a reminder of his authority, for example at 2 Cor. 2.17 and 12.19), but also more generally, of collections of individuals (e.g. Rom. 8.1 and 1 Thess. 2.14). At other times, he refers to congregations (ἐκκλησίαι) as being 'in Christ' (e.g. Gal. 1.22; 1 Thess. 1.1). In other words, this is an expression that applies both to individual Christ-followers and also to groups of them. This consideration pushes our reflections on 'in Christ' into the area of social identity. As a concept originating in social

---

[7] It also occurs in 5.19, although there in the different sense of God being at work in Christ.
[8] See Best 1955: 1-7, who identifies nine different usages.
[9] See Wedderburn 1985 and Parsons 1988.

psychology, social identity embraces both the individual and his or her psychological make-up and the group. Social identity is not predicated of groups but of individuals: it is the identity an individual gains by belonging to a particular group (especially in a context where there are other groups to which he or she does not belong). In this perspective 'in Christ' is not merely a theological concept (although it certainly is that), but one that bears directly on the character of Christ-groups and the nature of the identity individual members gained from belonging to them. At one level, it operates simply as a way to name a person as a member: if you are 'in Christ', you belong to a Christ-group, an ἐκκλησία, and 'those in Christ' (Rom. 8.1; 1 Thess. 2.14) is one way of saying 'Christ-followers'. Decades ago Günther Bornkamm, while recognizing a variety of ways the phrase was used, reached a view similar to this by identifying one of its functions as being to provide an equivalent of the word 'Christian' (1971: 154). It has a cognitive dimension, to remind the members that they belong to this group but also to tell them something of its core beliefs; an emotional dimension, how they feel about belonging to it; and an evaluative dimension, how they rate belonging to this group compared with other groups in their setting. The exalted character of the basis for belonging – being in Christ the son of God and sharing in the salvific effects of his death and resurrection that entailed a radical transformation in how the members lived their lives – means that levels of emotional satisfaction should be very high and the evaluation of this group compared to others extremely favourable. That was the ideal situation, inevitably, and problems arising from the context, or from within the group, might at times lessen or threaten the members' appreciation of the positive character of belonging, and require Paul's intervention. Nevertheless, situations of the latter kind do not detract from the overall picture of belonging to a group that put the members squarely in the centre of God's saving action for human beings and for creation itself.

The expression καινὴ κτίσις only occurs elsewhere in the New Testament in Gal. 6.15. While it may have been introduced to the Christ-movement by Paul, it was probably not formulated by him. Although there are some twenty instances of the word κτίσις ('creation') in the Septuagint, the expression καινὴ κτίσις is not to be found there. Yet on some rare occasions it does occur in extra-biblical texts, for example in 1 Enoch 72.1 (ግብር ሐዲስ; *gebr haddis*) and Jub. 4.26, and in certain Qumran documents (1 QS 4.25; 1 QH 9.10-14). The source for the idea of a new creation that in some sense replaces the original one first appears in Isa. 65.17 ('For behold, I create new heavens and a new earth') and Isa. 66.22 ('For as the new heavens and the new earth which I will make, shall remain before me . . .'), although in Isa. 43.19 we find 'Behold I do a new thing'.

Yet the words καινὴ κτίσις ('new creation') appear on their own, lacking both a subject and a verb. This means that they can be interpreted as 'he/she is a new creation' (the most common translation) or 'there is' or 'it is' a new creation. In favour of the latter alternative it has been suggested that 'something more inclusive than the new being of individual believers is in mind' (Furnish 1984: 314). Yet the rest of the verse renders this view unlikely, since it involves a sharp switch in meaning from the person mentioned at the start of the verse, and in the remainder of the verse, apparently in reference to a person in Christ, it states that the old order has been replaced by a new one. Paul's only other use of the expression, at Gal. 6.15, also has a reference to the Christ-follower: 'For neither circumcision counts for anything, nor uncircumcision, but a new creation.' So the probable reference of καινὴ κτίσις is to the prototypical Christ-follower. The position of such a believer is to be contrasted with how Paul will later describe that of the cosmos as a whole: it will be set free from its bondage only when the children of God have been glorified (Rom. 8.18-21).

In v. 17, the equivalence is drawn between being 'in Christ' and 'new creation.' Yet perhaps we should not be too ready (like Parsons 1988: 28) to apply the word 'eschatological' to what Paul is communicating here. Although Paul is drawing upon the rich body of Judean literature, biblical and extra-biblical, which spoke of the re-creation of the cosmos at the time of the last judgement, Paul is here applying that imagery to the transformation of those persons who are in Christ. From a social identity point of view, 'new creation' is an exalted way to describe the possible self that someone can realize by turning to Christ.

The final section of the verse uses an aorist tense for the old order that has passed away (παρῆλθεν) and a perfect for the new order that persists (for the Christ-follower) after this has happened (γέγονεν). This contrast underlines 'the radical discontinuity between the pre- and the post-conversion states' (Harris 2005: 434).

2 Corinthians 5.18-19 In vv. 18-19, Paul shifts his focus from the impact of Christ's redeeming death on his followers to an explanatory statement about God's role in this process. The opening statement, 'All things are from God', was widely articulated in Stoic and Judean writings (Furnish 1984: 316); it may have been something of a banality. If so, however, it is radically renewed in the remainder of v. 18 because of its specific reference to the benefits of the Christ-event described in vv. 14-17 and by Paul's use of the language of reconciliation in the form of the verb καταλλάσσω and the noun καταλλαγή. Paul alone uses these words in the New Testament, with the verb at Rom. 5.10 (bis); 1 Cor. 7.11 and 2 Cor. 5.18, 19, 20 and the noun at Rom. 5.11; 11.15; 2 Cor. 5.18, 19. Some commentators have seen in reconciliation the key to Paul's argument in 2 Corinthians (Vegge 2008), or even his thought as a whole (Martin 1981). The core meaning of καταλλάσσω is 'to replace a hostile relationship with a friendly one', 'to reconcile' (BDAG 521). The Vulgate uses *reconciliare* and *reconcilatio* in translating these two verses. In the Septuagint, the verb appears in Jer. 31.39 (LXX) and 2 Macc. 1.5; 7.33; 8.29 and the noun in Isa. 9.5 and 2 Macc. 5.20. In each of the three instances of the verb in 2 Maccabees, we find a passive form with God as the subject: the hope is expressed that God might be reconciled to his people. This latter usage is reversed in 2 Cor. 5.20, to mean his people might be reconciled to him. Nevertheless, it is possible that Paul has adopted the word from 2 Maccabees, even while radically modifying its connotation, since no exact parallels are known to his version 'reconcile (someone) to oneself' (Thrall 1994: 430). This unprecedented distinctiveness of Paul's usage is non-trivial, since it means that God has become an active party; even though angry and offended by human sin, he has taken the initiative in bringing about a reconciliation between himself and sinners (Porter 1994: 16). In v. 18, the 'us' that God reconciles to himself are probably all human beings, not just Christ-followers, because of its very general ambit and the reference to the κόσμος as the object of God's reconciliation in v. 19. For the same reasons, it is most unlikely to be an epistolary plural referring only to Paul (and Timothy). By saying that God achieved this result διὰ Χριστοῦ, 'through Christ', Paul makes clear that the relationship between God and Christ was one of principal and agent. This act of reconciliation in Christ must be co-incident with his having died on behalf of all (vv. 14-15).

The second part of v. 18, that God 'gave us the ministry (διακονία) of reconciliation', where 'us' must be restricted to Paul (and his fellow-workers), seems to strike a rather discordant note. If God has reconciled us to himself through Christ, what ministry of reconciliation remains to be undertaken? Yet this reflects a pattern of thought found elsewhere in Paul: Christ's death and resurrection were decisive but they do not represent the final act in the drama of the human experience of sin. Christ has died for us, yet an onus rests on us to cooperate with God's saving initiative. As far as v. 18 is concerned, 'Reconciliation is a fact, but it must be offered in proclamation and received by the hearer' (Harris 2005: 438). As Paul says in v. 20, 'Be reconciled to God.' Paul's ministry of reconciliation inserts him into the middle of an ongoing process whereby what God has done, really and actually done, must yet be accepted by human beings. At the same time, Paul's ministry and the fact that it was given to him by God forms a central plank in his case for leadership that he runs throughout 2 Corinthians. It is also central to his case to be an apostle.

Although v. 19 is largely a development of the thought in v. 18, its two opening words, ὡς ὅτι, somewhat cloud the connection between the two verses. The phrase is only found elsewhere in Paul in 2 Cor. 11.21 (and also in 2 Thess. 2.2). The three main possibilities are: (1) as causal, meaning 'because', with ὡς ὅτι equivalent to ὅτι; (2) as epexegetical, meaning 'namely that'; and (3) as introducing the content of something said or written with some doubt attending the accuracy of the message. Although not a great deal turns on this question, the causal explanation (adopted by the Vulgate in the translation *quoniam quidem* ['since indeed']) seems preferable. Thrall rejects the causal explanation for the reason that although v. 19b does 'provide some explanation of the reconciling process', 'the verse as a whole functions to repeat v. 18 rather than to provide its logical grounding' (1994: 432). Yet nothing in the closely reasoned and concentrated argument of 2 Corinthians suggests that Paul is in the habit of repeating what he has just written. And Thrall's view sets an unrealistically high bar for the meaning of 'causal'. There are aspects of v. 19 that do constitute 'grounding' for v. 18: (1) God is now said to be reconciling 'in Christ' and not 'through' him; (2) the process of reconciliation is explained as God's not holding people's transgressions against them; and (3) the 'ministry of reconciliation' is now interpreted as God's having placed 'the word of reconciliation' among us, which brings out the oral nature of the ministry (and implies the proclamation of the Gospel as the primary means by which the διακονία is operative). We must bear in mind that the notions of διακονία and διάκονος were being contested in Corinth by his opponents (2 Cor. 11.15, 23), and Paul cannot use the word here without communicating his claim against that of his rivals whom he will later describe, with savage invective, as διάκονοι of Satan pretending to be διάκονοι of righteousness (11.15).

That God is reconciling the κόσμος (here probably meaning human society, not the 'cosmos' as we understand it) 'in Christ' has attracted much scholarly attention. Lambrecht provides the bedrock insight for the discussion: 'the nuance of God's presence in Christ should not be overlooked' (1999: 99). Although it would be over-interpretation to find here a clear reference to Christ's divine nature, to say that God was reconciling 'in Christ' is very different from the bare agency that can be signified by 'through Christ'. This divine activity was manifested in God's not holding their trespasses against them, while the earlier reference to κόσμος suggests that this means the trespasses of all humanity.

In v. 19, Paul repeats the pattern of v. 18 in that a broad statement of God's salvific action is paired with an assertion of his special role in the economy of salvation thus effected; 'The parallelism ... is eye-catching' (Lambrecht 1999: 99). In v. 19, Paul insists that God has actually entrusted 'us' with the message of reconciliation (τὸν λόγον τῆς καταλλαγῆς). This 'us' could just convey Paul himself, or perhaps also Paul and Timothy. But it most certainly and transparently excludes the rival missionaries who have turned up in Corinth. Most commentators, insufficiently attuned to issues of group identity in the letter, typically overlook the sharply polemical nature of these two assertions relating to διακονία and λόγος within the context of the profound outgroup stereotypification in which Paul engages throughout the letter.[10]

2 Corinthians 5.20 Paul has previously described himself as a 'minister of the new covenant' (3.6) and now hits upon another way to encapsulate his leadership role. Since Paul has been entrusted by God with the word of reconciliation (v. 19), he is able to reason that this makes him 'function as an ambassador' (πρεσβεύειν) 'for' (ὑπέρ) Christ. Although Paul's letters are replete with his sending envoys on his behalf (and receiving them on their return), he does not use nominal terms such as ἄγγελος, πρεσβευτής or κῆρυξ of those envoys, nor indeed does he have a set term for the office or function of envoy.[11] This is the only instance of πρεσβεύειν in the genuine Pauline letters, with the only other example in the New Testament being found in Eph. 6.20, so it makes quite an impact here. The nominal form πρέσβυς does not occur in the New Testament, although it appears sixteen times in the Septuagint,[12] often with the rather less exalted meaning of 'messenger', but sometimes meaning the envoy of a king or political rule (Isa. 37.6; 39.1; 1 Macc. 9.70). Presumably, in using the word πρεσβεύειν Paul was able to rely upon the knowledge of his audience concerning this social role (Mitchell 1992). In fact, ambassadors were a very common phenomenon in the ancient Greek east, especially as between the cities and provincial governors, or the emperor himself. Margaret Mitchell has explained the two principal social and diplomatic conventions relating to the role of ambassador in the Greco-Roman world and related them to 2 Cor. 5.20. First, the proper reception of the envoy necessarily entailed the proper reception of the one who sent him. This factor is discernible in the use of πρεσβεύειν in 5.20 by virtue of his later requests to be received properly (6.11-13; 7.2). Secondly, envoys have significant power and authority to speak for those who sent them – in line with their instructions – because of the close relationship between the sender and the envoy. Paul makes much of his closeness to God and Christ in this

---

[10] The issue is overlooked, for example, by: Barrett 1973: 178; Furnish 1984: 320; Thrall 1994: 435-6; Witherington 1995: 396; Barnett 1997: 308-9; Garland 1999: 294; Lambrecht 1999: 99; Matera 2003: 141; Harris 2005: 445; Seifrid 2014: 258-9; and Guthrie 2015: 310.

[11] Mitchell 1992: 652. Long ago Richard Bentley conjectured that Paul employed the nominal form πρεσβευτής in Phlm. 9, rather than the standard reading πρεσβύτης ('old man'), in connection with Paul's work on Christ's behalf (BDAG 863).

[12] Num 21.21; 22.5; Deut 2.26; Ps. 67 (68).31; Hos. 5.13; Isa. 13.8; 21.2; 37.6; 39.1; 57.9; 63.9; 1 Macc. 9.70; 10.51; 11.9; 13.14; 4 Macc. 7.10 (in some versions).

letter, even in 2 Cor. 5.20 itself, with his insistence that God is making his appeal through him (Mitchell 1992: 645–51).

Paul's ambassadorial role provides a context for his beseeching them 'on behalf of Christ', with the phrase ὑπὲρ Χριστοῦ appearing for a second time in the verse, as an aspect of his appeal to them to be reconciled to God. The second-person plural, '(you) be reconciled (καταλλάγητε), here is surely targeted at the Corinthians, not at the world at large as Seifrid has suggested (2014: 259), nor to any audience beyond the Corinthians (Harris 2005: 448). The Corinthian Christ-followers are his audience throughout this section (and the letter generally) and a sudden communicative diversion to a wider group is not credible. A further reason to see here only the Corinthians is that Paul's urging them in 6.1 not to accept the grace of God in vain makes best sense as including, if not being identical with, 'the word of reconciliation' he has told them in v. 19 that God has given him. That Paul should counsel his audience to be reconciled to God shows that they have a role to play in the process and their role is not just one of passive receptivity. If Paul is to preach the word of reconciliation, they must hear, accept and respond to it. This is the way, or at least a sign, that their lives will be transformed since they no longer live for others (v. 15).

Yet in asking the Corinthians to be reconciled to God, is Paul also – at this point in the letter – wanting them to be reconciled to him? While this may not be the dominant note here, it is difficult to exclude the idea entirely. Certainly he does not give the idea direct expression. He has, moreover, just claimed that God has entrusted him with the 'word of reconciliation' (v. 19). By urging the Corinthians to be reconciled to God in v. 20, he is precisely implementing this divine charge. The thought that his role in the momentous drama of God's reconciliation with humanity could contract entirely to getting the Corinthians onside with him after the troubles of the recent past does not coincide with the substance of his task and would seriously detract from his communicative aims at this point. Nevertheless, he is Christ's ambassador, and, as we have just seen, in this setting it was assumed that there would be a close relationship between the sender and his ambassador. This means that reconciliation with the sender should also entail, at least to an extent, reconciliation with the envoy.

2 Corinthians 5.21 The two clauses of this verse contain an astonishing density of thought: 'For our sake he made him who knew no sin to be sin, so that in him we might become the righteousness of God.' Their primary rationale is probably to provide an explanation for, and expansion of, what Paul has said in v. 19 about God being in Christ reconciling the world to himself, not holding people's transgressions against them. It is clear that 'him who knew no sin' is Christ. 'Knowing' sin conveys not so much an intellectual knowledge but knowledge acquired by personal participation and experience (Harris 2005: 450). Such knowledge was alien to Christ. This is probably not a reference to Christ in his pre-existence but rather to his incarnate state; otherwise the efforts to which Paul goes elsewhere (e.g. Rom. 5.12-21) to present Christ as a second Adam, who undoes what Adam did, would make little sense (Matera 2003: 143). As Barnett has observed, 'the efficacy of Christ's redemption logically rests on a demonstrated sinlessness during his *earthly* ministry' (1997: 314; emphasis original).

The critical statement 'for our sake' (ὑπὲρ ἡμῶν) God made Christ to be sin (a statement similar to that in Gal. 3.13) has attracted close attention since the Patristic period, with views generally coalescing around two poles. First, some suggest that 'sin' means 'sin-offering', and, secondly, others propose that Christ in some way stood in for sinful humanity. Backing for the former alternative exists in the fact that in the Hebrew Bible the word חטאת means sin-offering in several places in Leviticus 4 and the Septuagint translates it as ἁμαρτία (Lev. 4.25, 32, 34). Paul's use of περὶ ἁμαρτίας in Rom. 8.3 could possibly derive from Isa. 53.10, where ἁμαρτία means 'sin-offering.' Yet a number of factors weigh against this possibility: it would entail that ἁμαρτία means 'sin' when it first appears in the verse and 'sin-offering' on its second appearance; Paul would more likely have written that God 'gave' (ἔδωκεν) or 'offered' (ἔθηκεν) Christ as a sin-offering than that he 'made' (ἐποίησεν) him such; ἁμαρτία could come from Isa. 53.9-11, where it means 'sin'; and, finally and most significantly, if, as seems likely, the audience was meant to take ἁμαρτία as antithetical to δικαιοσύνη, 'sin', not 'sin-offering', is appropriate.[13]

More promising is the second option, which offers a more personal and experiential meaning for ἁμαρτία and, above all, provides a suitable contrast to δικαιοσύνη. Although all attempts to interpret the meaning of being made sin involves a voyage into the unknown, it does seem likely that Paul meant that Christ assumed the whole burden of human sin so that the whole punishment for sin was inflicted on him instead. This means that the word 'substitution' probably comes closest to what Paul has in mind here, although this is a disputed subject with other commentators preferring the notion of 'representation', namely that Christ represents human beings on the cross, rather than substituting for them.[14]

The final part of v. 21 claims that the purpose of God's making Christ sin for us was that we might become the righteousness of God in him. This verse, therefore, encapsulates one version of the idea of 'interchange' to describe

---

[13] For these various factors, see Thrall 1994: 440–1; Matera 2003: 143; Harris 2005: 452–3.
[14] For a recent defence of substitution in explaining Paul's views on atonement, see Gathercole 2015.

the complex of the effect of Jesus' death and resurrection, as well explained by Hooker (1971). Yet the meaning of 'righteousness' here is hardly self-explanatory. Probably in the phrase 'the righteousness of God' the genitive is objective in nature: 'the righteousness that comes from God,' in the form of faithfulness and dependability (Matera 2003: 144; similarly, Hooker 2008: 370), not God's own righteousness, for how could the Corinthians, or any human beings, attain to that? Plainly a contrast is established with the sin (ἁμαρτία) that God made Christ for our sakes, so it is not possible to exclude the notion of proper behaviour,[15] or, in social identity terms, behaviour in line with group norms and identity-descriptors. Often commentators appeal to alleged 'forensic' or 'judicial' understandings of righteousness, where it means the state of acquittal. I have previously argued that such an understanding rests on a very shaky foundation, brought about by a misunderstanding and misinterpretation of the presentation of righteousness in the Hebrew Bible.

In my view, the key notion for understanding δικαιοσύνη is the quality designated by the epithet δίκαιος (on which Proverbs 10–15 are a rich source), and it originally refers to the condition of being a dedicated Israelite; that is, it is an identity-designator, and part of that identity comprises norms for appropriate behaviour. The verb (δικαιόω) means to be or to become δίκαιος, and the abstract noun δικαιοσύνη refers to the state of being δίκαιος (Esler 1998: 159–69). Paul has raided the collective memory of Israel in order to daringly reapply δικαιοσύνη, a glittering prize of being an Israelite, to the members of his congregations whether they were Judean or non-Judean (Esler 2006b). Directly in line with this approach, in 2 Cor. 5.21 δικαιοσύνη is primarily a way of describing the exalted identity of the Christ-movement, including a normative dimension, that comes from God via the redemptive work of Christ. This accords quite closely with the view of Ernst Käsemann, although coming at the matter from a very different direction, that in 2 Cor. 5.21 the expression 'the righteousness of God' means 'the reality of the redeemed community' (1969: 169), although 'identity' might be preferable to 'reality'. A critical point that Paul is making is that the righteousness he is offering comes from God; that is, for Christ-followers it does not derive from Judean ethnic identity. In saying this, he once again sharply differentiates the identity that comes from his version of the Gospel from that offered by his opponents, since when they claim to be 'ministers of righteousness', a false claim according to Paul (11.15), they have in mind the righteousness associated with being a Judean, as evident from their (no doubt proud) self-designation as Hebrews, Israelites and sons of Abraham (11.22).

---

[15] *Contra*, Thrall (1994: 443): 'It is doubtful whether Paul has in mind righteousness of moral character.'

2 Corinthians 6.1 As already noted, the sentiment in this verse – 'But working together, we also appeal to you not to receive the grace of God in vain' – is strongly tied to what was said in vv. 19-20. This constitutes one of the reasons to regard the section we have under consideration as ending at 6.2, rather than, as some propose (e.g. Thrall 1994: 449–50), at 5.21, with 6.1-2 also commencing the next section that runs to 6.13. 2 Corinthians 6.3 marks a transition, not as sharp admittedly as some imagine, to a recitation of Paul's apostolic hardships, whereas 5.11–6.2 concern, in the traditional language of scholarship, 'the essence and exercise of the apostolic ministry' (Harris 2005: 464). Or, more aptly in social identity terms, they concern 'the foundation and exercise of Pauline leadership'. The inclusion of ὑμᾶς ('you' plural) does not mean that 'Now, and not before, he specifically addresses the Corinthians' (Thrall 1994: 451), because they have already been addressed in the second-person plural form καταλλάγητε in the previous verse, but rather indicates that Paul has arrived at his summarizing conclusion to 5.11–6.2, comprising 6.1-2.

The identity of the other party or parties with whom he is 'working together' (συνεργοῦντες) is unclear. The main possibilities are: (1) God and/or Christ; (2) his Corinthian addressees; and (3) other evangelists. It is difficult to see what would impel Paul at this point to refer to other preachers of the Gospel, so that the choice really boils down to (1) or (2). In favour of the first option is that Paul has already told his audience in v. 20 that God is entreating them through him. The idea of God as principal and Paul as agent, given the close ties between sender and envoy in this setting, provides solid justification for Paul to refer to his as 'working together'. This is probably the majority view among commentators and translators (who often add 'with him' after 'working together' to bring out the point). Support for the second option, however, is found in Paul's designation of himself and the Corinthians in 1.24 as συνεργοί, co-workers', the nominal form of the verb used here. Συνεργοί is an expression of the cooperation that Paul works hard to achieve in the early part of the letter. Perhaps Paul had in mind here his work as preacher of the word of reconciliation (v. 19) and the imperative on them to accept it. If so, he has made a poor job of expressing the idea, with more required than just the use of συνεργοῦντες to produce this result. On balance, the factors in favour of the first option outweigh those in favour of the latter. Since in 1 Thess. 3.2 Paul calls Timothy a 'co-worker' (συνεργός) of God, he did not regard the idea as hubristic for preachers of the Gospel. Accordingly, this is one of those occasions where Paul exercises leadership not by emphasizing the relationship between himself and the Corinthians, hitherto the usual explanation offered by social identity theory, but by playing his trump card, his close relationship with God.

The appeal Paul enunciates in 6.1 is directed to countering the risk that the Corinthians might be receiving the grace of God in vain. The aorist form δέξασθαι may refer to a single action in the past as the occasion of their receiving God's grace, namely baptism but is more probably a 'timeless' aorist (after a verb of exhortation, παρακαλεῖν).[16] It carries the connotation that God's grace continues to be available in the present, as shown by the greeting in 1.2; that present is very much in view in this part of the letter (Harris 2005: 458), not least in the very next verse with its joyous affirmation, 'Behold, now is the acceptable time!'

The fear that Paul expresses here about their possible receipt of God's grace in vain corresponds with his earlier wish that they be reconciled with God, undoubtedly predicated upon the fear that they might not be. We must ask in what precise ways the Corinthians were in danger of letting God's grace come to nothing, although any answers are inevitably speculative. Possibilities include: failure to repudiate the world of idolatry and defilement (6.14-18; 7.1); being swayed by a different Jesus, spirit and gospel (11.4); engaging in group-disrupting behaviour (12.20-21); not recognizing the wickedness of Paul's opponents (11.3-15); and rejecting Paul's efforts at being reconciled to them (6.13; 7.2). All of these are possible, not just the last as has been suggested (Matera 2003: 150).

2 Corinthians 6.2 The final verse of this section begins with a quotation of the first part of Isa. 49.8. In line with the previous discussion of scriptural quotations in Paul, it is submitted that Paul assumed little or no familiarity with the context of this quotation on the part of his audience. As far as his communicative intention was concerned, it was enough for him that these were God's words, no doubt recorded somewhere in the scriptures of Israel. If his addressees had been aware of the original context of this quotation, they would have been rather puzzled. For they were addressed to the Servant of God some 500 years earlier (and not to the entirety of Israel), in what is the second of the Servant Songs (Isa. 49.1-13); it would have been necessary for Paul to have already explained to them why they applied to non-Judean Christ-followers. Even if some of them had heard this quotation before, for example by visiting Judean synagogues on the Sabbath, they would have required exactly the same explanation. It made Paul's communicative task far easier simply to have the Corinthians believe that these were God's words and that they had application to them (which in their original context they did not).

This conclusion aids in identifying the person or persons Paul wanted to identify to his audience as the beneficiaries of God's listening and help. For

---

[16] Furnish 1984: 341; Kistemaker (1997: 209) treats it as equivalent to a present. *Contra*, Barnett 1997: 316.

Mark Seifrid, the answer is that 'Paul interprets the text in reference to Christ, who also appealed to God and was delivered – yet not apart from his death on the cross', and he rejects rival explanations that find the referent in the Corinthians or Paul himself.[17] In support of this view Seifrid offers a detailed and intellectually elegant discussion linking numerous aspects of Isaiah 49 to the situation of Jesus Christ and his role in relation to the Corinthians. This is the first problem with his argument; it is simply not credible that Paul's Corinthian addressees would have had any idea of this, even if some of it (perhaps) had been in Paul's own mind. They were not clairvoyant; if Paul did not tell them, they were not going to know. Secondly, the course of what Paul has told them points in a different direction. He has just mentioned, in the previous verse, the grace (χάρις) they receive from God (with an emphatic 'you', ὑμᾶς, at the end of the verse. When Paul then offers an explanation – for (γάρ) he (i.e. God) says – to the effect, 'At the acceptable time I have listened to you, and on the day of salvation I have helped you', even though it is in the second-person singular, it is very hard to avoid the conclusion that the listening and helping are co-incident with the provision of grace just mentioned. The fact that Paul then asserts that 'Behold, now is the acceptable time! Behold, now is the day of salvation' makes it even clearer that he has the present moment and the Corinthians in mind.

---

[17] Seifrid 2014: 271; he cites Thrall (1994: 452–3) and Harris (2005: 461–3) for the view that Paul is applying this quotation to the Corinthians and Webb (1993: 138) for the view that Paul is referring to himself.

9

Leadership and ingroup identity (6.3–7.4)

In the next section of the letter, Paul moves from an expression of his leadership that, within the social identity approach, encompasses prototypical leadership that will include the reality of self-sacrifice (in 6.3-10), via a plea to the Corinthians for them to be receptive and responsive to his message (6.11-13), to an elaborate explanation of ingroup identity (6.14–7.1), which concludes with closing identity guidance (7.2-4). Issues of identity lock this material tightly together.

The hardships and triumphs of apostolic leadership (6.3-10)

Having described the substance of his ministry in 5.11–6.2, in 6.3-10 Paul proceeds to explain how he exercises that ministry, in relation both to the faultless manner of his doing so and to the trials that it entails, which together form the basis for his self-commendation. In reliance on the experiences he has endured as set out in vv. 4b-10, he will then plead with the Corinthians in vv. 11-13 to open their hearts to him.

2 Corinthians 6.3 Paul's disavowal of putting obstacles in anyone's way, so that no fault will be found with his ministry (διακονία), probably implies that there were people in Corinth who were doing just that. We know from earlier chapters that the Corinthians were upset with him for his changing his travel plans. In Chapter 7, it becomes clear they were also unhappy with his sending the painful letter. In Chapters 10–13, we will learn that rival missionaries in Corinth were critical of his ministry. Verse 3, therefore, functions as a form of suppressing fire aimed at all of those targets.

We have already observed the extent to which 'ministry' (διακονία) is a concept Paul uses in this letter to make crucial points about his leadership. His is a ministry of the Spirit (3.8), of righteousness (3.9) and of reconciliation (5.18), and he is a minister (διάκονος) of the new covenant (3.6). He is about to say that he is a minister of God (6.4), while later claiming to be a minister of Christ (11.23). It is not surprising, therefore, that the reason he offers in v. 3b for his disavowal of causing offence in v. 3a pinpoints its motivation not in any desire to defend himself but to protect 'the ministry'. While many translations insert 'our' before ministry here, the word is missing in the text and there is no justification for its insertion: the omission of 'our' (ὑμῶν) indicates 'that "the ministry" is prior to and more important than the one who exercises it' (Matera 2003: 150).

2 Corinthians 6.4-10 Verse 6.4a marks a further development in the abundant language of commendation and self-commendation in the letter. Paul appears to view self-commendation in an arguably negative light in 3.1 and 5.12 but states that he practises it in 4.2. Although Harris (commenting on 3.1; 2005: 259) claims that objectionable self-recommendation has the pronoun ἑαυτόν first (so 3.1 and 5.12), this is a questionable distinction. After all, 3.1 suggests that he engages in it or at least has done so in the past. Does Paul regard self-commendation negatively? Probably the only issue is whether there is a basis for self-praise. The instance at 5.12 does not seem to be negative; Paul is acknowledging that at that point he is praising himself but giving them the basis to praise him. The whole issue is whether justification exists for the praise. In 2 Corinthians 11 and 12, he makes honour-claims about himself, but only because he is forced to it and has a foundation for doing so. His self-praise in 6.4a is justifiable because he is about to explain his foundation for mentioning it, an explanation that occupies the long passage of vv. 4b-10.

Verses 4b-10 constitute the second catalogue of hardships in the letter, the others falling at 4.8-9, 11.23b-29 and 12.10. We have already commented on the connection between 4.8-9 and the *peristasis* catalogues of Hellenistic moralists in relation to 4.8-9 and will not repeat that material here. Paul has imposed a careful pattern on this material:

1. Three triads introduced by 'great endurance' (4b-5);
2. Two groups of four (6-7a);
3. Three contrasts (7b-8a); and
4. Seven antitheses (8b-10).

Part 1 of the catalogue is preceded by a word that differs from what follows in designating that aspect of Paul's character which typified his response to this whole panoply of difficulties, namely ὑπομονή ('endurance'), a reasonably common word in the Pauline letters.[1] After this, he proceeds to itemize them, and in each case they are introduced by the word ἐν ('in').

---

[1] Rom. 2.7; 5.3, 4; 8.25; 15.4, 5; 2 Cor. 1.6; 6.4; 1 Thess. 1.3

The first triad (in 4b) comprises:

*afflictions (θλίψεσιν)
*hardships (ἀνάγκαις), and
*dire straits (στενοχωρίαις).

These opening experiences are rather generic in nature and are suggestive, especially 'of a series of external situations of affliction, calamity, and trouble' that attend his ministry (Thrall 1994: 458), even if their emotionally draining aspects cannot be excluded (contra Thrall). The word θλίψις appears frequently in 2 Corinthians (1.4 (bis), 8; 2.4; 4.17; 7.4; 8.2, 13) and the participial form for the related verb commences the hardship list in 4.8-12. In 2 Cor. 1.8-11, he mentions a θλῖψις that beset him in Asia that left him despairing for this life. The second word in 4.8 is the passive participial form of the verb cognate with στενοχωρίαις. In addition, ἀνάγκαι and στενοχωρίαι are found in the short list of hardships in 12.10. So θλίψεις and στενοχωρίαι probably best encapsulate, at a general level, the hardships Paul encountered.

At this point Paul moves to the second triad (v. 5), also preceded by ἐν, which encompasses more specific trials, consisting of afflictions that had been imposed on him by others, which can often be related (in their nature if not necessarily in their exact circumstance) to events related in the Acts of the Apostles:

*beatings (πληγαῖς);
*imprisonments (φυλακαῖς); and
*riots (ἀκαταστασίαις).

As to beatings, he had received the thirty-nine lash beating by Judeans in their synagogues on five occasions (2 Cor. 11.24) and by Romans with rods three times (2 Cor. 11.25), while Acts mentions the instance at Philippi (16.22-23). He reveals later that he had been beaten far worse than his opponents (2 Cor. 11.23). Acts 16.23-40 describes how Paul was imprisoned, and Paul himself claimed to have been imprisoned far more than his opponents (2 Cor. 11.23). Acts (although without use of the word ἀκαταστασία) describes Paul being caught up in disturbances in Pisidian Antioch (13.50), Iconium (14.5), Lystra (14.19), Philippi (16.22), Thessalonica (17.5-7), Beroea (17.13), Corinth (18.12-17), Ephesus (19.23–20.1) and Jerusalem (21.27-36).

The third triad refers to difficulties that he had imposed on himself in the course of his ministry:

*labours (κόποις);
*sleepless nights (ἀγρυπνίαις); and
*fasting (νηστείαις).

Κόποι, and also ἀγρυπνίαι and νηστείαι, may refer to his working to support himself in a new missionary area (Matera 2003: 152). But they could also apply to the labours of active evangelism. Support for this view lies in Paul's distinguishing λιμός ('hunger') from νηστείαι in 2 Cor. 11.27, suggesting that the latter refers to voluntary hunger, fasting in a religious sense (Thrall 1994: 458; Harris 2005: 473).

By listing these difficulties that he had encountered in serving Christ and the Gospel through ministry to the Christ-groups themselves, both externally imposed and self-inflicted, Paul engages in leadership behaviour that social identity psychologists refer to as 'identity advancement'. By this is meant acting in the interests of the group, especially by taking action that prioritizes the needs of the group ahead of his or her personal needs and interests. There is no more persuasive way for a leader to do this than by putting his or her health, safety or even life on the line for the group, which is what Paul is providing evidence for his having done repeatedly here.

Next, Paul sets out the two groups of four, in each case also preceded by ἐν, but here meaning 'by' (6-7a). All of these are explicable as descriptors of Christ-movement identity. The first four are as follows:

*purity (ἀγνότητι);
*knowledge (γνώσει);
*forbearance (μακροθυμίᾳ); and
*kindness (χρηστότητι).

Three of these (purity, forbearance and kindness) are types of orientation and behaviour that individuals might possess but which Paul claims he embodies in a way that strongly implies he regards them as desirable for all Christ-followers. As Wayne Meeks has observed, even when Paul is asserting particular qualities in himself as part of his defensive mode, he also presents them as qualities that the community he is addressing should imitate (1993: 160). To return to a social identity perspective, purity, forbearance and kindness are normative descriptors of group identity. He is prototypical of the group in possessing these qualities, and the Corinthians will align themselves with the identity of the group if they follow him and also internalize them. This is the major way in which leadership is effective within a social identity perspective. Within a different framework, that of philosophical ethics, these three identity-descriptors are referred to as 'virtues'. Knowledge falls into a different category. It is not a form of behaviour but the practical or theoretical understanding of a particular subject. It connects with the two cognitive dimensions of social identity: first, the basic understanding and realization that one belongs to a particular group, and, secondly, understanding the beliefs characteristic of that group.

Considerable significance attaches to the prominence 'purity' enjoys from its first place among these four features, especially in view of the section 6.14-7.1 that is soon to follow, with Adewuya rightly regarding 2 Cor. 6.6 as an anticipation of 2 Cor. 6.14–7.1 (2001: 161). What does Paul mean by ἁγνότης? The question is difficult because of the limited use of this precise language elsewhere in the letter (Barnett 1997: 328). Ἁγνός appears in 2 Cor. 7.11 and 11.2 (a very significant instance) and in Phil. 4.8. It occurs on six other occasions in the New Testament and covers the range of meanings 'pure', 'holy' and 'innocent' (BDAG 13). A close synonym, ἁγιότης, might appear in 1.12, but is subject to textual uncertainty (the correct reading is probably ἁπλότης). In some versions, ἁγνότης appears in 11.3, but the preferable view is to exclude it. To begin with, there is no justification for restricting the word's meaning in 6.6 to 'the purity of his intentions' (so Thrall 1994: 459). 'Purity of morals and of intention' is better (Harris 2005: 474), but even that formulation is too constricted and too redolent of modern conceptualization. A better way to approach its meaning is by considering the antonyms to 'purity'. In 6.14-7:1, there is a long passage that begins with the need to avoid association with ἄπιστοι. Included in this passage is an injunction not to touch anything unclean (ἀκάθαρτος). The passage ends with a further direction: 'Let us cleanse (καθαρίσωμεν) ourselves from every defilement (μολυσμός) of body and spirit, perfecting holiness (ἁγιωσύνη) in the fear of God.' The negative injunctions here would very adequately indicate behavioural characteristics antithetical to purity, even if the word did not find a close synonym ἁγιωσύνη in the final clause.

We find this picture cropping up again later in the letter. In 11.2, Paul notes that he betrothed the Corinthians to one husband to present them as a 'pure (ἁγνή) virgin' to Christ. This is clearly a group-, not individual-oriented image of purity: 'It is the Christian community as a whole, and not any individual, that is the spouse of Christ' (Plummer 1915: 296). Paul warns his audience that this purity is imperilled by his opponents who have turned up preaching a different Jesus, spirit and gospel (11.3-6). In other words, his opponents and their teaching are inimical to the purity of the community, a point that can be made by 11.2 alone and does not require the addition of 11.3b, where there is probably another reference to ἁγνότη (see comment on 11.3). In short, however, Paul is explaining that 'the Corinthians were in danger of being corrupted (sc. by his opponents) and losing their purity' (Adewuya 2001: 162).

In addition, in 12.21 Paul reflects on the possibility that when he visits the Corinthians again, he may discover that that they have not repented of the impurity (ἀκαθαρσία), sexual immorality (πορνεία) and licentiousness (ἀσέλγεια) that they once practised. If this was how they once behaved (presumably before turning to Christ), it is unsurprising that Paul would prioritize purity among the features he lists in 6.6. Furthermore, the passage comprising 6.14–7.1 provides a detailed exemplum of what purity means shortly after he has mentioned that identity-descriptor and serves as a reminder of what they should aim at to avoid the problem he will later mention in 12.21.

Forbearance and kindness are characteristics of God. Μακροθυμία appears twice in Romans (2.4 and 9.22, both of the forbearance of God, and χρηστότης is also predicated of God at 2.4). But they are available to human beings courtesy of the Spirit: in Gal. 5.22, Paul lists the fruit of Spirit as love (ἀγάπη), joy, peace, μακροθυμία, χρηστότης, and so on. So when Paul mentions them both in 2 Cor. 6.6, they are not just qualities appropriate to himself who, for example, talks of sparing (φειδόμενος) the Corinthians in 1.23 (Thrall 1994: 459–60). Rather they are relevant to all Christ-followers, at least to the extent that they have been touched by the Spirit. Their presence is implied, for example, in the advice he has given the Corinthians previously, in relation to the malefactor for whom Paul urges forgiveness and love in 2.5-11. Although neither μακροθυμία nor χρηστότης occurs in that passage, the exercise of forgiveness and love are very closely connected to them. But their presence will also be felt soon after this, when he urges the Corinthians to open his hearts to him, just as his is open to theirs (6.11-13).

Probably the knowledge mentioned in 6.6 is that of God and Christ, the possession and dissemination of which Paul sees as an integral part of his ministry, as amply revealed earlier, in 2.14 and 4.6.

Then we have the second four:

*the Holy Spirit;
*genuine love (ἀγάπη ἀνυποκρίτῳ), which also appears in Rom. 12.9;
*the word of truth; and
*the power of God.

Except for 'genuine love', these are features of a different kind, and commentators go astray when they describe the eight features of vv. 6-7a as 'a list of Christian virtues' or 'an enumeration of moral qualities',[2] when

---

[2] As does Harris 2005: 475. Thrall describes them as 'human qualities; (1994: 460). Such views lead other commentators (such as Plummer 1915: 196-7) to seek to interpret

only four of them can be so described. The Holy Spirit, the word of truth and the power of God are not human characteristics but dynamic forces in the world – two of them (the Holy Spirit and the power of God) aspects of God's own being – which are active in his ministry. Only one of them, ἀγάπη, represents (like purity, forbearance and kindness) an identity-descriptor that encapsulates the distinctive orientation and behaviour of the Christ-movement. We know that ἀγάπη plays a pivotal role from elsewhere in his letters, especially from its first position among the list of fruits of Spirit in Gal. 5.22 and its similar place in the Rom. 12.9-21. The exact expression here, ἀγάπη ἀνυπόκριτος ('genuine love'), recurs in Rom. 12.9.

It is worth noting that whenever Paul refers to the Holy Spirit in his letters, he is not speaking about a theological category or making a statement about the divine ontology, but triggering a recollection among his audience of the dramatic presence of God among Christ-followers that is signalled by an explosion of charismatic gifts (1 Corinthians 12–14) and that brings forth fruit in forms of orientation and behaviour towards others (such as are listed in Gal. 5.22). These 'fruits' make up a large part of the identity of the Christ-movement. Paul prides himself on his being an agent of the Holy Spirit, as when he refers to (his) 'ministry of the Spirit' (2 Cor. 3.8).

By 'the word of truth' Paul is probably offering a restatement of 'the open statement of the truth' (φανέρωσις τῆς ἀληθείας), which pushes the 'word of truth' towards meaning 'the proclamation of the truth' (not merely 'a truthful word') that earlier in the letter he connected with his ministry (4.2). The truth embraces the Jesus, the Spirit and the Gospel that he preaches (11.4).

The final expression, 'the power of God', recalls his reference at 4.7 to 'the transcendent power is God's and not ours'. This is a subjective genitive, referring to the power that God supplies. Ending the list of eight features with the power of God reminds his readers of the ultimate force in the world while also conveying the implication that he is the servant of that power. The power of God is what ensures he is effective in spite of numerous obstacles (4.7-12). For an important dimension of this letter is encapsulated in the message that Paul later reports God gave to him: 'My grace is sufficient for you, for my power is made perfect in weakness' (12.9). Paul is totally dependent on God, as he learned when he nearly died in Asia (1.9). This experience of God's power in personal weakness sharply differentiates him from the self-sufficient and unconquerable Stoic sage (Harris 2005: 476). In

'Holy Spirit' as meaning a human spirit, even though whenever Paul refers to a spirit as holy, he has in mind the Holy Spirit (Harris, *loc. cit*). Matera (2003: 153) recognizes that this is not a list of 'human virtues'.

social identity terms, Paul is presenting himself as prototypical of the group identity in embodying qualities such as purity, forbearance, kindness and love, while also making a claim that he is dependent on the power of God in being able to do so.

Verses 7b-8a are structured as three contrasts each beginning with διά ('by', 'in'):

*by the weapons of righteousness (τῶν ὅπλων τῆς δικαιοσύνης) for the right hand and the left,
*amid honour (δόξης) and dishonour (ἀτιμίας),
*amid ill repute (δυσφημίας) and good repute (εὐφημίας).

The meaning of the first of these contrasts, the military metaphor 'weapons of righteousness', is debated. Many commentators regard it as a genitive of content, meaning 'weapons that consist of righteousness', that are righteousness, not weapons that righteousness provides (in which case the righteousness would be God's). For here the expression seems to have a human referent. It has a force equivalent to that of the virtually identical expression in Rom. 6.13: '(present) your (bodily) members to God as weapons of righteousness (ὅπλα δικαιοσύνης)', as opposed to presenting them as 'weapons of injustice' for sin. The human connection also appeared at 3.9 where Paul mentioned 'the ministry of righteousness' in a way that does not allow any doubt that he is speaking of his own ministry, and it will be even more apparent with the two instances of 'righteousness' in 9.9 and 9.10. Yet while this is a reasonable view, we must not neglect the connection that this righteousness has with God. For there is a principle used in the interpretation of legal documents that can be sensibly applied to biblical interpretation: it is that the document in which an expression occurs is the best guide to the meaning of that expression. Only a little earlier in the text Paul has observed of Christ that 'For our sake he made him who knew no sin to be sin, so that in him we might become the righteousness of God' (5.21). As I noted earlier in relation to 5.21, to say that Christ-followers become the righteousness of God is principally a means of referring to the exalted identity of the Christ-movement, which does embrace a normative aspect (although it is not primarily 'ethical'), but it comes from God as a result of the redemptive work of Christ. Accordingly, the phrase 'by the weapons of righteousness for the right hand and the left' is a way of referring to Christ-followers being equipped, through membership in this divinely sourced new identity in the world, for all eventualities. The fact that sometimes the arms of righteousness will be in the right hand, as with a spear or sword, and sometimes in the left, as with a shield, underlines the tension, also evident in the next two pairs, between being on the offensive (right hand) and being on the defensive (left hand), a contrast that presumably also conveys implications of success or failure, respectively.

The next two contrasted pairs, where the διά preceding each of them signifies attendant circumstances (in effect, meaning 'amid'; Harris 2005: 478), unambiguously testify that the culture of the ancient Greco-Roman east valorized the positive value of honour, the opposite of which was shame, in a way that is very different from the position in modern, individualistic cultures. The first pair of honour (δόξα) and dishonour (ἀτιμία) set out the position in the broadest terms, while the second, ill repute (δυσφημία) and good repute (εὐφημία), chiastically arranged with honour and shame, focus on a primary mechanism by which honour could be won or shame incurred, namely speech. Honour refers to the estimation one places on oneself but only if the local relevant public agrees with it. It is a kind of social credit rating. It can be increased or diminished, in the latter case with shame taking its place.[3] There are many signs of Paul being dishonoured in this letter, principally by his opponents whom he addresses primarily (but not exclusively) in chs 10–13. In this culture, persons of honour who are the subject of some form of negative comment or action, that is 'challenged', are duty-bound to reply, in the common social dynamic of 'challenge-and-response'.[4] Part of the aim of 2 Corinthians 10–13 is to provide a global reply to the various challenges that the opponents have been making to Paul where the relevant audience are his Corinthian Christ-followers who are being influenced by what the opponents are saying. He risks falling, or has to an extent already fallen, into δυσφημία, as a result of their criticism and needs to provide a strong response. That way he can replace δυσφημία with εὐφημία. In other words, Paul is taking action to restore his honour before the relevant local public. The broader context for this is Paul's intention to provide leadership in relation to the Corinthian Christ-followers, leadership that is being harmed by what is being said about him. It is part of the destiny of any leader to be subject to varying patterns of acceptance or rejection, high regard or low, praise or blame, as the context of the group and its inner dynamics change over time.

Finally, in vv. 8b-10, Paul sets out seven antitheses, each beginning with ὡς ('as'). They can be viewed as inspired by the closing antithesis of ill repute vis-à-vis good repute. In each case, Paul begins with a statement as to how he is perceived (often falsely), and follows this with a statement of the deeper

---

[3] See Malina 2001: 27–57 for a brief but magisterial treatment of this subject and one that introduced (in the book's first edition of 1981) biblical interpretation to ideas that are now omnipresent in the field.
[4] Malina 2001: 33–6 using the classic research into this phenomenon conducted by Pierre Bourdieu among the Kabyle of North Africa (1966).

reality of his life. The initial statements are, by and large, the sort of things people would say about him to generate ill repute. His replies seek to restore good repute. I will deal with them *seriatim*.

*as deceivers (πλάνοι) and yet we are true.

The gravamen of the charge in this letter that he was a deceiver (the Greek word πλάνος being not otherwise attested in Paul, although πλάνη appears in 1 Thess. 2.3), is almost certainly the fact that he had changed his travel plans (1.15-22), that he was a person who could say both yes and no. In 4.2, he insisted that he did not conduct himself with trickery (πανουργία), or by deceitfully falsifying (δολοῦντες) the word of God). In addition, there is the allegation of financial impropriety that he answers in 12.16-18, namely that being 'crafty I took you in by deceit' (πανοῦργος δόλῳ ὑμᾶς ἔλαβον). In 11.13, he claims his opponents were tricky (δόλιοι) and he clearly faced the same accusation. Apart from detailed denials on specific issues, his general answer to this charge is that he acted with 'divine sincerity' (εἰλκρίνεια τοῦ θεοῦ; 1.12), that he does not 'peddle' God's word but speaks with sincerity (εἰλκρίνεια; 2.17) and that he speaks the word of truth (6.7). Nor did he take advantage of anyone (οὐδένα ἐπλεονεκτήσαμεν; 7.2).

*as unknown and yet we are known,
*as dying and behold we live,
*as punished and yet not killed,
*as sorrowful, yet always rejoicing,
*as destitute but enriching many,
*as having nothing and yet possessing everything.

As Lambrecht observes (1999: 110), in the set of seven antitheses in vv. 8-10 Paul employs the language of paradox where the second term in each refers to a manifestation of God's power, with the last two instances, of 'enriching many' and 'possessing everything', needing to be understood in a metaphorical or spiritual sense.

A plea for receptivity and responsive action 6.11-13

2 Corinthians 6.11-13 is a short and clearly demarcated section in which Paul makes a plea to the Corinthians based on his heart being open to them and the need for theirs to be open to him. As we will see, this expression does not, as is almost universally assumed, relate to a demonstration of affection but to being receptive and responsive to the other, a responsiveness manifested in behaviour. The strong echoes of 6.11-13 in 7.2-4 only make sense on the

assumption that Paul always intended these two passages to frame 2 Cor. 6.14-7.1, since otherwise the repetitions would be otiose. As Lambrecht observes, '7:2-4 is not only the continuation, but also the resumption of 6:11-13. This seems to indicate that there was always an interruption after 6:13' (1999: 122). This circumstance sounds strongly against the unfortunate scholarly inclination to detach 6.14-7.1 from Paul's original letter (see the following).

2 Corinthians 6.11 The first phrase, 'Our mouth is open to you, Corinthians', conveys the frankness and confidence with which Paul speaks to the Corinthians. This may have particular reference to what he has just said in vv. 3-10. On the other hand, Paul's direct address to his audience as 'Corinthians' is highly unusual in his letters, and may well entail that Paul is referring not just to vv. 3-10 but to everything he has said in the letter concerning his ministry, his leadership, since his greeting to the church of God in Corinth in 1.1 (Thrall 1994: 468). Such a form of address probably indicates that he is drawing this initial section of the letter to a close before he pushes on to new topics. Earlier in the letter (3.12) he has claimed, in the course of contrasting himself to Moses, that he employs, παρρησία, frankness of speech. Having his mouth open to them has a similar meaning here in 6.11. Shortly after 6.11, moreover, in 7.4, he will affirm that he has great παρρησία with respect to them, and here there is debate as to whether meaning is either 'openness' or 'confidence'. The former is more likely, given the similar meaning of the word in 3.12 and the mention of his opening his mouth to the Corinthians in 6.11.[5] I will return to this link between 6.11 and 7.4 later.

Many commentators consider the expression 'our heart is open', literally, 'has been enlarged, (ἡ καρδία ἡμῶν πεπλάτυνται), the final expression in v. 11, concerns the demonstration of affection (Thrall 1994: 469; Matera 2003: 161; Guthrie 2015: 344), but without citing ancient evidence indicating that such a view is both sentimental and anachronistic. As I have argued elsewhere (Esler 2021d), the two Septuagintal instances of the notion of an 'open heart' (in Deut 11.6 and Psalm 118 [119].32) refer to receptivity, understanding and responsive action and that is Paul's meaning in 6.11.

Paul will revert to a virtually identical idea, using different but equivalent terms, in 7.2-4 when he says χωρήσατε ἡμᾶς. Although χωρέω (a *hapax legomenon* in Paul) has core meanings of 'go' or 'go forward', it also signifies 'have room for, hold, contain', such as of vessels holding a quantity of some product or of a space holding people. This meaning was also used figuratively, with χωρήσατε ἡμᾶς in 2 Cor. 7.2 often cited as an example, having the

---

[5]   BDAG 781 favours 'openness'.

meaning 'make room for us in your hearts' (BDAG 1094). But here again the meaning concerns receptivity, not affectionate expression. Then in 7.3 Paul will make explicit mention of 'hearts', when he reminds them that he has previously said that they were 'in our hearts'. So, we have a chiasmic arrangement:

6.11	7.2
Our mouth is open to you (πρὸς ὑμᾶς)	
Our heart is wide	Open your hearts to us
6.12	
You are restricted in your hearts (στενοχωρεῖσθε)	
6.13	7.3
Open (your hearts) (πλατύνθητε)	You are in our hearts
	7.4
	We have great freedom of speech (παρρησία) towards you (πρὸς ὑμᾶς)

2 Corinthians 6.12 Having just asserted that his heart is widened to them, Paul now persists with the same spatial imagery by insisting that they are restricted or narrowed, yet not by him but by their own hearts: 'You are not restricted (στενοχωρεῖσθε) by us, but you are restricted (στενοχωρεῖσθε) by your own inner parts (σπλάγχνοις)', where σπλάγχνα means pretty much the same as καρδία, 'heart' (BDAG 938). Apart from these two instances, Paul employs the word στενοχωρεῖσθαι, and its cognate noun, στενοχωρία in relation to the perils of ministry and discipleship (Rom. 2.9; 8.35; 2 Cor. 4.8; 6.4; 12.10).

2 Corinthians 6.13 Paul begins this verse with a phrase in the accusative case rather awkwardly inserted at the start of the verse: τὴν δὲ αὐτὴν ἀντιμισθίαν: 'with a view to the same recompense'. Paul is conveying the notion of reciprocity that was a prominent theme at the beginning of this letter. Most commentators assume that Paul is asking for affection and love from the Corinthians in return for his (e.g. Harris 2005: 491). All such views are based on a sentimental and unattested interpretation of the expression 'widen one's heart'. The implications of this expression rather concern receptivity, understanding, responsiveness and, ultimately, behaviour. (And this is what he also means at 7.3 when he says that they are in his heart.) When Paul adds in the remainder of the verse, 'I am speaking to you as children, widen (your hearts) also' (πλατύνθητε καὶ ὑμεῖς), *the implication is not that they need to show more affection but that they need to respond and act differently*, in particular, like him (as he has just set out). All this is preparation for the instruction about the identity of the Christ-movement and the behaviour appropriate to belonging to it to which he is about to proceed in 6.14–7.1.

An explanation of ingroup identity (6.14–7.4)

The introductory section (6.14-16b)

Many, if not most, commentators regard 2 Cor. 6.14–7.1 as a later interpolation in the text of the letter, and possibly not even written by Paul. This scepticism is a symptom of the wider scholarly inclination to chop the letter up into its alleged constituent parts, an inclination which, as we will see, is as misguided here as it is in relation to other parts of the letter. The main reasons for regarding 6.14–7.1 as an intrusion are: (a) its alleged awkward positioning between 6.13 and 7.2, (b) a number of expressions said to be non-Pauline or in a concentration not attributable to Paul and (c) a view that it does not fit into the overall course of Paul's argument. I will critique (a) in the following text, cover (b) in the course of the commentary and, in conclusion, respond to (c) by explaining the importance of the passage to the case Paul is making in 2 Corinthians.

2 Corinthians 6.14-16b This opening passage confronts us with the foundational interest of social identity theory. For here Paul situates his Corinthian addressees in a context of pronounced ingroup/outgroup differentiation. He distinguishes between πιστοί (meaning those who have accepted Christ and his Gospel, as Paul preaches them), on the one hand, and ἄπιστοι (meaning everyone else, including his opponents) on the other. Paul foreshadowed such a differentiation in 4.4 and now offers a detailed expansion of the position. The whole point of the passage is to insist upon the impenetrable boundary that does and must exist between the believing ingroup and the unbelieving outgroup in relation to the dimensions mentioned. This point is sharpened by juxtaposing five pairs of stark contrasts between πιστοί and ἄπιστοι with a recognition that elsewhere in human affairs communication and amity is possible across some boundaries, as seen in the existence of partnership, fellowship, concord, participation and agreement.

That is to say, there are settings where such phenomena occur, but not as between πιστοί and ἄπιστοι. Webb's attempt (1993: 60-2) to connect these words of communication and partnership with the covenant and the second Exodus is an unconvincing aspect of a creative thesis devoted to explaining all of 2 Cor. 6.14–7.1 on that fragile basis. The Paul who could speak so negatively of the Mosaic covenant and law in 3.1-18 is hardly likely to be reviving them for positive use later in the letter, while Webb's thesis places impossible demands on the Corinthian Christ-followers' knowledge of Israelite scripture or, alternatively, asks them to accept the applicability to them of texts that could have application only to ethnic Judeans.

In his opening statement (v. 14a), Paul delivers a direct prohibition of breaching the ingroup/outgroup boundary and then follows this with five antitheses that justify it. That verses 6.14-15 contain a number of Pauline *hapax legomena* and allegedly non-Pauline ideas has led many commentators to regard the whole section 6.14–7.1 as a later intrusion in the letter, possibly not even by Paul. These claims rest on very shaky foundations mainly because words cognate with the *hapax legomena* do appear in Paul, because the character of what he was saying pushed him to reach for words he did not normally employ and because claims that certain expressions are said to be non-Pauline do not withstand scrutiny (Fee 1977: 144–7; Esler 2021d).

He is not suggesting in v. 14a that the Corinthians are already misyoked, but rather warning them against that outcome (Furnish 1984: 361). Although ἑτεροζυγέω, appearing here in the present participle, ἑτεροζυγοῦντες, meaning 'being misyoked', occurs nowhere else in the New Testament, its substantival antonym, σύζυγος, is employed by Paul in Phil. 4.3 in the sense of 'true comrade' (literally 'yoke-fellow'). The substantival form ἑτερόζυγος appears in Lev. 19.19, in the context of a commandment against interbreeding different types of cattle, so that it is being deployed in a context of intimate, sexual associations. Not surprisingly, therefore, Philo deploys Lev. 19.19 against unlawful connections of a sexual type (*Special Laws*, 3.46). By contrast, ἑτερόζυγος is not employed in Deut. 22.10 where using an ox and an ass *to plough together* is prohibited. Whether Paul's Corinthian addressees would have appreciated the specific sexual reference of the one biblical verse where ἑτερόζυγος appears, especially when on its face it appears to relate merely to a shared activity involving close proximity in positive sense (here, ploughing), is highly unlikely. It is far more likely that they would have understood Paul as warning them broadly against a range of close associations with the wrong people. Nevertheless, Paul has a little earlier (2 Cor. 6.6) mentioned purity (ἁγνότης) first in a list of his personal qualities, and that may have triggered Lev. 19.19 in his recollection.

Although Paul designates the outgroup as 'unbelievers' (ἄπιστοι), determining whom he has in mind by that expression is a disputed issue. The word ἄπιστοι appears earlier in this letter, in 4.4. As I have observed earlier in this volume, Paul is there responding to charges that have been made against him, including that he falsifies the word of God (4.2), in a way that coincides with his implying that such behaviour is precisely what characterizes his opponents, as he will later elaborate upon in chs 10–13. In making his case in 4.2, Paul invokes every conscience of *human beings* (ἄνθρωποι) and thus impliedly encompasses members of all ethnic groups and, necessarily, Greeks, like the Corinthians, and Judeans. Then follows 4.3-4 with its statement that the god of this age has blinded the minds of the unbelievers (ἄπιστοι) to prevent them from seeing the light of the glory of the Gospel of Christ. In discussing 4.4, I concluded that the ἄπιστοι in that verse means all ἄνθρωποι, Judeans or non-Judeans, who fail to accept his Gospel and that this category therefore includes (idolatrous) Greeks, Judeans and Judean Christ-followers who do not accept his Gospel. In reaching this conclusion, his opponents are certainly to be included. After all, the god of this age (probably Satan) has blinded the minds of these unbelievers (4.4), and in 11.14-15 he will describe his opponents as the servants of Satan. A very similar understanding of ἄπιστοι has been reached by J. A. Adewuya (2001: 103) and Volker Rabens (2014). Webb, on the other hand, maintains an unconvincing interpretation of ἄπιστοι as 'non-Christians outside the church community' (1993: 199).[6]

In vv. 14b-16, Paul fashions an elaborate contrast between two realms akin to that implied in 2 Cor. 4.4. That contrast is expressed in five antitheses phrased as rhetorical questions assuming a negative answer: 'Can X have anything to do with Y?' The first antithesis (v. 14b) denies the possibility of righteousness (δικαιοσύνη) having any partnership (μετοχή) with lawlessness (ἀνομία). Righteousness is a reactive idea in Paul's letters, which he deploys when facing Judean opposition to this mission (Esler 1998: 153-9), but which he latches onto with great effect. Righteousness has already appeared three times in the letter. In 3.9 and 5.21, the word amplifies the identity of the redeemed Christ-movement communities. Its meaning in 6.7 is similar. It is a key identity-descriptor for Paul, especially as later in the letter he will speak of his opponents, servants of Satan, as disguising themselves as 'ministers of righteousness' (11.15). By including righteousness at a significant point in the list in 6.7 Paul announces his credentials in relation to this critical Christ-movement identity-descriptor; his prototypicality or exemplarity in this respect is central to his claim to leadership of the Corinthians. In view of the role of righteousness elsewhere in the letter, it is not surprising that it features at the beginning of what will be the great statement of Christ-movement identity that is 6.14–7.1. Its antonym is posited as ἀνομία, literally 'lawlessness', or 'iniquity', a word Paul will later use twice in Romans (4.7 and 6.19), in the latter case in conjunction with righteousness.

---

[6] For further details on this point, see Esler 2021d.

The second antithesis (v. 14c), 'What fellowship (κοινωνία) does light have with darkness?', is different in nature from the first. The word κοινωνία is quite common in Paul's letters.[7] Whereas the first antithesis provided substantive information about the two groups capable of observation in the course of human behaviour, the second really consists of employing the metaphors of light and darkness with the sole purpose of approbating the ingroup and derogating the outgroup without providing any details of either. Paul posited the same contrast between light and darkness earlier in the letter, in 4.3-6, so it is not surprising to find it here (Barnett 1997: 347).

The third antithesis, in v. 15a, asks, 'What concord (συμφώνησις) does Christ have with Beliar?' Although the word συμφώνησις only occurs here in Paul, σύμφωνος is found at 1 Cor. 7.5, while συμφωνία appears in Dan. 3.5 and 15 and 4 Macc. 14.3 and several times in Daniel Theodotion. Paul is looking for five abstract nouns meaning 'agreement', and the fact that he does not employ this word elsewhere is of little consequence in relation to his authorship of 2 Cor. 6.14–7.1. The word 'Beliar' is frequently found as a name for the devil in Judean extra-biblical literature, including the *Ascension of Isaiah* (passim), *Jubilees* (1.20) and the *Testaments of the Twelve Patriarchs* (*Reuben* 4 and 6; *Levi* 3, 19; *Daniel* 5). By Paul's time, Beliar was regarded as a Satanic spirit (Charles 1900: lvii). In the Hebrew Bible and in Hebrew texts from Qumran, the name appears as 'Belial', as in 11Q13 (or '11QMelch'), where he is described as the leader of the rebellious angels. In v. 15a, Beliar is probably another name, along with Satan (2 Cor. 2.11; 11.14; 12.7), for 'the god of this world' mentioned in 2 Cor. 4.4. This antithesis also develops the contrast between 'the god of this world' and Christ from earlier in the letter (4.4).

The fourth antithesis (v. 15a), 'What part (μερίς) does a believer (πιστός) have with an unbeliever (ἄπιστος)?', now makes explicit what was hitherto implied: πιστός as the opposite of ἄπιστος and therefore the designation of the ingroup. Ἄπιστος here has the same meaning as in 4.4 and the previous verse. The use of πιστός as a substantive is unique in Paul. Sometimes he uses πιστός of God (1 Cor. 1.9; 10.13; 2 Cor. 1.18; 1 Thess. 5.24) and sometimes of the trustworthy person (4.2, 17; 7.25) or of Abraham (Gal. 3.9), but always adjectivally.[8] Thus we have the πιστοί, here meaning those who have faith in Christ (as Paul understands it)[9] and the ἄπιστοι, who do not. The substantival

---

[7] Rom. 15.26; 1 Cor. 1.9; 10.16 (bis); Gal. 2.9; Phil. 1.5; 2.1; 3.10; Phlm. 6, and also in 2 Cor. 8.4; 9.13 and 13.13.

[8] Harris (2005: 503) comments that 'it was a natural development', on the analogy of ἄπιστος, for πιστός to come to be used substantively of a person who believed in Christ.

[9] Using different language but to very similar effect, Lambrecht (1999: 118) observes that '"Believer" is . . . a technical term for "Christian"'.

meaning of πιστός as 'believer' in 6.15 reappears later, in 1 Tim. 4:10, 12; 5.16, possibly inspired by that meaning here.

The fifth antithesis (v. 16a), 'What agreement (συγκατάθεσις) has the temple of God (ναὸς θεοῦ) with idols?', carries an explanatory statement (v. 16b) that needs to be read with it, 'For we are the temple of the living God . . .' which also points forward to what follows. Lim, in his fine treatment of the connection between Paul's use of metaphors and social identity, has argued (influenced by Lanci 1997) for seeing the pagan temples of Corinth as the context for this expression (2017: 140-8). Nevertheless, Paul clearly has the Jerusalem Temple in mind, given his use of the very Judean expression 'the living God' and the fact that the Temple was a central feature of Judean identity that his opponents must have been lauding among the Corinthians. The verbal form of the word συγκατάθεσις appears in Exod. 23.1, 32 and in Luke 23.51; it is unusual but Paul needs a fifth word meaning 'agreement' to maintain the pattern, and this is it. The contrast here is not quite so balanced as in the previous four antitheses; if it were, it would contrast 'the temple of God' with 'the temples of idols'. So two changes are introduced. The first is that the temple of God is personalized and now means 'us' (an idea he had already floated to the Corinthians in 1 Cor. 3.16-17). So this is a thoroughly Pauline idea. The reinterpretation of the Temple in this way shows how different Paul considered Christ-movement identity to be from Judean ethnic identity. The second change is that the entity posed as the opposite of God's temple consists of idols themselves, not a temple containing them. Yet the point is clear in spite of these two alterations to the pattern. Paul is excluding any association between (his) Christ-followers and idols, but without providing specific details of what that prohibition might entail.

6.16c-18: The biblical 'quotations'

2 Corinthians 6.16c-18 Verses 14-16b are followed by a catena of scriptural materials that is unique in 2 Corinthians. It is prefaced by the words 'just as God said' that are offered as a consequence of the statement in the fifth antithesis 'for we are the temple of the living God'. It is noteworthy that Paul makes no effort to identify the source of any of this material from the Septuagint; it has authority to the extent that it is what 'God said'. Although his addressees probably knew that such divine speech was to be found in Israelite scriptures, he does not tell them where and it is unsafe, as we will now see, to assume that they knew.

Making sense of this collection of biblical material necessitates taking a position in the current discussion in the field between researchers, inspired by Richard Hays' 1989 book *Echoes of Scripture in the Letters of Paul*, who consider that the context of scriptural echoes and quotations is important in interpretation, and those, especially represented in the writings of Christopher Stanley, who dispute this view. The position in this commentary is that if one is interpreting a Pauline letter in an attempt to discern what message Paul was seeking to convey to an *actual* audience in Corinth, as opposed to how he might have been understood by *implied* readers with extensive knowledge of the Septuagint, then Stanley's position is far more convincing (2004, 2008b). Paul's converts, admittedly, must have known he was a Judean and that Judeans possessed a substantial body of writing about their relationship with their God. On Stanley's view, moreover, Paul had probably explained certain broad features of Israelite scripture to the Corinthians (such as the story of Adam's fall, the Abraham narrative and certain key episodes in the Exodus narrative, as appear in 2 Corinthians 3) but illiteracy and lack of previous familiarity among non-Judean converts would have meant he could not possibly have expected them to understand points as fine as Hays and those influenced by him might notice. Moreover, as we will see, if the Corinthians had known the source of the quotations, they would have been thoroughly confused: What relevance to them were statements made in relation to Israel's return from Israel or of a promise that God made to Solomon? It is really enough for Paul simply for his audience to believe that God had uttered the statement he cites. To this extent this usage can be described as oracular (see Stanley 2004: 58; Eyl 2016; Esler 2021d).

2 Corinthians 6.16 Paul begins with this statement:

As God said, 'I will live and walk (ἐμπεριπατήσω) among them,
and I will be their God,
and they shall be my people'.

Webb argues that Paul had in mind Lev. 26.11-12 (LXX: 'And I will pitch my tent among you, and my soul will not abhor you, and I will walk [ἐμπεριπατήσω] among you. And I will be your God, and you will be my people') or Ezek. 37.27 (LXX: 'And my tent shall be among them, and I will be to them God and they will be to me my people') or both. According to Webb, 2 Cor. 6.14–7.1 is to be understood in the context of the new covenant and the second Exodus (1993: 33-40). But Ezek. 37.24-28 concerns the future re-establishment of Israel, under King David, on their land and observing God's laws, with God's dwelling place, that is, his temple, among them. This is a promise made to ethnic Israel and no one else. It could not have been Paul's interest as a leader seeking to communicate with his largely or totally non-Judean audience to draw their attention to a vision of future salvation from which they were necessarily excluded.

As it stands and understood as an oracular utterance, the alleged scriptural quotation in v. 16 serves to create an elevated identity for the members of the Christ-movement: it is they who are God's people, a statement that very much leaves the Judeans out in the cold as the old notion of Israel's election is, at the very least, heavily qualified if not jettisoned.[10] Not only that, but God dwells and walks among them, which also renders problematic the status of the Temple in Jerusalem.

2 Corinthians 6.17 The next verse bluntly reinforces the intergroup dimension of Paul's message:

> Therefore go out (ἐξέλθατε) from their midst
> and separate yourselves (ἀφορίσατε), says the Lord,
> and do not touch (μὴ ἅπτεσθε) anything/anyone unclean (ἀκαθάρτου);
> then I will welcome (εἰσδέξομαι) you.

Paul now informs the Corinthians that the God-chosen ingroup – the temple of the living God no less – exists among an outgroup from whom they must separate themselves. Being among them carries the risk of touching something or someone unclean (ἀκάθαρτον/ἀκάθαρτος); it is necessary to come out from among them to avoid such uncleanness. Commentators on this passage generally find Paul's inspiration in Isa. 52.11 (LXX):

> Depart (ἀπόστητε), depart (ἀπόστητε)! Go out from there (ἐξέλθατε ἐκεῖθεν)! Do not touch anything unclean (ἀκαθάρτου μὴ ἅπτεσθε); go out from her midst (ἐξέλθατε ἐκ μέσου αὐτῆς). Separate yourselves (ἀφορίσθητε), you who carry the vessels of the Lord. (Webb 1993: 40–3; Starling 2011: 67–9)

In Isaiah this passage is an exhortation to the Israelites to leave Babylon (as they once left Egypt) taking the Temple vessels with them, similar to the prophet's direction in Isa. 48.20. But even if Paul remembered the verse from Isaiah, it is unlikely that his addressees would have been able to identify it, or that he would have wanted them to. He also makes significant changes, for example by altering 'from out of her (that is, Babylon's) midst' (cities being regarded as feminine) to 'from out of their midst', with the plural pronoun linking the statement to the ἄπιστοι in v. 14. He generalizes the Isaianic passage, effectively erasing signs of its exilic provenance, so he can

---

[10] If it is jettisoned here, Romans 9–11 shows that Paul could not, in the end, deny to Israel election or the fulfilment divine promises and finally reached the (theologically satisfying) view that the Christ-movement and Israel would co-exist to the End.

deploy portentous biblical language in oracular fashion rather than evoking a picture of Israel departing from Babylon, which would only have confused his audience.

In this context, Paul probably meant the expression 'do not touch anything/anyone unclean (ἀκαθάρτου)' to have a wide scope that matches the similarly wide ambit of ἄπιστοι inv. 14 (and the ἄπιστος in v. 15). This extends to the practices of idolatrous neighbours, but must also be aimed at keeping away from Paul's opponents whom he presented as ministers of Satan. Confirmation of this interpretation comes from 7.1: 'Since we have these promises, beloved friends, let us cleanse (καθαρίσωμεν) ourselves from every defilement (μολυσμός) of the body (σάρξ) or spirit (πνεῦμα), making our holiness complete by the fear of God.' This suggests an ambit for what is unclean that embraces both the physical (things that can be touched) and the spiritual. For μολυσμός must designate the uncleanness of anyone who is not characterized by righteousness (δικαιοσύνη) but by lawlessness (ἀνομία), as mentioned in v. 14, and all who are under the power of Beliar as in v. 15.

The last statement in v. 17, with God still speaking (v. 16), is, 'And I will welcome (εἰςδέξομαι) you'. Commentators have sought to identify the specific biblical source for this statement, where εἰςδέξομαι has ὑμᾶς as its object. Webb notes six possibilities (1993: 44–5). But this is a fruitless quest, since the idea of God welcoming his people occurs very often in the Old Testament, either with 'them' or 'you'. The context here requires the second-person plural, and it cannot be attributed to a particular scriptural text. Paul simply adopts an expression often used of God to reinforce the theme of the close relationship between him and his people. There is no basis for attributing εἰςδέξομαι to any particular Old Testament text, such as Ezek. 20.34, which Webb chooses on account of its exilic setting (1993: 43–4).

2 Corinthians 6.18 Paul concludes these divine utterances with the following:

> I will be a father to you and you will be my sons and daughters (καὶ ἔσομαι ὑμῖν εἰς πατέρα, καὶ ὑμεῖς ἔσεσθέ μοι εἰς υἱοὺς καὶ θυγατέρας), says the Lord Almighty.

Most scholars believe that Paul was drawing primarily on 2 Sam. 7.14a for this statement (Webb 1993: 53). Here God tells David through Nathan that Solomon will build the Temple, before adding, 'I will be his father, and he shall be my son' (ἐγὼ ἔσομαι αὐτῷ πατέρα καὶ αὐτὸς ἔσται μοι εἰς υἱόν). This statement certainly provides the closest parallel of the possible sources that have been identified, the others being Isa. 43.6; 49.22; 60.4; Jer. 38[31].9; Hos.

1.10 (Webb 1993: 52). Yet this is not an exilic passage and offers no support to Webb's argument that Paul is evoking the exile in this passage. Moreover, the original context of the saying would have been completely irrelevant to the Corinthians, who would have been left scratching their heads wondering how a prophecy that it was to be Solomon who would build the Temple could possibly apply to them, and how it could be relevant to their lives if it did! If Paul did remember the source of this quotation, he has, rather, stripped it of its original reference and changed third-person singular pronouns to second-person plurals to make it suit his Corinthian audience in what was a decontextualized and oracular use of scripture.

The reason for Paul's inclusion of the statement in v. 18 as he sought to communicate with his Corinthian addressees has nothing to do with the Exile or the old covenant. It is related to the social identity of ingroup members. The social identity each of them derived from membership encompassed a cognitive dimension (the realization of belonging to *this* group, together with group beliefs), the emotional dimension (how they felt about belonging) and the evaluative dimension (how they rated themselves by membership of this group in distinction to that of other groups). Whereas in v. 16 he has resorted to the language of peoplehood (using λαός), he now uses the language of the dominant social institution in this world, that of kinship. Paul is reinforcing the intimate connection that exists between the almighty God, the Κύριος Παντοκράτωρ ('the All-Powerful Lord') and them: they are a family, with God their father and they his sons and daughters. This is highly charged language of belonging that certainly fosters the cognitive and emotional dimensions of their social identity and – even though it is unclear whether Paul means them to understand that they alone are God's sons and daughters (but he must include other Christ-believers who follow his Gospel) – the evaluative dimension as well.

2 Corinthians 7.1 Paul concludes this section by audaciously suggesting that the divine statements he has just 'quoted' represent promises to him and his Corinthian addressees (and Christ-followers loyal to his Gospel in other places).

> Since we have these promises (ἐπαγγελίαι), beloved friends, let us cleanse (καθαρίσωμεν) ourselves from every defilement (μολυσμός) of the body and spirit (σαρκὸς καὶ πνεύματος), making complete our holiness (ἁγιωσύνη) by the fear of God.

There are four divine promises in all: (a) that God will dwell and walk among them, (b) that He will be their God and they will be his people, (c) that he will welcome them (once they have separated themselves) and (d) that he will be their father and they will be his sons and daughters. These promises do not summarize the restoration theology of the exilic period, as Matera suggests (2003: 167). Paul did not intend the Corinthians to recognize the Exile here, and they were most unlikely to do so. Their original context in relation to ethnic Israel was irrelevant and would have confused the Corinthians. It was enough that these were divine statements and promises. He wanted to communicate a strong statement of identity for the ingroup, the πιστοί as opposed to the outgroup, ἄπιστοι, and he has selected from and modified Israelite scripture to do so. By asserting that they were the temple of the living God, he was proposing a means different from the Jerusalem Temple for God's being in the world, one that involved a non-ethnic group identity. The notion of holiness (ἁγιωσύνη) expresses the ultimate goal to which Paul refers, the exalted identity they will achieve once they have cleansed themselves, by separation from sinful outgroups.

Reiterative guidance (7.2-4)

2 Corinthians 7.2 Paul begins with a simple imperative, 'Make room for us (Χωρήσατε ἡμᾶς)', here meaning 'make room for us in your hearts' (see the aforementioned comment on 6.11). As previously argued, this signifies being receptive and responsive to Paul, not showing him love or affection. Consistently with this interpretation, he then excludes a number of possible modes of behaviour on his part that might persuade them not to do so: he has not wronged (ἠδικήσαμεν) anyone, corrupted (ἐφθείραμεν) anyone, exploited (ἐπλεονεκτήσαμεν) anyone. There is thus no reason why they should not be responsive to him, in particular by acting in a way he has suggested and of which he is prototypical. That this is the issue, not that they should be affectionate to him, as suggested by Thrall (1994: 480–1), for example, is confirmed by the next two verses.

There are strong connections, well explained by Matera (2003: 169), between the three critical words in the second clause of v. 2, just cited in Greek, and other parts of the letter. The verb used in his denial that he has not wronged anyone, ἀδικεῖν, reappears twice in 7.12 in relation to the offender and offended party, the former to be identified with the person mentioned in 2.5-11. Secondly, Paul's disavowal of having corrupted (φθείρειν) anyone may reflect a charge against him that he has corrupted people by the Gospel he preaches originating in the opponents he will excoriate in 2 Corinthians 10–13 but which he turns back on their heads in 2 Cor. 11.3-4. Thirdly, in denying that he has taken advantage (πλεονεκτεῖν) he employs a word that he later repeats in 12.17-18 when he asks if he or any of those he sent to the Corinthians had acted in this way towards them, a question obviously anticipating a negative reply. These connections provide further evidence for the integrated character of 2 Corinthians.

2 Corinthians 7.3 His discounting the idea that he is speaking to condemn them (πρὸς κατάκρισιν) indicates that such a notion might otherwise rise as an inference from what he has said. This confirms that the issue is their behaviour, not whether they are affectionate towards him or not, for it would be quite overbearing to condemn simply for not being affectionate towards him. As it stands, he has no complaints against them on this account.

When Paul states, 'for I have said before (προείρηκα γὰρ) that you are in our hearts, to die together and to live together', the reference can only be to 6.11: 'Our heart is open to you.' This observation further strengthens the case for 6.14–7.1 having formed part of his original conception of the letter, since it would be very odd to say προείρηκα of something mentioned only three verses earlier (on the assumption that 6.14–7.1 were not in the original text). His heart is open to them, and theirs must be open to him. This provides further evidence that the issue is not the expression of emotion but mutual receptivity and responsiveness. Thus, the mutuality that Paul was calling for in 6.12-13 now surfaces unambiguously in the statement that their being in his heart relates to their dying together and living together, thus evoking the partnership he affirmed in 1.24. His concern is mutual understanding and receptiveness, expressed in appropriate behaviour, not the expression of affection.

2 Corinthians 7.4 Verse 4, which is delivered in two pairs of stylistically similar assertions, brings 6.14–7.3 to a conclusion, while picking up themes earlier in the letter and providing a foundation for what is to come.

Great is my frankness towards you (πολλή μοι παρρησία πρὸς ὑμᾶς).
Great is the honour I claim in respect of you (πολλή μοι καύχησις ὑπέρ ὑμῶν).
I am filled with comfort (παράκλησις) and
I am overwhelmed with joy (χαρά) in all our affliction (θλῖψις).

The frankness (παρρησία) he mentions reasserts that quality which he explicitly claimed at 3.12 and, more importantly here, in 6.11, and also embodied in how he addresses them in 6.14–7.1 (Harris 2005: 519-20). The notions of comfort and joy also call to mind the related material in 2 Corinthians 1–2, including 1.24.

At the same time, however, in the second clause in v. 4 Paul is paving the way for his return to the autobiographical narrative of 7.5-16 he left off at 2.13. Thus, παράκλησις (or the verbal form παρακαλεῖν) appears in vv. 6, 7 and 13 and χαρά (or the verbal form χαίρειν) appears in vv. 7, 9, 13 and 16.

The verb θλίβω recurs in v. 5; indeed, in this verse it immediately takes up its cognate noun θλῖψις, which was the penultimate word in v. 4. The style of language use in v. 4 is also typical of Paul and should be not attributed to a redactor covering his tracks (Thrall 1994: 484). All of this indicates that Paul himself (not some unknown interpolator) is responsible for the intercalation of 2.14–7.4 (Esler 2021d).

10

Paul, Titus and the Corinthians (7.5-16)

2 Corinthians 7.5-16

In 2 Cor. 2.5-11, Paul provides the reasons for his having sent the severe letter to the Corinthians. In Chapter 5 of this volume, I set out a social identity approach to deviance to provide a theoretical framework for considering the relevant issues and then it applied to 2 Cor. 2.5-11. As noted during that discussion, Paul provides the balance of the material on this subject in 2 Corinthians 7. In 2 Cor. 2.12-13, Paul had related how he arrived in Troas to preach the Gospel, and, although a door was opened for him in the Lord, he could not rest because Titus was not there, so he had journeyed on to Macedonia. He returns to this narrative in 2 Cor. 7.5-16, by recounting his arrival in Macedonia and the difficulties he experienced there, which were assuaged by the coming of Titus and the good news he brought from Corinth. This good news subsisted in the positive reaction that his letter had engendered among the Corinthians. Presumably, Paul had asked Titus to deliver the painful letter to the Corinthians and had been anxiously looking forward to meeting him to learn of their response. This passage brings to an end the whole question of the ἀδικία that had prompted him to send the severe letter.

The arrival of Titus in Macedonia (7.5-7)

In these verses, Paul relates how his initial disappointment when he arrived in Macedonia only to discover Titus was not there (7.5) was turned to comfort and joy when he arrived with good news of the Corinthians' reception of the letter (7.6-7).

2 Corinthians 7.5 The first-person plural, ἐλθόντων ἡμῶν, may refer to Paul alone or it could indicate that one or more Christ-followers made the journey with him. Even if the latter, his focus immediately shifts to himself, by referring to his σάρξ that had no rest (ἄνεσις). By σάρξ, Paul probably has in mind not 'body' but 'the entirety of his person' (Thrall 1994: 488), which is also the meaning of πνεῦμα in 2.13, given the similar situations in 2.13

and 7.5 and the linkage of πνεῦμα and σάρξ to ἄνεσις in each case. Paul had no rest because 'outwardly there were disputes and inwardly fears' (ἔξωθεν μάχαι, ἔσωθεν φόβοι). The word μάχαι, used only here by Paul, conveys in the plural the meaning of conflicts without weapons, hence 'disputes', 'quarrels' or 'strife' (BDAG 622). These disputes were probably with outsiders, since he nowhere evinces any dissatisfaction with Macedonian Christ-followers and praises some of them, in Macedonia generally (2 Cor. 8.1-5). On the other hand, he had been shamefully treated, probably by outsiders, in Philippi in the past (1 Thess. 2.2). Paul's fears, on the other hand, would have included his fear for the safe arrival of Titus and apprehension at how his severe letter had been received by the Corinthians.

2 Corinthians 7.6 This is the first of two verses that demonstrate Paul's immense relief that the Corinthians had become reconciled to him as a result of his 'severe letter' (Barnett 1997: 371). In v. 6, Paul picks up the theme of comfort that is so prominent in 2 Corinthians 1–2. In particular, he comes close to repeating the image of God in 2 Cor. 1.4 as the God of all comfort. As numerous commentators note, Paul may have had in mind or was unconsciously recalling Isa. 49.13 (LXX): 'God has shown mercy to his people and has comforted (παρεκάλεσεν) the lowly ones (τοὺς ταπεινούς) amongst his people.' Yet it is fanciful to suppose that his audience would have recognized the allusion, still less that their attention would have been drawn to the exilic context of that verse, which would merely have confused them (see on 6.16-18 mentioned earlier). Ταπεινός occurs here and in 10.1 (and only elsewhere in Paul in Rom. 12.16), while the verb ταπεινόω is found in 2 Cor. 11.7 and 12.21 and nowhere else in Paul. The adjective, which reflects the centrality of honour and shame in ancient Mediterranean culture, has three main meanings: (1) 'of low social status', 'lowly', 'undistinguished' 'of no account'; (2) being servile in manner, subservient, abject'; and (3) 'unpretentious', 'humble' (BDAG 989). The first meaning is found in 7.6. In 10.1, however, Paul uses the word in the second meaning. The verb usually means 'to humble' or 'to humiliate' and carries that meaning in 11.7 and 12.21.

2 Corinthians 7.7 Here the language of comfort, but now passing from the divine to human realm, continues, as Paul explains that he drew comfort not merely by the arrival of Titus but by the Corinthians putting into practice, for the benefit of Titus, the comforting that Paul had earlier noted they had developed with his help (1.6-7): comfort now passes from the Corinthians, to Titus and then to Paul. We learn that the comfort Paul gained, and that led him to rejoice all the more, was derived from three aspects of the Corinthians' reaction to the letter: 'your longing (ἡ ὑμῶν ἐπιπόθησις), your mourning (ὁ ὑμῶν ὀδυρμός), your zeal (ὁ ὑμῶν ζῆλος) for me'. The repetition of ὑμῶν in each case emphasizes the closeness of the relationship between him and them. The longing mentioned can only be for Paul; the word will reappear, with 'zeal', in 7.11. This is the only Pauline use of ὀδυρμός, and the only other New Testament instance is Matt. 2.18 (from Jer. 38.15 [LXX]): 'A voice was heard in Ramah, wailing (κλαυθμός) and lamentation (ὀδυρμός).' It has a strong meaning and may suggest repentance for a wrong action. In context, it probably means their 'mourning' or 'grieving' over recent events that had distressed Paul, in particular their failure to act against the wrongdoer before the 'severe letter' arrived.[1] Although Paul has not previously deployed the words ἐπιπόθησις and ζῆλος in relation to his feelings for the Corinthians, he has come very close in stressing his love for them in 2.4, a sentiment he will repeat in 11.11 and 12.15, and he will use ζῆλος of his feelings for them in 2 Cor. 11.2. These features provide some basis for Harris (2005: 531), following Denney (1894: 778–89), seeing in the Corinthians' reaction to Paul a hint of 'a splendid new complementarity': the feelings he had for the Corinthians, the Corinthians now feel for him. Yet it is more accurate to view the reciprocity as renewed, rather than new – as he rebuilds his relationship with them – and as essential to Paul's task of strengthening his leadership credentials among the Christ-movement in Corinth.

Nothing in 7.7 provides evidence that the ἀδικία had something to do with Paul personally. Although his letter has elicited strong reactions from the Corinthians, their recognition that he was right in rebuking them by letter for their failing to address some wrongdoing in their midst unconnected with himself provides a perfectly adequate explanation for their emotions. In addition, although when Paul mentions their 'zeal *for me*' he is lapsing back into the first-person singular, and this continues through to v. 12 (Furnish 1984: 387), that transition is explicable on the same basis.

The reaction of the Corinthian Christ-followers to Paul's severe letter (7.8-13)

2 Corinthians 7.8 In this verse Paul begins to explain why he was joyful. Because of its difficult syntax, it is worth quoting in full[2]:

Because even though (Ὅτι εἰ καί) I caused you sorrow (ἐλύπησα ὑμᾶς) with my letter, I do not regret it (μεταμέλομαι). Although I did regret

---

[1] If Paul himself was the victim, which is not the view taken in this commentary, one could add to this factor sorrow for their disloyalty to him (Harris 2005: 530).
[2] This verse also has a difficult textual issue, namely whether to read βλέπω γάρ, βλέπω or βλέπων; I will follow the first option; see Thrall 1994: 490–1).

(μετεμελόμην) it, for I see that letter did cause you sorrow (ἐλύπησεν ὑμᾶς) even if (only) for a time).

Earlier in the letter (2.4) he stated that he sent the letter in the midst of abundant tears not that they might be caused sorrow (λυπηθῆτε), but that they might know the overwhelming love he had for them. Now he concedes that he did cause them sorrow. The concentration of the words λυπεῖν and λύπη in 2 Corinthians 2 (four and three instances, respectively) recurs here in connection with the same subject, his sorrowful letter (six and two instances).

Paul could only have learned of the Corinthians' sorrowful reaction to his severe letter from Titus. Presumably he felt regret for a time in Macedonia (μετεμελόμην is in the imperfect) after Titus had arrived, but that regret had faded by the time he was writing 2 Corinthians (Lambrecht 1999: 120; Harris 2005: 535; Guthrie 2015: 376–7).

2 Corinthians 7.9 Paul rejoices because they, in accordance with God's will, suffered sorrow that led to repentance (μετάνοια) and experienced no loss because of him. Here μετάνοια refers not to their initial conversion, but to their change of attitude towards Paul in a positive direction, and to their whole mentality, in response to their receipt of his severe letter about the perpetrator of ἀδικία (Lambrecht 1999: 130). Repentance on the part of the Corinthians necessitates that they had done some prior wrong. That is to say, the Corinthians' attitude towards the wrongdoer had a culpable dimension in relation to which Paul sought and obtained repentance from the Corinthians. But what was their wrong? It is highly likely that it consisted of their either having permitted the perpetrator to act with ἀδικία in the first place or in their having taken no action against him when he did. The latter option is far more likely, since it is deducible from 2.5-9 and 7.11, while there is no evidence suggesting the former. That culpability subsisted in their tolerating his misbehaviour until they had received the severe letter from Paul and repented. Their (initial) toleration of misbehaviour, but in another area, is what he is also going to accuse the Corinthians of in 2 Corinthians 10–13; in this respect there is a structural similarity in the two situations.

Later in the verse, Paul, having just admitted (v. 8) that he caused them sorrow, begins the task of involving God as a causative factor in that sorrow: he says, 'you were grieved in accordance with God's will', a connection he will repeat in vv. 10 (κατὰ θεὸν λύπη) and 11(τὸ κατὰ θεὸν λυπηθῆναι). At this point Paul is giving expression to an instance of what J. L. Martyn has called 'apocalyptic antimonies' (1997: 114), here the opposing two ways in which the Corinthians might grieve. Seifrid accurately notes, 'Their grief was caused by God and rested in his hand' (2014: 309). This is important for how we understand the loss they avoided suffering, in relation to which we glean more from v. 10. The ultimate source for Paul's positive understanding of grief and comfort (unlike the negative view of grief held by Stoics such as Epictetus) is likely to be Israelite tradition, as embodied in texts such as Lamentations 1 and 2 and Second Isaiah (Kaplan 2011).

In v. 9, 'because of us' (ἐξ ἡμῶν) is probably an allusion to Paul's sending of the letter (Harris 2005: 537). But what did Paul mean to convey by (ἐν μηδενὶ) ζημιωθῆτε, '(in no way) did you experience a loss'. Alternative translations for ζημιωθῆτε exist, especially 'suffer harm' (e.g. Harris 2005: 537) and 'suffer damage' (e.g. Thrall 1994: 427–8). The issue carries some weight, since these latter two options are possible outcomes of severe disciplining or punishment, but 'experience loss' far less so.

Although in the LXX the verb ζημιόω can mean 'punish' in a general sense (Prov. 17.26; 19.19; 21.11; 22.3), and the related noun ζημία can carry the same meaning (Prov. 27.12), it can also mean make a payment under legal compulsion, that is, sustain a legally compelled loss (the verb: Exod. 21.22; Deut. 22.19; 1 Esdras 1.36; the noun: 2 Kings 23.33; 1 Esdras 8.24). In the New Testament, however, the five instances of the verb additional to the one in question and the four instances of the noun all refer to suffering a loss, never to punishment, nor to harm or damage for that matter. Thus, in the two other Pauline instances where it occurs, ζημιόω means 'to suffer loss', as opposed to harm or damage (1 Cor. 3.15; Phil. 3.8). In the three other instances of the verb in the New Testament (Mt. 16.26; Mk 8.36; Lk. 9.25: loss of one's life), it has the same meaning. In the two instances of ζημία at Phil. 3.7 and 8, the word means 'loss' as opposed to gain (κέρδος), not 'harm' or 'damage'. The remaining two instances of this noun in the New Testament are in Acts 27.10 and 21 and here, again, the meaning is 'loss', in relation to the cargo on a boat and the lives of those on board. Accordingly, Pauline and other New Testament usage strongly favours this meaning here, and there is little justification for translating the verb to mean 'suffer harm' or 'suffer damage'.

This is a significant result in assessing Paul's attitude to the Corinthians expressed by this word. The word requires that on Paul's view, because they experienced godly grief, they did not suffer a loss in consequence of his sending the letter, even though he does not specify what sort of loss this might have been. This meaning for the word rules out the implication that he could have disciplined them severely if they had not responded positively, this latter possibility being noted by Thrall (1994: 492). Perhaps by his acting in such a way that they were deprived of something, by causing them to lose something, Paul could be exercising authority over them, but is this 'discipline'? In this letter, he indicates his intention to exercise discipline negatively: 'I will not spare' (οὐ φείσομαι; 13.2; also cf. 1.23). Yet it remains unclear as to what loss the Corinthians avoided. Suggestions include: Paul's decision not to return to Corinth (Héring 1967: 55); the forfeiture of future reward but not salvation (cf. 1 Cor. 3.14-15; Hughes 1962: 270); or the forfeiture of 'the rewards of the next life and their salvation' (Garland 1999: 355). Fortunately, an indication of what they did not lose because of his letter appears in the next verse.

2 Corinthians 7.10 Godly grief (κατὰ θεὸν λύπη) brings about a repentance that leads to salvation (σωτηρία), while worldly grief (τοῦ κόσμου λύπη) produces death. Accordingly, v. 10 specifies what the Corinthians did not lose as result of (the godly grief they experienced upon receipt of) Paul's letter: salvation (σωτηρία), which confirms Garland's view just mentioned. As noted earlier, not only do all other New Testament examples of ζημιόω involve loss but also in some of them the subject of the loss was life itself (Mt. 16.26; Mk 8.36; Lk. 9.25; Acts 27.10, 21). In v. 10, in developing the argument, Paul draws upon this probable meaning for ζημιόω. In this verse, Paul suggests two possible responses by the Corinthians on receipt of his letter: one would have been to plunge into worldly grief (presumably one that entailed no reconciliation with Paul) that would have led to their 'death', while the other (fortunately the response evinced by the Corinthians) was to experience godly grief leading to repentance and thence salvation. It was salvation – like life, the opposite of death – that the Corinthians could have lost by virtue of Paul's letter (ἐξ ἡμῶν; v. 9).

2 Corinthian 7.11a Paul details the reaction fuelled by their embracing godly grief in quite an emotional manner, both in the content and in the rhetorical structuring he employs:

> Just look at what (πόση) earnestness (σπουδή) this godly grief has brought about in you: what concern to clear yourselves (ἀπολογία), what indignation, what alarm, what longing, what zeal, what infliction of punishment (ἐκδίκησις)!

Here seven words are used to describe the Corinthians' response, beginning with πόση ('what, how great') preceding σπουδή ('earnestness'), the first of them, and the remaining six listed in staccato fashion, and in each case preceded by ἀλλά, meaning 'but also' or 'not only that' (Lambrecht 1999: 131). Their earnestness is not to be construed as the first in a list of seven elements of how they reacted. Rather, it serves as a general, umbrella statement of their reaction, followed by six specific dimensions. We know this not so much because of the transition from πόση to ἀλλά as intensifying expressions (although that is instructive), but because Paul introduces σπουδή again in v. 12, as a way to summarize their response.

Analysis of the six delineated aspects gives us reason to believe that they are posed roughly in the order that the severe letter elicited them from the Corinthians, although 7.15 states that they 'received' (ἐδέξασθε) Titus with 'fear and trembling', and this response probably covers both the time of his arrival and their attitude towards him thereafter (Harris 2005: 551). I will argue in the following text, in relation to 11b, that all seven of these characteristics contribute to Paul's estimation of the Corinthians as being ἁγνοί, which means that all of them must have a positive connotation as applied to the Corinthians, and I will assume that view here – in discussing the individual characteristics – pending my argument in the following.

Ἀπολογία comes a significant first in the list. It is the word for a defence mounted in legal proceedings (see Acts 25.16 and 2 Tim. 4.16) but it is also regularly used of a defence in a general sense, as employed by Paul himself in 1 Cor. 9.3 (personal defence) and in Phil. 1.7, 16 (defence of the Gospel) and with similar meaning in Acts 22.1 and 1 Pet. 3.15. There is no reason why the word could not have the meaning of a general defence here, although most commentators interpret it to mean 'concern to clear yourself' or similar expression. Its use certainly suggests that he had laid some charge against the Corinthians, probably in the letter but possibly also through Titus personally. In 1 Cor. 9.3, Paul uses the word in response to people who were interrogating him, obviously with a view that something he had done required a response. So we can imagine Titus arriving, with Paul's letter, and subjecting the Corinthians to a similar type of interrogation. Most commentators think the charge concerned a challenge to Paul's authority (e.g. Harris 2005: 542; Welborn 2011). As we have already argued, there is a paucity of evidence that the offence in question was against Paul. Whatever the charge, the Corinthians offered a defence. Now defence does not have to be effective to be a defence. Here, clearly, it was not fully effective, since they were soon reduced to grief and thence repentance. The Corinthians had a case to make, but recognized that it did not fully exculpate them. Nevertheless, that a defence can be made at least provides some justification for a course of action or inaction, and it is better that it be heard than not.

Ἀγανάκτησις, meaning 'indignation', occurs only here in the New Testament, although the verbal form appears seven times in the Synoptic Gospels. The word normally means to be indignant at someone or something else; the instance of the verbal form at Mark 14.:4 (ἀγανακτοῦντες πρὸς ἑαυτούς) is no exception, since it patently does not mean that the onlookers in the house of Simon the Leper in Bethany were indignant with themselves at the use of the spice but that they shared their indignation among themselves. Who were the Corinthians indignant at? Probably at the wrongdoer (as most commentators believe) because all of these characteristics must portray the

Corinthians in a good light. It is hardly likely that they were indignant at Paul and Titus for this reason and also because they were making their defence to the charge which they seemed to acknowledge had substance. It seems even less likely that they were indignant at themselves[3]; indeed, one would need proof that such a condition as self-indignation actually existed in the ancient world. Thus, having sought, albeit unsuccessfully, to give a favourable account of their conduct, the Corinthians now generate strong disapproval of the wrongdoer, perhaps on a 'better later than never' basis.

The third characteristic is φόβος ('alarm'). Presumably, having initially been relaxed about the wrongdoing, they came, either through the letter or Titus' explanations or both, to appreciate that it involved a breach of Christ-group norms and had placed them in some peril. The precise nature of the object of their fear is not, however, easy to determine (see Furnish 1984: 389; Thrall 1994: 494; Harris 2005: 542). Most probably, it was a fear that Paul might sever his connection with them. This is suggested by the fact that they 'received' Titus with fear and trembling (2 Cor. 7.15), which must embrace their first meeting with him, when he arrived with a letter from Paul. Alternatively, perhaps they feared that Paul might turn up to discipline them (perhaps with a 'rod' as in 1 Cor. 4.21); after all, if he spared them by sending a letter (1.23-2.4), perhaps he would revert to punishing them if the letter proved ineffective. Later in the letter (13.1-3) he reanimates the threat of his punishing them. This alarm could have related to their realization that the situation was a serious one requiring their attention, a possibility that requires more consideration than it receives, although Furnish suggests the most likely fear was 'a general state of apprehension (cf. *NEB*) and nervous concern' (1984: 389).

Listed fourth and fifth are ἐπιπόθησις and ζῆλος, which mean longing and zeal. Here we observe a shift of focus from the negative potential of the relationship to the positive. The longing and zeal are probably for Paul, since he mentions both features as characterizing the Corinthians' feelings for him in 2 Cor. 7.7 (Furnish 1984: 389). A more natural position for zeal in the list, if it meant zeal for taking action against the offender, would have been after 'indignation'.[4]

Sixth, and last, is infliction of punishment (ἐδίκησις). This word and the verb it comes from (ἐδικεῖν) are very common in the Septuagint, with the

---

[3] As Matera 2003: 176 and Harris suggest 2005: 542, with both also saying that indignation at the offender is also possible.
[4] Garland (1999: 357) mentions various objects of their zeal and fixes on the Corinthians' attention to the disciplinary matter, but without mentioning the closely relevant instance in v. 7. Meyer (1879: 333) regarded the zeal as a reference to their attitude towards the offender.

noun appearing six times in the New Testament and verb nine times. Paul employs the verb at Rom. 12.19 and 2 Cor. 10.6 and the noun here and at Rom. 12.19. The noun means the meting out of justice, frequently with the more precise meaning of punishment or retaliation for harm done, hence 'vengeance' (BDAG 301). This must refer to what they did to the wrongdoer, punishment Paul previously referred (in 2.6) to as ἐπιτιμία (Garland 1999: 357; Guthrie 2015: 381). No doubt this was what Paul wanted to result from his sending the severe letter, and, with this final word, he indicates that he was successful.

2 Corinthians 7.11b For reasons explained in the following, the last clause in 7.11 weighs heavily upon the interpretation of the whole letter: 'In every respect (ἐν παντί) you showed (συνεστήσατε) yourselves ἁγνοὺς εἶναι τῷ πράγματι.' The major critical issue thrown up by v. 11b is to explain the meaning of ἁγνοί. While its precise meaning will be considered in the following – with 'pure' or 'innocent' being the main options – the problem with these or any other translation is how to reconcile the very positive nature of whatever is here being predicated of the Corinthians with the fact that Paul has just asserted (in vv. 9–10) that their grief had led to repentance (μετάνοια). How could they be ἁγνοί in every respect if they had done something in the recent past of which they had now repented. Furthermore, if we wish to maintain the unity of 2 Corinthians, how are we to reconcile what Paul says about the Corinthian Christ-followers here with the (relatively, I will argue) negative things with which he taxes them in chs 10–13? The alleged inconsistency between Paul's attitude to the Corinthians here and in the final four chapters is one of the standard arguments used by those arguing that the letter is a composite. Answering these questions depends upon determining the context of συνεστήσατε, the ambit of ἐν παντί, the meaning of ἁγνοί εἶναι and the reference of πρᾶγμα.

Thrall notes three possible solutions to the alleged inconsistency between the Corinthians having been grieved into repentance (7.9) and the statement (7.11) that they proved themselves to be ἁγνοί in the matter, ἁγνοί regularly being translated as 'innocent' or 'guiltless' (1994: 495). First, Paul is referring to 'their state consequent upon receiving the letter and their favourable response to it' (suggested by Bachmann, Plummer and Martin). But she finds that 'this is not the natural way of understanding ἁγνοὺς . . . τῷ πράγματι', although without saying why. She then notes that the second alternative is possible: that ἐν παντί ('in every respect') is not to be taken too literally. But she comes down in favour of the third, tied to her own theory that the Corinthians were not guilty of the original deed which caused the problem (which is the πρᾶγμα of which they are ἁγνοί in every respect), on her view some financial misdemeanour, but only of failing to investigate the matter.

The first option, which Thrall rejects, is likely to be the correct one. The aorist tense for συνεστήσατε ἑαυτούς, 'you showed yourselves', is the tense used for every verb in this account of their interaction with Titus; Paul has in mind this particular occasion in the past (Barrett 1973: 212). Here the verb carries the meaning of providing 'evidence of a personal characteristic or claim through action', 'to demonstrate' or 'to show' (BDAG 973). But there was an audience for that demonstration, namely Titus, whom the Corinthians received with fear and trembling (v. 15) and set his heart at rest (v. 13). After the succession of seven named dimensions of their response to Paul's letter in v. 11 that the Corinthians expressed to Titus, the natural way to take ἐν παντί at the start of this clause is, 'in every respect', meaning those just mentioned.

The meaning of ἁγνοὶ εἶναι is highly significant. 'Innocent' is the most popular translation for ἁγνοί. Thus, Furnish, similar to many commentators, observes, 'In the context of 11:2 this same adjective (*hagnos*) describes the chastity of the bride, but here it has a more general (and probably legal) meaning: *innocent of alleged wrong*' (1984: 389). One must wonder whether so disregarding the meaning of the word in its only other occurrence in 2 Corinthians when it is uncommon in Paul (appearing only elsewhere in Phil. 4.8, where it also means 'pure') is a sound exegetical step. After all, its nominal form ἁγνότης occurs in 2 Cor. 6.6 (where it plays a very important role) and in 11.3 and nowhere else in Paul, or the New Testament for that matter. The use of ἁγνότης of Paul himself at 6.6 is matched by his message to the Corinthians in 6.14–7.1, which culminates in 7.1 with an invocation to keep themselves pure from all pollution and to bring about holiness (there using the noun ἁγιωσύνη) in fear of God (as discussed earlier in commenting on 7.1). Had Paul wanted to say that they were innocent – in the sense that they were never culpable for what happened – he could (and should) have used a word like ἀναίτιος. In the LXX, it appears four times in Deuteronomy (19.10, 13; 21.8, 9) and once in Susanna 62, always in connection with 'blood'. In the New Testament, it occurs in Matt. 12.5 and 7, unconnected with blood. Another possibility would have been ἀθῷος (which is very common in the Septuagint, and not just in connection with blood, while also appearing Matt. 27.4 and 24, of innocent blood). But Paul deploys another word entirely: ἁγνός, a word that appears in two other places in his letters. In 2 Cor. 11.2, it is used of the Corinthians as a chaste/pure virgin presented to Christ who is her one husband. In Phil. 4.8, of whatever is pure in a general sense. All other New Testament instances of the word have the meaning 'pure' (1 Tim. 5.22; Tit. 2.5; Jas 3.17; 1 Pet. 3.2; 1 Jn 3.3). The use of ἁγνός in 2 Cor. 7.11 conveys the meaning that at that time, by reason of what they said and the dispositions in favour of Paul that they exhibited to Titus, they were pure. It does not suggest that they were guiltless in the matter all along. Moreover, that Paul uses the present infinitive, εἶναι, instead of the aorist, γενέσθαι, with ἁγνοί strengthens the case that Paul was saying to the Corinthians that 'you are now pure', not that 'you were (always) pure' (Bachmann 1909: 304; Allo 1956: 198-9; Harris 2005: 543). There is, accordingly, no inconsistency between the idea that they were grieved into repentance for how they had acted initially and the purity they subsequently manifested, in the presence of Titus, in relation to the matter.

In this context, the statement that they showed themselves pure in the matter represents Paul's commending them for having acted in response to his severe letter in a way that typified the identity he had just set out for them in 6.14–7.1. It is difficult to find any commentator who has sought to relate the purity attributed to the Corinthians in 2 Cor. 7.11 with the purity Paul exhorts them to embody in 6.16–7.1. This neglect is one of the baleful consequences of the widespread view that 6.14–7.1 is not an integral part of the letter.

The argument so far on 7.11 has a bearing on the proper interpretation of πράγμα at the end of the verse. Its two possible interpretations are: first, the whole issue of the ἀδικία, including the arrival of the letter with Titus and the Corinthians' response to it; and, secondly, only the events surrounding Titus' arrival with the severe letter and the response of the Corinthians to it. In favour of the former option, Lambrecht suggests (1999: 131) that it becomes evident in v. 12 that the 'matter' refers to 'the incident that was already dealt with in 2.5-11'. In favour, the second option is that when Paul starts v. 11b by stating, 'In every respect' (ἐν παντί) you have shown yourselves . . .' with no particle connecting this clause to 11a, the 'respects' in view are the seven characteristics he has just listed as categorizing their reaction. But since all of them relate to the Corinthians' reaction to the arrival of the severe letter with Titus, it is to that episode, and it alone, that πράγμα refers. While the former option is more likely, since it would be odd for Paul to truncate the earlier aspects of the ἀδικία from its resolution, not much turns on this for the reason that in either case Paul has placed a very definite limitation on the ambit of ἁγνοὶ εἶναι. It is this: at the time they considered Paul's letter with Titus, the Corinthians became pure in relation to either that particular interaction with him or the whole affair of the ἀδικία including this resolution, *but nothing else*. In particular, it simply cannot be argued (although numerous commentators make the attempt) that the fact that Paul has patched up this issue with the Corinthian Christ-followers means he has no other issues with them, such as will appear in chs 8–9 and 10–13. To repeat, Paul is not saying that they were ἁγνοὶ in all respects and an ancient reader would not have been that surprised to find another area where Paul was unhappy with the Corinthians in Chapters 10-13.

2 Corinthians 7.12 This verse represents something of a jump in Paul's thought. He now asserts that he wrote the (severe) letter, not on account of the wrongdoer (τοῦ ἀδικήσαντος) or the one who was wronged (τοῦ ἀδικηθέντος), but so that the Corinthians would manifest their earnestness (σπουδή) towards him, with σπουδή being repeated from v. 11, where it formed the first of the seven characteristics of the Corinthians' response. Thus, he is asserting that the consequence of the receipt of his letter was actually the purpose for which he wrote it. Presumably, he is retrospectively reinterpreting the letter's purpose in the light of its effects (Thrall 1994: 495).

From the designation of the culprit as ὁ ἀδικήσας and the victim as ὁ ἀδικηθείς in 7.12, we may be sure that at the time he is writing Paul regarded the behaviour as constituting ἀδικία. And this is almost certainly how he characterized it all along, since there must have been something deeply troubling to him about the man's behaviour to stimulate him to send the stern letter in the first place. What did Paul mean by ἀδικία? It would have been extremely helpful if the word had a very specific meaning for him, but it does not, since he treats it as being of rather general import. There are seven instances of the verb in his genuine correspondence (1 Cor. 6.7 and 8; 2 Cor. 7.2 and 12 [bis]; Gal. 4.12; and Phlm. 18), nine instances of the noun (Rom. 1.18 [bis] and 29; 2.8; 3.5; 6.13; 9.14; 1 Cor. 13.6; and 2 Cor. 12.13) and three instances of the adjective (ἄδικος) (Rom. 3.5; 1 Cor. 6.1 and 9). In a transitive sense (as in 2 Cor. 7.12), the verb covers meanings such as 'to do wrong', 'to treat someone unjustly', 'to cause damage to', 'to mistreat', 'to injure' (BDAG 20). While it is true that for Paul it can mean the sort of wrong, in the form of fraud, that can result in legal proceedings (1 Cor. 6.7 and 8; possibly also Phlm. 18), his use of the word at Gal. 4.12 ('You did me no wrong'), where in context it means 'to scorn' or 'to despise', reveals its breadth. The noun ἀδικία can mean 'wickedness' in general for Paul, as in the instances from Romans just cited, so we should not underestimate its force. His ironic use of the word in 2 Cor. 12.13 confirms rather than militates against its impact for Paul.

The wrongdoer (τοῦ ἀδικήσαντος) is the person referred to in 2.5-8, who is not named but is a male. The reference to the one who was wronged (τοῦ ἀδικηθέντος) makes clear what was unclear in 2.5-8, namely that the victim of the wrong was an individual male. I will now discuss the main proposals for the identity of the wrongdoer and his victim and then interpret this section of the text using the social identity approach to deviance set out in Chapter 2 and applied to 2 Cor. 1.23–2.13.

Explanations for the identity of the wrongdoer and his victim

The identity of the wrongdoer and his victim in 2 Corinthians 2 and 7 have been of keen interest since the second century CE.[5] During the Patristic

---

[5] For a history of scholarship, see Welborn 2011: Chapter 2.

period, many interpreters, with John Chrysostom being the most eminent of them, took the view that the wrongdoer was the man Paul charged with incest because he was sleeping with this father's wife in 1 Cor. 5.1-2. Tertullian argued against this but his view was rejected as allegedly tainted by Montanism (Welborn 2011, Chapter 2). Chrysostom's explanation, which found favour until the early nineteenth century, no longer has much traction in the commentaries for a number of reasons (Thrall 1994: 61–5). This traditional explanation assumed that the letter mentioned in 2 Cor. 2.3-4 and 7, 8, 12 was 1 Corinthians. There are, admittedly, some similarities of language between the two situations, but these are too general to carry much weight. The argument of Tertullian against the identification has now come to be accepted: he contrasted the punishment Paul ordered in 1 Corinthians 5, namely permanent exclusion from the Christ-group, with the far less serious punishment in 2 Corinthians 2, which looks merely like a temporary and reversible exclusion from membership or the privileges thereof (*De pudicitia* 13; PL 2, Cols. 1003-1005). Another argument against the traditional view is that once 1 Corinthians is eliminated as the severe letter, too much has happened, notably Paul had made another visit to Corinth, for it to be plausible that the ἀδικία in 2 Corinthians 2 and 7 concerned the same issue as the problem mentioned 1 Cor. 5.1-2 (which had, after all, presumably ended with the man's permanent expulsion). In spite of these drawbacks, the Patristic view at least entailed the consequence that Paul himself was not the victim of the ἀδικία.

Modern discussion of the matter begins with Friedrich Bleek in 1830 who proposed: (1) The severe letter was not 1 Corinthians but a now-lost letter written between 1 and 2 Corinthians; (2) Paul must have visited Corinth for a second time before the severe letter; and (3) during that second visit, a painful one, Paul was the subject of a grave insult by a member of the congregation (Welborn 2011: Chapter 2). The broad thrust of this position has been widely adopted (Bruce 1971: 164). Of particular interest is the particular version proposed by Larry Welborn (2011), that the wrongdoer was Gaius and he accused Paul of embezzlement.

A variation on this approach has been to argue that it was not Paul himself who was insulted, but one of his representatives, so that what was said represented a grave challenge to his apostolic authority (e.g. Allo 1956: 55–6, 62).[6]

While the first and second points in Bleek's position are highly probable, the major problem with the suggestion that it was Paul himself who was insulted

---

[6] Bleek offered this as an alternative option that he himself did not favour; he preferred a version of the 1 Corinthians 5 identification (Thrall 1994: 65; Welborn 2011: Chapter 2).

is the very strong impression Paul gives that he has heard of the ἀδικία at a distance; that is why he says he does want to make another severe visit (which would be his third) but decides to send a letter instead (2 Cor. 1.23–2.4). If the problem happened during his second visit, why did he not rectify the situation then? Why does he need to receive further word of it before deciding to act, and then only via severe letter? A far more natural reading is that a new problem has arisen separate from whatever precipitated the second visit, and Paul is loath to return to Corinth to sort it out. Another obstacle to the proposal that the wronged party was Paul is that the mention of the victim in the third person in 2 Cor. 7.12 meant that it was not him (Windisch 1970: 238; Allo 1956: 199; Thrall 1994: 496). Many scholars, however, argue that the third-person form can be explained and that the injured party was indeed Paul, with Larry Welborn having devoted a powerfully argued monograph to that view (2011). Harris, who also believes it is Paul, cites 2 Cor. 12.2-10 as evidence that Paul could objectify his own experience and speak of himself in the third person. Yet that passage is quite different, in that Paul is doing this to avoid the impression of 'boasting'. He has no such motivation for disguising the fact that he is the victim in the current passage. The popular idea that the injustice Paul suffered was defamation met its match when Theodor Zahn demonstrated in 1909 that ἀδικεῖν is not used in the LXX or the New Testament to mean 'to slander' or 'to insult'. It means to cause voluntary injury in a manner contrary to law. If the incident in question had involved slander or libel (of Paul or someone else), Paul would probably have employed ὑβρίζειν or λοιδορεῖν (Zahn 1977: 349).

Margaret Thrall has proposed a solution that avoids the pitfall of casting Paul as the aggrieved party (1994: 68–9). This is that when Paul visited Corinth for the second time, one of the community members entrusted him with the money he had gathered for the collection. This money was then stolen by another member whose identity Paul suspected. Paul accused him of the theft; he denied it, and the community was divided, inducing Paul to believe that some of them were cognisant of the affair. On this view, Paul himself was not the aggrieved party. Unable to persuade them to take action, Paul left Corinth and later wrote the severe letter, which moved the community to repentance. The main problem with this theory is that it is composed of several elements for which there is no evidence, and for this reason almost all commentators have rejected it. Its major flaws, however, are that it assumes that the problem occurred when Paul was in Corinth for his second visit and that an issue that he could not sort out in person he could later solve via a letter.

The view taken in this commentary is that aggrieved party was not Paul, but that the evidence is not sufficient to allow us to identify him or the wrongdoer. Nevertheless, by approaching the issue from a social identity perspective on deviance, we open up important issues in new way.

A social identity explanation

The first issue when addressing the question from a social identity point of view is whether the behaviour was regarded as deviant. Although in using the expressions ὁ ἀδικήσας and ὁ ἀδικηθείς in 7.12 Paul does not convey the impression that such a categorization of whatever the man had done was likely to be disputed, he is writing after he has sent his severe letter and Titus had reported back to him that the Corinthians had accepted his chastisement. At this point, therefore, he does not need to argue for the appropriateness of employing the verb ἀδικεῖν in relation to whatever had happened, but can just casually slip the word in. But this does not appear to have been how the Corinthians saw the matter originally. Social identity theory predicts that even if what the man did was a breach of group norms, some ingroup members are likely to be more relaxed about troubling behaviour than others (as with British and US people being more tolerant of abuse of prisoners in Iraq than citizens of other countries). At the very least, such a difference of opinion was evident in relation to the perpetrator here, with the Corinthians reacting to his behaviour much more tolerantly than Paul.

For Paul had written to them to do something about the man who committed ἀδικία and that can only mean that they were not minded to do so themselves. In other words, some, perhaps a majority of the Corinthians, must have been inclined to overlook the ἀδικία, or even to regard the behaviour in question as not constituting ἀδικία, even though in time they came to regret this view, since Paul will later say that by his letter they were grieved into 'repentance' (μετάνοια; 2 Cor. 7.9). This probably entailed their regret for having initially tolerated the man's behaviour to his victim after Paul had pointed out the breach of group norms it involved, together with consequent action on their part to punish the offender.

If they had been active parties to the ἀδικία, it is hard to see why Paul speaks of one offender (ὁ ἀδικήσας). When Paul says at 2 Cor. 2.5 that the man caused sorrow (albeit only to a certain extent) to all the Corinthian Christ-followers, that relates to the position after they had accepted Paul's chastisement in his severe letter. It is less likely that the man caused all of them sorrow at a time when some or most of them were tolerating his behaviour.

The second issue is how the group chooses to treat the offender once it has decided to view his behaviour as an infraction of its norms. In his painful letter, it should be noted, Paul must have addressed both this and the previous issue: he must have insisted, first, that the behaviour was a breach of their norms and, secondly, proposed an appropriate punishment. In relation to the second question, as well, the social identity perspective set out in Chapter 4 of this volume posited that deviant behaviour within a group might be interpreted differently by different members. This is, in indeed, what we deduce has happened in relation to the offender. If they thought he had done anything wrong, they certainly had not punished him for it. Paul considered he had done wrong and wanted him punished. The Corinthians agreed to go along with the idea of punishment. But it is unclear whether Paul specified exactly what punishment he had in mind or whether he left it up to the Corinthians. In the event, they were split on what to do. The majority (οἱ πλείονες; 2 Cor. 2.6) imposed punishment, which a minority appear to have regarded as insufficient. Yet even this punishment seems to have run the risk of overwhelming the man with sorrow (2 Cor. 2.7), so perhaps it entailed exclusion from the group. But now that Titus has reported back to him, Paul is in favour of their forgiving the man and reaffirming their love for him (2 Cor. 2.7-11).

The social identity perspective allows useful interrogation of this data, which does indeed speak of different views among the members and of the change of such views over time. But the theory goes further, to suggest that those who strongly identified with the group tend to be more relaxed about negative behaviour than people who have a lower level of identification. Yet the initial reaction of the Corinthians and Paul was to the opposite effect! This is not, however, an argument against the utility of the theory. There are no social laws, and the social identity perspective can only disentangle the social interactions in play and suggest what might be their outcomes. In the present case, the Corinthians, surely less identified with the group than Paul himself, took a tolerant view to whatever the man had done while Paul's reaction was severe. Moreover, over the course of time the situation changed to one predicted by the theory. While a majority of the Corinthians would have persisted with the punishment, Paul urged them to forgive the man and reaffirm their love for him.

In addition, also as predicted by the theory, it is likely that some communication may have occurred between the perpetrator and the Corinthians, both in the period prior to the arrival of Paul's letter and while Titus was present in Corinth. Paul's pastoral concern that the man not be overwhelmed with sorrow (2 Cor. 2.7) must be based on Titus reporting back to him that that was a possible outcome and some communication between the offender and the group would have been necessary for Titus to form this view. Even after Titus left Corinth, however, some group members probably continued to talk to the offender.

2 Corinthians 7.13 The use of the language of comforting in the first clause ('Therefore we are comforted' [παρακεκλήμεθα]) connects this statement with the intense concentration of this language in 2 Corinthians 1–2, especially 2 Cor. 1.5-7. Paul's concern at the start of the letter that there be commonality of comfort between himself and the Corinthians in the area of comfort is confirmed by his being comforted here. But Lambrecht goes too far in suggesting (1999: 131) that this verse gives one the impression 'that the relations between Paul and the Corinthians are good again', since Paul's focus here is upon the particular matter raised by the offender and the severe letter he had felt compelled to write in relation to him, as the rest of the verse confirms. This is not a statement covering the entirety of relations between Paul and the Corinthians.

The remainder of v. 13 makes clear that Paul is still concentrating on the same issue of the severe letter. It is noteworthy that the spirit (πνεῦμα) of Titus, where πνεῦμα is 'a human faculty, the seat of one's inward life, perhaps simply the self' (Thrall 1994: 497), had been set at rest by *all* the Corinthians, and (as we will see in v. 15) all had been obedient. For many commentators, especially those who promote the idea of 2 Corinthians as a composite of letter fragments, this makes the subsequent deterioration in relations reflected in 2 Corinthians 10–13 hard to understand. Yet this position fails to acknowledge how what Paul says here is restricted to the matter currently under discussion – of the instance of ἀδικία and his correcting the Corinthians' response to it – while in chs 10–13 he presses on to completely different aspects of their relationship (the principal one, of the interlopers, having been introduced in 2 Cor. 2.17). But certainly at this point Paul is at pains to stress the unanimity of the community in Corinth in relation to the joy they gave Titus connected to the matter then at hand. This is probably intended to counteract somewhat the fact that earlier (2.6) Paul's mention of a majority (whose view on the punishment of the offender he endorsed) implied a minority who thought it was not sufficient, although it should be noted that they may all have been obedient to Paul in believing that some punishment was necessary.

Also, this section is a prelude to the request that Paul is about to make that they become active in regard to the collection; it suited his purpose to end this material on a high note, namely by describing the uniformly warm reception Titus had received from the Corinthians when Paul was about to send him back to Corinth to take up the collection (8.16-17). We recall the view of John Turner (2005) that a leader must establish himself as a prototype of group identity to the satisfaction of the members of a group if he or she wishes to be able to deploy its resources effectively. This section of the letter is integral to Paul's chances of success in relation to the collection in chs 8–9, to which he will soon proceed.

Paul, Titus and the Corinthians (7.14-16)

2 Corinthians 7.14 Paul begins by saying, 'If I have made some honour-claim (κεκαύχημαι) to him (sc. Titus) about you, I was not put to shame (κατῃσχύνθην).' This statement nicely illustrates the inappropriateness of translating κεκαύχημαι as, 'If I boasted' (with virtually all translations and commentaries). In a culture where honour is such a pre-eminent value, an honour-claim is acceptable as long as there is a basis for making it; if the claim is subsequently falsified, only then is its maker shamed. That did not happen here, the reason being that what he had said to Titus (*about them*) was true (as shown by the positive manner in which the Corinthians responded to his severe letter), just as everything he had said *to them* was true. By this latter statement, Paul is probably referring to the entirety of his previous communications with them, personally or by letter, as well as seeking to defend himself against charges of insincerity current against him in Corinth as he writes this letter, charges that he answered in more detail in its earlier chapters.

This verse therefore necessitates that Paul had said something favourable to Titus about the Corinthians, for which he was at least partly responsible, before he had sent him off to deliver the severe letter. Perhaps it related to the likelihood that they would do the right thing, which must have meant at the very least acknowledging that the action in question breached the norms of the Christ-movement in which he must have instructed them. Accordingly, as Thrall notes (1994: 498), it is unlikely that the community in Corinth was then in open revolt against Paul, which makes it equally unlikely such a state could have been the context for chs 10–13 (*contra*, Harris 2005: 549).

2 Corinthians 7.15 The opening expression at the start of the verse: καὶ τὰ σπλάγχνα αὐτοῦ περισσοτέρως εἰς ὑμᾶς ἐστιν (literally, 'his inward parts are all the more for you') may be translated as 'His feelings for you grow'. Once again Paul is at pains to express their unanimity, this time in relation to their obedience (ὑπακοή), but here with reference only to their response to the severe letter. At the same time, he makes clear that Titus feels love for them, just as Paul has said he does earlier in the letter (1 Cor. 2.4). That Titus' feelings for them grow as he remembers the Corinthians' obedience requires us to conjure a scene in which Paul and Titus are discussing the matter after Titus had met Paul in Macedonia.

The phrase 'fear and trembling', used of the Corinthians' response to Titus, derives from the Septuagint where its usual reference is to the 'fear and dread' that is felt when faced with hostile action that is threatened by an opponent, and hence to anxiety about one's death.[7] Paul applies the expression to

---

[7] Furnish 1984: 391, citing Exod. 15.16; Deut. 2.25; 11.25; Jdt. 2.28; 15.2; Isa. 19.6; 4 Macc. 4.10, and Ps. 54[55].5 (in relation to death).

himself to describe his own anxiety in 1 Cor. 2.3 and to the Philippians (to encapsulate their approach to working for salvation) in Phil. 2.12. The fear and trembling with which they received Titus was related to the obedience of the Corinthians. This suggests that they knew that they were in the wrong on the matter and were apprehensive about Paul's response. This suggests a reasonably high level of apprehension and not just 'nervous anxiety to do (one's) duty' (Plummer 1915: 228). The notion of 'fear and trembling' is clearly relevant to the question of whether Paul exercised coercion over the Corinthians.

2 Corinthians 7.16 Paul concludes this section of the letter with a verse that has great significance for the interpretation of the letter, not least because of its bearing on the unity of the text: 'I rejoice that in every respect (ἐν παντὶ) I have confidence in you (θαρρῶ ἐν ὑμῖν).' Although it lacks a connective with what proceeds, its effect is to carry forward Paul's leadership aims in the letter by concluding the passage comprising 7.5-15 and by preparing his readers for what follows, in both 2 Corinthians 8–9 and 10–13. It is a remarkable sign of the tenacity of those discerning the partition of the letter that a verse that does so much to integrate its contents as this has been construed as providing ammunition for their cause. According to Furnish, for example (1984: 398), who translates the verse as 'I rejoice, because I have every confidence in you', 7.16 is 'a statement . . . which could hardly have stood in the same letter with the worried polemic of chaps. 10-13 (contrast, e.g., 10.6, 9-10; 11.2-3; 12.11, 16, 20-21)'. Thrall (1994: 501), citing in support of Plummer (1915: 228) and Windisch (1970: 242), states, 'Whilst the ἐν παντί might be something of an exaggeration, what he says here must exclude the possibility that chaps. 10-13, which express profound anxiety about the readers' state, belong to the same letter.' Nor, she says, can you get away from this by saying that θαρρῶ means 'be bold' (as in 10.1); with ἐν, as here, it means 'have confidence in'.

Before assessing the function of the verse in the light of the partitionists' case, the meanings of two expressions require examination. What, first, does Paul mean by θαρρῶ ἐν ὑμῖν? When not followed by a preposition (as at 2 Cor. 5.6, 8; Heb. 13.6), the verb θαρρεῖν means 'to be confident, courageous'. The Stoics (e.g. Epictetus) used the language of confidence in relation to death, and Epictetus used both θαρρεῖν and πεποίθησις, the latter also occurring in this letter, at 2 Cor. 1.15; 3.4; 8.22 and 10.2 (Barnett 1997: 268). With the preposition ἐν, θαρρεῖν probably means 'to have confidence in', whereas with εἰς it probably means 'to be bold towards' (BDAG 444). In 2 Cor. 7.16, accordingly, Paul is likely to be expressing his confidence in the Corinthians, whereas in 2 Cor. 10.1, where the verb is followed by εἰς (and expresses the opposite of being ταπεινός), it means 'be bold towards'. Many commentators take this view, with Garland being a dissenting voice to the effect that the expression θαρρῶ ἐν ὑμῖν at 7.16 also means 'I am bold with you', given that it balances the noun παρρησία 7.4 (1999: 361). Yet at 7.4 the word probably means 'confidence' rather than the alternative possibility 'boldness' (BDAG 781). That is, in both 7.4 and 7.16, Paul's joy is generated because he is confident in the Corinthians, not because of his boldness in confronting them. Were Garland's view correct, the use of θαρρῶ in the same sense in both 7.16 and 10.1 would constitute a strong point of connection between 2 Corinthians 1–7 and 10–13 in that one could claim that at 10.1 Paul was referring to a topic that he 'parked' while he dealt with the collection in 2 Corinthians 8–9. Such an argument, however, is not necessary to maintain the unity of 2 Corinthians. Before explaining how, the meaning of ἐν παντὶ needs consideration.

The phrase ἐν παντὶ in 7.16 literally means 'in everything', 'in every respect'. In 2 Cor. 7.11, ἐν παντὶ appear but there reference is limited by the addition τῷ πράγματι, 'with respect to the matter', at the end of the verse, which tied the reference to the issue of ἀδικία. There is no such limitation on ἐν παντὶ in 7.16. On the contrary, 7.16 appears to look back to and largely replicate Paul's wide-ranging enthusiasm for the Corinthians that he expresses in 2 Cor. 7.4. Whereas Paul concluded one section of the letter with the buoyant joy of 7.4, here, at the conclusion of the affair of the ἀδικία, he concludes on a similarly high note.

He is about to begin a long section of the letter in which he asks the Corinthians to contribute for the poor Christ-followers of Jerusalem. In this context, a general expression of his confidence in his addressees, as a way of reminding him of their relationship, which critically includes his confidence in them, was, in line with Turner's approach to leadership (2005), absolutely essential. Reminding them of his boldness at this point, or of restricting his regard for them to the matters canvassed in the severe letter and in Titus' visit, would have been futile. On the other hand, the fact that these issues had been satisfactorily resolved and that the Corinthians were now 'pure' (ἁγνοί) in relation to them (7.11) provided a firm foundation for Paul's confidence in them with respect to other matters, in particular, that they would contribute to the collection (chs 8–9) and that they would respond appropriately to what he would have to say about the interlopers (chs 10–13). In other words, Paul has ultimate faith in their doing the right thing, even if they have in the past gone astray for a period. To similar effect is the view of Thomas Schmeller: 'Paul's statements of confidence (cf. esp. 7.5-16) serve to stabilize his relationship with the congregation – a relationship that has improved as a result of the letter of tears – and to further the process of reconciliation' (2013: 78).

This is really the answer to the commentators mentioned earlier who find the presence of 7.16 in the letter inconsistent with 2 Corinthians 1–7 having been joined with 2 Corinthians 10–13 in Paul's original form of the letter, rather than a case built on the occurrence of θαρρεῖν in both 7.16 and 10.1-2. Whatever Paul may say in criticism of the Corinthians in 2 Corinthians 10–13 – and we will see in the following that the outsiders who have arrived are his primary target, not the Corinthian Christ-followers – he is confident that they will do the right thing. Paul's position, in psychological terms, is not really much different from that of Mary in John 2.1-11, who, having indirectly asked her son Jesus help out with the wine problem and having been rudely rebuffed by him for the effort, then tells the servants, 'Do whatever he tells you' (John 2.5). On this view, the course of events surrounding the offender provide a model for the much more serious situation that Paul will address in chs 10–13. These are better explanations than that Paul is just offering 'a rhetorical overstatement' when he says he has confidence in them ἐν παντὶ (Lambrecht 1999: 132). After all, if Paul had not been of the view that he could persuade the Corinthians to do the right thing, he would never have written chs 10–13. The ultimate answer to the question, however, is that the course of events proved that Paul's confidence was not misplaced. For we know from Romans both that the collection was taken up in Corinth and that Paul successfully completed his work there (Rom. 15.23, 26).

Commentary: Part B

2 Corinthians 8–9: The collection

11

The collection (2 Corinthians 8–9)

Introductory issues

Paul's collection: Its rationale and history

On a number of occasions in his letters, Paul mentions a collection that he is undertaking for the Christ-movement in Jerusalem. His most extended discussion of the subject comes in 2 Corinthians 8–9 so that it is appropriate to consider the rationale and history of the collection prior to commenting on those chapters. The origin of the collection lay in Paul's crucial meeting with the leaders of the Christ-movement in Jerusalem recounted in Gal. 2.1-10. On that occasion, after he and Barnabas had reached an agreement (κοινωνία) with James, Cephas and John whereby apostleship to the 'uncircumcised' was allocated to Paul and Barnabas and the apostleship to the circumcised to these three 'supposed pillars', Paul also agreed to remember 'the destitute' (τῶν πτωχῶν). Paul refers to the collection again in 1 Cor. 16.1-4, there called, in the singular and plural, λογεία and λογεῖαι (see Arzt-Grabner 2014: 392) and targeted at 'the saints' (οἱ ἅγιοι) in Jerusalem. He notes he had previously instructed the assemblies of Galatia on the collection, which provides the context within which he had mentioned the agreement of Gal. 2.10 to the Galatian Christ-followers. Next we have the extensive treatment of the subject in 2 Corinthians 8–9. The final appearance of the collection in the Pauline letters comes in Rom. 15.25-31. This passage begins with his statement that he is going 'to Jerusalem ministering to the saints' (διακονῶν τοῖς ἁγίοις), since Macedonia and Achaia have resolved 'to make fellowship' (κοινωνίαν τινὰ ποιήσασθαι) with 'the destitute among the saints' (εἰς τοὺς πτωχοὺς τῶν ἁγίων) in Jerusalem (15.26). His failure to mention Galatia means that the Christ-groups there had, after all, not contributed to the collection. Even more remarkably, Paul ends by asking the Romans to pray that his 'ministry' (διακονία) for Jerusalem will be acceptable to the saints (15.31), which leaves hanging the large question of why it might not be. Although the overwhelming majority of commentators rightly regard these data as relating to the same collection, Downs (2008) and Longenecker (2010) adopt the less likely view that the arrangement recorded in Gal. 2.10 was not the same as the collection mentioned in 1 Cor. 16.1-4, 2 Corinthians 8–9 and Rom. 15.25-31.

The collection has attracted intense scholarly attention (Safrai and Thomson 2013). Much of this research has been directed at explaining why Paul undertook it. Many commentators regard it as a version of the Temple tax that Judeans sent yearly to Jerusalem (Malherbe 1959: 225–7; Nickle 1966: 74–89), as a sign either of the unity of the Christ-movement or of Paul's subordination to the Jerusalem church. Yet it is hardly likely that Paul would model his collection on the Temple tax. The Temple was a central feature of Judean ethnic identity to which Paul opposed subjecting his non-Judean Christ-followers, a position given concrete expression on the two occasions in the Corinthian correspondence he told them that they were God's temple (1 Cor. 3.16; 2 Cor. 6.16). He also unmistakeably distanced himself from the Temple in Rom. 9.1-5. In this passage, he not only declared his kinship with ethnic Israel but also made clear his sorrowful alienation from it, by saying, '(they) who are Israelites', not '(we) who are Israelites', so that when he listed features of their identity in vv. 4-5, he was maintaining a space between himself and those features, including the ἡ λατρεία, the Temple service, mentioned at 9.4.[1] Furthermore, as we will see in the following, Paul in no way regarded the agreement he reached with the leaders of the Jerusalem church in Jerusalem (Gal. 2.1-10) as a sign of his subordination to them, and it is most unlikely, especially after the incident in Antioch where they breached the agreement (Gal. 2.11-14), that he developed such an understanding later.

Other scholars consider that collection reflects the End-time pilgrimage of Judeans and non-Judeans to Jerusalem predicted in Israelite scripture (e.g. Pss. 22.27; 86.9; Isa. 2.2-4; 26.6; 66.23; Mic. 4.1-2; Zech. 14.16-19). Thus, Dieter Georgi argued that material aid was in view but so was something more comprehensive: the significance and achievements of the Jerusalem church were to be brought into remembrance by the Antiochene and 'Gentile' churches (1992: 41). This is another form of subordination of Paul's Gospel to the Jerusalem Christ-movement. Nickle also gave credence to the idea of eschatological pilgrimage but on a very different basis: that Judeans would be 'confronted with the undeniable reality of the divine gift of saving grace to the Gentiles and thereby be themselves moved through jealousy to finally accept the gospel' (1966: 142). The problem with the End-time pilgrimage approach is that Paul shows very little interest in the passages in Israelite scripture describing non-Judean nations coming to Jerusalem at the End-time, even bearing in mind impressive efforts lately by the 'Paul within Judaism' scholars to argue for this position (Esler 2021a). He hardly ever quotes these passages. When he cites Isa. 59.20 in Rom. 11.26, moreover,

---

[1] Esler 2003a: 272–3 for a more detailed discussion.

he makes a decisive change in having the redeemer come from Zion, not go to it. Paul's understanding of the Last Days is that it is not sited in Jerusalem and, hence, not ethnic, so that the End-time pilgrimage is irrelevant to it; this much is clear from 1 Thess. 4.13-18 (Esler 2021a).

Another long-standing approach has been to locate the collection within the traditions of Israelite almsgiving to the poor (Nickle 1966: 93–5). There is something to be said for this explanation, since it accords with the fact that on two occasions when discussing the collection Paul highlights aid for the destitute (πτωχοί; Gal. 2.10; Rom. 15.26). It also accords with the oldest extant interpretation of the collection, Luke's often-forgotten statement attributed to Paul in addressing Felix in Acts 24.17 that he came to Jerusalem to deliver alms (ἐλεημοσύναι) to his people (see the following). Tucker has recently revivified a close neighbour to this approach with his stress on Paul's interest in expressing the חן/חסד/χάρις/ἔλεος traditions of Israel in a kinship context in the collection (2014: 62–4).

The last three decades have seen the arrival of modes of New Testament interpretation that fix upon notions of reciprocity, patronage and benefaction that were omnipresent in the ancient Greco-Roman world. These forms of analysis find abundant responsive data in the Pauline texts concerning the collection (especially Joubert 2000) and other, closely related, issues such as 'grace' (χάρις; Harrison 2003; Barclay 2015). A particularly rich vein of analysis has recently been opened with John Kloppenborg's detailed comparison of Paul's collection and the various types of collection undertaken by the numerous voluntary associations in the Greco-Roman world (2017; 2019: 245–65). He finds a particularly close comparator in the practice of the ἐπίδοσις, a voluntary contribution individuals made to the state (257–64). The precise word Paul uses of the collection in 1 Cor. 16.1 and 2, λογεία ('collection'), was employed by voluntary associations with cultic dimensions, and Paul's use is comparable (Last and Harland 2020: 124–5, 144).

But in addition to such explanations has come a vigorously argued theological explanation in the form of Downs' view that the collection (without the Gal. 2.10 dimensions) is an act of cultic worship (2008). In 1995, Horrell had plausibly argued that Paul's main reason for the collection was to relieve poverty among the Jerusalem Christ-movement; this was a 'material' explanation. At the same time, however, Paul does at times (including in 2 Corinthians 8) suggest a theological under-girding for the project: it is an expression of gospel theology (1995: 76, 79). This is a more convincing way to integrate the cultural and theological dimensions of the enterprise than to explain it as having a primarily theological rationale.

Opposition to Downs' approach has come from commentators intent on demonstrating the way in which the collection aimed to provide material relief and was rooted in Mediterranean culture (following Joubert's lead). Thus, Ogereau (2012), partly building on Sampley (1980), focuses on the importance of κοινωνία in understanding the collection and concludes that it was aimed at establishing a new order of socio-economic equality and solidarity among emerging Christ-following communities, at both a local and a Mediterranean-wider level, and across sociocultural and ethnic divides. Welborn, who strongly opposes theological explanations (2019), has sought, in arguing for a material explanation, to illuminate the character of the collection with respect to the ideal of 'equality' (ἰσότης) in 2 Cor. 8.13-15 in relation to friendship, politics and the cosmos. He argues that Paul was attempting to create an economic structure – partnership in the collection – the goal of which was to achieve 'equality' between persons of different social classes through redistributive exchange.

A different tack has been taken by Tucker (2014) from a social identity perspective. He argues that Paul, rather than relying on discourses of reciprocity or obligation, wishes to see the Christ-followers demonstrate an ethic of mutuality, generosity and grace-filled regard for the other similar to that found in Israel's scriptural tradition in relation to its language of grace and compassion in a renewed discourse of kinship. All this should contribute to the formation of a salient 'in Christ' social identity with concomitant practices and social identifications.

The nature of the collection at its inception in the Jerusalem meeting has been seriously misunderstood in scholarship, as I have argued elsewhere (1998: 130–40). Its bitterly contested nature has been largely ignored. Nickle's observation (1966: 45) that 'Practically all commentators see in the giving of the right hand of fellowship a completely sincere expression of harmonious understanding' is still quite accurate fifty-five years later, and this indicates the depth of the problem. The Septuagint recognizes only one meaning for 'giving the right hand' (δεξιὰς διδόναι) and that is where, in a context of conflict, the superior party, by stretching out his right hand, offers mercy to the subordinate party – who is understood to be a suppliant in a kneeling or crouched position with a hand reached out seeking mercy. By 'taking' the hand of the suppliant, the gesture is completed. This is what *parcere subiectis* in Virgil's *Aeneid* 6.853 means and there is a picture of such a scene on one of the Flavian *Iudaea Capta* coins (Illustration 9, Esler 1995b: 252). In my earlier formulation of this view (1998: 130–40), I cited several Septuagintal passages in support (1 Macc. 6.58; 11.50, 62, 66; 13.45, 50; 2 Macc. 4.34; 11.26; 12.11; 13.22; 14.19). Gibson, in seeking to contradict my position (2013: 221), wrongly suggested that three of these did not carry this meaning (1 Macc. 6.58; 11.50, 62) and came up with three more instances that are actually to the same effect although he misunderstood their meaning. The act of Peter, James and John in offering their right hands to Paul and Barnabas was an act of condescension on their part, as if they were the victors in the conflict that had just been settled. Paul subverts this condescension by describing James, Peter and John as 'those who seem to be pillars' (οἱ δοκοῦντες στῦλοι εἶναι) immediately before mentioning that they 'gave their right hands' (Gal. 2.9). He had laid his Gospel defiantly before them and prevented Titus from being circumcised (Gal. 2.2-3), so that he was in no way subordinate to them.

In return for letting Paul operate in his own mission area among the non-Judeans, in a way that permitted commensality between Judean and non-Judean Christ-followers without the latter having to undergo ethnic translation – to adopt the useful formulation of Katherine Southwood (2014) – and become Judeans, James, Peter and John demanded a reciprocal act: the help of Paul's churches for the destitute Christ-followers of Jerusalem. Paul hastens to note that in agreeing to this he really gave nothing in return since he was eager to do it anyway. Later, in Antioch, Peter (and Barnabas, grievously betraying Paul) breached this agreement by withdrawing from mixed table-fellowship. Yet Paul insisted on keeping to his side of the bargain. This meant that every denarius he gathered for the Jerusalem Christ-movement was a reminder of the conduct of the Pillars. That is the main reason why he is later worried that the Jerusalem church might not accept the collection (Rom. 15.31). It is also why Luke later tries to cover up the fact that Paul's delivery of the collection on his final journey to Jerusalem was a major cause of controversy among the Christ-movement in the city. For Sweeney (2019: 142) errs in suggesting that 'Luke remains silent about the matter in recounting Paul's travels'. It is true that Luke does not mention the matter of the collection when describing Paul's arrival in Jerusalem and the events that ensued thereafter (Acts 21.15-23.30). Later in the narrative, however, Luke slips up, by having Paul disclose to Felix that 'after some years I came to give alms (ἐλεημοσύνας ποιήσων) to my people' (εἰς τὸ ἔθνος μου; Acts 24.17). This is the collection; Luke knew it was a bone of contention between Paul and the Jerusalem Christ-movement and that is why he failed to mention it in relation to Paul's arrival in Jerusalem. The collection was a continuing source of controversy, and that is how it will be understood in what follows.

Paul's collection in 2 Corinthians 8–9 from a social identity perspective

Paul's collection for the destitute Christ-followers in Jerusalem connects with the social identity approach in two ways. First, it can be explored in terms of a leader as 'impresario'. Secondly, the fact that it comes after Paul has rebuilt his relationship with the Corinthians in chs 1–7 aligns his instincts closely with the way John Turner (2005) has explained a leader exercises power in a group. I will now briefly reiterate from Chapter 2 of this volume the central issues in both aspects. 'Identity impresarioship' is concept developed by Haslam, Reicher and Platow (2011: 163–95). It refers to the way in which leaders promote activities and projects that help group members experience the realities of belonging to the group in a meaningful way. By active participation in such initiatives or by mere awareness that they are being carried forward, the members obtain a richer sense of the cognitive, emotional and evaluative aspects of group identity. This strengthens the bond between them and the leader. Paul's collection is eminently such an activity.

Secondly, that the collection was of such moment to Paul makes the fact that his treatment of it in 2 Corinthians 8–9 is so consonant with the approach to leadership and the exercise of power identified by John Turner all the more interesting. We must note initially that this material occurs more than half way through the letter. Paul does not mention it until he has taken great pains to rebuild his relationship with the Corinthians. More importantly, just as Turner argues that the old approach to the resources in leadership is incorrect in postulating that control of resources leads to power, the collection of 2 Corinthians 8–9 is not a resource under Paul's control that he can use to win influence over the Corinthians and have them do what he wants. First, he has to win their influence and trust as a leader who is prototypical and exemplary of Christ-movement values, and he does this in 2 Corinthians 1–7. Secondly, his manner of discussing the collection needs to make clear that this is not something over which he has power merely because of who he is. Thus, he expressly denies he is ordering them to take up the collection in 2 Cor. 8.8: 'I say this not as a command' (κατ' ἐπιταγήν). This is a matter on which he is only giving advice (γνώμη; 2 Cor. 8.10). The Corinthians must not feel that they are under any compulsion (ἀνάγκη; 2 Cor. 9.7). Moreover, Paul is entirely dependent on their cooperating with Titus when he sends him to undertake the collection. Even more notably, Titus will have two companions who will be able to vouch for the fact that nothing untoward has happened to the money collected (nor in the manner of its collection; it will not be 'an exploitative exaction', πλεονεξία; 9.5) but 'a willing gift' (εὐλογία; 9.5). Not only is Paul plainly saying that the money will not be under his control but the very fact of its being collected depends on his winning over the Corinthians with what he has said in the letter earlier. The fact that Achaia did, in the event, contribute to the collection (Rom. 15.26) indicates that Paul was successful with his Corinthian converts, even if he was not with those in Galatia (mentioned earlier). Thus, we have a successful instance of the approach to power, authority and leadership advocated by Turner. Only because Paul persuaded ingroup members in Corinth that it was right for him to exercise leadership over them in certain matters was he able to ensure the success of his strategy of having them contribute to the collection.

2 Corinthians 8–9 as integrated section of a unified letter

Many commentators who regard 2 Corinthians as a composite of Pauline letter fragments view 2 Corinthians 8–9 as comprised of the contents of two (or more) letters on the subject of the collection. Betz' 1985 Hermeneia commentary on these two chapters (subtitled 'A Commentary on Two Administrative Letters of the Apostle Paul') is probably the most prominent example of this trend, which is represented by other scholars such as Windisch (1970 [1924]: 242–3), Bornkamm (1971: 245–6), Georgi (1992: 75–9), Mitchell 2005, Roetzel (2007) and Welborn (2011: xix–xxvii). In spite of such impressive scholarly support, it is submitted that no element of the partitionist position on 2 Corinthians is so fragile as the notion that chs 8 and 9 represent originally separate documents. Instead, the view taken in this commentary is that they comprise a tightly unified and argued communication on the collection that Paul deliberately and for good reason placed at this point in the letter. Although a detailed discussion of this topic is beyond the compass of this volume, I will now address some of the main issues raised in partitionist theories, but in the course of discussing 2 Corinthians 8–9 in a way that will also serve as an introduction to the commentary on these chapters.

The setting

Paul is writing chs 8 and 9 from Macedon (8.1; 9.4). This provides a direct connection to 7.5 – his statement of his arrival in Macedon that was delayed from 2.13 – which necessarily conveys that 2 Corinthians 1–7 was also written from Macedon. This is a non-trivial link between chs 1–7 and 8–9, since Paul is writing about the collection in exactly the place you would expect him to be on the basis that 1–7 and 8–9 went together from the outset, not from any of the numerous other places in the eastern Mediterranean with which he was associated.

Not just the location, however, but also the narrative links these two sections of the letter. Although as he writes chs 8 and 9, Paul has Titus with him (8.6), Paul feels no need to explain to the Corinthians how this came to be. That is because he has just told them in 7.5-16. In addition, Paul's statement in 8.16 that God had put the same earnest care (σπουδή) for the Corinthians into Titus' heart (as into his, Paul's) only becomes explicable if set against ch. 7. For there Paul describes how Titus was comforted by the Corinthians (7.7) and how his affection for the Corinthians grew as he remembered their obedience and the fear and trembling with which they received him (7.15). The earnestness (σπουδή) of 7.11-12 reappears in the penultimate position in 8.7 (and is also used of the earnestness of the Macedonians in 8.8). In fact, 8.7 serves reasonably well as summarizing the attitude of the Corinthians and Paul in consequence of the severe letter and the visit of Titus. 2 Corinthians 7.2 contains a denial by Paul that he has financially exploited (ἐκπλεονεκτήσαμεν) anyone. This statement sounds like a response to criticism of him in relation to the collection, and it is directly paralleled by his statement in 9.5 that he was sending the brothers on ahead so that the collection would be a 'generous gift' (εὐλογία) and not an 'exploitative extraction' (πλεονεξία), the noun being cognate with the verb in 7.2, again presumably disavowing such behaviour on his own part.

Yet chs 8–9 are also joined to chs 10–13 by a striking feature of ch. 9. This is Paul's foreshadowing his impending visit to Corinth (9.4-6) that is echoed by his references to his imminent third visit in 2 Cor. 12.14 and 13.1. This is yet another sign of the narrative unity of chs 1–7, 8–9 and 10–13. What a coincidence it would be if chs 8 and 9, which (on the partitionists' argument) are fragments of letters written by Paul at some other time and very possibly in some other place(s), just happened to integrate so snugly with the narrative of chs 1–7 and 10–13!

Summary of 2 Corinthians 8–9 and their different topics

A central feature of the proposal that chs 8 and 9 were originally separate is that they 'contain two independent and complete presentations by Paul on the same theme' (Windisch 1970[1924]: 287), or that 'After a lengthy discussion of the collection in ch. 8, Paul introduces the subject anew in ch. 9, and treats it thoroughly, as if it had not previously been mentioned' (Welborn 2011: xx). The following summary of the two contents of the two chapters will reveal that this is not, in fact, the case. Neither ch. 8 nor 9 can stand alone; the material in both of them is needed to convey Paul's message.

8.1-6 Paul recounts the generosity of the Macedonian ἐκκλησίαι, in spite of affliction and poverty, in participating in 'the ministry for the saints' (τῆς διακονίας τῆς εἰς τοὺς ἁγίους), generosity that Paul has asked Titus to request the Corinthians to emulate by completing the collection that they had begun previously.

8.7-12 Paul makes a plea, not a command, for generous giving, to show others that they genuinely love him and to complete what they began a year before, in light of Christ becoming destitute for their sakes, and to show that their readiness (προθυμία) for the task is matched by their execution.

8.13-15 Paul explains how undertaking the collection would represent a desirable form of equality (ἰσότης).

8.16-24 Paul describes the particular delegates he is sending and the reasons for their selection: (1) Titus, already eager to go; (2) the brother famous among all the churches for his preaching of the Gospel and whom the churches have appointed and who will allay any doubts about Paul's administration of the collection; and (3) a brother Paul has chosen whom he has previously tested. Paul ends with an invocation to the Corinthians.

9.1-5 Paul says that it is superfluous for him to write to them about the collection, as he had already claimed honour for their readiness from the Macedonians the year before to encourage them to contribute. He is now sending the brethren so that he will not (later) be embarrassed lest, when he comes from Macedonia, he will not be humiliated before any Macedonians who accompany him.

9.6-15 This is a long section on the resources and beneficial results of generosity, with scriptural examples.

Summarizing the material in chs 8–9 leads to the inevitable conclusion that there is no repetition across the two chapters, although some issues in ch. 8 find counterpoints or are referred to (as context) in ch. 9. Thus, in 9.1-5 Paul surprises his readers by informing them that, whereas he had just been citing the Macedonians to spur them on, he had been using their earlier enthusiasm to urge on the Macedonians. It is extremely puzzling that anyone could find in this elegant rhetorical turn, which conveys entirely new information, a repetition of what he had said in ch. 8. On the other hand, 9.1-5 also link chs 8 and 9 in that the eagerness (προθυμία) of the Corinthians to take part in the collection in the previous year of which Paul reminds them in 8.11-12 is now unveiled in 9.2 (προθυμία) as also having been his stimulus to incite the Macedonians into action. Similarly, when Paul notes in 9.3 that he is sending (ἔπεμψα; an aorist with present meaning) the brothers, this is a reference to what he has said in 2 Cor. 8.6, 16-24 and only makes sense in a context where those brothers have already been mentioned. Again, these are not signs of repetition but of a developing and integrated argument. The extended mention of his impending visit in 9.4-5, however, is fresh information and is not mentioned in ch. 8. Lastly, 9.6-15, two-thirds of the chapter, is clearly a peroration for which there is no parallel in ch. 8. Thus, the doublets Windisch claimed to find in the two chapters are illusory.[2]

Other evidence that 2 Corinthians 8 and 9 constitute an integrated passage

There are other signs of this being an integrated passage. First, the expression χάρις τοῦ θεοῦ appears at the beginning and end of the passage (8.1; 9.15), thus forming an *inclusio*. Secondly, ἁπλότης ('generosity') is predicated of the Macedonian Christ-followers in 8.2 and then of the Corinthian Christ-followers towards the end of the passage, in 9.11 and 13. Paul is thus able to declare that the Macedonians' generosity he mentioned at the outset as a spur to their undertaking the collection will, in fact, be manifested by the Corinthians. In other words, he is confident that his citing the (ongoing) generosity of the Macedonians at the start of the passage as prototypical of Christ-movement values and behaviour for the benefit of the Corinthians will prove effective. In this vital respect, the Corinthian Christ-followers will embody the identity of the movement just like the Macedonians do. Thirdly, in the Greek of Paul's time the phrase Περὶ μὲν γάρ used at the start of 9.1 did not introduce a document or even come near the start of a document as had been claimed by Hans Dieter Betz (1985: 90). In a convincing riposte to Betz, Stanley Stowers has demonstrated (in reliance upon some ninety instances of the expression) that the phrase was regularly used to indicate a new dimension of an ongoing argument. It was also regularly followed by δέ to assist in setting up an 'on the one hand ... on the other hand' situation – as here, with the μέν covering vv. 1-2 and the δέ vv. 3-4. He has shown that in 9.1 the 'expression introduces the subtopic of the potentially embarrassing situation caused by Paul's boasting'. In addition, '9:1-4 provides a warrant and an explanation for Paul's exhortation in 8:24' (1990: 348). This conclusion also finds support in Paul's practice of commencing new sections in his letters with Περὶ δέ, not Περὶ μέν. The real division in these chapters comes not at 9.1 but at 9.6, which begins the peroration for 8.1–9.5.

The whole enterprise to separate chs 8 and 9 is deeply flawed and a troubling distraction from understanding what Paul was trying to say to his Corinthian addressees.

---

[2] They were: 9.1-2 and 8.1-5; 9.3-5 and 8.16-24; 9.6-7 and 8.12-15; 9.8-11 and 8.14; and 9.8 and 8.7 (Windisch 1970 [1924]: 286–7).

12

The collection (2 Corinthians 8–9)

The exemplary generosity of the Macedonian Christ-followers (8.1-6)

Towards the end of 1 Corinthians, Paul had outlined some instructions about the collection (16.1-4). In addition, we learn from 2 Cor. 8.6 that Titus had previously begun work on the collection, and he probably did this in the context of the Corinthians beginning the collection a year ago (ἀπὸ πέρυσι), as Paul mentions in 8.10. Paul uses the same highly unusual verb προενάρχομαι ('to-previously-make-a-beginning') – which occurs nowhere else in the New Testament, nor in the Septuagint – both of Titus and of the Corinthians beginning the collection (8.6, 10). Further evidence of this visit comes from 2 Cor. 12.17-18, where Paul, while asserting he had never taken financial advantage of them, denies that Titus (and another brother), whom he sent to the Corinthians, had done so, a disavowal surely pointing to Titus' inauguration of the collection. In all likelihood, therefore, after sending 1 Corinthians with the instructions about the collection (16.1-4), Paul despatched Titus in the previous year to help them get it under way. (As discussed in Chapter 1 of this volume, Titus probably carried 1 Corinthians to Corinth on the occasion of this visit.) This visit (see the following discussion) preceded the recent one by Titus that was concerned with the reaction of the Corinthians to the severe letter. So Paul was embarking on a discussion of a project with which the Corinthians were already well familiar, and he does so in the light of his current experience of how the Macedonians had been participating in the collection.

Paul begins his discussion of the collection in a manner readily consonant with social identity theory. In vv. 1-6, Paul calls upon the Corinthians to model their behaviour on that of other members of the Christ-following ingroup, in this case those in assemblies in Macedonia. This appeal represents an expression of the phenomenon where some group members are held up to the others as prototypical of the values and behaviour of the group. The task is for the Corinthian members to align their outlook and actions with those of Macedonia. In particular, Paul draws the attention of the Corinthians to the exemplary (meaning 'serving as a model') generosity of the Macedonians. This is a far more plausible explanation for introducing the Macedonians than the idea of Betz (1985: 48), who is (unwisely) supported by Thrall (2000: 527) and Vegge (2008: 219), that Paul was situating his thought in relation to alleged pre-existing ethnic and political rivalry between Corinth and Macedonia to engender a sense of competition between the two sets of Christ-groups. Paul is not encouraging competition but imitation. The purposes of a collection that 'is intended to bind the churches together in Christ' (Seifrid 2014: 324) could hardly be served by Paul's encouraging competition between the various Christ-groups, with all the negative connotations of competition in relation to honour prevalent in this culture.

2 Corinthians 8.1 The expression 'We want you to know' (Γνωρίζομεν) with which Paul begins goes beyond a conveying a mere wish to communicate information and is really a means of introducing a new and important topic (Matera 2003: 185). A very similar meaning is communicated using the different expression 'We do not want you to be ignorant' in 1.8. From 1 Thessalonians and Philippians, we know that the Christ-groups in view in Macedonia include those in Philippi and Thessalonica, and perhaps others whose involvement has not survived. The use of χάρις to refer to the collection occurs here and in vv. 6, 7 and 19. The word also appears in 2 Cor. 9.8, 14, 15, there in relation to the Corinthians; thus, chs 8–9 enact a transition from the God-given generosity of the Macedonians to that of the Corinthians, with χάρις forming an *inclusio* at the beginning and end of the whole passage. The perfect passive form δεδομένην, 'having been given', which qualifies χάρις entails that grace was given to the Macedonians and continues to be given.

2 Corinthians 8.2 This verse is structured around two paradoxes – joy in the midst of affliction and generosity amid poverty – which are the result of God's χάρις mentioned in v. 1 (Matera 2003: 186). While we do not know what particular affliction (θλῖψις) – meaning an episode of opposition from outsiders – Paul has in mind, affliction was a common problem for the Macedonian Christ-followers (cf. 1 Thess. 1.6; 2.14; 3.3-4; Phil. 1.27-30). Perhaps the fact that they have been reduced to extreme (κατὰ βάθους, literally, 'down to the depth') poverty is a consequence of the affliction. It is worth noting that πτωχεία probably does not carry the more extreme meaning of 'destitution' here, as it does in Luke's Gospel (Esler 1987: 180-1), since otherwise the Macedonians would have had nothing to contribute. Paul mentions this opposition to highlight the extraordinary character of their generosity in undertaking the collection.

Paul employs the word ἁπλότης here of the Macdeonians and in 9.11, 13 of the Corinthians. It is a nominal form of the adjective ἁπλοῦς, meaning 'motivated by a singleness of purpose so as to open and aboveboard, single, without guile, sincere, straightforward' (BDAG 104). Accordingly, ἁπλότης carries the primary meaning of 'simplicity, sincerity, uprightness, frankness' (BDAG 104). However, the word is unlikely to have that meaning here and in 2 Cor. 9.11, 13 and in Rom. 12.8, where it far more likely means 'generosity, liberality'. For the strong contrast in 8.2 between the deep poverty of the Macedonians and the abundance of their ἁπλότης seems to require that the word carries the connotation of generosity, as does the association of ἁπλότης with the Corinthians becoming rich in 9.11, a sense that carries over into the use of the word in 9.13. The link between almsgiving and ἁπλότης in Rom. 12.8 suggests a similar flavour to the word there. Harris cites two instances of the word meaning 'generosity' outside the New Testament, in *Testament of Issachar* 3:8 and Josephus, JA 7.332 (2005: 563).

Even if ἁπλότης did mean 'sincerity', the critical feature for the discussion is that the word is predicated of the Macedonians in 8.2 and then of the Corinthians in 9.11, 13, thus representing an *inclusio* that serves to unify the passage. It is worth noting that although the Macedonians are mentioned again in ch. 9, their ἁπλότης is not. This is the first of several issues that provide counter-evidence to Welborn's suggestion (2011: xx) that in ch. 9 Paul treats the subject of the collection 'thoroughly, as if it had not previously been mentioned'. Paul could hardly be treating the subject thoroughly in ch. 9 if he omitted reference to the ἁπλότης of the Macedonians.

2 Corinthians 8.3 Verse 3 begins a long sentence that only reaches its verb, 'they gave' (ἔδωκαν) in v. 5. The word Ὅτι ('Because') at the start of the verse (paralleling the same word at the start of v. 2) signals that the radical character of the Macedonians' contribution, here afforded further illustration, is a second aspect of God's grace that has been given to the Macedonians. Paul's use of the word αὐθαίρετοι (a compound of αὐτός and αἱρέω), meaning 'self chosen', 'of one's own freewill' in relation to their giving, forms part of an argument that the collection is not something he imposed on his Christ-followers but a project they voluntarily undertook. In 8.8, he will revert to this theme when he says that his views on the Corinthians and the collection are not uttered as a command (κατ' ἐπιταγήν). He has previously made clear that he will not 'lord it over their faith' (1.24). Even granting that Paul must have suggested the collection to them (Thrall 2000: 525), this is consistent with his not having directed them to participate. Αὐθαίρετος will reappear in 8.17 to describe Titus' willingness to return to the Corinthians.

2 Corinthians 8.4 The previous references to the generosity of the Macedonians now find their focus on the collection, here described as the ministry (διακονία) for the saints (εἰς τοὺς ἁγίους) in which the Corinthians are entreating participation (κοινωνία). Previously, κοινωνία appeared in the sense of 'close association' (6.14). Διακονία can be interpreted primarily as a service to other human beings (Furnish 1984: 401) or, more probably, as a service provided to others but ultimately performed for God (Collins 1990: 218, 336). The expression εἰς τοὺς ἁγίους is probably an abbreviation of the fuller expression 'for the poor among the saints in Jerusalem' found in Rom. 15.26 (Harris 2005: 567), and Paul's Corinthian audience would have so understood it.

Whereas in 8.1 the χάρις came from God, χάρις in v. 4 refers to a favour that Paul can bestow: participation in the collection. This expression reinforces Paul's previous statement that the Macedonians wanted to be involved of their own accord: Paul was not forcing them and, in fact, indicates that he had latitude as to whether to agree to it or not. 'Most earnestly' translates μετὰ πολλῆς παρακλήσεως, 'with a powerful appeal'. The other meaning of παράκλησις, namely 'comfort' or 'consolation', crops up frequently in 2 Corinthians 1–7 (1.3, 4, 5, 6 (bis), 7; 7.4, 7, 13).

2 Corinthians 8.5 Many commentators prefer to translate ἠλπίσαμεν as 'we expected' rather than literally as 'we hoped' because the Macedonians had gone beyond what Paul could have hoped for (Furnish 1984: 402). In any event, 'expect' is one of the usual meanings of ἐλπίζειν (BDAG 319). The unexpected feature of the Macedonians' response was that their generosity extended to the giving (not just of money) but of themselves. Presumably this giving of themselves means not their conversion (Seifrid 2014: 324), but rather their act of dedicating themselves to the Lord and to Paul through the will of God for the purpose of the collection. This may seem a bold collocation of the Lord and Paul, but Paul regularly presents himself as the Lord's agent for various purposes, beginning with his commission to preach the good news of Christ among the non-Judeans (Gal. 1.16).

2 Corinthians 8.6 Most translations treat v. 6 as beginning a new sentence, since although the long Greek sentence that started in v. 3 continues to the end of v. 6, there is a clear transition of thought at the start of his verse (a transition marked by an articular infinitive construction of resultative effect), from Paul's deliberations on the Macedonians' generosity to the conclusion that Paul draws from them, that Titus should help the Corinthians with their collection.

The second clause in v. 6, beginning with the word ἵνα ('in order that') that expresses purpose, is highly significant for understanding Paul's dealings with the Corinthians via Titus, yet also somewhat difficult to interpret. Literally translated, it means: 'so that just as (καθώς) he previously-made-a-beginning (προενήρξατο), so also (οὕτως καί) he might complete (ἐπιτελέσῃ) among you (εἰς ὑμᾶς) also (καί) this work-of-grace (χάρις)'. As noted earlier, the verb προενάρχομαι only appears here and in v. 10 and nowhere else in the New Testament, nor in the Septuagint. Since ἐπιτελεῖν also reappears in v. 11,

Paul is creating a connection between vv. 7 and 10-11: these almost certainly refer to the same occasion when Titus and the Corinthians previously made a beginning. The prefix προ- in προενήρξατο must designate a time prior to Paul's writing of this passage, and since in v. 10 this same (extremely rare) verb is applied to the action of the Corinthians ἀπὸ πέρυσι, 'in the previous year', we thus have the appropriate date for Titus' previous activity. Since Paul must have had in mind a calendar (perhaps the Roman one) in relation to which the visit occurred in the previous year (Harris 2005: 582-3), the possible date of the visit turns on how far advanced the current year was when Paul was writing and how far back into the previous year the visit took place. This means the visit could have occurred, at a maximum, two years before and, at a minimum, a few months before or even less. Yet ἀπὸ πέρυσι would be an odd way to refer to a very recent visit, and several months at least would appear to be required.

Although the position of the second καί immediately before χάρις might appear to suggest that there was something else Titus was to complete in addition to the collection, that possibility should be excluded because the context in vv. 1-5 solely concerns the collection (Thrall 2000: 528), and because that is also the subject of vv. 10-11. So Titus' mission was to complete among the Corinthians the work-of-grace he had begun in the previous year. This visit is unlikely to have been the recent one that Titus undertook at Paul's request in relation to the severe letter, since the purpose of that visit was entirely different and not easily reconcilable with work on the collection, and must have occurred sometime prior to it (with ἀπὸ πέρυσι suggesting a considerable period). A plausible solution to the chronological issues is that Paul had Titus convey the letter we know as 1 Corinthians to Corinth. This is very likely because Paul told them in 1 Cor. 16.1-2 to start work on the collection immediately, and here he is saying in v. 6 that he had sent Titus to make a beginning. As we will see later, 2 Cor. 12.18 suggests an unnamed brother accompanied him. Paul would later send Titus to Corinth with the severe letter and this provides confirmation that Paul regarded him as a suitable letter bearer, which is especially significant if it was Titus who read aloud and explained the letter. Titus' third visit to Corinth must have been as the bearer of 2 Corinthians.

A plea to the Corinthians for generous giving (8.7-12)

As previously noted, commentators who regard chs 8 and 9 as having originated in separate letters tend to regard the material in ch. 9 as repeating what is in ch. 8. There is nothing in ch. 9, however, parallel to 8.7-12, which is a rather serious omission, considering that it is only here, in all of chs 8 and 9, that Paul actually requests the Corinthians to participate in the collection. Although in 2 Cor. 9.6-15 Paul does expatiate, in part theologically, upon the resources and results of generosity, the foundational request for their involvement is limited to 2 Cor. 8.7-12.

2 Corinthians 8.7 Although some commentators regard v. 7 as the climax of vv. 1-6 (e.g. Barnett 1997: 402), the preferable view is that it begins a new section, since it addresses for the first time the need for the Corinthians to respond, both to the example of the Macedonians and to the imminent arrival of Titus. Having recounted the enthusiasm of the Macedonians for the collection – in a manner representing them as exemplary, not as a spur to compete with them – and the fact that he has urged Titus to go to Corinth to complete the collection, Paul now appeals directly to Corinthians to abound in this work just as they do in other areas of life (faith, speech, knowledge, eagerness and love). The faith of the Corinthians was mentioned in the important verse 1.24 and will reappear in 10.15 and 13.5.

Paul softens the force of the direction by expressing it not with an imperative of περισσεύειν but with the subjunctive mood: ἵνα . . . περισσεύητε. He has just mentioned how the Macedonians abounded (using περισσεία and ἐπερίσσευσεν) in joy and extraordinary generosity (8.2) and now turns to areas where the Corinthians do and might further abound. Paul is here establishing abundance in various types of virtuous behaviour as characteristic, indeed prototypical, of Christ-movement identity; where the Macedonians have led in this respect, the Corinthians should follow. A particular feature of the verse ties it closely to what Paul was saying at the end of Chapter 7, namely the reference to their σπουδή in the penultimate position in the list of characteristics, the quality that Paul had praised so highly in 2 Cor. 7.11-12.

2 Corinthians 8.8 Yet Paul now hastens to assure the Corinthians that this is not a command (ἐπιταγή). The word ἐπιταγή occurs on three other occasions in Paul: Rom. 16.26; 1 Cor. 7.6 (closest to here) and 25. Paul employs its cognate verb ἐπιτάσσω in Phlm. 8. Here its use coheres both with the presence of the subjunctive rather than the imperative mood in the previous verse and with his programmatic declaration in 1.24 that 'we do not lord it over your faith'. Clearly, Paul wants the Corinthians to be involved in the collection and thinks that would be an excellent thing, but he is not forcing them to take part. The matter is one of persuasion rather than compulsion (Harris 2005: 576). Throughout this letter Paul has taken great pains to emphasize that he is seeking cooperation with the Corinthians as together they work out the demands of Christ-movement identity: it is a matter of active discussion and engagement. As social identity psychologists

Nick Hopkins and Steve Reicher have written, 'people's talk of identity should be understood as having a performative and constitutive dimension, and as organized to encourage the forms of action that would realize a particular vision of how the social world should be' (2011: 38).

The social identity dimensions of the project also surface in the second part of the verse. Of considerable interest are the opening words: ἀλλὰ διὰ τῆς ἑτέρων σπουδῆς ('but through the eagerness of others'). In context, the others in view can only be the Macedonians; they are mentioned at the start of ch. 8 for their generosity and reappear in 9.2.[1] The mention of their 'eagerness' summarizes what Paul has said about them in 8:1-5. By use of the preposition διὰ with the genitive case (here functioning to mark instrumentality or circumstance, whereby something is accomplished, so 'by, via, through' [BDAG 224]), Paul seeks to align the experience and identity of the Macedonian Christ-followers with that of the Corinthians. The Macedonians are prototypical in respect of eagerness, and the Corinthians need to be so too.

The precise nature of that alignment depends on the words that follow 'but through the eagerness of others', namely 'δοκιμάζων the genuineness (γνήσιον) of your love'. The noun δοκιμή means a 'test' or the experience of being tested (as at 2.9 and 8:2), and its verbal equivalent, δοκιμάζω, means 'to put to the test', 'to examine' or to draw a conclusion on the basis of such a test, hence 'to prove' or 'approve' (BDAG 255-256). The adjective, γνήσιος, 'sincere' or 'genuine' (BDAG 202), which appears only elsewhere in the Pauline letters in Phil. 4.3 (of a genuine companion), is here employed in the nominal form to which is attached 'of your love'. Thus, we have Paul, the subject of the present participle δοκιμάζων, urging them to take part in the collection as a means of, or with a view to, his testing or proving the genuineness of their love. But does Paul mean testing or proving? Many commentators consider the latter, 'proving', is meant in 2 Cor. 8.8 (e.g. Furnish 1984: 404 ['verify']; Barnett 1997: 406; Harris 2005: 576; BDAG 255). Is that correct? Paul is certainly offering the Macedonians as an example of what the correct response to the collection entails. Yet that alone is not enough; he wants the Corinthians to make a positive response to that example. In other words, while proffering the Macedonians as exemplary in the matter might serve as a stimulus to their participation, as a *test* of their love, it cannot *tout court* go so far as to *prove* that love. For this reason, in 2 Cor. 8.8 δοκιμάζων means 'testing' not 'proving' (so also Bultmann 1987: 257 [*prüfen*]; Lambrecht 1999: 137; and Matera 2003: 190-1). As Matera astutely notes (2003: 191), this makes

---

[1] Thrall (2000: 532) rightly discounts the Christ-followers of Jerusalem as another possible candidate.

the collection the second 'test' (δοκιμή) Paul sets for the Corinthians in this letter, the first being in connection with their response to the severe letter (see 2.9). Implied, whether Paul means testing or proving, is an audience to whom such proof might be offered, an implication substantiated by the information Paul provides later (2 Cor. 9.2), to the effect that he is in the habit of praising the Corinthians to the Macedonians. Yet Paul does not introduce any sense of competition between the Macedonians and the Corinthians; in this culture, this would entail a battle over who emerges as most honourable from the encounter and that dimension is absent. Rather, Paul is speaking to a single Christ-movement that is broken into separate Christ-groups which are, nevertheless, in touch with each other, interested in each other's achievements and able to learn from one another. To that extent, they are like one group in this context (a family, for example) that share jointly in honour vis-à-vis outsiders and do not compete with one another.

2 Corinthians 8.9 Although he has previously mentioned the poverty of the Macedonians that abounded into the wealth of their generosity, Paul now, somewhat unexpectedly (Lambrecht 1999: 137), turns to Jesus Christ himself, who, 'although he was rich' (translating πλούσιος ὤν, 'being rich', where the participle is used concessively), became destitute so that the Corinthians might become rich. Among various possible senses of the Lord being rich and then becoming destitute, the most convincing is that which links the statement to Phil. 2.6-8, with its transition from his pre-existent glory to his incarnate state (Thrall 2000: 532–4). Taking this view means that Paul is not presenting the destitution of the Lord as prototypical (in the social identity sense) for Christ-followers (such as the Macedonians, whose πτωχεία was mentioned in 8.2), since it was of a kind that no other human being could share. This is one of many areas where it would be mistaken to assume that all aspects of Jesus Christ were prototypical for Christ-followers.

2 Corinthians 8.10 This verse begins with Paul's restatement of his denial in v. 8 that he was issuing a command; he is offering advice (γνώμη). The word γνώμη appears four other times in Paul, with the meanings 'purpose' (1 Cor. 1.10, 'opinion' (1 Cor. 7.25 and 40) and 'approval' (Phlm. 14). The word συγγνώμη appears once, in 1 Cor. 7.6, where it is contrasted with ἐπιταγή, as it is impliedly here, and with a similar meaning of 'advice', although BDAG offers 'concession', 'indulgence' rather than 'opinion', 'advice', 'judgment' (950). The sentiment in 8.10 is also informed by Paul's earlier statement that he is not seeking to lord it over their faith (1.24). Rather, he is working co-operatively and non-coercively with the Corinthians. He is reinforced in this approach by the fact that in the previous year the Corinthians had themselves become active in the collection, both in commencing action and in being willing to do so. The word 'this' (τοῦτο) starting the second clause refers to the fact that Paul is giving advice not a command; it is appropriate, he adds, because of their initiative in relation to the fact that they 'had-previously-made-a-beginning' (προενήρξασθε) on the collection the year before, which shows he has no need to command them to do it. The curious word order here, with the action mentioned before the intention to act ('not only in the execution but in the desire'), is perhaps to be explained as a way of suggesting that their decision to take part was their own, without compulsion by him (Thrall 2000: 536). This represents quite a change on his earlier position, because in 1 Cor. 16.1 he had, in fact, directed them to participate (διέταξα; 1 Cor. 16.1).

2 Corinthians 8.11 By 'now' (νυνί) Paul means in contrast to last year. He repeats the expression for 'execution' (ποιῆσαι) from v. 10, but now preceded by an injunction to complete it (ἐπιτελέσατε). This is the only imperative in 2 Corinthians 8-9, although the word is used in relation to Paul's request (in the subjunctive mood) to Titus to complete the collection in 8.6. In spite of the long scholarly interest in partitioning these two chapters, ch. 9 can hardly have existed separately from Chapter 8 without this imperative or some expression very like it. By restricting the scope of the giving by Corinthians to 'what you have' (ἐκ τοῦ ἔχειν), which is equivalent to 'according to whatever one has' (καθὸ ἐὰν ἔχῃ) in 8:12, Paul is giving them an easier burden than the Macedonians undertook, for they gave παρὰ δύναμιν ('beyond their means'; 8.3).

2 Corinthians 8.12 Having begun with 'If the readiness (προθυμία) is there', Paul continues with 'it is acceptable (εὐπρόσδεκτος) according to what one has, not what one does not have'. It is unlikely that εὐπρόσδεκτος is an adjective modifying προθυμία. As various commentators have suggested probably some word like χάρις ('gift') is implied here as modified by 'acceptable', since the point of v. 11 is execution not intention (Thrall 2000: 538). Paul is continuing the point made in v. 11 that the Corinthians are only being asked to contribute to the collection within their means. This is consistent with the advice he had previously given them, namely, that on the first day of each week they should put aside and save as much as they could (1 Cor. 16.2). Thus, they are to pay from their surplus and do not need to impoverish themselves for the collection. The Macedonians had adopted a different approach, by giving beyond their means (8.3). To that extent Paul is not presenting their actual practice as prototypical for the Corinthians, but their commitment to the cause; in that respect they are exemplary.

The aim of reciprocity (8.13-15)

2 Corinthians 8.13-15 The Greek in v. 13 is quite compressed and, translated literally, reads 'For not ἄνεσις ('relief') for others, θλῖψις ('affliction') for you, but from equality (ἰσότης). When Paul says 'others', he no longer means the Macedonians but has the recipients of the collection in mind. This identification and the nature of the 'equality' in view become clear in v. 14:

> During the present time, your surplus (περίσσευμα) should supply their deficiency (ὑστέρημα), so that their surplus (περίσσευμα) might supply your want (ὑστέρημα), in order that there might be equality (ἰσότης).

'Their deficiency' in the present time points to the poor or even destitute in the Christ-movement in Jerusalem, 'the πτωχοί' of Ga.l 2.10 and 'the πτωχοί of the saints in Jerusalem' in Rom. 15.26. Whereas at present the Corinthians have a surplus and the Jerusalem Christ-followers a deficiency, Paul envisages (at least for the sake of the argument, if not in actuality) a future time when their roles may be reversed.

In v. 15, Paul concludes this short section with a quotation from Exod. 16.18: 'The person having much did not have too much (ἐπλεόνασεν), nor did the one having little have too little' (ἠλαττόνησεν), which relates what happened when the Israelites were gathering manna in the desert. The Exodus of the Israelites from Egypt is one of those narratives with which Christopher Stanley has plausibly suggested that the Corinthians were generally familiar (2008b: 135). Nevertheless, while it is clear from 2 Corinthians 3 that Paul or perhaps his opponents had certainly told the Corinthians in general terms about the Exodus event, that they would recognize so granular a detail as this seems unlikely. In line with previous argument in this commentary, it is unlikely that Paul expected, let alone intended, his audience to recognize the original context of the quotation. His use of it is oracular; all they needed to know was that this was something to be found in Israelite scripture and that it had a direct bearing on their situation in Corinth and that of the potential recipients of their largesse among the movement in Jerusalem. The arrangement described in the quotation is not an ideal parallel if the Corinthians recognized its source, since it had nothing to do with a process of exchange; God provided the manna and the Israelites collected it. The quotation, in fact, works far better if the Israelites did not recognize its origin, because then they might suppose that here was a divine warrant for the type of process that Paul has just described in v. 14, where human action not divine intervention produces the equality in view. Paul's point is that as a result of the arrangements he has set out in the previous verses, Christ-followers in both places would always have what they needed; whether it was a lot or a little, it would suffice. If the Corinthians did recognize the referent of the quotation, they would realize the material nature of the substance being discussed. If not, they would assume that what was being discussed must have been similar to the monetary gift that Paul had been speaking about hitherto.

It is difficult to avoid the impression that Paul does have in mind monetary resources as what will move from surplus to deficiency. The view of Betz (1985: 68) that it is hard to imagine Paul ever expecting a material shortage in Corinth to be met from the church in Jerusalem is too speculative (after all, the poverty of the Macedonians was no restraint on their contribution) and is falsified by the contrary impression that v. 14 conveys in its context. Barnett suggests (1997: 414) the possibility of the Corinthians receiving both material help and the benefit of the Jerusalemites' loving and prayerful fellowship, for which he cites 9.14. That view might appear to draw some support from what Paul says at Rom. 15.27. Yet the idea that non-Judean Christ-followers are currently indebted to Judean Christ-followers for the blessings of the Spirit and should repay that debt in monetary form is missing from 2 Corinthians 8–9. In addition, 9.14 applies to the response of the Jerusalem Christ-group to the Corinthians in the present and does not represent a future transfer from their abundance to the Corinthians' dearth. The quotation from Exod. 16.18 in v. 15 has a material flavour whether or not the Corinthians recognized its source. Accordingly, the point Paul is making concerns the exchange of material help.[2] Paul does not suggest any theological motivation for the collection.

As commentators have observed, the notion of 'equality', the usual translation of ἰσότης, has a strong background in Greek thought.[3] Aristotle famously connected justice with equality (*Nichomachean Ethics*, 1129–31), and Philo said that equality was the mother of righteousness (*Spec. Leg.*, 4.231), sentiments clearly reflected in Col. 4.1, with the instruction to masters to give slaves what is 'justice and equality' (τὸ δίκαιον καὶ τὴν ἰσότητα). Larry Welborn has mounted a powerful argument that by using the idea of ἰσότης Paul promoted the ('economic') idea of 'the equalization of resources between people of *different* social classes through voluntary redistribution' (2013: 89; emphasis original).

Yet underlying this type of equalization may be a phenomenon very like what Ekkehard Stegemann and Wolfgang Stegemann have described as 'familial reciprocity', within their fourfold typology of reciprocity-oriented exchange (1999; Crook 2004: 56–9). The Stegemanns were indebted to Karl Polanyi for this idea. Family exchange can occur not only within a family but within other collectivities, such as clans within a tribe or, as

---

[2] To similar effect, see Lambrecht 1999: 138, Matera 2003: 192–3; Harris 2005: 592; and (above all) Welborn 2013; *contra*, Betz 1985: 68; Seifrid 2014: 334–5.
[3] See Furnish 1984: 407–8; Betz 1985: 67–8; Harris 2005: 590; Welborn 2013.

here, different parts of the one Christ-movement. It is to be distinguished from 'balanced reciprocity', which 'takes place between social equals and ... involves the mutual exchange of gifts with balanced value' and which can be seen in commercial transactions (Crook 2004: 56-7). There is no sense that the 'equality' that Paul has in mind in these verses involves the reciprocal payment of gifts of the same value, as in balanced reciprocity. Rather, as in familial exchange, one part of the Christ-movement that has a surplus will help another that has a deficiency, in the knowledge that it itself may be helped by the donee later, with the quantum of the respective gifts irrelevant. That the respective gifts were not expected to be quantitatively equal is clear from 8.15.

This is the rationale for the collection Paul offers the Corinthians. It was never likely, however, to be the way it was received by the Jerusalem Christ-movement for the reasons set out in the general discussion on the collection.

The mission of Titus and his companions (8.16–9.5)

There are strong links across the material in 8.16–9.5, and it is best to regard this as a distinct section (as do Furnish, Hafemann and Matera). Without 8.16-24 Paul's mention of 'the brothers' in 9.3 would not make much sense, and in the absence of 9.1-5 it would be hard to understand his reference in 8.24 to making an honour-claim about the Corinthians. In the first part of this section (8.16-24), Paul sets out the composition of the mission and commends it to the Corinthians (8.16-24), and in the second (9.1-5) he explains the reason for it (Matera 2003: 203), especially linked to his honour-claim just mentioned.

8.16-24 The delegates and their credentials

2 Corinthians 8.16-17 These verses represent the beginning of a new step in the argument, but one for which Paul has already paved the way by his discussion in 2 Cor. 7.5-16 of the recent interaction between Titus and the Corinthians. Here, then, is additional evidence of the integrated nature of 2 Corinthians and further reason to treat with scepticism the idea that chs 8 and 9 were originally one, let alone two, separate letters.

As with most sections of this letter, even a description of action such as we have here in 8.16-17 contains a number of issues requiring resolution. First, whom does Paul have in mind when he says in v. 16 that God has planted the *same* earnest care (σπουδή) in Titus' heart? Most commentators consider that Paul means Titus shares the earnestness that he, Paul, has for the Corinthians (e.g. Furnish 1984: 423; Harris 2005: 598). The advocates of this view recognize that 'same' appears to require a quality already mentioned. Yet up to this point σπουδή has not been predicated of Paul but twice of the Corinthians in their regard for Paul (7.11, 12) and once more generally of their disposition (8.7), and also of the Macedonians in relation to their commitment to the collection (8.8). Nevertheless, they typically point to the addition of the phrase ὑπὲρ ὑμῶν, 'for you', after 'the same earnestness' and suggest that the earnestness of neither the Corinthians nor the Macedonians was 'for the Corinthians' (Thrall 2000: 544–5). But this is to misinterpret the meaning of σπουδή by insisting that its object in any particular context forms part of its meaning, whereas in fact it is a general quality possessed by a person that is activated towards various other people depending on its context. Accordingly, the references noted earlier do indeed provide a strong argument for identifying the σπουδή mentioned here with that of the Corinthians and Macedonians. From a social identity perspective, by attributing to Titus the earnestness – a significant identity-descriptor – that he has already ascribed to the Corinthian and Macedonian Christ-followers, Paul underlines the importance of cooperation and mutuality that he has been working to promote in the letter from its outset. 'We are all in this together, sharing the same group values', Paul is implying, 'and Titus also embodies the same earnestness that you and the Macedonian Christ-followers have already demonstrated'.

Secondly, what is the meaning of the opening clause in v. 17: ὅτι τὴν μὲν παράκλησιν ἐδέξατο ('because he received the παράκλησις'), in particular what does παράκλησις mean and from whom has it been received? An appealing possibility, rarely, if ever, mentioned by commentators (probably because of their fixation upon partition theories), is that Paul actually has in mind here the fact that, when Titus visited the Corinthians in connection with the severe letter, he was 'comforted with comfort' from them (7.7), with παράκλησις having the same meaning as at 2 Cor. 1.3, 4, 5, 6 and 7. This reference would convey the meaning that 'Because Titus received this comfort from them, he was going back to them of his own accord'. Weighing against this interpretation, however, is that there is a more immediate context for the meaning of the clause in ch. 8. For this first clause in v. 17 is probably to be understood with reference to v. 6, where Paul stated that he had urged (using παρακαλέσαι, the verbal equivalent of παράκλησις) Titus to complete the collection. The word παράκλησις meaning 'appeal' also occurs in 8.4 of the Macedonians exhorting Paul to let them participate in the collection. In addition, in 9.5 Paul will note that he found it necessary to appeal (παρακαλέσαι) to the brothers to proceed to the Corinthians ahead of him, where the appeal in question covers Titus, the second brother mentioned in 8.18 and the third mentioned in 8.22, with the appeal in 9.5 thus also representing a sign of the integration of chs 8 and 9.

Paul's appeal to Titus needs to be reconciled with the effect of the second clause in the v. 17, the third interpretative question, where Paul states that Titus is very earnestly acting 'of his own accord' (αὐθαίρετος). The answer to this is that an appeal, as opposed to a command, allows its recipient to accept or refuse. It is Titus who decided that he would go to the Corinthians in relation to the collection, not Paul. Paul had previously stated that the Macedonians were contributing to the collection 'of their own accord' (αὐθαίρετοι; 8.3). Yet there is a strong theological dimension here, since in relation both to the Macedonians and Titus Paul attributes their response to the action of God (in 8.1 and 8.16, respectively). With good reason, therefore, Matera observes 'that here and throughout the chapter God is the one who inspires and enables the good that humans do' (2003: 196).

Fourthly, is ἐξῆλθεν an epistolary aorist – that is, one that denotes 'time contemporary with the writing or sending of letter, since the letter is written from the standpoint of an orally delivered message' (BDF §334) – or not: Is Paul saying Titus is setting off or (at some point in the past) set off? The same question arises in relation to 'we sent with' (συνεπέμψαμεν) in 8.18 and 8.22. It is highly likely that ἐξῆλθεν is an epistolary aorist: here 'something in the present is described as past because it will be concluded by the time this letter is received' (Furnish 1984: 422). The same applies to συνεπέμψαμεν in vv. 18 and 22. This interpretation entails the realistic view that Titus and his two companions were to bear the letter we know as 2 Corinthians to Corinth. Otherwise, we would have to assume that Paul sent the three of them off and, at some later time, despatched the letter borne by someone else, even though it contained a vital message about his three emissaries that Paul would surely have wanted the Corinthians to receive co-incident with their arrival in Corinth. If Paul had chosen to send the letter on after the three emissaries, he would not even have known for sure when, or indeed if, the letter would reach the Corinthians.

2 Corinthians 8.18-19 In v. 18, Paul begins by mentioning that the brother whom he is sending with Titus enjoys praise throughout all the Christ-groups (ἐκκλησίαι), which must embrace the Corinthians (and Achaia generally), whom Paul could hardly omit from the designation 'all the communities' without insulting them. In v. 19, on the other hand, there is mention of the appointment of this brother 'by the Christ-groups' as Paul's 'travelling companion' (συνέκδημος) for the purpose of the collection. This second group of Christ-groups appears to be a subset of their totality referred to in v. 18. Important issues of interpretation are linked to this narrowing of focus.

In v. 18, 'We are sending with' (συνεπέμψαμεν) is, as noted in discussing v. 17, an epistolary aorist and needs to be translated as a present tense. That Paul is sending the brother and he has not, like Titus, decided to go himself suggests that in Paul's eyes this brother has a lower status than Titus, which tends to confirm that Titus is the leader of the mission in Paul's eyes. He is also unnamed, yet the Corinthians, as just noted, must at least know of him by repute (and Titus will be able to introduce him to them). We may eliminate the (occasionally essayed) idea that his name (and that of the other emissary in v. 22) was omitted by a redactor, as a counsel of desperation (Lietzmann 1949: 136–7). It has been suggested that the anonymity of this man and the other emissary mentioned in v. 22 is explicable on the basis that the Corinthians, not Paul, had originally suggested that they accompany Titus (Betz 1985: 72–4). Yet this suggestion would appear to entail either a communication to Paul from the Corinthians after the arrival of Titus from Corinth and before his return there, of which there is no suggestion in the text, or that the collection was discussed with Titus during his visit in relation to the severe letter, of which there is equally no sign. The actual reason for his being unnamed is that when the Corinthians heard this letter read to them, this man was probably standing next to Titus and was already quite well known to the Corinthian Christ-followers.

Paul says that this particular brother has 'praise in the Gospel' among all the Christ-groups (ἐκκλησίαι). The brother's precise function in relation to the Gospel that has earned such praise is unstated; it need not entail preaching, as in many translations (e.g. RSV), but perhaps more administrative or pastoral work. Whatever it is, in the case of this emissary Paul is plainly arguing for the man having an honourable status among all the Christ-groups apart from his own view of him. This reminder of his status provides some reassurance to the Corinthians of his independence of judgement and action as far as Paul was concerned. Finally, the fact that Paul does not name him provides further support for the likelihood that Titus and his two companions were responsible for carrying the letter to Corinth – Paul would be able to rely on the Corinthians ascertaining the identity of this brother when they saw him either through an introduction from Titus or because they knew him already.

Also a matter of debate is the identity of the Christ-groups in the frame, since there is no mention of their geographic location, but they probably include Achaia and Macedonia as noted earlier. Nickle's interesting idea that Paul means here 'the churches of Judea' (1966: 20) would appear to be opposed by Paul's own practice, since in 1 Thess. 2.14 he provides the necessary specification: 'the Christ-groups of God that are in Christ Jesus in Judea', by which he meant the mixed Judean/non-Judean Christ-groups with whom he was aligned (Esler 2021c).

Paul notes that this man is his travelling companion 'in this work of grace that is being administered (διακονουμένῃ) by us'. The word διακονουμένῃ matches Paul's description of the collection as διασκονία in 8.4. Such administration is expressed to be 'for the glory of the Lord', which requires little comment, but also 'to show our readiness' (πρὸς . . . προθυμίαν ἡμῶν), which does. The readiness in question – προθυμία being a word that he has already applied to the attitude of the Corinthians to the collection (8.11, 12) and will soon do so again (9.2) – probably relates to the entirety of Paul's efforts for the collection, in which case the recipients of his readiness are the poor Christ-followers of Jerusalem (Barnett 1997: 422). This view is supported by the fact that Paul is not himself about to go to Corinth in relation to the collection, which suggests that he has in mind here his final delivery of the gift to Jerusalem (Thrall 2000: 249). Paul has the big picture in view here, the final delivery, not just the collection in Corinth. Thus, the basis for his readiness is not to be found in v. 20, as Furnish suggests (1984: 423). Verse 19 presents Paul as cooperating with the Christ-groups who have appointed this brother. Although how or when that happened is unclear,[4] his attitude fits in well with the note he struck very early in the letter of not wanting to lord it over the faith of Christ-followers (1.24).

2 Corinthians 8.20 In saying 'We are putting this arrangement in place' (στελλόμενοι τοῦτο) at the start of the verse, the τοῦτο could refer either to Paul's arrangement of Titus and the brother, or just to the latter aspect, with the former seeming better to reflect the running syntax of the passage.

Paul's reason for the arrangement – 'that no one might blame (μωμήσηται) us concerning this large gift we are administering' – seems highly likely to express his genuine apprehension that he will be, or already has been, accused of misbehaviour in relation to the collection. Otherwise, he would not express his concern in this way here, a statement that also follows on from what he has said in 6.3, 'We put no obstacle in anyone's way, so that no fault will be found with the ministry (μὴ μωμηθῇ ἡ διακονία)', where the verb μωμάομαι also occurs, and his even more closely related sentiment in 7.2: 'We have not wronged anyone, nor corrupted anyone, nor exploited (ἐπλεονεκτήσαμεν) anyone', where the last verb refers to fraudulent behaviour. The most likely charge was that he had siphoned off some of the contribution for his own purposes, as with Ananias in Acts 5.2 (Harris 2005: 605). Strong confirmation for the reality of the allegation being made against

---

[4] Betz opts for a formal election process (1985: 74–5); although that is speculative, since another appointment process could have been chosen. 2 Cor. 2.6 presupposes a vote by the Corinthian Christ-group on the punishment for the malefactor, a sign of the voting practices of the civic ἐκκλησία of the cities of the Greek East having permeated Paul's version of the Christ-movement (see Esler 2021c).

him will be found in 2 Corinthians 12 (another sign of the integral nature of the letter) when he asks, as rhetorical questions, whether he took financial advantage of them through anyone he sent to them or whether Titus had done so to anyone (vv. 17 and 18), using πλεονεκτεῖν in each case. This latter visit is the one referred to in 8.6.

The words 'concerning this large gift we are administering' translate the Greek ἐν τῇ ἁδρότητι ταύτῃ διακουμένῃ ὑφ' ἡμῶν (literally, 'in this abundance being administered by us'). This is the only appearance of ἁδρότης in the New Testament (and it does not occur in the LXX). While the phrase is equivalent to 'this work of grace being administered by us' in 8.19, here the emphasis falls on the large size of the gift.

2 Corinthians 8.21 It is often observed that effective leaders spend much of their time thinking about the future, that is, to use the language of management, thinking strategically. Here Paul makes the same claim, but specifying that the object of his thoughts is what is honourable before God and human beings. In so doing he is also acting in accordance with a proverb in Prov. 3.4: 'think ahead on what is honourable before the Lord and human beings' (προνοοῦ καλὰ ἐνώπιον Κυρίου καὶ ἀνθρώπων), which Paul closely reproduces except that he adds 'for', 'not only... but also' and an extra 'before'. He would later cite the proverb (without reference to 'before the Lord') in Rom. 12.17. As previously argued, there is no reason to think that the Corinthians would have been familiar with this proverb, and Paul does not even indicate that he is citing Israelite scripture. Rather, he is just making the point that the care he is taking over the collection is motivated by his concern to act honourably before his divine and human audiences.

2 Corinthians 8.22 Paul now adds mention of a third member of the mission to Corinth, another unnamed 'brother' who 'we are sending' (συνεπέμψαμεν) with Titus and the brother of vv. 18-19. Συνεπέμψαμεν is an epistolary aorist like those in vv. 17 and 18. But this time there is no direct mention of any appointment by the churches, although such may be implied in v. 23 (see in the following). This man is Paul's 'brother', thus suggesting a close relationship with him (Matera 2003: 198). Perhaps he is also a Judean by descent. Like the Corinthians (7.11-12; 8.7), the Macedonians (8.8) and Titus (8.16, 17), this third member of the team is eager (σπουδαῖος). Paul regards eagerness (σπουδή) as a central identity-descriptor in the business of the collection. Although this man has great confidence (πεποίθησις μεγάλη) in the Corinthians, we are left in the dark as to the circumstances in which he came to acquire it. Yet, following Thrall (2000: 552) we should be cautious about supposing that this confidence indicates his previously having visited Corinth, since perhaps he was relying on a report from Titus. Nevertheless, it is possible that he had previously been to Corinth, and perhaps is to be identified with the companion of Titus on his visit to the city that Paul mentions in 12.18, a visit probably to be identified with that in 8.6. This may have been one of the many matters in which Paul says here that he had tested him. But if so, why does Paul not say in words to the effect, 'You know X, who accompanied Titus when he came about the collection.' So it seems more probable to view his confidence as built on a report he has received from someone else than on his prior acquaintance with the Corinthians.

2 Corinthians 8.23 This verse addresses the credentials of the three emissaries. It is broken up into two statements, each starting with εἴτε. Normally two instances of εἴτε would be followed by finite verbs, but, if these are lacking, we have an ellipsis and the meaning in each case is 'if (someone asks)', 'or if (there is any question)'.[5] These statements, however, seem to be more than just summaries of the situation, as is sometimes suggested (so Thrall 2000: 553; Seifrid 2014: 345), for they also appear to be anticipating a possible objection, an example of the rhetorical practice of 'anticipation' (προκατάληψις or *praesumptio*). The author of the *Rhetorica ad Alexandrum* describes anticipation as 'the method by which we shall counteract the ill-feeling which is against us by anticipating the adverse criticisms or our audience and the arguments of those who are going to speak against us' (1423b).

Titus, the only one of the three named and described as Paul's partner (κοινωνός) and fellow worker (συνεργός) 'in your service' (εἰς ὑμᾶς), occupies the leading position. Partnership is a key concept in his efforts to lead the Corinthians by stressing their joint participation in the identity and actions of the Christ-movement, with συνεργός appearing at 1.24 and συνεργοῦντες at 6.1. Paul has also previously said that the Corinthians were partners (κοινωνοί) in his sufferings and comfort (1.7). In 8.4, he noted that the Macedonians begged him to allow them participation (or partnership: κοινωνία) in the collection. Now Paul draws Titus into this realm of partnership by describing him as his partner on behalf of the Corinthians. It is preferable, as Furnish suggests (1984: 424), not to translate εἰς ὑμᾶς as 'among the Corinthians' because there is no sign that Paul and Titus had worked in the city together, that is, at the same time. A good translation is the RSV's 'in your service', as adopted earlier.

Paul's description of the other two brothers as ἀπόστολοι is probably not used here in the same sense that Paul is an ἀπόστολος of Christ, a full-time position which came with a divine commissioning (e.g. 1 Cor. 1.1; 2 Cor. 1.1; Gal. 1.1), but in the secular sense of the time of 'messenger', 'emissary' or 'representative' (Harris 2005: 611). Yet an uncertainty arises in relation to

---

[5] See BDF §§446 and 454(3), and Harris 2005: 610.

Paul's description of the brothers as the 'ἀπόστολοι of the communities'. Does this imply that there has been a selection process, such as Paul mentions for the first brother but not the second? Or was it enough that Paul regarded them in this light, whether or not they had been formally appointed, so that the designation would then extend to the second brother whether the Christ-groups had selected him or not? The former (a selection process) seems more likely. It would hardly further Paul's communicative purpose if the Corinthians were to discover upon the arrival of the mission that the second of the brothers enjoyed authorization solely from Paul.

Finally, these two brothers, as well as being representatives of the assemblies, are also 'the glory of Christ'. Rather than pushing this too far, to suggest, for example, that they reflect the glory of Christ or come with his authority, which would be inappropriate in view of their subordinate (though valued) position compared with Titus, this probably means that they promote the glory of Christ (Thrall 2000: 554–5).

2 Corinthians 8.24 Paul completes this section with a direction to the Corinthians for which he uses a present participle instead of an imperative: literally, 'Providing proof, therefore (τὴν οὖν ἔνδειξιν . . . ἐνδεικνύμενοι), before the communities, of your love for these men and of the honour we claim in relation to you'. It used to be suggested that this expression showed Semitic evidence (Furnish 1984: 425). More recently, this has been doubted. But rather than following Verbrugge in seeing here the sign of an edited conclusion of a letter that originally contained only 2 Corinthians 1–8,[6] it is better to regard Paul as softening the force of his injunction in keeping with his general policy in the letter of not lording it over their faith (1.24). The two matters for which such proof is required are the Corinthians' love for the three emissaries and the substantiation of the honour-claim that Paul has made to them concerning the Corinthians. We have noted earlier in this volume that in ancient Mediterranean culture it was not inappropriate to make honour-claims (about yourself or others) so long as there was a factual basis for the claim. Now we see precisely this phenomenon here, and in relation to the second matter Paul wants proof.[7] We even have here express mention of another aspect of an honour-claim, namely the existence of a relevant public to hear it, here other communities of the Christ-movement. The οὖν indicates his belief that this proof is justified by what he has just said about

---

[6] Verbrugge 1992: 254–8, who is followed by Thrall 2000: 556, but convincingly disproved by Harris 2005: 613.
[7] Betz misconstrues the meaning (1985: 85) in suggesting that Paul wants the Corinthians to provide 'Paul an occasion to boast'. Paul has already 'boasted' to his emissaries before their departure to Corinth; now he wants the Corinthians to provide proof that he was justified in doing so.

Titus and the other two brothers. Paul has taken great care over his selection of the personnel for this important task and he wants the Corinthians to give them a positive welcome.

The reason for the delegation (9.1-5)

2 Corinthians 9.1 'For concerning the ministry (Περὶ μὲν γὰρ τῆς διακονίας) to the saints', Paul writes, 'it is superfluous (περισσόν) for me to write anything to you'. As noted earlier, Stanley Stowers (1990) has convincingly shown that the words Περὶ μὲν γὰρ that commence 9.1 cannot introduce a new document but rather a new dimension to an existing document. The material in ch. 9 was always connected with that in ch. 8.

Paul's statement that it is superfluous for him to write anything to the Corinthians about the collection is probably an example of the rhetorical device of *praeteritio*, by which one draws attention to a matter by apparently denying it (O'Mahony 2001: 60, 130). This adds to the effect of the contrast established by the μὲν . . . δέ construction that relates the two pairs of verses comprising vv. 1-2 and 3-4, both of which feature a statement of fact in the first verse and a causal or purpose clause in the second.

The precise aspect of the collection that Paul seeks to address here concerns the making of an honour-claim that he just mentioned in 8.24, specifically to ensure that there is a solid foundation for that claim concerning the Corinthians and that it does not collapse on inspection. That is to say, 8.24 is demonstrably and closely linked to 9.1-4 so that suggestions that chs 8 and 9 were originally separate letters are unsustainable.

2 Corinthians 9.2 In 8.24, Paul had spoken of honour-claims concerning the Corinthians that he had made to his three representatives. Now we learn that having previously encouraged the Corinthians to take part in the collection with reference to the enthusiasm for it shown by the Macedonians (8.1-5), he had previously fired up the Macedonians by making honour-claims about Corinthians' readiness for the project! So he has 'boasted' about the Corinthians to both his representatives and to the Macedonians. Paul knows of their readiness in the previous year because that was when Titus had begun the collection among them (2 Cor. 8.6) and subsequently reported their response to Paul. At that time they had shown readiness in commencing the work (8.11), with the same word, προθυμία, used there as here. Paul's praise of the Corinthians was effective among the Macedonians, since the zeal of the former spurred on most of the latter in the project of the collection.

Paul had addressed this letter to the Christ-group (ἐκκλησία) of God in Corinth and to all the saints in the whole of Achaia (1.1). Achaia was the name of the province in southern Greece of which Corinth was the capital. While directed primarily to the Corinthians, there were obviously other Christ-followers elsewhere in the province whom he anticipated would also receive this letter. While he probably returns to the word 'Achaia' here in v. 2 because of the implied reference to the province of Macedonia in the name 'Macedonians', the word reminds us that he does have the whole province in view, which is another sign of the integral nature of this letter. Later, in Rom. 15.26 he will make the point that both Macedonia and Achaia had contributed to the collection, further evidence that the collection involved more Christ-followers in southern Greece than those in Corinth.

Thrall, along with many scholars, finds an inconsistency between 8.10-11 and 9.3-4 on the basis that in the previous year they had only showed willingness and made some sort of beginning, whereas Paul now says that 'Achaia has been ready' (παρεσκεύασται) since last year (2000: 564–5). It might be thought that this alleged inconsistency fails in light of the fact that παρασκευάζω in the middle voice, as here, simply means someone is prepared for some task, not that the task is complete,[8] and that is precisely the situation Paul describes in 8.10-11, where he also makes clear that they still have to complete it. Yet this proves to be no answer since, as we will see, Paul does use forms of παρασκευάζω in vv. 3 and 4 and ἑτοιμή ('ready') in 9.5 in relation to the collection being already completed, that is, with the money collected. This pushes us to the conclusion that he may have exaggerated the scope of the Corinthians' devotion to the collection when speaking to the Macedonians and now finds himself in the embarrassing situation of possibly being caught out. From such embarrassment, he is about to argue, the Corinthians can save him by completing the collection now. Yet a more innocent explanation is available: perhaps when Paul made the claim that the collection was on course but the subsequent deterioration in his relations with the Corinthians had somewhat thrown it off course (Matera 2003: 202–3).

2 Corinthians 9.3 Now comes a crunch point, and, once again, it concerns the necessity of there being a factual foundation for any honour-claim. Paul starts by saying, 'I am sending (ἔπεμψα) the brothers', where ἔπεμψα is another epistolary aorist like συνεπέμψαμεν in 8.18 and 22. He had done this so that (the brothers would ensure) the Corinthians were prepared (παρεσκευασμένοι ἦτε) with the collection, just as he had previously 'boasted' to the Macedonians that they were. Here we see a very explicit statement of the need for honour-claims to have a factual basis. Paul does not mention Titus by name here, but we should regard him as included among

---

[8] See BDAG 771, citing the expressions such as παρασκευάζεσθαι ἐς μάχην, meaning 'prepared for battle', not that the battle has commenced.

'the brothers' Paul mentions; after all, the apostle calls Titus a brother earlier in this very letter (2.13).

2 Corinthians 9.4 Paul is foreshadowing that he will travel from Macedonia to Corinth. It should be observed that this fits with his writing chs 1–7 in Macedonia and with the fact that he mentions a future visit to Corinth in 2 Cor. 12.14 and 13.1 (which he notes will be his third visit to the city). In other words, all three parts of the letter (1–7, 8–9 and 10–13) are consonant in relation to Paul's current location and future movements.

With v. 4 we witness the consequence, in this honour and shame culture, of the collection not being complete by the time Paul arrives, at least in the event he is accompanied by some Macedonian Christ-followers (perhaps bearing the Macedonians' contribution to the collection) – he will be put to shame (καταισχυνθῶμεν ; for which the Vulgate has *erubescamus*, 'we will blush with shame'), but so too, he claims, will the Corinthians. The latter aspect is something of a stretch, since it was Paul who made the claim about the Corinthians, not the Corinthians themselves. Paul diplomatically downplays the likelihood that the Macedonians would find anything amiss when they reached Corinth by the very tentative introduction, μή πως ἐάν ('Lest perhaps if . . .') at the start of the verse (Thrall 2000: 567).

2 Corinthians 9.5 Paul now casts his sending the brothers on ahead of him to arrange the collection as a means for avoiding the shame that he and the Corinthians might otherwise have experienced. Paul had previously used the word παρακαλέσαι (8.6) and the nominal form παράκλησις (8.17) in relation to his asking Titus to go to Corinth to complete the collection, and its repeated use here represents one of the many features tying chs 8 and 9 together.

Yet, he appends a second reason for his despatch of the three brothers at the end of the verse: that the collection would appear to be a gift of blessing and not some exploitative extraction. Perhaps he has in mind keeping the Corinthians free of any charge of financial irregularity. But it seems more likely that Paul regards himself as the potential target of such a charge. After all, he would appear to mean that such a charge can be avoided so long as he absents himself from the process of the collection, and it is difficult to see how his so acting could clear the Corinthians of any charge of financial impropriety. In 12.17-18, moreover, Paul dismisses the idea that either he or Titus acting on his behalf (apparently in relation to Titus' work on the collection in the previous year), had acted in an extortionate way, with the cognate word πλεονεκτεῖν being used in each verse.[9] This suggests that,

---

[9] Thrall (2000: 572–3) argues in favour of the Corinthians, so that the εὐλογία and πλεονεξία refer to the same subject; but her argument against relating them to the

rather than ignoring the allegation, he decides to sidestep the whole issue by having the three people he is sending organize the collection.

God's enrichment of the giver (9.6-10)

These verses of the letter, which seem to constitute a reasonably circumscribed unit (O'Mahony 2001: 100-2), are characterized by a notable concentration of agricultural imagery, mainly to do with sowing and harvesting. They also feature a second semantic field relating to good deeds and righteousness. In addition, a number of quotations from scripture are discernible (at least to the modern scholar, if not to Paul's ancient audience).

2 Corinthians 9.6 The idea expressed here was a commonplace, with similar ideas appearing in both Israelite Wisdom texts and in Greco-Roman literature. It is found, for example, in Prov. 11.21, 24, 26, 30; 22.8; Job 4.8; Sir. 7.3 and in Aristotle and Cicero.[10] Paul has elegantly expressed the thought in his own way, however, by the use of two instances of chiasmus: 'My point is this: the one who sows sparingly, sparingly will reap, and the one who sows generously, generously will reap.' There is no reason to think that Paul has in mind a reward that will be received in the next world.

2 Corinthians 9.7 We have an ellipsis at the start of the verse, which contains no Greek equivalent for 'must give'. But the appearance of 'each' (ἕκαστος) in the singular shows that Paul is calling upon each individual Corinthian Christ-follower to contribute, as less directly suggested by the singular verbs and participles in v. 6. Paul's disavowal of any element of coercion (ἀνάγκη)[11] is in line with the efforts he has been making throughout the letter so far to achieve the outcomes he wants by persuading the Corinthians to accept his views, not by issuing orders to them (1.24). The final statement about the cheerful giver is a quotation from Prov. 22.8 (LXX), with 'blesses' changed to 'loves', but Paul does not signal its scriptural status and the Corinthians may not have recognized it as such. It comes just after a verse that mentions harvesting being proportional to sowing, so Proverbs 22 was obviously in Paul's mind when he crafted this section of the text.

2 Corinthians 9.8 The central idea of the verse is that God provides abundantly (περισσεῦσαι) to them so that from their sufficiency (αὐτάρχεια) they may contribute abundantly (περισσεύητε) to every good work –

---

recipient is not as compelling as the linkage between Paul and πλεονεκτεῖν in 12.17-18.
[10] Furnish 1984: 440. See the detailed examples in Betz 1985: 102-5, including Cicero, *De oratore* 2.65.261: 'As you have sown, so shall you reap' (*Ut sementem feceris, ita metes*).
[11] The word ἀνάγκη appears nine times in Paul, often associated with θλῖψις.

especially, by implication, the collection. This sentiment flows directly from the previous assertion that 'God loves the cheerful giver'. God's expression of that love takes the form of ensuring that such a person has the resources to reciprocate the divine generosity in the treatment of others. Αὐτάρχεια was a popular concept in Stoic and Cynic philosophy but went further than the economic focus it has here to embrace freedom from all external circumstances, even including other people, and was more a product of self-discipline than a result of divine assistance (Furnish 1984: 442, 447–8; Thrall 2000: 579–80). For Paul this type of sufficiency exists in the context of human relationships, not withdrawal. As is often the case, comparing Paul and Hellenistic philosophy is more interesting for the differences than the similarities.

2 Corinthians 9.9 By the opening statement, 'Just as it stands written', Paul signals that he is quoting Israelite scripture, yet he does not provide the source – from the Septuagintal form of Psalm 111.9 (= MT Psalm 112.9) that describes the practices of the righteous man to the poor. In the psalm before this, the expression 'his righteousness (δικαιοσύνη) endures forever' is attributed to God (Psalm 110:3 LXX [MT Psalm 111:3]). While Psalm 111:9 (LXX), on its face and out of context, could refer to God or to a human being, Paul's presumed knowledge of the psalm and the fact that its context is nicely cognate with his argument to this point push us to the conclusion that he intended the latter option.[12] His audience, however, who probably did not recognize the origin of the quotation, were not in a position to contextualize the statement; for them, accordingly, this was another oracular use of Israel's scriptures. They are, however, likely to have interpreted the quotation as involving a human not a divine agent, given that the previous verse contained an implied encouragement to them to give to the collection for the poor in Jerusalem and that the next verse speaks of 'the harvest of their righteousness', thus directly connecting that verse to v. 9. The reasons for seeing a human agent here are, as Harris suggests (2005: 640), 'compelling'. As a result, in social identity terms in v. 9 Paul is adumbrating for their benefit a group prototype that locates the benefit of generous giving in the form of righteousness that endures forever.

This latter dimension to this example of righteousness should probably be understood to mean both that their righteousness will persist as long as they live and that it will never be forgotten. The actual persistence of something of which it is said 'it will remain forever' is a feature of most of the dozen or so instances of this expression in the Septuagint, for example: God's plan (Psalm 32[33].11 and Prov. 19.21); David's descendants (Psalm 88[89].36); the Lord

---

[12] Critics who regard God as the agent include Betz 1985: 111–12; Barnett 1997: 440.

(Psalm 101[102].12); God's righteousness (Psalm 110[111].3) and God's truth (Psalm 116[117].2). But it is difficult to disentangle such persistence from its memorialization; after all, in Psalm 111 we also find the statement 'the righteous person shall be in everlasting remembrance' (εἰς μνημόσυνον αἰώνιον; v. 7). Thrall, who seeks to choose between actual and remembered righteousness, finds the latter alternative less likely 'at least if it is a matter of perpetual human remembrance or that its effects will influence generation after generation' (2000: 582). Yet this view appears to be falsified by the history of Christianity, in Paul's statement in Rom. 15.26: 'For Macedonia and Achaia have been pleased to make some contribution for the destitute among the saints in Jerusalem.'

Commentators usually reflect upon the meaning of righteousness in vv. 9 and 10; typical possibilities include: the justified status of a person who gives generously; general moral righteousness; or, perhaps the most popular option, righteousness expressed through benevolence, that is, almsgiving (Lambrecht 1999: 147; Thrall 2000: 502). Interpreters who adopt the far less likely view that regards God as the subject of the verbs in v. 9 tend to view righteousness as covenantal loyalty, his faithfulness to his people (Barnett 1997: 440). Yet almost entirely overlooked in commentaries is the extent to which Paul's repeated use of righteousness here forms part of the total communication in the letter that embraces chs 1–7 and 10–13. It should be recalled that only a little earlier in the letter, in 6.14, Paul has offered δικαιοσύνη as, in part, a summation of the behaviour to be expected of Christ-followers. In 9.9, he proposes participation in the collection as an exemplification of δικαιοσύνη and will repeat that theme in v. 10. Thus, he establishes a strong link between his great identity statement in 6.14–7.1 and the collection. Then, looking forward, in 2 Cor. 11.13-15 Paul excoriates the interlopers who have turned up in Corinth with a Gospel different from his in the following terms:

> For such men are false apostles, deceitful workmen, disguising themselves as apostles of Christ. And no wonder, for even Satan disguises himself as an angel of light. So it is not strange if his servants also disguise themselves as ministers of righteousness (διάκονοι δικαιοσύνης).

The critical point here is the last statement: they disguise themselves as ministers of righteousness (διάκονοι δικαιοσύνης). Righteousness was a fundamental aspect of Judean ethnic identity (a crucial 'identity-descriptor'), and in Galatians it was being offered by the interlopers to Paul's non-Judean converts as a glittering prize of becoming Judeans (Esler 1998:141–77). Paul meets this claim by insisting, to the contrary, that righteousness comes from his version of the Gospel, not from that of this opponents. In other words, in that letter righteousness is a field of lively intergroup contestation. Paul's opponents in Corinth appear to be proffering similar claims to those in Galatia, or at least insisting that they are representatives of righteousness, so that righteousness once again becomes a battleground between Paul and those hostile to him. This aspect of his communicative intention leapt from the page in 2 Cor. 3.9 when he characterized his own work as 'the ministry of righteousness' (διακονία τῆς δικαιοσύνης). He really is 'a minister of righteousness' unlike his opponents who merely disguise themselves as such. In this context, the references to the righteousness of the Corinthians in 2 Cor. 9.9-10 fall naturally into place as part of his integrated communicative aims in the letter. In v. 9 (and, as we will see, in v. 10), Paul provides part of the basis of his answer, namely that in contributing to the collection the Corinthians will also achieve or at least manifest righteousness. Accordingly, Paul is implying that by encouraging them to participate in the collection he solidifies the case he has already established in 2 Cor. 3.9 for his being the minister of righteousness. The collection has become an arena in which Paul's need not to be outdone by them in relation to ministering righteousness becomes evident. The fact that the text Paul has cited affirms that the righteousness in view will endure forever enhances its significance. Thus, righteousness emerges as a key feature of the conflict evident in Corinth. Should we classify this conflict as intergroup or intra-group? Paul portrays his opponents so negatively that he is unlikely to have regarded them as members of the same group as him, so the former term more aptly reflects his position. But perhaps his opponents were not so severe on him and viewed their dispute as what we would characterize as an intra-group conflict.

2 Corinthians 9.10 This verse expresses a point similar that of v. 8, but now using imagery from farming and food production, while also underlining what is said about righteousness in v. 9. Since the expression σπόρον τῷ σπείροντι καὶ ἄρτον εἰς βρῶσιν ('seed to the sower and bread for food ') occurs in Isa. 55.10 (LXX), except there we find σπέρμα instead of σπόρον, it is likely that what Paul says here is coloured by the Isaianic verse whether he realized that or not. On the other hand, he does not signal to his audience that he was citing scripture, and it is most unlikely that they would have recognized the source. It may have been a proverb at that time (Betz 1985: 113). In any event, his audience would have assumed that this was another way of saying that they would receive divine help in their making their contribution to the collection and in bringing it to a successful conclusion. The expression γενήματα δικαιοσύνης ('the harvest of righteousness') occurs in Hos. 10.12. Its appearance here means that Paul's mind was saturated with Judean scripture that he could draw on whenever he needed it; it does not mean that he imagined his audience would have recognized the source in Hosea 10, still less that they would have imported that source into how they understood what Paul was saying to them here. Nevertheless, the last statement in the verse, coupled with the point of v. 11, requires us to recognize that by the harvest of their righteousness Paul refers not only to the collection but to impact of that righteousness on the Corinthians themselves, as we will now see.

The offering of prayer to God (9.11-15)

2 Corinthians 9.11 This verse is transitional: it looks back to the section contained in vv. 6-10 and looks forward to vv. 12-15. As to the first aspect, the verse summarizes the position in which the Corinthians find themselves: they are 'being enriched (πλουτιζόμενοι) in every way for all generosity (εἰς πᾶσαν ἁπλότητα)'. This accepts the usual interpretation of πλουτιζόμενοι as a passive, which is most likely given the context, not a middle. As this enrichment is all embracing, it must also include their righteousness, mentioned in v. 10. So righteousness is a quality the harvest of which is not just confined to the size of the collection, although that is a vital index of their generosity, but to righteousness as a group value that they embody in how they live and behave. Many interpreters reject the translation of ἁπλότης as 'generosity', with Seifrid, for example, noting that this meaning is unattested (2014: 362). Danker also objects to the translation 'generosity', noting that here and in the other Pauline instances where it is proposed (Rom. 12.8; 2 Cor. 8.2; 2 Cor. 9.13) it is probably the case that 'the sense of *sincere concern, simple goodness* is sufficient' (BDAG 104). As noted earlier in relation to 2 Cor. 8.2, however, the context of the passage really demands the idea of 'generosity', not simply 'sincere concern'.

The last clause is reasonably straightforward and carries us forward into the remainder of the verse: the generosity of the Corinthians produces thanksgivings to God. That God deserves this generosity is manifest in his central role in the whole process as described in 9.6-11. A more difficult question is what Paul means when he says that their generosity produces thanksgiving διὰ ἡμῶν ('through us'). Probably the reference is to his role as the broker of the collection. 'Paul initiated this ministry', Barnett notes (1997: 443), 'and is now engaged in reinvigorating it, and he will oversee its fruits to Judaea (cf. 8.19-20)'. In this case the plural, 'through us' (διὰ ἡμῶν) could either be an epistolary plural or reflect the fact that a number of people will accompany the collection to Jerusalem.

2 Corinthians 9.12 This verse closely follows on v. 11, with ὅτι ('because') at its start marking the connection. The connective 'because' depends upon ἡ διακονία τῆς λειτουργίας ('the ministry of this service') not merely supplying the deficiencies (ὑστερήματα) of the saints but also overflowing with thanksgiving to God, with the latter element dominating what remains of ch. 9. In ch. 8, Paul had described the collection as a means for maintaining ἰσότης (equality or reciprocity) between the Christ-groups: if the Corinthians supplied the deficiency (ὑστέρημα) of the Jerusalem poor now, they would later find their own deficiency (ὑστέρημα) attended to by them (8.14). While here clearly referring back to what he said there (which provides further evidence for the integral nature of 2 Corinthians 8 and 9), Paul now fixes upon a related but different issue: the supplying of deficiency will also generate thanks to God.

Paul's centrality to the whole process of the collection, which is discernible in διὰ ἡμῶν in the previous verse, now comes to the surface. For he has previously used the words διακονία and διάκονος repeatedly of his ministry in general (διακονία: 3.8, 9; 4.1; 5.18; 6.3; διάκονος: 3.6; 6.4) and διακονία in chs 8 and 9 of this specific ministry relating to the collection (8.4; 9.1). By mentioning ministry in v. 12, he is once again reminding the Corinthians of his role in the whole venture. This stratagem is underlined by his introduction of the word λειτουργία, a word he only uses twice elsewhere (Phil. 2.17, 30), to designate the collection itself, which in 8.4 and 9.1 he had designated by διακονία. Speaking of the ministry of the service, the διακονία of the λειτουργία, brings out the salience of his role in the enterprise and its function within the larger framework of his proclamation of the Gospel: he is speaking once more of his ministry but at this moment in its specific manifestation of the collection. Here τῆς λειτουργίας is an epexegetical genitive offering a specific example of the larger category referred to by the main noun, διακονία. This point is usually overlooked by commentators,[13] in part because some of them regard chs 8-9 as constituting a different letter (or letters).

In the second clause in v. 12, we learn something more about Paul's ministry as exemplified in the collection, namely that it overflows through abundant thanksgiving to God. This largely reflects the assertion in v. 11, while adding the extra point of the connection between the supplying of the saints' needs and the expression of thanksgiving.

---

[13] The point is not noticed by Furnish (1984: 443); Betz (1985: 117-20); Barnett (1997: 443-5); Lambrecht (1999: 148-52); Thrall (2000: 586-8); Matera (2003: 208-9); Harris (2005: 648); and Roetzel (2007: 152-3). Seifrid is a rare exception who connects what Paul says here to his larger, apostolic mission and who recognizes the epexegetical character of the genitive (2014: 363-4).

2 Corinthians 9.13 Literally rendered, this verse runs: 'Because of the evidence of this ministry (διακονία) praising (δοξάζοντες) God for the obedience of your confession (ὁμολογία) concerning the Gospel of Christ and for your generosity (ἁπλότης) in sharing (κοινωνία) unto them (εἰς αὐτούς) and with everyone...' The subject of δοξάζοντες is almost certainly the (Jerusalem) saints referred to in the previous verse (Thrall 2000: 588), who are to be identified with αὐτούς in this verse, not the Corinthians.

The broad approach to interpreting the two instances of διακονία in v. 12 just advocated, where διακονία relates to Paul's ministry as it is expressed in the collection, so that his role, not just the activity of the Corinthians, comes into prominence, is fully justified by the sentiments expressed in v. 13. For the praise that others are directing to God with respect to the Corinthians covers not only their generosity but also their attachment to the Gospel of Christ. This is the only time Paul uses ὁμολογία (although the related verb, ὁμολογεῖν, occurs in Rom. 10.9, 10 in the sense of 'confess' or 'profess'). The likely meaning of ὁμολογία here is as an expression of allegiance as an action, meaning, 'confessing' or 'professing' as opposed to the expression of allegiance as the content of an action, 'confession', 'profession' (BDAG 709). Most importantly, 'the Gospel of Christ' is a characteristic Pauline description of the content of his ministry. It has already appeared in 2 Cor. 2.12 of his work in Troas, and later he will mention that he was the first to come all the way to them with the Gospel of Christ (10.14), a view also expressed in 1 Cor. 3.6. Their confession of the Gospel of Christ is the result of his proclamation of it, of his activity as a minister (διάκονος) of the new covenant (2 Cor. 3.6), as agent of the ministry (διακονία) of the Spirit (3.8) and of righteousness (3.9). This broadening of focus is also reflected in the otherwise puzzling expansion at the end of the verse, when after 'unto them' (presumably meaning the saints in Jerusalem) Paul adds 'and unto all' (εἰς πάντας), probably meaning, all Christ-followers (Furnish 1984: 445). This addition also suggests that the meaning of 'sharing' (κοινωνία) must go beyond the provision of money because there is no sign that Corinthian financial assistance was needed or envisaged for any Christ-followers apart from the poor in Jerusalem.[14] All of this requires that Paul has more than the collection in mind throughout this verse. Accordingly, we now have good reason to doubt Lambrecht's view that 'one could be a little surprised that the Corinthians' glorification of God will occur in the first place through their obedience and in the second place through their generous contribution' (1999: 148).

---

[14] Harris similarly notes (2005: 655) that it is better to give the term κοινωνία 'a broader sense such as "sharing" or "fellowship" or even (cf. BAGD 439b) "altruism"'.

The aim of Paul's insinuating himself and his ministry so firmly into a discussion of the collection, which will depend on the generosity of the Corinthians, is not likely to be a desire for honour on his part. Rather, it continues the theme of the letter that Paul and the Corinthians work closely together in the service of the Gospel and must continue to do so. It is essential to how he moulds the identity of Corinthian Christ-group and acts as a leader to guide them in particular directions.

2 Corinthians 9.14 The conclusion reached earlier as to the broad subject of δοξάζοντες, namely that it refers to the Jerusalem saints, is also pertinent here. These people now pray for the Corinthians and long for them on account of God's grace (χάρις τοῦ θεοῦ) on them. By so saying, Paul underlines yet again God's role in the whole process. Yet at the same time he creates an *inclusio* with 2 Cor. 8.1, where χάρις τοῦ θεοῦ in this sense also occurs (there in relation to the Macedonians generosity in relation to the collection). This is further evidence for the original interconnectedness of chs 8 and 9. The optimistic note that Paul strikes here as to the receptiveness of the Jerusalem Christ-followers to the Corinthians and their generosity stands in contrast to his asking the Roman Christ-folllowers not long afterwards (in Rom. 15.31) to pray that his ministry for Jerusalem might be acceptable to the saints. Was Paul so carried away by his enthusiasm for the project and the Corinthians that he over-egged the cake in 2 Cor. 9.14? Or did he later receive word that the Jerusalem Christ-movement had reservations about this gift.

2 Corinthians 9.15 These two chapters end with the apparently simple exclamation: 'Thanks be to God for his indescribable gift (τῇ ἀνεκδιηγήτῳ αὐτοῦ δωρεᾷ)!' But what is God's indescribable gift? Some interpreters tie it closely to the collection. For example, it could refer to the gift of love between Judean and non-Judean Christ-followers (Plummer 1915: 257, 267–8). Or possibly to the gracious action of God that resulted in the Macedonians' generosity and the anticipated generosity of the Corinthians (Furnish 1984: 452). But these seem too limited in scope for how Paul expresses himself here, especially in his description of the gift as indescribable (which is *hapax* for the New Testament). In Paul's two other uses of δωρεά, the word relates to God's gift of salvation: Rom. 5.15 ('the free gift') and Rom. 5.17 ('the free gift of righteousness'). So the word could be taken as referring to salvation in a general sense, the whole work of salvation (Lambrecht 1999: 148). Or it could point to Christ himself, the agent of that salvation, as numerous commentators believe. As Matera has noted, this ending entails Paul's again emphasizing 'the relationship of the collection to God's overall work of salvation' (2003: 210). Raising this issue, it should be noted, also carries an implied reminder of Paul's role in the process of redemption, as indicated in the widening out of the meaning of διακονία in vv. 12 and 13 and the mention of the Gospel of Christ in v. 13 to conjure up the wider character of Paul's ministry.

Commentary: Part C

2 Corinthians 10–13: Paul defends his leadership against his opponents and stiffens the Corinthians' identity in Christ

13

Paul's opponents and his response in a social identity perspective

Chapters 10–13 as an integral component of 2 Corinthians

Chapter 10 signals Paul's determined effort to address the remaining feature of the complex exigency that prompted him to write 2 Corinthians: the confusion being caused in Corinth by rival missionaries who have arrived with a gospel different from his and who are critical of him. But this subject is hardly a bolt from the blue. Paul has been preparing for the onslaught he is about to unleash earlier in the letter. These are the people who peddle the word of God (2.17), who come bearing letters of recommendation (3.1), who are preaching the importance of the law of Moses (3.2-18) and who have been raising insinuations about his financial probity (7.2). Titus had recently returned from Corinth to Paul in Macedonia (7.6-16) and had no doubt fully briefed him on the nature of the opposition. Many of the specific details that Paul raises in Chapters 10–13 no doubt have their source in that briefing. The nature of the opponents is covered in detail later in this chapter.

With the other pressing issues addressed, especially his relationship with the Corinthians – in the light of his change of travel plans and the man who acted wrongly – and the collection, he can now focus on this one. For unless he deals with these intruders, he risks the Corinthian Christ-followers succumbing to a Gospel different from his. So his need to solidify their in-Christ identity also surfaces in these chapters. The stakes are high and Paul, quite understandably, moves to an 'aggressive and even sarcastic argumentation' (Campbell 2014: 99) that has not been evident earlier in the letter. As noted in Chapter 1 of this volume, the greatest orator in the early Church, St John Chrysostom, considered that Paul handled the transition to this subject εὐκαίρως ('opportunely').

For many commentators, who believe 2 Corinthians is a composite of letter fragments, an alleged 'change of tone' at the start of ch. 10 signifies that 2 Corinthians 10-13 did not originally belong with the rest of the letter. As noted in the Introduction, weighed against the just-cited view of St Chrysostom, who possessed a first-hand familiarity of ancient rhetoric that modern commentators lack, this opinion cannot stand and, given the authority of Chrysostom as an opponent, cannot even realistically be offered.

One of the most influential arguments for 2 Corinthians being a composite letter is that chs 10–13 are actually the core of the severe letter Paul mentions in the text (2.3-4, 9; 7.12), as first proposed by A. Hausrath in 1870. The insurmountable obstacle to this idea is that the subject matter of the severe letter, Paul's direction to punish a single person who had committed ἀδικία on another, is nowhere to be seen in chs 10–13. An ingenious attempt to answer this has come from Francis Watson (1984). He argues, in brief, that the severe letter, properly understood, was not just about the man who committed ἀδικία but contained material about Paul's self-commendation, his apostolic status and his opponents. The answer to this proposal is that Watson's reconstruction of the severe letter depends on far too many suppositions deduced from 2 Corinthians 1–7 to establish a probable case.

Other approaches to separating chs 10–13 from the rest of 2 Corinthians rely on alleged inconsistencies between what is said here and in earlier sections of the letter. None of these is convincing, and I will deal with some of them as they arise.

Paul's opponents in 2 Corinthians

The issue

On numerous occasions in 2 Corinthians, especially but not only in chs 10–13, Paul refers to people who have arrived in Corinth and who are causing him trouble among his Corinthian addressees. These are usually, and reasonably, referred to as his 'opponents'. Modern discussion concerning who they were and what they stood for goes back to the writings of Ferdinand Christian Baur in 1831 and continues unabated to the present. C. K. Barrett once remarked of this issue that 'in the absence of new evidence it may well seem impossible to add to what has already been said on the subject' (1982b: 87). In this view he was mistaken, since knowledge does not advance only through the discovery of new data; sometimes a momentous new framework of understanding, one of Thomas Kuhn's paradigm shifts (1962), allows us thoroughly to reassess and reinterpret the evidence we already have. In what follows I will argue that the arrival of an intense interest in questions of group identity in New Testament studies in the last twenty-five years and the concomitant realization that the Ἰουδαῖοι of our sources (*Iudaei* in

Latin) were an ethnic group, not a 'religion', with the identity of the Christ-movement being of an altogether different character (Esler 2003a: 40–74; Mason 2007; Mason and Esler 2017), have provided just such a framework for a fresh investigation of Paul's opponents in 2 Corinthians.

Current discussion

Before undertaking that task, a brief summary of existing approaches is in order. Four major hypotheses have been advanced as well summarized by Sumney (1990: 13–73). The first was inaugurated by F. C. Baur himself, who viewed them (and I will use the terms employed in this scholarship, although they are now rendered problematic by the recent focus on identity) as 'Judaizers', meaning 'Jewish Christians' who demanded observance of the law of Moses by all 'Christians', including 'Gentile Christians', with circumcision the primary sign of such observance. In the twentieth and twenty-first centuries, variations of this approach have been published by D. Oostendorp (1967), C. K. Barrett (1982a: 60–86), J. J. Gunther (1973), G. Lüdemann (1989), Goulder (1994) and Harris (2005: 67–87). The second hypothesis construes the opponents as Gnostics; it had an early defender in Lütgert (1908) but has been principally advocated by Schmithals (1971). The third hypothesis, as advanced by Georgi (1987), is that they represented a 'divine man' (θεῖος ἀνήρ) viewpoint. The fourth hypothesis, associated with Käsemann (1942) and Sumney (1990), treats them as Pneumatics, in that the main point at issue between them and Paul is the Spirit. The second and third hypotheses (on the latter see Holladay 1977) have never found many followers, because of their strained use of the textual evidence and failure adequately to distinguish the very different situations underlying 1 and 2 Corinthians. The fourth hypothesis also depends on too thin a spread of textual data in 2 Corinthians to be convincing and, from a more recent perspective, inadequately addresses the signs of Judean ethnic identity being the dominant characteristic of the opponents.

Judean Christ-fearers requiring acceptance of Judean ethnic identity

Before proceeding to a new analysis along the lines mentioned earlier, it is useful to stress that there are really no methodological short-cuts in reaching a conclusion, such as the methods sought by Sumney (1990). Here, as anywhere in New Testament interpretation, our task is the detailed examination of textual data in their contexts using theoretical frameworks set out transparently at the outset. Nor is there any reason not to regard Paul as responding to things being said about him in Corinth. John Barclay's warnings against 'mirror-reading' (1987) were always more qualified and cautious than the meaning that they have subsequently acquired and more than meet their match in the ancient rhetorical practice of *prokatalepsis*, or *lepsis*, in Latin *praesumptio*, which meant the anticipation of counterarguments before they could be made. As Aristotle observed in *Rhetorica ad Alexandrum*, 1423b, *prokatalepsis* is 'the method by which we shall counteract the ill-feeling which is against us by anticipating the adverse criticisms of our audience and the arguments of those who speak against us'. Anyone who has argued a case in a court of law will know that Aristotle's advice is as applicable now as it was in his time. It is therefore remarkable that so many commentators are resistant to the idea that Paul understood and regularly acted upon the need to anticipate and answer the charges that were being made against him. In 2 Corinthians, he even had the benefit of a no-doubt-fulsome exposition of the situation in Corinth from Titus, who had only recently returned to him (2 Cor. 7.13-16). Nor, *contra* Stegman (2005: 40–1), is the effort to identify Paul's opponents 'doomed from the start' because of insufficient data. Paul provides abundant data on the subject.

In formulating the foundations of social identity theory, Henri Tajfel was very much alive to the prominence of ethnic groups as a source of such identity (1978: 1–2). At around the same time he was formulating social identity theory, ethnic identity was being placed on a more secure theoretical foundation by Fredrik Barth in a way that emphasized its ascriptive and processual dimensions and visualized the ethnic boundary as permeable, with some interactions across it permitted while others were proscribed (1969). In due course, the most common diagnostic indicators (not essentialist characteristics) of ethnic identity were identified as: (a) a common proper name for the group; (b) a myth of common ancestry; (c) a shared history or shared memories of a common past; (d) a common culture, embracing such things as customs, language and religious or cultic practices and beliefs; (e) a link with a homeland, either through actual occupation or by symbolic attachment to the ancestral land, as with diaspora peoples; and (f) a sense of communal solidarity (Hutchinson and Smith 1996: 6–7). In the late 1990s and early 2000s, the argument was beginning to be made that the Judeans were an ethnic group (Esler 1998: 77–92; 2003a: 62–74; 2009; Duling 2003, 2005; Elliott 2007), that 'religion' as we understand it was unknown in the ancient world (Esler 2003a: 7–8, adopting Smith 1991 [1962]) and that the Christ-followers' identity was of a very different type (Esler 2003a: 10–12, *passim*; 2006b; 2007a, 2011b, 2021b). Many of these ideas appeared in an article by Steve Mason in 2007 (written independently of Esler 2003a) and have recently been reasserted (Mason and Esler 2017) against attempts to minimize the boundary between Judeans and Christ-followers (Buell 2005; Horrell 2016). Subsequent research has abundantly substantiated the view that religion as we know it did not exist in the ancient Greco-Roman world (Nongbri 2015; Barton and Boyarin 2016). Accordingly, the *Ioudaioi* were an ethnic group, like the many others in their world (Esler 2009), though perhaps with a stronger cultic/religious dimension than most given the unique monotheism at its heart. Their name refers to their ethnic homeland (as with all other ethnic groups of the time) and is best translated 'Judean', not 'Jew'. To speak of them using the word 'Judaism', which is clearly a religion, is a category error. So too is the word 'Judaizing', which refers to the effort to impose 'Jewish' 'religion' of 'Judaism'. The word *Ioudaismos* in Gal. 1.13, 14 is thus egregiously mistranslated as 'Judaism', when it actually refers to ethnic indicator (d) mentioned earlier, namely the common culture (especially its customs and cultic rules derived from the law of Moses) of the Judean ethnic group.

According to Paul, when God revealed his son to him, it was so Paul could preach the Gospel about him among the non-Judeans (ἐν τοῖς ἔθνεσιν; Gal. 1.16). Paul understood this to entail that non-Judeans could join the Christ-movement without becoming Judeans, which meant without undergoing ethnic translation that involved, in part, circumcision for males (Gal. 2.10-14). But in every Christ-group Paul founded, there was at least one Judean, himself, present with non-Judeans, and this meant that the meals they shared (including the Lord's Supper, the κυριακὸν δεῖπνον of 1 Cor. 11.20) always involved commensality (not just meals in parallel) that offended a Judean rule current in the first century against this practice. This rule is known from Judean and Greco-Roman writers (Esler 1998: 93–116) and from Acts 10.28. It was probably based on the fear that idolatry could occur at such a meal. It, and a prohibition on Judeans marrying non-Judeans, were the two proscribed types of behaviour in the ethnic boundary between Judeans and non-Judeans that otherwise allowed interaction in other areas (as is abundantly clear in the documents of the Babatha archive (Esler 2017a]), in the manner explained by Fredrik Barth.

Thus, mixed table-fellowship was the problem and the answer from a Judean Christ-movement point of view was for the non-Judeans to become Judeans. That is why in the Jerusalem meeting (Gal. 2.1-10) Paul was under pressure (which he resisted) that Titus, his Greek companion, be circumcised (Gal. 2.3). Paul called the position that non-Judean Christ-followers did not need to become Judeans, which he presented as a form of enslavement, using the verb καταδουλόω (Gal. 2.4), 'the truth of the Gospel' (ἡ ἀλήθεια τοῦ εὐαγγελίου) in Gal. 2.5 and 2.14 (and he uses that phrase nowhere else).

The agreement reached in Jerusalem was to the effect that in his missionary areas Paul could continue with his version of the Gospel, meaning mixed table-fellowship. But Peter (and even Barnabas, a terrible betrayal of Paul) breached this agreement shortly afterwards in Antioch, at the behest of the 'circumcision party', meaning those insisting that all Christ-followers should be Judeans (Gal. 2.11-14). Thereafter, Christ-followers of this view tried to impose it on his Christ-groups in Galatia. The interlopers in Galatia were Judeans, since they were advocating the law of Moses (mentioned nearly thirty times in Galatians and often very negatively) and its particular embodiment in circumcision (Gal. 5.2, 3, 6, 11; 6.12, 13, 15), yet they were also Christ-followers, since they proclaimed a gospel, albeit different from Paul's (Gal. 1.6-7).[1] In seeking to persuade Paul's non-Judean Christ-followers in Galatia to become Judeans, moreover, they were offering them the glittering prizes of access to descent from Abraham and also righteousness. The appeal to Abraham is an illustration of ethnic indicator (b) mentioned earlier, a myth of common ancestry. Righteousness encompassed normative rules from the law of Moses and, in so doing, served as a Judean identity-descriptor. The appeal posed by these two dimensions of becoming a Judean (descent from Abraham and righteousness) is evident in Paul's (rather tortured) attempts to detach them from the Judean ethnic group and reattach them to his Galatian Christ-groups (Gal. 3.6-29), as I have elsewhere explained in relation to righteousness (1998: 169–78) and Abraham (2006b).

Paul was also apprehensive that people of this kind ('cutters') were going to arrive in Philippi (Phil. 3.2). Their pursuing Paul across his mission area, once they had broken the Jerusalem agreement, was not surprising. While Paul might derogate them as 'false brothers secretly brought in' to the Jerusalem meeting (Gal. 2.4), they (reasonably) saw themselves as both Christ-believers and as Judeans who needed to defend the ethnic identity of their people that was under threat wherever Paul proclaimed his gospel. It is 600 kilometres overland from Philippi to Corinth, or a journey of just over two weeks for an experienced walker. By sea the journey might only have taken a week.

All this sets the scene for understanding Paul's opponents in 2 Corinthians. Five factors deserve attention:

1. Like Paul himself, they were ethnic Judeans, or to use the proud self-designations they had provided to the Corinthians that Paul records in 11.22, no doubt on the basis of information received from Titus: 'Hebrews' ('Εβραῖοι), 'Israelites' ('Ισραηλῖται) and 'descendants of Abraham' (σπέρμα Ἀβραάμ). Whereas Ἰουδαῖοι was the word

---

[1] For my detailed views on this matter, see Esler 1998: 69–75.

outsiders used of them and Judeans used of themselves when other ethnic groups were in the frame (as in Gal. 2.15), Ἰσραηλῖται was an ingroup word, resonant both of an illustrious ancestor and possibly also of Israel as a specific land.[2] The fact of their being Judeans creates an initial link to the situation in Galatians.

2. More specifically, the valorization of Abrahamic ancestry implied in their claim to possess it (and no doubt to be able to share it) is a very significant link to the situation in Galatia. It was almost certainly being raised in Corinth as in Galatia as a benefit of becoming a Judean. The recognition of this connection (here perhaps for the first time) illustrates the benefits of moving to an ethnic understanding of Paul's opponents.

3. Paul's Corinthian opponents must have been claiming that they were Christ-followers, because they were referring to themselves as 'ministers of Christ' (διάκονοι Χριστοῦ; 11.23). They were also preaching Jesus, the spirit and the gospel, although all different from what Paul taught (11.4). The charge of preaching a different gospel (εὐαγγέλιον ἕτερον) is the same as he makes against his opponents in Gal. 1.6 (ἕτερον εὐαγγέλιον), noted earlier. It is a deeply serious allegation. Since the 'truth of the Gospel' was something that came from allowing non-Judeans into the Christ-movement without their becoming Judeans (Gal. 2.5, 14), the different gospel his opponents preached could not embody this truth. Indeed, they had necessarily set themselves against it.

4. There is probably a very direct reference to the breach of the agreement in Jerusalem in the fact of Paul's opponents not sticking to their agreed territory, but trespassing on his, in the implicit allegation in 2 Cor. 10.13-15 that this was exactly what they had been doing. Although this is a notorious crux in the letter, this seems to be the best interpretation (see the commentary on these verses).

5. The word Paul used for intentions of the false brothers in Gal. 2.4 bent on circumcising Titus, an enslavement (καταδουλόω), reappears in 2 Cor. 11.20 in relation to how his opponents are treating the Corinthians, its only other occurrence in Paul's letters.

Pursuing an ethnic approach to the data has thrown up such strong similarities between the opposition portrayed by Paul in Galatia and 2 Corinthians as to substantiate the case for their identity. But this conclusion runs up against the circumstance that commentators beyond number have denied that the

---

[2] See Elliott 2007.

opponents in 2 Corinthians were the same as those in Galatians by observing that neither circumcision nor Jewish customs are mentioned in the former (e.g. Lütgert 1908; Martin 1986: 107–8; Oropeza 2012: 113; Seifrid 2014: 102). While those who do so have all been labouring under the misapprehension that the issue was one of 'Judaizing', the question of circumcision and the Mosaic law is also significant within the new perspective adopted here in that it bears upon ethnic indicator (d), namely, a common culture, embracing such things as customs, language and religious or cultic practices and beliefs. The answer to this challenge is not that proposed by Barrett, that they 'were Jewish missionaries who did not insist on circumcision' (1982a: 80). Rather, the answer to this objection lies in the fact that while circumcision itself is not mentioned in the letter, the law of Moses is very prominent in 3.2–4.6 – especially in the unambiguous reference to the tablets of the law in 3.7 as 'the ministry of death, carved in letters of stone' – and this was the source of the rule on circumcising male infants (Gen. 17.10-13).

According to Oropeza (2012: 114), 2 Cor. 3.1–4.6 tells us virtually nothing specifically about the opponents' view of the law or their alleged 'Judaizing' tendencies, since to read their agenda into Paul's words in this passage 'would be to mirror-read the text'. As noted earlier, however, the advice of Aristotle in *Rhetorica ad Alexandrum*, 1423b, and confirmed by every advocate who has argued a case, is that is precisely what we must do. The essential point in understanding Paul's treatment of the law of Moses in 3.2–4.6 is that it comes immediately after he has, in successive verses, attacked people who peddle the word of God and people who come bearing letters of commendation (2.17–3.1). Peddling the word of God is Paul's derogatory way of referring to his opponents who expect to be paid for preaching the Gospel and who criticize him for not taking such support; that this is a big issue later in the letter (11.7-15) provides persuasive evidence of the integrity of the letter as we have it. It is highly likely that he introduces his discussion of the law of Moses that follows (3.2–4.6) at this point because these people have been recommending the merits of the law. Paul takes some pains (see the commentary) to draw a sharp and very negative distinction between the Mosaic law, a ministry of death (3.7) and of condemnation (3.9), the old covenant (3.14), with what he offers, a ministry (διακονία) of the Spirit (3.8) and of righteousness (3.9), that leads to freedom (3.17). Paul's attack on the law of Moses in 2 Corinthians is not as extreme as in Galatians, but this mention of freedom is reminiscent of his earlier claims that the law led to the 'enslavement' of non-Judean Christ-followers (Gal. 2.4; 4.3).

For Judean Christ-followers to have arrived in Corinth advocating the virtues of the law of Moses strongly indicates that they were doing so as part of a campaign that the non-Judean Christ-followers adopt that law, by becoming ethnic Judeans. Circumcision is not mentioned but taking on the Mosaic law inevitably entails circumcision. That this was what their campaign amounted to from Paul's perspective is virtually demanded by his use of καταδουλόω in 11.20 – where it heads the list of abuses to which Paul says his opponents are inflicting on the Corinthians – when its only other occurrence in Paul's letters is in Gal. 2.4 of the false brothers who want Titus circumcised. In addition, taking on the Mosaic law in the fullest sense inevitably entailed circumcision. It was not necessary expressly to mention circumcision. Thus, in Rom. 9.4-5 Paul carefully summarized the core of Judean ethnic identity characteristic of his 'brothers' (ἀδελφοί) and 'co-ethnics' (συγγενεῖς), 'Israelites', namely the sonship (υἱοθεσία), the glory, the covenants (διαθῆκαι), the giving of the law (νομοθεσία), the cultic worship (λατρεία), the promises (ἐπαγγελίαι) and the patriarchs. Here he did not need to mention circumcision, for it was covered by νομοθεσία. It is, however, possible that in singing the glories of the law of Moses the intruders did not start with the commandment concerning circumcision, and for obvious reasons. From their point of view, a glowing account of their law giver Moses (who would have reminded the Corinthian audience of figures like Solon and Lycurgus) and of his receipt of the law, plus an attack on Paul's authority, would have been a sensible rhetorical strategy to begin their task of persuasion. These factors weigh heavily against Matera's assertion that 'there is no indication that circumcision or the works of the law were an issue in Corinth as they were in Galatia' (2003: 257).

One other feature of the letter, rarely, it seems, hitherto mentioned in modern scholarship in this connection, confirms the extent to which they were trying to sell the law of Moses to the Corinthians. For the frequently heard claim that there is no reference to Mosaic regulations or Judean customs in the letter is entirely erroneous. For in 11.15 Paul says that they were disguising themselves as 'ministers of righteousness' (διάκονοι δικαιοσύνης). It would be untenable to deny that Paul's opponents in Corinth were, in fact, claiming to be such, since otherwise the real sting in Paul's rhetoric in that verse, that they were actually servants of Satan, would have no foundation. The δικαιοσύνη they were promoting can only be that derived from obeying the Mosaic law in the context of Judean ethnic identity. It embraced the ethical norms and prototypical behaviour characteristic of Judeans and encapsulated their privileged identity (Esler 1998: 159–69). Paul's opponents in Galatia had been making the claim that δικαιοσύνη came from obeying the law, which is why he takes pains to deny it (Gal. 2.21; 3.21). Now in Corinth Judean Christ-followers had begun making the same case to Paul's Christ-followers.

We conclude, therefore, that the opponents to whom Paul refers in 2 Corinthians were people who were naturally proud of their Judean ethnic identity but were also Christ-followers. They represented the same position that Paul had been combating his whole career, that non-Judean Christ-followers needed to undergo ethnic translation and become Judeans. Paul resisted this as contrary to 'the truth of the Gospel'. The battle lines were clear, and battle had been joined in Jerusalem, in Antioch and in Galatia. It is altogether unsurprising that such Christ-followers had arrived in Corinth to renew hostilities in the same cause. Perhaps most surprising is that, in the end, it was Paul and not his opponents who emerged victorious in Corinth (see Rom. 15.23-27).

It is worth noting that there turns out to be ancient precedent for this broad view of the situation that prompted Paul to write 2 Corinthians. Theodoret of Cyrrhus (c. 393-456/466 CE), an interpreter of the Antiochean school, as part of a work entitled *interpretatio in xiv epistulas sancti Pauli* (PG 82.376–7), wrote a commentary on 2 Corinthians. In the Prologue to this, he explained the occasion of the letter as follows:

> Yet once again some of those who had come to believe from among the Judeans (τινὲς τῶν ἐξ Ἰουδαίων πεπιστευκότων), welcoming a manner of life according to the Law (νομικὴ ... πολιτεία), and travelling around in all directions (πάντοσε), were slandering the Apostle's teaching, stigmatizing the divine Paul as an apostate and breaker of the Law, and commanding all to keep the Law. This was just what they had done in Corinth as well.[3]

Who were the super apostles?

One particular aspect of the discussion concerning Paul's opponents in Corinth requires separate consideration. In 2 Cor. 11.5, Paul observes that he does not consider himself 'the least inferior to the superlative apostles' (οἱ ὑπερλίαν ἀπόστολοι). He repeats the same sentiment in relation to these people in 12.11: 'For I am not at all inferior to the superlative apostles even though I am nothing.' Who are they? Scholarly discussion, succinctly summarized by Thrall, revolves around two possibilities (2000: 671–76). The first is that they are the Jerusalem Twelve, or a subset of them consisting of Peter, James and John. This idea, which goes back to John Chrysostom, has considerable support (e.g. Barrett 1973: 278; Käsemann 1942; Harris 2005: 75–7). Thus, Harris seeks to distinguish between the main group of Paul's opponents (whom he labels 'false apostles' in 11.13) from the 'superlative'

---

[3] I am grateful to Margaret Mitchell for having alerted me to the significance of Theodoret's views (by providing me with the pre-published version of Mitchell 2020).

apostles of 11.5 and 12.11. His main argument is that Paul would not claim both to be superior to his rivals but also 'in no sense inferior to them' (11.5) if he were talking about the same group. Harris also asks how Paul could call them apostles at all when he elsewhere says (of his actual opponents in Corinth) they are false apostles and minions of Satan (2005: 75).

The second possibility, which is probably the majority position, is that the phrase is merely another label by Paul for his rivals in Corinth. In other words, the false apostles and the superlative apostles are identical. Paul says what he does at 11.5 because he is being ironic. Garland understands the situation well: 'Paul deflates the boasts of his rivals as he insinuates, "Such a dwarf as I could not possibly compare with such giants." "I hardly rank with such luminaries." He thereby disparages their boasting with mock self-deprecation' (1999: 453). Similarly, as Philip Hughes notes, calling the opponents super apostles fits 'the satirical vein of the passage, and *is also germane to this immediate concern which is with these imposters rather than with any of the Twelve*' (1962: 380; emphasis added). Furthermore, to turn Harris' argument on its head, it is far more likely that Paul would call his opponents in Corinth false apostles and ministers of Satan than that he would apply such derogatory language to the Jerusalem Twelve (or, specifically, to Peter, James and John).

Bultmann argued that the false apostles and the super apostles were identical. Paul warns of their thoughts being led astray, just like the serpent misled Eve, in 11.3, and next talks of people who preach a different Jesus, spirit and gospel in 11.4. Then in 11.5 he says that he is not inferior to the superlative apostles. In 11.13, he is lambasting 'false apostles'. It just seems too much a stretch to think he suddenly shifts focus in 11.5 to a group of people different from those who are otherwise in his viewfinder throughout this passage. But the expression 'superlative apostles' works well if Paul is mocking their claims about themselves. Bultmann also notes that if Paul had meant to refer to the Twelve, he would have appealed to his call to justify his authority as he does in Galatians (1985: 203).

Further support for the super apostles just being the opponents in Corinth comes from 2 Cor. 10.13 and 15. Here, after differentiating himself from those who measure (μετροῦντες) themselves with themselves, Paul states that he will not make honour-claims beyond 'proper limits' (ἄμετρα), which carries the strong implication that his opponents have been doing so. Since ὑπερλίαν meaning 'exceedingly', 'beyond measure' (BDAG 1033), is almost identical in meaning to ἄμετρος, 'immeasurable' (BDAG 53), the case for equating the ὑπερλίαν apostles with Paul's Corinthian opponents finds significant support.

In addition, even if there were an argument for the superlative apostles in 11.5 referring to the Jerusalem leaders, there is no room for that view regarding the same phrase at 12.11, for it is immediately followed by Paul's mention of the signs he worked among them, which only makes sense if the contrast is with the intruders who did not work such signs when they were in Corinth, or at least deny that he did. Mentioning the Jerusalem apostles would make little sense here.

A social identity perspective on Paul's response to his opponents in Corinth

In this section of the letter, Paul often expresses anger, anger mainly addressed towards outsiders who have arrived in Corinth and are opposed to him and his Gospel in various ways. To an extent, he may also exhibit anger towards the Corinthians (see 11.4, where they are well disposed towards a different Jesus, spirit and gospel which does not necessarily imply a criticism of Paul personally, unless that is really an expression of frustration). In line with the social identity approach being taken towards the letter, especially as it relates to Paul's leadership of the Corinthian congregation, it will be helpful at the outset to set out some theoretical perspectives that seek to integrate research into emotions (such as anger) and social identity.

The early work on intergroup relations in social identity theory acknowledged the central role of the self. In his original formulation of social identity theory, Henri Tajfel (1978) defined social identity as having three dimensions: cognitive (the knowledge that one belonged to a group), emotional (how one felt about belonging to it) and evaluative (how one rated oneself compared to belonging to other groups). Yet social identity theory (amplified by self-categorization theory) in its early decades primarily emphasized the cognitive and evaluative dimensions (Smith and Mackie 2002: 286). Since the 1990s, however, there has been an increasing interest in the question of the emotions and their role in intergroup relations.

Eliot Smith did much to inaugurate investigation of this area, especially in two essays published in 1993 and 1999 in which he developed a model of intergroup emotions that was predicated upon social identification with the ingroup. This research entailed integrating the core of John Turner's self-categorization theory – namely that when social identity is salient, group members regard themselves as representatives of the group rather than as unique individuals so that, in effect, the group becomes part of the self – with social cognition research. Social cognition (another area of social psychology) focuses on how we process, store and then apply information about other persons and social situations; in short, it studies the way cognitive processes are operative in our social interactions. Smith's 1999 essay was part of a much wider movement to integrate the two fields, as indicated by its publication in a collection entitled *Social Identity and Social Cognition* edited by prominent social identity theorists Dominic Abrams and Michael Hogg (1999).

An important area of social cognition that Smith utilized in effecting this integration of the two areas (social identity and social cognition) was the appraisal theory of emotion. This holds, in brief, that to arouse an emotion in someone the object must be appraised as affecting that person in some way. Among social cognition theorists, this was viewed essentially as a response of the individual: the object affected him or her personally. Smith's distinctive contribution, in a 1993 essay, had been to argue that emotions can be based on appraisals that refer to the ingroup (the identity of which, as social identity theory has shown, can become a part of the self). This insight applies to a wide range of emotions: Smith's model 'goes beyond simple positive and negative feelings to hold that a host of specific emotions can similarly be based on group membership as well as the individual person' (Smith 1999: 185).

Smith showed that when the social identity of the ingroup is salient in this way, events that favour or harm the ingroup also favour or harm the individual selves of which it is composed, and, critically, these selves then experience affect or emotion on behalf of the ingroup. Even if members are not personally affected by the outgroup effect, they nevertheless experience emotions on the basis that their group might be helped or harmed by it. When this happens, the ingroup and the outgroup become targets of emotion. The force of such emotions at times leads to differentiated intergroup behaviour that responds to the opportunity or threat posed by the outgroup.

This approach allowed Smith to offer a new understanding of prejudice, which is a negative attitude towards an individual based solely on his or her membership of a particular social group. Existing approaches tended to focus on beliefs about an outgroup's attributes, but Smith saw the benefits of replacing beliefs with emotions:

> A *stereotype* is a set of appraisals of the outgroup in relation to the ingroup in the current situation. *Prejudice* is an emotional reaction to the outgroup triggered by its relevance to the perceiver's ingroup. Finally, *discrimination* is behavior driven by an emotional action tendency.[4]

This new approach makes it easier to see why, rather than a prejudice being based on a negative belief about an outgroup that was constant across

---

[4] Smith 1999: 185 (italics original). Note that an 'action tendency' is a state of readiness to achieve a particular kind of action, not a concrete behaviour (Mackie et al. 2000: 614).

situations or contexts, prejudice could be notably specific. Thus, a 'white' person in the southern states of the United States might strongly oppose integration of schools yet be very happy to employ an African American as a servant or gardener (Smith 1999: 185). It also helps us to understand 'the hot, affectively charged quality' often 'characteristic of prejudice ... A picture of prejudice as based on *emotions* rather than mere *negative evaluations* of an outgroup can give us some sense of why prejudice is sometimes hot' (Smith 1999: 188–9). This focus also allowed recognition of the fact that a wide range of distinct emotions (like fear, disgust, anger) could be triggered in the intergroup encounter and that these could lead to different reactions. At the same time, and most importantly for applying this approach to 2 Corinthians 10–13, the group-based emotion to prejudice does not militate against 'the importance of emotional reactions to individual outgroup members (as well as to the outgroup as a whole)'. Sometimes attitudes to an individual member and the outgroup as a whole will be similar, but on other occasions an individual might be regarded differently (typically, more favourably) than the outgroup (1999: 188).

This new emphasis found significant expression in an important article by Diane Mackie, Thierry Devos and Eliot Smith in 2000. The authors began by noting various types of negative behaviour towards outgroups and that hitherto the notion of prejudice had been used to understand the discrimination involved in such behaviour. Yet conceptualizing prejudice as a negative evaluation had not proved very helpful in explaining the wide variety of negative reactions to outgroups. They asked, 'Why does one out-group attract fear or contempt while another becomes the target of anger. If out-groups uniformly attract negative evaluation, what factors explain the impulse, desire, intention, or tendency to move against some groups and away from others?' (Mackie et al. 2000: 602). To answer this question, they relied on the new approach pioneered by Eliot Smith earlier (Smith 1993; 1999). They discovered over the course of three studies that when a particular social identity was salient, members experience emotions on behalf of the group that are based on how they appraise the intergroup situation, especially the respective strength of the ingroup vis-à-vis the outgroup. Moreover, they discovered (as Smith had predicted) that emotions generated in the process of intergroup encounters were differentiated depending on the situation; they did not subsist merely in some generalized negativity towards the outgroup. They focused on the emotions of anger, fear and contempt. Their results indicated that if the members of the ingroup perceived it was strong in relation to the outgroup, anger and, at times, contempt would be generated in response to an outgroup threat. There was also an effect observed in relation to action tendencies (which are states of readiness to achieve a particular kind of action): the emotion of anger was associated with a tendency to move against the outgroup, whereas emotions of exclusion were associated with a tendency to move away from the outgroup (2000: 612). Subsequent research showed that intergroup emotional reactions predicted not only the desire for intergroup behaviour (akin to an 'emotional action tendency') but also its actual occurrence (Dumont et al. 2003 and Iyer et al. 2007). In short, 'a wealth of evidence supports the idea that specific intergroup emotions produce both desires for and actual intergroup behaviors' (Mackie et al. 2008: 1875).

In 2006, Angela Maitner and colleagues undertook three studies in laboratory conditions to explore the function that emotions between ingroup and outgroup might have for intergroup behaviour. In particular, how were emotions felt by ingroup members when an outgroup acted negatively towards the ingroup, or modified such prior behaviour, and when ingroup members reacted to such initial and subsequent behaviour in various ways. Their first study showed that anger felt towards an offending outgroup is only discharged when the action towards which the anger is directed is successfully implemented. Their second study showed that participants in the experiment who received negative information about their ingroup were angrier when the ingroup responded unsuccessfully to the external threat than when it responded successfully. The experimenters induced anger towards the outgroup via its insulting the ingroup and then indicated, in one condition, that the ingroup had confronted the outgroup and, in the second condition, that it had not. They expected that ingroup anger towards the outgroup would decrease in the first condition (of effective response, causing the outgroup to relent) but would increase in the second condition (no or no effective response), and this is what they found to occur (Maitner et al. 2006). By 2008, it had become possible to speak of this integrated area of social psychological research as 'intergroup emotions theory', its principal tenet being that 'intergroup behavior is driven by emotions, but emotions of a uniquely social kind' (Mackie et al. 2008: 1867).

These studies play an important role in later research that takes us close to the question of leadership by assisting us to understand how someone (a group leader, for example) can manage identity successfully, or unsuccessfully. This recent research includes an analysis of how, within an ingroup threatened by an outgroup, reactions among ingroup members might differ and why. In 2014, Sarah Martiny and Thomas Kessler showed that, in line with social identity theory, a threat to positive social identity would elicit specific negative emotions (especially in the form of outgroup-directed anger) and motivate identity management. Moreover, where the identity management was successful, a positive social identity was restored and outgroup-directed anger was lessened. However, when successful identity management was blocked, the process was a failure and outgroup-directed anger remained at a higher level. Of particular interest was the discovery that this outgroup-directed anger was strongest for group members who highly valued their group (i.e. they had high group-based esteem). Members who were very busy with other things (whose 'cognitive resources' were stretched) showed more anger towards the offending outgroup than those with more time on their hands, perhaps because of the frustration encountered in not being able to fully engage in identity management. They also noted that, as postulated by social identity theory, group members 'have a strong collective motivation to protect their social identity'. However, as groups are made up of individual members, sometimes they will react to threats as individuals and sometimes they will act as a group. But whether they act individually or collectively, 'social identity threats trigger processes that take place within the individual group member' (Martini and Kessler 2014: 755).

All of this has considerable application to what Paul is seeking to communicate in 2 Corinthians 10–13.

14

Paul's assertion of his leadership against the claims of his opponents (2 Corinthians 10)

The power of Paul's leadership (10.1-11)

2 Corinthians 10.1 The expression with which he begins, 'I, Paul myself' (Αὐτὸς δὲ ἐγὼ Παῦλός), with its double pronoun, is a *hapax legomenon* and 'extraordinarily emphatic' (Barnett 1997: 457). It stresses the personal nature of what Paul is about to say, and, on the basis that chs 10–13 belong to the rest of the letter, it emphatically distinguishes Paul from his co-sender, Timothy. It also signals that he is about to embark on a new topic (Matera 2003: 219). He is about to defend his authority that had come under challenge and to remind the Corinthians of their identity in Christ. The double pronoun is not to be explained by his having written these chapters in his own hand (as some have suggested), since in that case he probably would have said so as he does elsewhere (1 Cor. 16.21; Gal. 6.11; Phlm. 19). *This clearly marks a major shift in the letter and Paul is being completely up-front about it. He emphatically announces he is moving into a new area of discussion and we should not be surprised when he arrives there.* That some modern critics (but no ancient writers) find this abrupt move after chs 1–9 difficult to accept, even though Paul is so emphatic he is making it, causes the partition edifice based on the 'change of tone' argument to shudder and fall.

The loaded self-description precedes Paul's statement 'I entreat you' (παρακαλῶ ὑμᾶς). As becomes more and more evident as he develops his argument, Paul has the same ingroup in view in 2 Cor. 10.1 as elsewhere in the letter. It consists of the people he addresses here in the second-person plural. This ingroup continues to include both sets of named addressees in 2 Cor. 1.1, 'the assembly of God which is in Corinth', and 'all the saints who are in the whole of Achaia', since the totality of Achaia is mentioned in 2 Cor. 11.10.

Although loudly signalling his transition to a new topic, where he will have some stern things to say (although not primarily to the Corinthians),

Paul lowers the volume somewhat by introducing the idea of the meekness (πραΰτης) and forbearance (ἐπιείκεια) of Christ. Such language is unusual for Paul. This is the only instance of πραΰτης in the letter, and elsewhere in Paul it appears only at 1 Cor. 4.21, while this is Paul's only example of ἐπιείκεια (although the adjectival form appears in Phil. 4.5). Gentleness and forbearance were seen as virtues of a calm and soothing disposition, especially appropriate to proper and moderate rule by those in authority (Garland 1999: .426–31). Paul is probably also referring to memories of the earthly Jesus (Roetzel 2007: 97). Paul's application of these qualities to himself and his dealings with the Corinthians evokes his earlier claim to leadership, but in the style to which he has already referred, especially in 2 Cor. 1.24 with its rejection of the blunt exercise of power and its replacement with joyful cooperation. And yet even here he emphasizes the exalted source of such meekness and forbearance: Christ himself. The ultimate foundation for Paul's leadership is his divine commissioning to the task.

In the remainder of v. 1, Paul refers to himself as 'I who am humble (ταπεινός) towards you when personally present (κατὰ πρόσωπον), but bold (θαρρῶ) towards you when I am absent (ἀπών).' This is a claim that was certainly being made against him in Corinth, and we should not be diverted by spurious complaints of 'mirror reading' in acknowledging this. Ancient rhetoric taught orators to anticipate and answer in advance charges that been made against them, and Paul's argument would collapse here if no such allegation had been levelled against him, by either the Corinthians or his opponents or both. Reason exists to regard his opponents as the source of this charge. In v. 9, Paul asserts that he does not want to frighten 'you' through his letters. This is probably a reference to their severity. Then, in 10.10 he explicitly quotes his opponents: 'Because, someone says (φησίν), "His letters are weighty and strong, but his physical presence is weak and his language (λόγος) amounts to nothing"'. He strongly demurs from this view in v. 11: 'Let such a person (ὁ τοιοῦτος) understand that we are the same both in the language (λόγος) of our letters when absent and also in action (ἔργον) when present.' Lurking behind the accusation made against Paul is how his opponents have interpreted the severe letter mentioned earlier in the letter from their knowledge of its effect on the Corinthians that Paul, in effect, concedes. Thus, in 7.8 he raises the possibility that it caused them grief (λυπή), and 7.11 he notes one of the reactions of the Corinthians to Paul, which must include at least their reaction to the letter, was 'fear', φόβος. Thus, his opponents have acknowledged the force of the severe letter (and of Paul's letters generally) while then seeking to differentiate the power of his letters from his allegedly unimpressive personal presence. That Paul makes this point is a sign of the connection of chs 10–13 to 1–9. The severe letter is still in the frame, but now with respect to a different issue: Paul's use of it to introduce the attack he is about to launch on the outsiders troubling the Christ-group in Corinth. The message conveyed here also prepares his audience for the mentions of his forthcoming visit that appear later in this section of the letter.

One can sense a measure of anger on Paul's part in this verse, but at this stage at least, it is not directed at the Corinthians. They are not the source of this accusation. He sharply differentiates ingroup from outgroup. Many of the difficulties that commentators have discerned in 2 Corinthians 10–13 that push them to view these chapters as not originally part of the letter originate in their failure fully to appreciate this differentiation. Paul's anger with the outgroup surfaces in his reaction to their attitude towards him that he implies in v. 1 and also in his expectation that he will display boldness towards them (v. 2). As discussed in ch. 13 of this volume, anger is commonly felt by members of an ingroup against an outgroup when the outgroup is not thought of as stronger than the ingroup (when fear might be a more appropriate emotional response). Where attempts by the ingroup or members of it, such as Paul, to engage in identity management in the confrontation have been unsuccessful, anger towards the outgroup can continue at a high level, and members of the ingroup (which must include its leaders) who highly value it are likely to be angrier than other members. Thus, Paul's anger is readily explicable. But he will also express frustration at the ingroup for not resisting the outgroup, especially in 11.3-4.

2 Corinthians 10.2 The first point to note is that Paul is envisaging a forthcoming visit, and this coheres closely with what he has already said in 9.2-5, that he is sending the brethren on ahead of him to Corinth, meaning he will be there himself in due course (possibly accompanied by some Macedonians, 9.4). Chapter 10 assumes the situation in ch. 9 and is therefore integrally connected with it.

The outgroups that are implied as the originators of the charge against Paul in v. 1 (when read with the extra details of vv. 10-11) also appear in this verse, and now explicitly; they are described as some (τινας) arguing (λογιζουμένους) that he behaves in a worldly fashion (κατὰ σάρκα περιπατοῦντας). Now Paul, in the course of foreshadowing another visit, denies the suggestion that he is not bold when he is present by saying that boldness is precisely the characteristic he may produce against these people, if provoked, when he returns to Corinth. That Paul intends behaving with the boldness in person he is alleged not to possess towards some who claim he lives in a worldly way strongly suggests that they are to be identified with the accuser mentioned in vv. 10-11. Although in those verses this view is attributed to one person ('someone says' [φησίν] and 'such a one' [τοιοῦτος]), too much weight should not be put on the singular number here (as some commentators are prone to do), since that would mean driving a wedge between people who raise the same accusation against Paul (even though they are described in the plural in v. 2 and the singular in vv. 10-11).[1]

The first statement creates a distinction between two groups, those to whom he does not wish to be bold and those (who are responsible for the criticisms of his speaking style in vv. 1-2) to whom he does. This is a distinction between one group who are only at risk of feeling his lash and another group who have already acted in such a way as to ensure that they will feel it. The former group are surely the Corinthians (even though the second-person plural pronoun, ὑμᾶς, is not supplied after 'I implore'). We may be confident on this point because the issue between Paul and the Corinthians in relation to the severe letter had already been resolved, as fulsomely recorded in 2 Cor. 7.11. It would be extremely odd if the Corinthians, despite having reached an accommodation with Paul in relation to the severe letter, one that involved its content, were now raising a new complaint that involved an issue with this character of his letters. That complaint makes far better sense coming from visitors from outside Corinth who are using the effect of Paul's severe letter on the Corinthians as the basis for the accusation. They may very well have been displeased by its effectiveness, as mediated by Titus, on the Corinthians, whom they had hoped to be winning over to their viewpoint. Indeed, it is likely that the outsiders were critical of the Corinthians precisely because they had succumbed to Paul's persuasion in the severe letter. They have, in effect, conceded the power of Paul's letters while trying to diminish the force of his personal presence. Accordingly, it is preferable not to follow commentators who consider that the outgroup also includes the opponents' Corinthian sympathizers (e.g. Lambrecht 1999: 154; Matera 2003: 222). This distinction of the Corinthian ingroup from the outgroup of interlopers is a pervasive theme in 2 Corinthians 10–13.

The second clause contains an accusation being levelled against Paul in Corinth, that he lives in a worldly fashion. Here it is safe to assume that the plural ('we live') is epistolary; Paul is only speaking for himself at this point in the letter. This has attracted numerous explanations. Although Thrall suggests seven possibilities (2000: 605–6), one that she does not mention is to relate what is said here to the detail in v. 10, even though it could go beyond that charge. One point of connection is that in vv. 5-6 he seems to answer in advance the negative view of his discourse expressed in v. 10.

It is very useful to range the accusation that his personal presence is weak against any notion that Paul exercises influence in a coercive way.

---

[1] Sometimes translators (e.g. the RSV) have 'they say' (φασίν) for 'someone says' (φησίν) in v. 10, but this is transparent attempt to solve a perceived (not an actual) problem.

His opponents are actually charging him with being unable to exercise his authority in person, not with exercising it coercively. Also they are merely saying he is bold when absent, not that he practises coercion.

But if boldness when he was absent can be seen in his directions in 1 Cor. 5.1-13 about the man committing incest and in the severe letter he sent with Titus, when had he been weak when present? Harris (2005: 671) suggests that perhaps this occurred during his recent 'painful' visit to discipline those guilty of immorality and bring them to repentance (2 Cor. 12.21; 13.2). This is possible for one mention of this visit (2 Cor. 2.1-2) suggests he caused them pain (λυπεῖν), and, in a later reference (13.2-3), he states that he warned them. Alternately, the weakness may refer to inadequacies in the actual manner of his oral discourse: his language that (allegedly) 'amounts to nothing' (v. 10).

2 Corinthians 10.3-6 These verses represent a notably bellicose outburst by Paul. He interprets his ministry with respect to a metaphor of a soldier who tears down fortresses that stand in his road, fortresses that consist of erroneous ideas and discourse. But this vehemence is not directed at the Corinthians. Here he intimates the boldness he will display when he arrives in Corinth, boldness that will give the lie to his opponents' claims (vv. 1 and 10) that he is weak in person.

'For although we live (περιπατοῦντες) in the human world (ἐν σάρκι),' he states in v. 3, 'we do not wage war (στρατευόμεθα) in a human manner (κατὰ σάρκα; v. 3).' Having in v. 2, in effect, denied that he 'lives in a worldly fashion' (literally: 'walks according to the flesh' [κατὰ σάρκα]), Paul now concedes that he does live 'in the human world' (literally: 'walks in the flesh' [ἐν σάρκι]). He is in the world but not of it. These two expressions must here have a different meaning, with the former being pejorative and the latter not (even though that is the case with this phrase in Rom. 8.8). His denial of living in a worldly fashion in v. 2 is now precisely matched by his denying he wages war in a human manner (κατὰ σάρκα), which perhaps includes the techniques of rhetoric, as Marshall suggests (1987: 391), even though Paul must have been familiar with basic rhetorical techniques, yet also extends to erroneous ideas. And wage war Paul does, but only in a manner focused on God, as we see in vv. 4-6.

Verses 4-6 comprise a passage replete with military imagery, specifically words relating to siege warfare: destroying fortifications, taking captives and punishing resistance. He starts with the explanation, 'For the weapons of our warfare are not those of the world but are powerful in God's cause[2] to knock down strongholds' (ὀχυρώματα). Although commentators have spilt much ink on what specific campaign might have inspired Paul, with

---

[2] Translating τῷ θεῷ as a dative of advantage.

Harris summarizing six possibilities (2005: 676–7), such speculation is rather pointless. The practices to which he alludes would have been so well known in the ancient Mediterranean from centuries of warfare, some of it recounted in Israelite scripture with which Paul was closely familiar, as to require no specific instance to fire Paul's imagination here or to convey his views to his audience. The more important issue is the reason that he has selected this field of imagery at this point; as already noted, the explanation lies in his need to rebut the outgroup's claims that he lacks boldness.

That they are firmly in his sights here is shown both by the use of 'arguments' (λογισμοί) in v. 4, which allude to the λογιζουμένους in v. 2 who oppose Paul (Furnish 1984: 458), and by the fact that it is likely to be their disobedience that he will be ready to punish (v. 5). He has some very severe charges to lay against them. They erect obstacles 'against the knowledge of God'. They have thoughts that are in some way disobedient. Thoughts (νοήματα) do not receive a good press in 2 Corinthians prior to this: they are wielded by Satan (2.11); the thoughts of the Israelites are hardened because when they read the law of Moses, it is covered by a veil (3.14); and the thoughts of unbelievers are blinded by God (4.4).

In what respect did those attacked here oppose the knowledge of God, a separate issue from their ad hominem attacks on Paul? First of all, they were preaching a different Jesus, spirit and gospel from Paul (11.4). Secondly, an important dimension must be implied from 2 Cor. 3.7-18: the critique of the Mosaic law in that passage requires that the intruders, armed with the letters of introduction mentioned in 2 Cor. 3.1, are pushing for its adoption. They are also disguising themselves as ministers of righteousness (11.15), which was a benefit Judeans could expect from having adopted the law of Moses (Esler 1998: 141–77 and 2006b).

In v. 6, Paul distinguishes between those whose every disobedience he stands ready to punish (no doubt when he arrives in Corinth) and others whose obedience he anticipates being complete at the time he punishes the disobedience of the previous group. That is, the completion of the obedience of the latter will be the sine qua non of, or even the trigger for, the punishment of the disobedience of the former. Who are those others? My view is that only the intruders are in view here (who are, after all, preaching a different Jesus, spirit and gospel to those he preaches; 11.4), and it is unnecessary to introduce anyone else. Many scholars take this view (e.g. Furnish, 1984: 461, 464; Martin 1986: 306–7). Barrett (1971: 239) makes the case like this:

> We hear of a παρακοή and a ὑπακοή; but whose disobedience, and whose obedience, and how are the two related? The obedience is undoubtedly that of the Corinthians, and the ὑμῶν that indicates this is so emphatic

that it can hardly be questioned that the disobedience is that of others. Paul is thus seeking complete obedience on the part of the Corinthians in order to take the next step of punishing... the disobedience of others, who, since they are not native Corinthians, must be outsiders who have intruded into the Corinthian church.

In a similar way, Harris reasonably notes that if the Corinthians were included in the disobedience, what would be the point of punishing their disobedience only after their obedience was complete? That would be when you would expect someone to remit punishment. Rather than following Garland (1999: 438) in seeing here a Corinthian (disobedient) minority and a Corinthian (obedient) majority, Harris suggests that 'it is better to assume that the disobedience is shown by persons other than the Corinthians, persons from outside the Corinthian congregation' (2005: 685).

Assuming the correctness of this view (which adheres closely with the argument I have been making about the presence of the outsiders in ch. 10 up to this point), two questions arise. First, in what sense can the interlopers be said to be disobedient? Barrett argues that it refers to their breach of the contract agreed in Jerusalem set out in Galatians 2, meaning their invasion of Paul's agreed area of missionary activity (1971: 239). While this is possible, another answer finds more support in the text. Since in v. 5 Paul states that he will capture every thought for obedience (ὑπακοή) to Christ, the disobedience (παρακοή) in v. 6 must equally be to Christ. That this is what he attributes to his opponents becomes patent a little later when we learn that they lead people astray from devotion to Christ (11.3), and that they do that by preaching a different Jesus, spirit and gospel from those taught by Paul (11.4). So, in part, while they have broken the Jerusalem agreement, this matters not so much in itself as that it entails disobedience to the Christ whom Paul preaches. In social identity terms, obedience to Christ is a central group belief, while also manifesting itself in action, such as the mixed table-fellowship of Judeans and non-Judeans, especially in the context of the Eucharistic meal.

This brings us to the second question arising from our acceptance of Barrett's view on the identity of the obedient and the disobedient: In what sense can the obedience of the Corinthians require some future fulfilment? As noted earlier, Garland (1999: 438) believes Paul is primarily concerned with correcting the disobedience of the Corinthians (and here he also points to 2 Cor. 12.21 and 13.2). Is it possible that Paul has in mind some of the Corinthians as disobedient? The textual evidence requires a negative answer to this question. We should not overplay the idea of the Corinthians' obedience requiring fulfilment. In 7.15, Paul commended their obedience to Titus. Here he is still talking about their obedience; the question is how to fulfil or perfect it. Although the question is considered in more detail in the following commentary, neither 12.20-21 nor 13.2 entail disobedient Corinthian Christ-followers, that is, Corinthians who are no longer obedient to Christ as Paul preaches him. Paul worries that they may have their faults (12.20) but there are more serious things, presumably, than quarrelling, jealousy, anger, selfishness, slander, gossip, conceit and disorder. Again these are things in relation to which their obedience will be made complete, after which he will punish the others. Paul is also concerned that they will not have repented (μὴ μετανοησάντων), in the sense of 'feel remorse' (BDAG 640), of the ἀκαθαρσία ('impurity'), πορνεία ('unchastity') and ἀσέλγεια ('licentiousness') that they previously practised (ἔπραξαν, in the aorist) (12.21). But that does not make them disobedient, even if one can agree that their obedience does require perfecting: they did not feel remorse for such things even though they were no longer engaged in them.

2 Corinthians 10.7 I interpret the verb βλέπετε in the first clause, 'Look at the facts in front of your face (Τὰ κατὰ πρόσωπον βλέπετε)', as an imperative. If, on the other hand, it is an indicative, it is something of a criticism of the Corinthians, meaning 'You are judging things by appearances'. But the imperative seems more likely on the basis of Pauline usage. As Garland notes (1999: 439-40), on each of the other eight occasions where Paul uses βλέπετε it is an imperative (1 Cor. 1.26; 8.9, 10.18; 16.10; Gal. 5.15; Phil. 3.2 [x3]).

Paul then makes the suggestion he has introduced with such emphasis: 'If anyone (τις) is confident in himself (πέποιθεν ἑαυτῷ) that he belongs to Christ (Χριστοῦ εἶναι), let him consider (λογιζέσθω) further in his own mind (ἐφ'ἑαυτοῦ) that just as he belongs to Christ, so also do I.' Who is this 'anyone'? Is it an actual or a notional person? Clearly Paul has in mind a Christ-follower, since no one else could even claim to belong to Christ. There is no need to read this to imply he only has one particular person in mind (the leader of the outgroup, for example). This is an instance of the collective (or generic) singular (BDF §139). Thrall plausibly suggests that the transition (from the second-person plural imperative in the first clause) to the third-person singular τις indicates that 'Paul is referring to the external opposition and not to any representative of the Corinthian congregation'. She notes the similar use of τις at 11.20 'where allusion to the rival missionaries is without doubt' (2000: 619). Thus, τις functions to refer to the whole outgroup of interlopers. This identification is strengthened by his using λογίζεσθαι to refer to their mental processes (as at 10.2). Paul's careful use of the expression πέποιθεν ἑαυτῷ here indicates that he is just reporting their view that they belong to Christ, not in any way vouching for its truth. In this regard the verse should be read with v. 6: Paul's view is that those who have come in from outside are disobedient to Christ; he is hardly, therefore, likely to concede that they belong to Christ.

A very important question here is the meaning of Χριστοῦ εἶναι. Many possibilities have been proposed but probably the most satisfactory is that it means 'a (special) servant of Christ', someone with distinctive authority from Christ. The evidence is as follows: (a) in 11.23, we learn that the opponents claimed to be 'ministers of Christ' (διάκονοι Χριστοῦ); (b) since in 11.13 Paul calls them 'false apostles' (ψευδαπόστολοι), they were probably claiming to be apostles; (c) in v. 8, Paul states that he has authority given to him by the Lord, who works to build up the community, and this gives substance to his claim to belong to Christ. So here Paul is acknowledging his opponents' claim to belong to Christ (while emphasizing that this is merely their view by use of ἐφ' ἑαυτοῦ), but later (11.13-15) he will reveal his own opinion, that his opponents are false apostles and belong to Satan (Harris 2005: 688–900).

It is worth noting here that Paul never names his adversaries in this letter. As Marshall has explained, this was a rhetorical technique, embedded in the Mediterranean honour and shame culture of his time, which had a number of advantages. According to the prevailing conventions of praise and blame, this was a method for dishonouring one's opponents (1987: 341–8). This forms part of Paul's policy of offering a *sunkrisis*, a comparison, of himself and his opponents in this last section of the letter (Witherington 1995: 429). In addition, and perhaps more pertinently, within a social identity framework, not naming the interlopers helps Paul to stereotype them as members of the outgroup. One aspect of stereotyping is the 'outgroup homogeneity effect', as opposed to the 'ingroup heterogeneity effect.' Whereas members of the ingroup know that, while enjoying the social identity that comes from belonging to the group, they are all distinct individuals, they tend to regard outgroup members as all being much the same, as all sharing the same outgroup characteristics that the ingroup views negatively. The reality of this phenomenon is recognized and mobilized in the current-day technique known as 'the contact hypothesis' whereby attempts are made to break down intergroup prejudice and tension by having members of rival groups meet and get to know one another as individuals. But in 2 Corinthians 10-13, Paul is working at the stereotyping stage of intergroup relations and is not interested in reconciliation as far as his opponents from outside are concerned. By not proffering their names, he begins a process of de-individualizing them that will later culminate in quite an extreme caricature of their negative characteristics.

2 Corinthians 10.8 The fact that in v. 7 Paul appeals to certain people also to consider that he belongs to Christ rather implies that they were suggesting he did not. In v. 8, he sets out a robust defence of his authority. He offers the following assurance: 'For if I claim honour (καυχήσομαι) a little too much in relation to my authority (ἐξουσία) which the Lord gave (ἔδωκεν) me for building you up (εἰς οἰκοδομὴν) and not for knocking you down (εἰς καθαίρεσιν ὑμῶν), I will not be put to shame (αἰσχυνθήσομαι).'

This is the first of many instances of καυχάομαι in this section of the letter (10.8, 13, 15, 16, 17 (bis); 11.12, 16, 18 (bis), 30; 12.1, 5 (bis), 6, 9 and the noun καύχησις appears in 11.10, 17). Although Paul has also reached for this semantic domain earlier in the letter,[3] its concentration in 2 Corinthians 10–12 is striking. As noted earlier in this volume, 'boast' is a poor translation of this Greek word, as it carries a negative connotation in our culture that was usually not present in the ancient world. Its meaning was to make a claim to honour; there was nothing wrong with that, since it was only if there was, or there turned out to be, no foundation for making the claim that it became problematic. Its use throughout the letter, especially in chs 10–13, is an index of the pressure Paul is under from his opponents as to his authority and connection with Christ. His answer is to make a claim to honour that is based on the authority (ἐξουσία) that the Lord had given him. Here it is virtually certain that by 'the Lord' Paul means Christ and not God (Thrall 2000: 624).

As numerous commentators have noted (e.g. Plummer 1915: 281; Thrall 2000: 624; Harris 2005: 693), the aorist (ἔδωκεν) points to a single occasion when the Lord gave him authority, namely his initial call (1 Cor. 1.1; Gal. 1.1, 15-16). Paul's authority is a key concept in ch. 10, even though the word appears only in v. 8; a very similar expression using it appears in 13.10. According to Lambrecht, 'it is Paul's apostolic commission to preach the gospel and to take care of the communities he founded' (1999: 156). But it is also fundamental for the effective exercise of Paul's leadership in Corinth given that an important part of his claim to exercise leadership is his divine commissioning for this task, in which he is unique. To this he adds the extent to which he is exemplary of Christ-movement values and behaviour.

Paul specifies that the Lord gave him this authority for building up (οἰκοδομή) the Corinthians, not for knocking them down. The sentiment that the Lord has given him authority (ἐξουσία) for building up (οἰκοδομή) and not destroying appears in very similar words (with) in 13.10. He also expresses his aim as their οἰκοδομή in 12.19. Social identity theory offers considerable assistance in Paul's strategy here. As will emerge throughout my discussion of chs 10–13, Paul is really aiming at his opponents, yet he does have some (fairly mild) criticism to make of the Corinthians too. In such a context, Jetten and Hornsey explain (2014: 475), 'In-group members who criticize the group are tolerated only when their message is intended

---

[3] καυχάομαι: 5.12; 7.14; 9.2; καύχημα: 1.14; 5.12; 9.3; καύχησις: 1.12; 7.4, 14; 8.24.

to be constructive and when it is clear that that have the best interests of the group at heart' (e.g. Hornsey et al. 2004). Paul satisfies this desideratum by his repeated references to his wanting to build them up; even when he is defending himself, a major theme in these chapters, it is only for this purpose (12.19).

This factor explains why Paul specified the purpose of this grant of authority as being 'for building you up', but why does he add 'and not for knocking you down'? The primary reason appears to be to differentiate the Corinthians from the troublesome outsiders. Thrall thought that Paul was possibly being inconsistent by saying he would engage in καθαίρεσις in 10.4 and disavowing that intent here (2000: 625). The flaw in this proposal is that it assumes that the Corinthians might be within the scope of v. 4. In reality, in v. 4 Paul spoke about knocking down (using the same word as here, καθαίρεσις) fortifications in a passage (vv. 4-5) where (as argued earlier) he had the outgroup of interlopers, not the Corinthians themselves, firmly in view. In v. 8, he further differentiates the Corinthians from the outsiders by making clear that they will not experience the destruction, he implies, that he has just promised for the position and ideas of the interlopers. The emphatic position of ὑμῶν, 'yours', (as opposed to theirs) at the end of verse further indicates this differentiation.

When he says he 'will not be put to shame' (οὐκ αἰσχυνθήσομαι), he means that he will never be in a situation where those present come to the view that his honour-claim was groundless (mentioned earlier); this could be in the immediate future, when he makes the visit that he foreshadows at (12.14; 13.1-2; cf 10.11) or, probably less likely here, it could be on the Last Day. The Vulgate very aptly translates *non erubescam* ('I will not blush with shame'). This clearly brings out the distinctive meaning of καυχάομαι. It does not mean 'to boast'; rather, making an honour-claim is only problematic if later on it emerges that the person had no basis to make the claim, in which case he or she will be caused public shame, as evidenced by the red colour of his or her face.

2 Corinthians 10.9 The syntax of this verse is difficult, as it begins with ἵνα μὴ ('In order that . . . not'): (I say this) in order that I might not seem to terrify (ἐκφοβεῖν) you with my letters. It is difficult to know how this goes with what has preceded it. But probably there is a connection between καθαίρεσις and ἐκφοβεῖν, which is why 'I say this' or something like it needs to be understood. Just as he was not given authority to destroy them, so too he does not write letters to terrify them. Later on (in 12.19) he will affirm that, in effect, in writing this letter he has been aiming at building them up, which coheres closely with this interpretation. This theme may well be related to his statement at 1.24 that he does not lord it over their faith, on that basis that generating destruction and applying terror were characteristics of the lords (κύριοι) in this world.

2 Corinthians 10.10 Paul claims that 'someone says' (φησίν) his letters are 'weighty and forceful' but his 'bodily presence is weak and his powers of speech contemptible'. The word φησίν is singular, and this probably signals a connection to, or perhaps even an identification of the speaker with, the person referred to as 'someone' (τις) in v. 7. The reference is probably to some notional person, but de-individualized for the reasons set out earlier, who serves as a representative of Paul's rivals in Corinth. Harris raises the possibility of the τις being a spokesman for Paul's critics, 'both Corinthians and intruders' (2005: 698). Later in connection with this verse and 11.6, he talks about 'the coalition of anti-Pauline Corinthians and the intruders from Judea' (2005: 748). Yet there is no sign of such a coalition in chs 10–13. Although at 11.4 they are well disposed towards a different, Jesus, spirit and gospel, that is not the same as subscribing to the personal criticism of Paul raised here. On the contrary, the ongoing logic of ch. 10 so far, which poses quite a sharp differentiation between Corinthians and interlopers, entails demurring from any suggestion that this figure could also be a representative of the Corinthians. The view Paul cites is what the outsiders are putting to the Corinthian Christ-followers; it does not originate with the latter.

'Weighty and forceful' (βαρεῖαι καὶ ἰσχυραί) probably have a positive meaning here (and thus express a concession by his rivals as to the power of his writing perhaps based on their observation of the effectiveness of the severe letter), since otherwise (a) the contrast which Paul seems to be establishing in the verse would not really exist and (b) he would not claim in v. 11 to be able to reproduce in his personal presence the same qualities that he expresses in his letters.

What do his rivals convey by saying that Paul's bodily presence is weak? Barrett suggested that 'bodily presence' was to be interpreted comprehensively, in terms of Paul's whole outward character and personality, not just his personal appearance (1973: 260–1). Yet personal appearance was also of some importance to ancient orators. To be 'weak' may have meant to be feeble and vacillating, but perhaps also physically unimpressive (Thrall 2000: 631).

2 Corinthians 10.11 'Let such a person (τοιοῦτος) consider (λογιζέσθω) this', Paul begins, and τοιοῦτος is certainly to be identified with the implied subject of φησίν in v. 10, and probably also with the τις of v. 7, with λογίζεσθαι occurring here, as in vv. 2 and 7 in connection with Paul's opponents. The view such a one must consider is that 'we will be just the same in our actions when we are present (παρόντες) as we are in speech through our letters when we are absent (ἀπόντες).' Verses 10–11 are inextricably connected.

Verse 11 represents, if not a repudiation, then certainly a qualification of, what he said in 10.1. Following in the example of Christ, he has admitted he is ταπεινός (10.1). But now he makes clear that this does not mean that he cannot produce the forceful quality of his letters when he is present. Somehow this forcefulness co-exists with the circumstance that, in some respects, Paul's physical presence is weak. This will be a big element later in the letter (11.21, 29, 30; 12.5, 9, 10; 13.3, 4, 9). Many commentators regard παρόντες as future, probably rightly, as Harris argues, because if, as is likely, ἀπόντες refers to recent letters (including the 'severe' letter), then παρόντες should refer to Paul's third, forthcoming visit to Corinth (12.14; 13.1-2). In addition, the expression here ties in closely with what Paul says in 13.10. (Harris 2005: 702-5). This conclusion necessitates that we recognize that Paul is issuing a threat in v. 11, and we can sense his anger seeping through, in a manner consonant with the social identity perspectives set earlier, at the way these outsiders have been troubling his Corinthian Christ-followers.

Paul's contestation of leadership claims(10.12-18)

In this section of the chapter, Paul responds to interlopers in his zone of evangelism and claims honour for the results of his work. They have commended themselves to the Corinthians and denigrated his authority (Garland 1999: 451). In the terms of Mediterranean culture, Paul's honour was at stake. In line with the social dynamic of challenge and response, his opponents, by belittling Paul and thus besmirching his honour, have issued a challenge to which he is honour-bound to reply but, in this case, not for his own sake but for the purposes of the Gospel. This is really a battle over who has the right to exercise leadership over the Christ-movement in Corinth. The whole of 2 Corinthians 10–13 concerns Paul eliminating the threat to the sort of leadership he has been seeking to exercise in Corinth in chs 1–9. These last four chapters of the letter are integrally linked to the question of his leadership.

2 Corinthians 10.12 The notion of self-recommendation (using the verb συνίστημι with a reflexive pronoun) is a prominent topic in the letter (Pawlak 2018). Most significantly, it occurs in chs 1–7 and in 10–13. Given that it appears nowhere else in the Pauline epistles, this is significant evidence for the integral nature of 2 Corinthians. On four earlier occasions prior to 10.12, Paul has raised the issue of commending himself. First, in 3.1 he asked if he was beginning to commend himself (ἑαυτοὺς συνιστάνειν) again or did he rather need letters of commendation, as some do, to the Corinthians or from them, before averring they were his letter of commendation. Since 3.1 follows immediately after the reference to those who peddle God's word in 2.17, the same group of people are in mind whom we have already argued are to be identified with his opponents in chs 10–13. Secondly, in 4.2 he commends himself 'to everyone's capacity to assess behaviour before God'. Thirdly, in 5.12 he repeats his question from 3.1: 'Are we commending ourselves to you again?' Fourthly, in 6.4 he commends himself as God's minister through the hardships he has endured for the Gospel. Pawlak has argued, perhaps somewhat too harshly, that Paul's use of self-commendation in the letter is inconsistent.

Paul begins 10.12 with a disavowal: 'We do not dare to classify (ἐγκρῖναι) or compare (συγκρῖναι) ourselves with any of those who commend themselves (ἑαυτούς)'. On the basis that those mentioned in 2.17–3.1 are to be identified with the opponents in chs 10–13, it is necessary to assume that the same people who have letters of recommendation (3.1) also engage in self-recommendation. These are the people Paul has in mind in 10.12. There is nothing surprising about this. If you have two ways to establish your position, why not use both? This is precisely Paul's approach; he will indulge in self-commendation if necessary, but he also has the Corinthians as a commendatory letter (3.2-3). In 12.11, he complains that they have not provided him with a commendation.

To understand what precisely is being said in v. 12 and in vv. 12-18 generally, it will assist if we take note of v. 18, which includes this section, at the outset: 'For it is not the person who commends himself (ὁ ἑαυτὸν συνιστάνων) who is approved (δόκιμος), but the person whom the Lord commends (συνίστησιν).' From this we observe an *inclusio* here in vv. 12 and 18: the section begins with Paul denying he compares himself with self-commenders and ends with his rejection of that practice in favour of the Lord's recommendation. Underlying and motivating such self-commendation (and the rival form advocated by Paul) is the issue of approval, of being δόκιμος (v. 18). What is ultimately at stake is to be approved, no doubt as a trustworthy minister of the Gospel who belongs to Christ; in order words, one's leadership credentials. The question of who must bestow that approval, if it is the Lord whose commendation of a person is the decisive factor to be taken into account in reaching a decision, is an interesting one. Probably Paul has in mind the Corinthian Christ-group. The process in view is rather like a personnel appointment process: a group will make a decision as to who should be approved for a particular leadership position where there are a number of applicants, but in making that decision the opinion of a very influential third party will be decisive. It is very much a competitive process and one in which Paul needs to be the successful candidate.

Having intimated in v. 11 that he is ready to act boldly against his critics, in v. 12, then, Paul launches an attack on the rival applicants for a leadership position among the Corinthian Christ-followers, an attack that begins ironically with the statement that he would not dare to do it. He characterizes them as self-recommenders, and, in the first clause, bashfully claims not to be able to compare himself with them. Aristotle had said, 'We compete with our equals' (*Rhetorica* 2.6). Paul is saying that he does not dare to put himself in the same class, which they obviously claimed was far higher than his, for the purposes of being classified with them (ἐγκρῖναι), nor does he compare himself with them. But this is said ironically, because soon it becomes clear that they are not in his league, which is actually higher than theirs. The verb ἐγκρῖναι means 'to make a judgment about something, and classify it in a specific group, to class' (BDAG 274). This is its only appearance in the NT (and it is not in the LXX). More significant is the word συγκρῖναι, which brings us face to face with the ancient rhetorical practice of σύγκρισις (*sugkrisis*), 'comparison'. As Peter Marshall has pointed out, σύγκρισις was often used as a form of invective; it allowed comparison to be drawn between two people on a range of issues, to determine which was the better or the worse (1987: 53–5). In a letter from the late first century CE, probably written from Alexandria, a young man complains to his father about a poor teacher he has, one Didymus, a mere provincial, who presumes 'to compare' (engage in *sugkrisis*) himself with better-qualified teachers.[4] Accordingly, σύγκρισις was apparently being used by Paul's opponents to praise themselves and 'to portray Paul as a socially and intellectually unacceptable person' (Marshall 1987: 325–39, 348). Unlike people like Didymus, Paul is saying that he would not dare to compare himself to these people, superficially suggesting he was inferior to them. The irony of 10.12 is that it allows Paul to hit back by conducting his own comparison with his opponents (Marshall 1987: 349).

In the second part of v. 12, Paul says of his opponents that 'when they are measuring (ἑαυτοὺς μετροῦντες) themselves with themselves (ἐν ἑαυτοῖς) or comparing themselves (συγκρίνοντες ἑαυτοὺς) with themselves (ἑαυτοῖς), they lack understanding.'[5] The two instances of ἑαυτοῖς, a reflexive pronoun, would probably make better sense as ἀλλήλοις, a reciprocal pronoun, because they seem to be comparing themselves with one another not with 'themselves'.[6] It is likely that they were engaging in the measuring and the comparing 'as a means of validating their ministry at Corinth in the eyes of the Corinthians' (Harris 2005: 708). Paul is presumably implying that

---

[4] P Oxy 2190; noted by Furnish (1984:470) on the basis of information provided to him by Edwin Judge.
[5] Some textual witnesses omit 'they lack understanding' (οὐ συνιᾶσιν) at the end of v. 12; the stronger textual tradition retains it.
[6] See Furnish 1984: 470 for a reflexive pronoun serving a reciprocal purpose, although usually with πρὸς ἑαυτούς not a dative plural; also Harris 2005: 708.

they are simply acting as a self-referential group, that is, there is no external verification for their claims (Thrall 2000: 641); this is the view he will express in v. 18, with the Lord being the verifier, and with other relevant discussion in vv. 13-17.

While Marshal considers that Paul is conducting his comparison 'with notable moderation and restraint', Paul is probably just feigning caution here. He indicated in v. 2 that he might dare (τολμῆσαι), now he says he will not, and at 11.21 he does indulge in some 'daring' behaviour. At 12.11 he will claim that he was forced to retaliate because the Corinthians failed to commend him.

2 Corinthians 10.13 The central image in the verse, that of measure and measurement, has been prompted by the reference to the opponents measuring (μετροῦντες) themselves with themselves in the previous verse. When Paul says that he will not claim honour 'beyond limit' (ἄμετρα), the necessary implication is that his opponents do. The statement that 'they lack understanding' in the previous verse may be an understatement for 'they are foolish', perhaps because they were exaggerating their abilities, presumably to Paul's detriment, in the course of making such comparisons. The situation is similar to that mentioned by Plutarch in *On Inoffensive Self-Praise*. Having noted that 'praise is frivolous which men are felt to bestow upon themselves merely to receive it', which is a behaviour close to what Paul attributes his opponents, Plutarch continues a little later by saying:

> But when they do not even seek to be praised simply and in themselves, but try to rival the honour that belongs to others and set against it their own accomplishments and acts in the hope of dimming the glory of another, their conduct is not only frivolous, but envious and spiteful as well. (3.1; ET Lacey and Einarson 1959: 117)

Although the remainder of the verse has several interpretative difficulties (Harris 2005: 709–16), what Paul says makes good sense in the context of rivals moving in on his reputation and his mission field (see v. 15 especially). Paul asserts that he will claim honour in accordance with τὸ μέτρον τοῦ κανόνος that God has allocated to him, a (μέτρον) that reaches (ἐφικέσθαι) even 'as far as you' (ἄχρι καὶ ὑμῶν).

A major issue is the meaning of τὸ μέτρον τοῦ κανόνος, which also appears in 10.15 and 16. The word κανών (*kanōn*) is related to the Hebrew *qāneh*, meaning a 'reed' or 'rod'. In classical Greek it can mean, inter alia, a straight edge used by masons or carpenters or a ruler, and it acquired the metaphorical meaning of 'rule' or 'standard.' It occurs three times in the LXX, as the rail of a bed or the bedpost (Judges 13.6), a rigid rule (Mic. 7.4) and a philosophical rule or principle (4 Macc. 7.21). In the New Testament, it is only found in Paul, in 2 Cor. 10.3, 15 and 16, and in Gal. 6.16, where it means the norm or principle of the new creation, although as in that verse it is something one walks by, the notion of a straight path, which is closely tied to its original meaning, does not seem far away. The preliminary observation to be made is that, whatever it means, Paul is laying claim to the possession of some dimension to his mission that God has given him and, by implication, not his opponents. There is an objective and God-given aspect of his ministry that the others lack. A wide range of meanings has been suggested, but given that there are so many indications of geographical position in vv. 13-16, it seems to have a geographical flavour. A bilingual Greek and Roman inscription dated 18–19 CE from Pisidia uses the word to mean an official schedule ('formula' in the Latin text) of transport services to be provided by the local community. The κανών is not a geographical concept, but the services it specifies are geographically limited (in commenting on the inscription, Edwin Judge says the services were geographically 'partitioned', but this is not quite accurate, since only one geographical reference is given, to two towns beyond which the services do not have to be provided). Judge (1981: 45) comments:

> It is reasonable to envisage that other governors were publishing similar definitions within their provinces. Paul and his colleagues who travelled the Roman roads will have been familiar with notices such as our edict, and took over from them the term which neatly expressed their understanding of the way God had measured out their respective territorial commitments.

This parallel suggests, therefore, that by κανών Paul means a schedule of services to be performed within a designated territory. Accordingly, it is appropriate to translate it as 'mission' or 'mission area'. Although Lambrecht (1999: 166) has critiqued this view, it does for the first time provide a meaning of κανών that has a geographical dimension that seems to be required by the immediate context (especially the word ἐφικέσθαι). Thrall plausibly regards it as the best interpretation yet offered (2000: 647). Numerous commentators (even before the publication of this inscription) had taken the view that the agreement of Gal. 2.9 lies behind what Paul says here and that view is confirmed by this particular meaning for κανών. This allusion to the Jerusalem agreement very strongly connects this material to 2 Corinthians 8–9, for it entails that Paul kept to his side of the agreement just as surely as the Jerusalem church did not.

Lying behind the statement that God allocated (ἐμέρισεν) a mission to Paul (taking οὗ with κανόνος since it is closest noun), one that he notes reached as far as the Corinthians, is almost certainly the great paradigmatic statement in Gal. 1.16 that God chose 'to reveal his son in me, so that I might preach the Gospel among the non-Judeans'. This meant that Paul would be working in areas outside Judea where the majority of the members of his Christ-groups would be non-Judeans but where there would often be some Judeans as well, meaning the issue of ethnically mixed communities sharing one loaf and one cup at the Lord's Supper would inevitably raise Judean hackles for the risk of idolatry it represented (Esler 1998: 93–116). Related to the issue of his call was the fact that the Jerusalem leaders – James, Cephas and John – had agreed that mixed table-fellowship would be permitted in his mission (Gal. 2.1-10) and then later reneged on the agreement (Gal 2:11-14). This reference to the core of the Pauline mission strengthens the case for the opponents representing the same type of opponent, namely those who wanted non-Judean Christ-followers to become Judeans, who had followed Paul to Galatia. This subject is covered in Chapter 13 of this volume.

2 Corinthians 10.14 By commencing with a disclaimer that he was overextending himself (ὑπερεκτείνομεν ἑαυτούς), the verb being a *hapax* in the New Testament, Paul probably implying that his opponents in Corinth were; that is, they were going beyond the proper limit. He, on the other hand, is staying within his limit, since God chose him to preach the Gospel to people such as the Corinthians. The phrase ἄχρι (γὰρ) καὶ ὑμῶν ('as far as you') is repeated from v. 13. Moreover, he was the first to reach them, (translating ἐφθάσαμεν as 'arrived first' not just 'arrived' since this seems the necessary implication, both from the wider context and from the replacement of ἐφικέσθαι with φθάνειν) so that he has primacy as the founder of their communities. This will begin a vehement complaint against the interlopers to the effect that they are trespassing on his mission, which Paul will develop in the remainder of this passage.

2 Corinthians 10.15a The initial assertion in this verse, 'we are not claiming honour (οὐκ . . . καυχώμενοι) beyond appropriate limits' (εἰς τὰ ἄμετρα), further develops this theme, that not only are the intruders trespassers in his mission area, but they also seek credit for what he has achieved. This clause, which is similar to v. 13, again implies that Paul's opponents are proceeding beyond appropriate limits and corresponds very closely to the point made by Plutarch quoted earlier in relation to v. 13.

2 Corinthians 10.15b Paul expresses the hope that as the faith of the Corinthians increases, he will be abundantly 'made great' (μεγαλυνθῆναι) among them in accordance with his mission area. Just what does μεγαλυνθῆναι convey? The RSV offers 'our field among you may be greatly enlarged'. Harris suggests 'our work may be enlarged' (2005: 720), while Thrall has 'increase, presumably, in apostolic achievement' (2000: 650). But in the

New Testament, μεγαλύνειν usually means 'magnify' in the sense of 'praise' (so Lk. 1.45; Acts 5.13; 10.46; 19.17). In the only other Pauline instance, at Phil. 1.20, the word has the similar meaning of 'honoured'. Only in the two remaining New Testament examples, Mt. 23.5 and Lk. 1.58, does it mean 'enlarge'. 'To be praised' is the meaning here, cohering closely with 'making an honour claim' at the start of v. 15, a word repeated three more times in vv. 16-17. The Vulgate runs along the same lines, translating the word as *glorificari*, 'to be awarded honour', and it is worth noting that it also employs the word *gloriari* ('to claim honour') to translate καυχᾶσθαι. Windisch, possibly writing in a context where honour was more important than it is to more modern commentators, also saw the point here, suggesting *unter euch verherrlicht zu werden*, while citing Phil. 1.20 and referring to 2 Cor. 5.12. He also linked this to the triumph that Paul was awaiting in Corinth (1970 [1924]: 312-13). It should be noted that what Paul says confirms that he has a positive view of the Corinthians; he hopes to be greatly honoured by them.

2 Corinthians 10.16 In this verse, Paul, by insisting that he will not claim the honour from work already done in someone else's mission area (κανών), is again implying that his opponents in Corinth are not as fastidious as he is in this respect. The Greek τὰ ἕτοιμα literally means 'the things that are ready' but here carries the meaning 'prepared by others'. An appropriate translation is: 'so as to preach the Gospel in regions beyond you and not to claim honour for work done by others in another's mission area.'

2 Corinthians 10.17 Here Paul is probably offering a shortened and modified version of what is said in the Septuagintal version of Jer. 9.23-24. The same 'quotation' appears in 1 Cor. 1.31. The 'Lord' here could be God, as in Jer. 9.23-24, or Christ, who is certainly the Lord mentioned in the next verse. Harris reasonably argues for the latter option and that Paul's point is that one must not claim honour for one's personal achievement but for the Lord, or for the fact that the Lord has worked these achievements through one (2005: 726; so also Thrall 2000: 652). Barnett (1997: 492) and Lambrecht (1999: 166) argue for the former option.

2 Corinthians 10.18 The reference to self-commendation here forms an *inclusio* with the similar sentiment in v. 12. Paul is obviously referring to the intruders in Corinth whom he has previously mentioned (in v. 12). The sting in the tail here is the implication that these people are not commended by God. What is implied here will be made brutally explicit in 2 Cor. 11.13.

15

Claiming honour as a fool (2 Corinthians 11)

A request for tolerance (11.1-6)

2 Corinthians 11.1 Paul is in a difficult position. He is about to start making honour-claims about himself even though he has just criticized his opponents for engaging in this behaviour. So he softens the blow by asking them to indulge him in a little foolishness (ἀφροσύνη). The word ἀφροσύνη appears in Paul's letters here and in vv. 11 and 21. It means the state of lacking prudence or good judgement (BDAG 159). The adjectival form (ἄφρων), meaning pertinent to the lack of judgement or prudence (and the opposite of φρόνιμος, as at 11.19), occurs in 11.16 (twice), 19; 12.6, 11 (and Rom. 2.20). Most commentators regard the appearance of ἀφροσύνη as inaugurating a passage that is centred on foolishness that will be prominent in chs 11 and 12. Opinions differ greatly, however, as to where the section ends, with 12.13 being perhaps the most likely place (Matera 2003: 237), not least because 12.14 inaugurates the treatment of his forthcoming visit to Corinth. Based on 2 Cor. 11.16 ('I say again, let no one think me foolish [ἄφρων]'), it seems that Paul's rivals were calling him ἄφρων, so that charge, which he will turn back on their heads, may have motivated this passage.

2 Corinthians 11.2 This is a quite remarkable image. Paul starts with the statement that he feels a divine jealousy (ζῆλος) for them, where ζῆλος means a zealous concern for one's own. He explains how in the second clause where he equates himself to a young woman's father who, in line with Israelite marriage practices, has betrothed his virginal daughter to a man (here Christ) and faces the period when she will actually enter her husband's house, during which time the father must protect her in her virginal state from other males (Furnish 1984: 499; Thrall 2000: 663). The verb is ἡρμοσάμην, from ἁρμόζω, meaning 'to join', here in the sense 'to betroth', in the aorist middle rather than active voice perhaps to emphasize Paul's role and interest in the matter (Furnish 1984: 486). The daughter is the Corinthian Christ-group and the period in question must be that from the present to the coming Day of the Lord. In other words, as Lambrecht notes (1999: 173), Paul's jealousy consists in his watching over the bride's conduct in the period between her betrothal (= baptism) and marriage (= the Parousia). Horsley observes that 'Paul's statement remains very bold; we have no analogy to a group of people being regarded collectively as a παρθένος' (1981: 71). This is actually quite a favourable view of the Corinthians since Paul is comparing them to a virgin in this interim period. For Paul as the father of his Corinthian converts, see 1 Cor. 4.15; 2 Cor. 6.13; 12.14.

2 Corinthians 11.3 Yet Paul is uncertain. He is afraid that just as the serpent tricked Eve with his cunning (πανουργία), their thoughts will be corrupted and 'turned away from single-mindedness (ἁπλότης) and purity (ἁγνότης) in relation to Christ'. If ἁπλότης is the correct reading at 2 Cor. 1.12, here we find Paul attributing to the Corinthians a quality he has also previously ascribed to himself (6.6). There is a textual problem over ἁγνότης, since it does not occur in some manuscripts, with the arguments for and against its inclusion fairly finely balanced. Yet the longer version, adopted here, is better attested and makes for better sense (Furnish 1984: 487). Paul's mention of ἁγνότης follows closely on the appearance of ἁγνή in v. 2. He has previously listed it among his own characteristics (6.6), and he has used a close synonym, ἁγιωσύνη, in 7.1 to bring his great identity statement in 6.14–7.1 to its conclusion. It is a key identity-descriptor for the Christ-movement. Accordingly, by his use of ἁπλότης and ἁγνότης Paul points to himself as prototypical of Christ-movement norms but also adduces another sign of the mutuality and reciprocity that are evident throughout this letter.

So here Paul, for the first time in 2 Corinthians 10–13, is saying something potentially unfavourable about the Corinthians, that he fears they may be corrupted from their pure devotion to Christ. But his inclusion of 'perhaps' (πως) in the opening statement 'I am afraid lest perhaps' (φοβοῦμαι δὲ μή πως) shows that he is only putting this suggestion forward very tentatively; it is a risk not a reality. The same will apply to his use of the same formula in 12.20. For the present, indeed, they are still characterized by single-mindedness (here in devotion to their one husband) and purity. It is possible that Paul had in mind a tradition where the serpent copulated with Eve (Thrall 2000: 662–3). Even without that dimension, however, it should be noted that there is no one else in the frame who could be the agents of such deception other than his opponents in Corinth. This means he is insinuating that they are diabolical. Their deception will presumably be perpetrated by a cunning (πανουργία) consisting, like that of the serpent, in what they are saying (Barnett 1997: 499; Matera 2003: 243). Paul had earlier disavowed the idea that *he* practised cunning (πανουργία; 4.2). Nor had *he* corrupted anyone (7.2), using the same verb as in this verse (φθείρειν). What he insinuates here will become blunt accusation in vv. 13–15, when he portrays the intruders as servants of Satan.

It is from this point that the earlier discussion about the deployment of anger in the context of external interference with the ingroup comes into its own. Here, to recall Smith's argument (1993), we see Paul attempting to arouse an emotion, anger most likely (but perhaps also fear and disgust), by assisting the Corinthians to appraise what the intruders have been saying to them as affecting the group and them as group members, and in a very negative way. They are at risk of succumbing to a form of diabolical cunning and deception.

2 Corinthians 11.4 The first clause of the verse confirms that problems are being caused for Paul by people arriving from outside Corinth. Although Paul complains of 'someone who comes', or 'the one who comes' (ὁ ἐρχόμενος), it is preferable to see this expression as a generic reference to the intruders and not to one particular person (Furnish 1984: 488). Paul has in mind a plurality of intruders (as is evident in v. 5), and does not isolate any of them for special attention as we would expect him to do if one in particular was causing him grief. These people have come to Corinth with a different Jesus, spirit and gospel (from his). The critical issue in the verse is what Paul means by 'another Jesus', 'a different spirit' and 'a different gospel', a question on which the most diverse opinions proliferate. The view adopted in this volume, as argued in Chapter 13, is that the outsiders who have arrived in Corinth are maintaining much the same programme as Paul's opponents in Galatia: they are Christ-following Judeans who want all Christ-followers to acquire Judean ethnic identity. This broad position is what Paul means by 'a different gospel'. It is also probable that the different spirit they preach does not come associated with charismatic phenomena as in Paul's mission, nor is their other Jesus one proclaimed in association with his humility, passion and death.

It is also noteworthy that in this verse Paul attributes something unfavourable to the Corinthians, that they are putting up with his opponents splendidly (καλῶς). Yet this is something apparently not bad enough that they have lost the single-mindedness and purity he attributes to them in v. 3. Even though they put up with these activities that they should not put up with, they are still the virginal betrothed. Yet, as Guthrie observes (2015: 511), there is a strong sense of irony in the verse: in v. 1, Paul beseeched the Corinthians to put up with him, now he asserts they put up with his opponents splendidly, in each case using the same verb (ἀνέχομαι).

We have seen in Chapter 13 of this volume that members of a group who received negative information about their ingroup were angrier with the outgroup when the ingroup responded unsuccessfully to the threat they posed than when it responded successfully (Maitner et al. 2006). This is precisely the position from Paul's point of view. Rather than rejecting out of hand the wrong Jesus, spirit and gospel proposed by the interlopers, the Corinthians had given them a tolerant hearing and thereby responded unsuccessfully to them. Social identity theory suggests that Paul's anger at the interlopers would have increased in consequence, and this is what we find with the way he characterizes them in the next verse.

2 Corinthians 11.5-6 As argued in Chapter 13 of this volume, the better view is that the 'superlative apostles' (οἱ ὑπερλίαν ἀπόστλοι) mentioned in v. 5 are to be identified with the intruders in Corinth and, accordingly, that they are not a reference to people such as Peter, James and John in Jerusalem or the Twelve generally. Paul expresses his anger at the interlopers by mocking them and their boasting about their mission by the use of mock self-deprecation (Garland 1999: 453).

This view is confirmed by his concession in v. 6 as to his lack of oratorical skill, since this connects with the claim – clearly made by the interlopers (not by the Jerusalem 'pillars') – that he is humble when in the presence of the Corinthians in 2 Cor. 10.1. Even more focused confirmation comes from his statement in 10.10, no doubt originating among the same people, that his powers of speech (λόγος) are contemptible. Harris has little justification for the suggestion (2005: 748) that 'perhaps the coalition of anti-Pauline Corinthians and intruders from Judea' were contending that his public speaking was contemptible. This was a charge made by the interlopers who were, in a prima facie way at least, qualified to make it. It should not be sourced to the Corinthians as well, even though Paul is distressed that they are paying too much attention to the interlopers' views. As far as the substance of Paul's statement is concerned, he is adamant, as he has abundantly made clear to them, that what counts is knowledge (γνῶσις) – of Jesus, Spirit and Gospel, for example – not the manner in which he delivers that knowledge.

Financial dependence and independence(11.7-11)

Turner's analysis of influence (2005), it will be recalled, posits that a leader first wins the confidence of the group, as Paul does in 2 Corinthians 1–7, and is then able to direct the use of resources, here with respect to the collection in 2 Corinthians 8–9. Yet Paul does not seek to benefit from his restored relations with the Corinthians in relation to seeking support from them. This may be because to take this money would involve him in patterns of social relationship in Corinth, especially to do with patronage (Chow 1992), in which he did not wish to be involved. Other reasons appear below.

2 Corinthians 11.7 The Greek text of this verse begins with the word Ἤ, meaning 'or', which serves to introduce a rhetorical question that anticipates a negative response (Guthrie 2015: 519), here to the suggestion that he sinned in not taking money from the Corinthians for his personal support as he preached the Gospel to them. Although there are many reasons why Paul preached gratis, Harris usefully summarizes three (2005: 765):

1. He did not want to be a financial encumbrance on his converts (2 Cor. 11.9; 12.13-14, 16; 1 Thess. 2.9);
2. By preaching for free, he was dramatizing in his own conduct the appeal of the Gospel as a free gift of God's grace (11.7; 1 Cor. 9.12b, 18); and
3. He wanted to distinguish himself from rivals who charged for their services (11.12).

The last factor probably carries the most weight. Throughout chs 10–13 Paul is at great pains to differentiate himself from the intruders especially since, as we will learn in 11.12, they attempt to align their missionary activities with his. Of critical important in understanding 2 Corinthians is that in 2 Cor. 2.17 Paul refers to many who are pedlars of God's word, thus identifying a group who now turn out to operate in a manner diametrically opposed to his practice. Paul is apparently writing in a context where his opponents are being supported by the Corinthians. In chs 10–13, he implies their practice of taking payment in 11.7, 12, 20, thus providing a link back to his 'pedlars of God's word' remark in 2.17. This means that the people whom he is attacking in chs 10–13 were present in Corinth all along (and have not arrived after he had written 1–9). The letter was a unified composition from the outset.

Paul is perhaps being ironic in asking a rhetorical question for which he expects a negative answer: 'Did I commit a sin?' But we must question whether this is really 'stinging irony' (Harris 2005: 754), and, in addition, whether it is irony at all. Whether ironic or not, Paul is certainly insisting that nothing he has done could possibly involve a breach of divine commandment.

His opponents were no doubt alleging that his practice of not being dependent on the community among whom he was conducting his ministry was sinful as in breach of the rule he quotes in 1 Cor. 9.14: 'The Lord commanded those who preach the Gospel to get their living from the Gospel.' Gerd Theissen has interpreted this as a rule of apostolic poverty, framing this dimension of the conflict between Paul and his opponents as one between the model of the wandering charismatic of rural Palestine and the role of community-organizer required in the cities of the Greco-Roman East (1982: 40-2). While this is a plausible view, we need to note the specific way Paul phrases his approach. He is 'humbling' (ταπεινῶν) himself. This may refer to his practice of working as this trade (in leather-working), since to work with one's hands was, in the view of the social elite of his world, a demeaning occupation (Hock 2007: 60). The counterweight to that view was the repeated assertions in Israelite tradition that God exalted the humble (Guthrie 2015: 519). On the other hand, in the present passage there is no explicit reference to his working (as there is in 1 Thess. 2.9), since the only source of funds he mentions is the Macedonians (vv. 8-9), even though it may have been that his failure to produce enough money by his own hands (in Corinth he was 'in a needy state' [ὑστερηθείς] in 11.9) meant that he needed the help the Macedonians supplied. It may be, however, that his humbling himself consists not of working with his hands but simply in his eschewing his apostolic right of support from the community among whom he is then preaching the Gospel (as suggested for Corinth by 1 Cor. 9.12b, 18). Support for this view comes from his not mentioning working with his hands, even though that can be implied from v. 9 (see in the following).

It is possible that underlying any negative feelings towards Paul among the Corinthians was the fact that the Corinthians did offer support and Paul rejected it. Wealthier members of the community would have interpreted this as Paul's rejection of patronage, a form of (admittedly asymmetrical) friendship. Yet while Paul may not have wanted to become anyone's client, his opponents in Corinth may not have been so fastidious, taking support and a client relationship when it was offered to them (Marshall 1987: 165–258).

In what might the exaltation of the Corinthians consist? It is presumably that by being active among them he has introduced them to the new economy of salvation in Christ. In other words, Paul is referring to the spiritual enrichment that he brought to the Corinthians by his work among them (Barrett 1973: 282; Thrall 2000: 684). But it is harder to see precisely how Paul's not taking any money from them has achieved this result. If, however, his humbling consisted rather in his simply giving up his right of apostolic support, their exaltation could take the form of a different style of leadership where he does not lord it over them (1.24) but cooperates with them in the Gospel.

2 Corinthians 11.8-9 There is an oxymoron in v. 8, since he is saying, 'I robbed (ἐσύλησα) other Christ-groups by accepting support' (ὀψώνιον), no doubt freely given (cf. 8.1-2), from them. The other churches in question probably included Philippi in Macedonia but others could have been involved as well. The verb can refer to the sack of a city and ὀψώνιον can be a soldier's pay, so Paul may be evoking a military setting here. It is not possible to identify the brothers who came from Philippi with the aid, although some commentators venture Silas and Timothy (Guthrie 2015: 522). Paul had received support from the Philippians earlier (Phil. 4.15-17), when they sent him money while he was in Thessalonika, but this was done as an expression of their sharing (ἐκοινώνησεν) their resources to assist the spread of the Gospel. As Matera has noted (2003: 250–1), this was a very different arrangement from the support apparently being offered to Paul by the Corinthians for his work among them, although Paul refrains from making this point, probably to avoid giving offence to the Corinthians by volunteering such a comparison.

We need to understand what is going on in terms of challenge and response. The Corinthians would probably have felt slighted by Paul's failure to accept their offer. But we need to reiterate that what Paul says here certainly presumes a willingness by the Corinthians to support him when he was with them and almost as certainly presumes this willingness was conveyed to him. Of course, Paul was only unwilling to accept financial support from people he was currently present among and evangelizing. He was perfectly happy to take money from a community if it was to be expended in preaching the Gospel somewhere else, typically when he accepted support to 'send him on his way' (προπέμπειν). He was happy to accept this kind of support from the Corinthians (1 Cor. 16.6) and also from the Romans (Rom. 15.24). He was disinclined to come under obligation to individuals where he was currently preaching the Gospel.

2 Corinthians 11.10 Paul now rams home the previous point by insisting, with an appeal to Christ's truth in him that is, in effect, an oath (Thrall 2000: 687), that (far from stopping, he implies) he will even make this practice of not taking support from them a basis for a claim to honour that he will shout throughout Achaia. He will not be silenced (φραγήσεται). Commentators (like Bachman 1909: 375) who suggest that it is the Achaians and not Paul who are doing the boasting are wide of the mark.

2 Corinthians 11.11 The question 'Why?' (διὰ τί) at the start of the verse relates to his failure to claim support (v. 9) not to his honour-claim for so doing (v. 10). From this verse, one deduces that the Corinthians were interpreting his refusal to accept support from them as a sign that he did not love them, so he needs to tell them that he does (Matera 2003: 249). This suggests that someone in Corinth (and there is no reason to suppose it was a Corinthian rather than one of the Judean interlopers) had suggested that Paul's lack of love for the Corinthians was shown by the fact that he failed to accept their (presumed) offer of financial support. In speaking of his love for them, he is really reassuring them of the love that he previously mentioned in 2.4 and will reiterate in 12.15. He has also previously noted that they love him (8.7).

False apostles (11.12-15)

2 Corinthians 11.12 This verse marks a transition from his not seeking assistance from the Corinthians to a direct attack on the intruders in Corinth who do. Some commentators see this verse as belonging to vv. 7-11 because of the number of links back to them it contains, rather than as beginning a new section that goes to v. 15 (Lambrecht 1999: 177; Harris 2005: 767). Probably the preferable approach, however, is to treat this as a verse that looks both backwards and forwards, but with the latter aspect having priority.

The trouble-makers in Corinth appear clearly in this verse; these are the people who are saying that Paul does not love the Corinthians because he does not accept their support. Paul gets quite personal in relation to his opponents here, possibly even petty. He will continue to practise financial independence so that his opponents, who depend on support from the Corinthians, will be deprived of the chance of saying they are equal to or the same as Paul in their work. Behind this is the insinuation that they recognize that Paul stands over them, and they want to bring him down to their level by having the Corinthians push him to turn to them for support.

The unstated basis for the intruders regarding themselves inferior to Paul deserves investigation. While Paul's refusal to accept local support differentiated his mission from that of the interlopers, he was also different from them in two other respects that they must have found irksome. First, it was Paul not his opponents who had planted the Gospel in Corinth (1 Cor. 3.6). Secondly, this formed part of his missionary area. This had been agreed with the Jerusalem pillars during the meeting in Jerusalem reported in Gal. 2.1-10, even though they later abrogated that agreement in Antioch, as recounted in Gal. 2.11-14 (Esler 1998: 131–40). Paul had alleged that he had stuck to his mission field, while they had trespassed upon it, as recently as 10.13-16. Thrall plausibly suggests the possibility that 'Paul's opponents had come to the city initially in furtherance of the Petrine mission'. Were Paul to change his practice, he would also 'align himself with the Petrine mission, and concede, symbolically, that Corinth is Petrine territory'. This would suggest his rivals' authority was equal to his (2000: 693). Paul's refusal to accept Corinthian aid thus served to symbolize the distance between him and them in a manner that also drew attention to these two issues.

2 Corinthians 11.13 Here Paul dramatically pulls the rug from under his opponents' claim to be in any way comparable to him in a particularly harsh and direct condemnation. There can be no doubt that 'such people' refers to those of whom he has just been speaking. The anger that he has been nursing since 10.1 in relation to them now bursts to the surface. His opponents obviously claim to be apostles of Christ; they are using this phrase as a self-designation (Harris 2005: 775). Paul is scathing about them on this point, asserting that these people are disguising themselves (μετασχηματιζόμενοι) as apostles of Christ when they are really false apostles (ψευδαπόστολοι) and deceitful workers (ἐργάται δόλιοι).

Ψευδαπόστολοι is *hapax* in the New Testament and may well be a Pauline coinage formulated for the very point he is making in vv. 13-15. Many commentators consider that it may have been inspired by the expression 'false prophets' (ψευδοπροφῆται) of Israelite tradition (Furnish 1984: 495; Thrall 2000: 694), a phrase that occurs in the Septuagint, Philo and Josephus and the New Testament (where ψευδοπροφῆται appears eleven times). Yet the expression 'false prophets' never appears in Paul's letters, and there is a more likely source much closer to home. For it is probable that ψευδαπόστολοι has been coined on the model of ψευδαδέλφοι, a word and a notion that were clearly on Paul's mind when he was writing this section of the letter, since the word appears a little later in 11.26, as one of the various hardships he had encountered in his ministry (11.23-29). The only other time Paul used this word was when he wrote Galatians, and its appearance in Gal 2.4-5 tells us precisely what he means by it. The ψευδαδέλφοι were Christ-followers who had been secretly brought into a meeting of the movement in Jerusalem, Paul says, 'to spy out the freedom that we have in Christ Jesus in order to enslave us'. But he did not yield to them for a moment, so that 'the truth of the Gospel might be preserved for *you*', meaning the Galatian Christ-followers to whom he was writing. The only other time Paul deployed the phrase 'the truth of the Gospel', as I have pointed out elsewhere (Esler 1998: 136), was when asserting that the Judean Christ-followers in Antioch were not walking according to it by breaking off table-fellowship with non-Judean Christ-followers (Gal. 2.14). False brothers, therefore, were false by opposing the Gospel truth that circumcision and the acquisition of Judean ethnic identity were not necessary for non-Judean Christ-followers. The false apostles in Corinth, while they were apostles rather than simply brothers, were false, inter alia, for the same reason: they wanted non-Judean Christ-followers to accept the law of Moses and become Judeans. Since the Gospel that Paul preached, which allowed his non-Judean converts freedom from becoming Judeans, embodied the truth, any other Gospel was false. Thus, the claims that his opponents were false apostles (11.13) and that they preached a different Gospel (11.4) were equivalent. Paul would probably also have allowed of them being false apostles in preaching a different spirit and another Jesus (11.4), in lacking apostolic authority (since they were trespassing on his missionary territory; 10.13-16) and in their manner of evangelism, in that they peddled God's word for money (2.17).

The expression 'deceitful workers' may not add much of substance to this damning verdict, but it certainly does reinforce the case for Paul's opponents being Judean Christ-followers who advocate the adoption by non-Judean Christ-followers of Judean ethnic identity (entailing, as it did, circumcision). For Paul's only other use of ἐργάται ('workmen') comes in Phil. 3.2-3:

'Beware of the dogs, beware of the evil workers (κακοὺς ἐργάτας), beware of the mutilation (κατατομή). For we are the circumcision (περιτομή), who worship God in spirit and claim honour in Christ and put no confidence in the flesh.' Here we see the contrast of actual and metaphoric circumcision.

2 Corinthians 11.14 With this verse Paul tightens the screws on his criticism, with the mordant comment that it is no wonder (οὐ θαῦμα) (i.e. that they do so) since Satan disguises himself (μετασχηματίζεται) as an angel of light. Paul was probably aware of specific texts where Satan had so disguised himself, such as the *Life of Adam and Eve* (9.1) and the *Apocalypse of Moses* (17.1-2; Furnish 1984: 494–5; Thrall 2000: 695). Yet there is no need to suppose the Corinthians were au fait with such traditions: it is enough for Paul's purposes that he just make the bald statement.

2 Corinthians 11.15 This is brutal criticism now: Paul asserts that his opponents are Satan's ministers (διάκονοι) and he can surely say nothing worse about them than that. In social identity terms, this is an extreme example of negative outgroup stereotypification. It also reveals just how angry Paul was with these people. The verse also means that he is conveying to the Corinthians the hard message that if they side with these people, they are siding with Satan (Harris 2005: 775).

But they also 'disguise themselves' (μετασχηματίζονται), the third use of this verb in three verses, as 'ministers of righteousness' (διάκονοι δικαιοσύνης). In the expression διάκονοι δικαιοσύνης, the genitive is probably objective, that is, it means 'ministers in the service of righteousness' (Harris 2005: 775). The repetition of sound in διάκονοι δικαιοσύνης also suggests that this is a self-designation by the intruders. As already mentioned in Chapter 13, the claim by Paul's opponents to be servants of righteousness (δικαιοσύνη) allows us a valuable insight into the dominant way in which their gospel differed from Paul's. To appreciate this, we refer by way of comparison to the situation in Galatia where the opponents were offering Paul's converts the glittering prize of righteousness if they were circumcised and became Judeans; their claim was, in effect, that 'righteousness is from the law' (Esler 1998: 170-1). His opponents are presenting themselves as advocates of righteousness, and given that their decidedly Judean character is soon about to appear (v. 22), there is no other form of righteousness that they would be propounding. Barnett reaches the same view (1997: 527), noting that 'righteousness' is most likely expressive of or connected with the Law of Moses for two reasons: first, Paul will soon describe the intruders as 'Hebrews, Israelites, descendants of Moses' (in v. 22), and, secondly, these must be the same people Paul has previously described as peddling God's word needing letters of recommendation (2.17–3.1) and ministers of the now-overtaken 'old covenant' written on tablets of stone (3.2-18).

Harris tries to avoid this conclusion and denies that righteousness can here mean the sort that depends on works or Torah observance, noting R. Tasker as a proponent of the former option and P. Barnett as a proponent of the latter.[1] He cites two reasons for his scepticism: first, it lacks a qualification such as 'from works' (ἐξ ἔργων) or 'from law' (ἐκ νόμου); and, secondly, because 'Judaizers' advocating this position would not be in disguise, an objection he has drawn from Windisch (1924: 343). Weighing against the first of these objections is that Paul can use righteousness without such qualifiers. Even if they were necessary, the very word ἔργα ('works') actually appears in the verse in connection with their activities. Secondly, the point is that they are using righteousness as a disguise for their being Satan's agents. (Judean) righteousness *is* their disguise! Moreover, righteousness is a field of contention. They were in disguise as far as Paul is concerned. It made perfect sense for him to claim that his opponents were disguising themselves as 'ministers in the service of righteousness' if the fact was that they were propounding a course of action that would not, in fact, produce righteousness. Paul has, moreover, previously described his own ministry as a ministry of righteousness (3.9). In his mission field, at least, there was only one valid ministry of this type and it was his, not that of his opponents. The verse concludes, as Thrall notes, 'with an ominous, though unspecified, threat of judgement, similar to those found elsewhere in Paul's letters' (2000: 698, citing Rom. 3.8; 1 Cor. 3.17; Phil. 3.19; 1 Thess. 2.16).

Martiny and Kessler (2014) provide evidence for the fact that when outgroup interference has obstructed the way a group is managing its identity, outgroup-directed anger is strongest for group members who highly value their group (i.e. who possess high group-based esteem). This was the position in which Paul found himself. The very foundations of the identity of the Christ-group he had founded in Corinth, its Gospel, were threatened by the interlopers, and no one valued that group and its identity more than him. These factors pushed him to the pitch of anger towards them that is plainly visible in the savage denunciation he expresses in this verse.

A justification for foolish boasting (11.16-21A)

2 Corinthians 11.16 As emphasized by 'again' (πάλιν), Paul returns to the theme of 11.1 – his request for tolerance for his foolishness (ἀφροσύνη) –

---

[1] Tasker 1958: 154 and Barnett (1997: 527), who also notes a connection between 'evil workmen' in Phil. 3.2 and righteousness in the law that I have already suggested earlier in relation to v. 13.

since, in spite of what he said there, he has not really started the honour-claim he apologetically indicated he was about to undertake. As previously noted, foolishness is a central notion in this section of the letter. In urging no one to consider him foolish, he probably has in mind his Corinthian addressees, rather than his rivals in Corinth (*contra*, Barnett 1997: 529). Paul apprehends that the former are at risk of accepting this estimation of his character as proposed by the latter. In asking them to accept him as they would a fool, he is probably implying that he would not be the first fool they had accepted, meaning the interlopers from Judea, an implication that becomes explicit in v. 19: 'For you gladly bear with fools.'

2 Corinthians 11.17 Paul's opening remark, 'What I am saying (ὃ λαλῶ)', has a future orientation in that Paul is, in a rather elaborate build-up, preparing the ground for what he is going to say, his claim for honour. This is a claim he is making in foolishness (ἀφροσύνη), and thus of his own volition, and not 'according to the Lord' (κατὰ κύριον). While the general meaning is clear, the precise connotation of κατὰ κύριον is difficult to determine (Harris 2005: 780-1). Lambrecht reasonably observes that translations such as 'at the Lord's command' or 'with the Lord's authority' 'seem to somewhat over-emphasize the Lord's activity in this matter' (1999: 188). The implication here is that Paul is not making the honour-claim as an apostle but as someone who has been driven to it because of what others have said. This action represents a temporary diversion into foolishness.

2 Corinthians 11.18 There is no reason to suggest, with Harris (2005: 782), that there may have been some Corinthians included in the 'many' who claim honour in a worldly way (κατὰ σάρκα), as he is about to do. The whole thrust of Paul's rhetoric since 11.1 (and earlier) has been that the virtuous Corinthians (v. 2) are at risk of falling prey to outsiders who are actually ministers of Satan, false apostles (v. 15). These same people are his target, his only target, in v. 18. They are the people he has already differentiated himself from in 2 Cor. 5.12 (Matera 2003: 257). This interpretation of the verse is confirmed by v. 19, where he distinguishes the Corinthians from the 'fools' they put up with, while being sensible themselves. Paul takes the rather risky step of saying he will make honour-claims just as they do, but his argument entails making clear that he realizes that it is foolishness to do so, indeed it is expressly not κατὰ κύριον (v. 17), whereas his opponents do not.

2 Corinthians 11.19 This is a verse of considerable significance in grasping Paul's attitude to the Corinthians. In starting with 'For you gladly bear with fools (ἡδέως γὰρ ἀνέχεσθε τῶν ἀφρόνων)', Paul uses the same verb for show tolerance that he used in relation to what he desired from the Corinthians (11.1), and in relation to his complaint of their tolerating his opponents (11.4). His designating them as 'fools' (ἄφρονες) is a further indication of his anger.

Most commentators regard the brief second clause, φρόνιμοι ὄντες, as causal: 'being sensible yourselves' or 'since you are sensible'. This view demands that Paul is being ironic towards the Corinthians (e.g. Plummer 1915: 315; Furnish 1984: 496; Lambrecht 1999: 189; Thrall 2000: 715–16; Harris 2005: 783). Such an interpretation accords with the common view (which I have critiqued earlier) that Paul is so hard on the Corinthians in 2 Corinthians 10–13 that this section of the letter must originally have been separate from chs 1–9.

The Greek, however, gives no indication that a causal meaning of φρόνιμοι ὄντες is required. Certainly at one point in 1 Corinthians Paul had spoken ironically when stating that the Corinthians were φρόνιμοι: 'We are fools on account of Christ, you are φρόνιμοι in Christ; we are weak, you are strong; you are honourable, we are dishonourable' (1 Cor. 4.10). Indeed, some commentators cite 1 Cor. 4.10 in support of reading φρόνιμοι ὄντες ironically here (Matera 2003: 257). In fact, the comparison, or, we should say, the contrast, with 1 Cor. 4.10 suggests precisely the opposite result. For 1 Cor. 4.10 shows the type of statement Paul would craft when he wanted to speak ironically of the Corinthians' wisdom. At one point in 1 Corinthians, moreover, Paul described his addressees as φρόνιμοι non-ironically: 'I speak as to people who are φρόνιμοι, judge yourselves what I say' (10.15). But there is nothing like the heavy irony of 1 Cor. 4.10 here, and his usage is closer to the simple statement in 1 Cor. 10.15. In particular, φρόνιμοι ὄντες is lexically unmarked for such a loaded meaning. Rather, the phrase has a concessive meaning: 'although you are wise'. Paul has employed a participial ὤν in a concessive sense a little earlier in this letter (πλούσιος ὤν in 8.9). The Vulgate (which astutely picks up the similarity in ἄφρονες and φρόνιμοι in the Greek) has: *Libenter enim suffertis insipientes, cum sitis ipsi sapientes.* The *cum* clause (with a present subjunctive) could be concessive or causal, but the addition of *ipsi* ('yourselves') is only compatible with a concessive sense.

We must ask why would Paul be ironic towards the Corinthians? Why risk alienating them unnecessarily? It is surprising that so few commentators have recognized the concessive force of φρόνιμοι ὄντες.[2] Following the irony route means missing the real point of Paul's attitude to the Corinthians in this verse, that he is expressing exasperation and hurt towards them in a way that makes for a much more powerful expression because of the actual

---

[2] A concessive meaning is seen in a few translations, such as the Twentieth Century New Testament (1904) and Montgomery (1929).

(as opposed to feigned) contrast it contains (as in the Vulgate's translation): 'How can sensible people like you put up with fools like them?'

2 Corinthians 11.20 This verse clearly requires no ironic reading of the second clause in the preceding verse to have its effect. Indeed, it carries far more force if there is no irony in the previous verse, for tolerating such behaviour is far worse for the Corinthians if they are sensible than if they are foolish. Here, as in the previous verse, Paul is expressing exasperation with the Corinthians, not deriding them as stupid. This verse also reads better if the previous verse has also expressed exasperation rather than irony for the further reason that there is nothing obviously ironic here, just a list of tolerated abuses.

So we have a series of five illustrations of what the Corinthians gladly put up with (even though they should know better). Larry Welborn has recently argued that tying the various abuses in this verse together is their dependence upon the common or stock figure in Greco-Roman comedy of the pompous and unpleasant guest who abuses his host and other guests alike (2009). Although that is a creative new suggestion, the seriousness of the behaviour Paul alleges would be rather undercut if he expected his addressees to regard such people as comic. Let us consider the five abuses specified *seriatim*.

As I noted in Chapter 13, the only other instance of the word used of enslavement, καταδουλόω, which (significantly) heads the list, in Paul is in Gal. 2.4. There it is used of false brothers who infiltrated the ranks of Paul and his group to deny the latter their freedom by requiring the imposition of Judean ethnic identity and the bondage of the law (especially by insisting upon circumcision). The presence of this unusual word, and the other factors I have outlined in Chapter 13 of this volume, strongly suggest that the law of Moses and, in due course, circumcision in particular formed part of the message of the intruders, who were thus essentially identical with those who troubled Paul in Galatia.

Commentators have proven remarkably resistant to this rather straightforward meaning of καταδουλόω. Lambrecht remarks that the meaning of καταδουλόω in Gal. 2.4 is 'not so obvious' here (1999: 189). Barrett, one of the few critics to entertain it, suggested that a 'Judaizing' party might lie in the background here as in 2.4 (1973: 291), a view that received short shrift from Thrall: 'But Judaizing as such is not the problem in Corinth' (2000: 716). Thrall suggests (2000: 716) that 'Metaphorically, these people "enslave" the Corinthian congregation, enforcing their own authority on the church', but how they manage this feat or what such 'enslavement' looks like she does not say (3262000: 716). On another view (Barnett 1997: 532, possibly influenced by Furnish 1984: 497), Paul has in mind 'the kind of domineering leadership that Paul himself was careful not to impose' (cf. 1.24; 12.14; cf.

4.5). But Paul never suggests he enslaves the Corinthians; indeed, he insists that he does not lord it over their faith (1.24). In fact, he makes himself their slave (4.5). The language used is very different. A final explanation is that καταδουλόω in the present context implies that the outsiders want to enslave the Corinthians *to themselves*, and this implication differentiates its use here from that in Gal. 2.4 (Harris 2005: 784–5). Yet there is no such implication in 2 Cor. 11.20, and there is also no indication of what such enslavement would entail in practice.

In sum, the alternative explanations fail and καταδουλόω has the same meaning as in Gal. 2.4. To revert to Thrall's view mentioned earlier, 'Judaizing' may not be *the* problem in Corinth – indeed the word is tied to a notion of 'Judaism' as the rival entity that many critics now regard as problematic. Nevertheless, the arrival of competing missionaries advocating Judean ethnic identity and the law of Moses for his converts, with circumcision the ultimate sign of the slavery that would result, was one of the *four* problems Paul sought to answer in writing this letter. This was the biggest problem the outsiders represented to Paul's Corinthian Christ-followers, their adherence to the very substance of his Gospel, and that is why καταδουλόω appears first in this list.

The second charge, that the Corinthians are being exploited, represents the Greek κατεσθίειν, literally, 'to eat down', 'to devour', and also with extended meanings such as 'to destroy' or 'to exploit'. The likely reference is to Paul's earlier mention of those who peddle the word of God (2.17), in other words, his opponents who, unlike Paul (11.8-9), seek financial support from the Corinthians (Furnish 1984: 497; Guthrie 2015: 540).

The meaning of λαμβάνει in v. 20 is probably similar to 'take in' in English, meaning to fool or deceive, since it has much this meaning in 12.16. There it is sharpened by the addition of δόλῳ, when Paul reports that the Corinthians were claiming that he took them in by a trick (δόλῳ ὑμᾶς ἔλαβον). A little before the current verse, in 11.13, Paul has already asserted that his opponents were 'tricky workmen' (ἐργάται δόλιοι).

As for the fourth charge, ἐπαίρεται literally (as probably, in the passive form, in 10.5) means 'to raise oneself up'. Here it must have a metaphorical, akin to 'be presumptuous' or 'put on airs'. In Sir. 11.4, it appears parallel to καυχᾶσθαι, 'to make an honour-claim'.

The fifth charge is that the Corinthians allow the interlopers to strike them in the face. It is unclear if such 'striking' is literal or figurative (meaning 'humiliate', since a red face was a physical sign of being dishonoured). John Chrysostom preferred the latter explanation. Nevertheless, there is some evidence that religious authorities did strike people or have them struck (Harris 2005: 706). Certainly v. 21a, at least if it relates solely to the last of the five phenomena and not to all five, seems to push us in the direction of a literal striking. Paul would need to be aware of only one such incident to be able to lay this charge. But that an interloper struck a Corinthian as one would strike a slave (Allo 1956: 290–1) is most improbable.

2 Corinthians 11.21a There are some difficulties here. Presumably these two clauses – 'I am ashamed to say (κατὰ ἀτιμίαν λέγω) that we have been too weak for that' – refer to the behaviour attributed to the intruders in v. 20; less probably the reference is to the last item, striking someone on the face. When Paul says that he speaks 'according to shame', it is probably his shame he has in mind, rather than that of the interlopers or the Corinthians since in such a case we would expect a pronoun, 'their' or 'your', or the definite article with ἀτιμίαν (Furnish 1984: 497; Harris 2005: 787). The notion of his being weak is no doubt meant as a response to such a claim being made about him by the intruders, such as he precisely records at 10.10 and alludes to in 11.1.

There can be little doubt that this verse is strongly ironic, but that does not mean that earlier material (especially v. 19) had that character. Moreover, even granted that Paul is now being ironic, we should not jump to the conclusion that the Corinthians were or would consider themselves to have been his target. It is pretty clear that this is a barb directed at the Judean interlopers, not the Corinthians. After all, here in 11.21 he is referring back to the accusation of weakness reported in 10.10 and, by implication, attacking those who make it: 'I may be weak in my personal presence but look at the sort of things I do not do but they do!' Back at 10.10, he did not deny he was weak and he essentially acknowledges the truth of his weakness. In 11.29-30, he will return to his being ἀσθενής, as he does at 12.10, and even more graphically at 13.3-4 and 9. His weakness recurs as a leitmotif in this letter. In Gal. 4.13, he noted that his ἀσθένεια was the reason for his preaching to the Galatians. So here Paul is being ironic as far as the Judean interlopers are concerned, but exasperated or perhaps rueful as far as his Corinthians are concerned.

Paul's identity and trials (11.21b-29)

Paul is finally about to begin making the honour-claims he has been signalling since 11.1. This section extends to 12.13, so a lengthy preparation was more than justified.

2 Corinthians 11.21b By 'anyone', in v. 21b (τις), Paul refers to someone from among his rivals in Corinth, not to the Jerusalem leaders, as Barrett suggests (1973: 292). It is likely that they have been making honour-claims to the Corinthians about their identity – namely that they are ethnic Judeans and also Christ-followers and ministers of Christ, as discussed in Chapter 13 of this volume – and also about the hazards they have encountered and the sufferings they have experienced. Paul's point is that whatever claims they make, he can equal and in some cases excel them. Continuing a theme he has made previously (vv. 11.1, 16-17) and will do again (v. 23), he apologizes for his foolishness in doing this. An admission of foolishness in making a series of honour-claims is Paul's way of mitigating the fact that he has previously criticized this type of behaviour (10.8. 11.1, 16).

2 Corinthians 11.22 With this verse, Paul begins his honour-claim that runs to 12.13. Verse 22 was considered in Chapter 13 of this volume as primary support for the argument that the intruders in Corinth represent essentially the same position as those in Galatia. They pride themselves on their Judean ethnic identity, here partially expressed in the claim to be Hebrews, Israelites and descendants of Abraham. These descriptors represent central features commonly associated with ethnic ancestry: a myth of succession, a shared history and an ethnic homeland. Their version of the Gospel insists that non-Judean converts become Judeans as well as accepting Christ. The totality of 11.22–12.13, however, stands to be considered as an instructive example of the Mediterranean social dynamic of challenge and response, first theorized by Pierre Bourdieu on the basis of his work among the Kabyle of North Africa (1966) and then applied to biblical interpretation by Bruce Malina in 1981 (30–3). The context was one in which people who were (at least approximately) social equals competed with one another for honour (the result being 'acquired honour') by making challenges to others who were bound to respond to them, else their honour be diminished in the eyes of the relevant public as a result. Here the interlopers have challenged Paul in several respects before an audience consisting of his Corinthian Christ-followers and he must reply, with the sense of social obligation upon him repeatedly stressed by his insistence that he has been forced to make the counter case, promoting his merits, because of the attack that they have launched against him. The first part of his honour-claim relates to his opponents' claim to Judean ethnic identity, a status that represents ascribed rather than acquired honour but which Paul includes here at the start of his response, since he also is such a Judean.

2 Corinthians 11.23 We now learn that his opponents also glory in their claimed status as 'ministers of Christ' (διάκονοι Χριστοῦ), which also necessarily implies their membership of the Christ-movement. Yet the point of v. 23 differs from that of v. 22. Paul's similarity of expression in vv. 22-23 is not a sufficient argument for Thrall's assertion that they must be 'ministers of Christ' just as much as they are Hebrews, Israelites and descendants of

Abraham (2000: 731). Whereas in the preceding verse Paul appears not to question the intruders' claim be ethnic Judeans, his response in v. 23 to their claim to be 'ministers of Christ' is more complex. The formal similarity of expression cannot entail that Paul endorses this claim tout court given that he has just described them as 'ministers' of Satan disguised as 'ministers of righteousness' (11.15).

Apart from a repetition of the theme that he is out of his mind (παραφρονῶν) to be articulating honour-claims vis-à-vis the intruders, he also adds a statement of his superiority over them that will be evidenced in the list of hardships that are to follow: ὑπὲρ ἐγώ. In this phrase, ὑπέρ is used adverbially to convey the meaning 'even more', a usage virtually unknown outside the New Testament (BDAG 1031). In any respect, claims Paul, 'I am even more so'. The comparative force of the expression suggests that Paul may allow that in some way they are ministers of Christ (in spite of 11.15), possibly when they are active in their own mission area, Judea presumably, and not in his, where their message is from Satan (Thrall 2000: 732).

Paul's contention that he is a better minister of Christ than they are then is substantiated by a long chain of evidence extending to 12.13. The first area of evidence is the catalogue of hardships he has endured (vv. 24-28). He lists labours, imprisonments, severe beatings and being often put at risk of death (θάνατος here meaning 'danger/risk of death'; BDAG 442). This is the third such catalogue in 2 Corinthians, the earlier examples being found at 2 Cor. 4.8-9 and 6.4-10, with a fourth, much shorter, instance to come in 12.10. I noted earlier, in relation to the first and second examples, the view of John Fitzgerald that these catalogues are similar to those found in other ancient authors, Stoics especially, often being deployed as a way of epitomizing the experience of the wise man as 'the suffering sage'. Unfortunately, Fitzgerald offered no treatment of the catalogues in 11.23-28 and 12.10 in his 1988 study.[3] Such catalogues functioned 'as rhetorical foils for the depiction and demonstration of the sage's various qualities as the ideal philosopher' (1988: 203). Yet they could also be used to distinguish true philosophers from false ones (1988: 206), and this comes close Paul's aim in 11.23-28. His intention is not to present himself as an ideal philosopher, but to reapply the catalogue tradition to argue, in a strongly agonistic context, that he is a superior minister of Christ than the intruders. Fitzgerald comes close to this view when he notes that the catalogue provided Paul 'with a tool of establishing himself as a true apostle and distancing himself from the superapostles' (1988: 206).

---

[3] He noted that their complexity required a longer study than he could include in the volume (1988: 3, fn. 7).

As discussed in Chapter 2 of this volume, social identity theorists refer to behaviour in which a leader puts the interests the group ahead of his own, as Paul pre-eminently claims he does here, as 'identity advancement'.

2 Corinthians 11.24 In this he proffers an example of the severe beatings mentioned in the previous verse, namely the distinctively Judean punishment – the scriptural basis for which was Deut. 25.1-3 – that provided for a maximum of forty lashes to be given to a person found guilty in legal proceedings before a court. Jesus had foretold this punishment for his followers (Matt. 10.17). The frequency with which Paul suffered such a lashing indicates that he must have had a very significant involvement with Judean synagogues in the diaspora, meaning that his mission in the Greco-Roman east outside of Judea extended to Judeans as well as non-Judeans. Rather surprisingly, none of these floggings is mentioned in Acts, even though they are consonant with Luke's Paul regularly speaking in synagogues in the cities he visits. His use of 'Judeans' (Ἰουδαῖοι) in v. 24 represents the standard designation for this ethnic group when other ethnic groups were in the frame, as they certainly were in the diaspora settings that Paul has in mind here.

2 Corinthians 11.25 Having just mentioned a beating that was peculiarly Judean, in v. 25 he begins with a distinctively Roman form of punishment meted out to *peregrini*; he says, 'I was beaten with rods' (ἐρραβδίσθην). Such beatings were administered by lictors, the servants of Roman magistrates. They could produce severe injuries, even death, such as was the fate of Gaius Servilius, on Verres' orders, as reported by Cicero (*Contra Verrem*, 2.5.139-142). If Paul was a Roman citizen, he should have been exempt from such a punishment, but sometimes Roman magistrates ignored these legal niceties (as with Verres and Gaius Servilius), and Paul may himself have chosen not to raise the issue of his citizenship. Acts 16.22-23, 37 claims that in Philippi Paul and Silas were beaten on the orders of Roman magistrates, even though they were Roman citizens.

The next two hardships in v. 25, being stoned and shipwrecked, satisfy the notion of 'danger of death' mentioned in v. 24. The type of stoning in view here was an extrajudicial punishment, a type of lynching, even though it was the form of punishment consequent upon the judgement that might be made by a duly constituted Judean court acting pursuant to laws against apostasy (Lev. 20.2; Deut. 13.6-11; 17.2-7) or blasphemy (Lev. 24.11-14, 16, 23). How Paul survived such experiences is a good question. Perhaps Paul has in mind the incident at Lystra recorded in Acts 14.19-20 where he was stoned by a mob stirred up by hostile Judeans from Antioch and Iconium. They thought they had killed Paul but he survived. Paul's claim to have been shipwrecked three times is not unreasonable given the number of sea voyages he needed to take to accomplish his missionary journeys and the acknowledged dangers of sailing the Mediterranean, especially in winter, in vessels that carried no life rafts (Casson 1974: 149–57). The dramatic date of the shipwreck Paul suffered as described in Acts 27 was after he wrote 2 Corinthians.

2 Corinthians 11.26 Of the eight dangers listed, some are natural hazards one was liable to experience crossing rivers, seas and deserts. But inhabited space, the city, could also be dangerous. The other four hazards relate to groups. First come bandits, who were likely to be encountered in isolated places, even if travelling on the main highways was reasonably safe (Furnish 1984: 517). Next, Paul mentions his fellow Judeans and non-Judeans and the references in vv. 24-25 to beatings in synagogues and by Roman officials and stoning (no doubt by Judeans) illustrate the most serious of these dangers. Finally, and one senses, climatically (Lambrecht 1999: 26; Harris 2005: 808), Paul mentions 'false brothers'. Their appearance in this list of typical dangers (κινδύνοι) indicates that were to be found in many locales and caused him great trouble as he conducted his mission to spread the Gospel. They were a persistent problem to him. The only other place, however, where the word ψευδαδέλφοι appears in the New Testament (and it may well be a coinage by Paul) is in Gal. 2.4, where it refers to the Judean Christ-followers who wanted non-Judean members to adopt the Mosaic law and be circumcised. Given, the essential identity between the opponents in Galatia and the ones who have followed him to Corinth, there is no reason to think the word has any other referent here. Indeed, it provides further evidence for the nature of the Christ-followers who trespassed on his missionary territory, in Corinth as elsewhere, in breach of the Jerusalem agreement (Gal. 2:1-10). Thrall (2000: 744) misses the precise meaning of ψευδαδέλφοι in v. 26 on account of the mistaken view (shared with many other commentators) that because circumcision is not specifically mentioned in 2 Corinthians, Paul's opponents did not represent the same position as those in Galatia.

2 Corinthians 11.27 By mentioning his labour and toil (κόπος καὶ μόχθος), Paul is probably here alluding to his work as a craftsman, since he uses the same phrase in 1 Thess. 2.9 to describe his hard work in Thessalonica to avoid being a burden on the Christ-followers there. Although an alternative view is that Paul is referring to the strenuous activity of his preaching, the use of the precise and unusual combination of κόπος with μόχθος as in 1 Thess. 2.9 pushes towards the former explanation being correct. Some of his frequent sleepless nights were probably spent on this activity, since he also observes in 1 Thess. 2.9 that he worked 'night and day'. Perhaps on other occasions he was preaching to those who worked during the day. Sleepless nights also feature among the hardships he lists earlier in the letter, at 6.4-10, at v. 5. The remaining items – hunger and thirst, lacking food and being cold and naked

– are more likely to relate to his experiences travelling between cities, but could perhaps also allude to occasions when he was imprisoned. It is possible that 'going without food' also refers to fasting that Paul voluntarily undertook (Guthrie 2015: 564–5).

2 Corinthians 11.28 The first phrase in the Greek is χωρὶς τῶν παρεκτός, where παρεκτός probably (its connotation is disputed) means 'additional' (Furnish 1984: 519), so the expression in total conveys 'apart from additional things'. It is not clear, however, what those other things are, and this has led to the suggestion that here we have an example of paralipsis, a rhetorical device by which a speaker proceeds to describe something he has said he would pass over (Zmijewski 1978: 264). But what follows does not really correspond with this idea grammatically (we would, for example, expect to see ἐπίστασις ('pressure') and μέριμνα ('anxiety') in the genitive in apposition to τῶν [Thrall 2000: 749]), so the better solution is probably that Paul meant that, although he could have gone on listing hardships, he has brought that process to an end, so he may proceed to two final issues. The first of these is in v. 29 and the second in vv. 30-33. Here ἐπίστασις is preferable to the textual variant ἐπισύστασις, meaning 'uprising' or 'disturbance'. 'All the Christ-groups' for which Paul feels anxiety must encompass not only those he has founded but all of the others as well, such as the Jerusalem Christ-group for which was organizing the collection and the Christ-groups in Rome to whom he would later write Romans.

2 Corinthians 11.29 The first clause brings to expression a powerful sense of reciprocity that coheres closely with the policy Paul adopted in chs 1–7 of stressing the mutuality that existed between him and the Corinthians: whenever a Christ-follower (presumably one of whom he is cognisant) is weak, so too is he. Paul emphasized this quite unequivocally in 1.24 when he said: 'Not that we lord it over your faith, but we are co-workers of your joy, since you stand by faith.' The precise nature of the weakness, however, is difficult, and indeed probably unnecessary, to determine. Verse 29 itself suggests that it has to be of a kind that Paul himself, at least in some sense, can and does share, and this excludes the weakness, meaning scruples with respect to food, that is referred to in 1 Corinthians 8–9 and Rom. 14.1-2 but are not an issue in 2 Corinthians (*Contra*, Thrall 2000: 750–2). Probably it means weakness in some general sense, perhaps some form of powerlessness. That Paul intended such a wide meaning is demanded by vv. 30-33. As discussed later, Paul there asserts that he will make an honour-claim in relation to matters of weakness, using in v. 30 the word ἀσθένεια (the nominal cognate of the verb ἀσθενεῖν that appears twice in v. 29), and the example he gives is escaping Damascus in a basket let down from the city's walls. Running through his head in this part of his letter, therefore, is the risk of being in someone else's power as a symptom of weakness.

The close parallel Paul draws between the two clauses in v. 29 means that, just as with the first clause, there must be some kind of parity between someone being caused to fall and Paul burning, a parity rendered unambiguously by the insertion of an emphatic ἐγώ ('I') before the verb. It is within this context that we must interpret 'I burn', translating Paul's πυροῦμαι, a middle or passive of πυρόω, 'to cause to be on fire', 'to burn'. The only other instance of πυροῦμαι in Paul is in 1 Cor. 7.9: 'It is better to marry than to burn.' Despite the argument of Barré, there is most unlikely to be any eschatological sense there or here (Barré 1975; see Thrall's critique 2000: 753). The figurative sense of the word must mean to burn with an emotion, and the most commonly cited candidate is anger or indignation. There are three instances of the word in 2 Maccabees, where it refers to burning with anger (4.38; 10.35; 14.45). But in each of those instances the presence of anger is signalled by the addition of τοῖς θυμοῖς, 'with outbursts of anger' (BDAG 461). The first example pertains to the anger of an evil character, Antiochus, the second and third to that of pious Judeans. To an extent, Paul recognizes that outbursts of anger can be problematic. Thus, Paul employs θυμοί later in the letter, of possible misbehaviour by the Corinthians (12.20), and in Gal. 5.20, where, however, the word acquires a negative connotation by virtue of its inclusion in catalogues of inappropriate behaviour. Yet anger is not necessarily a negative emotion for Paul. In Rom. 2.8, for example, he uses θυμός positively, in reference to God's righteous indignation (a word nearly always expressed in the Pauline letters, however, by the word ὀργή, 'anger'). In 2 Corinthians 10–13, he directs great anger at the interlopers. Accordingly, it is not impossible that anger is the explanation for Paul's burning. The major objection to this view is that we need the explanation for the burning to be in some way equivalent to being made to stumble, and as a sign of weakness. Anger does not satisfy this condition, since it is an expression of agency and strength. Shame, on the other hand, does, once we recognize the burning (without any other signifiers) as a concomitant of a blush: a face that suddenly turns red, as in a blush, also feels hot. Plummer is one of the few commentators to have reached this view (1915: 331). Catherine Hezser (2017: 206, also drawing on Barton 1999) has noted that 'References to blushing are very common in Greek and Roman texts, whether poetic, philosophical, or historical in character'. She also observes that, while a change of face colour could be interpreted in multiple ways, Aristotle explains that 'people who are ashamed blush (*eruthrainontai gar hoi aischunomenoi*), while those in fear of their lives turn pale' (*Nichomachean Ethics* 4.9). Virgil writes that Achilles grew red with shame (*erubuit*) at Priam's request to return the body of Hector (*Aeneid* 2.540-543). In one of the *Amores* Ovid notes that 'purple shame (*purpureus . . . pudor*)' appeared on a female lover's guilty face (2.5.34). On this view, when a Christ-follower is in some way made to stumble, itself both a humiliating experience and a sign of weakness, Paul himself also feels shame. Unstated, but lurking in the air, is the likelihood that the Christ-follower with whom he associates himself in this way was made to stumble by someone else, presumably someone opposed to Paul's Gospel. This dimension finds support in vv. 30-33 in the account of the opposition of Aretas' ethnarch to Paul.

11.30-33 Escape from Damascus

2 Corinthians 11.30 This verse has a retrospective and prospective function. It continues the previous theme of boasting and the introduction of the theme of weakness and shame in v. 29, and it inaugurates and looks forward to the (integrated) subject of boasting in weakness that will feature in ch. 12. The motivation for Paul's announcing an honour-claim lies in the general argument of this section, throughout which makes clear that he is compelled to do so (11.12, 16, 18), as here when he claims, 'If I must claim honour . . . .' Yet in line with what he has said in the previous verse about expressing solidarity with those who are weak and are caused to stumble, he now asserts that he will couch his claim in matters of weakness. This is a paradoxical reversal of the usual practice in an honour-centred culture such as this, but of a kind quite common to the frequently counter-cultural normative dimensions of Christ-movement identity. Paul will continue this theme of making honour-claims in respect of his weaknesses in 12.5 and 9, while in 12.10 he will include weaknesses among the hardships he accepts on account of Christ. There can be little doubt that by taking this line Paul differentiated himself from his opponents in Corinth who no doubt claimed honour in respect of their strengths (Barnett 1997: 551).

2 Corinthians 11.31 Prior to his recounting what might be regarded as a tall tale, Paul makes a solemn pronouncement with reference to God of his truthfulness, in a manner similar to what he says in Rom. 9.1 and Gal. 1.20. Moreover, vv. 32-33 follow directly on the statement 'I do not lie' and speak of quite remarkable circumstances in relation to which Paul might well have considered confirmation of their veracity was needed. It is thus preferable to regard this statement as primarily looking forward to the matter related in vv. 32-33 rather than to what he has just written. Yet it can hardly be denied that so decisive a statement as this, and in such general terms, also serves to strengthen what Paul has said previously (Lambrecht 1999: 193).

2 Corinthians 11.32-33 Commentators often make heavy weather of these verses, generally being puzzled by what they are doing here. Sometimes they are regarded as an interpolation, possibly having been moved here from an original position between Gal. 1.17 and 18, in relation to which Furnish has set out the main possibilities (1984: 540). There is, however, no textual support for such views. In fact, the mists clear once we realize that in a society where honour was a, if not the, dominant value, these verses present Paul behaving in a dishonourable way, as a sign of the weakness and shame he spoke of in v. 29. While we might be tempted to see in this incident an example of derring-do, that is not how Paul presents it since, as noted earlier, he categorizes it as an instance of weakness and humiliation, not one that portrays him as resolute and honourable. Edwin Judge has given a plausible explanation for this in the implied contrast between Paul being ignominiously let down from a city's wall with that of a valiant Roman soldier who received the great honour of the *corona muralis* ('wall crown') for being the first over the wall and into a besieged city, a decoration that would surely have been known to Paul's addressees in the Roman colony of Corinth (1968). Although Lambrecht sees in this incident an example of Paul's endurance as well as his humiliation (1999: 193), it is unclear how endurance could count as a weakness, especially of a type that would make Paul's face red with shame. The same argument also applies to the suggestion that this escape should be regarded as an act of daring (Windisch 1970 [1924]: 363), since we would need some indication that Paul had engineered his own escape, not that he had been lowered by fellow Christ-followers in a basket (Thrall 2000: 766).

There are numerous difficulties with the historical details of the account, not least because of the similar though different narrative in Acts 9.23-25, where no political authority is mentioned, and it is the Judeans from whom Paul makes his escape from Damascus, and where he is let down from the top of the wall, not from a window in it. The Aretas mentioned is without doubt Aretas IV, who reigned from 9 BCE to 40 CE (since he was followed by Malichus II, who reigned till 70 CE). Aretas IV was arguably the greatest Nabatean king, a man who claimed to be 'lover of his people'. For many details, however, we are reliant on information from his abundant coinage (Esler 2017a: 56–8). The 'ethnarch' is clearly the political authority in the city under the Nabatean king. This means that he is something more like a governor than an ethnarch, and the usual word used in Nabatean for this function was a slightly modified form of *strategos* (Esler 2017a: 111–16). An inscription is extant in which the same person bears the title of both ethnarch (perhaps meaning a tribal leader) and *strategos*. If this was common practice, as it may well have been, Paul has simply chosen one title rather than the other (Taylor 1992).

But what might Paul have done that necessitated the ethnarch's attempt to detain him? The most probable answer is that Paul's missionary activities had led to a civic disturbance. Two possible occasions for such a disturbance suggest themselves. Paul tells us in Gal. 1.16-17 that after God called him he went off, without talking to anyone, to Arabia, which certainly means the southern reaches of the Nabatean Kingdom from the region east of the Dead Sea and down to the northern parts of what is today Saudi Arabia. Then he returned (ὑπέστρεψα) to Damascus. This statement of a return indicates his call occurred in the proximity of the city, which is also the locale of the Acts account (9.1-9). So he could have precipitated a civic disturbance when he was in Arabia, and hence under Nabatean jurisdiction, immediately after his call (a period about which we most unfortunately know nothing). Secondly, however, his activities on behalf of the Gospel in Damascus on his return to the city might have provoked a disturbance, with Judeans presumably. This seems more probable. The different account in Acts 9.23-25 is to be explained on the basis of Luke's interest in minimizing the role of political authorities in the harrying of Jesus and Paul and heightening the involvement of the Judeans; in his Gospel, after all, Luke tells us that Pilate released Jesus to the Judeans 'to deal with as they pleased' as if to give the impression that it was them and not the Romans who were responsible for the crucifixion.

16

Paul's vision and his impending visit to Corinth

(2 Corinthians 12)

A vision and its aftermath (12.1-10)

There are notable issues of social identity – both intra-group and intergroup – in 2 Cor. 12.1-10. In general terms, they circle around the question of leadership, specifically, the balance between Paul's being prototypical yet also extraordinary, or 'charismatic' to use the term picked up by social identity theorists from Max Weber to analyse this dimension of leadership. It is likely that the explanation for Paul's need to claim honour (καυχᾶσθαι) in v. 1 lies in the pressure that had been placed on him by virtue of the arrival of outsiders who were denigrating him and his Gospel. This pressure was threatening his position vis-à-vis the Corinthians. The competition posed by these people has been evident from the beginning of 2 Corinthians 10, with the idea of his making honour-claims in relation to his authority commencing explicitly in 2 Cor. 10.8. That Paul's raising honour-claims in relation to himself was prompted by his opponents embarking on this practice themselves is suggested by his reference to them commending themselves in 2 Cor. 10.12. To commend oneself is to make an honour-claim about oneself. His opponents have been claiming honour for work they had done in another's mission field (10.15-16), certainly meaning his. He alleges that they seek an opportunity 'so that for what they claim honour they may be regarded as the same as us' (11.12). They disguise themselves as servants of righteousness (11.15) and claim honour from their ethnic lineage (11. 22) and connection with Christ (11.23). He is thus compelled to meet their honour-claims with some of his own, but claims only to do so in relation to his weakness (11.30).

2 Corinthians 12.1 'I must claim honour' (Καυχᾶσθαι δεῖ)[1] expresses Paul's sense that he has really no choice but to accept the challenge posed by

---

[1] Some manuscripts read easier and therefore are less likely δέ, instead of δεῖ.

his opponents' honour-claims by making his own. At the same time, rather unconvincingly, he claims that the practice is not beneficial. On this occasion, however, in what will be a climactic exercise in the genre, he will do so by revealing something quite remarkable about himself. The broad arena he will enter consists of visions (ὀπτασίαι) and revelations (ἀποκαλύψεις). The word ὀπτασία refers to an ecstatic experience with strong visual dimensions; it appears only here in Paul, and elsewhere in the New Testament in Lk. 1.22 and 24.23 and Acts 26.19. Indispensable to an understanding of charismatic phenomena in the Pauline letter from a cognitive science point of view, especially to the extent that they involve 'altered states of consciousness', is Shantz (2009).

Ἀποκάλυψις refers to a revelation of any kind. The visions and revelations in this verse are said to be 'of the Lord'. This is probably a subjective genitive, that is, the visions and revelations that come from the Lord. It is not an objective genitive, meaning their subject was the Lord, since Paul does not mention having seen the Lord in the vision he is about to describe and, in fact, only speaks of his hearing 'unutterable words'. Moreover, this experience is to be dated nearly ten years after his originary and unrepeatable vision recounted in Gal. 1.15-16 (see the following).

2 Corinthians 12.2 Although Paul has mentioned 'visions and revelations', he elects to mention only one. It is probably not necessary to suppose, as Lincoln (1981: 72, 76) and Lambrecht (1999: 200) suggest, that he initially intended to relate several visionary experiences but then decided to settle on one. Rather, in a context of oral communication, he grabs the attention of his audience with this reference to visions and revelations, thus forewarning them that they are about to hear something special, before setting out one particularly egregious example. He speaks of someone 'in Christ', probably here just meaning 'Christ-follower', though possibly also extending to 'in Christ's power' (Lambrecht 1999: 200). Paul chooses to relate the narrative of the revelation in the third-person singular, not directly of himself in the first-person singular. This is almost certainly because he wanted to mitigate the impact of the experience he will describe and the strength of the honour-claim it legitimated by putting a little rhetorical distance between himself and the beneficiary of the revelation. It has been suggested that Paul adopts the third-person approach because of some knowledge he possessed that the recipient of a vision had a sense of being separate from this body, that this was the 'self-transcendence' of the visionary (Dunn 1975: 214–15; Thrall 2000: 782; Guthrie 2015: 580). But this is unlikely. Paul is not interested in enlightening the Corinthians as to the psychological mechanics of a vision, but of informing them that he experienced one in a way that did not inflate his honour. In addition, such psychological awareness on Paul's part is inconsistent with his admissions not to know whether he had been taken up to heaven in or out of the body (vv. 2-3).

There can, it must be stressed, be no doubt that Paul is speaking of his own experience. First, the whole issue of his claiming honour for himself demands that he is the person in view. Secondly, the description in vv. 7-10 of the thorn he was given to bear would make no sense if this was not a divine response to 'the abundance of revelations' (v. 7) that he, Paul, had personally experienced, one of which is that described in vv. 2-4. This consideration also excludes the suggestion, made by Betz (1972: 73–100), that this was not a real experience, but that Paul was just parodying the claims made by his opponents. Furthermore, it is not at all clear that their honour-claims actually embraced visions and revelations; that Paul chooses this experience to bring the theme of claiming honour to a head rather suggests that they did not. Consistent with this view is that in an earlier letter to the Corinthians Paul claimed pre-eminence in another area of ecstatic experience: 'I thank God that I speak in tongues more than all of you' (1 Cor. 14.18).

Paul's mentioning that the experience occurred fourteen years before is likely to be significant but for reasons that are not self-evident. Assuming, as is likely, that he wrote 2 Corinthians in 55–56 CE, this vision occurred in 42–43 CE, many years after the occasion on which God chose to reveal his son to him (Gal. 1.15-16). One likely explanation for the period of fourteen years is that, since this is the first time Paul has told the Corinthians about this experience, his reference to its occurring fourteen years previously serves to underline the reluctance with which he is mentioning it now. The dating also gives the account the impression of verisimilitude.

In any event he speaks of the person being caught up (ἁρπαγέντα) into the third heaven, with the verb ἁρπάζω commonly used of God's action in carrying someone away (Acts 8.39) or to heaven (1 Thess. 4.17). 1 Enoch contains accounts of Enoch being taken up to heaven (14.8; 39.3). Among Israelite traditions in the first century CE, there was a variety of understandings as to how many 'heavens' or regions of heaven existed. The expression 'heaven and the heaven of heavens' (Deut. 10.14) and 'heaven and the highest heaven' (1 Kings 8.27; 2 Chron. 2.6; 6.18), followed by 'the heaven of heavens' in 1 Enoch 71.5, imply at least two levels of heaven. The original text of the *Testament of Levi* (2.7-10; 3.1-4) seems to have envisaged three heavens, but later Israelite works favoured seven (*Apoc. Moses* 35.2;) or even ten (*2 Enoch* 22; *1 Apoc. James* 26.2-19) (Furnish 1984: 525). Paul probably envisaged there were three, on the basis (see the following) that he equates the third heaven with Paradise mentioned in v. 4.

2 Corinthians 12.3-4 The partial repetition of language from v. 2 in vv. 3-4 has led some interpreters to think that here Paul is describing a second stage of his ascent. Plummer took this view, noting that many Patristic writers favoured either two ascents or two phases of one ascent (1915: 344). There is, however, no indication of any temporal transition between vv. 2-3 and 4. Rather, it is more likely, that vv. 3-4 represent a further exemplification of what he has said in v. 2, similar to the type of parallelism characteristic of Hebrew poetry (Harris 2005: 841). There is little point in speculating on the subject of the unutterable words (ἄρρητα ῥήματα) – Paul mentions their general character only so as to underline the extraordinary nature of his experience. The fact that he does not know whether he was taken up in the body or not reflects the phenomenon of somatic bewilderment that has been identified as a feature of altered states of consciousness by neurobiologists (Shantz 2009: 98).

2 Corinthians 12.5 In this verse, Paul continues his rather contrived effort to distance himself from the recipient of the vision lest he seem to be praising himself too highly. He also begins to draw the discourse into the issue of his weakness, since this seems to him the best way keep the extent of his self-praise under control.

2 Corinthians 12.6 The first half of the verse expresses Paul's insistence that he does have a sound basis to claim honour for himself (καυχήσασθαι). As noted earlier in this volume (in the commentary on 1.12), in the Mediterranean world of the first century CE making an honour-claim about oneself was not necessarily problematic unless one lacked the foundation for making it; if the foundation was lacking, the whole process would make the person concerned look foolish. Paul's reason for not claiming honour for himself appears in the second half of the verse: it is that the Corinthians may form an assessment of him based not on what he says about himself but on his actions and the content of his Gospel.

2 Corinthians 12.7 There is uncertainty as to whether the first clause of v. 7, 'and by reason the extraordinary character of my revelations' (καὶ τῇ ὑπερβολῇ τῶν ἀποκαλύψεων), begins the words that follow, or actually concludes v. 6. In the latter case, Paul would be asking the Corinthians to assess him on the basis of what he does or says and from the scale of the revelations he receives. Many authorities favour this approach, including the editors of Nestle-Aland, *Novum Testamentum Graece* (twenty-eighth edition), who insert a full stop in the text after ἀποκαλύψεων. Much of the discussion involves heavily contested issues of Greek style (Thrall 2000: 802-5; Harris 2005: 851-3). For example, in Paul διό ('therefore') usually commences its own clause, a factor that many find decisive for connecting this expression to v. 6 (e.g. Seifrid 2014: 444). There is, however, a stronger case for regarding the clause as beginning v. 7, a view that goes back as far as the Vulgate. The main reason for attaching these words to the start of v. 7 is one of content. In the second half of v. 6, Paul asks to be judged on what he has done and said, so that to add 'and by the magnitude of my revelations' would be redundant, since the only way the Corinthians could have learned of these experiences was by his telling him. It is far more plausible to regard his abundance of revelations as constituting the implied foundation of his honour-claims that he declines to mention in the first half of v. 6. That approach coheres closely with the way that v. 7 advances.

Accordingly, the first clause of v. 7 reads, 'And by reason of the extraordinary character of my revelations, therefore (διό), in order that I might not exalt myself . . . .' On this approach, διό serves to provide emphasis to the preceding phrase. After this comes a purpose clause: 'in order that I might not exalt myself (ὑπεραίρωμαι) . . . .' The cultural dynamic in view here is that by his receipt of such revelations Paul would truly have the basis for making honour-claims about himself such as he alludes to in the first clause of v. 6. The reality, however, is that he has been prevented from doing so by a very particular cause: he has been given a thorn in the flesh to torment him. Although in wider Greek usage the word for 'thorn', σκόλοψ, could refer to anything pointed, even a stake, its four appearances in the Septuagint (Num. 33.55; Ezek. 28.24; Hos. 2.8; Sir. 43.19) all mean 'thorn', and this is the most plausible translation. The thorn was both given by God (interpreting 'I was given' [ἐδόθη μοι] as a theological passive) and was also in some way a messenger of Satan. Paul is probably suggesting that God had a positive motive in giving Paul the thorn, to stop him exalting himself, but at the same time permitted Satan some latitude in its application – Satan's interest perhaps being to use it to dissuade Paul from carrying on his mission.

But what was the nature of this thorn? This question has inevitably attracted the interest of interpreters of the letter since the Patristic period. Three broad lines of approach have developed, as summarized by Thrall (2000: 809–18): (a) an internal psychological state, such as sexual temptation or grief at his previous persecution of the movement; (b) external opposition; and (c) physical illness or disability. There are significant interpretative objections to both of the first two options (e.g. the idea of sexual temptation may have arisen from a misinterpretation of the Vulgate's rendering *stimulus carnis meae*)[2], and the majority of commentators rightly consider that a physical illness or a disability offers the most likely solution. The case for this solution is strengthened if Paul's account of the physical weakness (ἀσθένεια τῆς σαρκός) that he suffered in Galatia (Gal. 4.13) refers to the same condition, which was a trial to the Galatians. This may have been connected with his

---

[2] Seifrid 2014: 447; v. 7 in the Vulgate reads: *Et, ne magnitudo revelationum extollat me, datus est mihi stimulus carnis meae, angelus Satanae, qui me colaphizet.*

eyes, since Paul asserts that the Galatians would have plucked out their eyes and given them to him (Gal. 4.15). The case for an ophthalmic theme is strengthened by Paul's earlier having accused the Galatians of succumbing to an evil-eye possessor: 'O foolish Galatians, who has put the evil eye on you, before whose eyes . . .?' (Elliott 2011). Nevertheless, even the physical illness solution faces an obstacle, namely that Paul here appears to be telling the Corinthians something that they did not already know about. From what type of debilitating condition could Paul have suffered that was not already visible to his Corinthians converts at least? Possibly it may have been a recurrent illness and had not manifested itself on the occasions he had been with them. Nevertheless, it is clear that the obstacles to reaching any firm view on the nature of the thorn are formidable indeed, and further investigation is likely to be fruitless.

2 Corinthians 12.8 When Paul says at the start of this verse, 'Concerning this' (Ὑπὲρ τούτου), it is more likely that τούτου refers to the thorn and not to the messenger of Satan (*contra*, Lambrecht 1999: 203), for it is the thorn that is the immediate cause of Paul's torment. In this verse, 'the Lord' must mean 'the Lord Jesus' on account of the way this verse connects with vv. 9-10, where Christ is directly in view. Probably Jesus has been in view from 12.1-2, where he is 'the Lord' who sends the visions and revelations. Apart from 1 Cor. 16.22, this is the only time in Paul's letters where he mentions praying to Jesus. It is likely that Paul has three separate and well-remembered events of entreaty in mind (Harris 2005: 861), but it is fruitless speculating on what they might have been.

2 Corinthian 12.9-10 Verses 9-10 represent the conclusion of the theme of claiming honour in weakness that Paul first enunciated in 2 Cor. 11.30 and repeated in 2 Cor. 12.5. In v. 9a, Paul quotes the answer that Christ has given (perhaps, as suggested by the perfect form εἴρηκεν, on more than one occasion) to his request for removal of the thorn, presumably in the course of a revelation or revelations: 'My grace is sufficient for you, for (my) power is made perfect in weakness.' Although it was a negative answer, it provided a different form of consolation: the grace of Christ was all Paul needed, because the power (of Christ) that accompanied it perfected Paul's weakness. In v. 9b, Paul makes the rather surprising statement that he claims honour on the basis of weakness *in order to* attract Christ's power.[3] This sentiment becomes less puzzling when we recall that in the honour and shame culture of his day a valid honour-claim depended on the existence of facts that could support it. Thus, to claim honour in relation to weakness presupposes the existence

---

[3] Although the best textual witnesses do not read 'my' with 'power' (some witnesses do), the word is implied; it is only Christ's power that is in view here.

of factors occasioning such a condition that are implied in the claim. This point becomes quite explicit in v. 10, where the (typical) causes of weakness in which Paul revels are itemized as insults, hardships, persecutions and difficulties. This brief list reads a little like a summary of the hardship lists that appear earlier in the letter (2 Cor. 6.4-10; 11.23-27). All of these he has endured ὑπὲρ Χριστοῦ, 'for Christ's sake'. Thus, Paul continues his emphasis in the letter on his working not for his own sake or for personal profit but for Christ's (e.g. 2.17). By his final statement, 'For when I am weak, then I am strong', Paul re-emphasizes the point: when he experiences weakness, he is nevertheless strong, that is, by the power of Christ that accompanies his grace. As Mark Seifrid has noted, this sentiment 'implies a real and effective *koinōnia* with Christ, in which the apostle shares in Christ's power' (2014: 453). Later in the letter, in 13.4, Paul will reveal that Christ himself manifested a similar pattern: 'For he was crucified in weakness, but lives by the power of God.' Yet, for some reason, Paul does not explicitly make this connection here. Nevertheless, in relation to Pauline leadership in the letter, this is one of those areas where Paul is asserting he has a particularly close relationship with Christ that is additional to any claim to be prototypical of Christ-movement identity: he is not saying he is a typical Christ-follower by virtue of his relationship with Christ, but an extraordinary one.

Peroration for 11.1–12.10 (verses 11-13)

2 Corinthians 12.11 The first statement in v. 11, 'I have become foolish', suggests that Paul is now winding up the fool's speech that he began in 2 Cor. 11.1 (Windisch 1970: 395). There he indicated he would indulge in a little foolishness, and here he asserts he has indeed become a fool. He now adds a further justification for what he has said: that it has been forced on him by the Corinthians. In ancient Greco-Roman rhetoric, one of the justifications for a speech made in praise of oneself was that it had been forced on the speaker who had to act to defend their good name. This is a point made by Plutarch in his treatise *On Inoffensive Self-Praise*, 540C-541E (Marshall 1987: 353-4). Here Paul asserts that the reason for this compulsion was that they had not commended him.

With this statement the explicit theme of recommendation in the letter using the word συνίστημι (3.1; 4.2; 5.12; 6.4; 7.11; 10.12, 18) reaches its climax. Since a commendation involves A saying something favourable about B to C, we need to ask, if A stands for the Corinthians and B for Paul, and here there was no such communication, who was C and when did the failure occur? The only possible identification for C consists of the Judean interlopers. He identifies them as 'the superlative apostles' (οἱ ὑπερλίαν ἀπόστολοι), a group he had mentioned earlier in this discourse (2 Cor. 11.5). No other party is in the frame here. Paul's complaint is thus that the Corinthians failed to sing his praises to the missionaries from outside, to whom, he insists, 'I was in no way inferior' (οὐδὲν ... ὑστέρησα). Within the group-oriented and honour-focused culture of his time this was both a severe breach of ingroup solidarity and also very shaming for him. Furthermore, the course of events is only explicable if Paul had demonstrated he was not inferior (giving the aorist form ὑστέρησα a past meaning) in ways to be discussed later both prior to the occasion when the Corinthians failed to commend him to the interlopers, no doubt in response to criticism by the latter of him, and in his absence. The Corinthians knew what he was like, and they should have defended him to these outsiders; but they did not. Disagreement exists as to whether the final statement in this verse, 'I am nothing', is meant to be taken literally (Guthrie 2-15: 603) or ironically (Martin 1986: 427). The preponderance of evidence probably favours the former alternative: for Paul makes no claim to personal adequacy and claims honour in the Lord. Fortunately, not much turns on which option is correct.

By his mention of 'the superlative apostles' in v. 11 and his declaration that he was in no way inferior to them, Paul signals that he is concluding this section, given the close similarity of his statements here to what he had said much earlier, in his discussion of honour-claims, at 2 Cor. 11.5, where he had affirmed, 'For I consider I am not in the least inferior (ὑστερηκέναι) to the superlative apostles' (οἱ ὑπερλίαν ἀπόστολοι). In both 11.5 and 12.11, he thus expresses the same sentiment about the superlative apostles – who are the interlopers in Corinth, not the leaders of the Jerusalem Christ-movement (as previously discussed) – and in the same language. The similarity of these two verses indicates that he is using them as an *inclusio* to demarcate a section in the letter devoted to comparing himself to them.

2 Corinthians 12.12 In spite of the views of some commentators (e.g. Matera 2003: 288; Harris 2005: 870), this verse does not provide a 'second reason' for Paul's statement that he was not inferior to the superlative apostles. Rather, in a highly competitive context, Paul feels it necessary at this point to remind the Corinthians of the primary evidence on the basis of which he denies that he is inferior to the interlopers: the signs of the apostle (τὰ σημεῖα τοῦ ἀποστόλου) were worked (κατειργάσθη) among them in all endurance, through signs (σημεῖα) and wonders (τέρατα) and marvellous acts (δυνάμεις). Here the use of the article (τοῦ) before ἀποστόλου shows this was a general concept (Barnett 1997: 579), probably preceding Paul's mission in Corinth. When he wrote Romans some years later, Paul also claimed, in a very similar way, to have won obedience from non-Judeans by what Christ worked (κατειργάσατο) through him by word and deed, and by the power of signs (σημεῖα) and wonders (τέρατα; Rom. 15.18-19). This similarity suggests that the implied object of κατειργάσθη in v. 12 is Christ, not (*pace* Matera 2003: 288) God. On both occasions, Paul is laying claim to having been the agent through which extraordinary activity happened in the cause of the Gospel. This activity must, at least in part, include the charismatic phenomena he describes in 1 Corinthians 12–14, since at one point he makes clear that both glossolalia and prophecy are signs (σημεῖα; 1 Cor. 14.22). The use of τέρατα, however, suggests phenomena that are more extraordinary, even miraculous. In 1 Cor. 12.29-30, he provides very revealing information: 'Are all apostles? Are all prophets? Are all teachers? Do all work miracles (μὴ πάντες δυνάμεις)? Do all possess gifts of healing (μὴ πάντες χαρίσματα ἔχουσιν ἰαμάτων)? Do all speak with tongues? Do all interpret?' Verses 28–29 make clear that there is a hierarchy in both leadership functions and in the magnitude of the gifts, which creates a linkage between apostles and miracle-working. This is not to say that apostles did not possess all of the other gifts (thus, Paul thanked God he spoke in tongues more than all of them; 1 Cor. 14.18). In Gal. 3.5, he mentions δυνάμεις being worked among the Galatians in a way that also suggests the extraordinary, or even miraculous. It should be noted that Paul is a little wary of affirming his having worked these signs among them, since he uses the passive form, 'were worked (κατειργάσθη)', to indicate their divine source and notes that this happened 'in all endurance' (ἐν πάσῃ ὑπομονῇ) to stress the hardships and difficulties that attended his missionary activity. He had catalogued those hardships a little earlier in the letter (11.23b-29).

That in v. 12 (and in 1 Cor. 12.29-30) Paul acknowledges the existence of external signs that one is an apostle necessitates that others apart from him also produced those signs as proof of their being apostles. Does the inference arise that such signs had been worked by Paul's rivals in Corinth, the people he ironically designates as superlative apostles? Some commentators deny this (e.g. Barnett 1997: 580; Harris 2005: 875), and we should not forget that Paul calls his rivals 'false apostles' in 11.13. Yet the collocation of the last statement in v. 11, his denial of inferiority to them, and v. 12, his assertion that he produced the signs of the apostles, rather produces the impression that his rivals had produced at least some of these signs. Otherwise there would be no context for his asserting he was not inferior to them. Moreover, if, as many commentators think likely, his rivals had charged Paul with not producing the signs of the apostle (Furnish 1984: 555), such criticism would have rung very hollow if they were in the same position.

2 Corinthians 12.13 The first clause of v. 13 sounds very like Paul is referring to a summative comment that the interlopers were making about the general position of the Corinthian Christ-group, namely that, because of Paul's activities among them, they were inferior to the other Christ-groups (ἐκκλησίαι). Only Christ-followers who had experience of ἐκκλησίαι elsewhere would have been in a position to raise this criticism. The rival missionaries in Corinth, Thrall observes, 'will have worked in other Christian communities prior to their arrival in Corinth' (2000: 842). Alternatively, it could be a formulation developed by the Corinthians on the basis of the interlopers' criticism of Paul. This suggestion is essentially disproved by what he has just said about the miraculous phenomena that attended his evangelism. Nevertheless, rather than seeking to answer the charge on this basis, Paul chooses to launch a rather surprising counterattack. He ironically concedes that the only way the Corinthians were worse off was because he did not burden them, meaning take money from them for preaching the Gospel. This is hardly a savage rebuke of the Corinthians; Paul is being gentle with them. In the phrase 'except that I myself' (ἐγὼ αὐτός), the words ἐγὼ αὐτός are emphatic and establish a strong contrast between himself and the many others, whom he has earlier in the letter accused of peddling the word of God (2.17); they are his real target throughout chs 10–13. He had dealt with his practice of not seeking support from them in some detail a little earlier (11.7-11). He was willing to receive help from a church he had worked in previously, but not from the one in which he was currently active. Perhaps this was to avoid getting caught up in patron–client dynamics that would complicate his claim to authority in the city where he was preaching the Gospel (Chow 1992).

It might be thought that when Paul says, 'Forgive me this injustice!' (for not being a burden to them), he appears to have become quite savage towards the Corinthians. But the problem, as Harris notes (2005: 879), is that in the absence of an oral performance of the letter, where the reader would introduce the tone that Paul intended, it is really difficult to be sure what connotation Paul was seeking to convey here. Was it, at the one extreme, acidic, mocking sarcasm (McCant 1999: 154–5)? Or, at the other, affectionate irony (Hughes 1962: 459)? Or something else? The fact that this verse is immediately followed by one related to it in subject matter that uses the image of parents saving their resources for their children (v. 14), which indicates his huge affection for the Corinthians, and then by another in which he expresses his love for them (v. 15), suggests we should not interpret the statement too severely. So a tone of affectionate irony seems appropriate.

To conclude, this whole effort on Paul's part in vv. 11-13 makes good sense within the social identity and cognitive approach to differential ingroup reactions to interference by outgroup members outlined in Chapter 13 of this volume. There is no doubt that Paul has been angry with the interlopers since the start of 2 Corinthians 10, for reasons set out earlier. In addition, however, in v. 11 we have further evidence of a strong emotional reaction on his part, but now with a different target, the Corinthians themselves. This emerges from his complaint that he should have been praised by the Corinthians (which would have obviated the need for him to engage in the foolish behaviour of praising himself). Yet precisely what emotion Paul is giving vent to here is not easy to determine: it could be anger, in this culture especially on account of the shame involved at being dishonoured by his own people, or personal hurt at their betrayal or, more likely, both. This is indeed the first unambiguous sign of Paul's being unhappy with the Corinthians (as opposed to the Judean interlopers) in chs 10–13. There are eighty-one verses in this, section and we have to work through fifty-nine of them (73 per cent of the total) before we get to Paul directly criticizing the Corinthians. Yet if Paul was angry in v. 11, as quickly as in v. 12, he has reverted to a more positive emotional attitude towards the Corinthians.

The position taken in this commentary, that 2 Corinthians is as Paul wrote it, requires that we reconcile the negative attitude he expresses towards the Corinthians at this point in the letter with what he says at 7.16 ('I rejoice because I have every confidence in you'). Briefly, the answer is that in that section of the letter Paul had been addressing an issue that is quite different from the one here. There, contrary to the popular view, the problem was one of the failure of the community to address ἀδικία in the community in which Paul himself was not personally involved. It is that issue he addresses in chs 1–7, as a prelude to his request in chs 8–9. He knows from Titus that the Corinthians had done what he asked in his letter (they had been obedient), but he had now had to write to them to relent a little. He needed to acknowledge just how well they had done and how happy with them he was in relation to that particular matter. But now a new issue has arisen. He has presumably learned from Titus of the arrival and activities of the Judean interlopers. If they were in the frame when he despatched Titus, his instructions would no doubt have extended to them too. Although there are unambiguous indications that he knew about them when he was writing the earlier section of this letter (see the aforementioned comments on 2.17–3.1), he withheld a full treatment till the end of the letter as this involved a separate issue, his authority vis-à-vis the false apostles, and he wanted to deal with the other matter uncomplicated by too much investment in this one.

Preparations for his third visit (12.14-18)

2 Corinthians 12.14 The Greek in the first clause of v. 14 could also be construed as meaning that this was the third time Paul had been ready to come to the Corinthians, not that he was about to make his third visit. The repetition of 'third' in relation to his forthcoming visit and not his readiness to make it in 13.1, however, excludes this possibility. The two earlier visits implied here were probably the time when he first came to Corinth preaching the Gospel (1 Cor. 2.1-5) and then the sorrowful visit that he mentions in 2 Cor. 2.1, which Paul may well have cut short when the offensive action (whatever it was and to whomever it was directed) occurred (Furnish 1984: 564).

Insufficiently appreciated, indeed, infrequently mentioned, by commentators, especially by those concerned to deny the unity of 2 Corinthians, is the close connection between what Paul says here and his earlier statements in 2 Cor. 1.15–3.13 as to why he had not visited them as he had said he would.[4] That would have been his third visit. His ultimate answer to not having made a third visit is to make it. Now, as he approaches the end of the letter, he returns to this issue to reassure them that he will soon be returning to them on this third visit. The relevance of this proposed third visit for the unity of the letter is also evident in that Paul would have hoped to receive the collection discussed in chs 8 and 9 (Matera 2003: 293). In 2 Cor. 9.3-5, Paul had indicated that he would be sending some Macedonian Christ-followers ahead of him. This confirms that Paul would be coming from Macedonia, which is the location from which he writes 2 Corinthians. Yet in chs 8 and 9, Paul does not actually promise a visit; he leaves that to 2 Cor. 12.14 and 13.1. Thus, chs 8–9 and 10–13 form part of the one letter. His third visit would also allow Paul to respond in person to the case that had been made against him by the Judean intruders.

Yet his first message for the Corinthians is that he would not be a burden on them. This repeats the point he made in the previous verse, even to the extent of his using the same unusual verb, καταναρκάω. Thus, he insists on maintaining a position that his opponents from outside Corinth taxed him with, presumably on the basis that a sign of the true apostle was the radical poverty that consisted of being supported by those to whom one preached the Gospel. Yet Paul moves beyond this competitive arena to set out what his practice means for his relationship with the Corinthians. He wants the Corinthians, not their money, which was viewed as a sign of genuine friendship in the ancient world: 'So you must love me myself, not my possessions, if we are to be genuine friends', wrote Cicero in his *De finibus* (2.26.85). He backs this up with another piece of folk wisdom from this culture, namely, that parents (γονεῖς) should accumulate property for their

---

[4] Guthrie (2015: 609) recognizes the importance of Paul's earlier references to the forthcoming visit (he cites 2.1, 3; 9.4; 10.6).

children, not vice versa (Furnish 1984: 558; Thrall 2000: 845). With this he appeals to what he regards as a fundamental aspect of his relationship with the Corinthians, that he was their spiritual father. He had made this point in his first letter to them, in 1 Cor. 4.14-15, where he vividly described the Corinthians as 'my beloved children' (τέκνα μου ἀγαπητά) and himself as their father who begot them in Christ Jesus through the Gospel. Moreover, earlier in this letter he alluded to his spiritual fatherhood over them (11.2).[5] This invocation of his parenthood/fatherhood has a particular point: it is directed to his insisting on his love for them, an issue that connects with earlier passages in the letter and surfaces in the next verse.

2 Corinthians 12.15 This verse represents in part a development of what Paul means by likening his attitude to that of parents (γονεῖς, the word used in v. 14). Although Harris suggests that here Paul is not merely interpreting fatherhood in terms of an education and admonishing role, or a disciplinary role, or a modelling role, but also in terms of a nurturing role (2005: 886), none of these suggestions captures Paul's aim. Rather, Paul is elaborating upon the nature of the relationship of parents (γονεῖς) and children (τέκνα) invoked in v. 14 with reference to the mutual love that should characterize it. In the first part of v. 15, Paul avers his intention to give his all for them, a form of self-sacrifice, with the verb 'spend' (δαπανάω) being used figuratively. In the second half of v. 15, he interprets this as a sign of how much he loves the Corinthians. Paul's offering to give his all on their behalf reflects that dimension of leadership social identity theorists all 'identity advancement'. The word for 'loves' is ἀγαπάω, the nominal form of which is ἀγάπη. For Paul, ἀγάπη was a central identity-descriptor for the Christ-movement, as can be seen in his great programmatic descriptions of it in 1 Corinthians 13 and Rom. 12.9-21, with the numerous mnemonic features in the Romans passage (alliteration and rhyme, for example) probably marking it as a precious fragment of Paul's oral proclamation (Esler 2003a: 316–19). Paul affirmed his love for the Corinthians as early as 2 Cor. 2.4, in relation to the severe letter he had sent them. That was in the wider context of chs 1–2 with their emphasis on mutual regard and mutual comforting, key aspects of Paul's understanding of Christ-movement identity. Paul's position was that this love was reciprocated; thus, in 8.8 he affirmed their love for him. In 11.11, he denied that his not burdening them (by requiring their financial support) meant he did not love them; he assured them he did. Now he makes a similar point; if he entirely expends himself for the Corinthians, it is a sign

---

[5] On the other hand, *contra* Harris 2005: 883, Paul does not appear to be referring to his 'spiritual paternity' over the Corinthians when he says at 2 Cor. 6.13 that he speaks to them 'as to children'.

of his love for them, which means he should not experience a lesser love (from them) in return. Paul is, accordingly, appealing to their shared identity as Christ-followers.

In the second clause, he is also reverting to the fact that his Corinthians have not taken his part against the interlopers. Because he loves them more, presumably than these false apostles who require to be supported, the Corinthians love Paul less. There seems to be real hurt here, yet not knowing the tone that would have accompanied the original oral delivery of these words makes it hard to assess. Paul is essentially suggesting a lack of reciprocity in this area (even though in chs 1–7 he praised them for their reciprocity in many respects).

2 Corinthians 12.16 The effect of 'So be it then' ("Εστω δέ) is to signal the end of the preceding discussion about his not taking support from them, with the words 'I did not burden you' constituting a closing reflection on this subject that was not contentious. As Windisch has suggested (1970: 402), citing Philo, *Embassy to Gaius* 357 and Epictetus, 1.29.2, it is probable that ἔστω δέ is an idiom used to express a point on which writer and the audience are in at least provisional agreement. No one, after all, was in doubt that Paul took no support from the Corinthians; the dispute concerned whether this policy was right or wrong.

After this, however, Paul launches on a new topic. He refers to a charge against him, probably raised by his opponents (his primary targets throughout 2 Corinthians 10–13), that he had been crafty (πανοῦργος) and tricked the Corinthians (Lit. 'captured them by trickery [δόλῳ]'). Paul has already gone to some lengths to neutralize in advance this accusation that arises from his allegedly being πανοῦργος. Thus, he denies that he conducts himself with 'craftiness' (πανουργία), or deceitfully falsifies (δολοῦντες) the word of God (2 Cor. 4.2). On the other hand, he aligns his rivals' preaching of a different Jesus, spirit and gospel with the actions of the serpent who deceived Eve with his πανουργία (11.3-4). He also claims that his opponents are false apostles, 'deceitful workmen' (ἐργάται δόλιοι; 11.13). So the accusations against him are false, since craftiness and deceitfulness characterize his opponents, not him. This verse contains no indication of the nature of the alleged craftiness; for that we must wait for the material that follows. We will see that it probably also, like the question of support, has a financial dimension.

2 Corinthians 12.17 While the Greek of v. 17 is very awkwardly expressed (Thrall 2000: 852), the meaning is clear: 'Did I take advantage of (ἐπλεονέκτησα) you through any of those I sent to you?' The keyword in the verse for understanding what it conveys is the verb: πλεονεκτεῖν, which means 'to take advantage of, exploit, outwit, defraud, cheat' (BDAG 824). The two instances in the LXX designate avaricious gain: Ezek. 22.27 and Hab. 2.9.

The word occurs earlier in the letter in 2.11, of being exploited by Satan (possibly in the sense of 'robbed' by Satan of a member of the group; BDAG 824), and in 7.2, where it ends a list of what Paul has not done: wronged, corrupted or taken advantage of anyone. The notion of denuding someone of one's possessions usually features when this word is deployed; indeed, the nominal form, πλεονέκτης, means a greedy person, someone who desires more than is his or her due, while the abstract noun πλεονεξία means 'greediness, insatiableness, avarice, covetousness' (BDAG 824). Given this semantic range, Paul is asking (in a manner expecting a negative reply) whether he had ever enlarged his money or possessions at the Corinthians' expense. Perhaps at this point he asks whether he did so through agents, since at 2 Cor. 2.11 he has already denied that he personally acted in this way. Having said only this much, Paul's audience would probably have surmised that he was in the process of denying any fiscal misconduct with respect to the collection. What he says next confirms this.

2 Corinthians 12.18 When did the visit of Titus and the other brother take place? In 1 Cor. 16.1-4, Paul had given the Corinthians directions about taking up the collection (λογεία) 'for the saints' that would be delivered to Jerusalem, including a direction that the collection be completed by the time he came. In 2 Cor. 8.6, Paul said, 'we have urged Titus that as he had already made a beginning, he should also complete among you this gracious work'. As noted in relation to 8.6 earlier, this means that Titus had previously visited the Corinthians to assist them with initiating the collection. In 2 Cor. 8.10, Paul also provides the valuable information that they had begun the collection a year previously (ἀπὸ πέρυσι). Furthermore, and as previously argued in this commentary, since Paul wanted the collection to begin when they received 1 Corinthians, Titus, accompanied by the other brother (unnamed because he was just Titus's travelling companion), was probably the bearer of that letter to Corinth. He both delivered the letter and also assisted the Corinthians to begin the collection. Accordingly, when Paul is writing 2 Corinthians, Titus has already visited Corinth at least twice, first to deliver 1 Corinthians and then to deliver the severe letter, and Paul is preparing to send him and two brothers back to Corinth to finalize the collection prior to his own arrival in the city (2 Cor. 8.16-24).

Commentators who believe that 2 Corinthians 10–13 was not originally attached to the earlier part of the letter, but was written later, are forced to construe these events in a particular way, by interpreting the visit proposed in 8.16-24 as the same as that described as having occurred in 12.18. On this view, chs 10–13 must have been written after chs 1–9 because in the former Paul is looking back as completed on a visit that is only foreshadowed in the latter (Bruce 1971: 251; Barrett 1973: 325). Few suggestions expose the problematic nature of partition theories more than this. For it is unarguable that the visit described in 12.18 is not the same as that in 8.16-24, and this for three reasons, either of which on its own would suffice for the purpose. First, the personnel are different; during the 12.18 visit, Titus had been accompanied by one brother, and during the 8.16-24 visit, he will have two brothers for company. Secondly, during Titus' previous visit mentioned in 8.6 (almost certainly to be identified with that of 12.18), he had been helping to inaugurate the collection, but his task in the forthcoming visit is to see to its completion (8.6). Thirdly, although it is possible (although a counsel of desperation) to interpret the first two aorist verbs in v. 18 as epistolary in character – 'I am urging Titus' and 'I am sending the brother' – the third verb, 'Did Titus take advantage of (ἐπλεονέκτησεν) you', only makes sense as a past tense (and it necessitates that the two previous aorists refer to the past as well).

Paul now urges upon the Corinthians the thought that just as Titus did not defraud them – using the same verb, πλεονεκτεῖν, as in v. 17 – nor did he. In fact, he walked in the same spirit and in the same tracks. Here Spirit probably means the Holy Spirit, as in the identical expression in Gal. 5.16, and not the human spirit (meaning a person's spiritual dimension or disposition). Paul is invoking a fundamental Christ-group belief here, not folk psychology. Margaret Mitchell has argued that Paul's envoys were not mere substitutes for Paul but played a complex role of mediation between him and his converts (1992). Paul's own understanding, however, seems somewhat different. The role of Titus as Paul describes it in ch. 7 might be thought to illustrate Mitchell's view, at least in relation to the level of interaction Titus appears to have had with the Corinthians during that visit. For he was probably called upon to respond to the Corinthians in ways not necessarily covered by the instructions Paul must have given him. Nevertheless, there is no sign that Titus diverged from his brief on any major point. Here in 12.18, moreover, Paul's position (whatever the reality of the situation) is that he and Titus were inseparably aligned on the requirements of the case; otherwise Paul's whole argument about his financial probity collapses. Describing this relationship (in Paul's view) as Titus being a mere substitute for Paul perhaps goes too far, but not by much.

Margaret Thrall takes some pains to explain how the idea that Titus had acted avariciously and fraudulently in some way might have arisen, focusing on the idea that they were suspected of misappropriation with respect to the collection (2000: 856). Yet such a factor would cripple Paul's argument. Paul is relying on there not being so much as a whiff of misconduct attributed to Titus in relation to the collection during his previous visit. His point is that since he and Titus are perfectly in agreement on such matters, how could the Corinthians possibly think he had behaved in a fraudulent manner?

That the Judean intruders might have raised false charges against Paul to interfere with the collection makes good sense in view of the negative attitude of the Jerusalem Christ-movement to this project. As explained in ch. 11 of this volume, Paul and the leaders of that group had agreed to allow Paul do things his way in his missionary area, and he, in turn, promised to arrange a collection for the poor in the Jerusalem church. Although the Jerusalem leaders breached their side of the bargain in Antioch, Paul continued to observe his, so that every coin he collected stood as a rebuke to the Jerusalem Christ-movement. That is why he was unsure that they would even accept the collection (Rom. 15.31).

Fears about the Corinthians' current state (12.19-21)

2 Corinthians 12.19 Given the fact that Paul has been defending his behaviour since 2 Corinthians 1-2 (there in relation to his change of travel plans and his severe letter) and even more intensely since the start of 2 Corinthians 10 as he strove to combat the false views of him and his mission being spread around by his rivals, it is hardly surprising that the Corinthians seem to have formed the view that he has, indeed, been defending himself. In 1 Cor. 9.3, after all, he had even asserted he was making a defence (ἀπολογία) to those who scrutinized him; so the idea was hardly alien to him, nor likely to be unexpected on the part of the Corinthians.

Yet Paul's point is that his *purpose* in speaking about himself is not to defend himself but to help them; he is not writing for his sake but for theirs. This is a central feature of the 'identity advancement' dimension to his leadership claims in the letter. He prefixes the particular way he will express this with a most solemn declaration that God and Christ are witnesses to the truth of what he says: 'we are speaking before God in the presence of Christ' (κατέναντι θεοῦ ἐν Χριστῷ λαλοῦμεν). Paul had used exactly this expression in 2 Cor. 2.17, when denying that he was not a pedlar of the word of God, but someone sent by God who spoke with sincerity. The repetition of this clause (which appears nowhere else in the Pauline correspondence) in close connection with attacks made on Paul by his opponents in relation to his refusal to take money from the Corinthians is hardly coincidental. It reveals the depth of his feelings on the matter and represents a strong point of connection between chs 1-9 and 10-13, thus providing further evidence (if more were needed) for the unity of 2 Corinthians.

Paul captures the real aim of his discourse in the notion of οἰκοδομή, 'building-up'. He used the idea of building-up earlier in this section of the letter (10.8), with the same meaning as here, averring this was his intention, not destruction. In both places, the word οἰκοδομή refers to the process of building, or building up, edification (although in 2 Cor. 5.1 it has the other meaning, of an actual building or edifice, admittedly there of one in heaven). It designates progress in the life and identity of Christ-followers, and includes both the cognitive dimension, such as core group beliefs (as explained by Bar-Tal), but also norms governing behaviour. In other words, it illustrates the social identity that members acquire by belonging to a group such as this. That Paul addresses them as beloved friends (ἀγαπητοί) in this verse coheres closely with this aim. Paul is appealing to ἀγάπη – a central identity-descriptor of the Christ-movement – and one that contributes significantly to its emotional attraction for members and one that he has just mentioned in v. 15.

The fact that Paul disclaims defending himself at this point signals that he is moving away from responding to the Judean false apostles to focus on the Corinthians and his relationships with them. Paul has now said enough about the false apostles and seeks to end the letter where he began it, with an emphasis on what it means to be a Christ-follower, the nature of this new identity in the world. In the last two verses of ch. 13, this will involve his delivering admonitions against the type of unacceptable behaviour and dispositions that would impede the Corinthians' growth in Christ-movement identity.

Many commentators consider that what Paul says to the Corinthians in vv. 20-21 is inconsistent with what he says about them in 2 Corinthians 7, especially their innocence (7.8-13) and the confidence he has in them (7.16), and they regard this alleged inconsistency as evidence against the literary integrity of the letter. At the end of the discussion of vv. 20-21, I will suggest reasons for why they are not inconsistent with what Paul says in ch. 7.

2 Corinthians 12.20 In this verse, Paul addresses his imminent (third) visit to Corinth (previously mentioned in 12.14). What Paul says in vv. 20-21, especially v. 21, entails that he will be meeting with the Corinthian Christ-followers as a group. This is a significant factor in these verses and also, as we will see, in ch. 13. He did not call Christ-following groups ἐκκλησίαι, literally 'assemblies' but for him and his readers 'Christ-groups', for nothing.

He begins by expressing some apprehension about what he might find in the city. Yet he does so very gently, both by the expression 'For I fear lest perhaps' (φοβοῦμαι γὰρ μή πως) and by the subjunctive mood of 'I might find' (εὕρω). The object of his fear in v. 20 is that he might find them not as he would wish and that he might be found by them to be not as they would wish. This indicates the depth of his commitment to reciprocity. He wants them to be to one another exactly as they would wish to be. Accordingly, the primary focus of Paul's anxiety is that the relationship between him and the Corinthians might be harmed by their disappointment with one another. This would mean damage had been done to the mutuality he had argued for so strongly in 2 Corinthians 1–2. Paul's position here corresponds to a recent social identity finding on leadership. As Jetten and Hornsey have explained (2014: 75), 'Those expressing criticism', as Paul is about to do here (although quite gently), 'can signal that their intentions are constructive by using inclusive language emphasizing their commitment to the group ("we have a problem" rather than "they have a problem") or by otherwise emphasizing their "groupy" credentials'. Paul's reaffirmation of the close and reciprocal relationship he has with the Corinthians immediately prior to his criticism of them closely reflects this dimension of leadership.

In the remainder of the verse he will go on to itemize the delinquencies that would cause them to be not as he would wish. It should be noted that this is not the first time he has expressed this kind of apprehension. In 11.3, he wrote:

> But I am afraid lest perhaps (φοβοῦμαι δὲ μή πως), just as the serpent deceived Eve by his cunning, your thoughts will be corrupted and turned away from single-mindedness and purity in relation to Christ.

The first clause here is essentially identical to that in 12.20. Even when Paul was in the midst of responding to his opponents, his thoughts were anxiously also fixed upon the Corinthians lest they succumb to the blandishments of the false apostles. The Corinthians would not have been surprised that, towards the end of the letter, when Paul was focusing upon them, he should give vent to his generalized concern for their commitment.

For many commentators, the vices that Paul mentions in v. 20 were known by him to be present in Corinth when he wrote this verse and, moreover, constitute evidence that 2 Corinthians 10–13 was not originally attached to 2 Corinthians 1–9 (or 1–7), for the reason that Paul's attributing this behaviour to them is inconsistent with the confidence he expressed in them in 2 Corinthians 7 (especially in 7.16). Harris, for example, assumes that these vices were present in Corinth 'at the time 2 Corinthians was written' and that Paul hoped the Corinthians would set their house in order in these respects before he arrived (2005: 897, 900), with Thrall expressing a similar view (2000: 862). Some commentators go further and argue that these vices were not only present but were due to the adverse influence of Paul's opponents (Barrett 1973: 329–30; Thrall 2000: 863; Matera 2003: 299–300). To this latter argument, there is a ready answer.

To make sense of the vice list on this hypothesis – with its reference to ἔρις, 'discord', especially – there must have one or more members of the Corinthian Christ-movement who were taking Paul's side and engaging in heated dispute with those who did not (Thrall 2000: 863; Matera 2003: 299–300). Yet Paul never mentions any such people in the whole course of 2 Corinthians 10–13. On the contrary, he gives the impression that the whole group had disappointed him. Thrall attempts to get round the problem by suggesting that there were some few who supported Paul and cites as evidence 2 Cor. 10.6, 'when your obedience may be fulfilled' (2000: 863). But that statement clearly applies to the whole group, not to a faction within it. Although 2 Cor. 12.21 may reflect a distinction in the group between those who repented of previous sins and those who did not (see the following), that distinction does not necessarily align with those who might have been for or against Paul on the issues raised by his opponents. But what of the primary question, namely whether Paul is suggesting these vices were present in Corinth or not?

Paul well knew from the experience of his two previous visits that there was potential for trouble to develop in Corinth. This is in spite of his having expressed complete confidence in them in relation to the specific matter Titus had dealt with (7.16). With time, the situation could change. *Paul is not saying that these negative phenomena currently exist in Corinth, only that he fears as time passes they may come to exist there by the time of his next visit.* The Corinthians were a rather labile group; he had seen the excitement that attended his first visit (1 Cor. 2.1-5) be replaced by serious difficulties that occurred after he left Corinth and that he confronted in 1 Corinthians and the further serious problem that occurred during his second visit (2 Cor. 2.1). Nevertheless, to reiterate, Paul (tentatively) fears these problems might exist in Corinth when he arrives; there is no suggestion in this verse that they are already there. This can be demonstrated by the list of pathologies he mentions.

The critical issue is that the vices mentioned are entirely conventional and have not originated in his knowledge of what was happening in Corinth. The evidence for this emerges in comparison with the longer list of 'works of the flesh' that appears in Gal. 5.19-21, where it is followed by a list of 'fruit of the Spirit' in 5.22-23. Hans Dieter Betz has pointed out that in the Greek east of the first century CE catalogues of vices and virtues formed a literary genre. These catalogues originated in Greek philosophy but were modified in Judean circles (e.g. in Wisdom and Philo). They were likely to have also been adapted for the catechetical instruction of the Christ-movement and may have formed part of Paul's original proclamation to the Galatians (Betz 1979: 281–3). To aid the comparison with 2 Cor. 12.20, here is the list in

Gal. 5.19-21 arranged in categories, slightly modified from that proposed by Matera (1992: 209-10):

1. Works of sensuality

   πορνεία   fornication
   ἀκαθαρσία   immorality
   ἀσέλγεια   licentiousness

2. Works of idolatry

   εἰδωλολατρία idolatry
   φαρμακεία   witchcraft

3. Works of group dissension

   ἔχθραι   enmities
   ἔρις   discord
   ζῆλος   jealousy
   θυμοί   outbursts of anger
   ἐριθεῖαι   contentiousness (or selfish ambition; BDAG: 392)
   διχοστασίαι dissensions
   αἱρέσεις   factions
   φθόνοι   occasions of envy

4. Works of self-indulgence

   μέθαι   drinking bouts
   κῶμοι   carousing

Leaping from the text of 2 Cor. 12.20 is that the first four vices mentioned are the same as four in the community dissension section of the Galatians, and they are given in the same order: ἔρις, ζῆλος, θυμοί and ἐριθεῖαι. While it is true that ἔρις and ζῆλος feature in 1 Corinthians (1.11 and 3.3), their presence is fully explicable here on the basis that Paul is quoting a stocklist. This is strongly indicated not just by the same vices appearing in the same order, but because there is no mention of ἐριθεῖαι or θυμοί in 1 Corinthians. Paul is just quoting a standarized list. The remaining four vices in 2 Cor. 12.20 also fit within the same broad category of fomenting or constituting dissension in the community. The first two, slander (καταλαλίαι) and gossip (ψιθυρισμοί), were not prompted by behaviour of which Paul complained in 1 Corinthians and seem to be taken from another, possibly larger list of vices. This view finds strong support in Rom. 1.29-30 where 'gossips' (ψιθυρισταί) and 'slanderers' (καταλάλοι) appear one after the other in a long catalogue of instances of wickedness occupying vv. 29-31. Paul mentions slander and gossip in 2 Cor. 12.20 because they are standard vices that can disrupt a group, not because he has heard of their occurrence among the Corinthian Christ-group. The final two vices in 2 Cor. 12.20, φυσιώσεις and ἀκαταστασίαι, also bear upon group disorder. Although the noun φυσίωσις, 'pride' or 'conceit', does not appear in 1 Corinthians, that meaning appears in the passive form of the verb, φυσιόω, meaning 'to become puffed up' or 'conceited' (BDAG 1069), of which there are five examples (4.6, 18, 19; 5.2; 13.4). Also making an appearance in 1 Corinthians is ἀκαταστασία, 'disorder, unruliness' (BDAG 35), when Paul denies it characterizes God (14.33) and without imputing it to the Corinthians. Both φυσίωσις and ἀκαταστασία are the sort of words that might have appeared in a vice list. Perhaps Paul ends here with ἀκαταστασία because it is similar to ἔρις and forms something of an *inclusio* with it.

Thus, for the vices mentioned here Paul is citing the conventional vices that could disrupt social harmony. While his previous experience of the Corinthians meant he knew they had been capable in the past of discord, jealousy and deceit, he is not accusing them of currently engaging in the eight forms of behaviour castigated in v. 20, merely offering them up as the sort of things in which he feared they might engage. It is extremely significant that Paul does not mention vices from the other three sections of the list in Galatians 5 as among those he apprehends he may find in Corinth. He is totally focused on the group and on the threat posed to its identity and existence by various forms of possible outgroup behaviour.

2 Corinthians 12.21 Before detailed examination of the contents of this verse, of considerable importance for interpreting the letter, it is necessary to settle some of its syntactical and grammatical features. To interpret v. 21, we need to observe its connections with v. 20. Verse 20 began with 'For I fear lest perhaps (φοβοῦμαι γὰρ μή πως) when I come', and after this came two verbs in the present subjunctive that were negatived by the μή: 'I might find' (εὕρω) and 'I might be found' (εὑρεθῶ). Verse 21 begins μὴ πάλιν ἐλθόντος μου, literally 'lest me coming again'. It is virtually certain that we must understand that these words hang upon φοβοῦμαι, 'I fear', in v. 20, which should be understood here, with ἐλθόντος having a conditional sense. Thus, we have: 'I fear that if I come to you again . . .'. Yet an alternative interpretation is to construe the πάλιν with the first of the two verbs that follow, ταπεινώσῃ, producing 'he (sc. God) might humble me again'. Probably a majority of commentators favour this latter option. If 'again' does go with 'humbling' and not 'when I come', the first humbling could well have happened during his second visit, which would constitute a reason to think it was Paul and not someone else who was treated unjustly. The (unanswerable) objection to that interpretation is that in this section of the letter Paul has fully settled that matter (7.16), and it would be inconceivable for him to open it up again here. On the other hand, Paul's forthcoming (third) visit to Corinth is very much on his mind in 2 Corinthians 10–13, and he mentioned it as recently as 12.14 and 20 (there also using the aorist participle ἐλθών). Πάλιν also occurs with ἔλθω two verses later (13.2). Accordingly, πάλιν qualifies ἐλθόντος not ταπεινώσῃ.

This verse captures Paul's foreboding that he might be humiliated, meaning publicly shamed, on this forthcoming visit to Corinth, a sentiment that resonates in the honour culture of the ancient Mediterranean. Rather surprisingly, Paul nominates God as the one who will humiliate him. Presumably, he means that God will either be the cause of his humbling or will permit it to occur (Harris 2005: 901). Public shaming of someone required an audience and here, if it occurs, the Corinthians will fulfil that role: it will occur in their presence (literally, πρὸς ὑμᾶς, 'before you'). Rather unexpectedly, the rival apostles are not mentioned, even though they would have had a keen interest in Paul's humbling.

Presumably, the cause of the humbling mentioned in the first clause is the issue set out in the rest of the verse. The 'and' before 'I will grieve' could indicate a separate issue, but this would leave the reason for Paul's potential humbling unexplained, while the nature of matter he is about to discuss, which seems unconnected with the rival missionaries, would explain their absence from the first clause.

Paul also has a foreboding that he will grieve on this next visit. The word πενθήσω, 'I would grieve', can cover a response to a wide range of misfortunes. Paul's only other use of πενθέω is at 1 Cor. 5.2, where it features as the appropriate response to a man living with his father's wife.

Considerable uncertainty attends the details of what Paul was worried might cause him to grieve. First, what did he mean by 'those who have sinned previously', represented by a perfect participle in the Greek, προημαρτηκότων, a word that only appears in the New Testament here and in 13.2? In Greek, the perfect tense 'denotes the continuance of a completed action' (BDF §340); in other words, it describes a completed action that had consequences which are continuing up to the present. Victor Furnish's view on the effect of the sinning that is referred to here, that it continues up to the time Paul is writing the letter, meaning that sexual immorality of the types mentioned is a current problem among the Corinthians,[6] seems to misconceive the effect of the

---

[6] Furnish (1984: 562, 568), who translates the participle as 'have continued in their former sinning'. Lambrecht also thinks the perfect participle means that the 'sinning has persisted until now' (1999: 215).

perfect. Rather, the sinning occurred previously but it has consequences in the present. Consistent with this position is the aorist tense of the other two verbs in the verse: the Corinthians in question did not repent (μὴ μετανοησάντων) of the impurity, fornication and licentiousness that they practised (ἔπραξαν). Accordingly, at some time in the past some of the Corinthians had sinned in these three ways, and, although they had since stopped, that had not repented of these sins.

Yet what does such a failure of repentance mean? It cannot mean that they failed to repent by continuing to sin. As just noted, the perfect participle προημαρτηκότων requires that the sinning was completed in the past, and Paul talks of three types of sinning which they practised, not which they are practising. Dieter Georgi takes a strong line: it means these people had never really become Jesus-believers and lacked faith (1987: 237). This view requires μετανοεῖν, 'repent', to be equivalent to 'become a Christ-follower'. Yet while in Acts repentance is used in missionary contexts of the fundamental turn to Christ (2.38; 3.19; 8.22; 17.30; 26.20), and 2.38 is explicitly connected with baptism, this is the only use of the verb in Paul and we cannot simply read the Acts usage onto this verse. Nevertheless, help is at hand from the three occasions when Paul uses the nominal form, μετάνοια. In Rom. 2.4 the word does carry the meaning of the basic reorientation to God that characterizes the instances in Acts. Yet the remaining two examples of μετάνοια occur in this very letter, in 2 Cor. 7.9 and 7.10, and they repay inspection. On the first occasion the word refers to the Corinthians' change of view to accord with Paul's approach to the man who had been punished. This change was associated with grief. So the context was not one of the Corinthians' decision for Christ but of their decision to align their views with those of Paul on a far less significant matter. Paul seeks to situate the Corinthians' change of mind in a wider context of repentance leading to salvation in 2 Cor. 7.10, but that effort cannot disguise the realities of the situation, namely that he is using μετάνοια to refer to their sorrowfully changing their minds to agree with him. This provides a means of interpreting 'repent' in v. 21 that is tied to Paul's usage in this letter: it connotes the fact that those concerned have not visibly shown sufficient, or any, regret for their pre-conversion sinfulness. Just having stopped sinning, Paul is saying, is not enough; signs of repentance are also necessary.

Lastly, we come to the three types of sinfulness mentioned – impurity (ἀκαθαρσία), fornication (πορνεία) and licentiousness (ἀσέλγεια). While these appear in the list of vices in Gal. 5.19 (although with the first and second in reversed order), it is unlikely that Paul is merely citing them here formulaically, as possible forms of misbehaviour, since he states bluntly in this verse that they practised them (i.e. in the past). In 13.2, he will issue a warning to those who have sinned before (using the same perfect participle), so we are certainly looking at actual, past behaviour. He had complained of similar activities in Corinth in 1 Corinthians 6. Πορνεία is mentioned in 1 Cor. 6.18. In 2 Cor. 6.17, Paul had instructed them not to touch anything ἀκάθαρτος in a passage that set up Christ-group identity in contradistinction to the pagan outgroup identity of Corinth.

Confrontation in Corinth and conclusion (2 Corinthians 13)

Warning of an impending confrontation (13.1-4)

2 Corinthians 13.1 There is debate as to whether the Greek at the start of v. 1 means that this is the third time Paul has formed an intention to come to Corinth or the third time that he is actually coming to Corinth. The latter alternative is to be much preferred. We know of his first visit to evangelize in Corinth that he mentions in 1 Corinthians and of the second, unfortunate visit he refers to in 2 Corinthians 2. This will be his third. Given the problems Paul had when he changed his intention to come to Corinth mentioned in 2 Corinthians 1, he was most unlikely to open himself up to exactly the same kind of criticism. He was going to come to Corinth, no ifs or buts.

The second clause, 'Every accusation (ῥῆμα) will be determined on the testimony of two or three witnesses', is a biblical citation from Deut. 19.15, but it is introduced very abruptly. In all of 2 Corinthians 10–13, Paul cites scripture only here and in 10.17, in neither case using an introductory formula. What is the point of this quotation? Let us consider the primary question of what the Corinthians might have made of it. Unless Paul had previously used this quotation in his dealings with them, they would almost certainly not have known that it was a quotation from Israelite scripture, or indeed from any text. Although the word ῥῆμα can mean 'an event that can be spoken about', 'object' or 'matter', as in Lk. 1.37, it usually means a 'word', 'saying', 'expression' or 'statement' (BDAG 905). Since this latter oral meaning of the word has appeared recently in the letter (2 Cor. 12.4) and recurs in the only other instances of ῥῆμα in Paul (Rom. 10.8, 9, 17, 18), it is adopted here, but modified a little, to 'accusation', as necessitated by the reference to witnesses. Thus, the Corinthians would presumably have gathered that Paul envisaged some occasion during the forthcoming visit in which rival claims would be made and any accusation had to be supported by two or three witnesses, an arrangement that clearly assists the person or people who are accused. This would indicate, at the very least, that Paul intended a discussion to occur on certain matters. But they would not have known whether that discussion would focus on his behaviour, or theirs, or both. This meant that they could not know the identity of the witnesses. Although, as we will see, the mists clear a little in vv. 2-3, it cannot be said that Paul was here at his communicative best.

Commentators have proffered a variety of ways to understand the quotation from Deut. 19.15. They point, for example, to the appearance of this quotation in Mt. 18.16, which suggests it may have had a transferred use in disputes within the Christ-movement. Its appearance in 1 Tim. 5.19 supports this view. Perhaps, then, Paul was planning to have a group disciplinary enquiry. Barnett argues that such an expectation can be deduced from his suggestion that he may grieve in 12.21, which is explicable as Paul's likely reaction to what would be a very difficult process (1997: 596). This type of proceeding, moreover, was hardly unknown to Paul (cf. 1 Cor. 5.1-5; 2 Cor. 2.6). Arguments against this proposal largely appeal to v. 2, which we will now consider.

2 Corinthians 13.2-3 One suggestion is that by 'witnesses' (μαρτύρων) in v. 1 Paul means his visits to Corinth. This idea was originally floated by Chrysostom and is now widely accepted, especially in line with C. K. Barrett's suggestion that 'The ordinals *third* and *second* in these two verses cannot fail to be connected with the cardinals *two* and *three* in the quotation'.[1] On the other hand, the alleged connection would certainly fail if the similarity were mere coincidence. Taking the view that the witnesses stand for visits entails a leap into metaphor. This is not impossible as a thought someone of Paul's remarkable intellectual acuity might have had. But is it seriously to be imagined that he intended his Corinthian audience, who would be hearing his letter read aloud, to make this connection, especially when 'third' appears before 'second' and 'second' is separated from 'third' by nineteen words? Moreover, as soon as one seeks to align Paul's visits with the notion of witnessing, problems, which have been amply documented by Larry Welborn (2010: 208–10), begin to proliferate. For example, if, as most agree, the first visit was Paul's initial period in Corinth and the second was the severe visit, what was there about the first visit that constituted it as a witness? Secondly, the Deuteronomy quotation requires the witnesses to testify in the same proceeding, but the visits were separated in time. Thirdly, Paul's visits to Corinth only involve a single person, himself, but Deut. 19.15

---

[1] Chrysostom PG 61, col. 506; Barrett 1973: 333. This view is also supported, for example, by Lambrecht 1999: 221; Thrall 2000: 874–6; Matera 2003: 305–6; Harris 2005: 908 (who favours 'warnings and visits').

requires two or three different people.² Larry Welborn has rightly added the further argument that the Deuteronomic rule was to protect the accused, not the accuser, whereas the view that Paul's visits were 'witnesses' means the Corinthians were the accused (2010: 210). Based on this insight, Welborm runs a powerful case that Paul had in mind that *he* would be the accused in Corinth.³ Yet while Welborn (2010: 214) sees Paul as preparing to answer charges against him of financial misconduct (a feature of 12.4–13.4), I will argue later in the chapter that Paul anticipated that a wider range of issues would be aired, but certainly including his defending himself in a number of respects.

In my view, however, the death knell for the theory that the witnesses are to be identified with visits sounds in v. 3, when Paul says, 'since you seek proof (δοκιμή) that Christ is speaking in me'. This is a textual feature that is largely but strangely ignored by those wanting to interpret witnesses as visits, even though it indicates an expectation on Paul's part that there is likely to be some form of hearing when he arrives. On this view, which adds an extra ground to Welborn's argument, the quotation from Deut. 19.15 refers to Paul and indicates his insistence that any case against him must be properly proven. He may well have had in his mind the previous part of Deut. 19.15, which stated: 'A single witness shall not prevail against a person or for any wrong in connection with any offence that he has committed.' At the same time, by saying 'I will not spare' in v. 2, Paul foreshadows that he will be holding the Corinthians answerable for their conduct and this also suggests some kind of proceeding. This brings us to the rest of vv. 2-3.

Paul is reminding the Corinthians that when he was paying them his second visit, he issued a warning to 'those who previously sinned' and 'all the rest' that if he came again he would not spare them. The use of the unusual word προημαρτηκόσιν identifies those to whom Paul is referring as the people badged with the same participle (προημαρτηκότων) in 12.21. These are not people who are still sinning, or Paul would have used the present participle of ἁμαρτάνω, as he does in 1 Cor. 8.12, not the perfect participle of προαμαρτάνω. This provides significant new information, both as to the past and as to his future dealings with the Corinthians. For the reasons set out earlier in relation to 2 Cor. 12.21, Paul is not suggesting that these people are still sinning but they have not, in some unspecified way, properly repented of their former life when they did. The situation would be far worse if they were

---

² Thrall (2000: 874–6) was aware of some of the problems but still clung to the visits = witnesses theory.
³ At the time he published the article, Welborn (2010: 213) was only aware of two other scholars who had suggested that Paul invoked the Deuteronomic rule in defence of charges brought against himself: Tasker 1958: 186 and Roetzel 2007: 118.

still sinning in the three ways mentioned in 12.21, but that is not what Paul is accusing them of. They are in the wrong, but certainly not in the worst way possible. Not enough, clearly, for Paul to have ceased loving them or to have given up on them. But now we learn that these people have not mended their ways even though Paul urged them to do so on his previous visit to Corinth. I say 'urged' here deliberately, because he does not say he ordered them to do what he said, merely that he warned them (προείρηκα). Firm advice perhaps, but still advice.

Paul also says that he has warned and is forewarning 'all the rest' (τοῖς λοιποῖς πᾶσιν). The identity of these people is uncertain. Two options present themselves. First, they are those other members of the Christ-group in Corinth with whom Paul is unhappy. Secondly, they are all remaining members of the Corinthian group other than those who 'have sinned before' (Windisch 1970: 415; Furnish 1984: 570; Matera 2003: 306; Harris 2005: 910; Guthrie 2015: 632). The former is more likely. The lack of any pronoun with 'those who have sinned before and all the rest', when combined with the appearance of the first group in the previous verse, suggests a third-person plural pronoun is implied. Yet in the next verse, where Paul certainly does appear to be addressing the whole congregation (as he was with πρὸς ὑμᾶς in the first clause 12.21), he says, '*you* are seeking . . . '. As Thrall has pointed out, if in 13.2 Paul had wanted to address the balance of the group, he would have said ὑμῖν πᾶσιν, 'to all of you' (2000: 877). Thus, Paul is indicating that his concern does not extend to all of the Corinthian Christ-followers, only those who 'sinned before' and certain other members.

While Paul says he warned them 'that if I come' (ὅτι ἐὰν ἔλθω), there can be no doubt that he is coming. Lambrecht explains that '[a]lthough *ean elthō* is an *eventualis* condition, its sense here is purely temporal and does not suggest uncertainty: "When I come"'(1999: 221). What is Paul about to do on the occasion of his forthcoming, third visit? To specify what this will involve, he says οὐ φείσομαι. The word φείδομαι can mean either 'to save from loss or discomfort, to spare' or 'to abstain from doing something, to refrain'(BDAG 1051), with the person or thing being spared taking the genitive case. The use of the verb on its own like this leaves hanging the question of what Paul is holding back from doing. Some guidance is available from the five other examples of the φείδομαι in his letters. In 1 Cor. 7.28, Paul informed the Corinthians that he wanted to spare them from the troubles of marriage. In Rom. 8.32, he notes that God did not spare his own son (i.e. from death), and in Rom. 11.21 he uses the verb twice of God not sparing the branches of the olive tree. Most relevantly, in 2 Cor. 1.23 (with 2.2) Paul asserted that he spared the Corinthians by not coming to Corinth for another painful visit. Accordingly, while the verb can embrace a wide range of possible outcomes, the last example indicates that one of them is Paul's refraining from being severe with the Corinthians. This may well be the meaning in 13.2 and could cover a range of behaviour from a public rebuke of the offenders to more extreme measures such as removal from the group (cf 1 Cor. 5.13; 2 Cor. 2.6; 10.6) or handing the offenders over to Satan for 'the destruction of the flesh' (1 Cor. 5.5).

The word 'since' (ἐπεί) at the start of v. 3 introduces the reason that Paul will not spare them: the Corinthians require proof that Christ is speaking ἐν ἐμοί 'in' or, we might say, 'through' me, an instrumental use of the pronoun ἐν (Furnish 1984: 570). As noted earlier, Paul's quotation of Deut. 19.15 in v. 1 indicates that any accusation made against him in connection with such a charge will require two or three witnesses. The connection between vv. 2 and 3 means that Paul is setting up a quid pro quo situation: he will take issue with them on various fronts because they intend challenging him to prove that Christ speaks through him. It is not the case that the Corinthians want this proof because he is not sparing the wrongdoers (Thrall 2000: 878); there is no sign of this elsewhere in the letter, and the proposal of a quid pro quo can be made merely because of the collocation of the two ideas in 2 Cor. 13.2-3. It is not clear what type of proof the Corinthians wanted from Paul. Perhaps they sought a vision or a miraculous sign, or perhaps they were just seeking a full and convincing account from Paul that answered all the matters that had been raised against him.

Why would the Corinthians want such proof? Presumably because the Judean false apostles had shaken their confidence in the extent to which, or if at all, Paul represented Christ. It is worth noting how much is at stake in the doubt the Corinthians have come to entertain, no doubt at the urging of the interlopers, concerning whether Paul is, in effect, 'Christ's mouthpiece' (Harris 2005: 912). If Christ does not speak through Paul, he can hardly be 'Christ's apostle' (1.1) or his ambassador (5.20); he could hardly share in Christ's sufferings and comfort (1.5); he could not be preaching the Gospel of Christ (2.12); he could not be the aroma of Christ (2.15); he could not be their servant for Jesus' sake (4.5); the love of Christ could not control him (5.14); he could not be appealing on behalf of Christ (5.20); he could not be taking every thought captive to obey Christ (10.5); the truth of Christ could not be in him (11.10). Taken together, these dimensions of his relationship with Christ that would be negated if Christ did not speak with him cover virtually every aspect of his leadership, including the collection. All of the questions that the text of 2 Corinthians suggests have been raised over Paul are subsumed into this fundamental issue. Since that is the case, it is not difficult to see why, when he came to Corinth, he wanted to tax the Corinthians with the various concerns he had with some of them. In relation to the social identity theory of leadership, this complaint against Paul relates to the extent that he is a prototypical apostle. Hogg and Reid (2006: 21) point out that marginal group members are less likely to influence the group as leaders: Paul's opponents are casting doubt on his prototypicality as apostle to diminish the influence he can wield over the Corinthians. They also point out, however, that in situations where a member is being challenged 'norm communication' comes into play, particularly through talk, where such a member will, like Paul here and throughout chs 10–13, engage in 'the rhetoric of justification of actions as being in the group's best interest and reflecting the essential identity of the group' (2006: 21). This is that dimension of leadership referred to in the social identity approach as 'identity entrepreneurship'.

There can, indeed, be no doubt that Paul expected that there would be some major occasion involving himself and the whole Christ-movement in Corinth when all of these issues, on their side and on his, would be ventilated. It is quite unnecessary to suppose that Paul envisaged convening a 'formal hearing', a possibility rejected by many commentators (e.g. Furnish 1984: 575). All that was needed was a meeting of the group at which members required Paul to prove that Christ was speaking 'through' him. On such an occasion the Corinthians could raise their complaints against Paul, although he was going to insist – as he launched a 'rhetoric of justification of actions' – that they had two to three witnesses for every accusation, and he, in turn, intended taking some of them to task, even if that would cause him personal grief. It was a meeting that was going to be not only a confrontation, during which Paul was concerned he might be humiliated, but also, hopefully, a clearing of the air and resolution of outstanding issues. Romans 15.23-27 indicates that Paul successfully completed the collection in Achaia and was about to go to Jerusalem to deliver it. He is plainly writing the letter from Corinth. This was most likely to have been at the conclusion of his third visit (Harris 2005: 53), so he finally and successfully resolved the issues in Corinth.

In the final clause of v. 3, Paul states that Christ is 'not weak in dealing with you but shows his power among you', and thereby initiates a train of thought that leads him into v. 4. In saying this, Paul offers his penultimate juxtaposition of strength and weakness that he includes in 12.5-10 and again in 13.9. This theme also connects with his mentioning weakness without words for strength in 1.8; 4.7; 10.10; 11.21, 29, 30; and strength without weakness in 6.7; 10.4. There is no suggestion that the Corinthians doubted Christ was powerful among them; the explosion of charismatic gifts that followed their conversion should have been enough to convince them. It is even possible that here Paul is actually quoting what the Corinthians themselves are saying (Thrall 2000: 881); if so, however, it may have been to draw an unfavourable comparison with Paul himself. In any event, Paul uses the apparent agreement on the strength of Christ to mount an argument that will strengthen his position, as v. 4 will reveal.

2 Corinthians 13.4 Commentators are divided about what Christ being crucified from weakness might mean. Two prime candidates are Christ's own personal human weakness and the weakness he shared with all other human beings (Matera 2003: 307). Perhaps we should bear in mind the extent to which anyone crucified was the passive victim of a monstrous exercise of power, violence and humiliation that certainly equated to weakness. But however this expression is to be understood, the first clause of v. 4 sets Christ up as someone who knew weakness in his crucifixion yet now experiences God's power. This enables Paul to align himself with this apparently paradoxical reality, thus invoking Christology as the basis of his authority. He affirms he is weak in Christ, but by God's power he will live with Christ, leaving till the very end the point that this will occur εἰς ὑμᾶς (the same expression as in v. 3) literally 'into/unto you', or 'in our relations with you'. The Corinthians have asked for proof that Christ speaks through him, and his response will come with a demonstration of how he shares with Christ a life lived by the power of God. The statement provides further enlightenment on what he meant by saying he would not spare in v. 2. It also brings to a climax the argumentative thread that Paul has been running on the connection in his ministry between strength and weakness: for example, the contrast between the effects he produces when present as opposed to when he is absent (10.4-6, 11) and the fact that, just as Christ's own power is made perfect in weakness (12.9), so when he is weak, then he is strong (12.10).

13.5-10 A plea for self-examination (13.5-10)

2 Corinthians 13.5 Paul has clearly been painfully shamed by the suggestion that he needs to offer proof that Christ spoke through him, meaning they wanted to cross-examine him on that matter. That was an insult, a challenge to his honour, and, in this honour-obsessed culture, it required that he reply (Malina 2001: 33–6). His first mode of response to this was to say (in vv. 2-3) that their request for proof was the reason he would not spare them. His second is to pick up the word the Corinthians have used against him, δοκιμή, 'proof' (v. 3), and turn the notion of examination and testing back upon them.

He begins with two verbs, πειράζειν and δοκιμάζειν, in v. 5, directing them to test themselves, to cross-examine themselves (ἑαυτούς), where the word ἑαυτούς is placed emphatically at the start of the verse, and repeated after each verb, thus implying they should not be cross-examining him.

Paul specifies the object of this examination as whether they are 'in the faith' (ἐν τῇ πίστει). Several solutions have been proposed for the meaning of being 'in the faith'. Examples include: adhering to the doctrine of the Christ-movement; obedience; and living the life of the Christ-follower in all its dimensions as opposed to that unbeliever (Thrall 2000: 888–9). The last answer seems the most convincing and coheres well with Paul's exposition of the identity of the movement in 2 Cor. 6.14–7.1.

The balance of v. 5 shows that Paul wants them to articulate a positive answer to the question of whether they are in the faith, because he asks them a parallel question – whether they recognize that Jesus Christ is in them – to which he undoubtedly also wants an affirmative answer, since not to provide it would mean that they had failed the test. He produces this result by recourse to words connected with δοκιμάζειν, a favourite semantic field for Paul. The word δοκιμάζειν in v. 5 inaugurates a passage in which words with the root δοκ- appear on five occasions like a riff, namely δοκιμάζειν itself, δόκιμος and ἀδόκιμος. Δόκιμος indicates that someone has been put to the test and has proved to be genuine (BDAG 256). Its antonym, ἀδόκιμος, refers to someone who has not passed the test, so 'unqualified, worthless, base' (BDAG 21). Paul's first gambit is to ask the challenging question: 'Surely you know this about yourselves, that Jesus Christ is in you?' Here 'surely' translates the Greek words ἢ οὐκ, which precede a question that expects an affirmative answer (Harris 2005: 920). This is confirmed by the follow-up question; 'Or do you fail the test (εἰ μήτι ἀδόκιμοί ἐστε)?' Failing the test would mean that they had not recognized Jesus Christ was in them when, in reality, he was. Paul's reminder that Jesus Christ was in them carried an implied corollary: the same must have been true for him, which indicated the folly of asking him for proof (δοκιμή) that Christ spoke through him (v. 3), an issue he brings to the surface in the next verse.

One final issue arising from v. 5 relates to the unity of the letter. Earlier in the text, Paul said to the Corinthians: 'You stand in the faith' (τῇ . . . πίστει ἑστήκατε; 1.24).' In spite of the occasional argument to the contrary,[4] it is likely that 'standing in the faith' and 'being in the faith' are equivalent. For some opponents of the literary integrity of the letter, Paul could not have told the Corinthians they 'stand in the faith' in 1.24 and then asked them to examine themselves to see if they are 'in the faith' in 13.5 (Plummer 1915: 376; Furnish 1984: 31; 572; Thrall 2000: 889.). The tension between

---

[4] Their equivalence is favoured, for example, by Matera 2003: 308; *contra*, Harris 2005: 920 (who narrows the meaning of πίστις in 2 Cor. 1.24 to 'personal trust' in Christ).

the two statements, however, is more apparent than real, and the appeal made to it by partitionists provides another indication of the fragility of the case for separating 2 Corinthians 1–9 from 10–13. Whereas in 2 Cor. 1.24 Paul is expressing his confidence that the Corinthians stand in the faith, in 13.5 he calls upon them to examine themselves so that they can reach this view for themselves; he knows it is true, the question that remains is whether they recognize this (Matera 2003: 308–9). We can press this issue a little more. In 2 Cor. 13.5, Paul assumes that they do stand in the faith: if they do not recognize that Christ is in them, they have failed the test. Yet the necessary foundation for Paul's confidence on this matter was expressed in 2 Cor. 1.24. In other words, the presence of the idea of standing or being in the faith in chs 2 and 13 is an argument for the letter's unity, not for its partition.

2 Corinthians 13.6 Paul now expresses the hope, 'you will find out that we have not failed the test'. The future tense of 'you will find out' (γνώσεσθε) points to the meeting Paul anticipates he will have with the Corinthians on his forthcoming visit, his third to the city. In context, this means that they will discover that Christ is in him (Lambrecht 1999: 6). At the same time, he seems to be implying that he expects that they will pass the test too. This recognition, that Christ is in Paul (as in themselves), will provide an answer to the issue they had already signalled as troubling them – whether Christ spoke through Paul. For if Christ was in Paul and in them, how could one doubt that Christ spoke through Paul. Since this was the case, no one could doubt that he was an apostle of Christ (whatever his opponents had been saying); as Harris has noted, 'The Corinthians' genuine faith and Paul's genuine apostleship were inextricably related; they stood or fell together' (2005: 922).

Accordingly, the theme in this letter that ties Paul and the Corinthians closely together is evident once more in this verse. Finally, this prophetic role for Paul was also a defence to any other accusation that might be made against him, of financial impropriety for example.

2 Corinthians 13.7 This verse contains a prayer containing two invocations, that the Corinthians will not do anyone wrong but will do what is right, each of which is accompanied by a qualifying clause that relates to the purpose of the prayer. The prayer is not consistent with the view of many commentators, which I have argued earlier is not justified by the evidence, that some of the Corinthians are currently immersed in various forms of sexual sinfulness. That view, if correct, would require Paul to pray that they cease committing the sins that he knows they are committing.

When Paul qualifies the first invocation with the statement, 'not so that we might appear to have met the test', he is referring to the test as to his authenticity as someone through whom Christ speaks. In other words, he does not want the Corinthians to eschew sinning in order to endorse his apostleship. He is interested in them, not in him. Here he is giving vent to the same sentiment as in 2 Cor. 12.19, namely everything he has done is for their building-up (οἰκοδομή), not for the defence of his own authority. No, he continues in the second invocation, his aim in praying is that they may do good. To this invocation, he attaches a more puzzling qualification: 'whilst we seem to have failed the test' (ἡμεῖς δὲ ὡς ἀδόκιμοι ὦμεν). Granted Paul is only allowing that he might seem to have failed the test, what test was it and in what respect did he fail? The primary test in view as far as Paul was concerned was the need for him to offer proof (δοκιμή) that Christ spoke through him. How he could fail to do so by virtue of the Corinthians doing good? For Matera, he will have failed in that there is no need for him to exercise his authority (2003: 309). Guthrie offers the same explanation, but usefully with more detail: Paul was only going to need to offer proof of his apostolic authority if the Corinthians refused to do the right thing. But in the event that they behaved properly and showed repentance for their past sins, there would be no need for Paul to offer the proof they had sought (2015: 642). And this is the course he prefers because, as noted earlier, he is concerned with their status in Christ, and with their edification, not with his authority. This verse also reflects the mutuality between him and them, which Paul has expressed earlier in the letter as a central feature of his style and exercise of leadership.

2 Corinthians 13.8 Verses 8-9 substantiate what he has said in v. 7. Scholarly opinion is divided on what Paul means by 'truth' (ἀλήθεια) in his assertion, 'For we are not able to do anything against the truth but only on behalf of the truth.' Meyer and Bultmann opted for 'the Gospel', with Meyer pointing to 2 Cor. 4.2 and 6.7 where he claimed that the word was used of the content of Paul's proclamation (Meyer 1879: 510; Bultmann 1985: 248). Yet while that may be the case for 4.2, the instance in 6.7 has a wider import: coming after 'genuine love' in a list of Christ-movement identity-descriptors, the phrase ἐν λόγῳ ἀληθείας, 'by truthful speech', embraces more than the proclamation of the Gospel; it means truth in everything Paul says. After all, Paul is someone who speaks the truth (12.6), which is hardly surprising when the truth of Christ is in him (11.10). In v. 8, too, the meaning 'the Gospel' seems too narrow, especially given the verse is meant as a comment on v. 7. This connection seems to demand that ἀλήθεια is interpreted to mean, in Thrall's astute formulation, 'Paul's ultimate lack of concern for his own personal interests (v. 7d), by contrast with his urgent desire that the truth the gospel should be visibly demonstrated in the lives of the Corinthians' (2000: 897). Whatever the precise meaning of ἀλήθεια here, however, Paul is certainly concerned that the truth should prevail at any cost (Barrett 1973: 339; Matera 2003: 309).

2 Corinthians 13.9 The first clause of this verse, 'We rejoice when we are weak and you are strong', is reprise of the qualifying statements in v. 7, and also points back to vv. 3-4. Also relevant is something he said earlier in the letter: 'So then death is at work in us, but life in you' (4.12). This web of reference suggests that we should take a broad view of Paul's weakness, so that it refers not only to his failing the test (v. 7) but to his general condition of being weak in relation to the crucified Christ (v. 4). This statement further reinforces the theme that his priority is not himself or his authority, but the Corinthians and the strength they will exhibit by doing good.

Paul has previously noted his interest in the οἰκοδομή, the building-up, of the Corinthians (10.8; 12.19) and will do so in the next verse. Now he encapsulates his prayer for them in relation to a new, but no doubt related, condition, κατάρτισις. This is the only appearance of the noun in the New Testament, although the cognate verb (καταρτίζειν) occurs thirteen times, with meanings ranging from 'to cause to be in a condition to function well, put in order, restore', to 'prepare for a purpose, prepare, make, create' (BDAG 526). While the former area of meaning is more appropriate here, it is not possible to know the Paul's precise communicative intention is using this word. Perhaps the best option is 'restoration', in the sense of a restoration of the relationships between Paul, the Corinthians and God. This aim, as Barnett points out (1997: 613), is also apparent in his earlier interest in reconciliation (5.18-20). This goal was central to Paul's whole effort to exercise leadership in relation to the Corinthians in this letter. This does not, however, exclude the possibility that Paul also needed a restoration in their behaviour, example, by repenting for past sins.

2 Corinthians 13.10 At this point Paul crisply encapsulates what he has been saying since 2 Cor. 13.1. Yet this does not provide 'a good reason for separating' chs 1–9 from 10–13, as Barrett (1973: 340), following Windisch, supposes. It merely reflects the fact that chs 10–13 include a concern with the fourth major issue that Paul needed to address in this long letter, namely, the adherence of the Corinthians to their new orientation to and identity in Christ. Moreover, it is likely that the Corinthians, when they heard this, would have understood that Paul was referring to the earlier parts of the letter as well.

In v. 10, Paul repeats the 'absent (ἀπών) now but present (παρών) soon' antithesis, although in the reverse order, from 13.2 and, thus, creates an *inclusio* that sets the context for this final explanation. When he comes to Corinth, he does not want to use the authority the Lord has given him in a severe manner against the Corinthians. For he holds that authority to build them up, not to knock them down (thereby reiterating the sentiment of 2 Cor. 10.8). That he can write in this way indicates that he is entirely open to the possibility that he will not need to exercise his authority against any possibly wayward Corinthians, that he will, in short, find them as he would hope to find them. On the other hand, the possibility of a severe exercise of his authority is a real one, and they need to take it seriously.

Conclusion (13.11-13)

Verses 11-13 bring the letter to its conclusion, a letter comprising the entirety of chs 1-13, a view founded both on the wider argument of this volume but also on the details of this section, as we will see. One can only breathe a sigh of relief that a majority of the commentators who believe chs 10-13 originated in a different letter at least regard 13.11-13 as the conclusion to that letter (Thrall 2000: 901-2). Worth noting is Jeff Weima's observation (1994: 209) that these verses contain all four of the usual elements in Paul's letter closings: (1) an exhortation (v. 11a); (2) a peace benediction (v. 11b); greetings (v. 12); and (4) grace benediction (v. 13).

2 Corinthians 13.11 The closing section ends with Λοιπόν ('finally'), before adding 'brothers ' (ἀδελφοί). This looks like a significant gesture of reconciliation on Paul's part, as this is only the third time in the whole letter that the word ἀδελφοί appears in the vocative (the others being in 1.8 and 8.1). There follows a string of five imperatives, in a manner similar to the ending of Philippians, which starts with τὸ λοιπόν and then has a number of directions in the imperative (Phil. 4.8-9). *Each of the imperatives in 2 Cor. 13.11 requires attention, as they have a summative function for major strands in this unified letter.*

First comes χαίρετε. This does not mean 'farewell' here, as suggested by Barrett (1973: 342). That notion would be quite out of place as initiating a list of imperatives directed towards the Corinthians. Secondly, its meaning of 'rejoice' is on display as recently as 2 Cor. 13.9. What is the word doing here? Paul could have just inserted χαίρετε at this point as expressing a sentiment generally appropriate to Christ-followers; thus, in the midst of list of instructions in the closing of 1 Thessalonians, he includes Πάντοτε χαίρετε, 'rejoice always' (1 Thess. 5.16). Yet more seems to be at stake with the appearance of χαίρετε in 2 Cor. 13.11 for two reasons. First, it has primacy in a very concise list of only five imperatives – much shorter than that in 1 Thessalonians 5, for example – and this affords it considerable prominence. Secondly, it recalls and responds to material from earlier in the letter. 2 Corinthians began in a very sombre tone, with Paul mentioning affliction (1.4, 8) and sufferings (1.5, 6, 7), for which comfort was needed. At the start of 2 Corinthians 2, he spoke of the grief (λύπη) that accompanied his most recent visit to them, grief he did not want to repeat (2.1-2). Nor did he write to them to cause them grief (2.4), but in 2 Corinthians 7 he acknowledged that his letter did cause them grief (7.8-11). In addition, although Paul often touches upon the sufferings of his ministry, he also repeatedly mentions his joy, either in the present or in prospect (1.24; 2.3; 6.10; 7.4, 13). His statement at 6.10 is of great import: here, after all, he made clear that rejoicing is the opposite of grief, when he said that he commended himself 'as sorrowful (λυπούμενοι), yet always rejoicing (ἀεὶ δὲ χαίροντες)'. Accordingly, by urging the Corinthians to rejoice in 13.11, Paul asks them, in effect, to put all such sorrow behind them. He has just told them he rejoices when he is weak (13.9), and now he wants them to rejoice in being strong. His thought here seems very similar to the one he expresses in Phil. 2.17b-18: 'I am glad and rejoice with you all. Likewise you also should be glad and rejoice with me.'

Second is καταρτίζεσθε. This verb recalls its cognate noun κατάρτισις in 13.9 and should probably be translated in the same way, and, in the passive voice, as a direction to the Corinthians to 'be restored', 'let yourselves be restored', that is, by God, a process that still requires cooperation on their part. Translating it as a middle would produce 'Pull yourselves together' (Barrett 1973: 341) or something similar. If it is a middle, and not much turns on whether it is passive or middle, the Corinthians would have a larger role in that restoration: 'aim for restoration' (Harris 2005: 933). Paul wants them to aim at restoration, virtually at perfection, and they have a way to go. Nevertheless, for the reasons advanced earlier, that distance is not as great as many commentators believe.

The third item in the list is παρακαλεῖσθε. One meaning of παρακαλεῖν is 'to urge strongly, urge, appeal to, exhort, encourage'. A second, at times hard to distinguish from this, is 'to make a strong request for something'. A third is 'to instil someone with courage or cheer, comfort, encourage, or cheer up' (BDAG 765). The first meaning occurs in 2 Corinthians, and on eight occasions (2.8; 5.20; 6.1; 8.6; 9.5; 10.1; 12.8, 18). The examples in 10.1 and in 12.8, 18 are plainly significant, as they are positioned in the letter close to the example in 13.11. All eight instances are in the active voice. The majority of commentators and translations favour this meaning for παρακαλεῖσθε in 13.11. Yet παρακαλεῖσθε is either in the middle or in the passive voice. As a middle, on this view, it would mean 'exhort one another' (Barrett 1973: 341) or 'encourage one another' (Witherington; 1995: 475; Matera 2003: 310-11).

This is most unlikely, however, since Paul would express this view in the active voice: παρακαλεῖτε ἀλλήλους, 'exhort one another'.[5] For this reason,

---

[5] Paul uses this expression in 1 Thess. 4.18 and 5.11, although there it means, not 'exhort one another' (so Furnish 1984: 582) but 'comfort one another'.

most commentators who favour this meaning treat παρακαλεῖσθε as a passive. A few boldly accept the oddity that results and offer translations such as 'be exhorted' (Plummer 1915: 308), 'be admonished' (Hughes 1962: 487) or 'be encouraged' (Guthrie 2015: 650), which leave awkwardly hanging the questions 'By whom?' and 'About what?' More commonly, commentators make circumlocutory suggestions that answer the first of these questions by inserting a first-person singular pronoun such as 'Pay attention to my appeals' (Furnish 1984: 582), 'Listen to my appeal' (Barnett 1997: 614), 'Heed my appeals' (Harris 2005: 933), 'Heed my appeal' (RSV) and 'Listen to my appeals' (GNB).

There is, however, a serious obstacle to translating παρακαλεῖσθε in this way. The word appears at the midpoint of five instructions, the other four of which refer to some specific disposition or behaviour the Corinthians should manifest: to rejoice, to restore themselves, to think the same and to be at peace. An instruction to 'listen to my appeal' or suchlike sits incongruously in this company because it recommends the Corinthians engage in a process without specifying the content of that process. That is why Harris (2005: 933) needs to speculate on 'What exhortations or appeals might Paul be thinking of?' This problem pushes us in search of another translation and fortunately one lies ready at hand.

There are nine other examples of παρακαλεῖν in 2 Corinthians, and they all have the third meaning mentioned earlier, namely 'to comfort' (1.4, 4, 4, 6; 2.7; 7.6, 6, 7, 13). In addition, there are eleven uses of the cognate noun, παράκλησις, nine of them conveying 'comfort' (1.3, 4, 5, 6, 6, 7: 7.4, 7, 13). There is, indeed, a remarkable focus on the issue of comfort in chs 1–2 and 7 of the letter, which balances the grief and pain very evident in those chapters. Of great moment is that on one occasion the verb is used in the passive voice: διὰ τοῦτο παρακεκλήμεθα, 'On account of this we have been comforted' (7.13). Those who have overlooked this translation have probably been influenced by the partition theories that so frequently separate chs 1–9 from 10–13. As soon as we resist this temptation, and recognize the letter for the unity that it is, the word παρακαλεῖσθε serves the valuable communicative purpose of linking this closing address to the theme of comforting, which was so dominant earlier in the letter and which still has relevance to the Corinthian Christ-followers. Paul's use of the passive form of the verb in 7.13 proves he was comfortable with this usage. Accordingly, the correct translation is 'be comforted'. Over the years a small minority of translations and commentators have adopted this translation.[6]

---

[6] The KJB has 'Be of good comfort', and Seifrid offers 'be comforted' (2014: 489), while also noting the connection to 2 Cor. 1.3-7.

In fourth place, we have τὸ αὐτὸ φρονεῖτε, literally 'think the same thing'. This injunction finds its context in the potential that the Corinthians possess for strife and division. This dimension to their community life was very apparent when Paul wrote 1 Corinthians (e.g. 1.10-13). Paul reminded them of this in 12.20, not, as argued in this commentary against the view of other commentators, because he knew these characteristics were already present in the Corinthian Christ-movement, but because he feared they would surface among the members. His direction 'to think the same thing' aimed to destroy the differences that lead to strife and divisions. It is quite similar to the sentiment he expressed to them earlier in their relationship, that they might 'be united in the same mind (νοῦς) and the same judgment (γνώμη; (1 Cor. 1.10)'. It is clear that this was a challenge not just for Corinthians because in his lengthy exposition of ἀγάπη in Rom. 12.9-21 he finds room for a very similar enunciation of the need for harmony in the group: τὸ αὐτὸ εἰς ἀλλήλους φρονοῦντες, 'thinking the same thing among one another' (Rom. 12.16).

Fifth and last is εἰρηνεύετε, 'live in peace'. It is somewhat wider in scope than the previous injunction and serves as a climactic statement leading to the blessing that follows. It is noteworthy that we find another use of this verb in Paul's ἀγάπη statement in Romans 12, in v. 18, shortly after his use of to αὐτὸ ... φρονεῖν just mentioned in 12.16, when he recommends – if it is possible for them – 'living in peace with all human beings' (i.e. even those outside the Christ-movement). In 1 Thess. 5.13, Paul says 'Live in peace amongst yourselves' (εἰρηνεύετε ἐν ἑαυτοῖς).

Verse 11 ends with a benediction, '(May) the God of love (ἀγάπη) and peace be with you', or a promise, 'the God of love and peace will be with you'. The uncertainty arises from the use of the future tense in ἔσται, 'will be', rather than the optative form, εἴη, 'may'. A decision on this point is not needed, however, to understand the broad point that Paul is making. As just noted, the last two injunctions reflect aspects of Paul's understanding of ἀγάπη, the distinctive love of the Christ-movement. This benediction serves to remind them that theirs is a God of love and peace who will help to enable them to live with one another in unity, love and peace (Barrett 1973: 343; Furnish 1984: 586; Matera 2003: 313).

2 Corinthians 13.12 The gesture of greeting one another with a holy kiss was a frequent feature of Pauline letter endings (Rom. 16.16; 1 Cor. 16.20; 1 Thess. 5.26; also cf. 1 Pet. 5.14). To interpret it as a gesture of reconciliation, as some do (e.g. Matera 2003: 313), is probably too restrictive since while this may have been appropriate for the Corinthians, and maybe in Rome, there is no sign that reconciliation was needed in Thessalonika. Probably, Paul meant this ritual act to take place at the conclusion of the reading of the letter to the group.

Rather than saying, 'All the saints (ἅγιοι) greet you', Paul could have said, 'all the brothers (ἀδελφοί) greet you' as in 1 Cor. 16.20 (which is followed by the same injunction concerning the holy kiss as here). Both ἅγιοι and ἀδελφοί are ingroup designations for Christ-followers conveying vital information about the identity of the group. 'All the saints' would certainly include the Macedonian Christ-followers, the people among whom Paul was located when he wrote the letter, possibly in Philippi. But it is also possible that Paul felt he could speak in the name of all Christ-followers in greeting the Corinthians (Barrett 1973: 343). In either case, however, the greeting would have reminded the Christ-followers of Corinth that they were part of a translocal movement, one indeed that stretched across the eastern Mediterranean, and conveyed that this was an unusual form of voluntary association, but still recognizable as such (Kloppenborg 2019).

2 Corinthians 13.13 This last verse in the letter contains a blessing rather than a declaration; that is, the missing verb is the optative of the verb to be (εἴη) not the indicative (Thrall 2000: 916). It is the most elaborate final blessing in the genuine Pauline letters, since all the rest of his closing blessings take the form, 'the grace of the Lord Jesus Christ' (Rom. 16.20; 1 Cor. 16.23; Gal. 6.18; Phil. 4.23; 1 Thess. 5.28; Phlm. 25). Why he has added the God and the Holy Spirit, and love and fellowship, on this occasion is a difficult question. In the expression 'the grace of our Lord Jesus Christ', it is highly likely that the genitive is subjective in nature: this is the grace that originates in Christ and which Paul prays will be experienced by the Corinthians. The 'love of God' probably also constitutes a subjective genitive: in the blessing it is God's love for them that is being evoked and invited, not their love for God, and this subjective genitive is parallel to the first. Whether 'the fellowship of the Holy Spirit' represents a subjective or objective genitive is more uncertain. If the former, it refers to the fellowship, or strong group identity, produced among believers by the Spirit. In this case, the focus would be on relationships between the members of the Christ-movement. If the latter option is correct, the expression refers to the participation of the believers in the Spirit. Here the focus would be on relationships between the Corinthians and the Spirit. In support of the former option is that this solution would maintain the succession of subjective genitives, and, most critically, that this type of fellowship would foster the harmony and unity in the group that Paul longed for (13.11). This would accord with Paul's intention to strengthen the interconnectedness and shared identity of the Corinthian Christ-followers that is evident throughout the letter. In favour of its being an objective genitive is the consideration that on most occasions when it is followed by a genitive in the New Testament, it usually has the meaning 'participation in'. Furthermore, as an objective genitive it can be related to the context: shared participation by group members in the Spirit might also be a solution to factionalism and strife. Although the case for these alternative approaches is finely balanced, a subjective genitive seems more closely aligned to the first part of the verse and to the rest of the letter.[7]

Finally, while it would be going too far to argue that this blessing contained a well-formulated Trinitarian theology, it certainly provided an important part of the New Testament evidence for the development of such a theology in subsequent centuries. As Matera has noted, 'this reflection on the divine economy of salvation is the proper starting point for such a theology' (2003: 314). Thus, a position that Paul reached as a response to the tumultuous experience of one part of the Christ-movement, experience locked into the social realities of his time, would ultimately inspire fundamental theological reflection. How then does one distinguish the theological from the social here?

---

[7] On the nature of the genitive, see the nuanced discussions by Thrall (2000: 917–19) and Harris (939–41), both of whom, however, find the case for an objective genitive slightly more convincing.

References

Abrams, Dominic and Michael A. Hogg (eds) (1999) *Social Identity and Social Cognition.* London: John Wiley & Sons.

Adewuya, J. Ayodeji (2001) *Holiness and Community in 2 Cor 6:14-7:1: Paul's View of Communal Holiness in the Corinthian Correspondence.* Studies in Biblical Literature, 40. New York: Peter Lang.

Allo, E.-B. (1956) *Saint Paul Seconde Épitre aux Corinthiens.* Ebib. Second edition. Paris: Gabalda (Reprint of the 1937 edition).

Arzt-Grabner, Peter (2013) *2. Korinther (Papyrologische Kommentare zum Neuen Testament, Band 4).* Göttingen: Vandenhoeck & Ruprecht.

Asano, Atsuhiro (2005) *Community-Identity Construction in Galatians: Exegetical, Social-Anthropological and Socio-Historical Studies.* Journal for the Study of the New Testament Supplement Series 285. London: T&T Clark.

Bachmann, P. (1909) *Der zweite Brief des Paulus an die Korinther.* Leipzig: Scholl.

Baker, Coleman A. (2008) 'New Covenant, New Identity: A Social Scientific Reading of Jeremiah 31:31-34', *The Bible and Critical Theory* 4, no. 1, 5.1–5.11.

Baker, Coleman A. (2012) 'Social Identity Theory and Biblical Interpretation', *Biblical Theology Bulletin* 42: 129–38.

Baker, William R. (2000) 'Did the Glory of Moses' Face Fade? A Reexamination of Καταργέω in 2 Corinthians 3:7:1-8', *Bulletin for Biblical Research* 10: 1–15.

Barclay, John M. G. (1987) 'Mirror-Reading a Polemical Letter: Galatians as a Test Case', *JSNT* 31: 73–93.

Barclay, John M. G. (1995) 'Some Applications of Deviance Theory to First-Century Judaism and Christianity', in Philip F. Esler (ed.), *Modelling Early Christianity: Social-Scientific Studies of the New Testament in Its Context*, 114–27. London and New York: Routledge.

Barclay, John M. G. (1996) *Jews in the Mediterranean Diaspora: From Alexander to Trajan (323 BCE-117 CE).* Edinburgh: T & T Clark.

Barclay, John M. G. (2011a) *Pauline Churches and Diaspora Jews.* Tübingen: Mohr Siebeck.

Barclay, John M. G. (2011b) 'Stoic Physics and the Christ-event: A Review of Troels Engberg-Pedersen, *Cosmology and Self in the Apostle Paul: The Material Spirit* (Oxford: Oxford University Press, 2010)', *JSNT* 33: 406–14.

Barclay, John M. G. (2015) *Paul and the Gift.* Grand Rapids, MI: William B. Eerdmans Publishing Company.

Barentsen, Jack (2011) *Emerging Leadership in the Pauline Mission: A Social Identity Perspective on Local Leadership in Corinth and Ephesus.* With a Foreword by Philip Francis Esler. Princeton Theological Monograph Series. Eugene, OR: Pickwick Publications.

Barnett, Paul (1997) *The Second Epistle to the Corinthians.* Grand Rapids, MI: William B. Eerdmans Publishing Company.

Barré, M. L. (1975) 'Paul as "Eschatologic Person": A New Look at 2 Cor 11:29', *CBQ* 37: 500–526.
Barrett, C. K. (1971) 'Paul's Opponents in II Corinthians', *NTS* 17: 233–54. Also in his essays on Paul (Barrett 1982).
Barrett, C. K. (1973) *The Second Epistle to the Corinthians*. HNTC. New York: Harper & Row.
Barrett, C. K. (1982a) 'Paul's Opponents in 2 Corinthians', in his *Essays on Paul*, 60–86. Philadelphia: Westminster/London: SPCK.
Barrett, C. K. (1982b) 'ΨΕΥΔΑΠΟΣΤΟΛΟΙ (2 Cor. 11.13)', in his *Essays on Paul*. Philadelphia: Westminster/London: SPCK, 87–107 (an essay originally published in 1970).
Bar-Tal, Daniel (1990) *Group Beliefs: A Conception for Analyzing Group Structure, Processes and Behaviour*. New York: Springer-Verlag.
Barth, Fredrik (1969) 'Introduction', in Fredrik Barth (ed.), *Ethnic Groups and Boundaries: The Social Organization of Culture Difference*, 9–38. London: George Allen and Unwin.
Barton, Carlin A. (1999) 'The Roman Blush: The Delicate Matter of Self-Control', in J. I. Porter (ed.), *Constructions of the Classical Body*, 212–34. Ann Arbor, MI: University of Michigan Press.
Barton, Carlin A. and Daniel Boyarin (2016) *Imagine No Religion. How Modern Abstractions Hide Ancient Realities*. New York: Fordham University Press.
Bass, B. M. (1990) *Bass & Stogdill's Handbook of Leadership: Theory, Research, and Managerial Applications*; Third Edition. NY: The Free Press.
Baur, Ferdinand C. (1831) 'Die Christuspartei in der Korinthischen Gemeinde, der Gegensatz des Petrinschen und Paulinischen Christentum in der Ältesten Kirche, der Apostel Petrus in Rom', *Tübingen Zeitschrift für Theologie* 3(4): 61–206.
Baur, Ferdinand Christian (1876) *Paul, the Apostle of Jesus Christ-His Life and Work, His Epistles and Doctrine: A Contribution to the Critical History of Primitive Christianity*. Vol 1. Second edition, trans. E. Zeller. London: Williams and Norgate.
Batey, Richard (1965) 'Paul's Interaction with the Corinthians', *JBL* 84: 139–46.
Best, Ernest (1955) *One Body in Christ*. London: SPCK.
Betz, Hans Dieter (1972) *Der Apostel Paulus und die sokratische Tradition: Eine exegetische Untersuchung zu seiner Apologie 2 Korinther 10–13*. Tübingen: Mohr Siebeck.
Betz, Hans Dieter (1979) *Galatians: A Commentary on Paul's Letter to the Churches in Galatia*. Philadelphia: Fortress.
Betz, Hans Dieter (1985) *2 Corinthians 8 and 9: A Commentary on Two Administrative Letters of the Apostle Paul*. Hermeneia Commentary. Philadelphia: Fortress Press.
Bieringer, Reimund (1994a) 'Teilungshypothesen zum 2. Korintherbrief. Ein Forschungsüberblick', in R. Bieringer and J. Lambrecht (eds), *Studies on 2 Corinthians*. BETL 112, 67–105. Leuven: Leuven University Press.

Bieringer, Reimund (1994b) 'Die 2. Korintherbrief als ursprüngliche Einheit. EinForschungsüberblick', in R. Bieringer and J. Lambrecht (eds), *Studies on 2 Corinthians*. BETL 112, 107–30. Leuven: Leuven University Press.

Bieringer, Reimund (1994c) 'Plädoyer für die Einheitlichkeit des 2. Korintherbriefes', in R. Bieringer and J. Lambrecht (eds), *Studies on 2 Corinthians*. BETL 112, 131–79. Leuven: Leuven University Press.

Bieringer, Reimund (2011) 'The Comforted Comforter: The Meaning of παρακαλέω or παράκλησις Terminology in 2 Corinthians', *HTS Theological Studies* 67/1.

Billig, Michael (1996) *Arguing and Thinking: A Rhetorical Approach to Social Psychology*. Second edition. Cambridge: Cambridge University Press.

Blass, F., Debrunner, A., and Funk, Robert W. (1961) *A Greek Grammar of the New Testament and Other Early Christian Literature*. A translation and revision of the ninth-tenth German edition. Chicago and London: The University of Chicago Press.

Bleek, Friedrich (1830) 'Erörterungen in Beziehung auf die Briefe Pauli an die Korinther', *Theologischer Studien und Kritiken* 3: 614–32.

Boers, Hendrikus (2002) '2 Corinthians 5:14-6:2: A Fragment of Pauline Christology', *CBQ* 64: 527–47.

Bornkamm, Günther (1971) *Paul*, trans D. M. G. Stalker. New York: Harper & Row.

Bosman, Jan (2009) *Social Identity in Nahum: A Theological-Ethical Inquiry*. Biblical Intersections 1. Piscataway, NJ: Georgias.

Bourdieu, Pierre (1966) 'The Sentiment of Honour in Kabyle Society', in J. G. Peristiany, (ed.), *Honour and Shame: The Values of Mediterranean Society*, 191–24. Chicago: University of Chicago Press.

Brawley, Robert L. (2020) *Luke: A Social Identity Commentary*. T & T Clark Social Identity Commentaries on the New Testament. London: T & T Clark.

Brown, Rupert (2020) *Henri Tajfel: Explorer of Identity and Difference*. European Monographs in Social Psychology. London and New York: Routledge.

Brubaker, Rogers (2006) *Ethnicity Without Groups*. Harvard: Harvard University Press.

Brubaker, R. and F. Cooper (2000) 'Beyond "Identity"', *Theory and Society* 29: 1–47.

Brubaker, R., M. Loveman and P. Stamatov (2004) 'Ethnicity as Cognition', *Theory and Society* 33: 31–64.

Bruce, Frederick F. (1971) *1 and 2 Corinthians*. NCB. Grand Rapids: Eerdmans.

Buell, Denise Kimber (2005) *Why This New Race: Ethnic Reasoning Early Christianity*. New York: Columbia University Press.

Burke, Trevor J. (2000) 'Pauline Paternity in 1 Thessalonians', *Tyndale Bulletin* 51: 59–80.

Bultmann, Rudolf Karl (1910) *Der Stil der paulinschen Predigt und die kynisch-stoische Diatribe*. FRLANT 13. Göttingen: Vandenhoeck 7 Ruprecht.

Bultmann, Rudolf Karl (1985) *The Second Letter to the Corinthians*. ET Roy A. Harrisville. Minneapolis: Augsburg.

Bultmann, Rudolf Karl (1987) *Der zweite Brief an die Korinther. Zweite Auflage*, edited by Erich Dinkler. Kritisch-exegetischer Kommentar über das Neue Testament. Göttingen: Vandenhoeck & Ruprecht.

Campbell, Douglas A. (2009) '2 Corinthians 4:13: Evidence in Paul that Christ Believes', *JBL* 128: 337–56.

Campbell, Douglas A. (2014) *Framing Paul: An Epistolary Biography*. Grand Rapids, MI: William B. Eerdmans Publishing Company.

Campbell, William S. (2016) 'Reading Paul in Relation to Judaism: Comparison or Contrast?', in Alan J. Avery-Peck, Craig Evans and Jacob Neusner (eds), *Earliest Christianity Within the Boundaries of Judaism: Essays in Honor of Bruce Chilton*, 120–50. Leiden: Brill.

Campbell, William S. (2018) *The Nations in the Divine Economy: Paul's Covenantal Hermeneutics and Participation in Christ*. Lanham, MA: Lexington Books/Fortress Academic.

Carlson, Stephen C. (2016) 'On Paul's Second Visit to Corinth: Πάλιν, Parsing, and Presupposition in 2 Corinthians', *JBL* 135: 597–615.

Casson, L. (1974) *Travel in the Ancient World*. London: Allen & Unwin.

Castelli, Elizabeth (1991) *Imitating Paul: A Discourse of Power*. Louisville, KY: Westminster/John Knox Press.

Charles, R. H. (1900) *The Ascension of Isaiah*. London: Adam and Charles Black.

Chow, J. K. (1992) *Patronage and Power: A Study of Social Networks in Corinth*. Sheffield: JSOT Press.

Cinirella, Marco (1998) 'Exploring Temporal Aspects of Social Identity: The Concept of Possible Future Social Identities', *EJSP* 28: 227–48.

Clarke, Andrew (2008) *A Pauline Theology of Leadership*. Library of New Testament Studies, 362. London: T & T Clark.

Collange, J.-F. (1972) *Énigmes de la Deuxième Épitre de Paul aux Corinthiens: Étude Exégétique de Cor. 2:14-7:4*. SNTSMS 18. Cambridge: Cambridge University Press.

Collins, J. N. (1990) *DIAKONIA: Reinterpreting the Ancient Sources*. New York: Oxford University Press.

Condor, Susan (1996) 'Social Identity and Time', in Peter Robinson (ed.), *Social Groups and Identities: Developing the Legacy of Henri Tajfel*, 285–315. Oxford: Butterworth Heinemann.

Cover, Michael (2015) *Lifting the Veil: 2 Corinthians 3:7–18 in the Light of Jewish Homiletic and Commentary Traditions*. Berlin: De Gruyter.

Crook, Zeba A. (2004) *Reconceptualising Conversion: Patronage, Loyalty, and Conversion in the Religions of the Ancient Mediterranean*. Berlin and New York: Walter de Gruyter.

Dalton, W. J. (1987) 'Is the Old Covenant Abrogated?' *ABR* 35: 88–94.

Dancy, Graham (2021) 'A Missional Reading of the Letter of James: Hearing the Voice of James in Mission', a doctoral thesis presented to the University of Gloucestershire.

Danker, Frederick William (ed.) (2000) *A Greek-English Lexicon of the New Testament and Other Early Christian Literature*. Third Edition. Chicago and London: University of Chicago Press.

Daugherty, Kevin (2011–2012) 'Naked Bodies and Heavenly Clothing: ΓΥΜΝΟΣ in 2 Corinthians 5.3', *JGRCJ* 8: 199–222.

Dean, J. T. (1938/1939) 'The Great Digression: 2 Corinthians 2:14–7:4', *Expository Times* 50: 86–9.

Denney, J. (1894) *The Second Epistle to the Corinthians*. The Expositor's Bible. London: Hodder. Reprinted by Eerdmans in 1943.

Downs, David (2008) *The Offering of the Gentiles: Paul's Collection in Its Chronological, Cultural and Cultic Contexts*. WUNT 2: 248. Tübingen: Mohr Siebeck.

Duff, Paul D. (2004) 'Glory in the Ministry of Death: Gentile Condemnation and Letters of Recommendation in 2 Cor. 3:6-18', *NovT* 46: 313–37.

Duff, Paul D. (2008) 'Transformed from Glory to Glory: Paul's Appeal to the Experience of His Readers in 2 Corinthians 3:18', *JBL* 127: 759–80.

Duling, Dennis C. (2003) '"Whatever Gain I Had . . .": Ethnicity and Paul's Self-Identification in Phil. 3:5-6', in D. B. Gowler, G. Bloomquist and D. F. Watson (eds), *Fabrics of Discourse: Essays in Honor of Vernon K. Robbins*, 222–41. Harrisburg, PA: Trinity Press International.

Duling, Dennis C. (2005) 'Ethnicity, Ethnocentrism, and the Matthean Ethnos', *BTB* 35: 125–43.

Dumont, M., V. Yzerbyt, D. Wigboldus, and E. H. Gordijn (2003) 'Social Categorization and Fear Reactions to the September 11th Terrorist Attacks', *Personality and Social Psychology Bulletin* 29: 1509–20.

Dunn, James D. G. (1970a) *Baptism in the Holy Spirit: A Re-Examination of the New Testament Teaching on the Gift of the Spirit in Relation to Pentecostalism Today*. London: SCM Press Ltd.

Dunn, James D. G. (1970b) '2 Corinthians III.17: The Lord Is the Spirit', *JTS* 21: 309–20.

Dunn, James D. G. (1975) *Jesus and the Spirit: A Study of the Religious and Charismatic Experience of Jesus and the First Christians as Reflected in the New Testament*. London: SCM.

Dunn, James D. G. (1988) *Romans 9-16*. Word Biblical Commentary, Volume 38B. Dallas, TX: Word Books.

Dunn, James D. G. (1993) *The Epistle to the Galatians*. Black's New Testament Commentary. Peabody, MT: Hendrickson.

Dunn, James. D. G (1998) *The Theology of Paul the Apostle*. Grand Rapids, MI: Eerdmans.

Ehrensberger, Kathy (2007) *Paul and the Dynamics of Power: Communication and Interaction in the Early Christ-Movement*. Library of New Testament Studies, 325. London: T & T Clark.

Ehrensperger, Kathy (2020) 'Trouble in Galatia: What Should Be Cut? (On Gal 5.12)', in Abel František (ed.), *The Message of Paul the Apostle within Second Temple Judaism*, 179–94. Lanham: Rowan & Littlefield.

Ellemers, N., T. C. de Gilder, S. A. Haslam, (2004) 'Motivating Individuals and Groups at Work: A Social Identity Perspective on Leadership and Group Performance', *Academy of Management Review* 29: 459–78.

Elliott, John H. (1981) *A Home for the Homeless: A Sociological Exegesis of 1 Peter, Its Situation and Strategy*. Philadelphia: Fortress Press.

Elliott, John H. (1993) *What is Social Scientific Criticism?* Guides to Biblical Scholarship New Testament Series. Minneapolis, MN: Augsburg Fortress.

Elliott, John H. (2007) 'Jesus the Israelite Was Neither a "Jew" Nor a "Christian": On Correcting Misleading Nomenclature', *Journal for the Study of the Historical Jesus* 5: 119–54.

Elliott, John H. (2011) 'Social-Scientific Criticism: Perspective, Process and Payoff. Evil Eye Accusation at Galatia as Illustration of the Method', *HTS Theological Studies*. 67.

Engberg-Pedersen, Troels (1990) *The Stoic Theory of Oikeiosis*. Aarhus: Aarhus University Press.

Engberg-Pedersen, Troels (2000) *Paul and the Stoics*. Edinburgh: T & T Clark.

Engberg-Pedersen, Troels (2005) 'The Relationship with Others: Similarities and Differences between Paul and Stoicism', *ZNTW* 96: 35–60.

Engberg-Pedersen, Troels (2010) *Cosmology and Self in the Apostle Paul: The Material Spirit*. Oxford: Oxford University Press.

Engberg-Pedersen, Troels (2011) 'Paul's Body: A Response to Barclay and Levison', *JSNT* 33: 433–43.

Esler, Philip F. (1987) *Community and Gospel in Luke-Acts: The Social and Political Motivations of Lucan Theology*. SNTSMS 57. Cambridge: Cambridge University Press.

Esler, Philip F. (1994) *The First Christians in Their Social Worlds: Social-Scientific Approaches to New Testament Interpretation*. London and New York: Routledge.

Esler, Philip F. (1995a) 'Making and Breaking an Agreement Mediterranean Style: A New Reading of Galatians 2.1-14', *Biblical Interpretation* 3: 285–314.

Esler, Philip F. (1995b) 'God's Honour and Rome's Triumph: Responses to the Fall of Jerusalem in 70 CE in Three Jewish Apocalypses', in Philip F. Esler (ed.), *Modelling Early Christianity: Social-Scientific Studies of the New Testament in Its Context*, 239–58. London and New York: Routledge.

Esler, Philip F. (1996) 'Group Boundaries and Intergroup Conflict in Galatians: A New Reading of Gal. 5:13-6:10', in Mark Brett (ed), *Ethnicity and the Bible*, 215–40. Leiden: E J Brill.

Esler, Philip F. (1998) *Galatians*. New Testament Readings. London and New York: Routledge.

Esler, Philip F. (2000) 'Jesus and the Reduction of Intergroup Conflict: The Parable of the Good Samaritan in the Light of Social Identity Theory', *Biblical Interpretation* 8: 325–57.

Esler, Philip F. (2001) '1 Thessalonians', in John Barton and John Muddiman (eds), *The Oxford Bible Commentary*, 1200–1212. Oxford: Oxford University Press.

Esler, Philip F. (2003a) *Conflict and Identity in Romans: The Social Setting of Paul's Letter*. Minneapolis, MN: Fortress.

Esler, Philip F. (2003b) 'Social Identity, the Virtues and the Good Life: A New Approach to Romans 12:1-15:13', *BTB* 33: 51–63.

Esler, Philip F. (2004) 'Paul and Stoicism: Romans 12 as a Test Case', *NTS* 50: 106–24.

Esler, Philip F. (2005) *New Testament Theology: Communion and Community*. Minneapolis: Augsburg Fortress.

Esler, Philip F. (2006a) 'Social-Scientific Models in Biblical Interpretation', in Philip F. Esler (ed.), *Ancient Israel: The Old Testament in Its Social Context*, 3–14. Minneapolis: Fortress Press.

Esler, Philip F. (2006b) 'Paul's Contestation of Israel's (Ethnic) Memory of Abraham in Galatians 3', *BTB* 36: 23–34.

Esler, Philip F. (2007a) 'From *Ioudaioi* to Children of God: The Development of a Non-Ethnic Group Identity in the Gospel of John', in Anselm C. Hagedorn, Zeba A. Crook and Eric Stewart (eds), *In Other Words: Essays on Social Science Methods and the New Testament in Honor of Jerome H. Neyrey*, 106–37. Sheffield: Sheffield Phoenix Press.

Esler, Philip F. (2007) 'Prototypes, Antitypes and Social Identity in First Clement: Outlining a New Interpretative Model', *Annali di storia dell'esegesi* 24: 125–45.

Esler, Philip F. (2009) 'Judean Ethnic Identity in Josephus' *Against Apion*', in Zuleika Rodgers with Margaret Daly Denton and Anne Fitzpatrick (eds), *A Wandering Galilean: Essays in Honour of Sean Freyne*, 73–91. Leiden: Brill.

Esler, Philip F. (2011a) *Sex, Wives, and Warriors: Reading Biblical Narrative with Its Ancient Audience*. Eugene, OR: Cascade.

Esler, Philip F. (2011b) 'Judean Ethnic Identity and the Purpose of Hebrews', in Andrew B. McGowan and Kent Harold Richards (eds), *Method & Meaning: Essays on New Testament Interpretation in Honor of Harold A. Attridge*, 469–89. Atlanta, GA: SBL.

Esler, Philip F. (2014a) 'An Outline of Social Identity Theory', in J. Brian Tucker and A. Baker Coleman (eds), *T & T Handbook to Social Identity in the New Testament*, 13–40. London: Bloomsbury T & T Clark.

Esler, Philip F. (2014b) 'Group Norms and Prototypes in Matt 5:3-12: A Social Identity Interpretation of the Matthean Beatitudes', in J. Brian Tucker and A. Baker Coleman (eds), *T & T Clark Handbook to Social Identity in the New Testament*, 147–72. London: Bloomsbury/T & T Clark.

Esler, Philip F. (2014) 'Second Corinthians and Ecclesiology: A Pauline Message for Church Organisation Today', *The Bible in Transmission: A Forum for Change in Church and Culture*, 23–26.

Esler, Philip F. (2017a) *Babatha's Orchard: The Yadin Papyri and An Ancient Jewish Family Tale Retold*. Oxford: Oxford University Press.

Esler, Philip F. (2017b) *God's Court and Courtiers in the Book of the Watchers: Re-interpreting Heaven in 1 Enoch 1–36*. Eugene, OR; Cascade.

Esler, Philip F. (2021a) 'The End-time in 1 Enoch, Paul and Matthew: Continuity and Discontinuity', in Meron Gebreananaye, Logan Williams, and Francis Watson (eds), *Beyond Canon: Early Christianity and the Ethiopic Textual Tradition*. Library of New Testament Studies 643, 9–22. London: T&T Clark.

Esler, Philip F. (2021b) 'Ethnic Identities in the Dead Sea Legal Papyri and Matthew: Reinterpreting Matthew 23:31-46', in Daniel Gurtner and Anders Runesson (eds), *Matthew Within Judaism: Israel and the Nations in the First Gospel*. Early Christian Literature, 197–211. Atlanta, GA: SBL.

Esler, Philip F. (2021c) 'The Adoption and Use of the Word Ἐκκλησία in the Early Christ-Movement: A Review Essay', *Ecclesiology* 17: 109–30.

Esler, Philip F. (2021d) 'Paul's Explanation of Christ-Movement Identity in 2 Corinthians 6:14-7:1: A Social Identity Approach', *BTB* 17: 109–30.

Eyl, Jennifer (2016) *Signs, Wonders, and Gifts: Divination in the Letters of Paul*. Oxford: Oxford University Press.

Falk, Carl, Steven J. Heine and Kosuke Takemura (2014) 'Cultural Variation in the Minimal Group Effect', *Journal of Cross-Cultural Psychology* 45: 265–81.

Fee, Gordon D. (1977) 'II Corinthians VI.14-VII.1 and Food Offered to Idols', *NTS* 23: 140–61.

Fitzgerald, John T. (1988) *Cracks in an Earthen Vessel: An Examination of the Catalogues of Hardships in the Corinthian Correspondence*. Atlanta, GA: Scholars Press.

Forbes, Christopher (1986) 'Comparison, Self-Praise and Irony: Paul's Boasting and the Conventions of Hellenistic Rhetoric', *NTS* 32: 1–30.

Forster, E. S. (1924) 'Rhetorica ad Alexandrum', in W. D. Ross (ed.), *The Works of Aristotle Translated into English under the Editorship of W. D. Ross*. Oxford: The Clarendon Press (not paginated).

Fredrickson, D. E. (1996) 'ΠΑΡΡΗΣΙΑ in the Pauline Epistles', in J. T. Fitzgerald (ed.), *Friendship, Flattery and Frankness of Speech: Studies on Friendship in the New Testament World*, 163–83, NovTSup 82. Leiden: Brill.

French, J. R. P. and B. H. Raven (1959) 'The Bases of Social Power', in D. Cartwright (ed.), *Studies in Social Power*, 150–67. Ann Arbor, MI: Institute of Social Research.

Furnish, V. P. (1984) *II Corinthians*. Garden City: Doubleday.

Gamble, Harry (1977) *The Textual History of the Letter to the Romans: A Study in Textual and Literary Criticism*. Grand Rapids: Eerdmans.

Garland, David E. (1999) *2 Corinthians*. NAC 29. Nashville: Broadman & Holman.

Gathercole, Simon (2015) *Defending Substitution: An Essay on Atonement in Paul*. Acadia Studies in Bible and Theology. Grand Rapids: Baker Academic.

Georgi, Dieter (1987) *The Opponents of Paul in Second Corinthians*. ET of 1964 German original. Edinburgh: & & T Clark. (Fortress edition published in 1986).

Georgi, Dieter (1992) *Remembering the Poor: The History of Paul's Collection for Jerusalem*. Nashville: Abingdon Press.

Gergen, Kenneth J. (1978) 'Experimentation in Social Psychology: A Reappraisal', *EJSP* 8: 507–27.

Gibson, Jack J. (2013) *Peter Between Jerusalem and Antioch: Peter, James and the Gentiles*. Tübingen: Mohr Siebeck.

Gleason, Randall C. (1997) 'Paul's Covenantal Contrasts in 2 Corinthians 3:1-11', *Bibliotheca Sacra* 154: 61–79.

Goodman, Felicitas D. (1972) *Speaking in Tongues: A Cross-Cultural Study of Glossolalia*. Chicago: University of Chicago Press.

Goodman, Martin (2010) 'The Qumran Sectarians and the Temple in Jerusalem', in Charlotte Hempel (ed.), *The Dead Sea Scrolls: Texts and Context*. Studies on the Texts of the Desert of Judah, 263–73. Leiden: Brill.

Goodrich, John (2012) *Paul as an Administrator of God in 1 Corinthians*. Society for New Testament Studies Monograph Series, 152. Cambridge: Cambridge University Press.

Goulder, Michael D. (1994) *A Tale of Two Missions*. London: SCM.

Gregory, C. R. and A. Harnack et al. (eds) (1997) *Theologische Studien: Herrn. Wirkl. Oberkonsistorialrath Professor D. Bernhard Weiss zu seinem 70. Geburtstage dargebracht*. Göttingen: Vandenhoeck and Ruprecht.

Griffin, Bruce W. (1996) 'The Palaeographical Dating of P-46', Paper presented at the Annual Meeting of the Society of Biblical Literature in New Orleans, November 1996. (http://www.biblical-data.org/P-46%20Oct%201997.pdF).

Grindheim, Sigurd (2001) 'The Law Kills but the Gospel Gives Life: The Letter-Spirit Dualism in 2 Corinthians 3:5-18', *JSNT* 84: 97–115.

Gunther, John J. (1973) *St. Paul's Opponents and Their Background: A Study of Apocalyptic and Sectarian Teachings*. Supplements to Novum Testamentum, 35. Leiden: E. J. Brill.

Guthrie, George H. (2015) *2 Corinthians*. Baker Exegetical Commentary on the New Testament. Grand Rapids, MI: Baker Academic.

Haenchen, Ernst (1971) *The Acts of the Apostles: A Commentary*. Oxford: Basil Blackwell.

Hafemann, Scott (1986) *Suffering and the Spirit: An Exegetical Study of II Cor. 2:14-3:3 Within the Context of the Corinthian Correspondence*. WUNT 2. Reihe 19. Tübingen: Mohr Siebeck.

Hafemann, Scott (1990a) *Suffering and Ministry in the Spirit: Paul's Defence of His Ministry in II Corinthians 2:14-3:3*. Grand Rapids, MI: Eerdmans.

Hafemann, Scott (1990b) '"Self-Commendation" and Apostolic Legitimacy in 2 Corinthians: A Pauline Dialectic', *NTS* 36:66–88.

Hafemann, Scott (1996) *Paul, Moses, and the History of Israel: The Letter/Spirit Contrast and the Argument from Scripture in 2 Corinthians 3*. Peabody, MA: Hendrickson.

Hafemann, Scott (2000) *2 Corinthians*, NIVAC. Grand Rapids, Mich.: Zondervan.

Hakola, Raimo (2015) *Reconsidering Johannine Christianity A Social Identity Approach*. Hoboken: Taylor and Francis.

Hall, David R. (2003) *The Unity of the Corinthian Correspondence*. London: T & T Clark International.

Harris, Murray J. (1983) *Raised Immortal: Resurrection and Immortality in the New Testament*. London: Marshall.

Harris, Murray J. '2 Corinthians' in F. E. Gaebelein (ed.), *The Expositor's Bible Commentary*, Vol. 10, 299–406. Grand Rapids: Zondervan.

Harris, Murray J. (2005) *The Second Epistle to the Corinthians*. The New International Greek Testament Commentary. Grand Rapids, MI: William B. Eerdmans.

Harrison, James R. (2003) *Paul's Language of Grace in Its Graeco-Roman Context*. Tübingen: Mohr Siebeck.

Harvey, Anthony E. (1996) *Renewal Through Suffering: A Study of 2 Corinthians*. Edinburgh: T & T Clark.

Haslam, S. Alexander (2001) *Psychology in Organizations: The Social Identity Approach*. Thousand Oaks, CA: Sage. Psychology Press.

Haslam, S. Alexander, Stephen D. Reicher and Michael J. Platow (2011) *The New Psychology of Leadership: Identity, Influence and Power*. Hove, East Sussex: Psychology Press.

Hausrath, A. (1870) *Der Fier-Capitel-Brief des Paulus an die Korinther*. Heidleberg: Bassermann.

Hayes, Christine (2002) *Gentile Impurities and Jewish Identities: Intermarriage and Conversion from the Bible to the Talmud*. Oxford: Oxford University Press.

Hays, Richard B. (1989) *Echoes of Scripture in the Letters of Paul*. New Haven and London: Yale University Press.

Hays, Richard B. (2002) *The Faith of Jesus Christ: The Narrative Substructure of Galatians 3:1-4:11*. Second edition. Grand Rapids, MI: Eerdmans.

Héring, J. (1967) *The Second Epistle of Saint Paul to the Corinthians*. ET of French original. London: Epworth.

Hezser, Catherine (2017) *Rabbinic Body Language: Non-Verbal Communication in Palestinian Rabbinic Literature of Late Antiquity*. Leiden: Brill.

Ho, Sin-pan Daniel (2016) *Paul and the Creation of a Counter-Cultural Community: A Rhetorical Analysis of 1 Cor. 5-11.1 in Light of the Social Lives of the Corinthians*. Library of New Testament Studies, 509. London: T&T Clark.

Hodgson, Robert (1983) 'Paul the Apostle and First Century Tribulation Texts', *ZNW* 74: 59–80.

Hock, Andreas (2007) 'Christ is the Parade: A Comparative Study of the Triumphal Procession of 2 Cor 2,14 and Col 2,15', *Biblica* 88: 110–19.

Hock, Ronald E. (2007) *The Social Context of Paul's Ministry: Tentmaking and Apostleship*. Minneapolis: Fortress.

Hogg, Michael A. (2001) 'A Social Identity Theory of Leadership', *PSPR* 5: 184–200.

Hogg, Michael A. and J. C. Turner (1987) 'Social Identity and Conformity: A Theory of Referent Informational Influence', in W. Doise and S. Moscovici, (eds), *Current Issues in European Social Psychology*, Volume 2, 139–82. Cambridge: Cambridge University Press.

Hogg, Michael A. and Graham M. Vaughan 2005. *Social Psychology*. Fourth Edition. Harlow: Pearson Education Ltd.

Hogg, Michael A. and S. A. Reid (2006) 'Social Identity, Self-Categorisation, and the Communication of Group Norms', *Communication Theory* 16: 7–30.

Hogg, Michael A. and Joanne R. Smith (2007) 'Attitudes in Social Context: A Social Identity Perspective', *ERSP* 18: 89–131.

Hogg, Michael A. and Howard Giles (2012) 'Norm Talk and Identity in Intergroup Communication', in Howard Giles (ed.), *The Handbook of Intergroup Communication*, 373–88. New York: Routledge.

Hogg, Michael A., Daan van Knippenberg, and David E. Rast III (2012) 'The Social Identity Theory of Leadership: Theoretical Origins, Research Findings, and Conceptual Developments', *ERSP* 23: 258–304.

Holladay, Carl R. (1977) *Theios Aner in Hellenistic Judaism: A Critique of the Use of This Category in New Testament Christology*. SBLDS 40. Missoula, Mon: Scholars Press.

Holmberg, Bengt (1978) *Paul and Power: The Structure of Authority in the Primitive Church as Reflected in the Pauline Epistles*. Coniectanea Biblica, New Testament Series, 11. Lund: CWK Gleerup.

Hooker, Morna D. (1971) 'Interchange in Christ', *JTS* n. s. 22: 349–61.

Hooker, Morna D. (2008) 'On Becoming the Righteousness of God: Another Look at 2 Cor 5:21', *NovT* 50: 358–75.

Hopkins, Nick and Steve Reicher (2011) 'Identity, Culture and Contestation: Social Identity as Cross-Cultural Theory', *Psychological Studies* 56: 36–43.

Horrell, David G. (1995) 'Paul's Collection: Resources for a Materialist Theology', *ER* 22: 74–83.

Horrell, David (1996) *The Social Ethos of the Corinthian Correspondence: Interests and Ideology*. Studies of the New Testament and Its World. Edinburgh: T & T Clark.

Horrell, David G. (2016) 'Ethnicisation, Marriage and Early Christian Identity: Critical Reflections on 1 Corinthians 7, 1 Peter 3 and Modern New Testament Scholarship', *NTS* 62: 439–60.

Hornsey, Matthew , M. Trembath and S. Gunthorpe (2004) '"You Can Criticise Because You Care": Identity Attachment, Constructiveness, and the Intergroup Sensitivity Effect', *EJSP* 34: 400–518.

Horsley, G. H. R. (1981) '"A Pure Bride" (2 Cor. 11.2)', in G. H. R. Horsley (ed.), *New Documents Illustrating Early Christianity, I: A Review of the Greek Inscriptions and Papyri Published in 1976*, 71–2. Sydney: The Ancient History Documentary Research Centre, Macquarie University.

Hubbard, Moyer (2016) 'Enemy Love in Paul: Probing the Engberg-Pedersen and Thorsteinsson Thesis', *Journal for the Study of Paul and His Letters* 6: 115–35.

Hughes, Philip E. (1962) *Paul's Second Epistle to the Corinthians*. New International Commentary on the New Testament. Grand Rapids, MI: William B. Eerdmans.

Hutchinson, John and Anthony Smith (1996) 'Introduction', in John Hutchinson and Anthony Smith (eds), *Ethnicity*, 3–14. Oxford: Oxford University Press.

Iyer, Aarti, T. Schmader and B. Lickel (2007) 'Why Individuals Protest the Perceived Transgressions of Their Country: The Role of Anger, Shame, and Guilt', *PSPB* 33: 587–96.

Iyer, Aarti, Jolanda Jetten and S. Alexander Haslam (2012) 'Sugaring O'er the Devil: Moral Superiority and Group Identification Help Individuals Downplay the Implications of Ingroup Rule-Breaking', *EJSP* 42: 141–9.

Janis, Irving Lester (1972) *Victims of Groupthink: A Psychological Study of Foreign-Policy Decisions and Fiascoes*. Oxford: Oxford University Press.

Jetten, Jolanda, Aarti Iyer, Paul Hutchinson and Matthew J. Hornsey (2011) 'Debating Deviance: Responding to Those Who Fall From Grace', in Jolanda Jetten and Matthew J. Hornsey (eds), *Rebels in Groups: Dissent, Deviance, Difference and Defiance*, 117–34. Oxford: Wiley-Blackwell.

Jetten, Jolanda and Matthew J. Hornsey (2014) 'Deviance and Dissent in Groups', *ARP* 65: 461–85.

Jewett, Robert (1979) *Dating Paul's Life*. London: SCM.

Johansen, Mark K., Nathalie Fouquet, Justin Savage and David R. Shanks (2013) 'Instance Memorization and Category Influence: Challenging the Evidence for Multiple Systems in Category Learning', *Quarterly Journal of Experimental Psychology* 66/6: 1204–26.

Johnson, Luke Timothy (1992) *The Acts of the Apostles*. Sacra Pagina Series, 5. Collegeville, MN: The Liturgical Press.

Jokiranta, Jutta (2013) *Social Identity and Sectarianism in the Qumran Movement*. Studies on the Texts of the Desert of Juda, 105. Leiden: Brill.

Joubert, Stephan (2000) *Paul as Benefactor: Reciprocity, Strategy, and Theological Reflection in Paul's Collection*. Tübingen: Mohr Siebeck.

Judge, Edwin A. (1968) 'Paul's Boasting in Relation to Contemporary Professional Practice', *ABR* 16:37–50.

Judge, Edwin A. (1981) 'The Regional κάνων for Requisitioned Transport', in G. H. R. Horsley (ed.), *New Documents Illustrating Early Christianity, I: A Review of the Greek Inscriptions and Papyri Published in 1976*, 36–45. Sydney: The Ancient History Documentary Research Centre, Macquarie University.

Kaplan, Jonathan (2011) 'Comfort, O Comfort, Corinth: Grief and Comfort in 2 Corinthians 7:5-13a', *HTR* 104: 433–45.

Käsemann, Ernst (1942) 'Die Legitimität des Apostels. Eine Untersuchung zu II Korinther 10–13', *ZNW* 41: 33–71.

Käsemann, Ernst (1969) 'The "Righteousness of God" in Paul', in Ernst Käsemann, *New Testament Questions of Today*, 168–83. London: SCM Press.

Keddie, G. Anthony (2015) 'Paul' Freedom and Moses' Veil: Moral Freedom and the Mosaic Law in Light of Philo', *JSNT* 37: 267–89.

Khan, Sammyh S., Nicholas Hopkins, Stephen D. Reicher, Shruti Tewari, Narayanan Srinivasan and Clifford Stevenson (2016) 'How Collective Participation Impacts Social Identity: A Longitudinal Study from India', *PP* 37: 309–25.

Kim, C.-H. (1972) *Form and Structure of the Familiar Greek Letter of Recommendation*. SBLDS, 4. Missoula: Scholars' Press.

Kim, Seon Yong (2016) 'Paul and the Stoic Theory of Οἰκείωσις: A Reply to Troels Engberg-Pedersen', *NovumT* 58: 71–91.

Kistemaker, Simon J. (1997) *II Corinthians*. New Testament Commentary. Grand Rapids, MI: Baker Books.

Kloppenborg, John S. (2017) 'Paul's Collection for Jerusalem and the Financial Practices in Greek Cities', in T. R. Blanton and R. Pickett (eds), *Paul and Economics: A Handbook*, 307–32. Minneapolis: Fortress Press.

Kloppenborg, John S. (2019) *Christ's Associations: Connecting and Belonging in the Ancient City*. New Haven and London: Yale University Press.

Klöpper, A. (1874) *Kommentar über das zweite Sendschreiben des Apostels Paulus an die Gemeinde zu Korinth*. Berlin: Georg Reimer.

Knox, John (1989) *Chapters in a Life of Paul. Revised Edition*. Revised by the author and edited and introduced by Douglas R. A. Hare. London: SCM.

Korner, Ralph J. (2017) *The Origin and Meaning of* Ekklêsia *in the Early Jesus Movement. Ancient Judaism and Early Christianity*. Leiden and Boston: Brill.

Kuecker, Aaron (2011) *The Spirit and the 'Other': Social identity, Ethnicity and Intergroup Reconciliation in Luke-Acts*. Library of New Testament Studies; 444. London: T&T Clark International.

Kuhn, Thomas (1962) *The Structure of Scientific Revolutions*. Chicago: University of Chicago Press.

Kümmel, Werner Georg, Paul Feine and Johannes Behm (1975) *Introduction to the New Testament. Revised and enlarged English edition*. Nashville: Abingdon.

Kwon, Yon-Gyong (2008) 'Ἀρραβών as Pledge in Second Corinthians', *NTS* 54: 525–41.

Lacy, Philip H. de and Benedict Einarson (1959) *Plutarch's Moralia*, Volume 7. Loeb Classical Library. London and Cambridge, MT: Heinemann and Harvard University Press.

Lambrecht, Jan S.J. (1986) 'The Nekrosis of Jesus: Ministry and Suffering in 2 Cor 4,7–15', *Bibliotheca Ephermeridum Theologicarum Lovaniensium* 73: 120–43.

Lambrecht, Jan S.J. (1999) *Second Corinthians*. Sacra Pagina, Volume 8. Collegeville, MN: The Liturgical Press.

Lambrecht, Jan S.J. (2008) 'A Matter of Method: 2 Cor 4,13 and Stegman's Recent Study', *ETL* 84: 175–80.

Lambrecht, Jan S.J. (2009) 'From Glory to Glory (2 Corinthians 3,18): A Reply to Paul B. Duff', *ETL* 85: 143–6.

Lambrecht, Jan S.J. (2010) 'A Matter of Method (II): 2 Cor 4,13 and the Recent Studies of Schenck and Campbell', *ETL* 86: 441–8.

Lambrecht, Jan S.J. (2013) 'The Paul Who Wants to Die: A Close Reading of 2 Cor 4,16–5,10', in Reimund Bieringer,Ma. Marilous S. Ibita, Dominika A. Kurek-Chomycz and Thomas A. Vollmer (eds), *Theologizing in the Corinthian Conflict: Studies in the Exegesis and Theology of 2 Corinthians*, 145–61. Leuven, Paris and Walpole, MA: Peeters.

Lanci, John R. (1997) *A New Temple for Corinth: Rhetorical and Archaeological Approaches to Pauline Imagery*. New York: Peter Lang.

Land, Christopher D. (2015) *The Integrity of 2 Corinthians and Paul's Aggravating Absence*. New Testament Monographs 36. Sheffield: Sheffield Phoenix.

Last, Richard (2018) '*Ekklēsia* Outside the Septuagint and *Dēmos*: The Titles of Greco-Roman Associations and Christ-Followers' Groups', *JBL* 137: 965–86.

Last, Richard and Philip Harland (2020) *Group Survival in the Ancient Mediterranean: Material Conditions and Mutual Aid in Associations*. London: Bloomsbury T & T Clark.

Lau, Peter H. W. (2011) *Identity and Ethics in the Book of Ruth: A Social Identity Approach*. BZAW 416. Berlin: de Gruyter.

Lee, Eun-Suk, Tae-Yoon Park and Bonjin Koo (2015) 'Identifying Organizational Identification as a Basis for Attitudes and Behaviors: A Meta-Analytic Review', *Psychological Bulletin* 141: 1049–80.

Levison, John R. (2011) 'Paul in the Stoa Poecile: A Response to Troels Engberg-Pedersen *Cosmology and Self in the Apostle Paul: The Material Spirit*', *JSNT* 33: 415–32.

Lieu, J. M. (1985) '"Grace to You and Peace:" The Apostolic Greeting', *BJRL* 68: 161–78.

Lietzmann, Hans (1949) *An die Korinther I/II. Fourth Edition*, edited by Werner G. Kümmel. HNT 9. Tübingen: Mohr Siebeck.

Lim, Kar Yong (2017) *Metaphors and Social Identity Formation in Paul's Letters to the Corinthians*. Eugene, OR: Pickwick Publications.

Lim, Kar Yong (2020) '2 Corinthians', in Brian J. Tucker and Aaron Kuecker, (eds), *T & T Clark Social Identity Commentary on the New Testament*, 327–54. London and New York: T & T Clark.

Lincoln, Andrew T. (1981) *Paradise Now and Not Yet*. SNTMSMS, 43. Cambridge: Cambridge University Press.

Lingård, Fredrik (2005) *Paul's Line of Thought in 2 Corinthians 4:6–5:10*. Tübingen: Mohr Siebeck.

Long, Frederick J. (2004) *Ancient Rhetoric and Paul's Apology: The Compositional Unity of 2 Corinthians*. SNTMSMS, 131. Cambridge: Cambridge University Press.

Longenecker, Bruce W. (2010) *Remember the Poor: Paul, Poverty, the Greco-Roman World*. Grand Rapids. MI: Eerdmans.

Longenecker, R. N. (1976) *Paul: Apostle of Liberty*. Grand Rapids, MI: Baker.
Lüdemann, Gerd (1989) *Opposition to Paul in Jewish Christianity*, trans. M. Eugene Boring. Minneapolis: Fortress.
Luomanen, Petri (2007) 'The Sociology of Knowledge, The Social Identity Approach and the Cognitive Science of Religion', in Petri Luomanen, Ilkka Pyysiäinen and Risto Uro (eds), *Explaining Christian Origins and Early Judaism: Contributions from Cognitive and Social Science*. Biblical Interpretation Series 89, 199–229. Leiden: Brill.
Lütgert, W. (1908) *Freiheitspredigt und Schwarmgeister in Korinth: Ein Beitrag zur Charakteristik der Christuspartei*. Gütersloh: Bertelsmann.
Mackie, Diane M., Thierry Devos and Eliot R. Smith (2000) 'Intergroup Emotions: Explaining Offensive Tendencies in an Intergroup Context', *JPSP* 79: 602–16.
Mackie, Diane M., Eliot R. Smith and Devin G. Bray (2008) 'Intergroup Emotions and Intergroup Relations', *SPPC* 2: 1866–80.
Maitner, Angela T., Diane M. Mackie and Eliot R. Smith (2006) 'Evidence for the Regulatory Function of Intergroup Emotion: Emotional Consequences of Implemented or Impeded Intergroup Action Tendencies', *JESP* 42: 720–8.
Malherbe, A. (1959) 'The Corinthian Contribution', *RQ* 3(4): 221–33.
Malina, Bruce J. (1981) *The New Testament World: Insights from Cultural Anthropology*. Third edition, revised and expanded. First edition 1981. Louisville, KY: Westminster John Knox Press.
Malina, Bruce J. (2001) *The New Testament World: Insights from Cultural Anthropology*. Louisville, KY: Westminster John Knox Press.
Malina, Bruce J. (2008) *Timothy: Paul's Closest Associate*. Paul's Social Network: Brothers and Sisters in Faith. Collegeville, MN: Liturgical Press.
Manstead, Antony S. R. and Gün R. Semin (2001) 'Methodology in Social Psychology', in Miles Hewstone and Wolfgang Stroebe (eds), *Introduction to Social Psychology: A European Perspective*. Third edition, 73–111. Oxford: Basil Blackwell.
Marohl, Matthew J. (2008) *Faithfulness and the Purpose of Hebrews: A Social Identity Approach*. Princeton Theological Monograph Series 82. Eugene, Ore: Pickwick.
Marshall, P. (1983) 'A Metaphor of Social Shame: Θριαμβεύειν in 2 Cor 2:14' 2 Cor 2:14', *NovT* 25: 302–17.
Marshall, P. (1987) *Enmity in Corinth: Social Conventions in Paul's Relations with the Corinthians*. WUNT 2/23. Tübingen: Mohr Siebeck.
Martin, Ralph P. (1981) *Reconciliation: A Study of Paul's Theology*. Atlanta: John Knox Press.
Martin, Ralph P. (1986) *2 Corinthians*. Word Biblical Commentaries. Waco, Texas: Word.
Martini, Sarah E. and Thomas Kessler (2014) 'Managing One's Social Identity: Successful and Unsuccessful Identity Management', *EJSP* 44: 748–57.
Martyn, J. Louis (1997) 'Apocalyptic Antimonies', in his *Theological Issues in the Letters of Paul*, 111–24. Nashville, TN: Abingdon.

Mason, Steve (2007) 'Jews, Judaeans, Judaizing, Judaism: Problems of Categorization in Ancient History', *JSJ* 38: 457–512.

Mason, Steve and Esler, Philip F. (2017) 'Judaean and Christ-Movement Identities: Grounds for a Distinction', *New Testament Studies* 63: 493–515.

Matera, Frank J. (1992) *Galatians*. Sacra Pagina. Collegeville, MN: The Liturgical Press.

Matera, Frank J. (2003) *II Corinthians: A Commentary*. NTL. Louisville, Westminster.

Mayer, Wendy and Pauline Allen (2017) 'John Chrysostom', in Philip F. Esler (ed.), *The Early Christian World*. Second Edition, 1054–71. London and New York: Routledge.

McCant, J. W. (1999) *2 Corinthians*. Sheffield: Sheffield Academic.

Meeks, Wayne A. (1993) *The Origins of Christian Morality*. New Haven: Yale University Press.

Meyer, H. A. W. (1879) *Critical and Exegetical Handbook to the Epistles to the Corinthians II*. ET by W. P. Dickson of 1870 German original. Edinburgh: T & T Clark.

Mills, C. Wright (1978) *The Sociological Imagination*. Harmondsworth: Penguin Books.

Mitchell, Margaret M. (1992) 'NT Envoys in the Context of Greco-Roman Diplomatic and Epistolary Conventions', *JBL* 111: 641–62.

Mitchell, Margaret M. (2005) 'Paul's Letters to Corinth: The Interpretive Intertwining of Literary and Historical Reconstruction', in Daniel N. Schowalter and Steven J. Friesen (eds), *Urban Religion in Roman Corinth: Interdisciplinary Approaches*. HTS 53, 307–38. Harvard: Harvard Divinity School.

Mitchell, Margaret M. (2020) 'Can It Work? (How?) Can Exegetical Studies of 2 Corinthians Talk Across the "Partition"?', in Eve-Marie Becker and Hermut Löhr (eds), *Die Exegese des 2 Kor Und Phil im Lichte der Literarkritik*, Biblisch-Theologische Studien, 103–44. Göttingen: Vandenhoeck & Ruprecht.

Moberly, R. Walter (1983) *At the Mountain of God: Story and Theology in Exodus 32-34*. JSOT Supplement Series, 27. Sheffield: Sheffield Academic Press.

Montgomery, H. B. (1929) *The New Testament in Modern English: Centenary Translation*. Philadelphia: Judson.

Munck, Johannes (1959) *Paul and the Salvation of Mankind*. London: SCM Press.

Murphy-O'Connor, Jerome (1996) *Paul: A Critical Life*. Oxford: Oxford University Press.

Murphy-O'Connor, Jerome O. P. (1983) *St. Paul's Corinth: Texts and Archaeology*. Good News Studies 6. Wilmington, Delaware: Michael Glazier.

Nickle, Keith F. (1966) *The Collection: A Study in Paul's Strategy*. Studies in Biblical Theology, No. 48. Naperville, Ill: Alec R. Allenson, Inc.

Nongbri, Brent (2015) *Before Religion: A History of a Modern Concept*. New Haven: Yale University Press.

Nosofsky, Robert M. (2011) 'The Generalized Context Model: An Exemplar Model of Classification', in Emmanuel M. Pothos and Andy J. Wills (eds), *Formal Approaches in Categorization*, 18–39. New York: Cambridge University Press.

Novick, T. (2011) 'Peddling Scents: Merchandise and Meaning in 2 Corinthians 2:14-17', *JBL* 130: 543-49.

Ogereau, Julien M. (2012) 'The Jerusalem Collection as Κοινωνια: Paul's Global Politics of Socio-economic Equality and Solidarity', *NTS* 58(3): 360-78.

O'Mahony, Kieran (2001) *Pauline Persuasion: A Sounding in 2 Corinthians 8–9*. Sheffield: Sheffield Academic Press.

Oostendorp, Derk (1967) *Another Jesus: A Gospel of Jewish-Christian Superiority in II Corinthians*. Kampen: J. H. Kok. (Not St A, but ordered Dec 09)

Oropeza, B. J. (2012) *Jews, Gentiles, and the Opponents of Paul: The Pauline Letters. Apostasy in the New Testament Communities*, Volume 2. Eugene, OR: Cascade.

Orton, David E. and R. Dean Anderson, eds (1998) *Heinrich Lausberg: Handbook of Literary Rhetoric: A Foundation for Literary Study*. With a Foreword by George A. Kennedy. English translation by Bliss, Matthew T., Jansen, Annemiek and Orton, David E. Leiden: Brill.

Otten, Sabine (2016) 'The Minimal Group Paradigm and Its Maximal Impact in Research on Social Categorization', *Current Opinion in Psychology* 11: 85–9.

Pandey, Kavita, Clifford Stevenson, Shail Shankar, Nicholas B. Hopkins, and Stephen D. Reicher (2014) 'Cold Comfort at the Magh Mela: Social Identity Processes and Physical Hardship', *BJSP* 53: 675-90.

Park, Young-Ho (2015) *Paul's Ekklesia as Civic Assembly*. WUNT 2, 393. Tübingen: Mohr Siebeck.

Parsons, Michael (1988) '"In Christ" in Paul', *Vox Evangelica* 18: 25–44.

Pawlak, Matthew C. (2018) 'Consistency Isn't Everything: Self-Commendation in 2 Corinthians', *JSNT* 40: 360–82.

Pfeffer, J. (1992) *Managing with Power*. Boston, MA: Harvard Business School Press.

Platow, M. J. and D. van Knippenberg (2001) 'A Social Identity Analysis of Leader Endorsement: The Effects of Leader Ingroup Prototypicality and Distributive Intergroup Fairness', *PSPB* 27: 1508–19.

Platow, M. J., D. van Knippenberg, S. Alexander Haslam, B. van Knippenberg and R. Spears (2006) 'A Special Gift We Bestow on You for Being Representative of Us: Considering Leadership from a Self-Categorization Perspective', *BJSP* 45: 303–20.

Plummer, Alfred (1915) *A Critical and Exegetical Commentary on the Second Epistle of St. Paul to the Corinthians*. New York: Scribner.

Polaski, Sandra (1999) *Paul and the Discourse of Power*. Sheffield: Sheffield Academic Press.

Porter, Christopher A. (2019) 'Building "One-of-Usness": Prototypicality and Shared Social Narratives in Epistolary Context', Paper delivered at the

'Writing Social-Scientific Commentaries Section' at the Annual Meeting of the Society of Biblical Literature, San Diego.

Porter, Stanley E. (1994) Καταλλάσσω *in Ancient Greek Literature, with Reference to the Pauline Writings.* Cordoba: El Almendro.

Portice, Jennie and Stephen D. Reicher (2018) 'Arguments for European Disintegrations: A Mobilization Analysis of Anti-Immigration Speeches by U. K. Political Leaders: A Mobilization Analysis of Anti-Immigration Speeches', *PP* 39: 1357–72.

Rabens, Volker (2014) 'Inclusion of and Demarcation from "Outsiders": Mission and Ethics in Paul's Second Letter to the Corinthians', in J. Kok, T. Niklas, D. T. Roth and C. M. Hays (eds), *Sensitivity Towards Outsiders: Exploring the Dynamic Relationship Between Mission and Ethics in the New Testament and Early Christianity.* WUNT II/364, 290–323. Tübingen: Mohr Siebeck.

Reicher, Stephen D. (2004) 'The Context of Social Identity: Domination, Resistance and Change', *PP* 25: 921–45.

Reicher, Stephen D. and Nicholas Hopkins (1996) 'Self-Category Constructions in Political Rhetoric: An Analysis of Thatcher's and Kinnock's Speeches Concerning the British Miners' Strike (1984–1985)', *EJSP* 26: 353–71.

Reicher, Stephen D. and Nicholas Hopkins (2001) *Self and Nation: Categorization, Contestation, and Mobilization.* London: Sage.

Reicher, Stephen D. and Nick Hopkins (2003) 'On the Science of the Art of Leadership', in Daan van Knippenberg and Michael A. Hogg (eds), *Leadership and Power: Identity Processes in Groups and Organisations,* 197–209. London and Thousand Oaks, CA: Sage Publications.

Reicher, Stephen D., S. A. Haslam and Nick Hopkins (2005) 'Social Identity and the Dynamics of Leadership: Leaders and Followers as Collaborative Agents in the Transformation of Social Reality', *The Leadership Quarterly* 16: 547–68.

Reicher, Stephen D., Clare Cassidy, Ingrid Wolpert, Nick Hopkins and Mark Levine (2006) 'Saving Bulgaria's Jews: An Analysis of Social Identity and the Mobilisation of Social Identity', *EJSP* 36: 49–72.

Reicher, Stephen D., S. Alexander Haslam, Russell Spears, and Katherine J. Reynolds (2012) 'A Social Mind: The Context of John Turner's Work and Its Influence', *ERSP* 23: 344–85.

Reicher, Stephen D. and S. Alexander Haslam (2017) 'How Trump Won', *Scientific American Mind* 28: 42–50.

Robinson, J. M. (1971) 'The Johannine Trajectory', in J. M. Robinson and H. Koester (eds), *Trajectories Through Early Christianity*, 232–68. Philadelphia: Fortress.

Roetzel, Calvin J. (2007) *2 Corinthians.* Abingdon New Testament Commentaries. Nashville: Abingdon Press.

Rosch, Eleanor (1978) 'Principles of Categorization', in Eleanor Rosch and Barbara L. Lloyd (eds), *Cognition and Categorization*, 27–48. Hilldale, NJ: Lawrence Erlbaum.

Safrai, Ze'ev and Peter J. Thomson (2013) 'Paul's "Collection for the Saints" (2 Cor 8–9) and Financial Support of Leaders in Early Christianity and Judaism', in Reimund Bieringer, Emmanuel Nathan, Didier Pollefeyt and Peter J. Tomson (eds), 132–20. Leiden: Brill.

Sampley, J. P. (1980) *Pauline Partnership in Christ: Christian Community and Commitment in Light of Roman Law*. Philadelphia: Fortress Press.

Sanders, E. P. (1977) *Paul and Palestinian Judaism: A Comparison of Patterns of Religion*. Minneapolis, MN: Fortress Press.

Sani, Fabio and Stephen D. Reicher (2000) 'Contested Identities and Schisms in Groups: Opposing the Ordination of Women as Priests in the Church of England', *BJSP* 39: 95–112.

Savage, Timothy B. (1996) *Power Through Weakness: Paul's Understanding of the Christian Ministry in 2 Corinthians*. SNTSMS, 86. Cambridge: Cambridge University Press.

Schenck, Kenneth (2008) '2 Corinthians and the Πίστις Χριστοῦ Debate', *CBQ* 70: 524–37.

Schlatter, Adolf (1969) *Paulus der Bote Jesu: Eine Deutung seiner Briefe an die Korinther*. Fourth edition (first edition 1934). Stuttgart: Calwer Verlag.

Schmeller, Thomas (2013) 'No Bridge Over Troubled Water: The Gap Between 2 Corinthians 1–9 and 10–13 Revisited', *JSNT* 36: 73–84.

Schmiedel, P. W. (1892) *Die Briefe an die Thessaloniker und an die Korinther*. HKNT 2.1. Freiburg: Mohr.

Schmithals, Walter (1971) *Gnosticism in Corinth: An Investigation of the Letters to the Corinthians*. ETJ. E. Seely. Nashville, Tenn.: Abingdon.

Schmitz, Otto and Gustav Stähin (1967) 'Παρακαλέω, παράκλησις', *TDNT* 5: 773–99.

Schnelle, Ugo (2005) *Apostle Paul: His Life and Theology*. ET of 2003 German original by Eugene Boring. Grand Rapids, MI: Baker Publishing.

Schowalter, Daniel and Steven J. Friesen, (eds) (2005) *Urban Religion in Roman Corinth: Interdisciplinary Approaches*. Cambridge. MT: Harvard University Press.

Schweitzer, A. (1953) *The Mysticism of the Apostle Paul*, trans. William Montgomery. London: Adam & Charles Black.

Scott, James M. (1998) *2 Corinthians*. NIBCNT. Peabody, MA: Hendrickson.

Schütz, John (1975) *Paul and the Anatomy of Apostolic Authority*. Cambridge: Cambridge University Press.

Seifrid, Mark A. (2014) *The Second Letter to the Corinthians*. The Pillar New Testament Commentary. Grand Rapids, MI: William B. Eerdmans.

Semler, Johann Salomo (1776) *Paraphrasis II. Epistolae ad Corinthios*. Halle: Hemmerde.

Shantz, Colleen (2009) *Paul in Ecstasy: The Neurobiology of the Apostle's Life and Thought*. Cambridge: Cambridge University Press.

Shaw, Graham (1983) *The Cost of Authority: Manipulation and Freedom in the New Testament*. Philadelphia: Fortress Press.

Shkul, Minna (2010) *Reading Ephesians: Exploring Social Entrepreneurship in the Text*. LNTS 318. London: T&T Clark.

Sloan, Robert B. (1995) '2 Corinthians 2:14-4:6 and "New Covenant Hermeneutics:" A Response to Richard Hays', *Bulletin for Biblical Research* 5: 129–54.

Smith, Eliot R. (1993) 'Social Identity and Social Emotions: Toward New Conceptualizations of Prejudice', in Diane M. Mackie and D. L. Hamilton (eds), *Affect, Cognition, and Stereotyping: Interactive Processes in Group Perception*, 297–315. San Diego, CA: Academic Press.

Smith, Eliot R. (1999) 'Affective and Cognitive Implications of a Group Becoming Part of the Self. New Models of Prejudice and of the Self Concept', in Dominic Abrams and Michael A. Hogg (eds), *Social Identity and Social Cognition*, 181–96. Oxford: Basil Blackwell.

Smith, Eliot R. and Michael Zarate (1990) 'Exemplar and Prototype Use in Social Categorisation', *Social Cognition* 8: 243–62.

Smith, Eliot R. and Diane M. Mackie (2002) 'Commentary', in Diane M. Mackie and Eliot R. Smith (eds), *From Prejudice to Intergroup Emotions: Differentiated Reactions to Social Groups*, 285–99. London and New York: Routledge.

Smith, Wilfrid Cantwell (1991 [1962]) *The Meaning and End of Religion*. Minneapolis: Fortress.

Southwood, Katherine E. (2014) 'Will Naomi's Nation Be Ruth's Nation?: Ethnic Translation as a Metaphor for Ruth's Assimilation Within Judah', *Humanities* 3: 102–31.

Stanley, Christopher D. (1992) *Paul and the Language of Scripture: Citation Technique in the Pauline Epistles and Contemporary Literature*. SNTSMS, 74. Cambridge: CUP.

Stanley, Christopher D. (2004) *Arguing with Scripture: The Rhetoric of Quotations in the Letters of Paul*. London: T & T Clark.

Stanley, Christopher D. (2008a) 'Charting the Course', in Stanley E. Porter and Christopher D. Stanley (eds), *As It Is Written: Studying Paul's Use of Scripture*, 3–12. Atlanta, GA: SBL.

Stanley, Christopher D. (2008b) 'Paul's "Use" of Scripture: Why the Audience Matters', in Stanley E. Porter and Christopher D. Stanley (eds), *As It Is Written: Studying Paul's Use of Scripture*, 125–55. Atlanta, GA: SBL.

Stargel, Linda M. (2018) *The Construction of Exodus Identity in Ancient Israel: A Social Identity Approach*. Eugene: Pickwick.

Starling, D. I. (2011) *Not My People: Gentiles as Exiles in Pauline Hermeneutics*. BZNW 184. New York: Walter de Gruyter.

Steffens, Niklas K., S. Alexander Haslam, Michelle K. Ryan and Thomas Kessler (2013) 'Leadership Performance and Prototypicality: Their Interrelationship and Impact on Leaders' Identity Entrepreneurship', *EJSP* 43: 606–13.

Steffens, N. K., S. A. Haslam and S. D. Reicher (2014) 'Up Close and Personal: Evidence that Shared Social Identity is a Basis for the "Special" Relationship that Binds Followers to Leaders', *LQ* 25(2): 296–313.

Steffens, Niklas K., S. Alexander Haslam, Stephen D. Reicher, Michael J. Platow, Katrien Fransen, Jie Yang, Michelle K. Ryan, Jolanda Jetten, Kim Peters and Filip Boen (2014) 'Leadership as Social Identity Management: Introducing the Identity Leadership Inventory (ILI) to Assess and Validate a Four-Dimensional Model', *LQ* 25: 1001–24.

Steffens, Niklas K., Sebastian S. Schuh, S. Alexander Haslam, Antonia Pérez and Rolf van Dick (2015) '"Of the Group" and "For the Group": How Followership Is Shaped by Leaders' Prototypicality and Group Identification', *EJSP* 45: 180–90.

Stegman, Thomas (2005) *The Character of Jesus: The Lynchpin of Paul's Argument in 2 Corinthians*. Rome: Pontificio Istituto Biblico.

Stegman, Thomas (2007) 'Ἐπίστευσα, διὸ ἐλάλησα (2 Corinthians 4:13): Paul's Christological Reading of Psalm 115:1a LXX', *CBQ* 69: 725–45.

Stegman, Thomas D. (2012) 'Reading ἔγραψα in 2 Corinthians 2:9 as an Epistolary Aorist', *NovT* 54: 50–67.

Stegemann, Ekkehard W. and Wolfgang Stegemann (1999) *The Jesus Movement: A Social History of Its First Century*. Minneapolis, MN: Fortress.

Stockhausen, Carol K. (1989) *Moses' Veil and the Glory of the New Covenant: The Exegetical Substructure of 2 Cor. 3:7-4:6*. Rome: Pontifical Biblical Institute.

Stowers, Stanley K. (1986) *Letter-Writing in Greco-Roman Antiquity*. Library of Early Christianity, 5. Philadelphia: Westminster Press.

Stowers, Stanley K. (1990) '*Peri men gar* and the Integrity of 2 Cor. 8 and 9', *NovT* 32: 340–8.

Striker, Gisela (1990) 'Ataraxia: Happiness as Tranquility', *The Monist* 73: 97–110.

Sumney, Jerry L. (1990) *Identifying Paul's Opponents: The Question of Method in 2 Corinthians*. JSNT Supp. Series, 40. Sheffield: Sheffield Academic Press.

Sweeney, Michael L. (2019) 'The Pauline Collection, Church Partnerships and the Mission of the Church in the 21st Century', *Missiology: An International Review* 48: 142–53.

Tack, Laura G. (2015) 'A Face Reflecting Glory: 2 Cor 3,18 in Its Literary Context', *Biblica* 96: 85–112.

Tajfel, Henri (1978) 'Introduction', in Henri Tajfel (ed.), *Differentiation between Social Groups: Studies in the Social Psychology of Intergroup Relations*. European Monographs in Social Psychology, 1–23. London: Academic Press.

Tajfel, Henri, M. G. Billig, R. P. Bundy and Claude Flamment (1971) 'Social Categorization and Intergroup Behaviour', *EJSP* 1: 149–78.

Tajfel, Henri and John C. Turner (1979) 'An Alternative Theory of Intergroup Conflict', in W. G. Austin and S. Worchel (eds), *The Social Psychology of Intergroup Relationships*, 33–47. Monterey, CA: Brooks/Cole.

Tasker, R. V. G. (1958) *The Second Epistle to the Corinthians*. TNTC 8. Grand Rapids, MI: Eerdmans/London: Tyndale.

Taylor, J. (1992) 'The Ethnarch of King Aretas at Damascus: A Note on 2 Cor 11.32-33', *RB* 99: 719-28.

Theissen, Gerd (1982) *The Social Setting of Pauline Christianity: Essays on Corinth*. Edited and Translated by John H. Schütz. Edinburgh: T & T Clark.

Thiessen, Matthew (2011) *Contesting Conversion: Genealogy, Circumcision and Identity in Ancient Judaism and Christianity*. Oxford: Oxford University Press.

Thorsteinsson, Runar M. (2006) 'Paul and Roman Stoicism: Romans 12 and Contemporary Stoic Ethics', *JSNT* 29: 139-61.

Thorsteinsson, Runar M. (2010) *Paul and Roman Stoicism: A Comparative Study of Ancient Morality*. Oxford: Oxford University Press.

Trebilco, Paul (2011) 'Why Did the Early Christians Call Themselves ἡ ἐκκλησία?', *NTS* 57: 440-60.

Thrall, Margaret E. (1981) '"Putting On" on or "Stripping Off" in 2 Corinthians 5:3', in E. J. Epp and G. D. Fee (eds), *New Testament Textual Criticism: Its Significance for Exegesis. Essays in Honor of Bruce J. Metzger*, 221-37. Oxford: Clarendon.

Thrall, Margaret E. (1987) 'The Offender and the Offence: A Problem of Detection in 2 Corinthians', in Barry P. Thompson (ed.), *Meaning and Method: Essays Presented to Anthony Tyrrell Hanson for His Seventieth Birthday*, 65-78. Hull: Hull University Press.

Thrall, Margaret E. (1994) *A Critical and Exegetical Commentary on the Second Epistle to the Corinthians. Volume I. Introduction and Commentary on II Corinthians I-VII*. The International Critical Commentary on the Holy Scripture of the Old and New Testaments. Edinburgh: T & T Clark.

Thrall, Margaret E. (2000) *A Critical and Exegetical Commentary on the Second Epistle to the Corinthians. Volume 2. Introduction and Commentary on II Corinthians VIII-XIII*. International Critical Commentary. London: T & T Clark International.

Triandis, Harry C. (1990) 'Cross-Cultural Studies of Individualism and Collectivism', in Richard A. Dienstbier et al. (eds), *Nebraska Symposium on Motivation*, 41-133. Lincoln: University of Nebraska Press.

Triandis, Harry C. (1995) *Individualism and Collectivism*. New Directions in Social Psychology: New York and London: Routledge.

Triandis, Harry C. (2001) 'Individualism-Collectivism and Personality', *Journal of Personality* 69: 907-24.

Tucker, J. Brian (2010a) *'Remain in Your Calling': Paul and the Continuation of Social Identities in 1 Corinthians*. Eugene, Oregon: Pickwick.

Tucker, J. Brian (2010b) *'You Belong to Christ': Paul and the Formation of Social Identity in 1 Corinthians 1-4*. Eugene, Oregon: Pickwick.

Tucker, J. Brian (2014) 'The Jerusalem Collection, Economic inequality, and Human Flourishing: Is Paul's Concern the Redistribution of Wealth, or a

Relationship of Mutuality (or Both)?', *Canadian Theological Review* 3(2): 52–70.
Tucker, J. Brian (2017) *Reading 1 Corinthians*. Cascade Companions 36. Eugene: Cascade.
Tucker, J. Brian (2018) *Reading Romans after Supersessionism*. New Testament after Supersessionism 6. Eugene: Cascade.
Tucker, J. Brian and Coleman A. Baker (eds) (2014) *T & T Clark Handbook to Social Identity in the New Testament*. London: Bloomsbury.
Tucker, J. Brian and Aaron Kuecker, eds (2020). *T & T Clark Social Identity Commentary on the New Testament*. London and New York: T & T Clark.
Turner, John C. (1981) 'Some Considerations in Generalizing Experiment in Social Psychology', in G. M. Stephenson and J. H. Davis (eds), *Progress in Social Psychology. Volume 1*, 3–34. Chichester: John Wiley & Sons.
Turner, John C. (1982) 'Towards a Cognitive Redefinition of the Social Group', in Henri Tajfel (ed) *Social Identity and Intergroup Relations*, 15–40. Cambridge: Cambridge University Press.
Turner, John C. (2005) 'Explaining the Nature of Power: A Three-Process Theory', *EJSP* 35: 1–22.
Turner, John C., with Michael A. Hogg, Penelope J. Oakes, Stephen D. Reicher, and Margaret S. Wetherell (1987) *Rediscovering the Social Group: A Self-Categorization Theory*. Oxford: Basil Blackwell.
Turner, John C. and S. Alexander Haslam (2001) 'Social Identity, Organizations, and Leadership', in M. E. Turner (ed.), *Groups at Work: Theory and Research*, 25–65. Mahwah, NJ: Lawrence Erlbaum Associates Publishers.
Turner, Nigel (1965) *Grammatical Insights Into the New Testament*. Edinburgh: T & T Clark.
Ulrich, J., O. Christ and R. van Dick (2009) 'Substitutes for Procedural Fairness: Prototypical Leaders are Endorsed Whether They are Fair or Not', *Journal of Applied Psychology* 94: 235–44.
van Dick, Rolf and Rudolf Kerschreiter (2016) 'The Social Identity Approach to Effective Leadership: An Overview and Some Ideas on Cross-Cultural Generalizability', *Frontiers of Business Research in China* 10: 363–84.
van Knippenberg, Daan (2011) 'Embodying Who We Are: Leader Group Prototypicality and Leadership Effectiveness', *LQ* 22: 1078–91.
van Knippenberg, Daan and Hogg, Michael A. (2003) 'A Social Identity Model of Leadership Effectiveness in Organizations', in R. M. Kramer and B. M. Shaw (eds), *Research in Organizational Behaviour*, Volume 25, 243–95. Amsterdam: Elsevier.
van Kooten, George (2012) 'Ἐκκλησία τοῦ Θεοῦ: The 'Church of God' and the Civic Assemblies (ἐκκλησίαι) of the Greek Cities in the Roman Empire: A Reply to Paul Trebilco and Richard A. Horsley', *NTS* 58: 522–48.
Vegge, Ivar (2008) *2 Corinthians — A Letter about Reconciliation*. WUNT 2: 239. Tübingen: Mohr Siebeck.

Verbrugge, V. D. (1992) *Paul's Style of Church Leadership Illustrated by his Instructions to the Corinthians on the Collection: To Command or Not to Command*. San Francisco: Mellen Research University Press.

Versnel, H. S. (1970) *Triumphus: An Inquiry inot the Origin, Development and Meaning of the Roman Triumph*. Leiden: Brill.

Watson, Francis (1984) '2 Cor. X-XIII and Paul's Painful Letter to the Corinthians', *JTS* 35: 326–46.

Weatherall, Margaret (1996) 'Constructing Social Identities: The Individual/Social Binary in Henri Tajfel's Social Psychology', in Robinson, W. Peter (ed.), *Social Groups and Identities: Developing the Legacy of Henri Tajfel*, 269–84. Oxford: Butterworth Heinemann.

Webb, William J. (1993) *Returning Home: New Covenant and Second Exodus as the Context for 2 Corinthians 6.14–7.1*. JSNT Supp. Series, 85. Sheffield: Sheffield Academic Press.

Weber, Max (1964 [1947]) *The Theory of Social and Economic Organization*. ET of *Grundriss der Sozialökonomik Wirtschaft und Gesellschaft* (1922) by A. M. Henderson and Talcott Parsons, edited by Talcott Parsons. New York and London: The Free Press and Collier Macmillan Publishers.

Wedderburn, Andrew J. M. (1985) 'Some Observations on Paul's Use of the Phrases "in Christ" and "with Christ"', *JSNT* 25: 83–97.

Weima, A. D. (1994) *Neglected Endings: The Significance of the Pauline Letter Closings*. JSNTSS 101. Sheffield: Sheffield Academic Press.

Weiss, Johannes (1937) *The History of Primitive Christianity*. Two volumes. ET by F. C. Grant. New York: Wilson-Fredrickson.

Weiss, Johannes (1959) *Earliest Christianity*. Two volumes. ET of German original of 1917 by F. C. Grant. New York: Harper.

Welborn, Larry L. (1995) 'The Identification of 2 Corinthians 10–13 With the "Letter of Tears"', *NovT* 37: 47–57.

Welborn, Larry L. (1997) 'Paul's Letter of Reconciliation in 2 Corinthians 1:1-2:13, 7:5-16 and Ancient Theories of Literary Unity', in Larry L. Welborn, *Politics and Rhetoric in the Corinthian Epistles*, 95–131. Macon: Mercer University Press. (Also in (1996) *NTS* 42: 559–83).

Welborn, Larry L. (2009) 'Paul's Caricature of His Chief Rival as a Pompous Parasite in 2 Corinthians 11.20', *JSNT* 82: 31–60.

Welborn, Larry L. (2010) '"By the Mouth of Two or Three Witnesses": Paul's Invocation of a Deuteronomic Statute', *NovumT* 52: 207–20.

Welborn, Larry (2011) *An End to Enmity. Paul and the "Wrongdoer" of Second Corinthians*. BZNW 185. Berlin: de Gruyter.

Welborn, Larry (2013) '"That There May be Equality": The Contexts and Consequences of a Pauline Ideal', *NTS* 59(1): 73–90.

Wenham, David (1995) *Paul: Follower of Jesus or Founder of Christianity?* Grand Rapids and Cambridge: William B. Eerdmans Publishing Company.

Windisch, Hans (1970 [1924]) *Der zweite Korintherbrief*. 9th edition (reprinted). KEK 6. Göttingen: Vandenhoeck & Ruprecht.

Witherington, Ben III (1995) *Conflict and Community in Corinth: A Socio-Rhetorical Commentary on 1 and 2 Corinthians*. Grand Rapids, MI: William B. Eerdmans Publishing Company.

Witulski, Thomas (2012) 'Der sogenannte "Midrasch" 2 Kor 3,7-18 und seine Funktion im Kontext der Argumentation des Paulus in 2 Kor 2,14-4,6', *Studien zum Neuen Testament und Seiner Umwelt* 37: 197-234.

Wypadlo, Adrian (2013) 'Paulus im Triumphzug Christi (2 Kor 2,14). Überlegungen zum Selbstverständnis des Apostels Paulus vor dem Hintergrund antiker Triumphzugspraxis', *Studien zum Neuen Testament und seiner Umwelt* 38: 146-87.

Yoon, David I. (2016) 'Ancient Letters of Recommendation and 2 Corinthians 3.1-3: A Literary Analysis', *JGRCJ* 12: 45-72.

Yuki, Masaki (2003) 'Intergroup Comparison Versus Intragroup Relationships: A Cross-Cultural Examination of Social Identity Theory in North American and East Asian Cultural Contexts', *Social Psychology Quarterly* 66: 166-83.

Zahn, Theodor (1977 [1909]) *Introduction to the New Testament*. Volume 1. English translation from the third German edition. Edinburgh: T & T Clark.

Zmijewski, J. (1978) *Der Stil der paulinischen 'Narrenrede': Analyse der Sprachgestaltung in 2 Kor 11, 1-12,10, als Beitrag zur Methodik von Stiluntersuchungen neutestamentlicher Texte*. BBB, 52. Köln: Peter Hanstein.

Index of authors

Abrams, Dominic 283
Adewuya, J. Ayodeji 185, 195
Allen, Pauline 18
Allo, E.-B. 88, 99, 150, 159, 215, 217, 218, 320
Anderson, R. Dean 76
Arzt-Grabner, Peter 229
Asano, Atsuhiro 28

Bachmann, P. 15, 88, 213, 215, 312
Baker, Coleman A. 28
Baker, William R. 118
Barclay, John M. G. 21–3, 25, 28, 52, 82, 115, 143, 231, 274
Barentsen, Jack 5, 6, 28, 29, 32, 36, 40
Barnett, Paul 69, 104, 106, 114, 132, 133, 137, 141, 145, 149, 158, 162, 167, 174, 179, 185, 196, 223, 245, 249, 254, 262, 263, 265, 266, 287, 305, 307, 315–17, 319, 328, 338, 339, 357, 366, 369
Barré, M. L. 327
Barrett, C. K. 12, 53, 55, 59, 78, 88, 92, 99, 101, 113, 174, 214, 272, 273, 278, 280, 292, 293, 298, 311, 319, 321, 345, 349, 357, 366–8, 370, 371
Bar-Tal, Daniel 34
Barth, Fredrik 274, 275
Barton, Carlin A. 275, 327
Bass, B. M. 42
Batey, Richard 78
Baur, Ferdinand C. 272, 273
Best, Ernest 169
Betz, Hans Dieter 4, 14, 41, 235, 238, 240, 249, 252, 254, 257, 261, 262, 264, 266, 350

Bieringer, Reimund 15, 53, 54
Billig, Michael 27
Bleek, Friedrich 78, 217
Boers, Hendrikus 163
Bornkamm, Günther 94, 170, 235
Bosman, Jan 28
Bourdieu, Pierre 189, 322
Boyarin, Daniel 275
Brawley, Robert L. 29
Brown, Rupert 6
Brubaker, Rogers 27
Bruce, Frederick F. 88, 96, 217, 345
Buell, Denise Kimber 116, 275
Bultmann, Rudolf Karl 20, 60, 94, 143, 245, 281, 365
Burke, Trevor J. 77

Campbell, Douglas A. 18, 78, 79, 147, 271
Campbell, William S. 114, 117, 125
Carlson, Stephen C. 78, 79
Casson, L. 325
Castelli, Elizabeth 6, 7, 31, 32
Charles, R. H. 196
Chow, J. K. 309, 340
Cinirella, Marco 148
Clarke, Andrew 6
Collange, J.-F. 125, 127, 130, 137
Collins, J. N. 242
Condor, Susan 67, 148, 149, 156
Cooper, F. 27
Cover, Michael 115
Crook, Zeba A. 249, 250

Dalton, W. J. 127
Dancy, Graham 36
Danker, Frederick William 265
Daugherty, Kevin 154
Dean, J. T. 96

Denney, J. 15, 207
Devos, Thierry 284, 285
Downs, David 229, 231
Duff, Paul D. 117, 131
Duling, Dennis C. 274
Dumont, M. 285
Dunn, James D. G. 55, 71, 114, 119, 332

Ehrensberger, Kathy 6, 7, 36, 53, 105, 146
Einarson, Benedict 62, 302
Ellemers, N. 37
Elliott, John H. 22, 37, 274, 277, 336
Engberg-Pedersen, Troels 143, 144
Esler, Philip F. 4-6, 10, 15, 20, 22, 25, 27, 28, 32, 34, 36, 37, 39, 50, 67, 71, 73, 89, 98, 105, 109, 119-21, 138, 141, 143, 144, 177, 191, 194, 195, 198, 204, 231, 232, 240, 253, 254, 263, 273-6, 279, 292, 304, 313-15, 329, 343
Eyl, Jennifer 198

Falk, Carl 25
Fee, Gordon D. 194
Fitzgerald, John T. 142, 143, 323
Forbes, Christopher 61
Forster, E. S. 66
Fredrickson, D. E. 124
French, J. R. P. 42
Friesen, Steven J. 8
Furnish, V. P. 11, 16, 76, 88, 98-102, 104, 123, 125, 127, 130, 134, 135, 137, 138, 149-51, 154, 155, 158, 159, 162, 166, 171, 174, 179, 194, 207, 212, 214, 222, 223, 242, 245, 249, 251, 252, 254, 256, 257, 261, 262, 266-8, 292, 301, 307, 308, 314, 315, 319-21, 325, 326, 329, 333, 342, 343, 353, 359-61, 363, 368-70

Gamble, Harry 17
Garland, David E. 15, 49, 55, 60, 66, 69, 104, 113, 114, 131, 155, 174, 210, 212, 213, 223, 281, 288, 293, 294, 299, 309
Gathercole, Simon 176
Georgi, Dieter 94, 111, 230, 235, 273, 354
Gergen, Kenneth J. 22
Gibson, Jack J. 232
Giles, Howard 40
Gleason, Randall C. 110
Goodman, Felicitas D. 73
Goodrich, John 6
Goulder, Michael D. 273
Griffin, Bruce W. 16
Grindheim, Sigurd 131
Gunther, John J. 273
Guthrie, George H. 69, 93, 96, 98-100, 131, 174, 191, 208, 213, 308, 311, 320, 326, 332, 338, 342, 359, 365, 369

Haenchen, Ernst 9
Hafemann, Scott 15, 98, 99, 111, 118
Hakola, Raimo 29
Hall, David R. 15, 79, 231
Harland, Philip 231
Harris, Murray J. 51, 52, 55, 57, 59, 64, 70, 75, 76, 85, 88, 92-4, 96, 98, 100, 101, 104, 106, 112, 114, 117, 119, 120, 122, 124, 126, 127, 130, 134, 137, 138, 140, 141, 144-6, 150, 152-6, 158, 163, 164, 167, 171, 172, 174, 176, 178, 179, 183, 185-7, 189, 192, 207-9,

211, 212, 215, 222, 242–5,
249, 251, 256, 257, 262,
266, 267, 273, 280, 281,
291–3, 295, 296, 298, 299,
301, 302, 304, 305, 309,
310, 313, 315–17, 320, 321,
325, 334, 338–40, 343, 349,
353, 357, 359, 360, 363,
364, 368, 369, 371
Harrison, James R.   231
Harvey, Anthony E.   5
Haslam, S. Alexander   26, 30, 32,
    38, 40
Hausrath, A.   12
Hayes, Christine   105
Hays, Richard B.   109, 110, 112,
    147, 197
Héring, J.   210
Hezser, Catherine   327
Ho, Sin-pan Daniel   28
Hock, Andreas   99
Hock, Ronald E.   311
Hogg, Michael A.   22, 23, 26, 30,
    32–4, 38–40, 283, 361
Holladay, Carl R.   273
Holmberg, Bengt   6
Hooker, Morna D.   177
Hopkins, Nicholas   25–8, 39–41,
    66, 245
Hornsey, Matthew J.   296, 297, 349
Horrell, David G.   96, 231, 275
Horsley, G. H. R.   307
Hubbard, Moyer   144
Hughes, Philip E.   88, 210, 281,
    340, 369
Hutchinson, John   274

Iyer, Aarti   83, 285

Janis, Irving Lester   19
Jetten, Jolanda   39, 82–4, 90,
    296, 349
Jewett, Robert   9
Johansen, Mark K.   35

Johnson, Luke Timothy   159
Jokiranta, Jutta   28
Joubert, Stephan   231, 232
Judge, Edwin A.   21, 22, 301,
    303, 329

Kaplan, Jonathan   53, 209
Käsemann, Ernst   177, 273, 280
Keddie, G. Anthony   114
Kerschreiter, Rudolf   25
Kessler, Thomas   285, 286, 316
Khan, Sammyh S.   26
Kim, C. -H.   103
Kim, Seon Yong   144
Kistemaker, Simon J.   125, 127, 130,
    137, 140, 158, 179
Kloppenborg, John S.   50, 231, 371
Klöpper, A.   15, 88
Knox, John   9
Koo, Bonjin   37
Korner, Ralph J.   50
Kuecker, Aaron   5, 28, 29
Kuhn, Thomas   272
Kümmel, Werner Georg   99
Kwon, Yon-Gyong   72, 156

Lacy, Philip H. de   62
Lambrecht, Jan S.J.   15, 70, 78, 80,
    93, 101, 106, 112, 127, 130,
    132, 134, 145, 147, 148,
    150, 151, 154, 155, 158,
    165, 167, 173, 174, 190,
    191, 208, 210, 215, 221,
    225, 245, 246, 249, 263,
    266–8, 290, 296, 303, 305,
    307, 313, 317, 319, 325,
    329, 332, 353, 357, 359, 364
Lanci, John R.   197
Land, Christopher D.   5, 15–18
Last, Richard   50, 231
Lau, Peter H. W.   29
Lee, Eun-Suk   25, 37
Levison, John R.   143
Lietzmann, Hans   15, 88, 252

Lieu, Judith M. 52
Lim, Kar Yong 5, 28, 67, 148, 197
Lincoln, Andrew T. 332
Lingård, Fredrik 151
Long, Frederick J. 4, 5, 15
Longenecker, Bruce W. 229
Lüdemann, Gerd 273
Luomanen, Petri 28
Lütgert, W. 273, 278

McCant, J. W. 340
Mackie, Diane M. 282-5
Maitner, Angela T. 285, 308
Malherbe, A. 230
Malina, Bruce J. 27, 37, 49, 64-5, 133, 135, 189, 322, 362
Manstead, Antony S. R. 25
Marohl, Matthew J. 28
Marshall, P. 61, 98, 103, 104, 291, 295, 301, 302, 311, 337
Martin, Ralph P. 213, 278, 292, 338
Martini, Sarah E. 285, 286, 316
Martyn, J. Louis 208
Mason, Steve 273-5
Matera, Frank J. 15, 66, 76, 92, 97, 98, 114, 117, 121, 122-3, 124, 129, 132, 134, 146, 147, 150, 153, 154, 159, 161, 164, 165, 167, 174, 176, 177, 179, 182, 184, 187, 191, 202, 212, 240, 245, 249, 252, 255, 259, 266, 268, 279, 287, 290, 307, 311-13, 317, 338, 339, 342, 349-51, 357, 359, 362, 365, 366, 368, 370, 371
Mayer, Wendy 18
Meeks, Wayne A. 184, 365
Meyer, H. A. W. 212
Mills, C. Wright 22
Mitchell, Margaret M. 15, 18, 20, 94, 174, 175, 235, 280, 346
Moberly, R. Walter 118

Montgomery, H. B. 318
Munck, Johannes 120
Murphy-O'Connor, Jerome 9, 81

Nickle, Keith F. 230-2, 253
Nongbri, Brent 275
Nosofsky, Robert M. 35
Novick, T. 101

Ogereau, Julien M. 232
O'Mahony, Kieran 19, 258, 261
Oostendorp, Derk 273
Oropeza, B. J. 278
Orton, David E. 76
Otten, Sabine 24

Pandey, Kavita 26
Park, Young-Ho 50
Parsons, Michael 169, 171
Pawlak, Matthew C. 299
Pfeffer, J. 42
Platow, M. J. 30, 32, 37, 38, 40
Plummer, Alfred 100, 185, 186, 213, 223, 268, 296, 327, 334, 363, 369
Polaski, Sandra 6, 7
Porter, Christopher A. 36, 50
Porter, Stanley E. 172
Portice, Jennie 26

Rabens, Volker 164, 165, 195
Raven, B. H. 42
Reicher, Stephen D. 23-8, 30-2, 39-41, 66, 245
Reid, S. A. 40, 361
Robinson, J. M. 97
Roetzel, Calvin J. 15, 17, 19, 235, 266, 288, 358
Rosch, Eleanor 32

Safrai, Ze'ev 230
Sampley, J. P. 232
Sanders, E. P. 114

Sani, Fabio   26
Savage, Timothy B.   5
Schenck, Kenneth   147
Schlatter, Adolf   13
Schmeller, Thomas   225
Schmithals, Walter   15, 273
Schmitz, Otto   53
Schowalter, Daniel   8
Schütz, John   6
Schweitzer, A.   169
Scott, James M.   15
Seifrid, Mark A.   15, 78, 101, 115, 123, 128–9, 134, 139, 147, 155, 158, 166, 169, 174, 180, 208, 240, 242, 249, 256, 266, 278, 334, 335, 337, 369
Semin, Gün R.   25
Semler, Johann Salomo   6, 14
Shantz, Colleen   73, 332, 334
Shaw, Graham   6
Shkul, Minna   18
Sloan, Robert B.   110, 112
Smith, Anthony   274
Smith, Eliot R.   33, 35, 282–5, 308
Smith, Joanne R.   33
Smith, Wilfrid Cantwell   274
Southwood, Katherine E.   120
Stähin, Gustav   53
Stanley, Christopher D.   109, 110, 115, 198, 248
Stargel, Linda M.   29
Starling, D. I.   199
Steffens, Niklas K.   26, 30, 31, 38, 39, 108
Stegman, Thomas   5, 91, 147, 274
Stegemann, Ekkehard W.   249
Stegemann, Wolfgang   249
Sterling, Gregory   105
Stockhausen, Carol K.   115
Stowers, Stanley K.   49, 238, 258
Striker, Gisela   144
Sumney, Jerry L.   273
Sweeney, Michael L.   233

Tack, Laura G.   131
Tajfel, Henri   6, 23–5, 274, 282
Tasker, R. V. G.   316, 358
Taylor, J.   329
Theissen, Gerd   104–5, 310
Thiessen, Matthew   105
Thomson, Peter J.   230
Thorsteinsson, Runar M.   143
Thrall, Margaret E.   3, 11, 12, 14, 15, 49, 52–5, 57, 59, 66, 69, 70, 72, 77, 79–81, 88, 90, 92, 98, 101, 106, 111–14, 117, 122, 125, 127–30, 132–9, 141, 144–7, 150, 152, 154–6, 158, 165, 166, 168, 172–4, 177, 178, 183–6, 191, 204, 205, 207, 209, 212, 213, 217, 218, 221–3, 240, 241, 243, 245–7, 251, 254–7, 259, 260, 262, 263, 266, 267, 280, 290, 294, 296–8, 302–5, 307, 311–16, 319, 322, 323, 325–7, 329, 332, 334, 335, 340, 343, 344, 346, 349, 350, 357–61, 363, 365, 367, 371
Trebilco, Paul   50
Triandis, Harry C.   37
Tucker, J. Brian   5, 28, 29, 231, 232
Turner, John C.   6, 15, 23–5, 32, 41–5, 51, 53, 60, 61, 66, 74, 95, 221, 224, 234, 235
Turner, Nigel   137

Ulrich, J.   26, 37

van Dick, Rolf   25
van Knippenberg, Daan   26, 32, 33, 37, 38
van Kooten, George   50
Vaughan, Graham M.   22, 23, 26
Vegge, Ivar   5, 78, 172, 240
Verbrugge, V. D.   257
Versnel, H. S.   98

Watson, Francis   272
Weatherall, Margaret   24, 25
Webb, William J.   180, 193, 195, 199, 200
Weber, Max   25
Wedderburn, Andrew J. M.   169
Weima, J. A. D.   367
Weiss, Johannes   15, 94, 143
Welborn, Larry L.   13, 17, 81, 85, 94, 97, 211, 216–18, 232, 235, 236, 241, 249, 319, 357, 358
Wenham, David   145

Windisch, Hans   218, 223, 235, 236, 238, 305, 316, 329, 337, 344, 359, 366
Witherington, Ben III   15, 93, 125, 174, 295, 368
Witulski, Thomas   131
Wypadlo, Adrian   98

Yoon, David I.   103
Yuki, Masaki   24

Zahn, Theodor   218
Zarate, Michael   33, 35
Zmijewski, J.   326

Index of ancient and biblical references

Ancient References

1 Apocalypse of James
26.2-19   333

Apocalypse of Moses
17.1-2   315
35.2   333

Aristotle
Nichmachean Ethics
4.9   327
1129-31   249

Rhetorica
2.6   301

Chrysostom, John
De pudicitia 13   217

Homily 21   18, 19

Cicero
Contra Verrem 2.5.139-141   324

De finibus 2.26.85   342

De oratore 2.65.261   261

1 Enoch
14.8   333
39.3   333
71.5   333
72.1   170

2 Enoch
22   333

Epictetus 1.29.2   344

Hippocrates
Art. 58   59

Josephus
Contra Apionem 2.16   115

JA
18.1.3   15
18.14   159

JW 2.163   159

Horace
Odes
4.2.50-51   99

Jubilees
1.20   196

Life of Adam and Eve
9.1   315

Lucian
Bis Accusatus 17   59

Martyrdom of Isaiah
2.4   139

Ovid
Amores
2.5.34   238

P Oxy 2190   301

Philo
De Virtutibus
76   155
102   105
102-103   105
108   105

Embassy to Gaius
357   344

Special Laws
3.46   194
4.231   249

Plutarch
Moralia
539 EF   62

540 CE   62, 337

1057 DE   143

On Inoffensive Self-Praise
3.1   302

1 QS
7.17-20   89

11Q 13   196

1 QH 9.10-11   170

1 QS 4.25   170

Rhetorica ad Alexandrum
1432b   66, 256, 274, 278
1436b-1437a   66

Testaments of the Twelve Prophets
Daniel 5   196

Levi
2.7-10   333
3   196
3.1-4   333
19   196

Reuben
4   196
6   196

Theodoret

Interpretatio in xiv epistulas sancti Pauli
PG 82:385   77
PG 82:376-377   280

Virgil
Aeneid
2.540-543   327

Biblical References (including the Apocrypha)

Gen.
1.3-4   141
1.26   140
8.1   99
17.10-13   278

Exod.
15.16   222
16.18   248, 249
21.22   209
23.1   197

23.32   197
29.8   99
31.18   109
34   115, 119, 126
34.27-28   116
34.29   119, 129
34.29-35   118
34.30   119
34.34   129
34.35   119, 122

Index of Ancient and Biblical References

Lev.
1.9   99
1.13   99
1.17   99
2.2   99
2.9   99
2.12   99
3.5   99
4.25   176
4.31   99
4.32   176
4.34   176
18.5   117
19.19   194
20.2   324
24.11-14   324
24.13   324
24.16   324
26.11-12 (LXX)   198

Num.
15.3   99
15.7   99
15.10   99
21.21   174
22.5   174

Deut.
2.25   222
2.26   174
4.13   109
5.22   109
9.9   109
9.10   109
9.11   109
10.1   109
10.3   109
10.14   333
11.25   222
13.6-11   324
17.2-7   324
18.18   113
19.10   214
19.13   214
19.15   356, 357, 358, 360

21.8   214
21.9   214
22.10   194
22.19   209
23.8   105
25.1-3   324
30.15-20   117
32.43 (LXX)   79

Judges
13.6   302

2 Sam.
7.14a   200

1 Kings
8.27   333

2 Chron.
2.6   333
6.18   333
32.8   110

Ez.
4.17   110

1 Esdras
1.36   209
8.24   209

Jdt.
2.28   222
15.2   222

1 Macc.
6.58   232
9.70   174
10.51   174
11.9   174
11.50   232
11.62   232
11.66   232
13.14   174
13.45   232
13.50   232

2 Macc.
1.5   172
4.34   232
4.38   327
5.20   172
7.33   172
8.29   172
10.35   327
11.26   232
12.11   232
13.22   232
14.19   232
14.45   327

4 Macc.
4.10   222
7.10   174
7.21   303
14.3   196

Pss
22.27   230
32[33].11   262
54[55].5   222
67[68]:31   174
86.9   230
88[89].36   262
101[102].12   263
110 (LXX).3   262
110[111].3   263
111 (LXX).7   363
111 (LXX).9   262
115 (LXX).1   147
116[117].2   263

Prov.
3.4   255
10-15   177
11.21   261
11.24   261
11.26   261
11.30   261
17.26   209
19.19   209
19.21   262
21.11   209
22   261
22.3   209
22.8   261
24.23   110

Wis.
5.25-26   140
9.15   152

Sir.
7.3   161
11.4   320
24.15   99, 100
39.13-14   99

Isa.
2.2-4   230
9.5   172
13.8   174
19.6   222
21.2   174
25.6   230
25.8   155
37.6   174
38.12 (LXX)   152
39.1   174
40.1   54
43.6   200
43.19   170
48.20   199
49   180
49.1-13   179
49.8   179
49.13 (LXX)   206
49.22   200
51.12   54
52.11 (LXX)   199
53.9-11   176
53.10   176
54.1   79
55 (LXX).10   264
57.9   174

59.17   121
59.20   230
60.4   200
63.9   174
65.17   170
66.22   170
66.23   230

Jer.
9.23-24   305
31.39 (LXX)   172
38   111
38.15 (LXX)   207
38.9 (LXX)   200
38.31 (LXX)   113
38.31-34 (LXX)   110
38.32 (LXX)   110, 113
38.33 (LXX)   110, 111, 113

Lam.
1   209
2   209

Ezek.
11.19   110, 111
20.34   200
22.27   344
36.26   110, 111
36.26-27   110
37.24-28 (LXX)   198
37.27 (LXX)   198

Dan.
3.5   196
3.15   196
12.2-3   159

Susanna
62   214

Hos.
1.10   200–1
5.13   174
10 (LXX).12   264

Mic.
4.1-2   230
7.4   302

Hab.
2.9   344

Zech.
14-16-19   230

Mt.
2.3   136
2.18   207
5.3-12   34
10.28   159
11.30   69
12.5   214
12.7   214
16.26   209, 210
18.16   357
20.25   76
20.28   108
23.5   305
25.31-46   159
27.4   214
27.24   214

Mark
8.34   36, 146
8.36   209, 210
10.42   76
10.45   108
14.4   211

Luke
1.22   332
1.37   356
1.45   305
1.58   305
9.23   36, 146
9.25   209, 210
22.25-26   76
22.27   108
23.51   197
24.23   331

John
2.1-11   225
2.5   225
5.28-29   159
14.2   152
16.30   153
20.29   157

Acts
2.38   354
3.19   354
4.33   64
5.2   254
5.13   30
8.22   354
8.38   333
9.1-9   330
9.23-25   329, 330
10.28   275
10.46   305
13.50   183
14.5   183
14.19   183
14.19-20   324
16.22   183
16.22-23   183, 324
16.23-40   183
16.37   324
17.5-7   183
17.13   183
17.26   136
17.30   354
18.5   8, 69
18.12-17   9, 183
19.17   305
19.23-20.1   183
21.15-23.30   233
21.27-36   183
22.1   211
22.22-29   52
24.15   159
24.16   153
24.17   231, 233
25.10-12   52

25.16   211
26.19   332
26.20   354
27   325
27.10   209, 210
27.21   209, 210

Rom.
1.1   50
1.2   52
1.17   120
1.18   216
1.29   216
1.29-30   351
1.29-31   352
2.4   186, 354
2.6   158
2.6-11   100
2.7   182
2.7-10   158
2.8   216, 327
2.9   192
2.16   160
3.5   216
3.8   316
3.21   167
3.21-22   120
4   5
4.7   195
4.19   145
5.1-21   176
5.3   182
5.4   182
5.8   164, 165
5.9   167
5.10   171
5.11   167, 171
5.12   155
5.15-19   164
5.18   164
6.1-11   169
6.3   55
6.3-4   145
6.3-6   146

6.3-11   165
6.11   146
6.13   188, 216
6.14   76
6.19   195
7   32, 120
7.1   76
7.7-11   120
7.7-12   117
7.12   114
7.14   114
7.22   149
8.1   167, 169, 170
8.1-2   117
8.2   146
8.3   176
8.6   146
8.8   291
8.9-11   130
8.18-21   171
8.32   146, 359
8.35   192
8.37   163
9-11   199
9.1-5   5, 230
9.4   230
9.4-5   230, 279
9.14   216
9.22   186
10.1-2   5
10.3   120
10.8   35
10.9   267, 356
10.17   356
10.18   356
10.10   267
11.1-2   5
11.13   107
11.15   171
11.17-24   5, 138
11.21   359
11.25   86
11.25-26   86
11.25-32   138

11.26   136, 230
11.30   167
12.7   107
12.9   186, 187
12.9-21   34, 187, 343, 370
12.16   206, 370
12.17   255
12.19   213
13.4   107, 108
13.11   167
14.1-2   326
14.9   76
14.10-11   159
15.4   182
15.8   71, 107
15.10   79
15.12-21   140
15.15   86, 107
15.22-29   14
15.23   225
15.23-27   7, 280, 361
15.24   86, 311
15.25   249
15.25-31   229
15.26   197, 225, 229, 234, 242, 248, 259, 263, 347
15.28   71
15.30   60
15.31   107, 229, 233
16.1   107
16.16   370
16.20   371
16.26   244

1 Cor.
1.1   49, 256, 296
1.3   52
1.6   64, 71
1.6-8   71
1.9   196
1.10   246, 370
1.10-13   370
1.11   11, 351
1.14-16   71

1.16 8	5.15 268
1.17 70, 88, 145	5.17 268
1.18 100, 145	6.1 216
1.23 145	6.6 139
1.26 294	6.7 216
1.30 121	6.8 216
1.31 140, 305	6.9 216
2.1 11	6.11 166
2.1-3 79	6.17 130
2.1-5 342, 350	6.18 355
2.2 145	7.5 196, 246
2.3 223	7.6 244, 246
2.4 73	7.11 171
2.8 145	7.12 139. 216
3.3 351	7.13 139
3.5 107, 108	7.14 139
3.6 8, 267, 313	7.15 139
3.10 8	7.25 244
3.14-15 210	7.40 246
3.15 209	8-9 226
3.16-17 197	8.9 294
3.17 316	9.1 328
3.19 140	9.1-18 102
4.6 352	9.3 123, 211, 347
4.10 318	9.9 140
4.13 53	9.12b 310, 311
4.14-15 343	9.14 310
4.15 307	9.18 310
4.16 36	10.1-5 109, 115
4.17 10, 11	10.7 140
4.18 352	10.9 140
4.19 10, 352	10.13 196
4.19-21 10, 11, 76	10.15 318
4.21 10, 212, 288	10.16 196
5 13, 81	10.18 294, 318
5-14 9	10.27 139
5.1-2 217	11.1 36
5.1-5 357	11.2 79
5.1-8 9	11.20 275
5.1-13 291	11.23 146
5.2 352, 353	11.25 110, 113
5.5 359	12-14 71, 73, 119, 163, 187, 339
5.9-13 9	12.3 130, 140
5.13 359	12.5 107

12.8	241, 265
12.27	123
12.28-29	339
12.29-30	339
13	343
13.4	352
13.6	216
13.9	123
13.10	123
13.12	123
14.2	139
14.14	163
14.18	73, 119, 163, 333, 339
14.19	163
14.22	339
14.23	139, 143
14.24	139
15	152, 153, 155
15.3	79, 165
15.8	168
15.9-10	112
15.23	152
15.25-31	230
15.31-32	155
15.37	154
15.44	152
15.45	140
15.51-58	155
15.52	152
15.54	155
16	14, 17
16.1	231, 247
16.2	231, 247
16.1-2	9, 243
16.1-4	229, 230, 239, 345
16.3-4	10
16.5-7	10
16.5-9	68
16.7	11
16.8	9
16.10	294
16.10-11	10, 11
16.15	8, 85, 107
16.17	9, 85
16.20	370, 371
16.21	287
16.23	371

2 Cor.

1-2	95, 206, 221, 343, 347, 349, 369
1-7	3, 14, 15, 19, 62, 97, 107, 122, 162, 224, 234, 235, 242, 260, 263, 272, 299, 326, 341, 343, 349
1-8	14, 144, 257
1-9	14, 15, 94, 134, 288, 310, 345, 347, 349, 364, 366, 369
1.1	49, 50–2, 53, 57, 70, 100, 102, 106, 112, 256, 258, 287, 360
1.1-2	49–53
1.1-2.13	19
1.1-22	74
1.2	51, 52–3, 179
1.3	53, 54, 242, 251, 369
1.3-4	53–5
1.3-7	53–8, 369
1.4	54–5, 58, 183, 206, 242, 251, 367, 369
1.5	55, 57, 59, 70, 145, 242, 251, 360, 367, 369
1.5-7	221
1.6	54, 55, 56, 57, 58, 144, 182, 242, 241, 369
1.6-7	206
1.7	56–8, 60, 67, 77, 88, 242, 251, 256, 367
1.8	141, 155, 361, 367
1.8-9	157
1.8-10	59
1.8-11	53, 58–60, 93, 183
1.11	53, 59–60
1.12	61–6, 67, 69, 73, 75, 102, 124, 125, 135, 185, 296, 307, 334
1.12-2.13	61
1.12-14	60–7
1.12-22	75
1.13	14, 61, 66–7, 90
1.13-14	86

1.14   67, 68, 123, 147, 148, 296
1.15   68, 78, 112, 223
1.15-3.13   342
1.15-16   11, 68, 93
1.15-22   14, 68-74, 190
1.17   67, 69, 73, 93, 167
1.17-18   68-9, 90
1.17-20   161
1.18   70, 196
1.19   8, 49, 69, 70
1.19-20   73
1.19-22   69-74
1.20   40, 70, 71
1.21   70, 71, 72
1.21-22   70-1, 73
1.22   71, 155
1.23   75-6, 186, 209, 359
1.23-2.1   12
1.23-2.11   93
1.23-2.13   75, 216
1.23-2.4   68, 212, 218
1.23-24   74
1.24   45, 56, 60, 76-7, 79, 80, 88, 91, 108, 141, 147, 178, 124, 288, 297, 363
2   208, 216, 217, 244, 246, 254, 256, 257, 261, 311, 319, 320, 326, 364
2.1   11, 76, 77-9, 342, 350
2.1-2   12, 368
2.1-4   80
2.2   78, 79, 85, 359
2.3   68, 78, 79-80, 91, 342
2.3-4   12, 217, 272
2.4   79, 80, 93, 183, 207, 208, 222, 312, 343
2.5   80, 85-9, 123, 219
2.5-8   216
2.5-9   208
2.5-11   68, 84-92, 186, 202, 205, 215
2.5-13   80-93
2.5-16   205-25
2.6   89, 213, 220, 221, 254, 357
2.6-8   85, 89-90

2.7   89, 91, 217, 220, 369
2.7-11   220
2.8   89, 91, 217, 368
2.9   13, 79, 87, 245, 246
2.9-10   90-1
2.10   88, 91, 92
2.10-11   91-2
2.11   92, 95, 196, 292, 345
2.12   61-6, 217, 267, 360
2.12-7.4   14
2.12-13   12, 92-3, 95, 205
2.12-14   61
2.13   75, 94, 95, 96, 98, 103, 205, 260
2.14   79, 94, 96, 98-100, 169, 186
2.14-6.10   94
2.14-6.13   103
2.14-7.4   19, 61, 94-8, 204
2.14-16   132
2.14-16b   102
2.14-17   98-103, 112, 132
2.15   99, 100, 360
2.15-16   166
2.15-16b   99-101
2.16   100, 101
2.16a   100
2.16c   99, 101
2.16c-17   101-3
2.17   95, 97, 99, 100, 101, 102, 122, 124, 125, 126, 131, 133, 134, 137, 138, 162, 169, 190, 221, 271, 300, 310, 314, 320, 337, 340, 347
2.17b-c   102
2.17-3.1   103, 124, 132, 139, 278, 300, 315, 341
2.17-3.6   162
2.17-3.18   19
3   3, 97, 116, 122, 248
3-6   49
3.1   101, 103-6, 111, 116, 122, 131, 134, 182, 271, 292, 299, 337
3.1-3   103-12
3.1-18   194
3.2   109, 113

Index of Ancient and Biblical References

3.2-3   112, 134, 300
3.2-4.6   278
3.2-18   271, 315
3.3   108, 109, 113
3.3-15   129
3.4   112, 223
3.5   76, 101, 112
3.5-6   112
3.6   101, 107, 111, 112–14, 115, 119, 132, 162, 174, 181, 266, 267
3.6-10   123
3.7   107, 114, 115, 116, 117, 119, 126, 127, 128, 278
3.7-11   115–24
3.7-18   115, 116, 132, 292
3.8   107, 119, 132, 181, 187, 266, 267
3.9   107, 108, 119–22, 132, 181, 188, 195, 264, 266, 267, 278, 316
3.10   122–3
3.11   123–4, 127, 128
3.12   124–5, 126, 134, 191, 203
3.12-13   129
3.12-15   137
3.12-18   124–31
3.13   125–7, 128, 137
3.14   127–8, 137, 169, 292
3.14-16   127
3.15   128, 137
3.16   128–30, 137, 230
3.17   114, 278
3.18   115, 118, 126, 130–1, 139, 149, 150
4.1   107, 142, 266
4.1-4   139
4.1-6   132–41, 142
4.2   102, 104, 133, 137, 138, 153, 161, 187, 190, 194, 195, 300, 307, 337, 365
4.3   137–8, 142
4.3-4   195
4.3-6   196
4.4   92, 138–40, 153, 193, 194, 195, 292
4.5   140, 142, 145, 288, 320, 360

4.6   140–1, 142, 186
4.6-5.10   149–60
4.7   141, 142, 151, 187, 361
4.7-8   149
4.7-11   59
4.7-12   146, 147, 157, 187
4.7-15   141–8, 149
4.8   183, 192
4.8-9   142–4, 149, 182, 323
4.8-12   183
4.10   144–6
4.10-12   144
4.10-15   144
4.11   145, 146
4.11-12   145
4.12   146, 147, 148, 366
4.13   140
4.13-14   147–8
4.14   147, 149, 159
4.15   141, 148
4.16   148, 149–50, 151
4.16-18   151–60
4.17   183
4.17   69, 149
4.18   150–1
4.19   145
5.1   131, 151–3, 156
5.1-5   73
5.1-10   151
5.2   152, 153–4, 155
5.3   153, 154–5
5.4   151, 154, 155
5.5   155–6
5.6   156
5.6-8   156–7
5.7   147, 156
5.7-8   156
5.8   154, 156, 157
5.9   157–8
5.10   147, 148, 154, 158–60, 161
5.10b   159
5.11   136, 161, 163
5.11-6.2   178, 181
5.11-15   161–6

5.12   104, 162, 163, 182, 296, 300, 305, 317, 337
5.13   162–3
5.14   158, 163, 165, 360
5.14a   167
5.14-15   159, 163–6, 167, 169, 172
5.14-17   171
5.16   167–9
5.16-6.2   167–80
5.17   166, 167, 169–71
5.18   107, 171, 172, 181, 266
5.18-19   171–3
5.18-20   366
5.19   158, 169, 171, 172, 174, 175
5.19-20   178
5.20   171, 172, 174–5, 178, 360, 368
5.21   121, 175–7, 188, 195
6.1   178–9, 256, 368
6.1-2   178
6.2   178–80
6.3   107, 178, 181–2, 254
6.3a   181
6.3b   181
6.3-10   59, 157, 181–90, 191
6.4   55, 104, 107, 113, 181, 182, 192, 266, 300, 337
6.4a   182
6.4-10   181–90, 323, 325, 337
6.4b-5   182
6.4b-10   182
6.5   183, 325
6.6   61, 185, 186, 194, 214, 307
6.6-7a   182, 184
6.7   121, 122, 195, 361, 365
6.7b-8a   182, 188
6.8b-10   182, 189
6.11   191–2, 202, 203
6.11-13   174, 186, 190–3
6.12   192
6.12-13   203
6.13   179, 191, 192, 307, 343
6.14   199, 200, 241, 263
6.14a   194
6.14b   195
6.14b-16   195
6.14c   196
6.14-7.1   15, 94, 97, 185, 191, 193, 191, 196, 203, 214, 215, 263, 307, 363
6.14-7.4   193–203
6.14-15   139, 194
6.14-16b   193–7
6.14-18   179
6.15   92, 158, 200
6.15a   196
6.16   200, 201, 230
6.16a   197
6.16-18   141, 206
6.16c-18   197–201
6.17   199–200, 355
6.18   200–1
7   53, 81, 84, 93, 95, 181, 200, 216, 217, 236, 244, 346, 348, 369
7.1   179, 201–2, 214, 307
7.2   174, 179, 190, 191, 192, 202–3, 216, 236, 254, 271, 307, 345
7.2-4   94, 97, 190, 191, 202–4
7.3   192, 203
7.4   97, 124, 125, 183, 191, 192, 203–4, 224, 242, 296, 369
7.5   94, 95, 96, 144, 203
7.5-6   97
7.5-7   205–7
7.5-15   223
7.5-16   12, 19, 75, 79, 81, 83, 85, 91, 96, 97, 203, 224, 250
7.6   203, 206, 369
7.6-13   87
7.6-16   271
7.7   56, 58, 203, 206–7, 212, 236, 242
7.8   79, 93, 207, 208, 288
7.8-9   12
7.8-11   12
7.8-13   207–16, 221, 348
7.9   12, 85, 87, 203, 208–10, 219, 354
7.9-10   213

Index of Ancient and Biblical References

7.10   208, 210, 354
7.11   104, 185, 207, 208, 213, 214, 215, 224, 251, 288, 290, 337
7.11-12   236, 244, 255
7.11a   210-13
7.11b   211, 213-15
7.12   12, 13, 68, 80, 81, 85, 86, 87, 88, 91, 202, 207, 215-16, 218, 219, 251, 272
7.12-13   68
7.13   58, 203, 214, 221, 242, 369
7.13-16   274
7.14   62, 222, 296
7.14-16   222-5
7.15   13, 211, 212, 214, 221, 222-3, 236, 293
7.16   203, 223-5, 341, 348, 349, 350, 353
8   10, 14, 15, 231, 235, 236, 237, 238, 243, 244, 245, 250, 252, 258, 260, 266, 342
8-9   3, 19, 57, 62, 74, 103, 107, 125, 215, 221, 223, 224, 229, 230, 234, 247, 249, 260, 266, 303, 341, 342
8.1   238, 240, 252, 367
8.1-2   311
8.1-5   206, 238, 243, 245, 258
8.1-6   236, 239-43, 244
8.1-9.5   238
8.1-24   19
8.2   125, 183, 238, 240-1, 244, 245, 246, 265
8.3   242, 247, 252
8.4   107, 196, 241-2, 251, 253, 256, 266
8.5   242
8.6   10, 236, 237, 239, 240, 242-3, 247, 251, 258, 260, 345, 346, 368
8.7   147, 236, 238, 240, 243, 244, 251, 255, 312
8.7-12   237, 243-7
8.8   234, 236, 241, 245, 251, 255, 343
8.9   246, 318
8.10   10, 234, 239, 242, 246-7, 345
8.10-11   243, 259
8.11   242, 247, 254, 258
8.11-12   237
8.12   247, 254
8.12-15   238
8.13   183, 247
8.13-15   232, 237, 247-50
8.14   238, 248, 266
8.15   248, 249, 250
8.16-9.5   250-61
8.16   250, 252, 255
8.16-17   221, 250-2
8.16-24   14, 237, 238, 345, 346
8.17   241, 251, 252, 253, 255, 260
8.18   252, 253, 255, 259
8.18-19   252-4, 255
8.19   107, 240, 254
8.19-20   265
8.20   107, 254-5
8.21   255
8.22   112, 223, 252, 255-6, 259
8.23   77, 255, 256-7
8.24   238, 257-8, 296
9   14, 15, 17, 235, 236, 237, 241, 243, 244, 250, 258, 260, 266, 289, 342
9.1   107, 238, 258, 266
9.1-2   238, 258
9.1-4   238
9.1-5   237
9.1-15   20
9.2   51, 237, 245, 246, 254, 258-9, 296
9.2-5   289
9.3   259-60, 296
9.3-4   238, 258, 259
9.3-5   238, 342
9.4   259, 260, 342
9.4-5   238
9.5   234, 236, 251, 252, 260-1, 368
9.6   161

9.6-7   238
9.6-10   261–5
9.6-11   265
9.6-15   237, 238, 244
9.7   234, 261
9.8   238, 240, 261–2, 264
9.9   121, 188, 262–4
9.9-8   238
9.9-10   264
9.10   121, 188, 263, 264–5
9.11   125, 238, 240, 241, 265, 266
9.11-15 265–8
9.12-15 265
9.12   107, 266, 337
9.13   107, 125, 196, 238, 240, 241, 265, 267–8
9.14   240, 249, 268
9.15   238, 240, 268
10   17, 271, 289, 296, 331
10-12   296
10-13   3, 4, 12, 14, 15, 17, 18, 19, 50, 55, 62, 63, 92, 94, 97, 98, 103, 107, 108, 122, 125, 131, 134, 162, 181, 189, 195, 202, 208, 213, 215, 221–3, 224, 225, 236, 260, 263, 271, 272, 286–9, 295, 296, 298–300, 307, 310, 327, 340–2, 344, 345, 347, 353, 356, 361, 363, 366, 369
10-13.10 14
10.1   18, 223, 224, 287–9, 299, 309, 368
10.1-2   167, 225
10.1-6   18
10.1-11 287–99
10.1-13.10 19
10.2   104, 112, 223, 289–91, 292, 294, 298, 302
10.3   291, 303
10.3-6   291–4
10.4   297, 361
10.4-5   297
10.4-6   362

10.5   292, 293, 320, 360
10.5-6   290
10.6   223, 293, 294, 342, 350
10.7   294–5, 298
10.8   55, 295–7, 322, 366
10.9   297–8
10.10   79, 288, 290, 291, 298, 309, 321, 361
10.10-11 289, 290, 298
10.11   297, 298, 299, 300, 362
10.12   104, 299–302, 305, 331
10.12-18 299–305
10.13   281, 296, 302–4
10.13-15 277
10.13-16 314
10.13-17 302
10.14   267, 304
10.15   147, 244, 281, 296, 302, 303, 304–5
10.15-16 331
10.16   296, 303, 305
10.16-17 305
10.17   63, 296, 305, 356
10.18   104, 300, 302, 305, 337
11   306
11.1   306, 316, 317, 321, 322, 337
11.1-6   306–9
11.2   185, 207, 214, 306–7, 317, 343
11.2-3   223
11.3   92, 125, 134, 185, 214, 281, 293, 307–8, 349
11.3-4   202, 344
11.3-6   185
11.3-15 179
11.4   102, 136, 137, 138, 140, 166, 179, 187, 277, 281, 292, 293, 308–9, 314, 317
11.5   50, 121, 280, 281, 308, 338
11.5-6   309
11.6   298
11.7   206, 310–11
11.7-9   102
11.7-11 104, 309–12, 340
11.7-15 278

Index of Ancient and Biblical References

11.8   107, 295
11.8-9   311–12, 320
11.9   310, 311, 312
11.10   51, 296, 312, 360, 365
11.11   207, 312, 343
11.12   296, 310, 312–13, 328, 331
11.12-15   126, 138, 312–16
11.13   35, 50, 102, 126, 134, 162, 190, 280, 295, 313–15, 316, 320, 339, 344
11.13-15   139, 162, 263, 295, 307, 314
11.14   126, 196, 314, 315
11.14-15   195
11.15   92, 107, 108, 111, 121, 126, 159, 162, 173, 177, 195, 292, 313, 315–16, 317, 323, 331
11.16   296, 306, 316–17, 322, 328
11.16-17   322
11.16-21a   316–21
11.17   296, 317
11.18   63, 296, 317, 328
11.19   118, 306, 317–19, 321, 361
11.20   114, 131, 279, 294, 310, 319–21
11.21   299, 302, 361
11.21a   320, 321
11.21b   321–2
11.21b-29   321–8
11.22   109, 116, 126, 276, 277, 315, 322, 331
11.22-12.13   322
11.22-23   322
11.23   107, 108, 109, 111, 173, 182, 183, 277, 295, 322–4
11.23-27   337
11.23-29   314
11.23b-29   182, 339
11.24   183, 324
11.24-28   323
11.25   183, 324–5
11.26   314, 325
11.27   184, 325–6
11.28   326

11.29   299, 326–8, 329
11.29-30   321
11.30   296, 299, 326, 331, 336, 361
11.30-33   326, 328–30
11.32-33   328–30
12   306, 328
12.1   163, 169, 296, 331–2
12.1-10   331–7
12.2   169, 334
12.2-3   333, 334
12.2-4   163, 333
12.2-10   218
12.3-4   333–4
12.3-10   333
12.4-13.4   357
12.5   296, 299, 328, 334, 336
12.6   296, 306, 334, 335, 365
12.7   92, 196, 333, 334–6
12.8   336, 368
12.9   187, 296, 299, 328, 362
12.9a   336
12.9b   336–7
12.9-10   336–7
12.10   182, 183, 192, 299, 321, 323, 328, 337, 362
12.11   50, 104, 223, 280, 281, 282, 300, 302, 306, 339, 341
12.11-13   337–41
12.12   35, 50, 55, 73, 338–9
12.13   216, 306, 321, 322, 323, 339–41
12.13-14   310
12.14   11, 14, 77, 78, 79, 169, 260, 297, 299, 306, 307, 319, 340, 341–3, 348, 353
12.14-18   102, 103, 341–7
12.15   207, 312, 340, 343–4, 348
12.16   133, 134, 223, 310, 320, 344
12.16-18   190
12.17   344–5, 346
12.17-18   10, 202, 239, 260, 261
12.18   243, 256, 345–7, 368
12.19   55, 103, 296, 297, 347–8, 365, 366

12.20   294, 307, 327, 348–52, 353, 370
12.20-21   78, 79, 179, 223, 294, 348
12.21   186, 206, 291, 293, 350, 352–5, 358, 359
13   12, 348, 364
13.1   11, 14, 78, 260, 342, 356–7, 366
13.1-2   78, 79, 297, 299
13.1-3   212
13.1-4   356–62
13.2   78, 209, 291, 293, 353, 355, 357, 362, 366
13.2-3   11, 76, 291, 294, 357, 362
13.3   106, 299, 363
13.3-4   321, 366
13.4   299, 337, 361, 362
13.5   147, 244, 362–4
13.5-10   362–7
13.6   364
13.7   364–5, 366
13.7d   365
13.8   365–6
13.9   299, 321, 366, 367, 368
13.10   55, 296, 299, 366–7
13.11   367–70, 371
13.11-13   14, 19, 367–72
13.12   370–1
13.13   196, 371–2

Gal.
1.1   50, 269, 296
1.2   52
1.4   165
1.6   277
1.6-7   276
1.6-9   166
1.8   137
1.11   137
1.11-17   72
1.13   133, 275
1.14   275
1.15-16   100, 113, 168, 296, 332, 333
1.16   73, 132, 141, 165, 242, 265
1.16-17   330
1.17   329
1.18   329
1.20   328
1.22   106, 169
1.23   133
2.2   137
2.2-3   233
2.1-5   120
2.1-10   105, 275, 304, 313, 325
2.3   275
2.4   114, 130, 131, 275, 276, 278, 279, 319, 320, 325
2.4-5   314
2.5   275, 277
2.9   196, 233, 303
2.10   229, 230, 231, 248
2.11-14   105, 120, 230, 275, 304, 313
2.12   105
2.14   275, 277, 314
2.15   277
2.17   107
2.20   146, 163, 167
2.21   279
3   5, 105
3.1   145
3.2   73
3.5   339
3.6-29   276
3.10-14   117
3.13   76
3.15   90
3.21   279
4.3   278
4.6   130
4.7   141
4.9   129, 167
4.12   216
4.13   11, 321, 335
4.27   79
5.1   131
5.2   276
5.3   276

5.6   276
5.11   145, 276
5.16   346
5.18   294
5.19-21   350
5.20   327
5.22   186, 187
5.22-23   34, 350
6.11   287
6.12   145
6.13   276
6.15   170, 171, 276
6.16   303
6.17   55
6.18   371

Eph.
2.21   136
6.20   174

Phil.
1.1   49, 107
1.2   52
1.5   196
1.7   211
1.16   211
1.19   130
1.19-26   157
1.20   124, 305
1.24   157
1.27-30   240
2.1   196
2.6-8   246
2.8   145
2.11   140
2.12   223
2.17   266
2.17b-18   368
2.30   266
3.2   121, 294, 316
3.2-3   314
3.4   112
3.6   133
3.7   209

3.8   209
3.9   120, 121
3.10   145, 196
3.10-11   55
3.12   155
3.18   145
3.19   316
4.2   245
4.3   194
4.8   183, 214
4.8-9   367
4.10   155
4.15-17   311

Col.
2.15   99
4.21   249

1 Thess.
1.1   52, 169
1.3   182
1.5   137
1.6   240
1.9   120, 129
2.2   206
2.3   190
2.9   310, 311, 325
2.14   106, 169, 170, 240
2.16   316
3.2   107, 108, 178
3.3-4   240
3.4   144
3.13   121
4.3   121
4.4   121
4.7   121
4.13-18   231
4.14-15   157
4.15   157
4.16   157
4.17   157, 333
4.18   368
5   367
5.11   368

5.12-22 34
5.13 370
5.16 367
5.18 121
5.23 121
5.24 196
5.26 370
5.28 371

1 Tim.
4.10 197
4.12 197
5.16 197
5.19 357
5.22 214
6.15 76

2 Tim.
4.16 211

Tit.
2.5 214

Phlm.
3 52
6 196
8 124, 244
9 174
13 107
18 216
19 287
25 371

James
3.17 214
5.11 36

1 Pet.
1.8 157
3.2 214
3.15 211
5.14 370

1 Jn
3.3 214

www.ingramcontent.com/pod-product-compliance
Lightning Source LLC
Chambersburg PA
CBHW052138300426
44115CB00011B/1424